THE UNIVERSITY OF CHICAGO

ORIENTAL INSTITUTE PUBLICATIONS

VOLUME LXXVII

THE UNIVERSITY OF CHICAGO
ORIENTAL INSTITUTE PUBLICATIONS
VOLUME LXXVII

STUDIES IN ARABIC LITERARY PAPYRI

III
LANGUAGE AND LITERATURE

BY NABIA ABBOTT

THE UNIVERSITY OF CHICAGO PRESS · CHICAGO AND LONDON

International Standard Book Number: 0–226–62178–2
Library of Congress Catalog Card Number: 56–5027

THE UNIVERSITY OF CHICAGO PRESS, CHICAGO 60637
THE UNIVERSITY OF CHICAGO PRESS, LTD. LONDON

Published 1972. Text printed in England by Stephen Austin and Sons Limited, Hertford. Plates printed in the United States of America by the University of Chicago Printing Department.

PREFACE

THE present volume concludes the series of studies in Arabic literary papyri as envisaged in the Preface to Volume I. The studies reveal a steadily accelerating literary activity in both the religious and secular fields throughout the Umayyad period. Poets and scholars in the various fields used concurrent oral and written transmission for the publication, transmission, and preservation of their literary products. The *isnād*, particularly in its multiple forms, was used to a much greater degree in the religious than in the secular fields. For poetry the family *isnād* took second place to that stemming from a poet's personal secretary, *kātib*, or from his transmitter, *rāwī*. A characteristically Arab approach and critical outlook mark Islāmic literature of this period and of the early decades of ʿAbbāsid rule.

Recent finds of Arabic papyri await processing and study. Inspection and classification of relatively small Arabic papyri collections that have lately found their way to the United States revealed several literary texts from the early ʿAbbāsid period itself. These include a leaf written in a schooled but small Kūfic script from an early, if not the earliest, version of the *Kalīlah wa Dimnah*, extracts from the poetry of Sayyid al-Ḥimyarī, Abū al-ʿAtāhiyah, and Abū Nuwās, and other verses yet to be identified. It is probable that other texts representative of early ʿAbbāsid literature are to be found among the rest of the extant collections.

In contrast to the comparative rarity of literary documents, Arabic papyri collections include large groups of private correspondence. The letters throw considerable light on several facets of the life and mores of middle-class urban society—an intriguing field that awaits an eager explorer.

In closing, I wish to express my appreciation to Director George R. Hughes of the Oriental Institute for his interest and encouragement, and again to our Editorial Secretary, Mrs. Elizabeth B. Hauser, for her skillful editing of the manuscript, and to her successor, Mrs. Jean Eckenfels, for cheerfully seeing the volume through the press.

NABIA ABBOTT

THE ORIENTAL INSTITUTE
CHICAGO, 1969

TABLE OF CONTENTS

LIST OF PLATES

ABBREVIATIONS

Abū Ḥayyān — Abū Ḥayyān Muḥammad ibn Yūsuf al-Andalūsī. *Manhāj al-sālik fī al-kalām 'alā alfīyat ibn Mālik*, ed. Sidney Glazer (New Haven, 1947).

Adāb al-Shāfi'ī — 'Abd al-Raḥmān ibn Abī Ḥātim al-Rāzī. *Adāb al-Shāfi'ī wa manāqibihi*, ed. 'Abd al-Ghānī 'Abd al-Khālī (Cairo, 1372/1953).

Aghānī — Abū al-Faraj al-Iṣfahānī. *Kitāb al-aghānī*. Vols. I–XX, ed. Naṣr al-Hūrīnī (Būlāq, 1285/1868); Vol. XXI, ed. Rudolph E. Brünnow (Leyden, 1888); Indexes, ed. I. Guidi (Leide, 1900).

Aghānī (1927——) — ———. *Kitāb al-aghānī* (Cairo, 1345/1927——).

AJSL — American Journal of Semitic Languages and Literatures (Chicago etc., 1884–1941).

Akhbār al-quḍāt — Wakī' Muḥammad ibn Khalaf ibn Ḥayyān. *Akhbār al-quḍāt*, ed. 'Abd al-'Azīz Muṣṭafā al-Marāghī (3 vols.; Cairo, 1366–69/1947–50).

Amālī — Ismā'īl ibn al-Qāsim Abū 'Alī al-Qālī. *Kitāb al-amālī* (3 vols.; Būlāq, 1324/1906).

Ansāb — Aḥmad ibn Yaḥyā al-Balādhurī. *Kitāb ansāb al-ashrāf*, ed. Muḥammad Ḥamīd Allāh (Cairo, 1379/1959——).

'Askarī, *Maṣūn* — Abū Aḥmad al-Ḥasan ibn 'Abd Allāh al-'Askarī. *Al-maṣūn fī al-adab*, ed. 'Abd al-Salām Muḥammad Hārūn (Kuwait, 1960).

Asrār — 'Abd al-Raḥmān ibn Muḥammad ibn al-Anbārī. *Asrār al-'arabīyah*, ed. Christian Seybold (Leiden, 1886).

Baihaqī — Ibrāhīm ibn Muḥammad al-Baihaqī. *Kitāb al-maḥāsin wa al-masāwī*, ed. Friedrich Schwally (Giessen, 1902).

Bevan — The Nakā'id of Jarīr and al-Farazdak, ed. Anthony Ashley Bevan (3 vols.; Leiden, 1905–12).

BGA — Bibliotheca geographorum Arabicorum, ed. Michael Jan de Goeje (8 vols.; Lugduni-Batavorum, 1879–1939).

Bughyah — Jalāl al-Dīn al-Suyūṭī. *Bughyat al-wu'āt* (Cairo, 1908).

Bukhārī — Muḥammad ibn Ismā'īl al-Bukhārī. *Al-jāmi' al-ṣaḥīḥ*, ed. Ludolf Krehl (4 vols.; Leyde, 1862–1908).

Concordance — A. J. Wensinck *et al.* Concordance et indices de la tradition musulmane (Leyden, 1936——).

Dhahabī — Muḥammad ibn Aḥmad al-Dhahabī. *Tadhkirat al-ḥuffāẓ* (4 vols; Ḥaidarābād, 1333–34/1915–16).

Dīnawarī — Abū Ḥanīfah Aḥmad ibn Dā'ūd al-Dīnawarī. *Akhbār al-ṭiwwāl*, ed. Vladimir Guirgass (Leiden, 1888).

EI — The Encyclopaedia of Islam (4 vols. and Supplement; Leyden, 1931–36 and 1938. New ed.; Leyden, 1920——).

Fāḍil — Muḥammad ibn Yazīd al-Mubarrad. *Al-fāḍil*, ed. 'Abd al-'Azīz al-Maimanī (Cairo, 1375/1956).

Fihrist — Muḥammad ibn Isḥāq al-Nadīm. *Fihrist al-'ulūm'*, ed. Gustav Flügel, Johannes Roediger, and August Mueller (Leipzig, 1871–72).

Fuḥūlat al-shu'arā'	Charles C. Torrey. Al-Aṣma'i's Fuḥūlat aš-Šu'arā'. *ZDMG* LXV (1911) 487–516.
Futūḥ	'Abd al-Raḥmān ibn 'Abd Allāh ibn 'Abd al-Ḥakam. *Futūḥ Miṣr,* ed. Charles C. Torrey (Yale Oriental Series—Researches III [New Haven, 1922]).
Futūḥ al-buldān	Aḥmad ibn Yaḥyā al-Balādhurī. *Kitāb futūḥ al-buldān,* ed. M. J. de Goeje (Lugduni Batavorum, 1866).
Gabrieli	Francesco Gabrieli. Al-Walīd ibn Yazīd, il califfo e il poeta. Revista degli studi orientali XV (Roma, 1935) 1–64.
GAL	Carl Brockelmann. Geschichte der arabischen Litteratur (2 vols.; Weimar etc., 1898–1902).
GAL S	———. Supplement (3 vols.; Leiden, 1937–42).
Griffini	*Shi'r al-Akhṭal,* ed. Eugenio Griffini. Printed by photolithography from a manuscript found in the Yemen (Beirūt, 1907).
Ḥājjī Khalīfah	Muṣṭafā ibn 'Abd Allāh Ḥājjī Khalīfah. *Kashf al-ẓunūn,* ed. Gustav Flügel (Oriental Translation Fund of Great Britain and Ireland. Publications XLII [7 vols.; London, 1835–58]).
Ḥusn	Jalāl al-Dīn al-Suyūṭī. *Kitāb ḥusn al-muḥāḍarat fī akhbār Miṣr wa al-Qāhirah* (2 vols.; Cairo, 1299/1882).
Ibn Abī Ṭāhir Ṭaifūr	Aḥmad ibn Abī Ṭāhir Ṭaifūr. *Balāghat al-nisā'* (Najaf, 1361/1942).
Ibn 'Asākir	'Alī ibn al-Ḥasan ibn 'Asākir. *Al-ta'rīkh al-kabīr,* ed. 'Abd al-Qādir Badrān (7 vols.; Damascus, 1329–51/1911–32).
Ibn Fāris, *Ṣāḥibī*	Abū al-Ḥusain Aḥmad ibn Fāris. *Al-ṣāḥibī fī fiqh al-lughah wa sunan al-'Arab,* ed. Muṣṭafā al-Shuwaimī (Beirūt, 1382/1963).
Ibn al-Jazarī	Muḥammad ibn Muḥammad ibn al-Jazarī. *Ghāyat al-nihāyah fī ṭabaqāt al-qurrā',* ed. Gotthelf Bergsträsse and Otto Pretzl (3 vols.; Leipzig, 1933–35).
Ibn Khallikān	Aḥmad ibn Muḥammad ibn Khallikān. *Wafayāt al-a'yān* (2 vols.; Būlāq, 1299/1882) and translation by Baron Mac Guckin de Slane (Oriental Translation Fund of Great Britain and Ireland. Publications LVII [4 vols.; Paris, 1843–71]).
Ibn al-Mu'tazz, *Ṭabaqāt*	'Abd Allāh ibn al-Mu'tazz. *Ṭabaqāt al-shu'arā' al-muḥdathīn,* ed. 'Abd al-Sattār Aḥmad Farrāj (Cairo, 1375/1956).
Ibn Rustah	Abū 'Alī Aḥmad ibn 'Umar ibn Rustah. *Kitāb al-a'lāq al-nafīsa* (BGA VII [1892] 1–229).
Ibn Sa'd	Muḥammad ibn Sa'd. *Kitāb al-ṭabaqāt al-kabīr,* ed. Eduard Sachau (9 vols; Leiden, 1904–40).
Ibn Ṭabāṭabā	Muḥammad ibn Aḥmad ibn Ṭabāṭabā. *'Iyār al-shi'r,* ed. Ṭāha al-Ḥājirī and Muḥammad Zaghlūl Sallām (Cairo, 1956).
Ibn Taghrībirdī	Abū al-Maḥāsin Yūsuf ibn Taghrībirdī. *Al-nujūm al-zāhirah fī mulūk Miṣr wa al-Qāhirah,* ed. T. W. J. Juynboll and B. F. Matthes (2 vols.; Lugduni Batavorum, 1852–61).
Ibshīhī	Muḥammad ibn Aḥmad al-Ibshīhī. *Al-mustaṭraf fī kull fann mustaẓraf* (2 vols.; Cairo, 1308/1890).
Inbāh	'Alī ibn Yūsuf al-Qifṭī. *Inbāh al-ruwāt 'alā anbāh al-nuḥāt,* ed. Muḥammad Abū al-Faḍl Ibrāhīm (3 vols.; Cairo, 1369–74/1950–55).

Inṣāf	ʿAbd al-Raḥmān ibn Muḥammad ibn al-Anbārī. *Al-inṣāf fī masāʾil al-khilāf*, ed. Gotthold Weil (Leyden, 1913).
Inṣāf (1961)	———, ed. Muḥammad Muḥyī al-Dīn ʿAbd al-Ḥamīd (2 vols.; Cairo, 1380/1961).
ʿIqd	Aḥmad ibn Muḥammad ibn ʿAbd Rabbihi. *Al-ʿiqd al-farīd* (7 vols.; Cairo, 1359–72/1940–53).
Irshād	Yāqūt ibn ʿAbd Allāh. *Irshād al-arīb ilā maʿrifat al-adīb*, ed. D. S. Margoliouth ("E. J. W. Gibb Memorial" Series VI [7 vols.; Leyden, 1907–27]).
Iṣābah	Aḥmad ibn ʿAbd Allāh ibn Ḥajar al-ʿAsqalānī. *Al-iṣābah fī tamyīz al-ṣaḥābah*, ed. Aloys Sprenger *et al.* (Bibliotheca Indica XX [4 vols.; Calcutta, 1856–88]).
Istīʿāb	Yūsuf ibn ʿAbd Allāh ibn ʿAbd al-Barr. *Kitāb al-istīʿāb fī maʿrifat al-aṣḥāb* (2 vols.; Ḥaidarābād, 1336/1917).
Jabbūr	Jibrāʾīl Sulaimān Jabbūr. *ʿUmar ibn Abī Rabīʿah* (2 vols.; Beirūt, 1935–39).
Jāḥiẓ, *Bayān*	ʿAmr ibn Baḥr al-Jāḥiẓ. *Kitāb al-bayān wa al-tabyīn*, ed. Ḥasan al-Sandūbī (3 vols.; Cairo, 1366/1947).
Jāḥiẓ, *Ḥayawān*	———. *Al-ḥayawān*, ed. ʿAbd al-Salām Muḥammad Hārūn (7 vols.; Cairo, 1356–64/1938–45).
Jāḥiẓ, *Maḥāsin*	———. *Kitāb al-maḥāsin* (Leiden, 1898).
Jāḥiẓ, *Tāj*	———. *Kitāb al-tāj*, ed. Aḥmad Zakī (Cairo, 1332/1914).
Jarḥ	ʿAbd al-Raḥmān ibn Abī Ḥatīm al-Rāzī. *Al-jarḥ wa al-taʿdīl* (4 vols.; Haidarābād, 1360–73/1941–53).
JNES	Journal of Near Eastern Studies (Chicago, 1942——).
Jumaḥī	Muḥammad ibn Sallām al-Jumaḥī. *Ṭabaqāt fuḥūl al-shuʿarāʾ*, ed. Maḥmūd Muḥammad Shākir (Cairo, 1952).
Jumal	ʿAbd al-Raḥmān ibn Isḥāq al-Zajjājī. *Al-jumal fī al-naḥw*, ed. Mohammed Ben Cheneb (Alger, 1927).
Khaṣāʾiṣ	ʿUthmān ibn Jinnī. *Al-khaṣāʾiṣ*, ed. Muḥammad ʿAlī al-Najjār (3 vols.; Cairo, 1952–56).
Khaṭīb	Abū Bakr Aḥmad ibn ʿAlī al-Khaṭīb al-Baghdādī. *Taʾrīkh Baghdād aw Madīnāt al-Salām* (14 vols.; Cairo, 1349/1931).
Khizānah	ʿAbd al-Qādir ibn ʿUmar al-Baghdādī. *Khizānat al-adab wa lub lubāb lisān al-ʿArab* (4 vols.; Būlāq, 1299/1881).
Kindī	Muḥammad ibn Yūsuf al-Kindī. *Kitāb al-umarāʾ wa kitāb al-quḍāt*, ed. Rhuvon Guest ("E. J. W. Gibb Memorial" Series XIX [Leyden and London, 1912]).
Lane	Edward William Lane. An Arabic-English Lexicon (London and Edinburgh, 1863–93).
Maʿārif	ʿAbd Allāh ibn Muslim ibn Qutaibah. *Kitāb al-maʿārif*, ed. Ferdinand Wüstenfeld (Göttingen, 1850).
Macartney	The Dîwân of Ghailân ibn ʿUqbah Known As Dhu 'r-Rummah, ed. Carlile Henry Hayes Macartney (Cambridge, England, 1919).
Majālis Thaʿlab	Aḥmad ibn Yaḥyā Thaʿlab. *Majālis Thaʿlab*, ed. ʿAbd al-Salām Muḥammad Hārūn (2 vols.; Cairo, 1948–49).
Majālis al-ʿulamāʾ	ʿAbd al-Raḥmān ibn Isḥāq al-Zajjājī. *Majālis al-ʿulamāʾ*, ed. ʿAbd al-Salām Muḥammad Hārūn (Kuwait, 1962).

Marātib — Abū al-Ṭayyib al-Lughawī al-Ḥalabī. *Marātib al-naḥwiyyīn*, ed. Muḥammad Abū al-Faḍl Ibrāhīm (Cairo, 1375/1955).

Marzūqī — Aḥmad ibn Muḥammad ibn al-Ḥasan al-Marzūqī. *Sharḥ dīwān al-ḥamāsah*, ed. Aḥmad Amīn and ʿAbd al-Salām Muḥammad Hārūn (4 vols.; Cairo, 1371–72/1951–53).

Maṣādir — Nāṣir al-Dīn al-Asad. *Maṣādir al-shiʿr al-jāhilī* (Cairo, 1962).

Masʿūdī — ʿAlī ibn al-Ḥusain al-Masʿūdī. *Murūj al-dhahab*, ed. C. Barbier de Meynard and Pavet de Courteille (9 vols.; Paris, 1861–1917).

Mubarrad — Muḥammad ibn Yazīd al-Mubarrad. *Al-kāmil*, ed. W. Wright (Leipzig, 1864–92).

Mufaḍḍalīyāt — Mufaḍḍal ibn Muḥammad al-Ḍabbī. *Al-mufaḍḍalīyāt*, ed. Charles James Lyall (3 vols.; Oxford, 1918–24).

Muḥāḍarāt — Ḥusain ibn Muḥammad al-Rāghib al-Iṣbahānī. *Muḥāḍarāt al-udabāʾ wa muḥāwarāt al-shuʿarāʾ wa al-bulaghāʾ* (2 vols.; Cairo, 1287/1870).

Muḥkam — Abū ʿAmr ʿUthmān ibn Saʿīd al-Dānī. *Al muḥkam fī naqṭ al-maṣāḥif*, ed. ʿIzzat Ḥasan (Damascus, 1379/1960).

Muʿjam al-shuʿarāʾ — Muḥammad ibn ʿImrān al-Marzubānī. *Muʿjam al-shuʿarāʾ*, ed. F. Krenkow (Cairo, 1354/1935).

Muslim — Muslim ibn al-Ḥajjāj ibn Muslim. *Ṣaḥīḥ Muslim bi sharḥ al-Nawawī* (18 vols.; Cairo, 1347–49/1929–30).

Muṭīʿ Babbīlī — *Dīwān Dhī al-Rummah*, ed. Muṭīʿ Babbīlī (2d ed.; Damascus, 1384/1964).

Muwashshaḥ — Muḥammad ibn ʿImrān al-Marzubānī. *Al-muwashshaḥ fī maʾākhidh al-ʿulamāʾ ʿalā al-shuʿarāʾ* (Cairo, 1343/1924).

Muzhir — Jalāl al-Dīn al-Suyūṭī. *Al-muzhir fī ʿulūm al-lughah wa anwāʿihā* (2 vols.; Cairo, 1954).

Namādhij — Cairo. Maʿhad al-makhṭūṭāt al-ʿarabīyah. *Al-kitāb al-ʿarabī al-makhṭūṭ ilā al-qarn al-ʿāshir al-hijrī*. I. *Al-namādhij*, ed. Ṣalāḥ al-Dīn al-Munajjid (Cairo, 1960).

Nuwairī — Aḥmad ibn ʿAbd al-Wahhāb al-Nuwairī. *Nihāyat al-arab fī funūn al-adab* (18 vols.; Cairo, 1342–74/1923–55).

Nuzhah — ʿAbd al-Raḥmān ibn Muḥammad ibn al-Anbārī. *Nuzhat al-alibbāʾ fī ṭabaqāt al-udabāʾ*, ed. Ibrāhīm al-Sāmarrāʾī (Baghdād, 1959).

OIP — Chicago. University. The Oriental Institute. Oriental Institute Publications (Chicago, 1924——).

OIP L — Nabia Abbott. The Rise of the North Arabic Script and Its Ḳurʾānic Development, with a Full Description of the Ḳurʾān Manuscripts in the Oriental Institute (1939).

OIP LXXV — ———. Studies in Arabic Literary Papyri. I. Historical Texts (1957). Cited throughout as "Vol. I."

OIP LXXVI — ———. Studies in Arabic Literary Papyri. II. Qurʾānic Commentary and Tradition (1967). Cited throughout as "Vol. II."

PERF — Vienna. Nationalbibliothek. Papyrus Erzherzog Rainer. Führer durch die Ausstellung (Wien, 1894).

Périer — Jean Périer. Vie d'al-Ḥadjdjâdj ibn Yousof (41–95 de l'Hégire = 661–714 de J.-C.) d'après les sources arabes (Paris, 1904).

Qudāmah — Qudāmah ibn Ja'far al-Kātib al-Baghdādī. *Kitāb naqd al-shi'r*, ed. S. A. Bonebakker (Leyden, 1956).

Qudāmah (1963) — ———. *Naqd al-shi'r*, ed. Kamāl Muṣṭafā (Baghdād, 1963).

Qurashī — Abū Zaid Muḥammad ibn Abī al-Khaṭṭāb al-Qurashī. *Kitāb jamharat ash'ār al-'Arab* (Cairo, 1308/1890).

Raba'ī — 'Abd Allāh ibn Zabr al-Raba'ī. *Al-muntaqā min akhbār al-Aṣma'ī*, ed. 'Izz al-Dīn al-Tanūkhī (Publications de l'Académie arabe de Damas, No. 7 [Damascus, 1355/1936]).

Rauḍ al-akhyār — Muḥammad ibn Qāsim ibn Ya'qūb. *Rauḍ al-akhyār al-muntakhab min rabī' al-abrār* (Cairo, 1280/1863).

Ṣāliḥānī, *Naqā'iḍ Jarīr wa al-Akhṭal* — *Naqā'iḍ Jarīr wa al-Akhṭal*, published for the first time from the Constantinople manuscript with commentary by Anṭūn Ṣāliḥānī (Beirūt, 1922).

Ṣāliḥānī, *Shi'r al-Akhṭal* — *Shi'r al-Akhṭal*, published for the first time from the St. Petersburg manuscript with commentary by Anṭūn Ṣāliḥanī (Beirūt, 1892–1925).

Ṣāliḥānī, *Shi'r al-Akhṭal* (1905) — *Shi'r al-Akhṭal*, ed. Anṭūn Ṣāliḥānī. Printed by lithography from manuscript found in Baghdād (Beirūt, 1905).

Ṣāliḥānī, *Takmilah* — *Al-takmilah li shi'r al-Akhṭal* from the Tehran manuscript with commentary by Anṭūn Ṣāliḥānī (Beirūt, 1938).

Sharḥ dīwān Jarīr — Muḥammad Ismā'īl 'Abd Allāh al-Ṣāwī. *Sharḥ dīwān Jarīr* (Beirūt, n. d.).

Shi'r — 'Abd Allāh ibn Muslim ibn Qutaibah. *Kitāb al-shi'r wa al-shu'arā'*, ed. Michael Jan de Goeje (Lugduni-Batavorum, 1902).

Sībawaih — 'Amr ibn 'Uthmān Sībawaih. *Al-kitāb*, ed. Hartwig Derenbourg (2 vols.; Paris, 1881–89).

Sīrāfī — Ḥasan ibn 'Abd Allāh al-Sīrāfī. *Akhbār al-naḥwiyyīn al-Baṣriyyīn*, ed. F. Krenkow (Bibliotheca Arabica IX [Paris, 1936]).

Sīrah — 'Abd al-Malik ibn Hishām (ed.). The *Sīrat rasūl Allāh* of Ibn Isḥāq, ed. Ferdinand Wüstenfeld (2 vols.; Göttingen, 1858–60) and translation by A. Guillaume (London, 1955).

Ṣūlī, *Adab al-kuttāb* — Muḥammad ibn Yaḥyā al-Ṣūlī. *Adab al-kuttāb*, ed. Maḥmūd Shukrī al-Ālūsī (Cairo, 1341/1922).

Ṭabarī — Muḥammad ibn Jarīr al-Ṭabarī. *Ta'rīkh al-rusul wa al-mulūk*, ed. M. J. de Goeje (15 vols.; Lugduni Batavorum, 1879–1901).

Tha'ālibī, *Ījāz* — 'Abd al-Malik ibn Muḥammad al-Tha'ālibī. *Al-ījāz wa al-i'jāz* in *Khams rasā'il* (Constantinople, 1301/1883).

Tha'ālibī, *Laṭā'if* — ———. *Laṭā'if al-ma'ārif*, ed. Ibrāhīm al-Abyārī and Ḥasan Kāmil al-Ṣairafī (Cairo, 1379/1960).

Tha'ālibī, *Thimār* — ———. *Thimār al-qulūb fī al-muḍāf wa al-mansūb* (Cairo, 1326/1908).

'Umdah — Abū 'Alī al-Ḥasan ibn Rashīq. *Al-'umdah fī ṣinā'at al-shi'r wa naqdihu ta'alīf Abī 'Alī al-Ḥasan ibn Rashīq al-Qairawānī* (2 vols.; Cairo, 1344/1925).

'Uyūn — 'Abd Allāh ibn Muslim ibn Qutaibah. *Kitāb 'uyūn al-akhbār* (4 vols.; Cairo, 1343–49/1925–30).

Waq'at Ṣiffīn — Naṣr ibn Muzāḥim. *Waq'at Ṣiffīn*, ed. 'Abd al-Salām Muḥammad Hārūn (Cairo, 1365/1946).

Wright, *Facsimiles* — Palaeographical Society, London. Facsimiles of Manuscripts and Inscriptions (Oriental Series), ed. William Wright (London, 1875–83).

Wright, *Grammar*	Carl Paul Caspari. A Grammar of the Arabic Language, trans. . . . and ed. with numerous additions and corrections by William Wright . . . 3d ed. . . . (2 vols.; Cambridge, England, 1896–98).
Yaʿqūbī	Aḥmad ibn Abī Yaʿqūb ibn Wāḍiḥ al-Yaʿqūbī. *Taʾrīkh,* ed. M. Th. Houtsma (2 vols.; Lugduni Batavorum, 1883).
Yāqūt	Yāqūt ibn ʿAbd Allāh. *Muʿjam al-buldān,* ed. Ferdinand Wüstenfeld (6 vols.; Leipzig, 1866–73; reprinted in 1924).
Yazīdī	Muḥammad ibn al-ʿAbbās al-Yazīdī. *Kitāb al-amālī* (Ḥaidarābād, 1368/1948).
Zambaur	E. de Zambaur. Manuel de généalogie et de chronologie pour l'histoire de l'Islam (Hanovre, 1927; reprinted in 1955).
ZDMG	Deutsche morgenländische Gesellschaft. Zeitschrift (Leipzig, 1847–1943; Wiesbaden, 1950——).
Zubaidī	Abū Bakr Muḥammad ibn al-Ḥasan al-Zubaidī. *Ṭabaqāt al-naḥwiyyīn wa al-lughawiyyīn,* ed. Muḥammad Abū al-Faḍl Ibrāhīm (Cairo, 1373/1954).

PART I

GRAMMAR

ORTHOGRAPHY AND SCRIPTS

REFERENCES in the sources to Muḥammad's concern with his scribes' careful and clear writing are not lacking, though Muslims prefer to overlook them or to explain them away because of their implication for the dogma of Muḥammad's illiteracy. This dogma is well illustrated by the fifth/tenth-century controversy that arose in respect to a tradition reported by Ibn Ḥanbal, Bukhārī, and Dārimī that Muḥammad "wrote with his own hand" some of the alterations in the preamble of the Treaty of Ḥudaibīyah.[1] Zaid ibn Thābit reported that Muḥammad instructed him in the correct writing of the letter *sīn* in the *basmalah* formula.[2] The caliph Mu'āwiyah instructed his secretary 'Ubaid ibn Abī Aws to make full use of diacritical points because as Muḥammad's secretary Mu'āwiyah had been instructed by Muḥammad to do so.[3] This statement reinforces my conclusions in favor of the pre-Islāmic use of diacritical points[4] and the belief that Muḥammad himself could at least read.[5]

Concern for correct speech and for good penmanship in reference to both the Qur'ān and administrative functions went hand in hand and increased as the great conquests of the first century of Islām led to an increasing number of non-Arab converts and called for more and more scribal work in the state bureaus of the capital and the provinces. 'Umar I wrote 'Abd Allāh ibn Mas'ūd in Kūfah to be sure that his public recitation of the Qur'ān was in the clear Arabic speech of the Quraish, in which the Qur'ān was revealed, and not in the dialect of the Banū Hudhail.[6] Both 'Umar and 'Abd Allāh ibn Mas'ūd preferred to have the Qur'ān dictated by young men of the Quraish and the Thaqaf, and Thaqafites were preferred by 'Uthmān as Qur'ānic copyists.[7] These preferences are reflected in the membership of the editorial committee that 'Uthmān appointed for the preparation of this standard edition of the Qur'ān.[8] Again, we find 'Umar I, who flogged his own son for incorrect speech,[9] ordering his governor of 'Irāq Abū Mūsā al-Ash'arī to flog a secretary who had committed a grammatical error in a letter and further instructing Abū Mūsā to have Abū al-Aswad al-Du'alī teach the Baṣrans grammatical reading of the Qur'ān (*i'rāb*).[10]

[1] Ibn Ḥanbal, *Al-musnad* (Cairo, 1313/1895) IV 291; Bukhārī III 133, 167; Dārimī, *Sunan* (Damascus, 1349/1930) II 237. For traditions that either modify or bypass the crucial phrase see *Concordance* III 338 صالح, V 413 قاضى and 523 قال المشركون لا نكتب. Muslim XII 135–39 covers the treaty but omits reference to Muḥammad's writing with his own hand; Nawawī's accompanying commentary covers typical arguments associated with the controversy that centered around the Spanish scholar Abū al-Walīd al-Bājī (403–74/1012–81) and involved scholars in the east as well (see e.g. Ibn 'Asākir V 248 f.; Dhahabī III 352; Maqqarī, *The History of the Mohammedan Dynasties in Spain . . .*, trans. Pascual de Gayangos [Oriental Translation Fund of Great Britain and Ireland, "Publications" LIII] I [London, 1840] 504 f.). Ibn Sa'd II 1, pp. 73 f., states emphatically that Muḥammad himself wrote in an additional treaty clause: كتب رسول الله صلعم فى اسفل الكتاب ولنا عليكم مثل الذى لكم علينا . *Sīrah* I 747 makes no reference to Muḥammad's writing on this occasion, but *Sīrah* I 235 implies that he wrote. Charles C. Torrey was convinced that Muḥammad was able to read and write Arabic and even argued that possibly he could read Hebrew also (see our Vol. II 257, n. 9).

[2] Ibn 'Asākir V 28 f.; for Zaid ibn Thābit see our Vol. II 19–21, 249–51, 256–61.

[3] Suyūṭī, *Tadrīb al-rāwī fī sharḥ Taqrīb al-Nawawī* (Cairo, 1307/1889) p. 152 (citing Ibn 'Asākir):
قال عبيد بن ابي اوس كتبت بين يدى معاوية كتابا فقال لى يا عبيد ارقش كتابك فاني كتبت بين يدى رسول الله صلعم فقال لى يا معاويه ارقش كتابك قلت وما رقشه يا امير المومنين قال اعطى كل حرفماينوبه من النقط.

[4] See *OIP* L 38, which has been overlooked by the able scholar Nāṣir al-Dīn al-Asad in a recent work where he assumes that he is the first to suggest the probable use of diacritical points in pre-Islāmic times (*Maṣādir*, p. 41). The key verb *raqash* in reference to writing is found in Abū al-Qāsim 'Abd Allāh al-Baghdādī (fl. 255/869), *Kitāb al-kuttāb*, ed. Dominique Sourdel, *Bulletin d'études orientales* XIV (1954) 134, along with a long list of synonyms said to mean حسّنه وزيّنه. Cf. Nabia Abbott, "Arabic paleography," *Ars Islamica* VIII (1941) 88 f., 101. The verb *raqash* is not found in the *Concordance*.

[5] See *OIP* L 46.

[6] Khaṭīb III 406.

[7] Cf. Ibn Fāris, *Ṣāḥibī*, p. 57.

[8] See e.g. *OIP* L 48 f. and Bukhārī II 383.

[9] *Khaṣā'iṣ* II 8; *Irshād* I 20 f.

[10] *Futūḥ al-buldān*, p. 346. Cf. Jāḥiẓ, *Bayān* II 220; Ṣūlī, *Adab al-kuttāb*, p. 129; *Inbāh* I 16.

The same concern eventually induced Abū al-Aswad al-Du'alī, encouraged or so ordered by Ziyād ibn Abīhi (Ziyād ibn Abī Sufyān), to use the dot or point to indicate by its position the three basic vowels in the written Qur'ān.[11] Both men showed general concern for correct Arabic, spoken and written, and Ziyād, some say, was motivated by both personal and official reasons since his sons spoke incorrectly and he demanded accuracy from his secretaries.[12]

Added motivation for mastery of the language came with the establishment of Arabic as the language of the state bureaus in the time of ʿAbd al-Malik (65–86/685–705) and his governor of ʿIrāq, the former schoolteacher Ḥajjāj ibn Yūsuf al-Thaqafī. Many are the anecdotes that throw light on the deep concern of both of these rulers for grammatically correct spoken and written Arabic. ʿAbd al-Malik regretted his own early negligence of Prince Walīd's education in this respect in that he was reluctant to send the youth to the desert to acquire correct speech from the eloquent among the Bedouins.[13] ʿAbd al-Malik developed a sharp ear for his heir's linguistic errors and reminded Walīd that he who would rule the Arabs must first have command of their speech.[14] Walīd therefore retired for six months with a number of grammar teachers in a belated effort to learn grammar but failed to master the subject. ʿAbd al-Malik himself credited his fast-graying hair to the tensions of his frequent public speeches and the fear of uttering a solecism,[15] for not even he nor Ḥajjāj was free from such errors. Perhaps Walīd's difficulty with grammar gave him full appreciation of the linguistic competence demanded of Qur'ānic-readers, for it was he who as caliph first put professional readers on the state payroll.[16] At least one scholar, who was anxious to avoid service under Ḥajjāj but dared not refuse an appointment, deliberately spoke incorrectly in Ḥajjāj's hearing in the hope that Ḥajjāj would cancel his appointment, and indeed he did.[17] ʿUmar II took ʿUmar I for his model and, like the latter, was extremely severe with members of his family and others who were guilty of incorrect Arabic.[18]

Numerous anecdotes involving the linguistic and grammatical errors of rulers and scholars have found their way into historical and biographical works[19] as well as into the *adab*[20] and linguistic literature.[21] The subject of incorrect Arabic itself gave rise to long series of interrelated works, the *laḥn* and *taṣḥīf* categories, covering errors in spoken and written Arabic made by the various professional groups, especially secretaries, linguists, grammarians, littérateurs, and scholars in general, as well as errors made by the general public (*laḥn al-ʿāmmah*). This subject has engaged the attention of Arabists intermittently for close to a century.[22] Here we find Kisā'ī (d. 189/805) heading the list, to be followed in the course of the third/ninth century by Ibn al-Sikkīt, Abū ʿUthmān Bakr ibn Muḥammad al-Māzinī, Abū Ḥātim al-Sijistānī, Dīnawarī, and Thaʿlab (d. 291/904) among others.

The same period saw a number of works written specifically for the education and guidance of state secretaries and for the younger members of the learned professions, religious and secular. This category

[11] See *OIP* L 39, with references cited in nn. 156–57. Several conflicting accounts credit now Abū al-Aswad and now Ziyād with the initiative in this matter (see e.g. *Marātib*, pp. 8–11; Sīrāfī, pp. 15 f., 19; Zubaidī, p. 14; *Aghānī* XI 105 f.; *Irshād* VII 200 f.; *Inbāh* I 15 f.).

[12] *Marātib*, pp. 8 f.; Ibn ʿAsākir V 417.

[13] E.g. Jāḥiẓ, *Bayān* II 210; ʿ*Iqd* IV 423.

[14] Ibn al-Ṭiqṭaqā, *Al-fakhrī*, ed. Hartwig Derenbourg (Paris, 1895), p. 173: لا يلي العرب الا من احسن كلامهم (cf. Jāḥiẓ, *Bayān* II 210 f.).

[15] Jāḥiẓ, *Bayān* I 149.

[16] Thaʿālibī, *Laṭā'if*, p. 18; see also our Vol. II 228.

[17] *Irshād* I 25.

[18] Ibn ʿAsākir I 25.

[19] E.g. *Irshād* I 8–27.

[20] E.g. Jāḥiẓ, *Bayān* II 159 f., 213–35; Ibn Qutaibah, *Adab al-kātib*, ed. Max Grünert (Leiden, 1900) pp. 29–34.

[21] E.g. *Fāḍil*, pp. 4 f.; *Khaṣā'iṣ* III 273–309; *Muzhir* II 396 f.

[22] See e.g. George Krotkoff, "The ʿ*laḥn al-ʿawām*' of Abū Bakr az-Zubaidī," *Bulletin of the College of Arts and Sciences in Baghdad* II (Baghdād, 1957) 1–15, which brings the current list of such works to 49, more than half of which have survived and some of which have been published.

is the familiar *adab al-kātib* or *adāb al-kuttāb*,[23] which, apart from covering the subject pertaining to each group, stressed for all groups the basic qualifications for the mastery of Arabic, namely correct use of orthography and good penmanship.

As state and private secretaries gained professional prestige and literary stature, they improved their penmanship and cultivated literary styles. This development is well illustrated by the career of Sālim ibn ʿAbd Allāh, the scholarly secretary of the caliph Hishām (105–25/724–43). A client of many parts, Sālim was known for his eloquence[24] as well as for his fine and accurate hand. He was also the teacher and son-in-law[25] of the better known Umayyad secretary ʿAbd al-Ḥamīd ibn Yaḥyā (d. 132/750), famed for his literary style and for his delineation of the power of the pen.[26] Others turned their attention to the art of penmanship itself and presently developed a series of "pens" or scripts for secular use as distinct from the earlier Qurʾānic scripts. The earliest of the professional script-men of ʿAbbāsid times is known simply as Quṭbah (d. 154/771). His significant contribution to calligraphic chancellery scripts as well as that of several of his successors has been detailed elsewhere by this writer.[27]

In the meantime Qurʾānic-readers and scholars as forerunners of professional grammarians devoted much attention to Qurʾānic orthography. We have no independent contemporary records as to the progress of linguistics and grammar in the Umayyad period. Dānī (371–444/981–1053), our fullest and best-informed author on the subject, was fully aware of the lack of adequate records for this early period.[28] The sources now available yield little more than the names of Qurʾānic-readers, copyists, and calligraphers. They present us with contradictions and give rise to questions that still remain to be answered and, all in all, leave much to be desired. We know little indeed of Abū al-Aswad al-Duʾalī as the first grammarian[29] and of his handful of leading pupils and of their pupils except that they too acquired some reputation as grammarians of Baṣrah.[30] Some of them paid special attention to the orthography of the Qurʾān, for we read that Naṣr ibn ʿĀṣim al-Laithī (d. 89/708) was the first to "point" vowels in the Qurʾān and mark off the verses in fives and tens.[31] But not until the generation of Ibn Abī Isḥāq (d. 117/735 or 127/744 or 745 at age 88) and Yaḥyā ibn Yaʿmar (d. 129/746 or 747) do bits of significant information become available. Yaḥyā is said to have been among the first to vowel the Qurʾān,[32] and Muḥammad ibn Sīrīn (d. 110/728) is reported as possessing a Qurʾān pointed by Yaḥyā himself.[33] Yet the Baṣrans did not consider Yaḥyā a leading grammarian.[34] That distinction was readily bestowed on Ibn Abī Isḥāq, who is credited with a basic role in the evolution of Qurʾānic orthography.[35] This could mean that Ibn Abī

[23] For a good sampling of this type of literature and for its usefulness down to our times see Walter Björkman, *Beiträge zur Geschichte der Staatskanzlei im islamischen Ägypten* (Hamburg, 1928). See also pp. 9 f. below.

[24] *Fihrist*, pp. 117, 125, 126, 353, credits him with *rasāʾil* of some 100 pages and lists him as a translator of Aristotle's epistles to Plato.

[25] *Fihrist*, p. 117; Ibn ʿAsākir VI 55.

[26] See e.g. *Fihrist*, p. 10; Ṣūlī, *Adab al-kuttāb*, p. 82; Abū Hilāl al-Ḥasan ibn ʿAbd Allāh al-ʿAskarī, *Kitāb al-ṣināʿatain al-kitābah wa al-shiʿr*, ed. ʿAlī Muḥammad al-Bajāwī (Cairo, 1371/1952) p. 138; Ibn ʿAbdūs al-Jahshiyārī, *Kitāb al-wuzarāʾ wa al-kuttāb*, ed. Hans von Mžik (Leipzig, 1926) p. 72; Abū Ḥayyān al-Tawḥīdī, *Thalāth rasāʾil*, ed. Ibrāhīm al-Kīlānī (Damascus, 1951) p. 39. See also Abū Ḥayyān al-Tawḥīdī's epistle on penmanship as edited and translated by Franz Rosenthal in *Ars Islamica* XIII–XIV (1948) 3–30; Ibn Khallikān I 387 (= trans. II 174).

[27] See *OIP* L 31–33; *Ars Islamica* VIII 88–90.

[28] *Muḥkam*, Intro. pp. 21 and 23 and text p. 47.

[29] See e.g. *Marātib*, pp. 5–11; Sīrāfī, pp. 13–20; Zubaidī, pp. 13–19; *Inbāh* I 13–16 and references there cited. See also John A. Haywood, *Arabic Lexicography* (Leiden, 1960) pp. 11–19.

[30] *Marātib*, pp. 11 f.; Sīrāfī, pp. 20–25; Zubaidī, pp. 19–25.

[31] *Muḥkam*, pp. 6 f.; *Inbāh* III 343 and references there cited; *Bughyah*, p. 403, credits him with a "book on Arabic."

[32] *Muḥkam*, pp. 5 f.; *OIP* L 38.

[33] Zubaidī, p. 23. Muḥammad ibn Sīrīn's brother possessed a copy of the *ḥadīth* of Abū Hurairah (cf. our Vol. II 17).

[34] *Marātib*, p. 25.

[35] *Muḥkam*, p. 7:

قال ابو حاتم السجستاني اصل النقط لعبد الله بن ابي اسحاق الحضرمي معلم ابي عمرو بن العلاء اخذه الناس عنه . . . والنقط لاهل البصرة اخذه الناس كلهم عنهم حتى اهل المدينة وكانوا ينقطون على غير هذا النقط فتركوه ونقطوا نقط اهل البصرة.

Isḥāq extended the point-voweling system, along perhaps with the use of colors, for other orthographic signs such as the *hamzah* and *shaddah*. Dānī reports that he himself acquired an old copy of the Qur'ān, dated Rajab 110/October 728 and written by Mughīrah ibn Mīnā, which had red dots for the *hamzah*, *shaddah*, and *tanwīn* "in accordance with the ancient practice of the east."[36] Whatever basic contribution was made by Ibn Abī Isḥāq, the point-orthography system continued to evolve and to develop regional variations.[37] The controversy as to the use of anything but the bare consonants in Qur'ānic codices shifted to consideration of the essential minimum of orthographic devices needed to insure ready and accurate reading of the sacred text.[38] With the general acceptance of the point-vowels, the "pointer" (*nāqiṭ*), whose exacting duty was to supply the consonantal text with the essential orthography, won early recognition[39] and achieved professional status relative to a Qur'ānic-reader comparable in a way with that of a *rāwī* to a poet.

It is readily to be seen that the development of the first steps of elementary grammar grew out of the needs of Qur'ānic-readers, secretaries, and teachers during the Umayyad period. The case of Muʿādh al-Harrā' is instructive. He started as a schoolteacher and soon clashed over methods of teaching grammar with Abū Muslim (d. 109/727), tutor to the sons of ʿAbd al-Malik. Their clash resulted eventually in the exchange of satirical verses between them.[40] Muʿādh is credited with being among the first to introduce accidence (*taṣrīf*), presumably of both the noun and the verb if we are to judge by the few examples of his teaching reported in later sources.[41] He is furthermore credited with having written books on grammar in the Umayyad period,[42] and presumably he wrote such books thereafter during his exceptionally long life.[43] He was the friend and advisor of the "poet of the Shīʿah," Kumait ibn Zaid (60–126/679–743), who at times failed to heed his advice only to regret it. Muʿādh, himself a productive poet of a sort, composed verses on these episodes, but his poetry was characterized later as "similar to the poetry of grammarians."[44] Whatever Muʿādh's accomplishments were, he was considered no more than a minor grammarian and was remembered as much, if not more, for having been the teacher of his paternal nephew Ru'āsī (d. 187/803) and of Kisā'ī (d. 189/805) and Yaḥyā ibn Ziyād al-Farrā' (d. 207/822), all three of whom were considered the founders of the Kūfan school of grammar.[45] Muʿādh's contemporary Qāsim ibn Maʿn al-Masʿūdī (d. 175/791), all-round scholar and Ḥanīfite but reluctant judge of Kūfah, was referred to as "the Shaʿbī of his time" because of his encyclopedic knowledge, which included poetry, language, and grammar, and he was also credited with grammatical works and a system of grammar that was rejected though Yaḥyā ibn Ziyād al-Farrā', Laith ibn Naṣr, and Ibn al-Aʿrābī were among his pupils.[46]

In the meantime some of Muʿādh's Baṣran contemporaries of the Umayyad period and some of his younger Kūfan contemporaries of early ʿAbbāsid times did produce among them all sorts of primarily

[36] *Ibid.* p. 87.

[37] *Ibid.* pp. 18–24.

[38] *Ibid.* pp. 10–13.

[39] See *ibid.* p. 9 for Nāfiʿ ibn Abī Nuʿaim (d. 169 A.H.) and his *nāqiṭ*.

[40] Zubaidī, pp. 136 f.; *Inbāh* III 293; *Bughyah*, p. 393.

[41] Suyūṭī, *Kitāb al-iqtirāḥ fī ʿilm uṣūl al-naḥw* (Ḥaidarābād, 1359/1940) p. 84; Ṭāshkuprīzādah, *Kitāb miftāḥ al-saʿādah* I (Ḥaidarābād, 1328/1910) 112–14, 125 f.

[42] E.g. *Fihrist*, p. 65; *Inbāh* III 290. Muʿādh's Medinan contemporary ʿAlqamah ibn Abī ʿAlqamah, traditionist and schoolteacher who died in the reign of Manṣūr (136–58/754–75), taught Arabic philology, prosody, and grammar; see Ibn Rustah, p. 216: كان له مكتب يعلم فيه العربيّه والعروض والنحو.

[43] His proverbial longevity gave rise to verses of younger rival poets in the reign of Hārūn al-Rashīd (see e.g. Jāḥiẓ, *Ḥayawān* III 423 f. and VI 327; *ʿUyūn* IV 59 f.; Masʿūdī II 130; *Inbāh* III 290 f.; Ibn Khallikān II 130 f. [= trans. III 372 f.]).

[44] E.g. *Fihrist*, p. 65; *Inbāh* III 288 f., 293–95.

[45] E.g. *Inbāh* II 270, III 288 and 290, and references cited.

[46] *Maʿārif*, p. 109; *Fihrist*, p. 69; Zubaidī, pp. 146 f., 219 f.; Khaṭīb X 245; *Inbāh* III 31 f.; *Irshād* VI 199–202; *Bughyah*, p. 381: صنف كتب في النحو وله فيه مذهب متروك.

lexical and grammatical works. Some of these works reflected the emergence and growth of these subjects as individual professional disciplines, while others served the practical needs of pupils, secretaries, copyists, and booksellers. So far as Qur'ānic orthography was concerned, Ibn Abī Isḥāq's contribution remained basic despite some additions and local variations reflected in a series of orthographic works in the titles of which *naqṭ* and *shakl* (or their derivatives) alone or in combination are the key words. Dānī, who himself wrote several such works,[47] mentions some of his predecessors, beginning with Khalīl ibn Aḥmad.[48] None of these early sources have come down to us, and of the extant sources not one gives a complete and integrated account of the system that was evolved by Khalīl, though Dānī provides us with many of its specific details.[49] Khalīl no doubt found the Qur'ānic orthography that was in use somewhat confusing and certainly too cumbersome for linguistic and literary purposes, particularly for grammar and poetry. We do indeed find his system specifically associated with poetry manuscripts as distinguished from the system used for the Qur'ān.[50] He probably worked out the basics of the new system of vowels in conjunction with his treatise on meters (*'arūḍ*), with which his name is more widely associated. Furthermore, the use of dots or points (*nuqaṭ*) as orthographic symbols even when they were differentiated by number, position, and color was neither adequate in scope nor suggestive phonetically or visually of their intended purpose. Khalīl's idea of using small letters for the three basic vowels and for some abbreviations as well as for distinguishing unpointed consonants was certainly an improvement in these respects. The *fatḥah*, *ḍammah*, and *kasrah* representing *alif*, *wāw*, and *yā'* were more explicit and meaningful as was also the use, for example, of a small *shīn* and a small *khā'* for *shadīd* and *khafīf* respectively.[51] It should be noted that Khalīl's Medinan contemporaries used the final *dāl* instead of the initial letter *shīn* for *shadīd*.[52]

Just when Khalīl introduced the new orthography is difficult to determine. I suspect it was quite early in his career and in that of his favorite pupil, Sībawaih, who is associated with him in its use.[53] Considering Khalīl's major role in the evolution of Sībawaih's *Kitāb* and the very nature of the work itself as to both its prime subject of grammar and its evidential poetry, it is probable that at first the use of the new symbols for the *Kitāb* and the use of some symbols of Qur'ānic orthography overlapped.[54] Second-century papyri give no evidence of and literary sources make no specific reference to the use in secular works of any vowel orthography prior to the time of the youthful Khalīl. Yet, a restrained use of Qur'ānic orthography probably served at first the needs of teachers, poets, traditionists, and particularly grammarians, whose specialty was prized by these others. The Umayyad poet Farazdaq (d. 110/728) finally expressed his own need and appreciation of the contribution of the linguist and grammarian Abū 'Amr ibn al-'Alā' (d. 154/771) in an eloquent verse[55] that is illustrative of a poet's need of the language specialist. Khalīl himself stressed his own decisive influence on the professional success or failure of the poets of his day in

[47] See *Muḥkam*, Intro. p. 25.

[48] *Ibid.* pp. 9, 47. See *ibid.* Intro. pp. 32 f. for a list of 17 authors of such works, beginning with Abū al-Aswad al-Du'alī and ending with 'Alī ibn 'Īsā al-Rummānī (d. 384/994); cf. *Fihrist*, p. 35.

[49] See *Muḥkam*, pp. 6, 9, 19 f., 22, 35 f., 42, 49, and, for applications of the system, pp. 209–60 *passim*; cf. *OIP* L 39 and references there cited.

[50] *Muḥkam*, Intro. p. 27 and text pp. 7 and 22: شكل الشعر هو الشكل الذى في الكتب الذى اخترعه الخليل.

[51] Whether or not Khalīl used an inclined stroke instead of a vertical one for the *fatḥah* is hard to say. Scripts with varying degrees of slant in the *alif* were and still are common. The *kasrah* is believed to be either the initial stroke of the letter *yā'* written in either of its two forms, the regular and the reversed *yā'* ى and ے respectively.

[52] In time the *khā'* lost its head and became a horizontal stroke; see *Muḥkam*, pp. 42, 49 f., 51 f., and, for further details of the early Medinan and Baṣran practices, pp. 49–53.

[53] E.g. *ibid.* pp. 49 f.

[54] Indirect evidence of such overlapping is seen even in printed editions of the *Kitāb* (see e.g. Sībawaih II 312 in connection with *ishmām* and see also Wright, *Grammar* I 71, 89).

[55] *Ma'ārif*, p. 268 (= Ibn Qutaibah, *Al-ma'ārif*, ed. Tharwat 'Ukāshah [1960] p. 540); *Marātib*, p. 15:

مازلت افتح ابوابا واغلقها   حتى اتيت ابو عمربن عمار

strong and colorful terms.[56] Equally well attested is the professional traditionist's acknowledged need of grammar. Ayyūb al-Sikhtiyānī (68–131/687–748), teacher of Khalīl, urged his followers to learn grammar.[57] Shuʿaib ibn Abī Ḥamzah (d. 162/779), court secretary to the caliph Hishām, for whom he wrote a large collection of *ḥadīth* from Zuhrī's dictation, was known for his fine and accurate penmanship.[58] Shuʿaib's manuscripts were later shown by his son to Ibn Ḥanbal, who praised them for their "beauty, accuracy, voweling," etc.[59] The leading Baṣran traditionist, Ḥammād ibn Salamah ibn Dīnār (d. 167/784),[60] who studied grammar early,[61] was a pupil of the Qur'ānic-reader ʿĀṣim al-Qārī (d. 127/744)[62] and of ʿĪsā ibn ʿUmar al-Thaqafī (d. 149/766) and Khalīl himself.[63] He won recognition as a grammarian in a class with Abū ʿAmr ibn al-ʿAlā'.[64]

Though sought out primarily as an expert in *ḥadith*, Ḥammād demanded correct speech from his pupils and corrected their grammatical errors as he is said to have done with the young Sībawaih, who then left Ḥammād to study grammar with Khalīl even as Ḥammād himself had done before him.[65] Ḥammād, like his father,[66] committed his materials to writing. The sources have not yet yielded a reference to the use of either system of orthography by Ḥammād, though they give evidence of the use of some orthographic symbols by his fellow Baṣran traditionist Abū ʿAwānah al-Waḍḍāḥ ibn Khālid (d. 170/786 or 176/792), who could read but not write and who therefore sought help with his manuscripts from one who paid special attention to the diacritical points and vowels so that he could read them correctly.[67] Ḥammād and Abū ʿAwānah had several pupils in common, at least three of whom became associated specifically with a comparatively liberal use of orthography in contrast to pupils who used vowel signs sparingly. The three pupils, namely ʿAffān ibn Muslim (134–220/752–835),[68] Ḥabbān ibn ʿĀmir,[69] and Bahz ibn Asad,[70] were closely associated with Ibn Ḥanbal as teachers and colleagues. It is from Ibn Ḥanbal that we learn of their use of orthography, while others simply mention their accurate manuscripts in which special attention was paid to names.[71] Ibn Ḥanbal, on the other hand, commented that no one escapes manuscript errors (*taṣḥīf*) and added that Yaḥyā ibn Saʿīd al-Qattān (120–98/738–813), a fellow pupil of the three mentioned above, used only the *tashdīd* while ʿAffān, Ḥabbān, and Bahz were given to the fuller use of orthography.[72] Inasmuch as the Qur'ānic point orthography was seldom used for non-Qur'ānic purposes,[73] not even when

[56] E.g. *Aghānī* XVII 16: انتم معشر الشعراء تبع لى وانا سكان السفينة اذا قرظتكم و رضيت قولكم نفقتم والا كسدتم (said to Ibn Munadhir [d. 199/815]). About a century later ʿUmārah ibn ʿAqīl ibn Bilāl, a great-grandson of Jarīr and a natural-born and ranking poet in his own right (see p. 147 below), expressed in verse the sentiment that were it not for the fear of Allāh he would curse the tomb of Khalīl because he introduced distressing problems in prosody:

الق مسائل في العروض تَغُمّنا   من فاعل مستفعل وفعول

(*Marātib*, p. 39).

[57] Jāḥiẓ, *Bayān* II 233: تعلموا النحو فانه جمال الوضيع وتركه هجنة الشريف. For Ayyūb as a traditionist see our Vol. II.

[58] Dhahabī I 205; Ibn ʿAsākir VI 321.

[59] *Jarḥ* II 1, p. 345: فاذا بها من الحسن والصحة والشكل ونحو هذا. For Shuʿaib see our Vol. II 177 f.

[60] For his activities as a traditionist see our Vol. II.

[61] *Irshād* IV 135; *Inbāh* II 105.

[62] *Marātib*, p. 24; Ibn al-Jazarī I 259.

[63] See *Marātib*, p. 66, for both teachers.

[64] E.g. *Maʿārif*, p. 252; Sīrāfī, pp. 42 f.; *Nuzhah*, pp. 25 f.; *Inbāh* I 329 f.

[65] *Maʿārif*, p. 252; *Marātib*, p. 66; Sīrāfī, pp. 43 f.; Zubaidī, p. 66; *Irshād* IV 135; *Inbāh* I 330.

[66] See e.g. Ibn ʿAsākir VI 216–28.

[67] *Jarḥ* IV 2, pp. 40 f.: صحيح الكتاب كثير الاعجام والنقط واذا حدث من حفظه غلط كثيرا. See also our Vol. II 61, 80, 226, 236.

[68] See e.g. Ibn Saʿd VI 52 f. and VII 2, pp. 51 and 78; Khaṭīb XII 276. Cf. our Vol. II 55.

[69] See e.g. Khaṭīb VIII 257.

[70] See e.g. *Jarḥ* I 1, p. 431; Dhahabī, *Mīzān al-iʿtidāl fī tarājim al-rijāl* (Cairo, 1327/1907) I 164.

[71] See e.g. Khaṭīb XII 275 f.

[72] *Jarḥ* I 1, p. 431; Khaṭīb XII 273 f.: كان يحيى بن سعيد يشكل الحرف اذا كان شديدا وغير ذلك فلا وكان هولاء اصحاب الشكل.

[73] See Vol. II, Document 5, for an example.

the Qur'ānic and Kūfic or semi-Kūfic scripts themselves were so used by Christians[74] or Muslims,[75] the logical conclusion is that these traditionists used the new small-letter vowels as devised by Khalīl. The advantages of Khalīl's letter vowel orthography over the older dot or point system was so evident that it is not surprising that it spread so quickly and was used at first by some even for Qur'ānic manuscripts, though most of the generally conservative Qur'ānic-readers either held on to the old point system or presently reverted to it "because it was the practice of the Companions and the Successors."[76] The Kūfan Kisā'ī (d. 189/805), well known as a Qur'ānic-reader, grammarian, and royal tutor, had Ṣāliḥ ibn ʿĀṣim as his private pointer (*nāqiṭ*). But, though Kisā'ī's variant readings and grammatical preferences are frequently cited, there is no specific indication as to which system he and Ṣāliḥ used. When we read that the people "pointed" their Qur'ān copies in accordance with Kisā'ī's public reading,[77] we wonder whether his large audiences in Kūfah and Baghdād used the old orthography to the exclusion of the new system. We know further that Kisā'ī was among the first to compose a work on spelling, *Kitāb al-hijā'*,[78] in which he must have taken note of the new system at least for non-Qur'ānic manuscripts. A younger Kūfan grammarian, Muḥammad ibn Ziyād, better known as Ibn al-Aʿrābī (*ca.* 150–231/767–846), definitely used the *fatḥah* in his manuscripts.[79]

The introduction and ready acceptance of Khalīl's system did not necessarily imply its full use in a given manuscript, whether it was Qur'ānic or secular. The use of either system in a particular field was controlled and selective for the most part in this early period, as both the sources[80] and the papyri indicate. Literary papyri that can be dated roughly from about the mid-second to about the mid-third century of the Ḥijrah do confirm practices indicated in the sources. While some use no orthographic signs whatsoever, not even the diacritical points, more do use them though in varying degrees; and some supplement the orthographic signs by use of small letters to distinguish unpointed consonants.[81] The letter vowels appear in fewer documents and are used more sparingly than the diacritical points, and both are more apt to be used with proper names or with particularly dubious words as evidenced in many of our prose documents[82] and also in a Heidelberg papyrus roll dated 229/844.[83] By contrast, and understandably enough, orthographic symbols were more freely used for poetry, as in our Documents 6 and 7 (see pp. 150 and 165).

Despite a mild controversy, inspired by cultural and social rather than religious motives, concerning the liberal or full use of orthographic symbols, individual teachers, secretaries, poets, linguists, and grammarians exercised their own judgment in the matter. As a rule they were guided by the intellectual or social level of their prospective readers relative to the latters' own professional or official positions.

[74] See e.g. Wright, *Facsimiles*, Pls. XX and XCV; Eugène Tisserant, *Specimina codicum orientalium* (Bonnae, 1914) Pl. 54; Agnes Smith Lewis and Margaret D. Gibson, *Forty-one Facsimiles of Dated Christian Arabic Manuscripts* ("Studia Siniatica" XII [Cambridge, England, 1907]) Pls. II and III; Georges Vajda, *Album de paléographie arabe* (Paris, 1958) Pl. 4.

[75] See e.g. Wright, *Facsimiles*, Pls. VI and XIX; *Namādhij*, Pls. 17, 19, 21, 64, but Pl. 7 illustrates a 5th-century heavy Kūfic Qur'ān which shows full use of the secular orthography.

[76] *Muḥkam*, pp. 22, 42 f. The older system continued to be used for Qur'ānic manuscripts for several centuries more. Scholarly works covering the subject of orthography primarily but not exclusively were produced by Qur'ānic scholars and grammarians of the period (see e.g. *Muḥkam*, Intro. pp. 32 f. and text p. 9; see also Abbott in *Ars Islamica* VIII 81, 83.

[77] *Muḥkam*, p. 13; Khaṭīb XI 409; *Inbāh* II 256, 264; Ibn al-Jazarī I 538.

[78] E.g. *Inbāh* II 271.

[79] Khaṭīb V 283.

[80] *Muḥkam*, p. 210, in a section headed in part مذاهب مقتدى اهل العربيّة وتابيعيهم من النقاط states explicitly اقتصر اكثرهم في نقط المتحرك على اواخر الكلم وهو مواضع الاعراب اذا فيه تقع الاشكال ويدخل الالتباس . . . وعلى ذلك اكثر العلماء.

[81] See e.g. Vol. II, Documents 5 and 12, and Documents 1–5 below.

[82] See e.g. Vol. I, Documents 1 and 3 and pp. 1 f.; Vol. II, Documents 2, 6–8, 11–13, and pp. 87–91; see also Documents 1 and 2 below.

[83] Carl H. Becker, *Papyri Schott-Reinhardt* I ("Veröffentlichungen aus der Heidelberger Papyrus-Sammlung" III [Heidelberg, 1906]) 8 f.; Gertrud Mélamède, "The meetings at al-ʿAḳaba," *Le monde oriental* XXVIII (1934) 4 plates between pp. 56 and 57.

Authors of textbooks for the young and handbooks for the relatively inexperienced would-be professionals were more apt to make liberal use of orthography. On the other hand, authors of manuscripts intended for the cultured class, for professional peers, and for official superiors would limit orthographic symbols to a minimum, thus tacitly flattering the recipient by implying his full command of the language. Inadvertent or intentional disregard of this guideline was likely to bring indignant protest or disapproval, as illustrated by the contemporary poets ʿAbbās ibn al-Aḥnaf and Abū Nuwās (d. 198/813)[84] and of ʿAbd Allāh ibn Ṭāhir (d. 230/844 or 845), governor of Khurāsān.[85]

The general secular concern with and approaches to correct lexical and grammatical forms and their practical and adequate representation in writing are reflected in a series of works usually titled *kitāb al-hijā'*, as was the work of Kisā'ī mentioned above, or more descriptively *kitāb al-khaṭṭ wa al-hijā'*. Such works were produced by leading Baṣran and Kūfan grammarians of the third and fourth centuries such as Abū Ḥātim al-Sijistānī, Mubarrad, Thaʿlab, Muḥammad ibn al-Qāsim ibn al-Anbārī, and Ibn Durustawaih, to mention a few in chronological order.[86] Furthermore, in the *adab al-kātib* or *adāb al-kuttāb* category[87] of secretarial "textbooks" chapters or whole sections were devoted to these problems. For instance, Ibn Qutaibah's *Adab al-kātib* has a section headed *taqwīm al-yadd* followed by one headed *taqwīm al-lisān* and thus stresses both written and oral spelling and grammar.[88]

Still another type of work, usually from the hands of state secretaries, dwelt on linguistic competence and literary style but stressed also the type, size, and quality of scripts as such. Works of this type were more apt to be titled *al-kitābah wa al-khaṭṭ* or *al-khaṭṭ wa al-kitābah*, for example those written by Ibn Thawwābah (d. 277/890) and Isḥāq ibn Ibrāhīm al-Tamīmī (d. 320/932).[89] Finally, there was a type of work with such titles as *al-khaṭṭ wa al-qalam* or *risālah fī al-khaṭṭ*. They were written generally by scholars or state secretaries who were renowned for their excellent penmanship and concerned mainly with the classification of scripts and calligraphic techniques. The basic role such authors played in the evolution of Arabic scripts—beginning with the Umayyad secretary ʿAbd al-Ḥamīd ibn Yaḥyā (d. 132/750), reaching a high peak during the reign of Ma'mūn with the state calligrapher Abū al-ʿAbbās Aḥmad ibn Abī Khālid al-Aḥwal and others, and climaxing with the calligrapher-wazir Ibn Muqlah (d. 328/940)—has been discussed elsewhere by this writer.[90]

In all these extensive and interrelated linguistic and scriptorial developments, despite the frequent references to the pious motives that led the aged Abū ʿAmr ibn al-ʿAlā' to destroy his roomful of linguistic and literary works, we find no true parallel to the initially heated controversy over committing *ḥadīth* to writing. As already seen, a controversy somewhat parallel to that over supplementing the bare consonants of the Qur'ānic text (*rasm al-Qur'ān*) with orthographic symbols[91] did arise but steadily subsided after the introduction of the letter-vowel orthography devised by Khalīl. For, in contrast to the rare use of the vowel symbols in early papyri, literary documents and other works dating roughly from about the mid-third century and later give evidence of the increasing use of orthographic signs, even to their full use in some scholarly works written in calligraphic scripts but mostly on paper or parchment. Excellent

[84] See Ṣūlī, *Adab al-kuttāb*, p. 61, for these and several other objectors; see also Franz Rosenthal's translation of Abū Ḥayyān al-Tawḥīdī's epistle on penmanship, *Ars Islamica* XIII–XIV 17 f., and Nuwairī VII 13.

[85] See *OIP* L 41, with references cited in n. 184.

[86] See e.g. *Inbāh* I 150, II 62, 113, 271, and III 208, 251. See also *Jumal*, pp. 269–81 and 290 f., where Zajjājī briefly covers the subject and refers to his own *Kitāb al-hijā'*.

[87] See e.g. Abbott in *Ars Islamica* VIII 85 and references there cited; Abū al-Qās'm ʿAbd Allāh al-Baghdādī, *Kitāb al-kuttāb*, ed. Dominique Sourdel, *Bulletin d'études orientales* XIV 115–53.

[88] See Ibn Qutaibah, *Adab al-kātib*, pp. 234–57 and 369–72; see also Ṣūlī, *Adab al-kuttāb*, pp. 243–59.

[89] See Abbott in *Ars Islamica* VIII 86.

[90] See *Ars Islamica* VIII 80–100, *OIP* L 30–38, and "The contribution of Ibn Muḳlah to the North-Arabic script," *AJSL* LVI (1939) 70–83.

[91] See e.g. *Muḥkam*, pp. 10–13, for prominent Companions and Successors who either opposed or permitted the use of these symbols.

illustrations of the combination of full orthography with fine Kūfic-*naskhī* and early Maghribī scripts are available on paper specimens from Abū ʿUbaid's *Gharīb al-ḥadīth*, dated 252/866,[92] Mālik ibn Anas' *Muwaṭṭa'* in bold *nashkī* and *thuluth* scripts of the Maghribī variety with all its lavish final-letter flourishes, dated 277/890,[93] Ibn Qutaibah's *Gharīb al-ḥadīth*, dated 279/892,[94] and Abū al-ʿAmaithal al-Aʿrābī's *Kitāb al-ma'thūr*, dated 280/893.[95] There are, on the other hand, codices from the second half of the third century, written on paper, papyrus, or parchment in different styles of scripts that vary in quality from poor to fine and that use both diacritical points and vowels in varying degrees of frequency. Furthermore, type of script, quality of penmanship, and use of orthographic symbols vary sometimes within a manuscript that is of considerable length. Known codices are a copy of Shāfiʿī's *Risālah* written on paper in a cursive hand, dated 265/878 and attested to by Rabīʿ ibn Sulaimān al-Murādī (d. 270/883 or 884),[96] a paper copy of the *Masā'il* of Ibn Ḥanbal[97] written in a rather poor hand and dated 266/879, a papyrus manuscript of the *Jāmiʿ* of Ibn Wahb[98] in a fine hand that varies from stiff to quite cursive *naskhī* and dated 276/889, and a parchment manuscript of St. Mark the Hermit dated 288/901 and now in the library of the University of Strasbourg.[99] In regard to orthographic symbols, our documents that date from about the mid-third century or after (Documents 1, 2, 6, 7) also vary from rare to all but full usage, as do a few others that have come to my attention but are not included in the present volume.[100]

A few works of the second century and a goodly number of the third and fourth centuries have survived in fourth-century copies written on paper or in rare instances on parchment. They are representative of scripts characteristic of both the eastern and the western varieties. Simple or elaborate Kūfic and *thuluth* scripts are used sometimes for titles and headings. Some of the manuscripts are written in a stiff style, while others are in a more cursive *naskhī*, and still others are in a Maghribī variety of this favorite book hand. A few are in the common nondescript *muṭlaq* hand, which is nevertheless reasonably legible. A rough survey of illustrations available to me revealed a variety of choice in the extent to which use was made of orthographic symbols. Though in some manuscripts they were used not at all or very rarely, in most of the manuscripts examined they were used either freely or to the full extent. The manuscripts available in reproductions cover a wide variety of subjects and represent leading authors in their respective fields. Though not all the copyists mentioned are readily identifiable, a few are well known scholar-copyists or scholar-booksellers. Christian and scientific manuscripts apart,[101] the extant dated manuscripts from the fourth century include the *Gharīb al-ḥadīth* (311/923) of Abū ʿUbaid,[102] the *Sirr*

[92] See Wright, *Facsimiles*, Pl. VI.

[93] See Vol. II 88.

[94] See *Namādhij*, Pl. 15.

[95] See 2 plates following Forwort in edition of F. Krenkow (London, 1925); *Namādhij*, Pl. 16.

[96] Shāfiʿī, *Al-risālah*, ed. Aḥmad Muḥammad Shākir (Cairo, 1358/1940) Intro. pp. 17–23 and Pls. 1–103; cf. B. Moritz, *Arabic Palaeography* (Cairo, 1905) Pls. 117–18. In his introduction to his translation of Shāfiʿī's *Risālah*, Majid Khadduri, *Islamic Jurisprudence* (Baltimore, 1961) p. 50, quotes me as "inclined to accept a fourth century dating" for the paper manuscript. Since my conversation with Professor Khadduri, paper manuscripts from the second half of the 3rd century have come to light (especially the above-mentioned *Muwaṭṭa'* of Mālik ibn Anas), including literary manuscripts written in cursive script. These new factors, while not conclusive in themselves, incline me to accept the earlier dating.

[97] See *Namādhij*, Pl. 14.

[98] See *Le djâmiʿ d'Ibn Wahb* I–II, édité et commenté par J. David-Weill ("Publications de l'Institut français d'archéologie orientale: Textes arabes" III–IV [Le Caire, 1939–48]).

[99] *Mélanges de l'Université Saint Joseph* XXVIII (1949–50) Pl. XVIII.

[100] E.g. Arabic papyrus No. 6686 in the University of Michigan Library, Oriental Institute No. A6964, Arabic papyrus No. P94 in the collection of Mr. H. P. Kraus of New York. Parchment and paper literary documents of the 3rd century tend to have fuller use of orthographic signs than do those written on papyrus.

[101] On the whole both groups show about as marked variations as to writing materials, variety of scripts, and extent of use of orthographic symbols. Parchment manuscripts are more frequent in Christian literature, and animal and human illustrations are more apt to occur in copies of *Kalīlah wa Dimnah* and in scientific works, especially those on zoology, medicine, and astronomy.

[102] See Moritz, *Arabic Palaeography*, Pls. 119–20.

al-naḥw (first half of 4th century) of Zajjājī,[103] the *Kitāb* (351/962) of Sībawaih,[104] and the *Ḥadhf min nasab Quraish* of Mu'arrij ibn ʿAmr al-Sadūsī, copy from the hand of Abū Isḥāq Ibrāhīm ibn ʿAbd Allāh al-Najīramī (d. 355/966), grammarian and scholar-copyist who was patronized by Kāfūr of Fāṭimid Egypt and who was a member of a family of three generations of scholar-booksellers.[105] The second half of the fourth century yielded many more dated manuscripts. These include the *Mukhtaṣar* (359/970)[106] of Abū Muṣʿab al-Zuhrī, the *Dīwān al-adab* (363/974) of Isḥāq ibn Ibrāhīm al-Fārābī,[107] the *Hidāyah* (364–66/974–76) of Ismāʿīl ibn ʿAbbād al-Ṣāḥib,[108] the *Sharḥ al-muʿallaqāt* (371/981) of Abū Jaʿfar Aḥmad ibn Muḥammad al-Naḥḥās,[109] the *Akhbār al-naḥwiyyīn al-Baṣriyyīn* (376/987)[110] of Sīrāfī written in beautiful calligraphic Kūfic and Kūfic-*naskhī* scripts by ʿAlī ibn Shādhān al-Rāzī, whose knowledge of Arabic left something to be desired, the *Dīwān Abī al-Aswad al-Du'alī* (380/990) in cursive vocalized script,[111] the *Kunā wa al-asmā'* (381/991)[112] of Daulābī, and the *Dīwān al-Mutanabbī* (398/1008).[113]

The ample manuscript evidence as to orthography and penmanship actually reflects the sustained concern of the intelligentsia in maintaining high standards for both. The biographical literature for the various professions, including the sciences, yields numerous references to scholars who themselves produced or searched for and acquired manuscripts known for their accuracy, legibility, and beauty of scripts. The libraries of the rich and powerful, especially those of caliphs and wazirs, frequently became the depositories of the choicest of such manuscripts, through commission and purchase or through confiscation and bequests.[114] The rank and file of students, young scholars, and laymen had to be content with the indifferent commercial products of the average copyists or booksellers, for whose services and stock of books there was ever increasing demand. Famed scholar-bibliophile-booksellers such as Nadīm, Yāqūt, and Qifṭī reveal in their works[115] a keen awareness of the quality of the manuscripts they acquired and described. Accuracy of text is their first concern, with stress now on legibility, now on beauty of scripts, or on the lack of either or both of these qualities as the case may be. They give special attention to manuscripts of lexical and grammatical works in these respects. Most of their descriptive terms are commonplace adjectives used alone or in various combinations.[116] Among the most frequently used terms that stress primarily accuracy of text are صادق الروايه والنقل and صحيح, مظبوط, those that stress legibility and quality of penmanship are مليح, جميل, حسن, خط جيد, and خط مرغوب به, while poor or careless manuscripts are described as ردى and قبيح. These are supplemented by terms that indicate the type and size of the scripts, the most commonly used being رقيق, محقق, رياسى, تعليق, and عتيق. Frequently reference to a well known and easily recognized hand of a famous scholar, copyist, or calligrapher is simply خطه معروف, "his handwriting is known."

[103] See *ibid.* Pl. 122.

[104] See *ibid.* Pl. 121; *Namādhij*, Pl. 17.

[105] See *Namādhij*, Pl. 64, and Mu'arrij ibn ʿAmr al-Sadūsī, *Kitāb ḥadhf min nasab Quraish*, ed. Ṣalāḥ al-Dīn al-Munajjid (Cairo, 1960) Intro. pp. 10 f. For the Najīramī family see *GAL* S I 201 f.; *Fihrist*, p. 87; *Irshād* I 278 f.; *Inbāh* I 170 f.; p. 39 below.

[106] See *Namādhij*, Pl. 18.

[107] See Wright, *Facsimiles*, Pl. LX.

[108] See *Namādhij*, Pl. 19.

[109] See *ibid.* Pl. 21.

[110] See Sīrāfī, Intro. pp. 8 f. and 3 plates; *Namādhij*, Pl. 22. See also p. 15 below.

[111] See Wright, *Facsimiles*, Pl. VII.

[112] See Vajda, *Album de paléographie arabe*, Pl. 18.

[113] See Wright, *Facsimiles*, Pl. XLVII.

[114] Qifṭī willed his magnificent library to his patron, the Ayyūbid ruler of Aleppo (*Inbāh* I, Intro. pp. 20 f.; Zubaidī, pp. 291 f.). See also p. 36 below.

[115] See e.g. *Fihrist*, pp. 7, 40, 107; *Irshād* I 81 f., II 266 f., and V 326; *Inbāh* I, Intro. pp. 13 and 20 and text, pp. 7–9.

[116] We are not concerned here with the profusion of literary expressions on the functions and power of the pen as against those of the sword, which start with Sūrah 96:4 and continue throughout Islāmic literature.

Nadīm, in a significant passage, reports having seen a large manuscript collection with autographs and written on leather, parchment, papyrus, and paper by scholars of the first and second centuries, beginning with Abū al-Aswad al-Du'alī and including such Qur'ānic scholars and grammarians as Yaḥyā ibn Yaʿmar, Abū ʿAmr ibn al-ʿAlā', Sībawaih, Kisā'ī, Abū ʿAmr al-Shaibānī, Yaḥyā ibn Ziyād al-Farrā', Aṣmaʿī and Ibn al-Aʿrābī (d. 231/846).[117]

However, in this as in a supplementary passage that concentrates on the manuscripts of Bedouin authors,[118] Nadīm does not characterize the penmanship of individual Umayyad scholars, apart from that of the Qur'ānic calligrapher Khālid ibn Abī al-Ḥajjāj, whom Walīd I employed to copy Qur'āns, poetry, and *akhbār*.[119] ʿAbd al-Malik's state secretary Rauḥ ibn Zinbāʿ is referred to as ʿIrāqī in his penmanship and Fārisī in his style,[120] which would indicate an angular Kūfic or Kūfic-*naskhī* script. Attention has been drawn (p. 5) to the fine and accurate hand of the scholarly Sālim ibn ʿAbd Allāh, secretary to Hishām. Specific details in references to the manuscripts and penmanship of ʿAbbāsid scholars are more readily available. Abū ʿAmr ibn al-ʿAlā' pointed out to Akhfash al-Akbar how easy it was to confuse carelessly formed *rā'* and *wāw* and hence misread a verse.[121] Khalīl, we are told, took pains with his manuscripts and disapproved of small light scripts (*khaṭṭ raqīq*),[122] usually associated with the love-sick because they too are emaciated[123] but used also by traveling scholars in the interest of light weight and paper economy.[124] The eloquent Bedouin scholar Abū Shibl al-ʿUqailī, patronized by Hārūn al-Rashīd and the Barmakids and teacher of Ibn al-Aʿrābī, wrote an ancient hand (*khaṭṭ ʿatīq*).[125] We know that Ibn al-Aʿrābī used the *fatḥah* in his manuscripts (see p. 9).

Descriptive references to the manuscripts and penmanship of third-century copyists, booksellers, and scholars are generally made on the basis of third-century manuscripts actually seen by Nadīm, Yāqūt, or Qifṭī. The bookshop of Ibn Waddāʿ al-Azdī of Baghdād was a rendezvous of scholars where many of their discussions and debates took place in the fourth decade of the third century. There was keen competition for Ibn Waddāʿ's hand copies, which soon became and for centuries remained highly prized collectors' items. Qifṭī, writing in 630/1232–33, reported that he examined critically several of Ibn Waddāʿ's copies, including a section of the *Dīwān al-Aʿshā* and a copy of Abū ʿUbaid's *Amthāl*, and found them to be the most carefully executed.[126] So far, I have found no references to Ibn al-Sikkīt's penmanship, a fine old ʿIrāqī, that is, Kūfic, hand, to judge by an excellent specimen from a copy of the *Ta'rīkh al-mulūk al-ʿArab* that is dated 243/857.[127] Muḥammad ibn ʿAbd Allāh al-Tamīmī, known as

[117] See *Fihrist*, p. 40; *Inbāh* I 7–9 reproduces the passage. See also *Ars Islamica* VIII 76 f., where I have dealt at length with the basically significant implication of this passage, namely the availability in the 3rd century and after of autograph manuscripts of 1st- and 2nd-century authors. I have since drawn attention to a considerable number of instances from the second half of the 1st century onward of an author's or a collector's manuscripts passing on to some member of his family, usually a son or a nephew and occasionally even a daughter, or to one or more of his leading pupils and transmitters (see e.g. our Vols. I 18 f. and 23–28, II 28 f., 37 f., 54 f., 156 f., 172 f., 175–78, 218, 227, 230 f.). Still other references to the survival of the manuscripts of several leading Umayyad poets and scholars will be noted in the present study. The number of specific references to the fate of 2nd- and 3rd-century manuscripts grew as competition for them increased among scholars, booksellers, and rulers. Rulers used their wealth and power, as seen above, to acquire especially desirable books or collections for their personal or state libraries. Bequests (*waṣiyah, tirkah*) of works or libraries became increasingly common in the 3rd century. The numerous benefits of such bequests for all concerned were listed and extolled at some length by the tireless author and bibliophile Jāḥiẓ in his *Ḥayawān* I 100 f.

[118] See *Fihrist*, p. 47.

[119] *Ibid.* pp. 9, 40; *OIP* L 54; Abbott in *Ars Islamica* VIII 76.

[120] Thaʿālibī, *Laṭā'if*, p. 42: عراق الخط فارسى الكتابة.

[121] *Muzhir* II 360 f., 363.

[122] *Rauḍ al-akhyār*, p. 24.

[123] Ṣūlī, *Adab al-kuttāb*, pp. 59 f.; *Muḥāḍarāt* I 60.

[124] See Vol. II 89.

[125] *Fihrist*, p. 46; *Muzhir* II 304.

[126] *Inbāh* I 53 and II 134: اقتنيتُ بخطه فرايته من الاتقان والتحقيق ما لا شاهدته فى غيره (see also *Fihrist*, p. 80).

[127] See Vajda, *Album de paléographie arabe*, Pl. 3, and *Namādhij*, Pl. 13. Note the free use of diacritical points and the absence of vowels.

Ḥazanbal, a transmitter from Ibn al-Sikkīt, receives high praise for his penmanship.[128] The autograph copy of the *Kitāb al-qabā'il* of Muḥammad ibn Ḥabīb (d. 245/860) that was written on Khurāsānian Ṭalḥī paper for the famous library of the wazir Fatḥ ibn Khāqān was seen by Nadīm, who was impressed with its accuracy.[129] Manuscripts from the prolific hand of Muḥammad ibn Ḥabīb's pupil Sukkarī (212–75/827–88) were desired for their accuracy.[130] Ibrāhīm ibn Muḥammad ibn Sa'dān ibn al-Mubārak, a third-generation scholar and bibliophile, was known for his accurate penmanship and faithful transmission. [131] Zajjāj sought to ingratiate himself with his patron the wazir Qāsim ibn 'Ubaid Allāh and with the caliph Mu'taḍid (279–89/892–902) by completing and recasting the *Jāmi' al-manṭaq* of Abū Ja'far al-'Askarī. He had Aḥmad ibn Ibrāhīm al-Tirmidhī, one-time teacher of Zajjāj's former Kūfan teacher Tha'lab and a penman in much demand, make but a single copy of the revised and completed *Jāmi'* on fine Khurāsānian Ṭalḥī paper for the caliph's library.[132] Several of the pupils and associates of Tha'lab were both scholars and booksellers known for their good penmanship. Among them were Abū Ḥasan al-Tirmidhī,[133] Abū Mūsā al-Ḥāmiḍ,[134] and Muḥammad ibn 'Abd Allāh al-Kirmānī al-Warrāq, whose copy of Ibn Qutaibah's *Ma'ārif* was acquired by Qifṭī, who describes the manuscript and its scholar-copyist in superlative terms.[135] Of Tha'lab's younger associates, the wealthy 'Alī ibn Muḥammad al-Asdī, better known as Ibn al-Kūfī (254–344/868–956), author and bibliophile, won high praise for his autographed manuscripts, which were seen and used by Nadīm, Yāqūt, and Qifṭī.[136] Mubarrad, who wrote a good hand,[137] considered himself a *warrāq* and had several close associates who were scholar-booksellers.[138] Mubarrad and Tha'lab as famed and rival leaders of the Baṣran and Kūfan schools of grammar had in common several enterprising pupils who were known for their knowledge of grammar and good penmanship. Among these pupils were Tha'lab's son-in-law Abū 'Alī al-Dīnawarī (d. 289/901), who settled in Egypt,[139] and the latter's stepson Muḥammad ibn Wallād (d. 298/910),[140] whose father, Walīd ibn Muḥammad al-Tamīmī al-Maṣādrī, better known as Wallād (d. 263/877), was the first to establish in Egypt a family of grammarians and scholar-booksellers.[141] Abū al-'Alā' al-Makkī (d. 317/929) made copies of the works of Zubair ibn Bakkār al-Zubairī (d. 256/870), one of which was seen by Qifṭī, who praised it highly.[142] 'Abd Allāh ibn Muḥammad, grammarian and tutor in the household of Muqtadir's (295–320/908–32) wazir 'Alī ibn 'Īsā, was known for his good hand.[143] The excellent penmanship of the

[128] *Fihrist*, p. 78; *Inbāh* I 339: له خط جيد معروف بين العلماء بالصحة والتحقيق متوافر القيمة.

[129] For the origin and early use by the Arabs of Khurāsānian paper and its Ṭalḥī variety, see Abbott, "A ninth-century fragment of the '*Thousand Nights*' " *JNES* VIII (1949) 146–49; Adolf Grohmann, *Arabische Paläographie* I (Österreichische Akademie der Wissenschaften, Philos.-hist. Kl., "Denkschriften," 94. Band, 1. Abhandlung [Wien, 1967]) 98 f. See also p. 149 below.

[130] *Fihrist*, p. 76; *Inbāh* I 292: كان السكرى مرغوبا فى خطه لصحته.

[131] *Inbāh* I 185: كان صحيح الخط صادق الرواية.

[132] *Fihrist*, pp. 60 f., 80; *Irshād* I 57 f.; *Inbāh* I 164 f. and III 232, where اليز يدى is a misreading for الترمذى.

[133] *Bughyah*, p. 103: خطه مشهور بالصحة مرغوب به.

[134] *Fihrist*, p. 79: يوصف بصحة الخط وحسن المذهب في الضبط وكان يورق (cf. *Inbāh* II 22).

[135] *Inbāh* III 155: مليح الخط صحيح النقط يرغب الناس بخطه وهو في غايه الحسن والصحة (cf. *Fihrist*, p. 79; *Irshād* VII 19).

[136] See e.g. *Fihrist*, p. 79. *Inbāh* II 305 f. adds a description of Ibn al-Kūfī's library; *Irshād* V 326 f. is more detailed on his penmanship:
رايت بخطه عدة كتب فلم ار احسن ضبطا واتقانا للكتابة منه فانه يجعل الاعراب على الحروف بمقدار الحرف احتياطا ويكتب على الكلمة المشكول فيها عدة مرار صح صح صح فكان من جماعى الكتب وارباب الهوى فيها . . . اسمه بخطه على عدة من كتبه.

[137] Zubaidī, p. 108; *Inbāh* III 242.

[138] *Fihrist*, p. 60, esp. n. 1; Tha'ālibī, *Laṭā'if*, p. 47.

[139] Zubaidī, p. 234: كان ابو على حسن المعرفة ثم قدم مصر والف كتاب فى النحو (cf. *Irshād* II 141).

[140] Zubaidī, p. 236: كان حسن الخط صالح (جيد) الضبط (cf. *Irshād* VII 133; *Inbāh* III 255; *Bughyah*, p. 112).

[141] See e.g. Zubaidī, p. 233, and pp. 35 f. below.

[142] *Inbāh* I 338: له خط حسن يرغب فيه لجودة ضبطه . . . رايت جزاء بخطه على نهايه الصحة وحسن الترصيع.

[143] *Ibid.* II 135: مليح الخط صحيحه.

wazir Ibn Muqlah (272–328/886–940) was too well known to be always described, though Nadīm makes frequent references to manuscripts from his hand.[144] Yāqūt comments also on the good penmanship of Ibn Muqlah's father and brother.[145] We read that Abū al-Faraj al-Iṣfahānī (284–356/897–967) frequented the flourishing book market (*sūq al-warrāqīn*) and bought good original sources, including manuscripts autographed by authors or copyists, which he used in his compositions,[146] a statement that is amply substantiated by the terms Abū al-Faraj uses in his "documentation" in the *Aghānī*.[147] Abū al-Faraj's rough copy of the *Aghānī* was written on the backs of discarded sheets or fragments (*ẓuhūr*) in the *taʿlīq* script,[148] a comparatively small and quite cursive script much used for memoranda, marginal notations, and rough copies. His contemporary Abū ʿAlī al-Qālī (288–356/901–67) wrote his rough copy of the *Bāriʿ* on the backs of discarded sheets,[149] probably also in the *taʿlīq* script or in a related comparatively small cursive hand. Abū ʿAlī al-Qālī's attachment to the autograph copy of the *Jamharah* of Ibn Duraid, which necessity forced him to sell, so touched the heart of the buyer that he returned the book with a gift of money.[150] Sīrāfī was an ascetic who provided for his personal needs by copying ten pages daily in a fine hand.[151] Several members of his family were scholar-booksellers[152] who probably employed copyists. Sīrāfī himself used some of his pupils as copyists for his works,[153] and reference has been made above (p. 12) to ʿAlī ibn Shādhān al-Rāzī's calligraphic copy of the *Akhbār al-naḥwiyyīn al-Baṣriyyīn*. ʿAlī ibn Muḥammad, better known as Abū Ḥayyān al-Tawḥīdī, who was a greatly appreciative pupil of Sīrāfī,[154] wrote a treatise on penmanship (*Risālah fī ʿilm al-kitābah*) which is cited above (see p. 5, n. 26). Sīrāfī's

144 *Fihrist*, pp. 42, 55, 69, 74, 80, *et passim*.

145 *Irshād* III 150 f.

146 *Fihrist*, p. 115, اكثر تعويله كان في تصنيفه على الكتب المنسوبة الخطوط او غيرها من الاصول الجياد. The phrase الكتب المنسوبة الخطوط, could possibly refer to manuscripts written in proportioned script (*khaṭṭ al-mansūb*), which was regularized by Ibn Muqlah, but hardly so in the present context and in the light of Abū al-Faraj's source terminology, which reveals his great reliance on manuscript sources.

147 A quick spot-check of *Aghānī* XI to XXI showed that Abū al-Faraj's most frequently used term is "I copied," which occurs 60 times, while "I found" occurs 10 times, and "he mentioned" only 4 times. These terms, in the order of their frequency, are used in the formulas وجدت بخط فلان, نسخت من بعض الكتب, نسخت من كتاب فلان بخطه, نسخت من كتاب فلان, وجدت بكتاب بخط فلان, وجدت ببعض الكتب بلا اسناد, ذكر فلان في كتاب الفلاني, ذكر فلان. Furthermore, the oral-transmission terms قال, اخبرني, حدثني, اعطاني فلان are also used and refer roughly as often to booksellers as to scholars.

148 E.g. *Aghānī* (1927——) I, Intro. pp. 33 f. The term *ẓuhūr al-dafātir* was used in literary circles in two concurrent yet distinctly different senses. In one sense it refers to the practice of needy or frugal students and scholars who used the blank spaces of discarded sheets or manuscripts for their notes and the rough copies of their works, as we know the Kūfan judge Sharīk ibn ʿAbd Allāh (95–177/714–793) and Shāfiʿī to have done in their youth (for Shāfiʿī see Khaṭīb IX 280; for Sharīk see Nabia Abbott, *Two Queens of Baghdad: Mother and Wife of Hārūn al-Rashīd* [Chicago, 1946] pp. 56–58, and *Irshād* VI 369). Sometimes a scholar would hastily or pointedly jot down his answer to a note or a letter at the foot or on the back of a page, as we know Ḥammād ibn Salamah and Shāfiʿī to have done (see Nawawī, *Bustān al-ʿĀrifīn* [Cairo, 1348/1929] pp. 32 f., and *Irshād* VI 384–86 respectively). Such practices came to be frowned upon in cultured circles as small economies that exposed writer and reader to trouble or embarrassment and, above all, "encouraged the destruction of older manuscripts, which is madness" (Ṣūlī, *Adab al-kuttāb*, p. 149; cf. *Inbāh* III 83). Papyrus fragments give evidence of such uses of earlier manuscripts (see e.g. our Vol. II 59 and Documents 9 and 12 and Documents 1 and 4–5 below).

In its second sense the term *ẓuhūr al-dafātir* refers to the writing of pithy remarks, bits of wisdom, epigrams, or appropriate quotations in prose or verse such as are placed on the cover or on the flyleaf or at section headings of a book. For we read that Abū Zaid al-Anṣārī, after listening to a certain well read and cultured man whose memory was stocked with choice reports and who quoted nothing but the best, exclaimed: "It is, by Allāh, as though all his knowledge is on the backs of books." On this remark the narrator comments: "He means that nothing but the best is written on the backs of manuscripts" (*ʿalā ẓuhūr al-dafātir*; see Khaṭīb al-Baghdādī, *Taqyīd al-ʿilm*, ed. Yūsuf al-ʿAshsh [Damascus, 1368/1949] p. 141). So impressed was Qifṭī with this type of literary product that he made an anthology of it which he titled *Nuhzat al-khāṭir wa nuzhat al-nāẓir* (see *Inbāh* I, Intro. p. 23, No. 26, and text pp. 53 f., see also Khaṭīb, *Taqyīd al-ʿilm*, p. 134, and *Irshād* III 151).

149 E.g. Zubaidī, pp. 203 f.: كتاب البارع يشتمل على خمسة آلاف ورقه . . . توفى قبل ان ينقّحه فاستخرج بعده من الصكوك والرقاع.

150 E.g. *Muzhir* I 95.

151 Khaṭīb VII 342; *Irshād* III 85, 101; *Nuzhah*, p. 184; *Inbāh* I 313.

152 E.g. *Inbāh* III 227; *Bughyah*, p. 53.

153 E.g. *Irshād* III 105.

154 See Abū Ḥayyān al-Tawḥīdī, *Risālah fī al-ṣadāqah wa al-ṣadīq*, ed. Ibrāhīm al-Kīlānī (Damascus, 1964) pp. 69 f.

contemporary the secretary, grammarian, and literary critic Āmidī of *Muwāzanah* fame used a fine ancient script.[155] ʿAlī ibn Naṣr al-Barnīqī, active in Egypt in 384/994, copied many books that became collector's items, among them a copy of the *Jamharah* of Ibn Duraid.[156] Jurjānī (d. 392/1002), judge, poet, essayist, literary critic, and author of the *Wasāṭah*, was described as combining the poetic talent of Buḥturī with the prose style of Jāḥiẓ and the penmanship of Ibn Muqlah.[157] Ibn Jinnī, author of the well known *Khaṣāʾiṣ*, was not only himself a good penman but supervised the penmanship of his three sons[158] and counted among his pupils the artist and "matchless" calligrapher Ibn al-Bawwāb (d. 423/1032).[159] Abū Naṣr al-Jawharī (d. *ca.* 398/1007), author of the *Ṣiḥāḥ*, was teacher, scholar, and calligrapher who taught penmanship and himself used the proportioned scripts in the style of Ibn Muqlah.[160] His pupil the bookseller Ibrāhīm ibn Ṣāliḥ, who completed and made the final copy of the *Ṣiḥāḥ* after Abū Naṣr al-Jawharī's death, was also known for his scholarship and good penmanship though he was not of the caliber of the master in either field.[161]

In contrast to the numerous references to scholars, copyists, and booksellers who wrote fair, good, or excellent hands, references to poor penmen in the literary fields seem to be quite rare.[162] I have so far found but six such references, and three of these were made with some qualifications. The hand of Aḥmad ibn Muḥammad al-Ḥulwānī (d. 333/944), pupil and transmitter of Sukkarī (see p. 14), is described as extremely poor yet schooled.[163] The hand of Aḥmad ibn Aḥmad, known also as Ibn Akhī al-Shāfiʿī, a bookseller patronized by Ibn ʿAbdūs al-Jahshiyārī (d. 331/942), is described as not good-looking but appreciated by scholars for its accuracy.[164] Ibn al-Marāghī (d. 371/981), realizing that he lacked artistry in his script, wrote verses on the back of his commentary on the *Jumal* of Zajjājī apologizing for his poor though accurate hand.[165] Ṣūlī mentions three secretaries who wrote poor or extremely bad hands but observes elsewhere that ambiguity or uncertainty occurs even in fine and good penmanship "and as for deplorable penmanship, its case is difficult (and even) impossible,"[166] an observation that can readily be confirmed by papyrologists and editors of ancient manuscripts, especially such manuscripts as are written in a bare consonantal script.

155 *Inbāh* I 287: كان يكتب خط حسنا من خطوط الاوائل وهو اقرب خط الى الصحة.

156 See *Irshād* V 433, رايت بخطه كتبا ادبيه لغوية ونحويه فوجدته حسن الخط متقن الضبط, and *Inbāh* II 323, وكان كتب بخطه الكثير الناس يتنافسون في خطه وتحصيله وذلك الى زماننا هذا . . . وكان خطه قاعدا عاقلا بين الخطوط كثير الضبط في غاية التحقيق والتنقيب والتصحيح.

157 Thaʿālibī, *Yatīmat al-dahr fī maḥāsin ahl al-ʿaṣr*, ed. Muḥammad Muḥyī al-Dīn ʿAbd al-Ḥamīd (Cairo, 1366/1947) IV 3–26; cf. *Irshād* V 249–52.

158 *Irshād* V 19: خرّجهم وحسّن خطوطهم فهم معدودين من الصحيحين الضبط وحسن الخط (cf. *Inbāh* II 385).

159 *Khaṣāʾiṣ* I, Intro. p. 55; *Irshād* V 445–51, esp. p. 446: كان فى اول امره مزوقا يصور الدور ثم صور الكتب ثم تعانى الكتابة ففاق فيها المتقدمين واعجز المتاخرين. For Ibn al-Bawwāb see also *OIP* L 30, 36, 38, with references cited in nn. 97 and 126–30. Cf. Abbott in *AJSL* LVI, 71–78.

160 *Irshād* II 266 f.; *Inbāh* I 194 f.: مقيم بنسابور على التدوين والتاليف تعلم انخط الانيف وكتابه المصاحف والدفاتر اللطائف وخط يضرب به المثل في الحسن الخطوط المنسوبة بخط ابن مقلة.

161 *Irshād* II 269; *Inbāh* II 90; *Bughyah*, p. 195.

162 References to manuscripts written in poor hands, without identification of the writers, are found e.g. in *Fihrist*, p. 77.

163 *Fihrist*, p. 80: له خط في غاية القبح والردأة الا انه خط عالم (cf. *Irshād* II 58; *Inbāh* I 98).

164 *Irshād* I 81 f.: رايت جماعة من العلماء يفتخرون بالنقل من خطه ورايت خطه وليس بجيد المنظر لكنه متقن الضبط.

165 *Inbāh* III 83:

اعذر اخاك على ردأة خطه   واغفر رداته لجودة ضبطه
فالخط ليس من تعظيمه   ونظامه الا إقامة شمطه
واذا ابان عن المعاني خطه   كانت ملاحته زيادة شرطه

166 Ṣūlī, *Adab al-kuttāb*, p. 45: التشبيه يقع كثيرا بالخط الجيد الحسن اما الخط الردى فحكايته صعبة ممتنعة. See his pp. 52 f. for the three cases mentioned above and pp. 42 and 186 f. for secretaries and others who deliberately wrote poor and difficult hands or in code in the interest of secrecy.

It is clear from the foregoing representative list that the qualities desired in secular manuscript copies were faithful transmission, grammatical accuracy, and good penmanship. In order to meet the first two requirements an author's private copyist and the commercial copyist who functioned also as a bookseller had to have command of the language and be familiar with, if not indeed well versed in, the discipline he served.[167] Good penmanship for all general purposes of the literary fields involved careful execution of each consonant, adequate but not excessive orthography, uniformity in the style of scripts[168] and in any use of colors, and abbreviations to indicate source and correctness.[169] Furthermore, the good secretary and penman in the literary fields as a rule had to avoid the extremes represented by the hasty careless work of inferior commercial copyists and the marked artistry of the professional calligraphers who utilized their skills to adorn Qur'ānic manuscripts, special state documents, and royal diplomatic correspondence.[170]

[167] See e.g. Nuwairī IX 214–17.
[168] Ṣūlī, *Adab al-kuttāb*, p. 50; Nuwairī VII 15.
[169] See e.g. Sībawaih I vi; cf. our Vol. II, Document 7, Tradition 7, and Document 11, Traditions 2–4.
[170] Ṣūlī, *Adab al-kuttāb*, pp. 50, 57.

TWO GRAMMATICAL DOCUMENTS

Our two grammar fragments, without *isnād*'s or names of scholars, give no clue as to their dates or authors, and the literary sources have not provided a close enough parallel to the text of either document to permit positive identification. The approximate dating of both documents is, therefore, based partly on their scripts and partly on the progress of grammatical studies in Egypt and North Africa in the second–third/eight–ninth centuries. The script of Document 1 has affinities with north Arabic types in which the open *ʿain* appears as late as the eight/fourteenth century.[1] The more cursive script of Document 2, with its comparatively liberal use of diacritical points and vowels, is in keeping with the scripts of late third-century literary papyri, such as that of the second part of the *Jāmiʿ* of Ibn Wahb,[2] which is about as different from the script of the first part as the script of Document 2 is different from that of Document 1.

Different as the scripts of these two documents are, in their careful execution both reflect the increasing emphasis that scholars of the second and third centuries, particularly grammarians and philologists, placed on good penmanship. They appreciated accuracy and legibility from their colleagues and, as a rule, demanded it from their pupils, copyists, and booksellers.

[1] See Vajda, *Album de paléographie arabe*, Pl. 53 (dated 770/1368).
[2] See *Le djâmiʿ d'Ibn Wahb*, ed. David-Weill, I iv–xi and plates.

DOCUMENT 1

Oriental Institute No. 17619. Late third/early tenth century.

Fine papyrus, broken at top, 12 × 17 cm. (Pl. 1). The text is written on the verso of a late third/late ninth-century legal document of which only the names of some witnesses remain.

Script.—The closely written somewhat angular book hand yields to a smaller and very cursive one for the familiar formulas of line 3 but to a less cursive hand for line 14, which ends the section. Characteristic letter forms are the final *kāf* and the open medial *ʿain*, though the latter is not consistently used. Medial *ṣād* is sometimes indicated by a small *ṣād* below it. The pen was lifted, so that generally the vertical strokes were written downward. Diacritical points and vowels are sparsely used. A semicircle is used for the *hamzah*. The vowels and other orthographic signs are not always carefully placed in relation to the letters to which they belong. Scribal errors are canceled with neat lines as in lines 7, 9, 11, and 12.

TEXT

1 [traces only]

2 مبنى الا الرفع على ما اعلمتك

3 والحمد لله كثيرا بسم الله الرحمن الرحيم

4 وقد يكون الجر مانعا للرفع كقولك أعجبنى اكلُك

5 رغيفا واعجبنى اشباعِك رغيفٌ واذا قلت اكلك رغيفا

6 كانت الكاف فى موضع الفاعل فمنعتها الاضافة

7 الى الجر فمنع الرفع الى الوقوع عليها واذا قلت

8 اشباعك رغيف كانت الكاف فى موضع المفعول

9 المنصوب فمنعتها الاضافة من النصب وذلك

10 لان العامل قد يعومل فى العامل ولو لا ذلك ابقى الجر

11 اقوا من الرفع والنصب الاترى انك تقول رايت

12 زيداً ضارباً عمراً فتنصب ضارباً لوقوع فعلك به وفيه

13 ضمير فعلى وقع بعمرٍ و فلم يمنعه ان كان عامل ان يعمل

14 فيه عامل فافهم ذلك ان شأ الله

Comments.—The vowels and other orthographic signs are not so liberally used nor so carefully formed or placed as one might expect in a text of this nature. The writer or copyist was concerned mainly with desinental syntax, إعراب الآواخر or حركة إعراب, as against حركة بناء. He relied less on vowel signs than on sentences to explain the grammatical analysis and to clarify the governance of the declinable noun as used in verbal sentences with more than one object. The technical terminology is mainly that of the Baṣran school of grammar, as shown by the consistent use of الجر as against الخفض, favored by most Kūfans, to indicate the genitive case. On the other hand, line 12 has the phrase لوقوع فعلك به, which reflects the Kūfan term الفعل الواقع, as against the Baṣran term الفعل المتعدّ, to indicate the transitive verb.

Lines 1–2. These lines end a section that dealt with the indeclinable noun. The traces at the end of line 1 could be ذكر سيبويه or هذا قول سيبويه. The first word of line 2, مَبْنِىٌّ, indeclinable, was written with a final *alif* which was corrected to *yā'*. Didactic expressions such as "as I have informed you" of line 2 and "understand that (well), Allāh willing," of line 14 were carried over from oral instruction into teachers' written works. A wide variety of such expressions appears, with varying degrees of frequency, in for example the *Kitāb* of Sībawaih, the *Majālis* of Tha'lab, and the *Khaṣā'iṣ* of Ibn Jinnī, who uses فتامله تحظ به بعون الله تعالى or فتأمله وابحث عنه or فاعرف ذلك وقس به or فاعرف ذلك واكتفي به or فاعلم ذلك (*Khaṣā'iṣ* I 186, 256, 300). Sībawaih and Ibn Jinnī sometimes combine pious or didactic phrases with cross-references, using such expressions as وقد كتبنا ذلك فيما مضى or وستراه فيما تستقبل ان شأ الله and وسترى ذلك مشروحا بحسب ما يعين الله عليه وينهض به (Sībawaih I 125 and 151, II 239; *Khaṣā'iṣ* I 96, 101).

Line 3. The use of pious formulas at the beginning or end of a section, though they are not always given a separate line, seems to have been a common practice from the start. They are freely used in the works mentioned in the preceding comment.

Lines 4–10. Simple illustrative sentences beginning with such verbs as اعجبني or سرني and followed by a noun or a pronominal phrase in the nominative case, for example اعجبني الثوبُ or سرني حسنه, are commonly used in most grammatical works. Complex sentences beginning with these verbs where a relative clause or a subordinate sentence is called for, as in our text, are also readily used. The initial اعجبني frequently alternates with عجبتُ من by way of clarification as to the virtual meaning of the sentence (*ma'na taqdīrī*). Commentators on earlier grammatical works dwell at length on such sentences. They dwell on the possible changes in the word order and the introduction of various particles that in turn affect the end-voweling which may or may not change the initial meaning of the sentence (see e.g. Sībawaih I 79–81; *Jumal*, pp. 25, 37 f., 45, 133, 135 f.; Ibn Fāris, *Ṣāḥibī*, p. 118; *Khaṣā'iṣ* I 279–84, for an instructive chapter on في الفرق بين تقدير الاعراب وتفسير المعنى; Abū Ḥayyān, pp. 137, 304–24; Ibn Ya'īsh, *Sharḥ mufaṣṣal al-Zamakhsharī*, ed. G. Jahn [Leipzig, 1882–86] I 817 f. and II 1192–94; Wright *Grammar* II 47 f., 59, 252, 286).

Lines 10–11. The relative strength of the three cases is indicated in the declension of the noun, where the genitive of some of the triptote or first declension takes the accusative ending, and even more so in the diptote or second declension, which is characterized by this regulation. The greater ease in pronouncing the *fatḥah* resulted in its wider general use than either the *ḍammah* or the *kasrah*, alone or in succession (see e.g. *Khaṣā'iṣ* I 69–73; *Asrār*, p. 99).

Lines 11–14. This illustrative sentence, used in part to elucidate the syntax of the preceding one, stresses the fact that the direct object of the initial verb, رايتُ, is itself the subject of the following gerundial or verbal-noun action, which in turn takes a direct object. The sentence itself is used by practically all of the grammarians, some of whom point out that since all three nouns are in the accusative this word order is essential to the preservation of the subject-object relationship of the nouns "Zaid" and "'Amr." The ألا ترى of our text alternates with ألا تَرَ in the sources (see Wright, *Grammar* II 24 and 307, on this use of the indicative and jussive moods).

Line 14. See comment on lines 1–2.

DOCUMENT 2

PERF 735. Late third/early tenth century.

Papyrus fragment, 12 × 16 cm. (Pl. 2). A rough estimate of the original width of the page is about 22 cm. (see comment on recto 8).

Script.—Readily legible *naskhī* book hand. Many of the vertical strokes start with a hooked head, and some have a slight wave. The lower end of a few of the *alif's* turns slightly to the left or to the right. Most of the ligatured vertical strokes were written downward, showing that the pen was lifted frequently. Diacritical points are more liberally used here than in Document 1. Except in نـِعم of verso 2, vowels are used only in connection with desinental syntax, as in Document 1. The *hamzah* is not indicated. The circle is used for sectional punctuation.

TEXT

Recto

1 [هذا باب ما ○ عمل ما الحجازية رفع ونصب و] ذلك ق[ولك اذا بدأت بالاسم]
2 [ما عبد الله منطلقا ولا] زيدٌ [قائ]ما نصبت منطل[ق وقائم فاذا أدخلت]
3 [في الخبر إلا بطل عملها نحو قو]لك ما زيدٌ إلا قائمٌ. وقل[ت ما زيدٌ إلا بقائمٍ]
4 [اذا ادخلت حرف الجر بالخبروذ] لك لو انك قلت مازيدٌ إ[لا] بم[نطلق]
5 [تجرّ منطلق بالباء. ور]فعت على كل حال نحو قولك ما خارجٌ
6 [عبد الله وما قائم زيدٌ] ولا جالسٌ عمرٌ وكل هذا رفع اذا
7 [قدمت الخبر ○]
8 [هذا باب التنازع في العمل] تقول ضربث وضربني زيدٌ اذا اخرت
9 [المـُضْمـَر على الظاهر وتقول ضرب]ت وضربني اخوك
10 [واذا قدمت المضمر قلت ضربنى وضربت اخا]ك الا فقلت
11 [في التثنية ضربت وضربنى الزيدان وضر]بنى وضربت

Verso

1 [الزيدين وفى الجمع ضربت وض]رب[وني] إُخوانـُ[لك وضربوني وضربت]
2 [اخوانك فافهمه ○] هذا باب نـِعم و[بئس هما فعلان ضعيفان لايتصرفان]
3 [وذلك قولك نعم الرجلُ ز]يدٌ اوقعنا على نعم [النصب وعلى الرجل]
4 وز[يد الرفع و]ذلك قولك نعم الرجلُ زيدٌ [وبئس الغلام غلامُ]
5 زيدٍ وتقول فى النكرة نعم رجلاً زيدٌ [وبئس غلاماً غلامك فالفاعل]
6 نعم وبئس والاسم الذي تقعان عليه خب[ر وزيد خبر لمبتدا محذوف]
7 وذلك قولك نعم الرجلُ زيدٌ فنعم الر[جلِ خبراصله زيدٌ نعم الرجل]
8 وذيدٌ ابتداء فافهمه ○ فان ذكر[ت مـُؤَنـّثا الحقت]
9 فى اخره التاء وان شئت لم تثن[ى فتقول نعمت المراة هندٌ]
10 وبيست المراة جارية[لك وتقول في التثنية نعمت المراتان الهندان]
11 وذلك قول مبدا [فاذا اخرت قلت زيدٌ نعم الرجلُ و]

Comments.—The text consists of concise statements of "rules" that govern three controversial grammatical themes: the negative particle ما (recto 1–7), verbs indicating reciprocal action (recto 7–verso 2), and بِـئْس and نِـعم as irregular verbs of praise and blame (verso 2–11). The reconstruction of the missing text is perforce conjectural to a certain degree. Nevertheless, it is based largely on clues and phrases found in comparable works dating from the late second/late eighth to the early fourth/early tenth century. The order in which the above-mentioned three themes are treated varies in the sources on hand. The sources most pertinent to the concise text of our papyrus are Sībawaih's *Kitāb* and Zajjājī's *Jumal* and his *Īḍāḥ* and to a lesser extent Zamakhsharī's *Mufaṣṣal* and Ibn al-Anbārī's *Asrār*. Lively controversy among rival grammarians centered on numerous points, including those involved in the three themes of our text. The nature and method of such discussions are reflected in Thaʿlab's *Majālis* and Zajjājī's *Majālis al-ʿulamāʾ*. A brief but studied presentation is to be found in Zajjājī's *Īḍāḥ*. Fuller treatment by Abū ʿAlī al-Fārisī and by his pupil Ibn Jinnī is reflected in the latter's *Khaṣāʾiṣ*. A more systematic and detailed account of the reasons underlying the various methods and points of view is provided by Ibn al-Anbārī in his all but exhaustive *Inṣāf*. Later grammarians, despite some voluminous works, tend to multiply the illustrative examples but lack system and clarity in the elucidation of the *ʿilal* and, all in all, add little that is basic to the three themes of our papyrus.

Recto 1–2. The heading هذا باب ما is in keeping with the wording of the heading in verso 2. The rest of the reconstruction is suggested by Zajjājī (*Jumal*, p. 119): هذا باب ما — اعلم ان ما في لغة اهل الحجاز ترفع الاسم وتنصب الخبر اذا كان الخبر مؤخراً منفياً. The space available in the papyrus does not allow for this comparatively lengthy statement. The reconstruction is therefore according to the sense (معنى) rather than the wording (لفظ) of Zajjājī's text, for this particular sense is called for by the very fragmentary text of the papyrus.

Recto 2–3. The Ḥijāzians and the Baṣrans followed Qurʾānic usage in likening the particle *mā* to the irregular weak verb *laisa* as in the case governance indicated in recto 1–2. On the other hand, the Tamīmites, except those who were aware of the Qurʾānic usage of *mā*, disputed its similarity to *laisa* and insisted that it called for the nominative case for both subject and predicate, and their view was upheld by the Kūfans. The Baṣrans conceded the logic of the Tamīmite-Kūfan position but nevertheless held to the Qurʾānic usage when *mā* was used alone. However, when *mā* was combined with *illā* the Ḥijāzians and the Baṣrans followed the Tamīmite-Kūfan usage. The reconstruction of our text is based on *Jumal*, p. 119, line 5 (see also e.g. Sībawaih I 21–23 and *Asrār*, p. 59).

Recto 3–5. Baṣran and Kūfan grammarians agreed on the use of the genitive in this construction but disagreed on the reason for its use.

Recto 5–7. Sībawaih in emphasizing the general use of the nominative in such verbal sentences justifies constructions of the type found in recto 1–2 as differentiating nominal from verbal sentences, again as in the case of *laisa* (Sībawaih I 22 f.).

Recto 8. The line probably starts with a heading that begins with هذا باب as in verso 2. The heading used by Sībawaih for sentences indicating reciprocal action is very long and all but self-explanatory. That used by Zajjājī is not much shorter. A modern editor of Ibn al-Anbārī's *Inṣāf*, Muḥammad Muḥyī al-Dīn ʿAbd al-Ḥamīd, supplies the heading القول في اولى العاملين بالعمل في التنازع. Abū Ḥayyān Muḥammad ibn Yūsuf al-Andalūsī uses the heading التنازع في العمل, which in combination with هذا باب fits well in the space available for the reconstruction of the first part of recto 8 (see Sībawaih I 28; *Jumal*, p. 123; *Inṣāf* [1961] I 83; Abū Ḥayyān, p. 131).

Recto 8–verso 2. In this type of verbal sentence the Baṣrans and the Kūfans agreed that both verbs should precede the noun but disagreed as to which of the two verbs governs the expressed noun. The Kūfans argued in favor of the governance of the first verb since it starts the sentence and, with the exception of Kisā'ī (d. 189/805), limited the first verb to the first person singular. Their reconstruction of the basic reciprocal verbal sentence ضربتُ وضربني زيداً is ضربتُ زيداً وضربني. The Baṣrans took a more inclusive view. They accepted the governance of the first verb but without limiting it to the first person singular. Furthermore, they definitely preferred the governance of the second verb, for they considered the noun originally governed by the first verb to have been supressed. They therefore reconstructed the statement to yield in each case two verbal sentences, as for example ضربتُ (زيداً) وضربني زيدٌ and ضربني (زيدٌ) وضربتُ زيداً. The second point of controversy between the Baṣran and the Kūfan grammarians centered around the agreement in person and number of the governing verb and the noun. Here again the Baṣrans allowed a more inclusive usage of the dual and plural forms of the verb than did the Kūfans, whose more limited use of these forms was in keeping with their view that the initial verb of the sentence was the governing verb. Our text supplies clues sufficient to indicate that it represents the more inclusive Baṣran view on the two major points of difference stated above. The reconstruction is borrowed largely from Sībawaih and Zajjājī (Sībawaih I 28–31; *Jumal*, pp. 123–25; *Inṣāf* [1961] I 83; Abū Ḥayyān, pp. 131–33).

Verso 1. It is clear from the surviving text in verso 3–11 that the papyrus represents the Baṣran view that نعم and بئس are verbs and not the Kūfan claim that they are nouns. Sībawaih, in his *Kitāb*, covers the subject in Chapter 145, which is more comprehensively titled هذا باب ما لايعمل في المعروف إلا مضمراً. His is the earliest available Baṣran exposition of these two terms as weak verbs of praise and blame respectively. Some of his successors, whether of the Baṣran or the Kūfan school of grammar, define these two terms in both the lexical and the grammatical sense while others are concerned only with the latter, as in our text. Zajjājī (d. 337/949) has the simple heading باب نعم و بئس. He follows the lexical definition with هما فعلان ضعيفان غير متصرفين, which fits quite well in the space available in our papyrus. Ibn al-Anbārī (d. 577/1181) uses هما فعلان ماضيان لا يتصرفان, which fits equally well in the available space. Zajjājī's statement is used in the reconstruction because it is much closer in date to the probable date of our text (see Sībawaih I 256 f.; *Jumal*, p. 121; *Inṣāf* [1961] I 97; *Asrār*, p. 42).

Verso 3–6. The sources briefly point out that نعم and بئس as verbs that begin a sentence must take their subject, if defined (*muʿarraf*), in the nominative case and, if undefined (*munakkar*), in the accusative case. This statement is usually followed by another brief but not so obvious statement, namely that the second noun of the sentence is always placed in the nominative case for one of two reasons (لامرين or such variants as لوجهين, في اعرابه وجهان, and فيه مذهبان). The explanation of these two reasons or views is, as often as not, deferred until after the presentation of illustrative verbal sentences whose subject is either a single noun or two or more nouns in conjunction or two nouns in the construct state, that is, illustrative sentences similar to those in verso 3–6 (see Sībawaih I 258 f.; *Jumal*, p. 121; *Khaṣā'iṣ* I 395 f.; *Asrār*, p. 45; Ibn Yaʿīsh, *Sharḥ mufaṣṣal al-Zamakhsharī* II 1034 f.; Abū Ḥayyān, pp. 396, 399).

Verso 6–8. These lines return to the two reasons mentioned in verso 3–4, either of which requires that the noun, "Zaid," be put in the nominative case. The first reason is that نعم الرجل زيدٌ is a contraction of نعم الرجل هو زيدٌ, which consists of the two verbal sentences نِعم الرجلُ and هوزيدٌ. These two verbal sentences, though linked in meaning, are independent in their grammatical construction and therefore "Zaid" as the predicate of the second sentence must be put in the nominative. The second reason for "Zaid" to be in the nominative is stated in the briefest possible terms, that is, وزيدٌ ابتداء of verso 8, the full sense of which can be better grasped when it is followed by an explanatory statement such as فنعم الرجل خبر مقدم اصله زيدٌ نعم الرجل فزيد مرفوع بالابتداء or, in the words of Zajjājī فجعلتَ زيداً رفعاً بالابتداء وجعلتَ ما قبله خبره (see Sībawaih I 259; *Jumal*, p. 121; *Asrār*, p. 45; Ibn Ya'īsh, *Sharḥ mufaṣṣal al-Zamakhsharī* II 1034 f.; 'Abd Allāh ibn Yūsuf ibn Hishām, *Al-mughnī al-labīb* [Cairo, 1299/1882] II 44).

For the فافهمه of verso 8 and other didactic expressions see comment on lines 1–2 of Document 1.

Verso 8–11. Note the careful pointing of تثنى in verso 9 to prevent misreading of the word with its three consecutive similarly formed letters. On the other hand, the careful pointing of بيست in verso 10 reflects a preference for the use of *yā'* instead of *hamzah*, a practice reported by Akhfash al-Awsaṭ (d. 215/830 or 221/835) and by Abū 'Alī al-Fārisī (d. 377/987) as being favored by some of the Arabs (Abū Ḥayyān, p. 388, details the progressive steps in the emergence of this form).

Though generally indeclinable, these verbs of praise and blame do occur in the third person masculine and feminine. Sībawaih draws attention to and accepts the wide use of the singular forms even when the subject is dual or plural. The reconstruction called for in verso 9 and 10 reflects the use of the feminine singular نعمت for both a singular and a dual subject. Furthermore, the use of the masculine singular dominates even when the subject is feminine, but more so for the feminine plural than for the singular and the dual. The dominance of the masculine—not reflected in our text—is noted and explained with varying degrees of elaboration on the generally greater strength of the masculine forms of indeclinable verbs and of declinable verbs whose subject is collective or generic (see Sībawaih I 260; *Jumal*, pp. 121 f.; *Khaṣā'iṣ* III 244; *Inṣāf*, pp. 104, 107, 111; Ibn Ya'īsh, *Sharḥ mufaṣṣal al-Zamakhsharī* II 1028, 1035–37; Abū Ḥayyān, pp. 389 f., 400 f.; cf. Khalaf al-Aḥmar, *Muqaddimah fī al-naḥw*, ed. 'Izz al-Dīn al-Tanūkhī [Damascus, 1381/1961] pp. 95–97 [باب المذكَّر والمؤنَّث], and Wright, *Grammar* I 97 and II 290).

Verso 11. The text returns to the construction of nominal sentences referred to at the beginning of verso 8 (see comment on verso 6–8). The Baṣrans permitted this construction, though they generally preferred verbal sentences.

THE EVOLUTION OF GRAMMAR

TEXTBOOKS

The texts of Documents 1 and 2 can be safely said to represent the views of the Baṣran grammarians on the subjects covered in these fragments. Furthermore, the almost too concise presentation of the points involved indicates that both documents represent brief introductory grammars. We shall follow the development of this type of grammar as one phase of the general progress and expansion of the linguistic and literary sciences to about the mid-fourth/mid-tenth century. ʿIrāq's leading role in this development is basic to our understanding of its progress in Egypt and farther west.

The supply of brief elementary grammars increased steadily to meet the demands of teachers (*muʿallimūn*) in the mosque schools as well as those of private tutors (*muʾaddibūn*) and their charges at court and in the homes of the nobility and the wealthy. We know of several teachers and tutors who were active in the reigns of Muʿāwiyah and ʿAbd al-Malik and most of whom are said to have been older or younger students of Abū al-Aswad al-Duʾalī. But, as far as I have been able to discover, only the Baṣran Ibn Abī Isḥāq and the Kūfan Muʿādh al-Harrāʾ were credited with writing and dictating grammars in Umayyad times. Ibn Abī Isḥāq's family *isnād* traces back through his father and grandfather to ʿAlī ibn Abī Ṭālib.[1] The family produced several more generations of scholars, among them a uterine nephew and pupil, Maslamah ibn ʿAbd Allāh, who in his old age was tutor to Prince Jaʿfar, son of the caliph Manṣūr.[2] Ibn Abī Isḥāq himself was a pupil of Naṣr ibn ʿĀṣim al-Laithī and Yaḥyā ibn Yaʿmar. We find him together with his pupil and colleague ʿĪsā ibn ʿUmar al-Thaqafī (d. 149/766) attending the sessions of Ḥasan al-Baṣrī (d. 110/728), and both wrote notes from Ḥasan's dictation.[3] Ibn Abī Isḥāq's own teaching circle in the mosque was situated next to that of Muḥammad ibn Sīrīn (d. 110/728), who disliked Ibn Abī Isḥāq's interpretation of poetry but was eventually reconciled to his orthodox use of poetry.[4] As a grammarian and Qurʾānic-reader Ibn Abī Isḥāq was credited with a basic role in the development of Arabic orthography (see pp. 5–7). As a teacher he dictated the *Kitāb al-hamz* and was active in formal discussions with his contemporaries.[5] He was frequently compared and contrasted with his former pupil who came to be considered as his rival, Abū Amr ibn al-ʿAlāʾ (*ca.* 70–154/*ca.* 689–771), one of the famous seven Qurʾānic-readers and teacher of both Khalīl ibn Aḥmad and Sībawaih.[6] Eventually Khalīl's estimate of their respective scholarly merits, namely that Ibn Abī Isḥāq was the better grammarian and Abū ʿAmr the better philologist, came to be generally accepted.[7] A second contrast drawn between these two Baṣrans was that Ibn Abī Isḥāq was more given to analogy and accidence than was Abū ʿAmr and that the former was, indeed, the first to make a real breakthrough in grammatical theory.[8] His enthusiastic pupil Yūnus ibn Ḥabīb (d. 182/798 at age close to 100) went as far as to declare that, for his

[1] Ṭāshkuprīzādah, *Kitāb miftāḥ al-saʿādah* I 127; see also pp. 3–6 above. For Abū al-Aswad al-Duʾalī's leading pupils as students of grammar see e.g. *Irshād* VII 200 f. and *Inbāh* I 21 and II 381 f., III 337 f., 343 f.

[2] Jumaḥī, p. 14; Zubaidī, p. 41; *Inbāh* III 262; Ibn al-Jazarī I 410.

[3] *Fihrist*, p. 41; Sīrāfī, p. 80; *Irshād* VI 70.

[4] E.g. *Inbāh* II 106.

[5] Jumaḥī, pp. 14 f.; *Marātib*, pp. 12 f.; Zubaidī, pp. 25 f.

[6] Sīrāfī, pp. 25 f.; *Majālis al-ʿulamāʾ*, pp. 243, 247; *Inbāh* II 105 f. For Abū ʿAmr as a Qurʾānic-reader see e.g. *Fihrist*, p. 28, and Ibn al-Jazarī I 288–92.

[7] E.g. *Marātib*, p. 14.

[8] E.g. Jumaḥī, p. 14. See also Zubaidī, p. 25, هو اول من بعج النحو ومدّ القياس وشرح العلل, and *Marātib*, p. 12, يقال عبد الله (بن ابي اسحاق) اعلم اهل البصرة واعقلهم فرّع النحو وقاسه وتكلم فى الهمز حتى عُمل فيه كتاب مما املاه.

day, Ibn Abī Isḥāq and grammar were synonymous.[9] Furthermore, these two scholars were different in temperament, tribal origin, and social standing. Ibn Abī Isḥāq was more forthright, while Abū ʿAmr was more politic, especially with those in authority.[10] Ibn Abī Isḥāq, a *mawlā*, made sharp verbal thrusts at upper-class Arabs and drew in return from the sharper-tongued Farazdaq verses of seething satire.[11] Abū ʿAmr, on the other hand, gloried in his South Arab origin and the role of the South Arabs in the establishment of Islām.[12] He drew largely on those of eloquent speech among the city Arabs and the Bedouins for his knowledge of Arabic, its dialects, and its poetry.[13] Yet he, too, was at first satirized by Farazdaq, who on coming finally to realize his need for the niceties of grammar and philology made peace with Abū ʿAmr, whom he then praised in eloquent verse (see p. 7). The families of each of these leading Baṣrans produced a number of scholars. Ibn Abī Isḥāq's descendants were Qur'ānic-readers well versed in grammar, especially his grandson Yaʿqūb ibn Isḥāq al-Ḥadramī (d. 205/820 at age 88), a grammarian who ranked eighth in the list of the ten most famous Qur'ānic-readers in Islām and who counted among his pupils Abū Ḥātim al-Sijistānī and Abū ʿUthmān Bakr ibn Muḥammad al-Māzinī.[14] Three of Abū ʿAmr's brothers seem to have been overshadowed by him,[15] but two of his sons won recognition, Khalaf as a student of Bashshār ibn Burd and transmitter of his poetry[16] and Muʿāwiyah as a poet.[17] Even a daughter (not named) is mentioned as attending her father's lectures along with Aṣmaʿī among others.[18] Abū ʿAmr's grandson Jahm ibn Khalaf (n.d.) was a versatile scholar who was compared for his knowledge of poetry and its obscurities to Khalaf al-Aḥmar and Aṣmaʿī and who typified for the poet Ibn Munādhir the entire family.[19]

Even before the passing of the aged Abū ʿAmr, Khalīl ibn Aḥmad and his star pupil, Sībawaih, had become dominating figures in the fields of philology and grammar in Baṣrah, while in Kūfah Kisā'ī had joined forces with Muʿādh al-Harrā' and Ru'āsī. It is at this time that the sources first mention the composition of a brief general grammar called the *Faiṣal* (or *Faṣīl*) *fī al-naḥw*, which according to some was "composed by the Kūfans"[20] and according to others was the work of Ru'āsī,[21] the then leading Kūfan grammarian and teacher of both Kisā'ī and Yaḥyā ibn Ziyād al-Farrā'. If we are to consider the *Faiṣal* a joint Kūfan venture, then Muʿādh, Ru'āsī's uncle and teacher, must have had a hand in it (see p. 6). The work itself was written no later than the second decade of ʿAbbāsid rule, since according to Kisā'ī's own statement he was already studying the book in the lifetime of the Qur'ānic-reader Ḥamzah

[9] E.g. Jumaḥī, pp. 14 f., Sīrāfī, p. 26, and *Inbāh* II 105, read هو والنحو سواء, but Zubaidī, p. 26, and *Nuzhah*, p. 12, read هو والبحر سواء.

[10] *Majālis al-ʿulamā'*, pp. 13 f.

[11] E.g. Sīrāfī, p. 27; *Marātib*, pp. 12 f.; Zubaidī, p. 27:

فلو كان عبد الله مولى هجوته ولكن عبد الله مولى مواليـــا

To this verse Ibn Abī Isḥāq retorted: "You erred; you should have said مولى موالٍ" (cf. *Nuzhah*, p. 13; *Bughyah*, p. 282).

[12] E.g. *Majālis al-ʿulamā'*, p. 233.

[13] Jāḥiẓ, *Bayān* I 157–59, 308 f.; *Majālis al-ʿulamā'*, p. 262; Sīrāfī, pp. 25 f.; Zubaidī, p. 28; *Nuzhah*, p. 12; *Inbāh* II 105.

[14] *Fihrist*, pp. 30, 36; *Majālis al-ʿulamā'*, pp. 63 f., 156; *Marātib*, pp. 12, 27, 77 f.; Zubaidī, pp. 51, 102; Khaṭīb VII 436 f.; *Irshād* VII 302; Ibn al-Jazarī II 386–89.

[15] See *Majālis Thaʿlab* I 138; Zubaidī, p. 31; *Bughyah*, p. 423.

[16] *Aghānī* III 44 (= *Aghānī* [1927——] III 189 f.).

[17] Jumaḥī, Intro. p. 13.

[18] Zubaidī, p. 32.

[19] E.g. *Fihrist*, p. 47:

سمَّيتُمُ آل العلاء لانكم اهل العلاء ومعدن العلمِ

ولقد بنى آل العلاء لمازن بيتا احلّوه مع النجمِ

(cf. *Inbāh* I 271; *Irshād* II 427; *Bughyah*, p. 213).

[20] E.g. *Majālis al-ʿulamā'*, pp. 266, 269.

[21] *Nuzhah*, p. 32; *Irshād* VI 480; *Bughyah*, p. 33; *Muzhir* II 400.

al-Zayyāt (d. 156/773).[22] Kisā'ī found the work unsatisfactory and sought answers to some of his questions from Khalīl and among the Bedouins,[23] and later he himself wrote a *Mukhtaṣar fī al-naḥw*.[24] There is, furthermore, the often repeated statement of Ru'āsī that Khalīl borrowed his book the *Faiṣal* from him and made use of it and passed some of the borrowed materials to his pupil Sībawaih, who in his *Kitāb* cites Ru'āsī simply as "the Kūfan."[25]

During the period of the Baṣrans Khalīl and Sībawaih and the Kūfans Ru'āsī and Kisā'ī, the production of books in the fields of Arabic language and literature kept pace with that of books on Qur'ānic studies, Tradition and history and accelerated rapidly for some two centuries, as the long lists of such works credited to grammarians, philologists, lexicographers, poets, and literary critics readily attest. Many of the leading grammarians of Baṣrah, Kūfah, and Baghdād wrote several grammatical works ranging from elementary textbooks to lengthy, sophisticated volumes covering the history and theories of language. Many of the leading grammarians began their professional careers as teachers or private tutors, and a comparative few of these rose to the enviable position of royal tutor. More of their fellow "graduates" hired out as copyists or copied and marketed their own works, while still others as copyist-booksellers started family businesses which grew and prospered for several generations. Most of them, in whichever capacity, seem to have been motivated by the specific needs of their charges or by the lure of personal recognition and prestige or by the rewards of a lucrative market or by a combination of these motives. For here, again, we find no parallel to the initially heated controversies over the writing-down of *ḥadīth* and the "sale of religious knowledge" (*bai' al-'ilm*) either through fees for instruction or sale of Qur'ānic and *ḥadīth* manuscripts.[26] Even the initial opposition to the transmitting and writing of wounding satirical poetry was soon disregarded as the ancient satires were more than matched in the *naqā'iḍ* of Jarīr and Farazdaq (see pp. 132 ff.). The formal study of grammar and language, having been associated from the start with the correct reading and interpretation of the Qur'ān, acquired a religious overtone among pious Companions and Successors who taught these subjects without fees as personal contributions to the cause. But, when 'Abd al-Malik made Arabic the official language of the state and Walīd I put Qur'ānic-readers on the public payroll, command of the language became a *sine qua non* in both the religious and the secular fields, especially for the increasing number of largely Persian converts who sought professional careers in religious or administrative positions. Thereafter any scruples about charging modest fees for language instruction and copying of manuscripts and the sale of language books was limited to a few who for reasons of personal piety or temperament neglected the economic rewards of their profession. Two outstanding instances of such an individualistic outlook that readily come to mind are provided by Abū 'Amr ibn al-'Alā' and Khalīl. Abū 'Amr, who equated knowledge of Arabic with knowledge of the faith,[27] wrote down everything and counseled others to do so[28] but burned his large and valuable library in his old age.[29] The gifted and dedicated Khalīl was so engrossed in his original studies that he preferred poverty to lucrative patronage[30] though his students and colleagues were exploiting his

[22] *Majālis al-'ulamā'*, p. 266.

[23] *Majālis al-'ulamā'*, pp. 266, 171; Khaṭīb XI 404; *Inbāh* II 258.

[24] *Majālis al-'ulamā'*, p. 269; *Fihrist*, p. 65; *Nuzhah*, p. 42; *Inbāh* II 271. See Ṭāshkuprīzādah, *Kitāb miftāḥ al-sa'ādah* I 121, for Kisā'ī's verses on the necessity of knowing grammar.

[25] *Fihrist*, pp. 64 f.; *Irshād* VI 480; *Nuzhah*, p. 33; *Muzhir* II 400.

[26] See Vols. I 24 and II 227–29.

[27] *Irshād* I 8: علم العربية هو الدين بعينه. See Zajjājī, *Al-īḍāḥ fī 'ilal al-naḥw*, ed. Taḥqīq Māzin al-Mubārak (Cairo, 1378/1959) pp. 95 f., for early representative views on the benefits of knowing grammar.

[28] See e.g. *Marātib*, p. 15; *Majālis al-'ulamā'*, p. 115; *Muzhir* II 304. Cf. Aḥmad Farīd Rifā'ī, *'Aṣr al-Ma'mūn* (Cairo, 1346/1927) III 114.

[29] E.g. Jāḥiẓ, *Bayān* I 308 f.; *Irshād* IV 217. Cf. our Vol. II 52.

[30] E.g. Sīrāfī, pp. 38 f.; *Inbāh* I 344.

contributions for their own profit.[31] On the other hand, when Sībawaih's foremost pupil, Akhfash al-Awsaṭ, known as "the path to the *Kitāb*,"[32] set out to defend Sībawaih's reputation after the deplorable treatment the latter had received at the hands of the Kūfan grammarians led by Kisā'ī in the famous but still controversial affair of the *zunbūrīyah*,[33] Akhfash was won over by Kisā'ī, who paid him a handsome fee for reading Sībawaih's *Kitāb*[34] with him and employed him as tutor to his sons.[35] Furthermore, with an eye to personal prestige and profit Akhfash stopped short of complete clarity in his grammatical works so that he would be sought out for personal instruction.[36] The more dedicated and pious Abū ʿAmr Ṣāliḥ ibn Isḥāq al-Jarmī (d. 225/840) and Abū ʿUthmān Bakr ibn Muḥammad al-Māzinī (d. 249/863), fearing lest Akhfash's "monopoly" on the transmission of Sībawaih's *Kitāb* might tempt him to claim it as his own work, persuaded him, for a fee (amount not stated), to read it with them, and they then made it readily available to the public. Both scholars were much occupied with the study of the *Kitāb*, Abū ʿAmr with the identification of its more than a thousand verses of poetry,[37] while Abū ʿUthmān declared that he who would write a large grammar after Sībawaih should be ashamed of himself.[38] Both scholars were sought after as transmitters of the *Kitāb*, as teachers, and as authors of brief grammars among other works, and both attained first rank as leaders of the Baṣran school[39] and received the accompanying material rewards[40] though no amount of money could induce Abū ʿUthmān to read the *Kitāb* with a Jew because it contained over three hundred citations from the Qur'ān.[41]

Linguistic studies progressed rapidly from the time of the Umayyads and the first handbooks of orthography and accidence to the basic contributions of the Baṣrans Ibn Abī Isḥāq[42] and Abū ʿAmr ibn

[31] E.g. *Nuzhah*, p. 29; *Irshād* IV 182: كان النضر بن شميل يقول اكلت الدنيا بعلم الخليل بن احمد وكتب وهو فى خص لا يشعر به.

[32] *Fihrist*, p. 52; Sīrāfī, p. 50; *Nuzhah*, p. 84. See also *Marātib*, p. 69.

[33] *Majālis al-ʿulamā'*, No. 4, pp. 8–10. See Zubaidī, pp. 68–73, for several accounts of this episode, especially pp. 71–73 for Akhfash's own account, which is repeated in part in *Inbāh* II 36 f.; see also *Inbāh* II 348 and 358 f. and *Inṣāf*, No. 99, pp. 292–95 (= *Inṣāf* [1961] II 702–6). The long-standing controversy is centered on a difference of opinion between the Baṣrans and the Kūfans as to the correct case called for in a certain sentence construction involving compound pronouns. The several accounts, differing considerably as to what actually took place when the question was debated by Sībawaih and Kisā'ī and as to the other persons involved, including in particular the role played by the Bedouins, gave rise to a secondary controversy that has engaged Arabists for a century. Kisā'ī's or his partisans' conspiracy with the Bedouins is accepted by such scholars as Johann Fück, August Fischer, and Régis Blachère, minimized or denied by others such as John A. Haywood and Joshua Blau, while the entire episode is considered a legend by Sidney Glazer. See e.g. Gustav Flügel, *Die grammatischen Schulen der Araber* (Leipzig, 1862) pp. 45–51; *Inṣāf* (1913) Intro. pp. 79 f.; Abū Ḥayyān (1947) p. xlii; Fück, *Arabiya: Untersuchungen zur arabischen Sprach- und Stilgeschichte* (Sächsische Akademie der Wissenschaften zu Leipzig, Philol.-hist. Klasse, "Abhandlungen" XLV 1 [Berlin, 1950]) p. 30 and references there cited; Blachère, *Histoire de la littérature arabe des origines à la fin du XVᵉ siècle de J.-C.* I (Paris, 1952) 90 f., 127; Haywood, *Arabic Lexicography* (1960) p. 17 and references there cited; Blau, "The role of the Bedouins as arbiters in linguistic questions and the *mas'ala azzunburiyya*," *Journal of Semitic Studies* VIII (1963) 42–51.

While I am not convinced of Kisā'ī's personal participation in a conspiracy with the Bedouins against Sībawaih, yet I am inclined not to minimize the influence of the eloquent Bedouins (*fuṣaḥā' al-aʿrāb*) who were sought out by such pioneer scholars as Abū ʿAmr ibn al-ʿAlā', Kisā'ī, Abū ʿAmr al-Shaibānī, Abū Zaid al-Anṣārī, and Aṣmaʿī, or of Bedouins who, like leading and aspiring poets of their day, awaited an audience with early ʿAbbāsid wazirs or caliphs, or of others who were enticed into the provincial courts, especially that of ʿAbd Allāh ibn Ṭāhir, governor of Khurāsān, or of still others who were sought out by such major lexicographers as Ibn Duraid and Abū Naṣr al-Jawharī.

[34] The stated amount of the fee, or gift as it is also referred to, varies from 50 dinars (e.g. *Marātib*, p. 74; Sīrāfī, p. 51; *Inbāh* II 40) to 70 dinars (e.g. Zubaidī, p. 74; *Inbāh* II 37, 350).

[35] E.g. Zubaidī, p. 74; *Inbāh* II 36. Akhfash's younger Kūfan contemporary Ibn al-Aʿrābī, described as a distinguished teacher received 1,000 dirhems a month (*Irshād* VII 7).

[36] Jāḥiẓ, *Ḥayawān* I 91 f.; Sīrāfī, pp. 50 f.; *Inbāh* II 40 f.; *Nuzhah*, p. 84.

[37] E.g. Zubaidī, p. 77.

[38] E.g. Sīrāfī, p. 50; *Irshād* II 388; *Bughyah*, p. 203.

[39] See e.g. *Marātib*, p. 84; Sīrāfī, pp. 71, 96.

[40] E.g. *Inbāh* II 82; *Marātib*, p. 79; Sīrāfī, p. 76; Zubaidī, p. 59; *Fihrist*, p. 57.

[41] E.g. Ibn Khallikān I 115 (= trans. I 265); *Bughyah*, p. 202. See our Vol. II 9–10 for early aversion to teaching or learning from Christians and Jews. See *Nuzhah*, p. 21, and *Bughyah*, p. 406, for an earlier converted Jew who was a good grammarian.

[42] Yūnus ibn Ḥabīb (d. 182/798), who greatly appreciated Ibn Abī Isḥāq's intellectual gifts and in particular his contribution to the science of grammar, registers the rapid progress since Ibn Abī Isḥāq's day as follows: " If any one today knew no more than he did, he would be a laughingstock" (Sīrāfī, p. 26; see also pp. 25 f. above).

al-ʿAlāʾ, which led to the magnificent contributions of Khalīl and his intellectual heirs and particularly Sībawaih in his *Kitāb*.[43] The same period saw an increasing number of books on specific topics relating to language and grammar and an increasingly lengthy and sophisticated approach to the theories and principles of language and grammar—an approach concerned primarily with *fiqh al-naḥw*, *uṣūl al-naḥw*, and *ʿilal al-naḥw* to the neglect of the needs of beginners and literate laymen. This situation was fully grasped by Khalaf al-Aḥmar (d. *ca.* 180/796), who set out to help remedy it, as he tells us in the brief preface to his *Muqaddimah fī al-naḥw*, which can be summed up as follows: "When I saw that all the grammarians and Arabic experts have resorted to lengthy volumes and much theory and analysis, forgetting in the meantime the needs of beginners and laymen for lighter materials, easy to memorize, absorb, and understand, I gave thought to writing a brief book . . . that would enable the beginner to dispense with such lengthy works. So I composed these pages . . . so that whoever reads, memorizes, and studies the text will know the basis of all the grammar he needs for correct speech and writing or for reciting poetry or for composing a formal speech or epistle."[44]

Khalaf al-Aḥmar's *Muqaddimah fī al-naḥw* and Kisāʾī's *Mukhtaṣar fī al-naḥw* may have met the needs of their own generation but hardly those of the next century, during which the science of grammar continued to progress and the differences between the Baṣran and Kūfan schools became more marked as literacy and culture reached new peaks. Many leading grammarians of the Baṣran, the Kūfan, and the so-called Baghdād mixed school produced elementary or intermediate textbooks, which must have varied considerably in extent and quality. The key word in the titles of most such text books is *mukhtaṣar* or *muqaddimah*, while *mudkhal*, *muqarrib*, and *mūjaz* are infrequent alternatives. These key words in contrast to others such as *kāmil*, *jāmiʿ*, *uṣūl*, or *ʿilal*, all frequently appearing in long lists of titles of the works of many leading grammarians, indicate the level and the nature of each work. The following list though not exhaustive gives an adequate picture of the continued production of comparatively brief introductory and secondary grammars, most of them authored by leading grammarians, from late in the second to about the end of the fourth century of Islām.

Yaḥyā ibn al-Mubārak al-Yazīdī (*ca.* 126–202/744–817) was the first of a family of four generations of scholars, poets, royal tutors, and courtiers. He, as the Baṣran tutor of Prince Maʾmūn, found himself in competition for Hārūn al-Rashīd's favor with Prince Amīn's Kūfan tutor Kisāʾī[45] and like him wrote a *Mukhtaṣar fī al-naḥw*.[46] Hishām ibn Muʿāwiyah al-Ḍarīr (d. 209/824), a pupil of Kisāʾī and a Kūfan tutor, also wrote a work with this title,[47] while the more famous Akhfash al-Awsaṭ (d. 215/830 or 221/835) wrote an intermediate textbook titled *Al-awsaṭ fī al-naḥw*.[48] Abū ʿAmr al-Jarmī (see p. 28) attempted an abridgement of Sībawaih's *Kitāb* in addition to producing his own *Mukhtaṣar naḥw al-mutaʿallimīn*,

[43] Khalīl's major contribution to Sībawaih's *Kitāb* was not lost on their contemporaries and immediate successors and subsequent grammarians and their biographers nor were the lesser contributions of some "forty" others; see *Fihrist*, p. 51 (repeated in *Inbāh* II 347): قرات بخط ابي العباس ثعلب اجتمع على صنعة كتاب سيبويه اثنان واربعون انسانا منهم سيبويه والاصول والمسائل للخليل. See also Sīrāfī, p. 40; Zubaidī, p. 49 (repeated in *Bughyah*, p. 366): قيل ليونس بن حبيب صنف سيبويه كتابا فى الف ورقه من علم الخليل. The great extent of Khalīl's contribution and the lesser contributions of others have been dramatized in a statistical study of the *Kitāb* by Wolfgang Reuschel, *Al-Ḫalīl ibn-Aḥmad* (Deutsche Akademie der Wissenschaften zu Berlin, Institut für Orientforschung, "Veröffentlichung" Nr. 49 [Berlin, 1959]).

[44] Khalaf al-Aḥmar, *Muqaddimah fī al-naḥw*, ed. ʿIzz al-Dīn al-Tanūkhī, pp. 33 f.

[45] See e.g. Abbott, *Two Queens of Baghdad*, pp. 174–79 and 182–84 and references cited.

[46] E.g. *Fihrist*, pp. 50 f.; *Irshād* VII 290; *Inbāh* III 240; *Nuzhah*, p. 50.

[47] E.g. *Fihrist*, p. 70; *Irshād* VII 254.

[48] E.g. *Fihrist*, p. 53; *Irshād* IV 244; *Inbāh* II 42. The title is not a play on "the Awsaṭ" attached to his name since he was known as "the Aṣghar" in his own lifetime to distinguish him from Sībawaih's teacher Akhfash al-Akbar (see *Muzhir* II 453 f. and 456 and *Bughyah*, p. 436; cf. *Inbāh* II 36).

which was well received[49] and, despite its title, considerably advanced since it called for several commentaries (*shurūḥ*) in succeeding generations.[50]

Two sons of Yaḥyā ibn al-Mubārak al-Yazīdī, Muḥammad (d. 214/829) and ʿAbd Allāh (n.d.), followed in his footsteps as courtiers and tutors, and each wrote a *Mukhtaṣar fī al-naḥw*,[51] as did Yaḥyā's grandson ʿAbd Allāh ibn Muḥammad (n.d.),[52] pupil of Yaḥyā ibn Ziyād al-Farrā', and his great-grandson Muḥammad ibn al-ʿAbbās (d. 310/922), tutor to the sons of the caliph Muqtadir.[53] Among their contemporaries who wrote a *Mukhtaṣar fī al-naḥw* were the schoolteacher and bibliophile Muḥammad ibn Saʿdān ibn al-Mubārak (161–231/777–845) and his son Ibrāhīm[54] as well as the then ranking Baṣran grammarian Abū ʿUthmān al-Māzinī.[55] Abū Ḥātim al-Sijistānī (d. 255/869), a bibliophile and probably a bookseller,[56] inferior as a grammarian to Abū ʿAmr al-Jarmī and Abū ʿUthmān al-Māzinī[57] and a severe critic of the Kūfan grammarians,[58] was ordered by Yaʿqūb al-Ṣaffār to write and forward to him a *Mukhtaṣar fī al-naḥw*.[59] Ibn Qādim (d. after 253/867), pupil of Yaḥyā ibn Ziyād al-Farrā' and Abū ʿAmr al-Jarmī, teacher of Thaʿlab, and tutor of Prince Muʿtazz, whom he feared as caliph because he had disciplined him, also wrote a *Mukhtaṣar fī al-naḥw*.[60] Ibn Qutaibah (d. 276/889) and his son Abū Jaʿfar Aḥmad (d. 332/943 or 944) each produced a short grammar entitled *Al-naḥw al-ṣaghīr*.[61] Mubarrad (d. 285/898), ranking Baṣran scholar of his day, fee-exacting teacher of Zajjāj, tutor and courtier, produced a short grammar titled *Mudkhal* (or *Muqarrib*) *fī al-naḥw*.[62] On the order of Muwaffaq, brother and regent of the caliph Muʿtamid (256–79/870–92), Mubarrad's Kūfan counterpart, Thaʿlab (d. 291/904), wrote a short grammar which he titled *Al-Muwaffaqī mukhtaṣar fī al-naḥw*.[63]

The next generation of grammarians, most of them pupils and avowed partisans of either Mubarrad or Thaʿlab and some of them pupils of both, produced brief grammars along with more sizable linguistic and literary works. Among them were Muḥammad ibn Aḥmad ibn Kaisān (d. 299/912),[64] Abū ʿAlī al-Dīnawarī (d. 289/901),[65] Mufaḍḍal ibn Salamah (d. 305/917 or 918), Abū Mūsā al-Ḥāmiḍ (d. 305/917 or 918), who achieved Kūfan leadership after the death of Thaʿlab and who marketed his own works,[66] Zajjāj (d. 311/923), who was leader of the Baṣrans after Mubarrad,[67] Zajjāj's fellow pupil Abū Bakr ibn al-Sarrāj (d. 316/928) and the ranking scholar after him,[68] their Baghdādian contemporaries ʿAbd Allāh ibn Muḥammad ibn Shuqair (d. 317/929),[69] Muḥammad ibn ʿAbd Allāh al-Kirmānī al-Warrāq (d. 329/941),

[49] E.g. *Fihrist*, p. 56 f.; Zubaidī, p. 77; *Irshād* II 82 and IV 268; *Inbāh* II 81; *Nuzhah*, p. 90.

[50] E.g. *Nuzhah*, p. 200; *Inbāh* III 165; Ḥājjī Khalīfah V 78, 450. See pp. 153–58 below for *tafsīr* and *sharḥ* literature.

[51] E.g. *Inbāh* II 151 and III 240.

[52] E.g. *ibid.* II 134.

[53] E.g. *ibid.* III 199.

[54] *Fihrist*, pp. 70, 79; *Irshād* I 286 and VII 12; *Inbāh* I 185. For Ibrāhīm see also p. 14 above.

[55] *Irshād* VII 19, line 18: شرح مختصر المازني.

[56] The uncertainty stems from the unpointed سحر which is rendered يبحّر or يتبحر in some sources and يتجر in others (see e.g. *Fihrist*, p. 58; Sīrāfī, p. 94; *Inbāh* II 59; *Bughyah*, p. 265).

[57] E.g. *Nuzhah*, p. 116; *Inbāh* II 59.

[58] See e.g. *Marātib*, p. 24, 26 f., 74 f.

[59] Zubaidī, p. 100.

[60] E.g. *Fihrist*, p. 68; *Irshād* VII 16; *Bughyah*, p. 59.

[61] E.g. *Fihrist*, pp. 77 f.; *Inbāh* II 146; *Bughyah*, p. 291.

[62] E.g. *Fihrist*, p. 59; *Irshād* VII 144; *Inbāh* III 252; Ḥājjī Khalīfah V 88. For the unusual and eventually mutually profitable financial arrangement between Mubarrad and Zajjāj see e.g. Khaṭīb VI 90 and *Inbāh* I 159–62 and III 249 f.

[63] E.g. *Fihrist*, p. 74; *Inbāh* I 150; Khaṭīb V 210.

[64] *Fihrist*, p. 81; *Irshād* VI 281; *Inbāh* III 59.

[65] E.g. *Irshād* I 382 f.

[66] *Fihrist*, p. 79; Khaṭīb IX 61; *Irshād* IV 254; *Inbāh* II 22; *Bughyah*, p. 263.

[67] *Fihrist*, p. 61; *Inbāh* I 165; Ibn Khallikān I 13 f. (= trans. I 28 f.); Ḥājjī Khalīfah V 450.

[68] *Fihrist*, p. 62; Zubaidī, p. 122; *Inbāh* III 145, 149.

[69] *Fihrist*, p. 83; *Nuzhah*, pp. 150 f.; *Irshād* I 411; *Bughyah*, pp. 130 f.

whose manuscript copies Qifṭī praised so highly,[70] and Muḥammad ibn ʿUthmān al-Jaʿd (d. *ca.* 320/932),[71] an associate of Muḥammad ibn Aḥmad ibn Kaisān. Among Zajjāj's leading pupils who, like him, wrote a *Mukhtaṣar fī al-naḥw* may be mentioned Muḥammad ibn ʿAlī al-Marāghī al-Warrāq (n.d.),[72] the Persian Abū ʿAlī Lughdah (n.d.),[73] and the Egyptian Abū Jaʿfar Aḥmad ibn Muḥammad al-Naḥḥās (d. 337/949).[74] Abū al-ʿAbbās Aḥmad ibn Muḥammad, better known as Ibn Wallād (d. 332/943), was also a pupil of Zajjāj, who considered him superior to Abū Jaʿfar al-Naḥḥās.[75] Either Ibn Wallād or a contemporary Egyptian grammarian also named Abū al-ʿAbbās Aḥmad ibn Muḥammad (al-Muhallabī) or both men wrote a *Mukhtaṣar fī al-naḥw.*[76] Ibn Wallād, third-generation member of a family of grammarians and booksellers, in all probability wrote a short grammar in competition with Abū Jaʿfar al-Naḥḥas, his foremost rival in Egypt.[77]

The more basic and well received of the textbooks listed above no doubt represented progress in grammatical science. Those of Mubarrad and Zajjāj, like those of the earlier Abū ʿAmr al-Jarmī and Abū ʿUthmān al-Māzinī, later called for commentaries.[78] The steady production of elementary and secondary grammars continued to engage leading scholars such as Sīrāfī (d. 368/979), who, unlike the mercenary Akhfash al-Awsaṭ, made his works so simple and clear that they needed no commentary from him or others.[79] Ibn Fāris (d. 395/1004 or 1005)[80] and Abū Naṣr al-Jawharī (d. *ca.* 398/1007) are each credited with an introductory or brief grammar.[81]

THE PROGRESS OF LINGUISTIC STUDIES IN EGYPT

The foregoing list of textbooks brings us to the latest probable limit of the age of papyrus in Egypt, its homeland, where it continued to be used after the imported and superior Khurāsānian and Chinese papers began to be supplemented by the local paper products of ʿIrāq toward the end of the second/eighth century.

We now turn our attention to progress in the study of Arabic philology and grammar in Egypt itself. ʿIrāq's and particularly Baṣrah's priority and sustained leadership in both fields is enthusiastically upheld by Abū al-Ṭayyib al-Lughawī in contrast to the poor picture he gives for the Ḥijāz. Yet, it is he who reports the authoritative role of the Meccan ʿIkrimah ibn Khālid al-Makhzūmī (d. 115/733), to whom Abū ʿAmr ibn al-ʿAlāʾ, the then leading Baṣran philologist, from time to time wrote inquiring about *ḥurūf al-Qurʾān.*[82] Furthermore, Abū ʿAmr believed that ignorance of Arabic philology went hand in hand with heresy.[83] In Medina, as in Baṣrah, traditionist-jurists were aware of the significance of grammar for their professions. The encyclopedic Shaʿbī encouraged grammatical transmission of *ḥadīth.*[84] The Medinan Zuhrī, committed to the writing-down of *ḥadīth*, is credited with saying that "the people have not initiated

[70] E.g. *Fihrist*, p. 79; *Bughyah*, p. 60. See also p. 14 above, with references cited in n. 135.

[71] Khaṭīb III 47; *Nuzhah*, p. 185; *Irshād* VII 40; *Inbāh* I 269.

[72] *Fihrist*, p. 86; *Irshād* VII 47; *Inbāh* III 196.

[73] *Irshād* III 83; *Inbāh* III 43; *Bughyah*, pp. 222 f.

[74] *Inbāh* I 101; Ibn Khallikān I 35 (= trans. I 81).

[75] Zubaidī, p. 238; *Inbāh* I 998.

[76] *Fihrist*, p. 84; *Irshād* II 58 f.; *Bughyah*, pp. 169 f.

[77] Zubaidī, pp. 238 f.; *Inbāh* I 99–101; *Bughyah*, p. 169. See also p. 37 below.

[78] See e.g. *Inbāh* III 165; *Bughyah*, p. 344; Ḥājjī Khalīfah V 78, 88, 450 f.

[79] E.g. *Irshād* III 86: كان ابنه يوسف يقول وضع ابي النحو في المزابل بالاقناع.

[80] E.g. *ibid.* II 7; Ḥājjī Khalīfah V 70.

[81] E.g. *Irshād* II 268.

[82] *Marātib*, p. 15.

[83] *Nuzhah*, p. 16: اكثر من تزندق بالعراق لجهلهم بالعربية (cf. *ibid.* p. 77; see also p. 27, n. 27 above).

[84] *Irshād* I 26: اعربوا الحديث فلا باس به.

a manly practice more pleasing to me than learning grammar and eloquent speech."[85] Shāfiʿī's earlier studies were in philology, poetry, and eloquence of style, all of which he later used in the Ḥijāz as well as in ʿIrāq and Egypt in his career as traditionist-jurist (see pp. 33–35). Mecca in the second half of the second century was still the prime convention center during pilgrimages for exchange of political intelligence and literary knowledge,[86] and Medina with its Nāfiʿ ibn Abī Nuʿaim and Mālik ibn Anas had great drawing power for Qur'ānic-readers, traditionists, and jurists.[87] But with the passing of such leaders and the emigration of other outstanding scholars, including Shāfiʿī, to ʿIrāq and other provinces, the Ḥijāz lost what cultural leadership it had had. Aṣmaʿī was disappointed with Mālik because of his neglect of grammar, for which Mālik offered the surprising excuse that Rabīʿah al-Ra'ī was even worse in that respect.[88] Mālik's attitude may have influenced some of his followers to some extent, just as Abū Ḥanīfah's reputed neglect of *ḥadīth* influenced some of his followers.[89] Had these two scholars, with their basically different intellectual approaches and outlooks, been primarily grammarians, Abū Ḥanīfah would have been in the front ranks of the Baṣran grammarians and Mālik a leader among the Kūfans. But in Abū Ḥanīfah's younger days the study of grammar was still in its infancy as a distinct discipline, and even in Mālik's last decades the Baṣran grammarians' emphasis on analogy (*qiyās*) had yet to be challenged from within and to play a significant role in the stabilizing of the rival Kūfan school with its emphasis on tradition and usage. Abū Ḥanīfah's outstanding pupil Abū Yūsuf al-Qaḍī was taught an embarrassing lesson on the value of grammar by Kisā'ī,[90] while his distinguished fellow pupil and colleague Muḥammad ibn al-Ḥasan al-Shaibānī patronized not only traditionists and jurists but also grammarians and poets, among whom he divided his inheritance equally,[91] and Mālik's young pupil Shāfiʿī was already proficient in philology and poetry. The loss of its political power, the migration of its enterprising young scholars, and the great progress of linguistics in ʿIrāq combined finally to relegate the Ḥijāz to a minor role in the study of linguistic sciences. Abū al-Ṭayyib al-Lughawī (d. 351/962 or 963) stated emphatically that he knew of no Medinan master philologist.[92] His view was tacitly endorsed by the cosmopolitan Spanish scholar Zubaidī (d. 379/989), who bypassed the Ḥijāz in his list of provinces. The originality and contribution of the ascetic Arab genius Khalīl ibn Aḥmad and the receptivity and vast industry of his favorite and star pupil, the Persian Sībawaih, were quickly recognized throughout Islām and unanimously confirmed in Mecca itself. For ʿAbd Allāh ibn Muḥammad al-Tawwazī (d. 230/845 or 238/852), pupil and close associate of Aṣmaʿī and Abū ʿUbaidah,[93] reported that at a general gathering in Mecca of literary scholars from all the provinces (probably during a pilgrimage) all agreed, despite provincial pride and rivalry, that Khalīl excelled all the Arabs in intelligence and that he was the key to the sciences and their skillful diversifier.[94]

We have approached Egypt through the roundabout way of the Ḥijāz because of the especially close cultural relationship that existed between these two provinces in the first two centuries of Islām. We can safely assume that Egypt was represented at the above-mentioned Meccan gathering by scholars

[85] *Ibid.* I 20 and 22: ما احدث الناس مروة احب اليى من تعلم النحو (والفصاحة) (for Zuhrī see our Vol. II, esp. Document 6).

[86] See e.g. *Adāb al-Shāfiʿī*, pp. 44, 58, 102–5, 128, 179.

[87] See *ibid.* pp. 195–97 and 200–202 for Shāfiʿī's confidence in Mālik and the Medinans.

[88] Ṣūlī, *Adab al-kuttāb*, p. 133; cf. Fück, *Arabiya*, p. 39.

[89] As jurists the Mālikites were generally referred to as *ahl al-ḥadīth* as against the Ḥanīfites, who were known as *ahl al-ra'y* (see Vol. II 2, 12, 16, 19, 35, 62, 82, 113).

[90] *Majālis al-ʿulamā'*, p. 121: فنظر ابويوسف بعد ذلك فى النحو. See also Zubaidī, p. 139: فكان ابو يوسف بعدها لا يدع ان ياتى الكسائى. Aṣmaʿī's contemporary Sufyān ibn ʿUyainah had no use for analogy in any field since he considered it a device of the devil (see e.g. Thaʿālibī, *Laṭā'if*, p. 6, and cf. our Vol. II 35).

[91] Dhahabī, *Manāqib al-Imām Abī Ḥanīfah* (Cairo, 1366/1947) p. 54.

[92] *Marātib*, pp. 98–101: فاما المدينة فلا نعلم بها اماما في العربية.

[93] *Fihrist*, pp. 57 f.; Sīrāfī, p. 71; *Nuzhah*, pp. 107 f.; *Inbāh* II 126.

[94] *Marātib*, p. 29: اجتمعنا بمكة أدباء كلّ افق . . . فلم يبق احدا إلا قال الخليل أذكى العرب وهو مفتاح العلوم ومصرّفها.

whose interest in philology and grammar as well as in belles-lettres was ancillary to their profession as Qur'ānic-readers and to a lesser extent as traditionists and jurists (see pp. 6 f.), Egypt had a fairly good number of such scholars even though she had yet to produce a full-fledged professional philologist or grammarian. Zubaidī was the first to include Egyptians, none of whom were earlier than the third century, among the scholars in these two closely related sciences. Grateful as we are for his contributions, his generally brief entries leave much to be desired. Six of the thirteen Egyptians listed receive three lines at most, and dates are frequently lacking.[95] Suyūṭī's coverage of Egyptian philologists and grammarians starts with Ibn Hishām, famed as editor of the *Sīrah* of Ibn Isḥāq and an expert also in the linguistic sciences. He had settled in Egypt, where Shāfiʿī, whom he considered an authority on language,[96] later joined him and the two exchanged many citations from the poetry of the Arabs.[97] Both Zubaidī and Suyūṭī are misleading since they give the impression that grammar and philology were all but totally neglected in Egypt until the third century. Actually second-century Egypt made considerable progress in the fields of Qur'ānic readings and law, both of which disciplines called for a workable knowledge of Tradition and the linguistic sciences. For Egyptian scholars kept in close touch with the cultural developments first in Mecca and Medina and later in ʿIrāq. Scanty as our sources are on these cultural contacts, they yield significant evidence of the influence of the Ḥijāz and ʿIrāq on second-century Egypt, particularly in the religious and related linguistic sciences. As a result of the Arab migration westward, which started with the conquest of Egypt, many of the Companions settled in Egypt and were followed by a greater number of the Successors. Among the latter was a group of *ʿulamā'*, many of whom were Medinans. We read for instance that ʿUmar II sent Nāfiʿ ibn Hurmuz, client and pupil of Medina's leading traditionist ʿAbd Allāh ibn ʿUmar ibn al-Khaṭṭāb, to Egypt to instruct the people in the *sunnah*.[98] ʿAbd al-Raḥmān ibn Hurmuz al-Aʿraj (d. 117/735), considered by some as the first to introduce formal study of language in Medina, settled in Egypt and died in Alexandria.[99]

The Egyptian ʿAmr ibn al-Ḥārith (94–148/712–65), client of the Anṣār, pupil of Zuhrī, and teacher of Mālik and Laith ibn Saʿd, was appointed tutor in 133/750 in the household of Egypt's governor Ṣāliḥ ibn ʿAlī, whom he accompanied to Syria in 137/755.[100] ʿAmr was a versatile scholar who held public discourse on Qur'ānic readings, Tradition, and law as well as on philology and poetry.[101] His Egyptian pupil Laith, though known primarily as a jurist, was as versatile.[102] ʿUthmān ibn Saʿīd, better known as Warsh (115–97/733–812), was of Coptic origin. He studied Qur'ānic readings with Nāfiʿ ibn Abī Nuʿaim, achieved leadership in that field, and was an expert in Arabic.[103]

In the meantime Shāfiʿī's career and life had all but run their course in the Ḥijāz, the Yemen, and ʿIrāq before he settled in Egypt in 198 A.H. His early and intensive training was that of a well rounded gentleman, with emphasis on language and literature.[104] Having spent many years (17 according to the record) in the desert with the Banū Hudhail, famed as the most eloquent of the Arabs, he returned to Mecca as an expert in poetry, history, and accounts of the battle days of the Arabs (*ayyām al-ʿArab*) among

95 See Zubaidī, pp. 233–41.

96 *Adāb al-Shāfiʿī*, p. 136; *Bughyah*, p. 315.

97 *Adāb al-Shāfiʿī*, p. 136; *Ḥusn* I 306.

98 See *Ḥusn* I 162 for Nāfiʿ ibn Hurmuz and several others.

99 *Fihrist*, p. 39; Sīrāfī, pp. 21 f.; Zubaidī, pp. 19 f.; *Nuzhah*, p. 10. See our Vol. II for his activities as a traditionist.

100 Kindī, pp. 84, 89, 105, 357; Zambaur, p. 26.

101 Dhahabī I 173:
كان يخرج فيجد الناس صفوفا يسألونه عن القرآن والحديث والفقه والشعر . . . والعربية والحساب . . . وكانً اخطب الناس وابلغهم وارواهم للشعر . . . ولم يكن بعد عمرو بن الحارث مثل الليث بمصر.

102 *Ḥusn* I 164: قال يحيى بن بكير ما رايت احدا اكمل من الليث كان فقيه النفس عربي اللسان يحسن القرآن والنحو ويحفظ الحديث والشعر (for Laith as traditionist-jurist see our Vol. II, esp. Document 6).

103 *Ḥusn* I 277. See also *ibid.* I 167, 255; Ibn al-Jazarī I 502; *Muḥkam*, pp. 87, 94, and, for some of Warsh's pupils, p. 224.

104 *Adāb al-Shāfiʿī*, pp. 136 f., 214; *Irshād* VI 268 f.

D

his several other accomplishments. To these he now added the study of Tradition and law, beginning with the *Muwaṭṭa'* of Mālik.[105] In Mecca he studied Qur'ānic readings with the reader Ismā'īl ibn 'Abd Allāh ibn Qusṭanṭīn (d. 170/786 or 190/806).[106] Ismā'īl was said to have composed a grammar which he himself discarded after a visit to Baṣrah and which he replaced with a second work that was considered by the biographers as of no account.[107] Since Shāfi'ī was himself a poet of sorts and a prose stylist, poetry and grammar were no mere tools for use in his other intellectual pursuits but subjects to be cultivated independently. When law eventually captured his imagination and occupied his great talents, he did not neglect the intellectual interests of his youth. Among his literary admirers were Ibn Hishām, Abū 'Ubaid, and Aṣma'ī.[108] Aṣma'ī sought him out in Mecca for his transmission of the poetry of the Banū Hudhail and Shanfarā.[109] Mālik recognized his young follower's intellectual gifts,[110] and Ibn Ḥanbal bore witness to his clarity of thought and eloquent diction[111] in addition to considering him a godsend for the preservation of the *sunnah*.[112]

When Shāfi'ī settled in Egypt, it did not take the leading Egyptian scholars long to appreciate his worth. Aḥmad ibn Yaḥyā al-Miṣrī (171–250/787–864), the leading Egyptian scholar of his day, had almost as many interests as did Shāfi'ī, with whom he associated.[113] Yūnus ibn 'Abd al-A'lā (170–264/786–877), who studied Qur'ānic readings with Warsh and *fiqh* with Shāfi'ī, felt that whenever Shāfi'ī discoursed on Arabic, poetry, or law it would be said that he was most learned in that subject.[114] Sarj al-Fūl, known for his knowledge of language and poetry, had frequent sessions with Shāfi'ī,[115] and other philologists attended his lectures just to enjoy his command of the language.[116] Shāfi'ī's sustained interest in these many fields was attested to by his foremost pupil, Rabī' ibn Sulaimān al-Murādī (d. 270/883 or 884), who describes the master's teaching day from dawn to noon as consisting of four successive seminars, beginning with Qur'ānic science, followed by Tradition with commentary and a period for discussion and study, and ending with philology, prosody, grammar, and poetry.[117] It is in the light of his great versatility that Shāfi'ī's own terse expressions on the effects of the various disciplines on an individual's standing and character yield their full significance.[118] Ḥarmalah ibn Yaḥyā (166–243/783–857), Egyptian pupil and close associate of Shāfi'ī, reports him as saying: "Philologists are the jinns of mankind; they comprehend what others fail to perceive."[119]

[105] Young Shāfi'ī's first interest was in poetry: قال محمد بن ادريس (المكى) وراق (عبد الله بن الزبير) الحميدى (d. 219/834) سمعت الحميدى يقول سمعت الشافعى يقول كنت اطلب الشعر وانا صغير واكتب . . . فكنت اطلب العلم واكتبه على الخرق واطرحه فى الزير حتى امتلا (Abū Nu'aim, *Ḥilyat al-awliyā' wa ṭabaqāt al-aṣfiyā'* [Cairo, 1351–57/1932–38] IX 74 f.).

For Shāfi'ī's subsequent studies in the religious sciences see *Irshād* VI 369 f.; see also our Vol. II 54–56 and 81.

[106] *Adāb al-Shāfi'ī*, pp. 142 f.

[107] *Marātib*, pp. 100 f.

[108] *Adāb al-Shāfi'ī*, pp. 136 f.; *Irshād* VI 379 f., 388 f.

[109] *Irshād* VI 380, 387; *Muzhir* I 160, 176.

[110] *Adāb al-Shāfi'ī*, pp. 27 f.; *Irshād* VI 370 f. See *Irshād* VI 195–203 for Shāfi'ī on Mālik.

[111] *Adāb al-Shāfi'ī*, p. 136; *Irshād* VI 379, 381.

[112] *Adāb al-Shāfi'ī*, p. 86; *Irshād* VI 389; *Ḥusn* I 166.

[113] *Irshād* II 155; *Inbāh* I 152; *Bughyah*, p. 174: كان من اعلم اهل زمانه بالشعر والادب والغريب وايام الناس وصحب الشامغى وتفقه له.

[114] *Irshād* VI 380. For Yūnus ibn 'Abd al-A'lā, see e.g. *Jarḥ* IV 2, p. 243; Dhahabī II 98 f.; *Ḥusn* I 169.

[115] *Bughyah*, p. 252.

[116] *Irshād* VI 380.

[117] *Ibid.* VI 383.

[118] See Māwardī, *Adab al-dunyā wa al-dīn* (Cairo, 1343/1925) p. 23: من تعلم القرآن عظمة قيمته ومن تعلم الفقه نبل مقداره ومن كتب الحديث قويت حجته ومن تعلم الحساب جزل رايه ومن تعلم اللغة رقّ طبعه ومن لم يصن نفسه لم ينفعه علمه (cf. Yūsuf ibn 'Abd Allāh ibn 'Abd al-Barr, *Jāmi' bayān al-'ilm wa faḍlihi*, ed. Muḥammad 'Abduh Aghā [Cairo, n.d.] II 169, and see our Vol. II 56, with references cited in n. 216).

[119] *Adāb al-Shāfi'ī*, p. 150: اصحاب العربية جنّ الانس يبصرون ما لا يبصر غيرهم.

Thus, in second-century Egypt intellectual interests were expanding, being stimulated first by learned visitors and settlers from the east who represented practically all of the Islāmic and the linguistic and literary disciplines, as Suyūṭī and his predecessors recorded so diligently. The easterners were soon followed by eager and inquiring students and scholars from the western provinces of North Africa and especially from Umayyad Spain. North Africa had its ʿIyāḍ,[120] son or brother of ʿAwānah ibn al-Ḥakam (d. 158/775), grammarian and teacher of the better known Abū al-Walīd al-Mahrī (d. 253/867).[121] Among the early Qur'ānic-readers to visit Egypt was the Cordovan Ghāzī ibn Qais (d. 199/814), who was already a well known tutor when ʿAbd al-Raḥmān I (138–72/756–88) entered Cordova. Ghāzī's journey eastward was made no later than 150/767 since he transmitted *ḥadīth* from Ibn Juraij, who died in that year, and he also transmitted from Awzāʿī (d. 157/773). He studied Qur'ānic readings with Nāfiʿ ibn Abī Nuʿaim, the *Muwaṭṭa'* with Mālik himself, and language with Aṣmaʿī and men of like caliber.[122] A second Spanish scholar, Shamir ibn Mundhir, poet, philosopher, and grammarian, journeyed (*raḥal*) to the east and settled in Egypt, where Ibn Wahb (d. 197/812) was among his pupils.[123] A third Spaniard, Muḥammad ibn ʿAbd Allāh, while on his journey to the east sought out the Egyptian Warsh for study of Qur'ānic readings and returned to Spain to serve as tutor to the sons of Ḥakam I.[124] Egypt's role as a halfway center where scholars from the east and the west met for instruction and discourse is well illustrated in the case of Abū al-Ḥasan al-Aʿazz, a former pupil of Kisā'ī. Abū al-Ḥasan was sought out in 227/842 by a group of Spanish scholars who were instructed by him.[125] He is one of only three entries in Zubaidī's first group (*ṭabaqah*) of Egyptian grammarians, the other two being Wallād (see below) and Maḥmūd ibn Ḥassān (d. 272/885 or 886). All that Zubaidī tells us about Maḥmūd is that he was the teacher of the son of Wallād. Qifṭī adds that he was an early and leading grammarian who, like Wallād and others, followed the path of Khalīl, and Suyūṭī supplies his death date.[126]

It is clear from the foregoing brief survey that Egypt was alert to the developments in the linguistic sciences in both the Ḥijāz and ʿIrāq, particularly in the religious branches of these disciplines, and that her own participation increased progressively before, during, and after Shāfiʿī's brief residence in that province until his death in 204/820.

Walīd ibn Muḥammad al-Tamīmī al-Maṣādrī, better known as Wallād (d. 263/877), was Egypt's first full-fledged professional philologist-grammarian. He was of Baṣran origin but grew up in Egypt and returned east as a youth in search of knowledge. He studied grammar in Medina with a former pupil of Khalīl, known only as Muhallabī, who was not skillful or thorough. Wallād then journeyed to Baṣrah to study with Khalīl himself, with whom he stayed for some time and from whom he "took much."[127] This could have been no later than 175/791, the latest accepted date for the death of Khalīl. If Wallād was about sixteen[128] at the time, his birth date would fall about 159/776, which would make him over a hundred years old at his death and allow him some three-quarters of a century for industrious intellectual pursuits. The length of Wallād's stay in ʿIrāq is not stated.[129] We do know that, being of Baṣran origin,

[120] Zubaidī, pp. 246–48; *Inbāh* II 361–63.

[121] See Zubaidī, pp. 249–53: . . . شيخ اهل العربية والنحو والرواية. Zubaidī's entire entry is repeated in *Inbāh* II 209–11.

[122] Zubaidī, pp. 276 f.; *Muḥkam*, pp. 8 f.; Ibn Farḥūn, *Al-dībāj al-mudhahhab fī maʿrifat aʿyān ʿulamā' al-madhhab* (Cairo, 1351/1932) p. 219; Ibn al-Jazarī II 2; *Bughyah*, p. 371. Ghāzī returned to Spain "with great knowledge" and became tutor to the sons of ʿAbd al-Raḥmān I, Hishām I (172–80 A.H.), and Ḥakam I (180–206 A.H.). He established a family of three generations of scholars; his son and grandson also made the journey to the east (see Zubaidī, pp. 277, 282, 289).

[123] Zubaidī, pp. 279 f.; *Inbāh* I 75 f.; *Bughyah*, p. 267.

[124] Zubaidī, p. 293.

[125] *Ibid.* p. 233.

[126] *Ibid.*; *Inbāh* III 264.

[127] Zubaidī, p. 233: سمع منه ولازمه; *Inbāh* III 354: ادرك الخليل ولقيه واخذ عنه واكثر بالبصرة وسمع منه الكثير ولازمه.

[128] The age at which Thaʿlab (200–291 A.H.) began to study linguistics (*Fihrist*, p. 84; Khaṭīb V 205).

[129] *Inbāh* III 354: سمع من علماء العراق وقتا من كتبهم الحسان.

he had family connections there. This fact, along with ʿIrāq's political and cultural leadership at the time, the young man's own ambition, and his reputed accomplishment while he was in ʿIrāq, would indicate that he spent several years in that province, as one of his young sons was to do several decades later (see below). Before returning to Egypt, Wallād revisited Medina and debated his former teacher, who had to concede his superiority.

Wallād's contribution to linguistic studies in Egypt encompasses three related categories. He imported books from ʿIrāq, starting with books for his own personal study. He speeded up the dissemination of knowledge and the sale of books by establishing a family of three generations of scholar-booksellers (see below). He achieved personal leadership as a teacher-transmitter in philology and grammar, thus laying the foundation for Egyptian authorship of works in these fields.[130] Nevertheless, despite the general acknowledgment of his enterprising role, the sources yield few details of his long career. We do not know what books he studied in ʿIrāq and with whom he studied them, nor do we know what books he introduced into Egypt or which ones he himself transmitted. He is seldom referred to as a bookseller (*warrāq*) though a son and a grandson are each referred to as the son of the bookseller.[131]

Wallād had two sons, Aḥmad and Muḥammad. Little is known of Aḥmad besides the fact that he was a grammarian of Baghdād who lived in Egypt and there transmitted material on the authority of Mubarrad.[132] Muḥammad (d. 298/910), on the other hand, was much better known despite a comparatively short life of fifty years as against his father's advanced age. He and at least one of his sons were known as scholar-booksellers (see p. 14). Muḥammad in all probability started his education with his aged father. Be that as it may, we find him, while he was still a youth, studying with the Egyptian grammarian Maḥmūd ibn Ḥassān (d. 272/885 or 886)[133] and with Abū ʿAlī al-Dīnawarī (d. 289/901), who had settled in Egypt.[134] Like his father before him and drawn by the same forces, Muḥammad went east to ʿIrāq to complete his education and stayed for eight years.[135] He sought out both Mubarrad and Thaʿlab, among others (not named), and in time became tutor to the sons of an influential land-tax collector in Baghdād. He was particularly anxious to make a copy of Sībawaih's *Kitāb* from Mubarrad's personal copy, something which Mubarrad permitted no one to do. Story has it that Muḥammad bribed Mubarrad's son to make the manuscript available to him in small sections at a time. When Mubarrad discovered this he took Muḥammad to court and demanded his imprisonment, from which fate he was rescued by his government employer. Eventually Muḥammad did get to read the *Kitāb* back to Mubarrad, presumably for the latter's usual fee of 100 dinars.[136] Muḥammad's personal copy of the *Kitāb*, written no doubt with his reputed accuracy and good penmanship (see p. 14), became a family heirloom and a collector's item that eventually graced the library of Ibn al-Furāt, known also as Ibn Ḥinzābah (308–91/921–1001), the Ikhshīdid wazir who paid handsomely for any manuscript he desired.[137] We do not know the details of Muḥammad's personal contacts with Thaʿlab, whose views he probably acquired in part from Thaʿlab's son-in-law Abū ʿAlī al-Dīnawarī, who had settled in Egypt and who was Muḥammad's stepfather. Abū ʿAlī also had a personal copy of Sībawaih's *Kitāb*, which he had read first with Abū ʿUthmān Bakr ibn Muḥammad

[130] Zubaidī, p. 233, and *Inbāh* III 354: لم يكن بمصر كبير شى من كتب النحو واللغة قبله . . . عاد الى مصر ومعه كتب التى استفاد علمها وتصدر بمصر وافاد. See also *Bughyah*, p. 405, citing the Egyptian historian Ibn Yūnus (281–347/894–958): كان نحويا مجودا روى كتب اللغة والنحو وكان ثقة.

[131] *Bughyah*, p. 435.

[132] *Ibid.* p. 172. The earlier sources have no entries on Aḥmad.

[133] Zubaidī, p. 233; *Inbāh* III 264.

[134] Zubaidī, p. 234; *Irshād* VII 133; *Bughyah*, p. 112.

[135] Zubaidī, p. 236.

[136] *Ibid.*; *Inbāh* III 224; *Irshād* VII 133; *Bughyah*, p. 112.

[137] *Inbāh* III 224 f. See Ibn Khallikān I 131 (= trans. I 320) for Ibn Ḥinzābah's general interest in copies of manuscripts.

al-Māzinī and again with Mubarrad.[138] Both Abū ʿAlī and Muḥammad were recognized leaders in Egypt in the study of language and grammar according to the Baṣran school, but their reputation rested more on their study and teaching of the *Kitāb* and its dissemination through pupils' copies and other book sales than on the single work by Muḥammad and the two by Abū ʿAlī which Zubaidī dismisses as either of no account or as lacking in originality.[139]

A second basic work that we know Muḥammad took back with him to Egypt was a copy of the *Kitāb al-ʿain*, the work having been first brought from Khurāsān to Baṣrah by a bookseller in 248/862. The immediate and heated controversy that followed, alike among the Kūfans and the Baṣrans, led by the staunch Abū Ḥātim al-Sijistānī (d. 255/869), as to Khalīl's authorship of the work,[140] did not hinder its intensive study and quick distribution in ʿIrāq and the eastern provinces or its early transmission to Egypt, North Africa, and Spain. Muḥammad ibn Wallād transmitted the *Kitāb al-ʿain* on the authority of the poet and littérateur ʿAlī ibn Mahdī al-Kisrawī (d. 283/896 or 289/902),[141] tutor in the household of the better known poet and scholar ʿAlī ibn Yaḥyā ibn al-Munajjim (d. 275/888), whose great and famous library was stocked with books on many subjects, including the natural and physical sciences.[142] ʿAlī ibn Mahdī no doubt had ready access to ʿAlī ibn Yaḥyā's rich and growing library, to which he may even have contributed a copy of the *Kitāb al-ʿain*, since he was a recognized authority on the work and it was he who later transmitted it to Ibn Durustawaih (258–346/871–958).[143]

Further stimulation from ʿIrāq was provided by ʿAlī ibn Sulaimān, better known as Akhfash al-Aṣghar (d. 315/927), who was in Egypt in the years 287–300/900–912,[144] and by the controversial Muʿtazilite Abū al-ʿAbbās al-Nāshī, whose legal and linguistic theories forced him to flee from ʿIrāq to Egypt, where we find him in 280/893 and until his death in 293/906.[145]

Muḥammad ibn Wallād had two sons, Abū al-ʿAbbās Aḥmad, who was better known as Ibn Wallād (d. 332/943), and the younger Abū al-Qāsim ʿAbd Allāh (n.d.), both of whom transmitted Sībawaih's *Kitāb* from their father.[146] ʿAbd Allāh, considered the less able of the two brothers, is the last member of the family reported to have inherited his father's autograph copy of this work, which was used by the visiting Spanish scholar Muḥammad ibn Yaḥyā al-Rabāḥī (d. 358/969),[147] who furthermore transmitted from ʿAbd Allāh bits of the Wallād family history to his own pupil Zubaidī.[148]

The family tradition of scholar-booksellers was carried on by Ibn Wallād, whom we have already met along with his fellow pupil and rival Abū Jaʿfar al-Naḥḥās and as the probable author of a brief grammar (see p. 31). The rivalry between these two scholars was accentuated partly by their different professional emphases and partly by their personalities. Though both were of the Baṣran school of grammar, Ibn Wallād was a stricter follower of Sībawaih, as the title of his *Intiṣār Sībawaih ʿalā al-Mubarrad* indicates, while Abū Jaʿfar al-Naḥḥās leaned toward the views of Mubarrad and Akhfash al-Aṣghar, with both of whom he had studied in ʿIrāq and again with Akhfash during the latter's long stay in Egypt (287–300 A.H.).[149] We have record of but one public confrontation between the two rivals, in the presence of an

138 Zubaidī, p. 234.

139 *Ibid.* pp. 234, 236; *Inbāh* I 34 and III 225.

140 Haywood, *Arabic Lexicography*, p. 26, places too much emphasis on Kūfan propaganda in this controversy; see e.g. *Muzhir* I 83 f.: قال ابو على القالى لما ورد كتاب العين من بلد خراسان في زمن ابي حاتم انكره ايو حاتم واصحابه اشد الانكار ودفعه بابلغ الدفع.

141 *Fihrist*, pp. 43 and 150: كان مودبا اديبا حافظا عارفا بكتاب العين خاصة (cf. *Irshād* V 427 f.; *Bughyah*, p. 356). For a list of ʿAlī ibn Mahdī's works and samples of his poetry see *Irshād* V 428–32.

142 Kūrkīs ʿAwwād, *Khazāʾin al-kutub al-qadīmah fī al-ʿIrāq* (Baghdad, 1367/1948) pp. 205–7.

143 *Fihrist*, p. 43; Stefan Wild, *Das Kitāb al-ʿain und die arabische Lexicographie* (Wiesbaden, 1965) pp. 20 f., n. 65.

144 Zubaidī, pp. 125 f.; *Nuzhah*, p. 149; *Inbāh* II 276–78; Ibn Khallikān I 418 (= trans. II 244–46); *Bughyah*, p. 338.

145 *Marātib*, p. 85; Khaṭīb X 92 f.; ʿ*Umdah* I 134; *Inbāh* II 128 f.

146 Zubaidī, pp. 236, 239.

147 *Ibid.* p. 236; *Bughyah*, p. 172.

148 See e.g. Zubaidī, pp. 233, 238. See *ibid.* pp. 335–40 for Zubaidī's entry on this teacher of his; cf. *Inbāh* III 231, 233.

149 E.g. *Inbāh* I 99, 101; *Nuzhah*, p. 175; *Ḥusn* I 306.

Egyptian ruler (not named), and Ibn Wallād was declared to be in the right, a decision that was upheld later by Zubaidī.[150] The two rivals were both students and transmitters of poetry. Ibn Wallād is reported as saying that he transmitted the *dīwān* of Ru'bah ibn al-ʿAjjāj (d. 145/762) on the authority of his father on the authority of his grandfather,[151] who stated that when he was still a schoolboy he heard the poet in person. If we take the statement literally, the grandfather would have to be Wallād, who grew up in Egypt and died there in 263/877, that is, some 118 years after the death of the poet. If the report is to be accepted, "grandfather" (*jadd*) would have to mean an "ancestor" who was contemporary with Ru'bah. Ibn Wallād's own compositions were comparatively few,[152] but they and the man himself were well received. Abū Jaʿfar al-Naḥḥās, on the other hand, was a more prolific author with some fifty titles to his credit, but his poor delivery, mean disposition, and miserly habits made him more acceptable in his works than in his person, though many sought him out for his store of knowledge.[153] Among those who sought him out was the Cordovan chief justice and bibliophile Mundhir ibn Saʿīd (265–355/878–966), whose personality was in marked contrast to that of Abū Jaʿfar since he is described as having good presence and delivery in addition to being an expert debater and a born poet.[154] He did not hesitate to correct, in public, Abū Jaʿfar's dictation of the poetry of Qais ibn Muʿādh and thus roused his displeasure, so that Abū Jaʿfar refused to permit him to use his copy of the *Kitāb al-ʿain* for collation with the copy which Mundhir had made in Qairawān.[155] Mundhir was then directed to Ibn Wallād, whom he found to be both learned and agreeable and who made his copy of the *Kitāb al-ʿain* available to Mundhir. Abū Jaʿfar later relented and made his copy of the book also available to the visitor, who on his return to Spain to grace the court of ʿAbd al-Raḥmān III (300–350/912–61)[156] transmitted the *Kitāb al-ʿain* on the authority of Ibn Wallād only.[157]

Among other contemporaries of Ibn Wallād and Abū Jaʿfar al-Naḥḥās who either visited or settled in Egypt to teach or study should be mentioned Jāḥiẓ' nephew Yamūt ibn al-Muzarraʿ (d. 304/916 or 917), who made several visits to Egypt, the last being in 303 A.H.[158] He was followed later by Ibn Qutaibah's son Abū Jaʿfar Aḥmad, who was appointed deputy judge for Egypt in 321/933 and who died there the next year. Ibn Qutaibah's works had already made their way into Egypt and the west.[159] Abū Jaʿfar Aḥmad had inherited his father's numerous manuscripts, which he claimed to have memorized.[160] His own reputation as a scholar had preceded him to Egypt, where he dictated all of his father's works to large audiences which included both Ibn Wallād and Abū Jaʿfar al-Naḥḥās.[161] His son ʿAbd al-Wāḥid, who had served him as legal secretary, remained in Egypt and transmitted materials on the authority of his father

[150] Zubaidī, p. 238; *Inbāh* I 100.

[151] *Inbāh* I 99:
كان يقول ديوان رؤبه رواية لى عن ابي عن جدى . . . كان رؤبه بن العجاج ياتى مكتبنا بالبصرة فيقول اين تميمنا فاخرج اليه ولى ذوابة فيستنشدنى شعره.

The report may have come from Ibn Wallād's uncle Aḥmad ibn Wallād (see p. 36 above), who transmitted on the authority of Mubarrad and who had among his transmitters the Egyptian poet ʿAbd Allāh ibn Yaḥyā ibn Saʿīd (*Bughyah*, p. 172).

[152] See *GAL* S I 201 for his surviving works.

[153] Zubaidī, pp. 239 f.; *Inbāh* I 102 f.; *Irshād* II 72–74; Ibn Khallikān I 35 (= trans. I 81 f.); *Bughyah*, p. 157. See *GAL* S I 201 for surviving manuscripts.

[154] E.g. *Inbāh* III 325.

[155] Zubaidī, p. 240; *Irshād* VII 178–83; *Muzhir* I 83.

[156] Zubaidī, pp. 240, 319; *Irshād* II 73 and VII 178; *Inbāh* I 103 and III 325; *Muzhir* I 911; Maqqarī, *History of the Mohammedan Dynasties in Spain* I 240 f., 375–79, and esp. 470–75.

[157] E.g. Zubaidī, pp. 240, 319.

[158] *Ibid.* pp. 235 f.; Masʿūdī VIII 35–37; Khaṭīb III 308 and XIV 358–60; *Nuzhah*, pp. 144 f.; *Irshād* VII 305 f.; Ibn Khallikān II 453 (= trans. IV 390).

[159] Kindī, p. 547; *Inbāh* III 216. See also Gérard Lecomte, "Les disciples directs d'Ibn Qutayba," *Arabica* X (1963) 282–300.

[160] E.g. Kindī, p. 547; *Inbāh* I 46.

[161] Kindī, pp. 547 f.; *Irshād* I 160.

on the authority of his grandfather.[162] An even more distinguished scholar, the philologist Abū ʿAlī al-Qālī, visited Egypt during his long journey on the way to Spain (328–30/940–42) though details of his stay in Egypt are not given in the sources at hand.[163]

In the meantime a number of native Egyptians had attained recognition and leadership in various branches of linguistic studies. Among these may be mentioned ʿAbd Allāh ibn Fazārah (d. 282/895)[164] and Abū Ṭāhir Aḥmad ibn Isḥāq (d. 301/913 or 914),[165] each covered by Zubaidī in a one-line entry which is repeated with little or no added information by later authors. A better known Egyptian grammarian, ʿAlī ibn Ḥasan al-Hunāʾī (fl. 309/921), had studied both the Baṣran and Kūfan systems but leaned toward the former. He was credited with several compositions that were in demand and that he copied in a fine and accurate hand and marketed himself.[166] There were also Abū Bakr al-Malāṭī (d. 330/941), imam of the Mosque of ʿAmr ibn al-ʿĀṣ in Cairo and tutor to sons of nobility,[167] Ibn Isbāṭ, who had been a pupil of Zajjāj,[168] the Shīʿite ʿAllān al-Miṣrī (d. 337/949),[169] Muḥammad ibn Mūsā (d. 351/962), a scholar-bookseller who copied many manuscripts of Tradition and grammar,[170] Aḥmad ibn ʿAbd al-Raḥmān (d. 356/967), who flourished in the days of Kāfūr,[171] and the much better known Muḥammad ibn Mūsā al-Kindī, known also as Ibn al-Jubbī (284–358/897–969), whose pre-occupation with grammar was so intense and extensive that he came to be called "Sībawaih."[172] Many of the scholars who visited or settled in Egypt were patronized by the Ikhshīdids and their major-domo and regent Kāfūr (d. 357/968) but not always with happy results for all concerned, as the final relationship of Kāfūr and the poet Aḥmad ibn al-Ḥusain al-Mutanabbī (d. 354/965) illustrates. Abū Isḥāq Ibrāhīm ibn ʿAbd Allāh al-Najīramī (d. 355/966) of Baghdād, pupil and colleague of Zajjāj, from whom he had learned much, was well received and duly honored by Kāfūr, and many Egyptians transmitted from him.[173] He was among the first to write a biographical work about grammarians, and such works by Sīrāfī and others followed.[174] The Najīramī family settled in Egypt, where Abū Isḥāq's own works and autograph copies of literary manuscripts continued to circulate[175] and some were later put to good use by Suyūṭī.[176] A second member of this family of scholars, Abū Yaʿqūb Yūsuf ibn Yaʿqūb (345–423/957–1031), whose specific family relationship to Abū Isḥāq is not stated, built for himself a solid reputation in the field of language and literature and as a copyist-bookseller. Though their penmanship was not much to see, Abū Yaʿqūb and his associates were extremely accurate and much sought after to the extent that Abū Yaʿqūb's autograph copy of the *Dīwān Jarīr* cost ten dīnārs.[177] Furthermore, most of the ancient works on philology, poetry, and the battle days of the Arabs that circulated in Egypt were through his expert transmission.[178] Other linguists and grammarians, settlers or native Egyptians of the second half of the fourth century include

162 Kindī, p. 546; Khaṭīb II 8 f.: سکی مصر وروی بها عن ابيه عن جده کتبه.

163 Zubaidī, p. 132; *Irshād* II 351–54; *Inbāh* I 204–9; Ibn Khallikān I 93 f. (= trans. II 210–12); *Bughyah*, p. 198.

164 Zubaidī, p. 236; *Inbāh* I 125; *Bughyah*, p. 286.

165 Zubaidī, p. 237; *Inbāh* I 29; *Irshād* I 376; *Bughyah*, p. 128.

166 *Fihrist*, p. 83; *Irshād* V 112; *Inbāh* II 240: كتبه في مصر مرغوب فيها وكذلك في المغرب وكان خطه حسنا صحيحا قليل الخطاء وكان يورق تصانيفه.

167 See *Ḥusn* I 306, which names several more.

168 Zubaidī, p. 241; *Inbāh* III 68.

169 Zubaidī, p. 241; *Inbāh* II 240.

170 *Bughyah*, p. 109.

171 *Inbāh* I 86.

172 *Irshād* VII 110 f.; *Bughyah*, p. 108; *Ḥusn* I 306.

173 E.g. *Irshād* I 278 f.; *Inbāh* I 170 f.; *Bughyah*, p. 181.

174 *Fihrist*, p. 87.

175 *Irshād* I 277–79 and II 233. See also p. 12 above.

176 For entries see e.g. *Muzhir*, Index. See *GAL* S I 201 f. for Abū Isḥāq's surviving works.

177 *Inbāh* I 46; *Bughyah*, p. 425.

178 Ibn Khallikān II 462–64 (= trans. IV 409–11).

Ḥasan ibn ʿAlī (d. 379/989), already a leading grammarian in the days of Kāfūr and teacher of both Egyptian and visiting scholars,[179] and Abū ʿAdī al-Miṣrī (d. 381/991), who had studied with Abū Jaʿfar al-Naḥḥās.[180] There was also Abū Bakr al-Adfuwī (304–88/916–98), still another pupil of Abū Jaʿfar al-Naḥḥās and transmitter of his works. He was the leading Egyptian Qur'ānic-reader and commentator of his day, whose works were praised alike by Egyptians and non-Egyptians[181] and whose leading pupil, ʿAlī ibn Ibrāhīm al-Ḥaufī (d. 430/1039), was in turn the leading Qur'ānic scholar of his day and produced comprehensive works on the Qur'ān and on grammar.[182]

We have covered enough of Egypt's promotion of and participation in the basic linguistic sciences and have examined most of the pertinent surviving manuscripts, both as to writing materials and scripts, from the second through the fourth century—the end limit of the age of papyrus—to justify certain conclusions. Egypt though not a pioneer in these fields—perhaps partly because of her predominantly non-Arab, non-Muslim population for the greater part of the period—was nevertheless constantly in touch with the linguistic developments first in the Ḥijāz and then in ʿIrāq. Aware of the difference in approach of the Baṣran and Kūfan schools, Egyptian grammarians and philologists sought out the leaders of both schools but eventually leaned heavily toward the Baṣran school, though not without some intergroup differences. Egypt in addition to being the geographic center of the Muslim world served also as a cultural halfway center for students and traveling scholars from the eastern and western provinces. In book importation and the local book trade, the close ties among scholar, copyist, and bookseller, early and firmly established in ʿIrāq, were as firmly established in Egypt, as the multiple roles of the Wallād and Najīramī families adequately illustrate. It is to these factors that we owe the survival of the majority of literary manuscripts from the second through the fourth century, whether they are of papyrus, parchment, or paper and whether or not the original works or their surviving copies originated on Egyptian soil.

[179] *Inbāh* I 317; *Irshād* III 149.
[180] *Ḥusn* I 280; Ibn al-Jazarī I 349 f.
[181] *Inbāh* III 186–88; *Bughyah*, p. 81; *Ḥusn* I 280, 306; Ibn al-Jazarī II 198 f.
[182] *Inbāh* II 219 f.; *Irshād* V 80 f.; *Bughyah*, p. 325.

PART II

LITERATURE

DOCUMENT 3

A SPEECH OF ʿAMR IBN AL-ʿĀṢ AND DESCRIPTIONS OF THE IDEAL MAIDEN

PERF. No. 712. Mid-second/third quarter of eighth century.

Medium quality papyrus, 17 × 14 cm. The fragment is the lower part of a single sheet with several large and some smaller lacunae (Pls. 3–4). There are narrow margins all around. The cleanness of the cut at the top suggests that it is the work of a modern dealer.

Script.—The *naskhī* script shows the early characteristic of the lifting of the pen so that most of the vertical strokes were written downward. On the other hand, liberal use of hooked verticals, characteristic of the later formalized *naskhī* book hand, was not common before the mid-second/mid-eighth century. The total absence of diacritical points and other orthographic signs represents the practice of a conservative minority of scholars. The circle is used for punctuation. The double circle of verso 5 may indicate collation.

TEXT

Recto

1 قال عمرو بن العاص ان لكل شجرة اصلا ولكل اصل
2 فرعا ولكل جبل سهلا ولكل خبر اهلا وان امير المومنين
3 اصل الفروع وفرع الجذوع قد استخصكم بمحسنة
4 واستخصكم لنفسه فاختاركم للقود وصيركم للسيور
5 فاخلصوا طليبته واطلبوا بقاه بالسمع والطاعة
6 وحسن النوا[ة] في وقت السر والعلانية [ ]
7 وقال يعق[وب بن عط]ا إلا وقد اخذوا في الذى فيكن فتولاكن خذوا
8 في معنىٰ سوّا هذا في الكتاب من النساء واللذات ○
9 قال الاحنف بن قيس ان الذل لله اسر وافضل الصفات
في منزل احمر
10 لجاريه عذرىٰ في حلة خضرا في قرقر الجهر في بيت مبخر

Verso

1 قال جارية بن قدامه بل جارية حضور ساكنة في القصور من خوات الخدور
2 تنكا نقية عجرة مُهية جوف علية ان انضرتها اشتهيت وان
3 قبلتها اشهيت وان كنت صادر رويت ○
4 قال نصربن الحجاج بل جارية اديبة مشبعة العقل لبيبة كريمة في اهلها
5 حسينة ابنت عم اوبنت خالة قريبة الي حيبى تاتى حبيبة ◎
6 [قال فلان بن فلان ب]ل [ج]ارية [ ]
7 [○]

8 قال زيدبن جَبلة بل جارية ضرابة هلابة جلابة للقلب سلابة للصلب

9 خلابة للهم ذهابة للنفس طرابة ○

10 قال هاني بن عروة بل جارية عروف في بيتها تطوف مشيا شبه

11 الولق قد رابها السيوف ○

Comments.—The lost upper part of the recto probably contained a short speech or speeches of ʿAmr ibn al-ʿĀṣ or some other contemporary political and military leader or leaders, the unifying feature being the *khuṭbah.* The lost upper part of the verso must have contained more individual descriptions of a desirable maiden. The lost text of recto 6, of which very few traces remain, may have alluded to either the protection of or the abstinence from women during wartime, or more probably it contained a brief heading for the second section of the text. On the other hand, abrupt transition from one theme to another was not uncommon in early literary collections and modern editors of even later book-length manuscripts frequently feel the need to supply sectional headings.

Though all the men named in the text are identifiable, the sources on hand have as yet yielded no parallel to any of their statements. The text of the statements of recto 9 to verso 11 can be pointed and voweled in various ways to give different slants in meaning. It is sometimes difficult to decide which of the possible readings the writer had in mind. On the whole, the general character of all these statements reflects remarkable restraint for this category of Arabic literature. This restraint can perhaps be explained partly by the character of the speakers and partly by the implication that the maiden each speaker describes is desired as a prospective Arab wife of equal social status rather than as a non-Arab concubine.

Recto 1–6. The *amīr al-muʾminīn* of recto 2 must be either ʿUmar I or Muʿāwiyah. The relationships of both these caliphs with ʿAmr ibn al-ʿĀṣ is discussed below, along with pertinent comment on the papyrus text (see pp. 47–53).

Recto 7–8. Space and remaining traces best fit reconstruction of the name as Yaʿqūb ibn ʿAṭāʾ. The only such person in the early sources is Yaʿqūb ibn ʿAṭāʾ ibn Abī Rabāḥ (n.d.), of whom little beyond his name seems to be known though his father (d. 114/732 at age 88) was a well known Meccan schoolteacher and traditionist (Ibn Saʿd V 360, 344–46; Ibn Rustah, p. 221; Jāḥiẓ, *Bayān* I 251; *Maʿārif,* p. 271; Dhahabī I 92; see also our Vol. II 16, 112, 149, 153).

Yaʿqūb is citing a book which advocates the taking of enjoyment of women and of other pleasures without allowing any of these to master one. The second sentence, with its key word خذوا, alludes loosely to the Qurʾānic permission of such pleasure-taking (see e.g. Sūrahs 3:13, 4:3, 7:31). For the enjoyment of similar pleasures in the world to come see e.g. Sūrahs 37:46, 43:71, and 47:15. The theme of this section brings to mind the description of the cloistered houris, good and comely, who await the martyrs and the true believers in the world to come (see e.g. Sūrah 55:54–76 and cf. *Concordance* I 526 حور).

Recto 9–10. Note the crowding of line 10, the last on the page, and the interlineal phrase.

Aḥnaf ibn Qais al-Tamīmī of Baṣrah (d. *ca.* 68/688) was the acknowledged leader of his tribe, which had settled in ʿIrāq. The four men mentioned after him in the text were his contemporaries who, either as tribesmen or as South Arabs, were at times associated with him. As an able general Aḥnaf played no small part in the conquest of Khurāsān and in the First Civil War of Islām. As an active statesman Aḥnaf played significant roles from the time of ʿUmar I until his death in the reign of ʿAbd al-Malik (see e.g. Ṭabarī II 2565–68, 2680, 2867, 2897–2900, 2903 for Aḥnaf's early campaigns). His association with ʿAlī and Muʿāwiyah is discussed below. History has accorded Aḥnaf an enviable reputation as a man of wisdom, integrity, and, above all, patient forbearance which became proverbial. Nature, on the other hand, stinted him as to physical endowment. He was clubfooted—hence the name Aḥnaf—and narrow shouldered, had buck teeth and a receding chin. He lost an eye in battle or through smallpox and was bald-headed. These and a few other deformities were no doubt responsible for his limited family. He had but one son, who proved to be weak, lazy, and of no account, and a granddaughter who died young (e.g. *Maʿārif*, pp. 216 f., 284; *ʿUyūn* IV 35; Thaʿālibī, *Laṭāʾif*, pp. 105, 109; Ibn Khallikān I 291 [= trans. I 641]; see Ibn ʿAsākir VII 18–23 for a long and fairly representative list of Aḥnaf's qualities and of his sayings, followed by a list of his physical deformities). He was known to have come to the aid of women, especially widows and victims of war, and to have counseled Muʿāwiyah on great forbearance toward one's children (e.g. Āmidī, *Al-muwāzanah baina shiʿr Abī Tammām wa al-Buḥturī*, ed. Aḥmad Ṣaqr [Cairo, 1961] p. 194; *ʿIqd* II 437).

In view of Aḥnaf's physical deformities and sterling qualities, it is not surprising that his is the most restrained of the statements in our text. His reluctance to dwell on physical pleasures is confirmed by relevant statements, some of which are quite outspoken (see e.g. Ibn ʿAsākir VII 21; Ibn Khallikān I 289 [= trans. I 637]; Ibn al-Ṭiqṭaqā, *Al-fakhrī* [1895] p. 79: جنبوا مجالسفا ذكر الطعام والنساء فاني ابغض ان يكون الرجل وصافا ليطنه مداحا لفرجه مائلا بصغوه الى النساء; but see also *ʿUyūn* IV 96). He was generally against seeking women's counsel and against levity (Ibn ʿAsākir VII 18). He gave orders that no woman was to follow his bier. But a prominent elderly woman of his tribe, described as his maternal cousin in some of the sources, passed by his burial and stopped to deliver an impromptu eulogy that covered his many commendable qualities, including his consideration for women, much to the embarrassment of Muṣʿab ibn al-Zubair, in whose cause Aḥnaf had fallen (e.g. Jāḥiẓ, *Bayān* II 312; Ibn Abī Ṭāhir Ṭaifūr, pp. 50 f.; *Amālī* III 28; Ibn ʿAsākir VII 24).

Verso 1–3. Note the use of the verb نضر in verso 2 rather than نظر. The unpointed personal name of verso 1 is sometimes pointed to read Ḥārithah, but more often the man is identified as the Baṣran Jāriyah ibn Qudāmah al-Tamīmī, especially in the earlier sources, all of which, however, can be safely assumed to be later than the papyrus text. In tribal and local politics, Jāriyah was second only to Aḥnaf, who addressed him as "uncle" and "cousin," as a mark of respect since they were not such close relatives as some thought (Ibn Saʿd VII 1, p. 38; *Istīʿāb* I 94; *Iṣābah* I 444). Both men were leading ʿAlīd generals who took part in the First Civil War of Islām as a last resort, and both were appeased by Muʿāwiyah sometime after the abdication of Ḥasan ibn ʿAlī in 41/661 (see pp. 54 f.). Aḥnaf, officiating at the funeral of Jāriyah (after 50/670), concluded his prayer with these words: "May Allāh bless you! You envied not the rich nor despised the poor" (*ʿIqd* II 321).

Jāriyah's stipulation for a personable noble maiden, protected and chaste, of a specified figure, attractive, responsive, and considerate could hardly be objected to by his companions, even though they had ideas of their own.

Verso 4–5. Naṣr ibn al-Ḥajjāj (fl. *ca.* mid-first century A.H.) is identified as the son of Ḥajjāj ibn ʿIlāṭ al-Tamīmī, who witnessed Muḥammad's victory at Khaibar, after which he converted to Islām. Ḥajjāj returned to Mecca with the false report that Muḥammad had been defeated and taken prisoner and that he, Ḥajjāj, wished to collect what money his wife had and what debtors owed him so that he could return in time to trade in the spoils of Khaibar. His real objective, however, was to secure his capital and return to Muḥammad. He was with Muḥammad at the time of the conquest of Mecca and is said to have died during the reign of ʿUmar I (Ibn Saʿd IV 2, pp. 14 f.; Yaʿqūbī II 57 f.; *ʿUyūn* I 274; *Istīʿāb* I 129 *Iṣābah* I 641). His son Naṣr does not seem to have figured prominently in any political role but is known to have accompanied Abū Mūsā al-Ashʿarī on his campaign to Persia and was present with him at the conquest of Tustar in 17/638 as was also Aḥnaf (Ṭabarī I 2542, 2551; Yāqūt I 847–49; *Khizānah* II 111). A poet of sorts, he is remembered rather as an extremely handsome young man who was attractive to the matrons of Medina. Some of these ladies, including, it is said, Hind bint ʿUtbah, mother of Muʿāwiyah, and Fāriʿah, the literate mother of Ḥajjāj ibn Yūsuf, addressed romantic verses to him (see Nabia Abbott, "Woman and the state on the eve of Islam," *AJSL* LVIII [1941] 269–79, for a historical biography of the aggressive Hind). When ʿUmar heard a woman reciting some of these verses, he, ever concerned for the morals of the City of the Prophet (see Ṭabarī I 2745 f. and our Vol. II 108–10), summoned Naṣr, ordered his head shaved, and exiled him to Baṣrah and soon exiled a second Tamīmite for much the same reason "to join his cousin in Baṣrah" (Ibn Saʿd III 1, pp. 204 f.; Jāḥiẓ, *Maḥāsin*, pp. 236 f., 286–89; *ʿUyūn* IV 23 f.; Mubarrad, p. 333; Masʿūdī IV 98 f.; *Aghānī* IV 98; *ʿIqd* II 463 and VI 119; see *Khizānah* II 108–12 for later authors who give the story with some variations). Baṣran women, orthodox or Khārijite, were known for their freedom of action, which presently induced Ziyād ibn Abīhi (Ziyād ibn Abī Sufyān), as Muʿāwiyah's governor of ʿIrāq, to take drastic action against them (see Mubarrad, p. 582; *ʿIqd* VI 96 f., 101; see also Abbott, "Women and the state in early Islam," *JNES* I [1942] 352).

In Baṣrah, Naṣr again got into trouble, this time with Mujāshiʿ ibn Masʿūd al-Tamīmī, illiterate Bedouin general and deputy-governor of Baṣrah under ʿUqbah ibn Ghazwān (15–16/636–37; see Ṭabarī I 2238; Yaʿqūbī II 166; Yāqūt I 241 f.; Zambaur, p. 39). In the presence of Mujāshiʿ, Naṣr wrote in the sand his declaration of love to be read by Mujāshiʿ's beautiful and literate wife Shumailah and she responded by doing the same. Mujāshiʿ dismissed Naṣr and either had someone read the love messages for him or forced the truth out of his wife, whom he then divorced. Naṣr is said to have composed some verses denying any wrongdoing, but Ibn Qutaibah suspected the verses to be spurious. The beautiful Shumailah later married Ibn ʿAbbās. Mujāshiʿ, a Zubairid partisan, fell in the Battle of the Camel (*Ansāb* I 137; *ʿUyūn* IV 24; Dīnawarī, p. 156; *Aghānī* XIX 143). We hear of Naṣr once again when he strove in vain to have the caliph Muʿāwiyah recognize the paternity of his half-brother ʿAbd Allāh ibn al-Ḥajjāj, even as Muʿāwiyah had already recognized the paternity of his half-brother Ziyād ibn Abī Sufyān in 44/664 (*ʿIqd* VI 133 f.; Ṭabarī III 480). The caliph Mahdī, in 159/776, condemned Muʿāwiyah's decision and reversed it.

Naṣr's statement is the only one in the document to include culture and intelligence as desirable qualities in a maiden. Such an outlook no doubt rendered the handsome Naṣr doubly attractive to such high-placed, aggressive, and literate women as those mentioned above. One should keep in mind that, despite the one-man moral censorship by ʿUmar I, the high-born Arab woman was still for the most part a free and outspoken agent in a changing society in which the veil and seclusion had yet to take hold of her and thereafter leave a clear field for the accomplished songstress and the slave-concubine (see Abbott in *JNES* I 106–26 and 341–68, esp. pp. 113 f., 123, 351 f.; see also Jāḥiẓ, *Qīyān* in *Thalāth rasāʾil*, ed. Joshua Finkel [Cairo, 1344/1926] pp. 56–59, and *ʿIqd* VI 96 f.).

Verso 5. First-cousin and other interfamily, intertribal marriages, though generally practiced and approved for the sake of economic and tribal numerical strength, were nevertheless recognized as having the drawback of limiting the choice of wives and, in the case of first cousins, of ultimately debilitating the health of the families and hence of the tribe. Arguments, on individual and tribal bases, for and against such marriages are readily available (see e.g. *ʿUyūn* II 67 and IV 3, 6, 71; Ibn Abī Ṭāhir Ṭaifūr, p. 107; *ʿIqd* VI 103, 117; *Amālī* III 47; Khālidīyān, *Kitāb al-ashbāh wa al-naẓāʾir*, ed. Sayyid Muḥammad Yūsuf, I [Cairo, 1958] 228–31; Jāḥiẓ, *Nisāʾ* in *Rasāʾil*, ed. Ḥasan al-Sandūbī [Cairo, 1352/1933]).

Verso 6–7. In all probability the speaker is another Tamīmite or else a member of a South Arab tribe (see comment on verso 10–11).

Verso 8–9. Zaid ibn Jabalah al-Tamīmī was another associate of Aḥnaf. He admired Aḥnaf and considered him in some respects superior to himself and for that very reason felt justified in asserting himself against Aḥnaf's provocative behavior (*ʿUyūn* I 285; *Aghānī* XXI 20; Ibn ʿAsākir V 451). Both men were in the ʿIrāqī delegation to ʿUmar I. When Aḥnaf made a favorable impression on that caliph, Zaid attempted to counteract it but was rebuked by ʿUmar. Aḥnaf's eloquent argument at the time persuaded ʿUmar to send more colonists to ʿIrāq and to order its governor, Abū Mūsā al-Ashʿarī, to undertake an irrigation project in the interest of that province's economy (e.g. *ʿIqd* II 62 f.). When, after the First Civil War, the Banū Tamīm, led by Aḥnaf, made peace with Muʿāwiyah, Zaid served for some time as chief of police under ʿAbd Allāh ibn ʿĀmir, Muʿāwiyah's governor of ʿIrāq (41–44/661–64; see Ṭabarī II 15; Ibn ʿAsākir V 450; Zambaur, p. 39). Though there are occasional references to Zaid's wisdom, very few of his sayings have survived in contrast to the numerous citations credited to Aḥnaf (see e.g. *ʿUyūn* I 245, 285; *ʿIqd* IV 203). The papyrus text's long list of intensive verbal adjectives in addition to expressing Zaid's desire for a highly gifted, vivacious, captivating, exciting, anxiety-vanquishing, and pleasure-giving maiden does credit also to his eloquence.

Verso 10–11. Hānī ibn ʿUrwah al-Murādī al-Mudhḥijī (d. 60/680) is identified as a Yemenite partisan of ʿAlī, on whose side he and his son fought, as did Aḥnaf, in the Battle of Ṣiffīn in 37/657 (see *Waqʿat Ṣiffīn,* pp. 153 and 231). Hānī remained a staunch Shīʿite, and his headquarters in Kūfah became a gathering place for local partisans and a refuge for fellow tribesmen in flight from Muʿāwiyah or his governors (Mubarrad, pp. 71 f.; Ṭabarī II 229–31, 244–56, 268–71; *ʿIqd* I 136). After the fall of Ḥusain ibn ʿAlī at Karbalāʾ (61/680) Hānī and Muslim ibn ʿAqīl, to whom Hānī had given refuge, plotted the death of ʿUbaid Allāh ibn Ziyād, who, on discovering the plot, executed both men (Ibn Saʿd IV 1, p. 29; Dīnawarī, pp. 245 f.; Ṭabarī II 229–32, 244–60; *ʿIqd* IV 378).

Hānī, it should be noted, is the only one to use a simile in his description. A swift walking pace was and still is admired in a young maid. The verb *walaqa,* "to hasten," though used for humans, is generally used to describe the vigorous swift pace of a she-camel (*nāqah walqā*). A slow measured step was and still is generally preferred in a mature woman. The walk and talk of women, young and old, have received much attention in Arabic poetry and prose literature (see e.g. *ʿUyūn* IV 81–84; Ibn Abī ʿAwn, *Kitāb al-tashbīhāt,* ed. ʿAbd al-Muʿīd Khān [London, 1950] pp. 101 f.; Yazīdī, pp. 151 f.; Khālidīyān, *Kitāb al-ashbāh wa al-naẓāʾir* I 50 f., 53–59, 102, 200–205). Women were readily compared to swords or associated with swords as being slender and well formed or well tempered, or acquainted with and quick to face danger, or sharp tongued (Jāḥiẓ, *Nisāʾ* in *Rasāʾil,* pp. 274 f.; *Amālī* I 233; see also Lane, سيف, pp. 1485 f.). Figures of speech apart, in pre-Islāmic and early Islāmic times, women accompanied men on raids and to battle. Enough of them took part in the actual fighting, using clubs and daggers or whatever they could lay their hands on, to call for clarification of their legal status as "warrior women" (see e.g. Muslim XII 187: النساء الغازيات). The simile was the most widely used figure of speech in describing not only the walk and talk but almost any feature or characteristic of women. It was used more frequently in poetry than in prose and in the latter more in the ʿAbbāsid than in the Umayyad period—a development that has some bearing on the dating of our document (see p. 78).

HISTORICAL BACKGROUND

I

The *amīr al-muʾminīn,* "commander of the believers," of recto 2 must be either ʿUmar I, who was the first caliph thus addressed, or the caliph Muʿāwiyah. Both caliphs placed ʿAmr ibn al-ʿĀṣ in command of large expeditionary forces, ʿUmar I for the initial conquest of Egypt and Muʿāwiyah for its reconquest from Muslim rebels during the First Civil War of Islām. My first reaction to the text of recto 1–6 was that the unnamed caliph referred to was probably Muʿāwiyah. Research into the relationships of ʿAmr ibn al-ʿĀṣ with ʿUmar I, ʿUthmān ibn ʿAffān, and Muʿāwiyah strongly reinforced my first impression even though a parallel to the papyrus text in an explicit historical context, which alone can provide certainty, is yet to be found.

A brief sketch of ʿAmr's military and political career is in order. His family, like that of Muʿāwiyah and other leading Quraishites of Mecca, was strenuously opposed to the mission of Muḥammad.[1] It is well known that ʿAmr's conversion, generally placed shortly before the conquest of Mecca, took place only after he and such other notables as Khālid ibn al-Walīd and ʿUthmān ibn Ṭalḥah had come to realize that Muḥammad was within reach of ultimate victory.[2] Muḥammad, sensing ʿAmr's military qualities and Muʿāwiyah's political acumen, placed ʿAmr in command of sizable expeditionary forces that included both Abū Bakr and ʿUmar,[3] and used Muʿāwiyah as his secretary.[4] What is not so well known is ʿAmr's struggle to come to terms with his own immediate family situation. His mother, a war captive used by several men, "assigned" him to ʿĀṣ ibn Wā'il, who, according to ʿAmr himself, showed little interest in him in contrast to the attention he paid to his younger half-brother Hishām.[5] Later, ʿAmr compared himself unfavorably with Hishām because Hishām had accepted Islām early and had died in its cause during the conquest of Syria.[6] Political rivals and gossipers seldom allowed ʿAmr to forget either the shadow over his birth or his late conversion.[7]

Furthermore, ʿAmr harbored a deep-seated and long-lasting resentment against ʿUmar on social, political, and personal grounds[8]—a resentment that was reciprocated by ʿUmar both before and during his caliphate. Though kept under control for the most part, the undercurrent of mutual resentment and mistrust flared on occasion into harsh words and accusations between the authoritative caliph and his ambitious general,[9] even though both men realized the need and the advantage of co-operation between them in the momentous first decades of Islām. ʿUmar I saw to it that ʿAmr, though appointed governor-general of Egypt, did not for long have sole control of that rich province, particularly its financial administration and the distribution of its large revenues.[10]

There was not much love lost between ʿUmar I and Muʿāwiyah either. But Muʿāwiyah had the advantage of a clear-cut birthright and was, moreover, more restrained and politic with ʿUmar I as with most people, including ʿAmr. After their successful campaigns in Syria and Egypt, Muʿāwiyah and ʿAmr as governors-general of Syria and Egypt respectively presented conflicting claims before ʿUmar I. ʿAmr, realizing that he was losing the argument, did not hesitate to disrupt the meeting by interrupting and slapping Muʿāwiyah in the face.[11]

ʿUmar I's suspicions and fears of ʿAmr were reinforced by ʿUthmān ibn ʿAffān, who is said to have induced ʿUmar to call a halt on ʿAmr's march on Egypt and to curtail his powers as governor of that

[1] See e.g. *Sīrah* I 167, 187 f., 234 f., 261 f., 272 for this group's mocking taunts of Muḥammad and his followers and the Qurʾānic revelations called forth thereby.

[2] See Vol. I, Document 6, esp. p. 85, with references cited in comment on recto 16–verso 1; see also Yaʿqūbī II 28 f.; Zubairī, *Kitāb nasab Quraish*, ed. E. Lévi-Provençal (Le Caire, 1953) p. 322; *Ansāb* I 232 f.; Ṭabarī I 1600–1605; *Istīʿāb* II 434 f.

[3] See e.g. *Sīrah* I 984–87; Ibn Saʿd VII 2, pp. 188, 192; *Ansāb* I 529 f.; Yaʿqūbī II 85; Ṭabarī I 1894–96; Ibn Taghrībirdī I 71:
قلت لعمرو بن العاص مات رسول الله صلعم وهو يحبك وقد استعملك قال عمرو بلى فوالله ما ادرى احبا كان لي منه او استعانه بي.

[4] See e.g. Yaʿqūbī II 87 and ʿ*Iqd* IV 168, where both ʿAmr and Muʿāwiyah are listed among the secretaries of Muḥammad, but ʿAmr functioned as such only occasionally.

[5] See e.g. *Ansāb* I 215; *Istīʿāb* II 595; ʿ*Iqd* II 289 and IV 11.

[6] E.g. Ibn Saʿd II 2, p. 8; *Istīʿāb* II 434, 595; *Iṣābah* III 1–4, 1243–45; *Fāḍil*, p. 50.

[7] E.g. *Waqʿat Ṣiffīn*, pp. 444, 562, 583, 624; Ṭabarī I 3335, 3357, 3405; ʿ*Uyūn* I 284; *Istīʿāb* II 434; Jāḥiẓ, *Bayān* III 223; *Fāḍil*, pp. 49 f.; ʿ*Iqd* IV 11–13, 39.

[8] *Futūḥ*, p. 146:
قال عمرو بن العاص قبح الله يوما صرتُ فيه لعمربن الخطاب واليا فلقد رايت العاص بن وائل يلبس الديباج المزرّر بالذهب وان الخطاب بن نفيل ليحمل الحطب على الحمار بمكة.

[9] *Ibid.* p. 79; Jāḥiẓ, *Bayān* II 291.

[10] *Futūḥ al-buldān*, p. 219; *Futūḥ*, pp. 147 f.; ʿ*Iqd* I 47 f.

[11] ʿ*Iqd* I 17. The sequel to this episode is not reported. ʿAmr, however, was to use the element of "shocking surprise" on several later occasions in the interest of himself and Muʿāwiyah, who came to recognize the ruse as characteristic of ʿAmr (see n. 24 on p. 50 below).

province.[12] Even on his deathbed ʿUmar rebuked ʿAmr severely for being overly ambitious, as the Oriental Institute's unique papyrus fragment from Ibn Isḥāq's *Taʾrīkh al-khulafāʾ* revealed.[13] In his rebuke, ʿUmar assumed that ʿAmr expected to stay in power through co-operation with Muʿāwiyah as a prospective caliphal candidate.[14] The implication is that ʿAmr himself would not aspire to the caliphate, because he was the son of a captive woman. ʿUthmān as caliph, motivated partly by nepotism and partly by mistrust of ʿAmr, soon removed the latter from the governorship of Egypt.[15] The indignant ʿAmr, feeling much wronged, went into political retirement throughout the rest of the caliphate of ʿUthmān—a fact which in itself reflects the deep antipathy between the two men. ʿUthmān, threatened by the Egyptian rebels, appealed to ʿAmr among others to use his influence with them, and ʿAmr in turn urged the troubled caliph to mend his own ways.[16] Though ʿAmr at heart favored the Medinan opposition, he remained neutral through the election of ʿAlī, the subsequent outbreak of the First Civil War, and ʿAlī's victory in the Battle of the Camel in 36/657.

The sources differ as to who took the initiative in the alliance that was soon formed between ʿAmr and Muʿāwiyah, though the weight of evidence points to Muʿāwiyah.[17] ʿAmr, accompanied by his sons ʿAbd Allāh and Muḥammad and his secretary Wardān, having first discussed the situation with them, journeyed north to meet and bargain with Muʿāwiyah on a basis of partnership,[18] in which ʿAmr was ultimately to play the role of caliph-maker in return for the still coveted governorship of Egypt from which ʿUthmān had removed him. ʿAmr and Muʿāwiyah had several qualities of leadership in common along with others that were complementary. Muʿāwiyah, the astute politician with proverbial patience, genuine or not, in the face of great provocation contrasted sharply with the comparatively quick-tempered ʿAmr. But in war strategy and the use of the element of surprise at a critical moment to avert a defeat if not, indeed, to turn it into victory, ʿAmr had much the advantage over Muʿāwiyah. Muʿāwiyah himself, during the caliphate of ʿUmar I, had been the unfortunate victim of this strategy of ʿAmr's. Now ʿAmr, allied with Muʿāwiyah against ʿAlī, was to use the element of surprise in their common interest on at least three occasions. The first was in a preliminary encounter with ʿAlī prior to the Battle of Ṣiffīn (37/657) when ʿAmr deliberately exposed himself and caused the shocked ʿAlī to turn away in disgust.[19] The second occasion was during that battle, in which ʿAmr's sons ʿAbd Allāh, who was but thirteen years younger than his father, and the younger Muḥammad were active[20] along with Wardān, ʿAmr's secretary and standard-bearer.[21] As he sensed that the battle was going against him, ʿAmr sprung the surprise of the well known episode of raising Qurʾānic manuscripts on spearheads and demanding that the Book arbitrate

[12] See Nabia Abbott, *The Ḳurrah Papyri from Aphrodito in the Oriental Institute* ("Studies in Ancient Oriental Civilization," No. 15 [Chicago, 1938]) pp. 80–82 and references there cited; see also Ibn Taghrībirdī I 6 f.: قال عثمان ان عمرو امروا لمجرم وفيه اقدام حب الامارة . . . .

[13] Vol. I, Document 6.

[14] *Ibid.* recto 16–verso 4 and comments on p. 85.

[15] Ṭabarī I 2813 f., 2817–19: فغضب عمرو على عثمان عضباً شديدا وحقد عليه. See also e.g. *Futūḥ*, pp. 173 f.; Masʿūdī IV 298; ʿ*Iqd* II 462 and IV 24; Ibn Taghrībirdī I 75.

[16] Ṭabarī I 2932–34; Yaʿqūbī II 202 f.

[17] See Ibn Saʿd IV 2, pp. 2–8; Yaʿqūbī II 214–16; Dīnawarī, p. 167; Ṭabarī I 3249–54; Masʿūdī IV 339 and V 54 f.; ʿ*Iqd* IV 345; Ibn Taghrībirdī I 128 f.

[18] Ibn Taghrībirdī I 128 f. states this very clearly: قال عمرو ان اتيتُ عليا قال لي انت رجل من المسلمين وان اتيت معاوية يخلطني بنفسه ويشركني في امره (cf. *Ibid.* I 72).

[19] *Waqʿat Ṣiffīn*, pp. 463, 482; Masʿūdī IV 370 f.; ʿ*Iqd* IV 12 and 339 f., VI 150.

[20] *Waqʿat Ṣiffīn*, pp. 233, 255, 386, 441 f.; *Ansāb* I 168; Dīnawarī, pp. 183 f.; Ṭabarī I 3256 f.; *Istīʿāb* I 234, 370; Ibn ʿAsākir VI 293. Muḥammad is generally characterized as more warlike than ʿAbd Allāh, who was more inclined to diplomacy and is said to have joined in the battle only in obedience to his father, for whom he had acted as deputy-governor of Egypt during ʿAmr's visit to Medina at the end of the caliphate of ʿUmar I (*Ansāb* I 168 f.; Ṭabarī III 2540; Kindī, p. 10; ʿ*Iqd* II 375 f.; Ibn Taghrībirdī I 75, 128 f.). ʿAbd Allāh came to be much better known as a traditionist (see our Vol. II).

[21] Wardān was ʿAmr's secretary and standard-bearer in ʿAmr's first conquest of Egypt also (e.g. Ibn Taghrībirdī I 21–23).

their differences.[22] The third occasion of surprise was at the subsequent Arbitration of Adhruḥ, when ʿAmr outwitted ʿAlī's representative Abū Mūsā al-Ashʿarī, who declared ʿAlī deposed while ʿAmr reaffirmed Muʿāwiyah as caliph.[23] The resulting quick disorganization of ʿAlī's forces, followed by a schism within his party, did more damage to ʿAlī's cause than all of Muʿāwiyah's intrigues and ʿAmr's reputed military generalship. It was at this point that Muʿāwiyah himself pointed out to ʿAmr and others of his leading supporters the advantages of an immediate march on Egypt, the coveted governorship of which he had already promised to ʿAmr as the reward for his services. Muʿāwiyah accepted ʿAmr's military plan for the invasion and quick conquest of the province and at the same time corresponded with key figures in Egypt urging them to support ʿAmr.[24]

This last occasion seems to be the most logical background for the speech of ʿAmr ibn al-ʿĀṣ that is recorded in recto 1–6 of our papyrus, and analysis of the text yields the same conclusion. Conceivably ʿAmr could have used the figurative phraseology of recto 1–3 to apply to any one of the three caliphs under whom he served—ʿUmar I, ʿUthmān, and Muʿāwiyah.

If we assume that the papyrus text refers to ʿUmar I, then the most probable occasion for ʿAmr's speech would have been either prior to his initial march to ʿArīsh or on the arrival of the reinforcements under four commands that ʿUmar I later sent him.[25] Impatient and suspicious of the delay in this first conquest of Egypt, ʿUmar wrote ʿAmr a letter accusing him of purposeful delay for personal reasons, reminding him that Allāh grants victory only to those who are true and sincere and ordering him to address the people and urge them on to a whole-hearted and united effort, to give public support to the four commanders previously sent him, and to attack the enemy as one man.[26] But even without such constant stress and strain between caliph and general, ʿAmr would hardly have used the first sentence of recto 4, "and he has chosen you exclusively for himself," to apply to ʿUmar. For to ʿUmar, as to Abū Bakr before him and ʿAlī later and as ʿAmr himself had come to realize, allegiance was owed first to Islām and the community of believers and not to any one person, caliph or general. This was dramatically illustrated by ʿUmar's removal from military command and trial of Khālid ibn al-Walīd, whose generalship in the conquest of ʿIrāq and Syria had won him the title "The Sword of Allāh."[27]

ʿUthmān, in view of his personal relationship with ʿAmr (see pp. 48 f.), need hardly be considered as the *amīr al-muʾminīn* referred to in our papyrus text.

Thus, we come back to Muʿāwiyah as the caliph most probably referred to in our document. For there is ample evidence that, despite their public declarations, ʿAmr and Muʿāwiyah each had at heart primarily his own self-interest (see e.g. n. 18 above). Furthermore, ʿAmr's forces for the Battle of Ṣiffīn (37/657) and for his second conquest of Egypt (38/658) were Syrian troops provided by Muʿāwiyah for the specific purpose of opposing ʿAlī and transferring Egypt's allegiance from ʿAlī to himself, pending the outcome of the proposed arbitration.[28] For following the truce agreement to arbitrate, the Syrians took the oath of

[22] *Waqʿat Ṣiffīn*, pp. 545–47, 555; Ibn Saʿd IV 2, pp. 3 f.; Yaʿqūbī II 219; Ṭabarī I 3333–38; Masʿūdī IV 381; Dīnawarī, p. 201. Dīnawarī, pp. 206–10, gives full details of the drafting of the truce agreement and the most detailed text of the treaty itself, which is dated Wednesday, the 15th of Ṣafar 37/3rd of August 657.

[23] Ibn Saʿd III 1, p. 21; Jāḥiẓ, *Bayān* I 183, 271; Ṭabarī I 3356 f.; Yaʿqūbī II 221 f.; Dīnawarī, pp. 213 f.; Masʿūdī IV 391–98; ʿ*Iqd* IV 346–49.

[24] Ṭabarī I 3396–98: قال معاوية انك يا ابن العاص امرؤٌ بورك لك في العجلة وانا امرو بورك لي في التوّدة. *Ibid.* I 3400 gives Muʿāwiyah's parting words to ʿAmr as follows: ...اوصيك يا عمرو بتقوى الله والرفق فانه يُمن وبالمهل والتودة فان العجلة من الشيطان

[25] *Futūḥ*, pp. 61 f.; Ibn Taghrībirdī I 9.

[26] *Futūḥ*, p. 79.

[27] Khālid's son ʿAbd al-Raḥmān was with Muʿāwiyah at the Battle of Ṣiffīn as one of ʿAmr's standard-bearers and high in Muʿāwiyah's counsel. He was inspired by his father's reputation to engage in several courageous single combats against some of ʿAlī's leading supporters, including Jāriyah ibn Qudāmah of verso 1–3 of our papyrus (see *Waqʿat Ṣiffīn*, pp. 233, 412, 450, 482, 485, 489; Dīnawarī, pp. 197, 209). Later, when ʿAbd al-Raḥmān was suggested as Muʿāwiyah's successor, Muʿāwiyah, it is said, had him poisoned to clear the way for his own son Yazīd (*Aghānī* XIV 12).

[28] E.g. Yaʿqūbī II 226; Ṭabarī I 3400, 3406; Kindī, p. 29; Masʿūdī IV 421.

allegiance to Muʿāwiyah in Dhū al-Quʿdah 37/April 658.[29] Moreover, the text of recto 4–6 is addressed not to a general assembly of troops but to their commanding officers. Some of ʿAmr's trusted commanding officers who accompanied him on his second conquest of Egypt had served under him in his first conquest of that province[30] and thus were given a fresh and impressive demonstration of ʿAmr's resourcefulness in accomplishing his aims.

The phrase "in private or in public" of recto 6 was already current in the time of Muḥammad and occurs in both the Qur'ān and the standard *ḥadīth* collections.[31] It occurs also in the literary sources in contemporary reference to ʿAmr himself and to Ziyād ibn Abī Sufyān, among others, as being the same in private and in public.[32] The phrase "with hearing and obedience" of recto 5, along with several variants, was also current in the time of Muḥammad and after and is likewise found in the Qur'ān[33] and even more frequently in the *ḥadīth* collections in reference to several religious duties and military commands with the emphasis on absolute obedience to the commands of Allāh as revealed through Muḥammad.[34] The extension "to hear is to obey" in reference to the commands of a caliph came first to be associated with Muʿāwiyah, who was soon to be generally accused of turning the caliphate into an absolute monarchy. Moreover, even before he claimed the caliphate, Muʿāwiyah, in negotiating the initial alliance with ʿAmr, had insisted on ʿAmr's allegiance and obedience in return for the governorship of Egypt for life, though Egypt was yet to be reconquered.[35]

After his second conquest of Egypt (36/658) ʿAmr left his son ʿAbd Allāh as deputy-governor of Egypt and returned, along with his secretary Wardān, to be Muʿāwiyah's representative at the arbitration which followed in Shaʿbān 38/January 659. After ʿAmr had outwitted Abū Mūsā al-Ashʿarī, who declared ʿAlī deposed, and reaffirmed Muʿāwiyah as caliph, there developed renewed stress and strain between ʿAmr and Muʿāwiyah. Wardān, who usually drew up the agreements between them, had previously pointed out to ʿAmr that the governorship of Egypt for life was not much of a reward since ʿAmr was already an old man.[36] The Shīʿite Naṣr ibn Muzāḥim (d. 212/827), author of *Waqʿat Ṣiffīn*, reports that at the Battle of Ṣiffīn Muʿāwiyah accused ʿAmr of coveting the caliphate for himself[37] and that during the conference between ʿAmr and Abū Mūsā al-Ashʿarī preliminary to the fateful Arbitration of Adhruḥ Abū Mūsā had suggested his son-in-law ʿAbd Allāh ibn ʿUmar ibn al-Khaṭṭāb as their common choice, to which ʿAmr countered by suggesting his own son ʿAbd Allāh.[38] It is not surprising, then, that after his unexpected reaffirmation of Muʿāwiyah as caliph, the aging ʿAmr felt that more was due him for his great services than the lifetime governorship of Egypt. Masʿūdī reports that ʿAmr stayed away from Muʿāwiyah, who eventually called on him. Realizing ʿAmr's trend of thought, Muʿāwiyah tricked him by first isolating him from

[29] Ṭabarī II 199.

[30] E.g. *Futūḥ*, pp. 61 f. See *Ḥusn* I 113 for Khārijah ibn Ḥudhāfah, who accompanied ʿAmr on both conquests, after the second of which ʿAmr appointed him chief of police and called on him at times as his substitute in leading the public prayer service. In the latter function he was mistaken for ʿAmr and was murdered in the well known triple assassination plot of 40/661 in which the intended victims were ʿAlī, Muʿāwiyah and ʿAmr himself (see e.g. Yaʿqūbī II 251 f.; Dīnawarī, pp. 227–29; Ṭabarī I 3457–65; Masʿūdī IV 426 f.).

[31] E.g. Sūrahs 2:274, 13:22, 14:31, 35:29; *Concordance* II 447 and IV 340. See also e.g. Ibn Ḥanbal, *Al-musnad* II 256, 363, 459 and esp. IV 309, which refers to Muḥammad as being the same in private and in public.

[32] Ibn ʿAsākir VI 424; Ibn Taghrībirdī I 72 f.

[33] Sūrahs 4:59, 64:12 and 16.

[34] Concordance II 540 f. and IV 35–37. See also e.g. Bukhārī III 5 f. and IV 401–3, 419; Muslim XII 222–28; Ibn Ḥanbal, *Al-musnad* IV 130, 202. The phrase is absent in ʿUmar's speeches (see e.g. Ṭabarī I 2137 and 2144, for his brief inaugural speech; *ibid.* I 2757–62, esp. pp. 2757 f.; *Sīrah* I 1017; Ibn Saʿd III 1, pp. 196 f.).

[35] *Waqʿat Ṣiffīn*, pp. 43–46; Ibn Saʿd VI 2, pp. 2 f.; Dīnawarī, pp. 167–69; Ṭabarī I 3249–54. For further references see n. 17 on p. 49 above.

[36] Yaʿqūbī II 263. ʿAmr's age at the time of his death in 43/664 is variously given as 78, 90, 98, and 100 (see e.g. Ibn Saʿd VII 2, pp. 188 f.; Masʿūdī V 60; *Istīʿāb* II 435; Ibn Taghrībirdī I 130 f.).

[37] *Waqʿat Ṣiffīn*, pp. 358, 463 f., 621; Dīnawarī, p. 189.

[38] *Waqʿat Ṣiffīn*, pp. 621, 623, 626; Dīnawarī, pp. 211–13; Ṭabarī I 3355 f.; Masʿūdī IV 396. ʿAbd Allāh's mother was ʿAmr's legal Arab wife (see e.g. Ibn Saʿd IV 2, p. 8).

his followers and then threatening his very life until ʿAmr was forced to declare anew his own allegiance publicly and to call on the people to accept Muʿāwiyah as the best available caliph.[39] In a written agreement drawn at this time, Muʿāwiyah specified *al-samʿ wa al-ṭāʿah* in return for no more than the previously agreed-on governorship of Egypt for life,[40] which had already begun officially in Rabīʿ I 38/July 658.[41] On his return to Egypt late in 39/spring 660[42] ʿAmr could hardly have been well enough disposed toward Muʿāwiyah to be urging wholehearted support of his cause in any of the subsequent military engagements.[43] The next year brought ʿAlī's assassination followed by Muʿāwiyah's public inauguration of his own reign. Ḥasan ibn ʿAlī's short reign ended in Rabīʿ I 41/July 661 with his abdication, which finally brought Muʿāwiyah the allegiance of all the provinces of the empire.[44]

Ibn Saʿd's entry on ʿAmr ibn al-ʿĀṣ, though only briefly covering his early alliance with Muʿāwiyah, reports yet another rift and reconciliation between them, which led to a new agreement at about the end of 39/early 660.[45] The account states that when the affair (*amr*) was in Muʿāwiyah's hand—and the *amr* must refer to the Syrians' acceptance of Muʿāwiyah as their caliph—Muʿāwiyah felt he had given ʿAmr too much in a lifetime governorship of Egypt with total control of its revenues and that ʿAmr saw to it that Muʿāwiyah drew no profit from the great wealth of Egypt.[46] ʿAmr, for his part, felt that Muʿāwiyah should be willing in the event of complete victory[47] to add the governorship of Syria to that of Egypt, which Muʿāwiyah refused to consider. The bitter quarrel that followed would have severed their alliance but for the mediation of Muʿāwiyah ibn Ḥudaij, who had served both men well at the Battle of Ṣiffīn and later and who now brought about the reconciliation and new written agreement between them. The significant clauses of this agreement were Muʿāwiyah's explicit insistence on ʿAmr's allegiance and obedience and a change in the tenure of ʿAmr's governorship of Egypt from life to seven years.[48] This change would seem, on the face of it, to be a complete victory for Muʿāwiyah, particularly in view of ʿAmr's advanced age. There is, however, some evidence that the seven-year clause was perhaps intended as a concession to the aging ʿAmr and his son ʿAbd Allāh. For we find that Muʿāwiyah's triumphal entry into Kūfah in 41/661 was followed by his appointment of ʿAbd Allāh as governor of that city. But on second thought Muʿāwiyah either canceled the appointment before it took effect or soon removed ʿAbd Allāh from the governorship in order to eliminate any possibility of being caught in Syria between "ʿAmr in Egypt and his son in Kūfah,"[49] these two provinces being the most strategic, geographically and politically, of Muʿāwiyah's hard-won empire. ʿAmr himself may have helped to bring about the annulment of his son's appointment or else to have hastened his removal from the governorship of Kūfah. For Muʿāwiyah soon found himself short of funds to distribute as largess to the members of the numerous delegations from ʿIrāq and the Ḥijāz that came to his court in Syria during the first year of his uncontested

[39] Masʿūdī IV 402–6.

[40] *Ibid.* IV 405: مصر لك ما عشت.

[41] Ṭabarī I 3400, 3443; Kindī, p. 31.

[42] Ibn Saʿd IV 2, pp. 5 f.; Ṭabarī I 3464.

[43] Ṭabarī II 206 f. gives an instance of ʿAmr's attempts to belittle Muʿāwiyah as a new caliph. In contrast, ʿAmr himself had addressed Muʿāwiyah as *amīr al-muʾminīn* while the Battle of Ṣiffīn was in progress (*ʿIqd* I 26).

[44] Masʿūdī V 14; Ṭabarī I 199.

[45] Ibn Saʿd IV 2, pp. 5 f.:
لما صار الامر في يدى معاوية استكثر طعمة مصر لعمرو ما عاش ورأى عمرو انّ الامر كله قد صلح به وبتدبيره . . . وظنّ ان معاوية سيزيده الشام . . . .

[46] Yaʿqūbī II 263, 277. See Masʿūdī V 61 and Kindī, pp. 33 f., for divergent accounts of the extent of ʿAmr's estate.

[47] Both men must have felt this to be more than ever probable, knowing the rapidity with which ʿAlī's strength was being sapped by political factions and the Khārijite revolt.

[48] Ibn Saʿd IV 2, p. 6:
على انّ لعمرو ولاية مصر سبع سنين وعلى ان على عمرو السمع والطاعة لمعاوية . . . ثم مضى عمرو بن العاص على مصر واليا عليها وذلك في آخر سنة تسعة وثلاثين فوالله ما مكث بها الا سنتين او ثلاثا حتى مات.

[49] Ṭabarī II 10 f.; Zambaur, p. 42.

caliphate. He appealed to ʿAmr for funds from Egypt's revenues, and ʿAmr's only answer was to remind Muʿāwiyah of the terms of their agreement.[50] On the other hand, ʿAbd Allāh did in fact succeed his father in 43/664 as governor of Egypt for at least a brief period,[51] which in Wāqidī's report, however, extends to some two years.[52] But Ṭabarī reports the curious statement that Muʿāwiyah removed (*ʿazala*) ʿAbd Allāh ibn ʿAmr from the governorship of Egypt in the year 47/March 667–February 668,[53] that is, at the very time that the agreement of late 39/early 660, which stipulated the seven-year clause, was due to expire. We have already seen that early in the alliance between ʿAmr and Muʿāwiyah, Wardān had pointed out to ʿAmr that his reward of lifetime governorship of Egypt was unsatisfactory. Wardān had suggested further that ʿAmr bargain for the succession of his heirs. ʿAmr had then spoken to Muʿāwiyah about this but had been turned down.[54] Nevertheless, ʿAmr himself did not dismiss the idea of a family succession. His son Muḥammad was primarily a soldier with no taste or talent for politics. That left ʿAbd Allāh, who had on several occasions acted as his father's deputy-governor, as ʿAmr's political heir. ʿAmr, as we have seen above, at one time in his talks with Abū Mūsā al-Ashʿarī had even suggested ʿAbd Allāh as a caliphal candidate. In view of all these facts, it seems not at all improbable that Muʿāwiyah, faced with a total break between himself and ʿAmr when as yet only Syria and Egypt acknowledged him as caliph, did indeed make a concession to ʿAmr and his son ʿAbd Allāh in the seven-year agreement, which he ignored shortly after ʿAmr's death in 43/664 until its formal expiration in 47/667. Here we must leave this tantalizing question until new source materials provide more clear-cut information. In any event, the several near-breaks between the fairly well matched and primarily self-seeking ʿAmr and Muʿāwiyah, each keenly aware of the other's strong and weak points, illustrate each one's awareness of his own capabilities. Muʿāwiyah one day asked ʿAmr: "What is the measure of your intelligence?" "I have not undertaken anything ever from which I could not extricate myself," answered ʿAmr. "As for me," countered Muʿāwiyah, "I have not undertaken any matter whatsoever from which I wish to be extricated."[55] On still another occasion Muʿāwiyah characterized himself as one who uses not his sword where his whip serves his purpose, nor his whip where his tongue is sufficient, adding that he would not permit matters between him and the people to get so out of hand as to reach the breaking point even if no more than a hair held them together.[56] These self-appraisals, one must concede, were certainly borne out in the relationships of both ʿAmr and Muʿāwiyah so that they came to be counted in the foreranks of shrewd men and astute and wily politicians.

All in all, the foregoing survey of ʿAmr's ups and downs with the first four caliphs, on the one hand, and with Muʿāwiyah, on the other, points to the latter as the most probable *amīr al-muʾminīn* of our papyrus text. Furthermore, in view of the increasing stress and strain between ʿAmr and Muʿāwiyah in the post-arbitration period, the over-all tone of ʿAmr's speech best reflects their relationship in the period between the truce agreement with ʿAlī and the fateful arbitration itself. For this was the period in which discipline deteriorated markedly in ʿAlī's camp but held fast among Muʿāwiyah's well disciplined forces,[57] as it was also the exhilarating period during which Muʿāwiyah was first acknowledged by the Syrians as their caliph and ʿAmr, with troops supplied by Muʿāwiyah, achieved his second conquest of Egypt and received the long-coveted governorship as his well earned reward.

50 Dīnawarī, pp. 235 f.
51 Yaʿqūbī II 264; Masʿūdī V 61; *Istīʿāb* II 436; Ibn Taghrībirdī I 139. Zambaur, p. 25, does not record this event.
52 Ṭabarī II 28, citing Wāqidī.
53 Ṭabarī II 84.
54 Yaʿqūbī II 262 f.
55 *ʿIqd* II 242: قال معاوية لعمرو ما بلغ من عقلك قال ما دخلت في شي قط خرجت منه فقال معاوية لكني ما دخلت في شي قط اريد الخروج منه.
56 *ʿUyūn* I 9; *ʿIqd* I 25.
57 *Waqʿat Ṣiffīn*, pp. 529 f., 614; Ṭabarī I 3283 f.; Masʿūdī V 80. See also p. 59 below.

II

We have seen (pp. 44–47) that in addition to Ya'qūb ibn 'Aṭā', who is the author or transmitter of our papyrus text, five other men are mentioned in the second section, which begins with recto 7, and that these five were close contemporaries. The sources reveal Aḥnaf ibn Qais al-Tamīmī as the central figure, with whom the others were closely associated on various occasions as fellow tribesmen and co-delegates or as 'Alīd supporters. Aḥnaf's guiding principles seem to have been to serve and safeguard the interests of his tribe, the Tamīmites, and to support the regularly constituted caliphal authority. He advocated the settlement of political disputes by negotiation and compromise, failing which he took refuge in neutrality. But he did not stop short of participating in rebellion and civil war as a last resort in the interest of justice as he saw it. He remained neutral in the rebellion against 'Uthmān and throughout the first stages of the First Civil War that ended with 'Alī's victory in the Battle of the Camel.[58] The continuation of the rebellion against 'Alī, headed this time by Mu'āwiyah in formidable alliance with 'Amr ibn al-'Āṣ, came as a shocking and ominous surprise. Aḥnaf's natural inclination toward 'Alī, as representing the Prophet's family and as the duly elected caliph who had already fought on the battlefield for the right to his office, was enough to convert him from a neutral to a whole-hearted supporter of 'Alī for the remainder of the First Civil War.[59] The Tamīmites fought well under his command in the ensuing Battle of Ṣiffīn.[60] He was among those who questioned 'Amr's and Mu'āwiyah's motives in raising the Qur'ānic manuscripts, and he strenuously opposed the truce that followed.[61] He was on hand at the drawing of the truce agreement and cautioned 'Alī repeatedly to be wary of the wily 'Amr and Mu'āwiyah and specifically warned him in the strongest terms possible not to yield to 'Amr's demand to delete the *amīr al-mu'minīn* appended to his name in the drafting of the truce agreement.[62] When it was time for the Arbitration of Adhruḥ, Aḥnaf, realizing that Abū Mūsā al-Ash'arī was no match for 'Amr and convinced that he himself was more than a match for the latter,[63] entreated 'Alī in vain to appoint him or any other of Muḥammad's Companions as a counselor to Abū Mūsā. All he could then do was to give the departing Abū Mūsā his advice, which, like that offered 'Alī, went unheeded.[64]

After the death of 'Alī and the abdication of Ḥasan ibn 'Alī, Aḥnaf and his Tamīmites took the oath of allegiance to Mu'āwiyah and co-operated with his successive governors of Baṣrah. Mu'āwiyah was a firm believer in keeping communications open between the ruler and the tribal leaders as his counselors and helpers (*wuzarā'*).[65] It took the patient yet dignified prudence (*ḥilm*) for which he was proverbially famed

[58] E.g. Ṭabarī I 3148, 3168 f., 3178 f. See also Nabia Abbott, *Aishah, the Beloved of Mohammad* (Chicago, 1942) pp. 150, 161, and references cited.

[59] *Waq'at Ṣiffīn*, pp. 28–31; Ṭabarī I 3226.

[60] E.g. *Waq'at Ṣiffīn*, pp. 231, 440, 462.

[61] E.g. *ibid.* pp. 573 f., 582; Ṭabarī I 3329–36.

[62] E.g. *Waq'at Ṣiffīn*, pp. 582 f.: لاتمح اسم امير المومنين عنك فاني اتخوّف ان محوتها الاترجع اليك ابداً لا تمحها وان قتل الناس بعضهم بعضاً. But 'Alī cited the example of Muḥammad at the drafting of the Treaty of Ḥudaibīyah (Ṭabarī I 3334 f.).

[63] *Waq'at Ṣiffīn*, pp. 573 f.; Ṭabarī I 3334 f.

[64] *Waq'at Ṣiffīn*, p. 617; Dīnawarī, pp. 205 f.: فقال الاحنف بن قيس لعليّ . . . فان شئت ان تجعلنى حكما فافعل والا فثانيا اوثالثا فان قلت انى لستُ من اصحاب رسول الله صلعم فابعث رجلا من صحابته واجعلنى وزيرا له ومشيرا فقال على ان القوم قد ابوا ان يرضوا بغير ابي موسى والله بالغ امره. 'Alī's first choice was 'Abd Allāh ibn 'Abbās, but objections were raised to having two North Arabs as the arbiters (Ṭabarī III 2363). The term *wazīr* was applied to Abū Bakr as Muḥammad's burden-bearer, and 'Umar I applied it to 'Abd Allāh ibn Mas'ūd when he sent him to Kūfah, and Ziyād ibn Abī Sufyān was referred to as *wazīr* of Mu'āwiyah.

[65] Ibn 'Asākir VII 22, in passages collected to illustrate Aḥnaf's political sagacity, quotes him thus:
راس سياسة الوالى خصال ثلاث اللين للناس الاستماع منهم والنظر في أمورهم ورأس مرؤة الوالي خصال ثلاث حب العلم والعلمآء ورحمة الضعفآء والاجتهاد في مصلحة العامة ولا يتم أمر السلطان إلا بـالوزرآء والأعوان ولا ينتفع الوزرآء والأعوان إلا بالمودة والنصيحة ولا تنفع المودة والنصيحة إلا بالرأي والعفـاف وقال أعظم الأمور على الملوك خاصة وعلى النـاس عامة أمران أحدهما أن يحرموا صالح الوزرآء والأعوان والآخر أن يكون أعوانهم ووزرآؤهم غير ذوي مروءة ولا حيآء وقال ليس شيء أهلك للوالي من صاحب يحسن القول ولا يحسن العمل وقال حلية الولاة وزينتهم وزراؤهم . . . وقال يجب على الخلق من حق اللّٰه التعظيم له والشكر ويجب على الرعية من حق السلطان الطاعة له والسمع والمناصحة ومن حق الرعية على السلطان الاجتهاد في أمورهم.

for Aḥnaf to hold his own with Muʿāwiyah as caliph. Muʿāwiyah, for his part, aware of Aḥnaf's powerful influence in ʿIrāq and aspiring to that same quality of *ḥilm*, having first angrily provoked his erstwhile enemy,[66] came in time to court, use, and admire him,[67] even as ʿUmar I had done some three decades earlier. When Aḥnaf and Jāriyah ibn Qudāmah came in 50/670 with a Baṣran delegation to Muʿāwiyah, they and two other leaders each received a gift of 100,000 dirhems.[68] Aḥnaf's independent spirit combined with his sense of loyalty was well illustrated on several occasions when Muʿāwiyah sought his support for the succession of his son Yazīd. Unimpressed with the youthful Yazīd and opposed to dynastic succession, Aḥnaf remained silent while a group of influential leaders summoned by Muʿāwiyah praised Yazīd and favored his succession. ʿAmr ibn Saʿīd's high praise of Yazīd was considered excessive even by Muʿāwiyah. It included the metaphor *jadhaʿ qāriʿ*,[69] which is closely related to one used earlier by ʿAmr ibn al-ʿĀṣ (see recto 3 of our papyrus text) to describe presumably Muʿāwiyah himself. When in 53/673 Muʿāwiyah called on Aḥnaf to speak his mind, all Aḥnaf would then say was: "I fear Allāh too much to speak falsehood and I fear you too much to speak the truth."[70] But on another occasion he is reported as saying to Muʿāwiyah: "You know Yazīd better than any one of us—how he conducts himself by night or day in private or in public. Do not feed him this world while you are on your way to the next one."[71] It took Muʿāwiyah several years, beginning in 53/673, to win enough support so that he could actually appoint and reaffirm Yazīd as his heir in 56/676.[72] Once this step was taken, Aḥnaf accepted it and remained loyal to Yazīd as heir and as caliph.[73] But even after Yazīd was appointed as heir, Muʿāwiyah continued to seek support for him from those who had remained neutral and especially from those who

66 Ibn Khallikān I 288 (= trans. I 635 f.). At an early meeting after Muʿāwiyah's caliphate had been firmly established, Muʿāwiyah expressed his lasting anger at the very thought of the Battle of Ṣiffīn. Aḥnaf minced no words in assuring Muʿāwiyah that should he renew the war Aḥnaf and his followers would be more than ready to meet him in battle again; then Aḥnaf rose and walked out. Muʿāwiyah commented: "That is the man who, if angered, has one hundred thousand of the tribe of Tamīm to share his anger without asking him the reason for it." A second angry exchange of words between Aḥnaf and Muʿāwiyah took place when Aḥnaf protested the cursing of ʿAlī (*Waqʿat Ṣiffīn*, p. 636; *ʿIqd* IV 28, 366; Nuwairī VII 237 f.).

67 Muʿāwiyah even took Aḥnaf into his confidence in a harem affair, with the result that Aḥnaf received a tongue-lashing and rough handling from one of Muʿāwiyah's wives. For this episode see Ibn Qaiyim al-Jauzīyah, *Kitāb akhbār al-nisāʾ* (Cairo, 1319/1901) pp. 93 f.; Mr. Joseph Bell drew my attention to the fact that Ibn Qaiyim al-Jauzīyah's authorship of this work has been questioned and that it is now believed by some to be the work of Ibn al-Jauzī (see e.g. Khair al-Dīn al-Zirkilī, *Al-aʿlām* [2d ed.] IV [Cairo, 1374/1954] 90, n. 1, and VI [1374/1955] 281, n. 1; ʿAbd al-Ḥamīd al-ʿAlwajī, *Muʾallafāt Ibn al-Jauzī* [Baghdād, 1385/1965] p. 66, No. 14.

68 Ṭabarī II 96. ʿAmr ibn al-ʿĀṣ, it will be recalled, had refused to supply Muʿāwiyah with Egyptian funds for a similar purpose. ʿAmr's able secretary Wardān was retained in charge of the taxes and was presently ordered by Muʿāwiyah to increase the head tax. When Wardān pointed out that this was against the treaty agreement with the Egyptians, he was removed from office. The *dīwān al-kharāj* was then brought under the control of Muʿāwiyah's brother ʿUtbah, governor-general of Egypt; see *Futūḥ*, pp. 85 f., 98, and Kindī, p. 34, from which it may be inferred that Wardān served in the *dīwān al-kharāj* under ʿAbd Allāh ibn ʿAmr (Yāqūt III 195; Maqrīzī, *Kitāb al-mawāʿiẓ al-iʿtibār bī dhikr al-khiṭaṭ wa al-āthār* [Būlāq, 1270/1854] I 79). Thereafter Egyptian revenues were at Muʿāwiyah's disposal and were probably used for some of his large gifts to key personalities (Yaʿqūbī II 277; ʿ*Uyūn* III 40). Wardān remained in Egypt at his headquarters and fought in subsequent campaigns. He fell in 53/673 at Barallus, near Alexandria, fighting against the Byzantines (Kindī, p. 38; Yāqūt I 593; Ibn Taghrībirdī I 149 f.).

Wardān was of Greek origin and multilingual. We have already seen how well he served ʿAmr ibn al-ʿĀṣ with pen and sword. His linguistic and intellectual gifts, his integrity, and his comparative disinterest were brought home to ʿAmr on several occasions (see e.g. *Waqʿat Ṣiffīn*, pp. 40–42, 425; Dīnawarī, p. 290; Wāqidī [pseudo], *Futūḥ al-shām* [Cairo, 1316/1899] II 28; Ṭabarī I 3257). His good qualities did not go unnoticed by Muʿāwiyah; for, when in relaxed and intimate conversation these three expressed their fondest wishes, Muʿāwiyah on several occasions acknowledged Wardān's greater humanity and altruism (Ṭabarī II 212 f.: فقال معاويه (لعمرو) هذا العبد غلبنى وغلبك; Masʿūdī V 58–60: قال وردان الافضال على الاخوان فقال معاويه انا احق بهذا منك; see also Yāqūt III 195).

69 E.g. ʿ*Uyūn* I 95; *Amālī* II 73.

70 Ibn Saʿd VII 1, p. 67; ʿ*Iqd* I 59 with variations, II 472, IV 368 f. Ibn Khallikān I 289 (= trans. I 636) adds: "Well," said Muʿāwiyah, "may Allāh reward you for your obedience toward Him," and then he ordered a large sum of money to be given to Aḥnaf.

71 ʿ*Uyūn* II 211 (فلا تلقمه الدنيا وانت تذهب الى الاخرة); see also ʿ*Iqd* IV 370.

72 ʿ*Iqd* IV 368; *Majālis Thaʿlab* II 519–21; Masʿūdī V 69 f.; see also Abbott, *Aishah*, pp. 194–96 and references cited.

73 Ṭabarī II 437: انه كان ليزيد في اعناقنا بيعة.

still opposed him either because they were opposed to the principle of dynastic succession or because they were themselves caliphal aspirants.[74] Aḥnaf's influence in this matter must have had its effect during these critical succession years.

In his own province, ʿIrāq, Aḥnaf supported Ziyād ibn Abī Sufyān and his son ʿUbaid Allāh. He advised Muʿāwiyah and Ziyād against eliminating some of the ever increasing and increasingly bold *mawālī*, pointing out to Muʿāwiyah that they were maternal relatives and to Ziyād that the Qurʾān and the practice of Muḥammad were against such a step, and he added that the *mawālī* class rendered lowly but needed services in the market place.[75] Aḥnaf's support of ʿUbaid Allāh was not affected by the latter's coolness toward him. When Muʿāwiyah was considering the appointment of a governor of Baṣrah to replace ʿUbaid Allāh, he asked for nominations from the Baṣran delegation. Several of the men spoke in favor of their candidates, but Aḥnaf remained silent until Muʿāwiyah called on him to speak. "If you appoint one of your family," said Aḥnaf, "we consider no one the equal of ʿUbaid Allāh." And ʿUbaid Allāh, already governor of Kūfah, had Baṣrah restored to his jurisdiction, but not without an admonition from Muʿāwiyah for his failure to appreciate Aḥnaf.[76] Later, when the Second Civil War broke out soon after the death of Yazīd I (64/683) and ʿUbaid Allāh himself had to flee Baṣrah, Aḥnaf alone stood by him.[77] But when ʿUbaid Allāh fell in battle and the Khārijites turned from allies to rivals of ʿAbd Allāh ibn al-Zubair, Aḥnaf threw in his lot with the latter. Aḥnaf remained a soldier and a general to the end. He was with ʿUbaid Allāh on the expeditions to Khurāsān[78] and fought and fell in ʿIrāq on the side of Muṣʿab ibn al-Zubair.[79]

LITERARY BACKGROUND

I

The over-all literary style of the speech of ʿAmr ibn al-ʿĀṣ is appropriate for any period of his life. Brief terse prose was generally characteristic of pre-Islāmic, early Islāmic, and Umayyad times. This is well illustrated by the extant papyrus manuscripts representative of administrative correspondence from the time of ʿAmr's first conquest of Egypt to the first decades of ʿAbbāsid rule.[80] Extant historical and literary works of the second and third/eighth and ninth centuries further attest the preference throughout the Umayyad period for elegantly concise prose in conversation, oratory, and correspondence.[81] The use of rhymed prose, as in recto 1–2 of our document, and an occasional figure of speech, primarily a simile or a metaphor involving familiar desert flora and fauna such as the palm tree of recto 2–3 and the camel of verso 10–11, were equally characteristic of the literary taste of the time. However, one has to keep in mind that, though oratory was cultivated, the much admired literary figure of pre-Islāmic and Islāmic times was not so much the orator as the poet. The poet who was also a master orator ranked at the very

[74] Ṭabarī II 196–98; Masʿūdī V 72 f.; *Amālī* III 177 f.; *Ḥusn* II 115.

[75] ʿ*Iqd* III 413; Ibn ʿAsākir VII 15: فهم يقيمون اسواق المسلمين افتجعل العرب يقيمون اسواقهم قصابين وقصارين وحجامين. See our Vol. II 34 for Muʿāwiyah's and Zuhrī's attitude and for the *mawālī's* increasing participation in the learned professions.

[76] Ṭabarī II 190–92; Ibn Khallikān I 289–91 (= trans. I 640).

[77] Ṭabarī II 192, 432–38; Ibn Khallikān I 291 (= trans. I 640).

[78] Ṭabarī II 156, 170; Ibn Khallikān I 2.

[79] Ibn Saʿd VII 1, p. 69; *Maʿārif*, p. 217; Ṭabarī II 682–85, 720, 750; Ibn Khallikān I 291 (= trans. I 640); see also pp. 44 f. above.

[80] See the many documents published in Becker, *Papyri Schott-Reinhardt* I, Adolf Grohmann, *Arabic Papyri in the Egyptian Library* I (Cairo, 1934), and Abbott, *The Ḳurrah Papyri from Aphrodito in the Oriental Institute.*

[81] Iḥsān al-Nuṣṣ, *Al-khiṭābah al-siyāsīyah fī ʿaṣr Banī Umayyah* (Damascus, 1965), has brought together some representative speeches for various occasions of this period.

top of the literary class.[82] Certainly in the campaigns of Muḥammad and the conquests of the Umayyads the primary propagandists were the poets who accompanied the armies. It was they, whether reciting ancient poetry or improvised verses suited to the occasion, who upheld the morale of the troops and taunted the enemy. They were reinforced by the political and military leaders on hand, most of whom quoted ancient verse and many of whom were poets of a sort and recited their own poetry. Formal military speeches were brief as a rule and comparatively rare. These literary ideals and practices help in part to explain the abundance of poetry, spurious or otherwise, in Ibn Isḥāq's *Sīrah*[83] and Naṣr ibn Muzāḥim's *Waqʿat Ṣiffīn,* dating respectively from the first and the second half of the second/eighth century. It is therefore not surprising that Jāḥiẓ and his contemporaries and their predecessors paid more attention to poets and their poetry than to prose literature, including public speeches of various categories, but took special note of orators who were also poets or men of wisdom and learning.[84] Jāḥiẓ was aware that he had not done the orators justice as to classification according to time, tribe, and merit—a treatment he shirked in order to content himself with general references only,[85] though he did later give a brief account of some tribal and regional orators, especially those who were South Arabs,[86] and he did touch on oratory in connection with other subjects, especially *akhbār.*[87]

Yet, despite the comparative neglect of rhetoric as such, the private discourse and public speeches of outstanding personalities, beginning with Muḥammad, attracted special attention and seem to have been early committed to writing and collected along with some official correspondence. Some of these materials, oral or written, must have been available to Ibn Isḥāq, Naṣr ibn Muzāḥim, and Wāqidī and his secretary Ibn Saʿd, all of whom have preserved for us scattered samplings of this type of early prose literature.[88] Certainly their successors, including Jāḥiẓ, had access to such collections, especially well known collections devoted to the speeches of Muḥammad and the first four caliphs.[89] The court secretary of Maʾmūn, Sahl ibn Hārūn (d. 215/830), himself a poet, orator, and author and the librarian largely responsible for the great collection of Maʾmūn's famed library, the Dār al-ḥikmah, produced several types of anthologies, including poetry and public speeches.[90] Jāḥiẓ lists and comments on a number of orators,[91] while Ibn Qutaibah and Ibn ʿAbd Rabbihi each devote a section to a collection of speeches going back to the time of Muḥammad.[92] Some classification of formal speeches, such as Friday sermons in the mosques and inaugural speeches of caliphs and governors, seems to have been made early in Umayyad times to judge

[82] Jāḥiẓ, *Bayān* I 25 f., 62, and 244 (citing Abū ʿAmr ibn al-ʿAlāʾ) and III 372 f. (citing Abū ʿUbaid and Yūnus ibn Ḥabīb), takes up this theme and gives reasons for the relative positions of poet and orator in these early times. Jāḥiẓ' own day, when poets had become largely mercenary and prose literature had developed in style, saw the reversal of the positions of poet and orator and produced the highly cultured court secretary, with his polished prose, who became a rival of both until still later when prose literature itself became too flowery and verbose. Formal treatises on rhetoric came in the wake of poetics, both being more or less under Greek influence (see e.g. Qudāmah, Intro. pp. 36–44; Ibn Sīnā, *Al-khiṭābah* [*Al-shifāʾ: Al-manṭiq* VIII] ed. Muḥammad Salīm Sālim [Cairo, 1373/1954]).

[83] See Vol. I 9–17 for the earlier ʿUbaid ibn Sharyah's *Akhbār* and esp. pp. 14 f. for the use of poetry in it.

[84] Jāḥiẓ, *Bayān* I 55–66, gives representative lists of pre-Islamic and early Islāmic orators and points out that poets outnumbered orators and that those who combined both talents were few, the best among them being Kumait, Baʿīth, and Ṭirimmāḥ (cf. *ibid.* III 372 f.).

[85] *Ibid.* I 295: لما عجزتُ . . . تكلفت ذكرهم في الجملة.

[86] *Ibid.* I 332–45; ʿ*Uyūn* II 231–56. *Fihrist,* p. 125, gives an unclassified list of *khuṭabāʾ*, drawn up by Ibn Muqlah, which starts with ʿAlī and carries through to the reign of Maʾmūn.

[87] Jāḥiẓ, *Bayān* I 131–35.

[88] Muḥammad's speech and style received special attention in the works of these and later scholars (see e.g. Qudāmah, pp. 18 f.).

[89] Jāḥiẓ, *Bayān* I 208: هذه خطب دسول الله صلعم مدونة محفوظة ومخلدة مشهورة وهذه خطب ابوبكر وعمر وعثمان وعلى رضى الله عنهم.

[90] *Ibid.* I 68 f. For Sahl ibn Hārūn see *Fihrist,* p. 120, and *Irshād* IV 258 f.

[91] Jāḥiẓ, *Bayān* I 312–20, 332–38.

[92] ʿ*Uyūn* II 231–56; ʿ*Iqd* 54–154, where pp. 54–96 take us through Umayyad times.

by their frequent appearance in subsequent literature.[93] We do know that Khālid al-Qaṣrī (d. 126/744), governor of Baṣrah and later of Mecca and finally Hishām's governor of both Baṣrah and Kūfah (105–20/723–38), who was himself an orator, as were his son and grandson, reported that his father had made him memorize a thousand speeches as a very effective part of his liberal education and that he himself had a large collection, including speeches made at weddings,[94] and we know also that he sought historical and genealogical manuscripts from Zuhrī.[95]

The Umayyad family produced no master orator, and the only ones mentioned as having some oratorical talent are Muʿāwiyah's brother ʿUtbah, his half-brother Ziyād, and ʿAbd al-Malik, who believed the responsibility of the Friday sermons in the mosque turned his hair gray.[96] The Quraish as a whole, though proud of their Arabic as the language spoken by Muḥammad and chosen for the Qur'ānic revelations, produced comparatively few master orators. Though ʿAlī and ʿAbd Allāh ibn al-Zubair were considered as such by their partisans,[97] their speeches do not measure up in ideas and style to those of such men as Ziyād ibn Abī Sufyān, Ḥajjāj ibn Yūsuf,[98] or Khālid al-Qaṣrī.[99]

The three leading personalities of our papyrus text, ʿAmr ibn al-ʿĀṣ, presumably Muʿāwiyah, and Aḥnaf ibn Qais, represent a larger group of orators of lower rank. Aḥnaf was much more renowned for his pithy sayings and pearls of wisdom than for his few short speeches that are recorded.[100] Muʿāwiyah, too, seems to have been more effective in private or small-group discourse than in public oratory if we are to judge by the style and effect of his speeches as compared to those of ʿAmr during their long period of association.[101] ʿAmr seems to have had the advantage over Muʿāwiyah in his readiness to address large gatherings, in his effective delivery, and in his rapport with his audiences, qualities which Muʿāwiyah recognized and put to use. When Muʿāwiyah first heard of ʿAlī's speech urging his followers on the march to give him battle, he was disturbed and called on ʿAmr for advice. The practical ʿAmr, more of a soldier than Muʿāwiyah, advised speedy preparation of the Syrian forces and speeches to rouse in them burning desire to avenge the blood of ʿUthmān. ʿAmr's own speech played on the weakness, both political and military, of ʿAlī's army, which had not yet fully recovered from the Battle of the Camel.[102] Muʿāwiyah's speeches then and at other times placed more stress on ʿAlī's role in the death of ʿUthmān and his own right to avenge him.[103] In the course of the battle, which lasted for several days, Muʿāwiyah scolded his followers for lack of enthusiasm in word and deed and pointed out that ʿAmr alone could lay claim to both,

[93] The speeches of governors most frequently recorded are those of Ziyād ibn Abī Sufyān, Ḥajjāj ibn Yūsuf, and Khālid al-Qaṣrī. Jāḥiẓ, *Bayān* II 255, gives instances of men who experienced "stage fright" (*ḥaṣr al-manābir*) and either could not deliver their speeches or bungled them.

[94] See Ibn Ṭabāṭabā, p. 10, حفظّنى ابى الف خطبة ثم قال لى تناسها فتناسيتها فلم أرد بعد ذلك شيئا من الكلام إلا سهل علىّ, which is followed by Ibn Ṭabāṭabā's comment فكان حفظه لتلك الخطب رياضة لفهمه وتهذيبا لطبعه وتلقيحا لذهنه ومادة لفصاحته وسببا لبلاغته ولسنه وخطابته (see also *Fihrist*, p. 125). ʿ*Uyūn* IV 72–76 gives a representative collection of wedding speeches. Length of speech varies from one line to five lines, with an occasional citation from the Qur'ān or a verse of poetry. These, like other categories of speeches, grew longer with time (see e.g. Baihaqī, p. 483).

[95] See Vol. II 33 and *Aghānī* XIX 59.

[96] *Amālī* I 240 f. and 245, II 149 and 132; Ibn Taghrībirdī I 139; ʿ*Uyūn* II 239 f., 241–43; ʿ*Iqd* IV 55, 81–86, 90, 110–13, 137–39. ʿ*Iqd* IV 55 and 81–96 covers speeches made by Umayyad caliphs and most of their governors.

[97] Shīʿite literature dwells on a variety of ʿAlī's literary gifts. For example, *Waqʿat Ṣiffīn*, p. 759, lists 20 of his speeches in connection with the Battle of Ṣiffīn and its aftermath, some of which are found also in e.g. Ṭabarī I 3262, 3282 f., 3290, 3301, 3360, 3411; ʿ*Uyūn* IV 66–81; ʿ*Iqd* II 235–37. For ʿAbd Allāh ibn al-Zubair see e.g. ʿ*Uyūn* II 240 f. and ʿ*Iqd* IV 107–10; Ibn ʿAsākir VII 401 f. compares him as an orator with his maternal grandfather, the caliph Abū Bakr.

[98] See e.g. Jāḥiẓ, *Bayān* II 124 f., 147, 176 f., 318–21; ʿ*Uyūn* II 243–47, 251. See ʿ*Uyūn* IV 119–24 for a collection of Ḥajjāj ibn Yūsuf's speeches.

[99] See e.g. ʿ*Iqd* IV 135 and V 30 f.

[100] Jāḥiẓ, *Bayān* II 140; ʿ*Iqd* II 64 f. and IV 134; *Amālī* II 73; Nuwairī VII 237 f.; see also p. 55 above.

[101] See *Waqʿat Ṣiffīn*, pp. 36, 91, 143, 210, 250, 332 f.; Ṭabarī I 3397; ʿ*Uyūn* II 237; ʿ*Iqd* IV 81–83, 87–89.

[102] Ṭabarī I 3256 f.; Ibn ʿAsākir VI 293 f.

[103] *Waqʿat Ṣiffīn*, p. 143, also pp. 36 and 91; Dīnawarī, p. 194.

but he only angered several of the leaders.[104] Again, after the discouraging results of the fifth day of the battle, Muʿāwiyah counseled with ʿAmr, who first pointed out ʿAlī's familial and political advantages and then cautioned Muʿāwiyah against personal laxity but urged him to lose no time in easing discipline and austerity among the Syrians and leading them to greater exertion by raising their hopes for future comforts and rewards. Muʿāwiyah prepared and delivered a short speech with these points in mind and was reinforced by a similar speech from ʿAmr.[105] Both men are said to have delivered somewhat longer speeches before the last day of the battle.[106]

A few other speeches of ʿAmr have survived and are scattered in a wide variety of sources, but the occasions that called them forth are seldom specified. A few datable exceptions are of special interest. The first is a speech made in Syria in the year 17/638, known as the "year of the plague." Unlike most of his leading contemporaries, who looked on the plague as willed by God and therefore not to be deliberately avoided, the hard-headed ʿAmr urged the people to flee to the hills to avoid the plague, which, once started, spread like wildfire.[107] Two of Amr's Friday sermons in the mosque, delivered during his first governorship of Egypt, seem patterned for content more or less after those of Abū Bakr and ʿUmar I, particularly the latter, whose traditions from Muḥammad ʿAmr quoted in regard to religious duties, family, social behavior, and considerate treatment of the Copts.[108] ʿAmr's facility with words and his smooth delivery were appreciated by ʿUmar I, who whenever he heard a speaker grope for words or stammer would marvel at how the same God created both such a speaker and the fluent ʿAmr.[109] ʿUmar's admiration for ʿAmr's vivid description of Egypt is well known, as is his appreciative remark on reading it.[110] Not so well known is ʿAmr's terrifying description of the sea written in reply to ʿUmar's request and said to have influenced that caliph's refusal of Muʿāwiyah's request for an aggressive naval policy.[111]

Several of Muʿāwiyah's speeches during his caliphate have come down to us.[112] They are more labored in style, and their tone progresses from an effort at conciliation in the first year of his caliphate,[113] to a threatening assertion of his authority, particularly in reference to the succession of Yazīd as his heir (see pp. 55 f.), to reflection on his long reign and its effects on the people, to his readiness to depart this world in the hope of a favorable reception by Allāh.[114]

Of the three leading personalities of our papyrus text, the sources report Aḥnaf's familiarity with classical poetry but cite hardly any verses of his own. Muʿāwiyah was readier with quotations from the

[104] *Waqʿat Ṣiffīn*, pp. 527 f.:
جمع معاوية كل قرشي بالشام فقال العجب يا معشر قريش انه ليس لاحد منكم في هذه الحرب فعال يطول به لسانه غدا ما عدا عمراً فما بالكم وابن حمية قريش.

[105] *Ibid.* pp. 250 f., 332 f.; Jāḥiẓ, *Bayān* II 293; Ṭabarī I 3256 f.

[106] *Waqʿat Ṣiffīn*, pp. 333, 358 f.

[107] E.g. Ṭabarī I 2519.

[108] *Futūḥ*, pp. 139–41, which starts with a description of ʿAmr's physical traits, his attire, and his bearing as he delivers his sermon.

[109] Ibn Taghrībirdī I 72, citing Jumaḥī.

[110] See e.g. Ibn Taghrībirdī I 33 f.: قال عمر بن الخطاب درك يا ابن العاص لقد وصفتَ لي خبرا كاني اشاهده. Interesting are ʿAbd Allāh ibn ʿAmr's description of Egypt's strategic location and his praise for the character of the Egyptians and their friendliness to the Arabs (*ibid.* I 30 f.). ʿAbd Allāh's appraisal is in sharp contrast to that of some of his younger contemporaries, especially Ibn al-Qirrīyah (d. 84/703), from whom we have the fullest early comparative descriptions of the peoples and provinces of the empire (*ibid.* I 54 f.; Yūnus al-Mālikī, *Kanz al-madfūn* [Cairo, 1358/1939] p. 287).

[111] Ṭabarī I 2820 f.; Jāḥiẓ, *Bayān* II 115 f. But see *Futūḥ*, p. 165, where ʿAmr is shown to have had ulterior motives for exaggerating the dangers of the sea.

[112] See e.g. *ʿUyūn* II 237 f.; *ʿIqd* IV 55, 81–89; Ibn ʿAsākir VII 251.

[113] *ʿIqd* IV 81; Ibn Taghrībirdī I 137.

[114] *Amālī* II 315. For reflective and remorseful statements by ʿAmr during his last illness see e.g. Ibn Saʿd IV 2, pp. 6–8, Jāḥiẓ, *Bayān* I 383, Masʿūdī V 60 f., and Ibn Taghrībirdī I 71.

poets and is credited with a number of impromptu verses of his own.[115] There are reports of several instances when these two discussed some poets or verse.[116] We find that ʿAmr was as ready with citations as Muʿāwiyah and more productive of original verse, both as to number and length of poems.[117] ʿAmr is mentioned among the pagan Quraishite poets who satirized Muḥammad and the Anṣār.[118]

We have no direct evidence that ʿAmr himself made a point of committing his verses to writing except those which he included in his correspondence with Muʿāwiyah and others.[119] The practice of including poetic citations and original verses in personal and political correspondence was already much in evidence among ʿAmr's leading associates and contemporaries.[120] There is, for instance, the earlier episode of ʿUmar I and Naṣr ibn al-Ḥajjāj ibn ʿIlāṭ, when both Naṣr and the mother of Ḥajjāj ibn Yūsuf sent ʿUmar written verses avowing their innocence.[121] A little later, ʿUmar received anonymously written verses complaining of the rule of ʿAmr in Egypt.[122] ʿAmr is, furthermore, credited with knowledge of the dialects of the Qur'ān[123] and with transmitting traditions from Muḥammad.[124] There is some evidence that, if neither ʿAmr nor his secretary Wardān kept copies of ʿAmr's correspondence and his other literary output, then his son ʿAbd Allāh[125] and the latter's grandson Shuʿaib ibn Muḥammad did so, at least for some of ʿAmr's traditions and poetry.[126]

II

Turning now to the immediate background of the second section of our papyrus text, in which Aḥnaf ibn Qais of Baṣrah and his companions express their views on the ideal maiden, we note that these men, whatever their individual distinction or interest as wisemen, statesmen, politicians, or poets, were all South Arabs and also warriors of one rank or another who were already active in the reign of ʿUmar I. Though all, including eventually Naṣr ibn al-Ḥajjāj, had either Baṣrah or Kūfah as their headquarters, their political and military careers ran their course in ʿIrāq and points to the east and in the Ḥijāz and Syria. From the literary sources on hand we have already ascertained that except for Naṣr these men all participated in the First Civil War. Furthermore, they are not otherwise associated in the sources. Therefore, our papyrus text, which shows them all together, including Naṣr, must indicate that this war was the background of their conversation. This fits well with the most logical background for ʿAmr's speech, namely the period following the Battle of Ṣiffīn (see p. 50), which in turn suggests that in all probability

[115] For Muʿāwiyah's interest in classical poetry see Vol. I 14 f. in connection with his constant demand for poetry from ʿUbaid ibn Sharyah. For samples of poetry credited to Muʿāwiyah see e.g. *Waqʿat Ṣiffīn*, pp. 726–39, which cites him 14 times; *ʿUyūn* II 169, III 159, and IV 55; Masʿūdī V 31 f., 55; Ibn ʿAsākir VII 328. Muʿāwiyah's patronage of poets and his use of them for political propaganda is well illustrated in the role played by Miskīn al-Dārmī in the succession of Yazīd (see e.g. *Shiʿr*, p. 347; *Aghānī* XVIII 69 f.).

[116] Thaʿlab, *Sharḥ dīwān Zuhair ibn Abī Sulamā*, ed. Aḥmad Zakī (Cairo, 1363/1944) Intro. pp. 14 f.; *ʿIqd* II 462.

[117] See e.g. *Waqʿat Ṣiffīn*, pp. 726–39, which cites him 16 times; Yaʿqūbī II 215 f.; Ṭabarī I 3257; Masʿūdī V 28, 30 f., 55, 60 f.; *ʿIqd* IV 15, 344 f.; Ibn ʿAsākir VI 293 f.

[118] E.g. *Sīrah* I 272, 621, 623; Yaʿqūbī II 143; *Aghānī* IV 4.

[119] E.g. *Waqʿat Ṣiffīn*, pp. 396, 467–69, 630; Yaʿqūbī II 214–16; *ʿIqd* IV 344 f.

[120] E.g. *Waqʿat Ṣiffīn*, pp. 57, 59, 176–78, 470 f., 473 f.; *Futūḥ*, pp. 147 f.; Jāḥiẓ, *Maḥāsin*, pp. 288, 341 f., 204; *Aghānī* XVII 57 and 59, XXI 23 f. and 37; *Irshād* VII 67 f. One must keep in mind, however, the question of the authenticity of such poetry.

[121] See e.g. *Khizānah* II 108–12 and other references cited on pp. 45 f. above.

[122] ʿUmar I prohibited the Muslims from taking the initiative in satirical verse against the Anṣār and the still pagan Quraish but permitted the Muslims, should they be so attacked, to retaliate by composing and committing such verse to writing. The Anṣār had a written collection of such verse (*Aghānī* III 5 f.). Furthermore, in 21/642 ʿUmar wrote his governor of Kūfah to send him written copies of the poetry of contemporary poets in his province (Yazīdī, p. 100) and also instructed Abū Mūsā al-Ashʿarī to order those who were with him to study poetry because it leads to high morality, good judgment, and knowledge of genealogy (*ʿUmdah* I 10).

[123] Ibn al-Jazarī I 601.

[124] Nuwairī, p. 479, credits him with 37 traditions.

[125] See Vol. II, esp. pp. 36, 41, 58, 66.

[126] Ibn Ḥanbal, *Al-musnad* II 158; *Jarḥ* II 1, pp. 351 f.; *Aghānī* IX 58; *ʿIqd* IV 43; Ibn ʿAsākir VI 324.

the conversation of Aḥnaf and his companions took place during the truce period. Relieved of actual fighting and awaiting the outcome of the pending arbitration, these warriors, it would seem, passed their evenings in light conversation as their thoughts turned to home and maidens, as soldiers' thoughts are wont to do—a setting similar to that which started the Persian *Hazār Afsāna* on its way as the forerunner of the *Arabian Nights*.[127]

For the literary background of this section of our papyrus text we must keep in mind the racial origin as well as the tribal and socio-cultural status of our speakers and must consider further the stage of development of Arabic literary prose in the first half of the first century of Islām. The speakers, being all Arabs from either shortly before the advent of Islām or soon thereafter, reflect in part long-established pre-Islāmic concepts of the ideal maiden and in part the recently imposed Islāmic ideal. The combination of the two concepts is reflected in Aḥnaf's opening statement (recto 9–10), which stipulates humility before Allāh as his first requirement and a homebody as his second, but the "home" is no more than a tribal leader's tent. We may safely assume that Aḥnaf's companions tacitly accepted his first, if not his second, stipulation as basic, since humility before Allāh is required of Muslim men as well. This raises the question of the significance of the particle *bal* in this context in respect not only to Aḥnaf's statement but also to each successive statement, that is, whether it is still being used in its less common copulative conjunctival sense or in its more common restrictive or adversative adverbial sense.[128] In other words, does each speaker negate the preceding statement in favor of his own specifications or does he add his specifications to those already mentioned? There are no inherent contradictions in the successive statements, and hence it is possible that they were meant to be cumulative so that they would cover physical, mental, and personality characteristics. The ideal maiden, in that case, would have to be a paragon of sorts. The alternative would be to consider the particle *bal* as put to use first as a conjunction, where each speaker supplements Aḥnaf's statement, and second as an inceptive particle of digression, where each speaker, irrespective of what has already been said, stresses his own basic desire in a maiden and displays at the same time his own eloquence. A case can be argued for either of these two alternatives in so far as the pertinent content of the literary sources is concerned.

The earliest recorded and best known description of the ideal maiden is that which traces back to the Kūfans and to Ḥammād al-Rāwiyah, Abū 'Ubaidah, and Hishām ibn Muḥammad ibn al-Sā'ib al-Kalbī, whose accounts are sometimes combined.[129] Briefly, the story behind the description is as follows. A Lakhmid king of Ḥīrah, Mundhir IV (A.D. 576–80),[130] is said to have sent a gift of an Arab maiden along with a written description of her to Khusrau Anūshirwān (A.D. 531–79), who was delighted with the maiden and so impressed with the description that he ordered it filed in his state bureau. Later, when Khusrau II (A.D. 590–628), looking for a wife for his heir, was studying the same description, he was assured by Zaid ibn 'Adī, his Christian Arab secretary,[131] that the family of the Ḥīran king Nu'mān ibn al-Mundhir (A.D. 580–602) had a score or more of young girls who answered that description. Khusrau sent Zaid to Nu'mān with a request for the hand of one of these girls for the Persian prince, which was indignantly refused. The angered Khusrau later imprisoned Nu'mān and brought about his death. The episode is said to have set the background for the Battle of Dhū Kār, which was fought in Muḥammad's time but is dated variously from A.D. 604 to 620. The description of the maiden covers almost a page of Ṭabarī's printed text, and about half of it is devoted to the maiden's physical charms, item by item and

[127] See Abbott in *JNES* VIII 129–64.

[128] See e.g. Wright, *Grammar* II 334; Lane, pp. 243 f.

[129] See e.g. Ṭabarī I 1016, 1025–29; *Aghānī* II 29–31; *Aghānī* (1927——) II 120–27.

[130] See *OIP* L 5–8 and 17–19 for the Lakhmid kingdom of Ḥīrah, whose rulers were vassals of the Persian empire, and its use of Arabic in pre-Islāmic diplomatic correspondence.

[131] For the role of Zaid's father, 'Adī ibn Zaid (d. *ca* A.D. 590), and his family in pre-Islāmic poetry see e.g. Jāḥiẓ, *Ḥayawān* IV 197–99, 205, 375 f., and *Khizānah* I 184–86.

feature by feature, from head to toe. The rest of the description stresses mostly mental and personality traits. The language involves rare words and unfamiliar terms that call for explanatory comments. Rhymed prose is freely used along with an occasional figure of speech.[132] Some sources, early and late, mention the episode but do not give the text of the description as such.[133]

Ibn ʿAbd Rabbihi (246–328/860–940), citing only his contemporary Abū Muḥammad al-Faraghānī, general and historian, pupil of Ṭabarī,[134] reports a second pre-Islāmic Arab description of the ideal woman, this time given to Khusrau II and credited to Ḥārith ibn Kaladah al-Thaqafī. Ḥārith was known as a "physician of the Arabs," who had acquired some of his medical knowledge in Persia and about whom several medical anecdotes are available.[135] Khusrau begins his interview with Ḥārith by belittling the Arabs as uncultured. Ḥārith's defense of and pride in his Arab heritage soon convince Khusrau that Ḥārith himself is a cultured man. Khusrau proceeds next to test Ḥārith's medical competence and plies him with questions about disease, medicine, diet, and sex. Ḥārith's prescription for good health, in brief, involves the concept that prevention is better than cure and calls for moderation in food and sex.[136] Khusrau finally asks for a description of the woman most pleasing to eye and heart. Ḥārith's answer, devoted entirely to a physical description, is in rhymed prose. It starts with simple two-word phrases and ends with a series of longer phrases in which the girl is said to be softer than butter, sweeter than sugar, more fragrant than jasmine and rose, and more pleasing even than paradise.[137] The only other comparable account of the conversation between Khusrau and Ḥārith is provided by Ibn Abī Uṣaibiʿah,[138] who cites no initial single or composite authority for it but reports several additional anecdotes of Ḥārith, some of which are traced to early transmitters readily found in Ibn Saʿd and Ṭabarī, such as the Companion ʿAmr ibn ʿAwf,[139] ʿAbd al-Malik ibn ʿUmair al-Lakhmī (*ca.* 33–136/653–753),[140] and Abū ʿAwānah al-Waḍḍāḥ ibn Khālid (d. 170/786 or 176/792).[141] He supplies two details not found in Ibn ʿAbd Rabbihi's account, namely that Ḥārith informed Khusrau that he had read some books of the *ḥukamā*ʾ and that Khusrau ordered Ḥārith's speech to be committed to writing, which Ibn Abī Uṣaibiʿah assumes was done by Ḥārith himself.[142] We find Ibn Abī Uṣaibiʿah's account to have grown by about a fourth so far as the basically descriptive phrases are concerned but to have omitted two non-descriptive phrases. There is also an appropriate word substitution or correction of the earlier text, which could well have been called for by a scribe's paleographic error. The order is the same in both texts. Considering the three centuries that separate Ibn ʿAbd Rabbihi and Ibn Abī Uṣaibiʿah, we can understand the discrepancies in their versions. Their sources probably drew on variant manuscript copies which are now lost or still undis-

[132] See e.g. Ṭabarī I 1025 f.; *Aghānī* II 29 f. *Aghānī* (1927——) II 122–24 gives the pointed text with the editor's lexical commentary and a few emendations and minor textual variations, which text and the author's comments thereon form the basis of the account in Nuwairī XV 326–28, where further references are given.

[133] E.g. Jāḥiẓ, *Ḥayawān* IV 375–77; *Maʿārif*, p. 319; Masʿūdī III 205–8; *Khizānah* I 185.

[134] See Vol. I 109, 115 f.

[135] See e.g. *ʿUyūn* II 65 f., III 218 and 272, IV 131–33; *ʿIqd* IV 263 and V 4 f.; Ibn Abī Uṣaibiʿah, *Kitāb ʿuyūn al-anbā*ʾ, ed. August Mueller, I (Cairo, 1882) 113. Ḥārith and his family, especially his son Naḍr, physician, musician, and storyteller, were among those who persisted in their opposition to Muḥammad. Naḍr was executed after the Battle of Badr, and his sister's (or daughter's) elegy is said to have touched Muḥammad. Ḥarith is said to have lived until the time of Muʿāwiyah; for samples of his knowledge and skill see e.g. *Sīrah* I 187–91, 235, 262, 400, 457 f., 539, 874; Mu'arrij ibn ʿAmr al-Sadūsī, *Kitāb ḥadhf min nasab Quraish*, pp. 46, 48; Jāḥiẓ, *Bayān* III 339; Ṭabarī I 1230, 1304, 1335; Masʿūdī IV 184; *Adāb al-Shāfiʿī*, p. 257 and references cited; Ibn Abī Uṣaibiʿah, *Kitāb ʿuyūn al-anbā*ʾ I 109–16.

[136] Ḥajjāj ibn Yūsuf asked his personal physician Bādhūn for health rules and received much the same advice, some of it in phrases very similar to those used by Ḥārith (*ʿIqd* VI 306).

[137] *ʿIqd* VI 373–76.

[138] *Kitāb ʿuyūn al-anbā*ʾ I 109–13.

[139] Ibn Saʿd IV 2, p. 79.

[140] *Ibid.* VI 220 f.

[141] See *ibid.* VII 2, pp. 43 f., and p. 65 below. See also Ṭabarī for all three men.

[142] Ibn Abī Uṣaibiʿah, *Kitāb ʿuyūn al-anbā*ʾ I 112, line 12, and 113, lines 18–19.

covered. It should be further noted that portions of varying lengths of the conversation between Khusrau and Ḥārith appear scattered in earlier literary and in other medical works (see n. 135 above).

Thaʿālibī[143] recorded another demand by Khusrau II for a description of the most desirable maiden. The demand was met this time not by an Arab but by a most knowledgeable young Persian administrator of the *dihqān* class in Khusrau's service. The maiden's description again concludes a lengthy conversation, preceded, however, not by a medical theme but by a discussion of the best of all kinds of luxuries. It is reasonable to assume that the entire conversation was in Persian and that what we have is but an Arabic version of it. The description is physical except for the stipulation that the maiden be few of words and very modest. Khusrau, we are told, considered it perfect. Its literary style is less harmonious and flowing than that of the two descriptions already covered. Rhymed phrases are less frequent, and all but one of the phrases sustain the two-word measure, which soon grows monotonous in such a lengthy description. Similes are more freely used but are not unusual in character. The maiden must be almond-eyed, pearl-toothed, apple-breasted, wasp-waisted, and so forth.

In sampling this type of Arabic prose literature in its pre-Islāmic Arab setting we have to rely on the samples that were committed to writing later. Concern with the relationship of the sexes was much in evidence in pre-Islāmic and early Islāmic times and was not limited to the erotic or romantic. It covered, in addition to general attitudes, numerous specific relationships of fathers and daughters, of mothers and sons, of brothers and sisters, of husbands and wives, and of youths and maidens. We need not go into all these relationships nor be limited to men's statements in order to gain an idea of the content and style of this type of prose, particularly in reference to the appearance and qualities of a prospective wife or husband. Advice given to prospective brides by fathers and mothers or by elderly women of the immediate family reflected the general attitude as tested and either accepted or modified by their personal experience or by the experience of a larger unit of the tribe. Nor need we limit ourselves to either desert or city dwellers since the basic social mores in a mobile society that as yet knew not the veil and segregation of the sexes was much the same in the desert and the town through the greater part of the Umayyad period.

Almost all of the pre-Islāmic descriptions of young girls are comparatively brief and consist for the most part of a series of one-word or two-word phrases in rhymed prose. Many of these start and end with physical descriptions. Many others, though they list primarily physical characteristics, include some personality trait or moral quality. Still others, though not so many, further stipulate some intellectual qualities. The affinity of such descriptions with those in our papyrus text is obvious. There is on the whole a set of physical requirements that serves as a common denominator for all types of descriptions. The maiden must be good-looking and healthy, physically strong and well knit in form yet soft and yielding, not too tall nor too short, not too thin nor too fat. As to specific features, those most frequently desired are a fair complexion, heavy black hair, large black eyes, pearly teeth, slender neck, firm round breasts, small wrists, small waist and feet, and large hips.[144] There is still considerable leeway for description not only of the remaining parts of the body but for further delineation of the features specified. The fair complexion, for instance, is further defined as white or creamy white or eggshell white or white and rosy or light yellow touched with red—specifications which bring to mind complexions compared to cream and roses and to cream and peaches. The common denominator for personal and ethical traits involves little more than obedience, patience, responsiveness, and fidelity. Lists of individual specifications, on the other hand, though seldom longer, cover a wider range. For, while one prospective husband looks for a cheerful and playful maid, another specifies a dignified household manager who would husband the family resources. Or, while one desires a maiden of proud bearing and descent, another wishes for a self-

[143] *Ghurar akhbār mulūk al-Furs*, ed. H. Zotenberg (Paris, 1900) pp. 705–11, esp. pp. 710 f.

[144] For a recent study of feminine beauty as conceived in pre-Islamic and early Islāmic times see Aḥmad Muḥammad al-Ḥūfī, *Al-ghazal fī al-ʿaṣr al-jāhilī* (Cairo, 1381/1961).

effacing girl of humbler background. Varying combinations of traits reflect further the wide variety of individual taste and status. For the less often stipulated intellectual requirements, the list is even shorter and the statements are more general and less varied. The qualities most frequently sought are eloquence (*faṣāḥah*), intelligence or wisdom (*ʿaql*), and perfection (*kamāl*). They are graduated in degree and called for either singly or in combination.

Most of the well known transmitters and authors of the third and fourth centuries of Islām, such as Jāḥiẓ, Ibn Qutaibah, Ibn ʿAbd Rabbihi, and Abū ʿAlī al-Qālī, frequently cite Bedouins on the ideal maid or wife. More frequently than not they omit context and *isnād*. Where an *isnād* is given, it usually traces back to such well known authors as Abū ʿAmr ibn al-ʿAlāʾ, Haitham ibn ʿAdī, Hishām ibn Muḥammad ibn al-Saʾib al-Kalbī and his father, Abū ʿUbaid, Abū ʿUbaidah, Aṣmaʿī, Abū Zaid al-Anṣārī, Madāʾinī, and Ibn al-Aʿrābī. Only in cases where Abū ʿAmr ibn al-ʿAlāʾ (d. 154/771) is the ultimate source can we safely assume the possibility that the Bedouin in a contextless statement reflects late pre-Islāmic attitudes since the long-lived Abū ʿAmr is said to have drawn, in his earlier days, on Bedouins contemporary with the younger generation of Companions. For the rest, Bedouin concepts of the ideal maid and wife were not much affected by the advent of Islām, even during the early Umayyad period. Furthermore, there are few instances where the context indicates the speaker, Bedouin or not, to be of either the pre-Islāmic or the early Islāmic period.

There is, to begin with, Hind bint al-Khuss, the earliest of this group, who is herself described as eloquent, wise, shrewd, and ever ready with marvelous answers to questions put to her.[145] She seems to have been asked about every phase of life, including the various relationships of the sexes. Her answers came in crisp, short, rhymed phrases no matter what the subject. Her opinions characterizing the best and the second-best of all types of men and the best and the second-best of all types of women are followed by her characterization of the worst types of men and women.[146] Ibn Abī Ṭāhir Ṭaifūr (204–80/819–93) reports on the authority of Ibn al-Aʿrābī the longest account of a contest held in Sūq ʿUkkāẓ between Hind and her sister. The contest ended in a tie and showed both girls to be ready with extempore verses.[147] Hind describes herself as a young girl,[148] states her own basic requirements in a husband,[149] and answers a prospective husband's request for advice as to what type of girl he should marry, in each case in a few short rhymed phrases.[150]

Abū ʿAlī al-Qālī provides us with an account very similar in its scheme and literary style to that of the contest between Hind and her sister. The contest this time is between two Ḥimyarite princes, ʿAmr and Rabīʿah, who are being tested by their aged father (not named). Qālī's impressive *isnād* starts with Ibn Duraid and traces back to Abū ʿAmr ibn al-ʿAlāʾ. Comparison of the two accounts shows that the two sisters' answers to questions in reference to good and bad men and women dwelt less on the physical and stressed more the practical qualities desirable in either a wife or a husband, while the cultured princes' answers, though much concerned with physical appearance, stressed moral and intellectual qualities for both men and women. But when describing the worst types of women, both accounts stress undesirable personality and character traits more than either physical defects or intellectual shortcomings,[151] as do

[145] Abū Zaid al-Anṣārī, *Kitāb al-nawādir fī al-lughah*, ed. Saʿīd ibn Khūrī (Beirūt, 1894) p. 251; Jāḥiẓ, *Bayān* I 300 and II 166; Jāḥiẓ, *Ḥayawān* V 94, 105, 459. See also *Majālis Thaʿlab* I 343. Jāḥiẓ and Abū ʿAlī al-Qālī provide some lexical comments, and in *Muzhir* II 540–45 is brought together much of what the earlier authors have on Hind and considerable attention is given to their *isnād*'s.

[146] *Amālī* III 108 f., 120; Ibn Abī Ṭāhir Ṭaifūr, pp. 55–57; *Muzhir* II 541.

[147] Ibn Abī Ṭāhir Ṭaifūr, pp. 53–58; Jāḥiẓ, *Bayān* III 34; *ʿUyūn* II 214. Most of Hind's answers to the many questions put to both girls are found widely scattered in later sources.

[148] Jāḥiẓ, *Ḥayawān* V 94; Thaʿālibī, *Thimār*, p. 460.

[149] *ʿUyūn* IV 11.

[150] *Amālī* II 260 f.

[151] *Ibid.* I 152–55, esp. pp. 153 f.; *Muzhir* II 512–17, esp. pp. 513 f.

most sources that give considerable attention to women of any period.[152] We do, indeed, find an early if instinctive appreciation of the "golden mean" which later came to be more formally stated and defended, perhaps under Aristotelian influence. Most men felt that the extremely beautiful and highly intelligent and literate woman was to be avoided because they believed that as a wife she would all but inevitably be independent in social and moral matters.[153] This brings to mind the high-placed, beautiful, and literate women who addressed Naṣr ibn al-Ḥajjāj of our papyrus text (see verso 4–5 and comments on pp. 45 f.).

There is, furthermore, some evidence of expected reciprocity of unselfish devotion between husband and wife. This is best illustrated by the instructions given to Umm Iyās (fl. *ca.* A.D. 550), daughter of the Shaibānid chief ʿAwf ibn Muḥallim, on the eve of her marriage to the Kindite king ʿAmr ibn Hujr or his son Ḥārith, ancestors of the poet Imruʾ al-Qais: "Be to him a bondswoman and he will be to you a slave and," added the mother, "observe ten points of conduct which will lay up for you with him a treasure store." The ten points, grouped in five pairs of instructions in rhymed prose, may be summarized as follows. Be content in his company and ever ready to obey him; be always personally tidy and sweet smelling when with him; watch out for the proper time of his food and be quiet while he sleeps; husband his resources carefully without, however, stinting his family or retainers;[154] and do not ever oppose him or reveal his secrets; and—as an afterthought—always match your mood to his.[155] These instructions soon became proverbial, and fathers, including some of the Companions, used them for the benefit of their daughters.[156] Again content and style are compatible with our text. Not so is an added description of Umm Iyās credited to ʿIṣām, a South Arab female agent of the Kindite king. So far as I have been able to discover from the sources available to me at present, the story, including the long and detailed description of Umm Iyās, was recorded in varying degrees of fullness by three writers. The first is the third-century Mufaḍḍal ibn Salamah, who mentions the Baṣran Abū ʿAwānah al-Waḍḍāḥ ibn Khālid (d. 170/786 or 176/792)[157] as his source. Later, Ibn ʿAbd Rabbihi split the story into two parts, citing ʿAbbās ibn Khālid al-Sahmī[158] as his source for the first part and presumably also for the second or descriptive section. The third version is by the fifth-century Maidānī, who gives Mufaḍḍal ibn Salamah as his source[159] but does not mention Abū ʿAwānah. The three accounts, apart from the outline of the story and the basic content of its two units—instructions and description—are far from identical. Mufaḍḍal's account is the shortest. Ibn ʿAbd Rabbihi's account has single-word variations, mostly acceptable synonyms but occasionally a word with a different meaning such as "be humble" for "be content." It also omits some items but has more short additions interspersed in the text and longer ones at the end

152 Such as Jāḥiẓ' several *rasāʾil* on women, Ibn Abī Ṭāhir Ṭaifūr's *Balāghāt al-nisāʾ*, Ibn al-Sāʿī's *Nisāʾ al-khulafāʾ*, and the sizable sections devoted to women in such works as Ibn Qutaibah's *ʿUyūn*, the *Aghānī* of Abū al-Faraj al-Iṣfahānī, the *ʿIqd* of Ibn ʿAbd Rabbihi, and in works intended for secretaries such as Ibn Qutaibah's *Adab al-kātib*.

153 Jāḥiẓ is credited with stating the extreme point of view in this respect. See Jāḥiẓ *Maḥāsin*, p. 223, where he reports a wise man of Medina as saying اياك والجمال البارع, and *Irshād* VI 63, where Jāḥiẓ himself is reported as saying اذ كانت المرأة عاقلة ظريفة كاملة كانت قحبة . . . لانها تاخذ الدراهم وتمتع بالناس والطيب وتختار على عينها من تريد والتوية معروضة لها متى شائت. Elsewhere, however, Jāḥiẓ debates the opposite point of view, as was his custom, in coming to the defence of womanhood and draws freely on examples of beautiful women of pre-Islāmic and early Islāmic times who though intellectually gifted and non-segregated were yet virtuous.

154 A housewife's duty to husband the family resources was as frequently emphasized as love of money and free spending were condemned. See Bukhārī I 227 and III 441, 446 f.; Muslim XII 213 f.; Concordance VI 187 المرأة راعيه . . . بيت زوجها. See also e.g. *ʿIqd* VI 82 (citing Solomon), 112; *Muzhir* II 173; but cf. n. 199 on p. 70 below.

155 See *ʿIqd* VI 83, where the mother is said to have made the entire speech. Jāḥiẓ, *Ḥayawān* I 329, makes passing reference to the episode.

156 E.g. *ʿIqd* VI 84 f.; *ʿUyūn* IV 77.

157 See Vol. II 61, 80, and 226 for Abū ʿAwānah's manuscripts.

158 I have been unable to identify him.

159 Mufaḍḍal ibn Salamah, *Al-fākhir*, ed. C. A. Storey (Leyden, 1915) pp. 151–53 and ed. ʿAbd al-ʿAlīm al-Taḥāwī and Muḥammad ʿAlī al-Najjār (Cairo, 1380/1960) pp. 184–87; *ʿIqd* VI 83 f., 110 f.; Maidānī, *Al-majmaʿ al-amthāl* II (Cairo, 1353/1934) 216 f. Ibn Rustah, pp. 199 f., makes passing reference to the story and cites another of its proverbs: ترك الخداع من كشف القناع.

of each of the two units. Maidānī's account has some minor variations, a few deletions, and some additions. The additions are mainly in reference to the origin of the proverb ما وراءك يا عاصم, which he himself accepts as having originated with the story of Umm Iyās. He states further that Abū ʿUbaid reported the proverb as having been first addressed to a man, namely by Nābighah al-Dhubyānī to ʿIṣām ibn Shahbar, chamberlain of the Ḥīran king Nuʿmān ibn al-Mundhir, as reported also in the *Fākhir* of Mufaḍḍal ibn Salamah but without mention of Abū ʿUbaid.[160] Neither the proverb nor the story of Umm Iyās is in the *Amthāl* of the still earlier Mufaḍḍal ibn Muḥammad al-Ḍabbī[161] of *Mufaḍḍalīyāt* fame or in Bakrī's fifth-century commentary on Abū ʿUbaid's collection of proverbs.[162] We have dealt at length with the story of Umm Iyās because the style of its prose has some bearing on the dating of our papyrus (see pp. 75–78). Close analysis of the three versions as to content and style points to the final stabilization of the story in the second half of the second/eighth century at the earliest. In particular, the section describing Umm Iyās has marked affinities with the more labored prose of that half century and after and with the style of the secretarial class. This style is reflected in its longer phrases and its profuse use of similes, including such scribe-oriented comparisons as "eyebrows as though drawn with a pen, belly wrinkle like rolled papyrus, legs like the stems of the papyrus plant." For, while any one of these similes could have been used alone in earlier prose or poetry,[163] their simultaneous use in close succession points to scribal circles. Furthermore, with all due recognition of the contribution to Arabic literary prose and the secretarial arts by such early and gifted secretaries as Sālim ibn ʿAbd Allāh, his pupil ʿAbd al-Ḥamīd ibn Yaḥyā, and Ibn al-Muqqaffaʿ, it was not until the time of the Barmakids and the Banū Sahl under Hārūn al-Rashīd and Maʾmūn that the secretarial class as such attained any literary distinction, and that of a type peculiarly its own. At that time linguistic and literary studies, like other intellectual activities, took a long leap forward into the golden age of Islām, the period in which the pupils and younger contemporaries of Sībawaih and Khalīl ibn Aḥmad explored and exploited all phases of linguistic and literary studies, including classified vocabularies and the collection of proverbs. Works in both of these categories were produced more often than not by the same person, for instance Naḍr ibn Shumail's *Kitāb al-ṣifāt* and his *Amthāl*, Abū ʿUbaidah's *Kitāb al-khail* and his *Amthāl*, Abū Zaid al-Anṣārī's *Nawādir* and his *Amthāl*, Aṣmaʿī's *Kitāb al-ṣifāt*, his *Khalq al-insān*, and his *Amthāl*. All of these were available to if not used by Abū ʿUbaid in his *gharīb* works and in his *Amthāl*.[164] The *ṣifah*, or descriptive vocabulary relating to humans, comprised two somewhat overlapping types, an objective list of words and expressions covering anatomical terms and a vocabulary intended primarily for æsthetic, moral, and intellectual characterization,[165] such as the descriptive terms of our papyrus text.

[160] Mufaḍḍal ibn Salamah, *Al-fākhir* (1380/1960) p. 187; Maidānī, *Al-majmaʿ al-amthāl* II 216 f.

[161] See Mufaḍḍal al-Ḍabbī, *Amthāl al-ʿArab* (Constantinople, 1300/1883).

[162] See Bakhrī, *Faṣl al-maqāl fī sharḥ kitāb al-amthāl lī Abī ʿUbaid*, ed. ʿAbd al-Majīd ʿĀbidīn and Iḥsān ʿAbbās (Khartum, 1958) p. 122. This work, according to the editors (p. 306), omits or overlooks many proverbs of Abū ʿUbaid's original collection, which is not available to me.

[163] For example the expression كأنما خصرها طى الطومار was used in verse during the caliphate of Sulaimān (Yazīdī, pp. 151 f.). For an even more scribe-oriented description of a maid who was herself a secretary see e.g. *ʿUmdah* II 35. In other contexts, figures of speech involving the pen and writing were used in pre-Islāmic times, frequently in the Qurʾān, and by Umayyad secretaries and poets, though nowhere to the same extent as later under the ʿAbbāsids (see e.g. Ṣūlī, *Adab al-kuttāb*, pp. 21–28, 41, 45–53, 61–68, 78 f., *et passim*; *Muzhir* II 351 f.).

[164] See e.g. *Marātib*, pp. 92 f.; Khaṭīb XII 404; *Irshād* VI 162 f. For a comprehensive survey of the early development of the *amthāl* literature, see Rudolph Sellheim, *Die klassisch-arabischen Sprichwörtersammlungen insbesondere die des Abū ʿUbaid* (Gravenhage, 1954) esp. Chapters I–III.

[165] Early descriptive vocabularies were cast and recast by each successive generation of scholars, who augmented and organized them into chapters or sections or separate monographs under such headings as خلق الانسان, صفة النساء, and صفة بنية الرجل والمرآة. These vocabularies were put to use in sections of books or separate works devoted to the description and characterization of women—a category of literature which in its turn paralleled the growth and evolution of the linguistic and *akhbār* literature, as the numerous sources on women cited in the present study readily attest, not to mention many other similar works that have not survived (see pp. 75–78).

Moving into Islāmic times, we find Muḥammad himself citing the story of the Yemenite Umm Zarʿ and her husband Abū Zarʿ as a model for his own relationship with ʿĀʾishah. The story is one of several usually grouped under such headings as "women's descriptions of their husbands" or "women who praised their husbands" as against women who found fault with their husbands.[166] In the story of Umm Zarʿ, eleven women agreed to give frank descriptions of their husbands. Five of them were critical of their husbands, but in varying degrees, and five others praised their husbands in varying degrees. The eleventh, Umm Zarʿ, could not praise Abū Zarʿ enough even though he had divorced her to marry another and she herself had since married a good man.[167] Muḥammad, in relating the story to ʿĀʾishah, prefaced it with "I am to you as Abū Zarʿ is to Umm Zarʿ," and some sources add that he closed the story with: "Furthermore, I will not divorce you." ʿĀʾishah is said to have answered: "Truly, you treat me better than Abū Zarʿ treated Umm Zarʿ."[168] The story serves to dramatize certain qualities of desirable husbands as well as the full appreciation by wives of the good qualities of their husbands. Because of its association with Muḥammad and ʿĀʾishah, the story is often repeated in early and late sources, with or without an *isnād*, but, where an *isnād* is given, it traces through various chains back to ʿĀʾishah, though the earliest extant written form known to us is that in the *Gharīb al-ḥadīth* of Abū ʿUbaid (d. 223/838).[169] As in the case of the story of Umm Iyās, the outline of the tale and most of the vocabulary are stable but no two versions are identical. The fullness of the women's statements varies, as does the order except that Umm Zarʿ is always the last speaker. Furthermore, and again because of its association with Muḥammad and ʿĀʾishah, the story is reported by both Muslim and Bukhārī among other leading traditionists[170] and, where found in either religious or secular[171] sources, it is more apt than not to be accompanied by an extensive lexical commentary.

The story of Umm Zarʿ is of interest for several reasons apart from its association with Muḥammad and ʿĀʾishah. Umm Zarʿ eulogizes not only her husband but also other members of the family, including a marriageable daughter, whose description has bearing on our papyrus text. The girl emerges as a dutiful and obedient daughter, beautiful of face and figure to the point of being the envy of her neighbors, generous, chaste, intelligent, and cultured—in short, perfect, as some commentators assure us.[172] Our further interest in the story is the character of its prose. All versions, whether stemming from a single source or a composite account, include a large number of strange words that call for explanation. To what extent, if any, the strange words can be attributed to the fact that all of the eleven women involved were Yemenites is hard to tell. Their statements are in short series of one-word rhymed phrases or in rhymed phrases of two or three words each except the statement of the tenth woman, who uses longer rhymed phrases or sentences. On the whole the style is straightforward, the few similes and metaphors being familiar ones associated with desert life and animals. That is, apart from the strange vocabulary, the style of the piece in respect to brevity (*ījāz*), rhyme (*sajʿ*), and figures of speech (*tashbīhāt*) is in harmony with that of our papyrus text.

[166] See e.g. Ibn Abī Ṭāhir Ṭaifūr, pp. 76–123. Other frequent groupings include women who remained faithful to their husbands even after divorce or death, girls who described and praised their fathers, girls who described desirable prospective husbands, parents' advice to their children on choice of a mate and family life (see e.g. Jāḥiẓ, *Maḥāsin*, pp. 223 f.; Ibn Abī Ṭāhir Ṭaifūr, pp. 88 f., 93, 114; *Majālis Thaʿlab* I 45; Mufaḍḍal ibn Salamah, *Al-fākhir* [1380/1960] pp. 109 f., 171 f., 253; *Amālī* I 17, 80 f. and II 222 f.).

[167] See Ibn Abī Ṭāhir Ṭaifūr, pp. 76–86; *Concordance* V 541 وتعاقدن ان لا يكتمن من اخبار ازواجهن شياء.

[168] *Muzhir* II 535.

[169] For manuscript copies see pp. 10–11, with nn. 92 and 102.

[170] See Muslim XV 212–22, with Nawawī's lengthy commentary; Bukhārī III 441 f.; *Concordance* V 541.

[171] See e.g. Ibn Abī Ṭāhir Ṭaifūr, pp. 76–86; *Muzhir* II 532–36.

[172] E.g. Muslim XV 219. Nawawī's terms are حسنها وجمالها وعفتها وادبها. Ibn Abī Ṭāhir Ṭaifūr, p. 82, stresses her physical beauty and perfection: حسنها وكمالها; *Muzhir* II 534 stresses her pleasing and generous personality, her modesty and graciousness, and other qualities: مؤنقة منفقة قنواء كريمة الخِلّ . . . .

The Qur'ān expressly states that Muslim men are to marry Muslim women only and that a Muslim concubine is to be preferred to a polytheist even though the latter may be more pleasing.[173] I have elsewhere detailed some of the factors that influenced Muḥammad's choice of each of his wives.[174] Tradition credits him with the following brief formula for selection of a wife, be she maid, divorcée, or widow: "Marry a woman for her wealth, her beauty, and especially for her faith."[175] Other traditions expand this formula to include noble or respectable descent.[176] Khadījah was singled out as meeting all four requirements, while 'Ā'ishah and Umm Salamah lacked only wealth.[177] But for most of Muḥammad's contemporaries and successors the combination most sought after in a wife, presumably apart from her faith,[178] was beauty and suitable descent. Rich women continued to find husbands, but a poor man or one with modest means was cautioned against marrying a rich woman. For it was assumed or feared that her wealth would give her the upper hand in family and social affairs,[179] all the more so if she was also beautiful and well-born, as was indeed illustrated by the conduct of "the two pearls of the Quraish," 'Ā'ishah's niece and namesake 'Ā'ishah bint Ṭalḥah and Sukainah the granddaughter of 'Alī.[180] Both these women were married to the rich, handsome, and well-born Muṣ'ab ibn al-Zubair,[181] and they had successive well-born husbands during the lifetime of several of the leading characters of our papyrus text. Therefore, descriptive prose by or about these several women and their contemporaries should be of interest in connection with both the content and the style of our papyrus text.

There seem to be no statements by Khadījah pertinent to our theme in contrast to the many that are available about her, beginning with Muḥammad's eulogistic characterization of her.[182] Umm Salamah and 'Ā'ishah, Muḥammad's two most prominent wives after Khadījah, were both described as beautiful, graceful, and independent. Umm Salamah was well known for faithfulness, innate intelligence, and mature wisdom, while the young 'Ā'ishah was more often described as playful, witty, eloquent, ambitious, and, later, as a woman of great knowledge with a memory well stocked with poetry.[183] However, no one early source gives a complete formal description of either Umm Salamah or 'Ā'ishah. The earliest formal description of 'Ā'ishah bint Ṭalḥah ibn 'Ubaid Allāh, who strongly resembled her Aunt 'Ā'ishah, is that recorded by Abū al-Faraj al-Iṣfahānī with the following *isnād*: "Ḥusain ibn Yaḥyā informed me on the authority of Ḥammād on that of his father on the authority of Ṣāliḥ ibn Ḥassān al-Baṣrī."[184] What follows tells how Muṣ'ab ibn al-Zubair, 'Abd Allāh ibn 'Abd al-Raḥmān ibn Abī Bakr al-Ṣaddīq, and Sa'īd ibn al-'Āṣ, having asked for the hands of 'Ā'ishah bint Ṭalḥah, Umm al-Qāsim the granddaughter of Ṭalḥah, and 'Ā'ishah the daughter of the caliph 'Uthmān respectively, wanted detailed descriptions of the three women. They sent 'Azzat al-Mailā', a woman of Medina said to be knowledgeable about women, to inspect the ladies.[185] 'Azzat al-Mailā' visited the three women and returned to give an enthusiastic

[173] Sūrah 2:221. Some of the later sources show familiarity with biblical views of the good and the evil wife (e.g. *'Iqd* VI 82, 111 f.).

[174] See Abbott, *Aishah*, and *JNES* I 121–23.

[175] E.g. Bukhārī III 442; Muslim X 51 f.; Ibn Ḥanbal, *Al-musnad* III 80, 302; see also *Concordance* I 373 جمال and cf. *Aghānī* XV 21.

[176] Muslim X 51 f.; Bukhārī II 133 f.; see also *Concordance* VI 551 تنكح المرأة على اربعة.

[177] For the remarkable qualities of Khadījah and 'Ā'ishah see e.g. Muslim XV 197–212; see also citations in n. 174 above.

[178] See e.g. *'Iqd* VI 100; Ibn al-Jauzī, *Ta'rīkh 'Umar ibn al-Khaṭṭāb* (Cairo, 1924) p. 195.

[179] See e.g. *'Iqd* VI 102, 115; *Amālī* II 260. *'Iqd* VI 96–98 cautions even noble wealthy men against marrying rich women.

[180] See Abbott, *Aishah*, pp. 207 f., *JNES* I 347 f., 363 f.

[181] *'Uyūn* IV 21 f., 25, 90; Jāḥiẓ, *Maḥāsin*, pp. 221–23; *'Iqd* IV 412 and VI 109 f., 119 f.; *Aghānī* III 122 f. and XIV 168 f.

[182] E.g. *Sīrah* I 119, 154–56, 277; Ibn Sa'd I 35, III 1, pp. 12 and 27, VIII 35; *Istī'āb* II 717–21; *Iṣābah* IV 537–42.

[183] For both women see Abbott, *Aishah*, esp. pp. 12–16 and 53 f., and *JNES* I 123 f. 'Ā'ishah's favorite poet was Labīd.

[184] *Aghānī* X 55 f. The Ḥammād of the *isnād* is Ḥammād ibn Isḥāq al-Mauṣalī. Ṣāliḥ ibn Ḥassān al-Baṣrī was known as an *akhbārī* but was considered weak as a traditionist, as was also Haitham ibn 'Adī, who transmitted Ṣāliḥ's materials. For Haitham's role and manuscripts see p. 76, n. 246.

[185] It seems that they sent one other woman to inspect their prospective brides, but the second report gives no detailed descriptions (*Fāḍil*, pp. 117 f.).

item-by-item description of ʿĀʾishah bint Ṭalḥah, whose only defects, she said, were large ears and big feet. She found no defects in the other two women, whom she briefly described in general terms except for the comment that ʿĀʾishah bint ʿUthmān was too aloof. The story ends with three marriages. The handsome Muṣʿab was ever proud of his ʿĀʾishah's beauty and talents, as he was of the beauty of his other wife, Sukainah (see references in n. 181). It is noteworthy that the descriptions of all of these women are cast in more or less the same literary style, that is, a comparatively simple vocabulary grouped mostly in two-word rhymed phrases with now and again a few one-word or three-word rhymed phrases. Figures of speech are rarely used. It is interesting also to note here that ʿĀʾishah's phrases describing the character of Muḥammad and that of her father, the caliph Abū Bakr, are cast in short measured sentences but not necessarily always in simple vocabulary or rhymed phrases and with few, if any, figures of speech.[186]

The role of the independent and gifted woman, royal or otherwise, of the Umayyad period has been detailed elsewhere.[187] Muʿāwiyah's often very cordial reception of leading tribal women and gifted poetesses[188] reflects his more or less balanced outlook on and approach to the opposite sex from his youth onward as expressed in his own words.[189] Ṣaʿṣaʿah ibn Ṣūḥān, a staunch supporter of ʿAlī, was taken prisoner by Muʿāwiyah, who appreciated his vast knowledge, eloquence, and wit. Ṣaʿṣaʿah was politically less powerful than Aḥnaf ibn Qais of our text but far more outspoken, alike in his defense of the Shīʿah and his personal conversation with Muʿāwiyah.[190] Muʿāwiyah once asked Ṣaʿṣaʿah what type of woman he desired most and what type least, to which he answered tersely: "She who does what pleases you and she who does not." "This is a hasty criticism," said Muʿāwiyah. "But a just one," countered Ṣaʿṣaʿah.[191] At another time Ṣaʿṣaʿah was bold enough to ask Muʿāwiyah: "O Commander of the Faithful, how can we consider you wise when but half a human being has the mastery over you?" He was referring to Muʿāwiyah's wife Fākhitah bint Qarẓah, and Muʿāwiyah answered: "Women surpass men in nobility and are surpassed in ignobility."[192]

A curious tale[193] involving the proverbially romantic Banū ʿUdhrah, Marwān ibn al-Ḥakam as governor of Medina (41–49/661–69 and again briefly in A.H. 56–57), and Muʿāwiyah runs as follows. When a loving ʿUdhrite couple fell on hard times, the father-in-law, who was the uncle of the husband (neither one named), took his daughter, Suʿdā, back home even though the husband had refused to divorce her. The unhappy man appealed to Marwān, before whom the girl and her father were brought for questioning. Marwān lost his heart on first sight to this girl of surprising beauty. He bribed the father for the promise of her hand, imprisoned and flogged the unfortunate husband until, despairing of his very life, he divorced Suʿdā, whom Marwān then married. The distraught ʿUdhrite appealed next to Muʿāwiyah, who ordered Marwān to divorce Suʿdā and send her north. When the girl appeared before Muʿāwiyah, he in turn lost his heart and mind to the delicate and perfectly beautiful young woman with an eloquent tongue.[194]

186 See e.g. Khaṭīb VI 158 f.; Nuwairī VII 230 f. For some of her other public speeches see Abbott, *Aishah*, pp. 131, 146, 157, with references there cited.

187 See Abbott in *JNES* I 341–68.

188 See e.g. ʿ*Iqd* II 102–21.

189 See e.g. *ibid.* IV 363: لم يكن فى الشباب شى الا كان مني مستمتع غير اني لم اكن صرعة ولانكحة ولاسباً. A poisoned wound received at the Battle of Ṣiffīn necessitated an emergency operation that rendered Muʿāwiyah sterile but not impotent (Ṭabarī I 3464). See *Waqʿat Ṣiffīn*, pp. 416 f., for his comprehension of a woman's lasting memory of her first love and of the murder of her first-born, to which he compares his own lasting anger against the murderers of ʿUthmān.

190 See e.g. Masʿūdī V 91–93, 98–112.

191 ʿ*Iqd* VI 106: قال معاويه هذه النقد العاجل فقال صعصعه بالميزان العادل. ʿ*Uyūn* IV 10 credits this to ʿAqīl ibn Abī Ṭālib.

192 ʿ*Iqd* VI 106: انهن يغلبن الكرام ويغلبهن اللئام. For Fākhitah see e.g. Ṭabarī II 204, ʿ*Iqd* VI 18, Masʿūdī VIII 148, and Ibn Qaiyim al-Jauzīyah, pp. 93 f.

193 Ibn Qaiyim al-Jauzīyah, *Kitāb akhbār al-nisāʾ* pp. 4–8 (for uncertainty as to the author of this work see n. 67 on p. 55 above).

194 *Ibid.* pp. 6 f.: فاذا بجارية رعبوبة لا تبق لناظرها عقلا من حسنها وكمالها . . . فاستنطقها فاذا هى افصح لسان العرب.

In exchange for her, he offered the ʿUdhrite three young girls and much wealth and pensions for all. But the ʿUdhrite vowed that not for all of Muʿāwiyah's kingdom would he exchange Suʿdā and cited verses of Majnūn Lailā to express his devotion to her. Muʿāwiyah then reminded the ʿUdhrite that he had already divorced Suʿdā, yet Muʿāwiyah offered to give her the choice between himself and her former husband. Suʿdā declared her choice of her husband in verse reinforced by prose reminiscent in part of the Christian marriage vow: "I am not, O Commander of the Faithful, about to forsake him because of the accidents of fortune. For I have had a good life with him and I, above all, ought to bear with him patiently in happiness and misfortune, in poverty and wealth, in sickness and health as Allāh has ordained for me with him." Muʿāwiyah and his court marveled at her good sense, perfection, and humanity.[195] Muʿāwiyah not only honored her choice but presented her with 10,000 dirhems and placed her on public welfare. Touched up or not by a late and gossipy author, our only source, the story is nevertheless consistent in its general description of Suʿdā's qualities and its literary style of one and two-word rhymed phrases. Furthermore the open appreciation of Suʿdā's moral qualities reminds one of the pagan Shanfarā (d. *ca.* A.D. 510) and his verses in appreciation of noble womanhood.[196]

During the reign of ʿAbd al-Malik (65–86/685–705) the moral tone sought by ʿUmar I and Ziyād ibn Abī Sufyān receded in an indulgent society exposed increasingly to slave girls of many races and varied endowments.[197] The women of prominent tribes and families long known for the beauty and spirit of their women continued to be in demand at court and among men of position and wealth. This is well illustrated in the case of the Anṣār, the Banū Taim and descendants of the caliph Abū Bakr, the family of ʿAqīl ibn ʿUllafah, who would even reject ʿAbd al-Malik's son because he was born of a non-Arab mother,[198] and the Banū Makhzūm,[199] particularly the family of ʿAbd al-Raḥmān ibn al-Ḥārith ibn Hishām al-Makhzūmī, whose daughter Zainab rejected even ʿAbd al-Malik himself.[200] ʿAbd al-Malik and his son and successor Walīd I (86–96/705–15) frowned on public mention, let alone detailed descriptions, in verse or prose, of the members of their large harems. And, though the female marriage agent (*dallālah*) still enjoyed a lucrative profession, her descriptions of marriageable Arab girls or women seem to have been no longer as frequently recorded. Furthermore, she now met competition from male marriage brokers who mixed freely with the rising class of songstresses and courtesans and were considered more knowledgeable than women as to what qualities in a woman, other than the primarily physical, appealed most to men.[201] She faced competition also from the expert slave dealer who picked, trained, described, and displayed his

[195] *Ibid.* pp. 7 f.: عقلها وكمالها ومروتها. The word order of the second part of Suʿdā's statement reflects the measure and rhyme of her prose: قالت وانا احق من صبر معه على السراء والضراء وعلى الشدة والرخاء وعلى العافية والبلاء وعلى القسم الذي كتب الله لي معه.

[196] See Reynold A. Nicholson, *A Literary History of the Arabs* (2nd ed.; Cambridge, England, 1930) p. 90, for translation and reference for one passage: Aṣmaʿī, who had received Shanfarā's poetry from the younger Shāfiʿī (see p. 34 above), considered Shanfarā's one-line physical description of a woman the best of its kind (*Muzhir* I 160; Thaʿālibī, *Ījāz*, p. 30). See ʿ*Uyūn* IV 79 f. for Shanfarā's verses on long-suffering passion.

[197] See Abbott in *JNES* I 351 f.

[198] ʿ*Uyūn* IV 12, 78; *Aghānī* XI 86, 90 f.; ʿ*Iqd* II VI 98 and 191 f.

[199] Masʿūdī V 364; Thaʿālibī, *Thimār*, pp. 238 f.: بنو مخزوم سُمي ريحانة قريش لحظوة نسائها عند الرجال . . . The terms *rīḥān* and *raiḥānah*, any aromatic plant and also chrysanthemum, were applied to women by Muḥammad in a playful and complimentary sense, and "Raiḥānah" was used also as a girl's name (see *Concordance* II 318 ريح). We find that Ḥajjāj ibn Yūsuf and later Ibn al-Muqaffaʿ, both strong believers in the subjugation of women, refer to a woman as a fragrance to be enjoyed and not as a helper to be burdened with one's affairs (Ibn Abī Ṭāhir Ṭaifūr, pp. 128 f.; ʿ*Uyūn* IV 78 f.: انما المرآة ريحانة وليست بقهرمانة). In time, however, unfavorable connotations arose with the use of the metaphor, such as a woman is but a flower to be enjoyed while fresh and like a wilted flower she is to be cast away (e.g. Jāḥiẓ, *Qīyān* in *Thalāth rasātil*, pp. 55 f.; Thaʿālibī, *Thimār*, p. 215; Washshāʾ, *Kitāb al-muwashshā*, ed. Rudolph E. Brünnow [Leyden, 1886] pp. 122 f.). Or, again, a woman is but a doll to play with and discard when worn out (see *Concordance* VI 121 النساء لعبة). And, finally, in rarer but more derogatory terms, a woman is but a slipper to be worn out and thrown away (Ibn Abī ʿAwn, *Kitāb al-tashbīhāt*, p. 316).

[200] ʿ*Iqd* VI 99; see also Abbott in *JNES* I 348 f.

[201] Jāḥiẓ, *Nisāʾ* in *Rasāʾil*, pp. 274 f.

choicest articles of trade—beautiful and gifted young girls and handsome youths—to meet the increasing demands of court and society.[202] Since these brokers and slave dealers and their patrons are frequently named, it is possible to date roughly their statements. The interest in women of a particular family and tribe, not always with happy results,[203] was presently expanded to interest in foreign women, who soon came to be classified by preference and function. Greek girls, for instance, were frowned on by ʿAbd al-Malik for their moral laxity but were favored by his son Yazīd II (101–5/720–24).[204] ʿAbd al-Malik noted the patience of Indian women and recommended Berber girls for pleasure, Persian girls for fine offspring, and Russian girls for service.[205] A description of the women of Ṭabaristan is traced back to Abū ʿAmr ibn al-ʿAlāʾ.[206] The Bedouins also were a source of descriptions of desirable women. They either described specific women or volunteered their opinions of the ideal maiden. But more often than not these Bedouins are nameless since second- and third-century transmitters and authors cite them simply with the expression *wa qāla aʿrābī* and the particular Bedouin may or may not have been contemporary with the transmitter or author. Thus, even rough dating of Bedouin statements is risky. Nevertheless the liberal supply of their statements in almost any work or section devoted to women enables us to observe that, though their statements present various views, they share a common style, namely brief descriptions in either ordinary or rather strange but generally rhymed prose with here and there a simile or a metaphor.[207]

ʿAbd al-Malik himself was not only knowledgeable about women but also passionately devoted to them until old age overtook him.[208] He had in all at least ten wives, not to mention unnumbered concubines.[209] He asked for the opinion of his confidant Rauḥ ibn Zinbāʿ on one of his royal wives, the mother of his heir Walīd, and received a frank though uncomplimentary answer with which he himself readily agreed.[210] He ordered Ḥajjāj ibn Yūsuf, his governor of ʿIrāq, to secure three lovely slave girls for him. Ḥajjāj did so, and in his brief rhymed description of one of these girls the only simile used compares her coloring to that of gold and silver.[211] ʿAbd al-Malik was interested in the opinions of poets on women, particularly that of his court poet ʿAdī ibn al-Riqāʿ, whose ideal woman, described in two verses, combined the best physical characteristics of the women of the tribes of Quḍāʿah, Kindah, Khuzāʿah, and Ṭayy with the wisdom of Luqmān, the beauty of the biblical Joseph, the diction of David, and the chastity of the Virgin Mary.[212] ʿAdī is credited with being the first poet to compare a groom and his bride to the moon and the sun respectively, the occasion being a royal wedding at the court of ʿAbd al-Malik.[213] ʿAbd al-Malik once ordered a man of the North Arab Banū Ghaṭafān to describe for him the most beautiful of women. The description given was limited to physical traits and started, for a change, with the feet and moved upward. It covers seven lines of printed text and is cast in smoothly flowing rhymed prose of two-word phrases

202 See e.g. Abbott in *JNES* I 351 f.; Masʿūdī V 344–47, 394–96; *Aghānī* VI 133 (= *Aghānī* [1927——] VII 67).

203 See *JNES* I 346; *Aghānī* XIV 141; *ʿIqd* VI 98 f., 104 f., 114 f.; *Amālī* III 47.

204 Khalīl Mardam, *Dīwān al-Walīd ibn Yazīd* (Damascus, 1355/1937) p. 21; cf. *ʿUyūn* IV 8 f.

205 E.g. *ʿIqd* VI 103, 120; Ibshīhī II 203.

206 Thaʿālibī, *Bard al-akbād* (in *Khams rasāʾil* [Constantinople, 1301/1883]) p. 121.

207 E.g. *ʿUyūn* IV 5 f.; *ʿIqd* VI 107, 112 f.; *Amālī* II 81, 260; Abū Zaid al-Anṣārī, *Kitāb al-nawādir fī al-lughah*, p. 170.

208 *Aghānī* XXI 9; Ibn ʿAsākir VII 311 f.

209 See Abbott in *JNES* I 348–51.

210 See *ʿIqd* VI 114, where she is compared by both men to a rough and prickly object. Rauḥ could barely hold his own with a high-born Arab wife (*ibid.* VI 114 f.).

211 Ibshīhī II 148 f.

212 *Ibid.* II 205:

قضاعية الكعبين كندية الحشاء   خزاعية الاطراف طائية الفم
لها حكم لقمان وصورة يوسف   ومنطق داودِ وعفة مريم

See Ibn Abī Ṭāhir Ṭaifūr, pp. 73–75, for a female genealogist's characterization of the various tribes in the time of Muʿāwiyah.

213 *ʿUyūn* III 69; Thaʿālibī, *Thimār*, p. 239. For ʿAdī's figurative reference to the "pen and ink" see e.g. Ṣūlī, *Adab al-kuttāb*, pp. 78 f., and for other such comparisons see p. 66 above. See e.g. *Shiʿr*, pp. 391–94, and *Aghānī* VIII 179–84 for ʿAdī's biographical entries.

without a single simile or metaphor. The specifications are so exacting that ʿAbd al-Malik is said to have exclaimed: "Woe to you! And where is she to be found?" "You find her," came the unhesitating answer, "among the pure-blooded Arabs and the pure-blooded Persians."[214] ʿAbd al-Malik's governor of North Africa sent him a gift of a maiden (probably Berber; see p. 71) who arrived when he was about to go on an expedition against the rebellious Ibn al-Ashʿath (80–82/699–701). She is described as beautiful, elegant, and utterly charming, all that one could ever hope for or desire. ʿAbd al-Malik cited a verse of Akhṭal which placed the business of war before pleasure and then sent the girl away to await his return.[215] A decade earlier, his favorite wife, the glorious ʿĀtikah, granddaughter of Muʿāwiyah, had sought in vain to dissuade him from taking to the field against Muṣʿab ibn al-Zubair. As she and her attendants burst into tears at his parting, ʿAbd al-Malik recalled a verse of Kuthaiyir which aptly fitted the situation.[216] Thus, unlike some others before and after him, his passion for women was not allowed to interfere with his caliphal duties, and when, like other passions, it subsided in old age, his one remaining pleasure, he said, was conversation with his friends on a moonlit night in the desert[217]—conversation interspersed no doubt with citations from the poets.

ʿAbd al-Malik's and Walīd's major-domo Ḥajjāj ibn Yūsuf (d. 95/714) was by contrast not much of a lady's man. His marriages were made with an eye to politics and improvement of his social status but frequently boomeranged, for he was ordered to divorce a high-born wife and driven to divorce another such wife because of her persistent disregard of or open aversion to him.[218] He nevertheless believed in always having the full quota of four wives and advised others to do the same.[219] One group of four wives presented Ḥajjāj with an enviable variety. One was playful, another regal, the third a Bedouin versed in Bedouin speech and poetry, and the fourth a scholar versed in law.[220] He called on Ibn al-Qirrīyah (d. 84/703), whose literary style and judgment about women impressed him, to act as marriage agent and ask for the hand of Hind bint Asmāʾ in no more than three sentences.[221] Later, when he wished to divorce Hind, who had no use for him, he sent Ibn al-Qirrīyah to inform her in no more than two words that he had divorced her.[222] At another time he wrote Ibn al-Qirrīyah to find his son a wife with the following specifications: "beautiful (of form and coloring) from afar, pleasing (in face and feature) when near, from

[214] ʿ*Iqd* VI 108; cf. Khālidīyān *Kitāb al-tuḥaf wa al-hadayā*, ed. Sāmī al-Dahan (L'Institut français d'archéologie orientale du Caire, "Textes et traductions d'auteurs orientaux" XII [Cairo, 1956]) pp. 101–4; Ibshīhī II 204. The Persians rejected mixed breeds and considered children of ordinary concubines as slaves, as Aṣmaʿī learned in conversation with Yaḥyā al-Barmakī (ʿ*Iqd* VI 129; Zubaidī, pp. 187 f.).

[215] Jāḥiẓ, *Tāj*, p. 175; Jumaḥī, p. 459; Masʿūdī VI 64 f.; ʿ*Iqd* IV 407. Akhṭal's verse reads

قوم اذا حاربوا شدوا مآزرهم   دون النساء ولو باتت باطهار

[216] E.g. *Aghānī* VIII 35 and XVII 162; *Amālī* I 14; Ibn al-Ṭiqṭaqā, *Al-fakhrī* (1895) p. 169:

نهته فلما لم تر النهى عاقه   بكت فبكى مماشجلها قطينها

For ʿĀtikah and her influence on ʿAbd al-Malik see Abbott in *JNES* I 349–51. For an earlier ʿĀtikah who kept ʿAbd Allāh ibn Abī Bakr from his civil and military duties see Abbott, *Aishah*, p. 87, and *Khizānah* IV 350–52.

[217] Abū Ḥayyān al-Tawḥīdī, *Risālah fī al-ṣadāqah wa al-ṣadīq*, p. 32. For thumbnail characterizations of the youthful ʿAbd al-Malik by Muʿāwiyah and ʿAmr ibn al-ʿĀṣ and later by ʿAbd al-Malik himself see e.g. Jāḥiẓ, *Bayān* II 35, 248 and *Muwashshaḥ*, p. 32.

[218] See e.g. Abbott in *JNES* I 347, 349, 353 f.; ʿ*Uyūn* II 209; ʿ*Iqd* 122, 130; Ibshīhī I 50 f. Ḥajjājwas not above rewarding a staunch supporter by scaring his social superiors into giving him their daughters in marriage (Masʿūdī V 331–33).

[219] *Amālī* III 48.

[220] ʿ*Iqd* VI 104 f., 122.

[221] ʿ*Uyūn* III 69 gives the three sentences: جئتُ من عند من تعلمون والامير يعطيكم ما تسئلون أفتنكحون ام تردّون (cf. Jāḥiẓ, *Maḥāsin*, pp. 239 f.).

[222] ʿ*Uyūn* II 209; ʿ*Iqd* VI 107. The two words were كنتِ فبنت, and Hind answered كنا فما حمدنا وبنا فما ندمنا and rewarded Ibn al-Qirrīyah with 10,000 dirhems for bringing her the good news. Mubarrad, pp. 291 f., gives a supposed reason for this divorce.

a noble family, humble in spirit and obedient to her husband."[223] Ibn al-Qirrīyah's response to Ḥajjāj's inquiry as to what he thought of married life was to describe the type of woman with whom one could live a serene and happy life. In the description, which covers seven lines of printed text, physical charms are subordinated to religious, ethical, and personality traits. The simple rhymed prose consists for the most part of series of one-word, two-word, or longer units but includes also a series of four similes.[224] He used the same style in a two-line description of a woman who would render life miserable for all around her and who is compared to a heavy load being dragged by a weak old man.[225] In a weak moment Ibn al-Qirrīyah supported the ill-fated rebellion of Ibn al-Ashʿath against ʿAbd al-Malik and Ḥajjāj. He was later captured, bound, and brought before Ḥajjāj. He begged to be allowed to plead his case "in just three sentences," and his plea was granted. One word led to another until finally Ḥajjāj ordered his head struck off but soon regretted that he had thus deprived himself of Ibn al-Qirrīyah's company and conversation.[226]

A youthful contemporary of Ibn al-Qirrīyah and Aḥnaf ibn Qais of our papyrus text was the latter's fellow tribesman Khālid ibn Ṣafwān al-Tamīmī of Baṣrah (d. 135/752), who early won a reputation as an orator with a style distinguished for its clarity and eloquence. He, like Aḥnaf, was known to extol the excellence of Baṣrah and of ʿIrāq.[227] Like Aḥnaf, Khālid ibn Ṣafwān had the ability to win the confidence of those in power. In his home province of ʿIrāq he was in favor with the governor Khālid al-Qaṣrī and his successor Yūsuf ibn ʿUmar ibn Shubrumah (120–26/738–44). The latter included Khālid ibn Ṣafwān in a delegation to the court of Hishām, whom he found at a desert resort. He regaled the caliph with stories of the Khusraus and stressed the transience of wealth and power and of life itself.[228] His theme and eloquence so touched Hishām that he broke camp and returned with his retinue to his palace. When an opportunity presented itself, he ventured to plead with Hishām on behalf of the fallen Khālid al-Qaṣrī, only to be told that the treatment meted out to the latter was no worse than he actually deserved.[229] Hishām as prince once called for the opinions of some of his companions on the relative merits of Farazdaq, Akhṭal, and Jarīr and was dissatisfied with the views expressed. He then asked Khālid ibn Ṣafwān to give his opinion of the three poets and was quite satisfied with the answer.[230]

Khālid ibn Ṣafwān lived a simple life, perhaps because of a streak of piety[231] though most of his contemporaries credited it to extreme miserliness.[232] He advocated small families as a safeguard for one's peace of mind and freedom from financial pressures.[233] Proposing to a woman, he felt it only fair that she should know his temperament before giving her answer and proceeded to describe himself as one whose wife would weary him coming and afflict him going and would have no access to his money. He added that there were times when he felt so afflicted that were his own head in his hand, he would fling it away.

[223] ʿ*Iqd* VI 107: جميلة من بعيد مليحة من قريب شريفة في قومها ذليلة في نفسها مواتية لبعلها. The implied distinction of جميل and مليح is that offered by Khālid ibn Ṣafwān (see ʿ*Uyūn* IV 23 and cf. ʿ*Iqd* VI 117). Ibshīhī II 204 f. has confused Ḥajjāj's son ʿAbd al-Malik with the caliph ʿAbd al-Malik.

[224] Jāḥiẓ, *Maḥāsin*, p. 239; the good woman is described as كالريحانة والنخلة لمن يجتنيها وكاللولوة التى لم تثقب والمسكة التى لم تفتق. For other specimens of Ibn al-Qirrīyah's prose see e.g. *ibid.* pp. 9 f., 263–67; Masʿūdī V 323 f.; and references in n. 110 on p. 59 above.

[225] Jāḥiẓ, *Maḥāsin*, p. 239: المرأة السوء كالحمل الثقيل على الشيخ الضعيف يجره في الارض جراً. See Masʿūdī V 394–96 for Ibn al-Qirrīyah's longer descriptions of the best and the worst women.

[226] *Maʿārif*, p. 206; Ṭabarī II 1127–29; Masʿūdī V 323.

[227] Jāḥiẓ, *Bayān* II 90; Yāqūt I 97, 649 f.

[228] See *Aghānī* II 35–37 and XVIII 139 and *Irshād* IV 161–64 for this and similar instances of his preachments.

[229] *Aghānī* XIX 63. For the fall of Khālid al-Qaṣrī and his family see e.g. Ṭabarī I 1641–58.

[230] *Aghānī* VII 73; *Irshād* IV 160 f. See also p. 141 below.

[231] He was one night, he said, contemplating the world's riches until in his imagination he saw the green sea covered with red gold but realized that all he really needed was two loaves, two jugs, and two old garments, to which another version adds the worship of the merciful (Allāh); see Jāḥiẓ, *Bayān* III 147; Jāḥiẓ, *Maḥāsin*, p. 221: رغيفان وكوزان وطِمران وعبادة الرحمن.

[232] He came to be considered one of the four most miserly Arabs (*Aghānī* II 46; *Irshād* IV 164).

[233] Masʿūdī VI 114 f.; Jāḥiẓ, *Maḥāsin*, p. 221.

The woman answered that she would not consider him acceptable even for the daughters of Iblīs and dismissed him with Allāh's blessings.[234] He commissioned agents to find him a wife, but his specifications were so exacting that the agents could do no more than assure him he would find her in heaven.[235] He must have eventually sweetened his proposals with a promise of due consideration and a legacy,[236] for wives he did have and also at least one son and a daughter. But home was not always peaceful, for we find him declaring that the best night of his life was that in which he divorced his two wives.[237] When among a group of men the conversation centered on women—a frequent pastime—Khālid listened attentively to each speaker, city dweller or Bedouin.[238] He was an admirer of Bedouin verse and prose and particularly of Bedouin oratory.[239]

Khālid's attitude toward women and even some of the phrases he used in describing them seem to have remained more or less constant to judge by a comparison of his earlier with two of his later, if not indeed his last, statements, which were made to the first ʿAbbāsid caliph, Abū al-ʿAbbās al-Saffāḥ (132–36/750–54), who enjoyed Khālid's company.[240] The caliph, commenting on the growth of people's harems, asked Khālid what type of woman he preferred most. Khālid answered that his preference was for one not too young nor too old, of impressive beauty of form from afar and still attractive when near, slender from (the waist) up and full from (the waist) down, one who had experienced both wealth and poverty. This description all but duplicates earlier instructions given a marriage agent.[241] On a second, and probably later occasion, Khālid suggested to the caliph, who in being monogamous provided the proverbial exception to the rule, that he should enlarge his harem. He proceeded to tantalize the caliph's imagination by referring to the many types of women, slave or freeborn, that were available in his vast empire. Among those mentioned were Berber girls and other girls of foreign extraction but born and bred in Medina and trained to amuse and please, free women whose conversation was delightful, and girls of all descriptions who were born and bred in Baṣrah and Kūfah.[242]

Once again, in analyzing Khālid's descriptions of women, we find that the physical attractions predominate, with here and there a reference to personality and training but hardly any emphasis on intellectuality. As for Khālid's style, some choice of vocabulary apart, it is very similar to that of his predecessor Ibn al-Qirrīyah. Rhymed prose is the rule, with one-word or two-word phrases predominating. Khālid's descriptions tend to be somewhat shorter and even less given to the use of figures of speech. Once again we find marked similarity of content and style between the text of our papyrus and comparable texts that later literary sources have preserved from the Umayyad period.

It is both interesting and instructive to conclude our sampling of this type of literature by drawing attention to yet another description of a paragon of a woman. It comes from early ʿAbbāsid times, when descriptions of beautiful and gifted slave girls were more readily available than those of high-born free

[234] ʿ*Uyūn* IV 14. See *ibid.* IV 23, where he describes himself as short, dark, and bald.

[235] ʿ*Iqd* VI 107; Jāḥiẓ, *Maḥāsin*, pp. 220 f.

[236] See ʿ*Uyūn* IV 5, where his specification ends with إن عشتُ اكرمتها وان مت ورّثتها. The effeminate male agent he employed had a reputation for success (ʿ*Iqd* VI 105).

[237] ʿ*Uyūn* IV 127. One distressed wife sent him his bedding, and the other sent his daughter with a basket of food. The sequel is not reported.

[238] See e.g. ʿ*Iqd* VI 107 and *Amālī* III 34 f., where a Bedouin describes in verse the desirability of women according to their ages and Khālid replies لقد اتيت على ما في نفوسنا.

[239] Jāḥiẓ, *Bayān* I 184. When a barefooted Bedouin surpassed Khālid in eloquence, the latter exclaimed كيف نسابقهم وانما نجرى على ما سبق الينا من اعراقهم.

[240] See e.g. Jāḥiẓ, *Bayān* I 324 f.; Yaʿqūbī II 433. Abū al-ʿAbbās al-Saffāḥ preferred to spend most of his evening leisure time in the company of men and could not understand why some men left such company for that of women, where they hear nonsense and see shortcomings (Masʿūdī VI 118, 137).

[241] ʿ*Iqd* VI 107, lines 10–13, as compared with lines 16–17, and both passages as compared with ʿ*Uyūn* IV 23, lines 1–4.

[242] Masʿūdī VI 110–18. For more background, details, and the sequel see Abbott, *Two Queens of Baghdad*, pp. 13 f.

women. Muḥammad ibn Manṣūr ibn Ziyād, an influential Barmakid secretary in the reign of Hārūn al-Rashīd,[243] was widely known for his generosity. This prompted an (unnamed) admirer to write him requesting the gift of a slave girl whose qualifications he specified at length along with interspersed comments giving his reasons for a particular physical or personality specification. The requirements are exhaustive, and the style is mixed. Short and longer rhymed phrases intertwine with a series of similes and a verse of poetry. The sophisticated Barmakid secretary replied that he too was looking for such a maid but did not think she was to be found even in the next world. Nevertheless he inclosed a gift of 1,000 dinars and directed his correspondent to employ a professional agent to look for the desired girl, whose full price he promised to pay should she indeed be found.[244]

DATING OF THE DOCUMENT

A summary of the results of our research as detailed above is called for so that we may appraise its significance for the dating of the papyrus. We found that the two types of prose literature represented by the two sections of our text—a speech and descriptions of the ideal maiden—were well developed in pre-Islāmic times and continued to be popular thereafter. The ideas and the prose styles of both oratory and descriptive compositions through the Umayyad period were closer to those of pre-Islāmic times than to those of the new literary style (*badīʿ*) that was emerging in early ʿAbbāsid times. The simpler idiom and the briefer phraseology of the pre-ʿAbbāsid prose stylists contrasted with the more florid idiom and the lengthier phrases of their successors. Pre-ʿAbbāsid eloquence with its characteristic desert idiom was first infiltrated and then all but supplanted by the labored eloquence of the city dweller as molded largely by the influential secretarial class, whose idiom and figures of speech in both prose and poetry reflected progressively life in the heterogeneous metropolis. The characteristic rhymed phrases, retained by ʿAbbāsid stylists, grew longer for the most part and hence complicated the elements of weight and balance. True, this process, which began roughly in the mid-second/mid-eighth century, had as yet far to go to reach completion. Nevertheless, its growth, analysis, and critical appraisal are reflected in the works of such leading authors from the second/eighth century onward as Jumaḥī (d. 231/845), Jāḥiẓ, Ibn al-Muʿtazz, Ibn Abī ʿAwn, Qudāmah ibn Jaʿfar, and Ibn Rashīq (d. 463/1071). Still later, Ḍiyāʾ al-Dīn Naṣr Allāh ibn Muḥammad ibn al-Athīr (558–637/1163–1239), surveying the long history of literary prose, which by his time had reached its verbose and florid peak, summed up the argument that literary prose, being the medium of the Qurʾān, was not only superior to poetry but demanded greater effort and skill on the part of the stylist.[245] Few would question the rigor of late ʿAbbāsid prose, but none can fail to see that it is far removed from the brief and simple yet eloquent prose of our papyrus text.

The third-century authors who figure most significantly in our study of the historical and literary backgrounds of our document are Jāḥiẓ, Ibn Qutaibah, Ibn Abī Ṭāhir Ṭaifūr, Yaʿqūbī, Dīnawarī, and Ṭabarī. Their sources, in reverse chronological order, are Ibn al-Aʿrābī (d. 231/846 at age 81), ʿUtbī, Madāʾinī, Abū ʿUbaid, Aṣmaʿī, Abū ʿUbaidah, the Shīʿite Naṣr ibn Muzāḥim, Naḍr ibn Shumail, the

[243] Ṭabarī III 688; *Aghānī* XV 141.

[244] Khālidiyān, *Kitāb al-tuḥaf wa al-hadayā*, pp. 101–4. Muḥammad ibn Manṣūr himself owned an accomplished slave girl named Fauz, with whom the romantic court poet ʿAbbās ibn al-Aḥnaf became enamored and for whom he wrote verses (see *Aghānī* XV 141 f.; see also *Dīwān al-ʿAbbās ibn al-Aḥnaf*, ed. ʿĀtikah al-Khazrajī [Cairo, 1373/1954]). *Fihrist*, pp. 306–8, gives a long list of popular tales, some of which were authored by Hishām ibn Muḥammad ibn al-Sāʾib al-Kalbī and Haitham ibn ʿAdī, including a *Kitāb ʿAbbās wa Fauz* whose author is not named. Contemporary poets praised Muḥammad ibn Manṣūr for his generosity but more during his lifetime than in their elegies (e.g. Ibn al-Muʿtazz, *Ṭabaqāt*, pp. 253, 293 f., 296, 437; *ʿIqd* III 291–93 and V 327).

[245] Ḍiyāʾ al-Dīn Naṣr Allāh ibn Muḥammad ibn al-Athīr, *Al-jāmiʿ al-kabīr fī sināʿat al-naẓm min al-kalām al-manthūr*, ed. Musṭafā Jawād and Jamīl Saʿīd (Baghdād, 1375/1956) pp. 73–75.

Khārijite Haitham ibn ʿAdī, and Hishām ibn Muḥammad ibn al-Sāʾib al-Kalbī (d. 204/819 or 206/821).[246] Their *isnād*'s trace back in turn to Abū ʿAwānah al-Waḍḍāḥ ibn Khālid (d. 170/786 or 176/792), Mufaḍḍal ibn Muḥammad al-Ḍabbī, Ḥammād al-Rāwiyah, Abū ʿAmr ibn al-ʿAlāʾ, Muḥammad ibn al-Sāʾib al-Kalbī, ʿAwānah ibn al-Ḥakam, and Ibn al-Muqaffaʿ (d. *ca.* 139/757 or 142/759). Two significant observations about all of these authors[247] are, first, that they used manuscripts with or without accompanying oral transmission[248] and, second, that all of them, though some more than others, drew on the more knowledgeable and eloquent Bedouins, both those in their midst and others whom they sought out in the desert—men and women whom they cited for the most part anonymously.[249] Furthermore, these several groups of authors reflect the early literary interests as they developed in the Ḥijāz and Syria and the subsequent dominance of ʿIrāq in the linguistic and literary fields. They reflect also the early participation of both North and South Arab scholars, orthodox or otherwise, who were soon joined by non-Arab colleagues mainly from the eastern provinces. Moreover, early ʿAbbāsid sources provide some evidence that secular prose literature was already in circulation in Umayyad times, particularly literature of the *ansāb*, *akhbār*, and *amthāl* categories and a wide variety of *nawādir* for the most part from the history and folklore of the Persians and the Arabs.[250] This should surprise no one, considering the rapid increase in literacy[251] and the absence of injunctions against or hesitancy about committing such literature to writing. Even more significant is the realization that such early objections as had existed to committing sacred literature to writing, other than the Qurʾān itself, had been overcome by the time of Zuhrī (d. 124/741) and his pupils, as already detailed in our Volume II. And Zuhrī was contemporary with the Meccan schoolteacher and scholar ʿAṭāʾ ibn Abī Rabāḥ and his son Yaʿqūb of our papyrus text (see recto 7 and comment on p. 44), as also with Ibn al-Qirrīyah, Shaʿbī, Khālid ibn Ṣafwān,[252] ʿAbd al-Malik ibn ʿUmair (d. 136/753 at age 103),[253] and Ibn al-Muqaffaʿ, all of whom have roles in our understanding of the literary background of our papyrus text.

Still another factor that must be taken into consideration is the wide range of interest of the Umayyad and early ʿAbbāsid scholars no matter what their particular fields of specialization. Stirring speeches and

[246] Hishām and Haitham were severely criticized as traditionists but recognized, nonetheless, as knowledgeable authors in the fields of history, genealogy, racial and tribal customs and manners (see e.g. *Jarḥ* II 397 f.; Khaṭīb XIV 50–54; *Irshād* VII 261–66; Dhahabī, *Mīzān al-iʿtidāl fī tarājim al-rijāl* III 265 f.). Nadīm credits Haitham with 52 titles that, though fewer than those he credits to Madāʾinī, indicate a wide range of subjects. One covers intermarriage between Arabs and non-Arab clients, and another is titled *Kitāb al-nisāʾ*. Haitham's pupil and transmitter Ḥafṣ ibn ʿUmar produced a like work, a copy of which in the handwriting of Sukkarī (212–75/827–88) was seen by Nadīm (*Fihrist*, pp. 35, 99 f., 110, 306; *Irshād* VII 265 f.). Haitham is frequently cited by Jāḥiẓ and Ibn Qutaibah, as the indexes to their works readily reveal, and also by Ibn Abī Ṭāhir Ṭaifūr, pp. 95, 116, 156, 166 f., 172 (no index in edition here cited), who probably used written sources since he did use the *wijādah* method of transmission as indicated on his pp. 25 and 65.

For Jāḥiẓ' critical estimate of the role of some of these scholars and their contemporaries see e.g. his *Bayān* I 321, 342, II 146, 150, 242, and III 297.

Fourth-century authors, particularly Masʿūdī, Abū al-Faraj al-Iṣfahānī, Abū ʿAlī al-Qālī, and Ibn ʿAbd Rabbihi, whose works have been used freely in our study, rely for the most part on this group of earlier scholars and their still earlier sources.

[247] For some of their contributions to the type of literature under consideration see pp. 61 f. and 65 f.

[248] I.e., through the accepted *munāwalah*, *mukātabah*, or *wijādah* method, for which see Vol. II.

[249] Jāḥiẓ, *Bayān* I 134 f.; *ʿUyūn* IV 5; Ibn Abī Ṭāhir Ṭaifūr, pp. 41, 92 f., 105, 107, 108 f., 141 f. For Jāḥiẓ' estimate of the significant role of the Bedouins in the study of language and literature see his *Bayān* I 158 and III 252, 322–24, 347–49. See also pp. 71 and 74 above.

[250] See Vol. I 9–19, 29; see, further, Masʿūdī V 77 f. and *Fihrist*, pp. 89 f.

[251] See e.g. *ʿIqd* IV 45, which indicates that even older illiterate Companions were expected to learn to read the Qurʾān and to write copies of it. ʿUmar I ordered a Bedouin to do the same (Ṣūlī, *Adab al-kuttāb*, p. 30, n. 3).

[252] His speeches and sayings were in wide circulation and were no doubt recorded in Madāʾinī's *Kitāb Khālid ibn Ṣafwān* and in part at least in some two dozen "books" that Madāʾinī devoted specifically to women (see *Fihrist*, pp. 102, 104, 115, 125, and Jāḥiẓ, *Bayān* I 324–26: لكلام خالد كتاب يدور في ايدى الوراقين; see also *GAL* S I 93 and 105). Later still, Julūdī (d. after 330/942) also produced a book on Khālid ibn Ṣafwān (*Fihrist*, p. 115). For Khālid as a literary critic see p. 141 below.

[253] He had access to Muʿāwiyah's state bureau and library (*dīwān*), where he saw a letter from the king of China to Muʿāwiyah (Jāḥiẓ, *Ḥayawān* VII 113). For some of his transmission see Ibn Saʿd VI 220 f.; Jāḥiẓ, *Ḥayawān* VI 352; Ṭabarī II 200, 314.

lively anecdotes[254] held a certain fascination for all. The subject of women intrigued poet, scholar, and layman alike. Under the Marwānid branch of the Umayyads, the rulers and courtiers indulged in such quick turnover of wives and concubines that Walīd I is said to have married and divorced sixty-three wives during his reign.[255] Sulaimān was so openly preoccupied with his bountiful table and his women that the members of his court and his wealthier subjects, taking their cue from him, "became excessively preoccupied with conversation and exchange of opinion about the marrying of free women and the enjoyment of slave girls."[256] This trend, despite an attempted reversal during the brief reign of ʿUmar II, continued on its widening course in the plural society of the golden age of the early ʿAbbāsid empire (see p. 74) though not without a few marked exceptions, particularly among dedicated scholars.[257] Finally, we need to keep in mind that literate families such as those of ʿUmar I, ʿAmr ibn al-ʿĀṣ, ʿAlī ibn Abī Ṭālib, ʿAbd Allāh ibn ʿAbbās, ʿAbd Allāh ibn al-Zubair, and both branches of the Umayyads each included at least one person, of the blood or a client, who was primarily concerned with the history and deeds of the family. We read, for instance, that Saʿd (or Saʿīd) al-Qasīr, a client of Muʿāwiyah's full brother ʿUtbah ibn Abī Sufyān, transmitted Umayyad family history. Saʿd himself fell at Mecca in the Second Civil War of Islām but his materials were transmitted and the family history continued by other members of the family and put to good use by the family poet, historian, and scholar ʿUtbī (d. 228/842), who transmitted from his scholarly father, ʿUbaid Allāh al-ʿUtbī, among others.[258] ʿUtbī was no narrow or formal political-military historian. His interests included genealogy, anecdotes, poetry, and ethics—*ansāb*, *manāqib*, *ashʿār*, and *akhlāq*—as reflected in the titles credited to him: *Kitāb al-akhlāq*, *Kitāb al-aʿārīb*, and a collection of the poetry of women whose love turned to hate.[259] Both Ibn Saʿd and Abū Ḥātim al-Sijistānī transmitted from him, and the latter reported the use of ʿUtbī's books after his death.[260] Furthermore, inasmuch as poetry continued to be a source of political and social history there were those, poets or not, who collected and transmitted contemporary or nearly contemporary poetry. We read, for instance, that Walīd II collected the records of the Arabs covering their poetry, history, genealogy, and dialects and made use of the manuscript collections of Ḥammād al-Rāwiyah and Jannād. We find, moreover, that not much later a grandson of ʿAbd Allāh ibn ʿAbbās, namely ʿAbd Allāh ibn ʿAlī, who witnessed the fall of the Umayyads, collected the *dīwān*'s of the Marwānids and declared that of Hishām the most accurate and the best for subject and ruler alike.[261] The poetry in such *dīwān*'s, even if incomplete, could

[254] See e.g. Jāḥiẓ, *Bayān* I 158.

[255] Ibn Abī Ṭāhir Ṭaifūr, p. 145. Mughīrah ibn Shuʿbah is said to have contracted 80 marriages in all (ʿ*Uyūn* IV 37).

[256] Ṭabarī II 1272 f.; Thaʿālibī, *Laṭāʾif*, pp. 116 f.: اغلب عليه حب الطعام والنساء فكان الناس في ايماه . . . يستكثرون من الحرص على احاديث النساء ويتسآءلون عن تزويج الحرائر والاستمتاع بالسرارى. See e.g. Masʿūdī V 401 f. for Sulaimān's appetite and table manners as described by Aṣmaʿī to Hārūn al-Rashīd, who was amazed at the scholar's intimate knowledge of the Umayyads.

[257] Such as Yūnus ibn Ḥabīb (*Fihrist*, p. 42; *Bughyah*, p. 426), Kisāʾī (see ʿ*Uyūn* IV 81 but see also *Inbāh* II 266 f.), Kulthūm ibn ʿAmr al-ʿAttābī (*Irshād* VI 214), Jāḥiẓ (Ḥasan al-Sandūbī, *Adab al-Jāḥiẓ* [Cairo, 1931] pp. 203–5), Ṭabarī (*Irshād* VI 434), and Muḥammad ibn al-Qāsim ibn al-Anbārī (Zubaidī, pp. 172 f.; *Inbāh* III 204 f.).

The family trials and tribulations of some dedicated scholars who did marry are reflected in anecdotes about or statements by, for instance, Zuhrī (see our Vol. II 183, esp. n. 114), Khālid ibn Ṣafwān (see pp. 73 f. above), Laith ibn Naḍr, who was involved in the *Kitāb al-ʿain* controversy (see pp. 37 f. above), and Aṣmaʿī (ʿ*Uyūn* IV 125; *Rauḍ al-akhyār*, pp. 185 f.: قال الاصمعى النكاح فرح شهر وترح دهر وكسرظهر والزام مهر). Such matters bring to mind I Cor. 7:32–34, Sūrah 64:14–15, and Francis Bacon's essay "Of Marriage and Single Life."

[258] *Maʿārif*, p. 267; *Fāḍil*, p. 67; *Fihrist*, pp. 90, 121; Khaṭīb III 324–26; Ibn Khallikān I 661 (= trans. III 106 f.); Ibn Abī Ṭāhir Ṭaifūr, p. 127.

[259] E.g. *Fihrist*, pp. 90, 121.

[260] *Amālī* II 81 f.; Ibn Abī Ṭāhir Ṭaifūr, pp. 70, 118, 153, 159, and see *ibid.* pp. 25, 116, and 172 for reports which cite ʿUtbī simply as قال العتبى and which could have been taken from his manuscripts alone since Ibn Abī Ṭāhir Ṭaifūr did use the *wijādah* method of transmission (*ibid.* pp. 25 and 65).

[261] Ṭabarī II 1732 = Ibn al-Athīr, *Al-kāmil fī al-taʾrīkh*, ed. C. T. Thornberg (Lugduni Batavorum, 1851–76) V 196: جمعت دواوين بنى مروان فلم ارى ديوانا اصح ولا اصلح العلمة وللسلطان من ديوان هشام.

The word *dīwān* is here an inclusive term used in reference to both state archives and personal libraries.

hardly have been intrusted to memory alone. That poets of the Umayyad period committed to writing at least some of their own poetry, apart from such few verses as they included in their correspondence or sent as love messages,[262] is indicated by the controversy over whether such compositions should begin with the *basmalah* formula. Shaʿbī was against the use of the formula, but Saʿīd ibn Jubair (d. 95/714) insisted on it and the public as a rule followed his example, though there was a choice in the matter.[263] The judge and poet Muḥārib ibn Dithār, hearing of the death of ʿUmar II and wishing to compose an elegy for the occasion, summoned his secretary to write down his verses. The secretary automatically wrote the *basmalah* formula but was ordered to erase it "for it is not to be used with poetry."[264]

We have learned that prose literature of the type represented by the two sections of our papyrus text, in both content and literary style, was popular in Umayyad times and that some of it was available in writing to a number of second/eighth-century ʿAbbāsid scholars who were known to have committed their own works to writing. On the basis of its script and of the name Yaʿqūb ibn ʿAṭā' in recto 7 we can place our document about the middle of this century. Yaʿqūb may or may not have long survived his aged scholarly father, ʿAṭā' ibn Abī Rabāḥ, who died in 114/732. Nevertheless, the papyrus could as well be from Yaʿqūb's hand as from that of a younger second-century transmitter. The omission of *isnād*'s was common for this type of *akhbār* literature, as *ḥadīth* critics later saw fit to point out. And Jāḥiẓ was probably not alone in appreciating the political and literary accomplishments of the Umayyads and in realizing that the greater part of their secular literature was lost, neglected, or corrupted by the time of such leading ʿAbbāsid scholars as Abū ʿUbaidah, Madā'inī, Hishām ibn Muḥammad ibn al-Sā'ib al-Kalbī, and Haitham ibn ʿAdī.[265] We have here an actual literary specimen from the Umayyad period.

[262] See Ibn Abī Ṭāhir Ṭaifūr, p. 151; *Akhbār al-quḍāt* I 185, 192 f. See also n. 122 on p. 60 above and pp. 115 f. and 170 below.

[263] ʿ*Umdah* II 237 f.; Samʿānī, *Adab al-imlā' wa al-istimlā'*, ed. Max Weisweiler (Leiden, 1952) p. 169; Aḥmad ibn ʿAbd Allāh ibn Ḥajar al-ʿAsqalānī, *Fatḥ al-bārī fī sharḥ al-Bukhārī* I (Cairo, 1319/1901) 5.

[264] Abū Nuʿaim, *Ḥilyat al-awliyā' ṭabaqāt al-aṣfiyā'* V 321. For Muḥārib see Ibn Saʿd VI 214.

[265] Jāḥiẓ, *Bayān* III 297: فلم يدركوا إلا قليلا من كثير وممزوجا من خالص.

DOCUMENT 4

ANECDOTES FROM AṢMAʿĪ

Oriental Institute No. 17639. First half of third/ninth century.

Coarse papyrus, 25 × 16 cm. The piece has several lacunae, almost no vertical margins, and horizontal margins of 2 cm. (Pl. 5). The verso is blank except for a brief undated entry of an unspecified amount of rent still due from Jahm al-Jazzār(?) for the five months from Dhū al-Ḥijjah to Rabīʿ II.

Script.—Nondescript, common, cursive hand, closely written and carelessly executed both as to the letter forms and the placing of some of the diacritical points. The latter are used freely especially in the verses cited. Vowels and the *hamzah* are not used. The circle with a dot indicates the end of a verse of poetry. The script of the notation on the verso is similar but more carefully written.

TEXT

1 بسم الله الرح[ـمـ]ـن ا[لرحيم]
2 قال الاصمعي
3 مررت بقوم فاذا انا بعرابي خفا خيام قام عنها
4 فقلت له يا اعرابي ما اوقفك هاهنا في هذه الناحية
5 قال عشق جارية في هذا الحي قلت وما يمنعك عنها
6 قال الكسل قال فهل قلت في كسلك شياء
7 قال نعم فانشاء يقول سالت الله ياتيني بسلمى اليس الله يفعل
8 ما يشاءُ ⊙ فياخذها فيطرحها بارض زي قدها
9 وينكشف الكساء ⊙ وياخذني فيطرحني عليها ويوقظنا
10 وقد قُضِّيَ القضاء ⊙ وتاتى ديمة فنحن سجاما [فتغ]سلنا
11 وقد ذهب العناء ⊙ يا طيب ما يكون بخفض عيش بلاصيف
12 ولا شتاء ⊙ وقالـــ
13 امرة الحجاج بن يوسف باخراج العراب من واسط قال فاتاه عرابي
14 فقال له اطال الله بقا الامير لِمَ امرت باخراجي من عملك قال لانك
15 لا تقرأ القرآن قال بلا والله اني قد اقرأ قال فاقرأ
16 قال فما تريد ان اقرأ لك قال اقرأ لى اذا جاء نصر الله
17 قال فانشاء الاعرابي يقولـــ

Comments.—The text consists of two anecdotes reported by Aṣmaʿī, in the first of which (lines 2–12) he himself is a participant. The second (lines 12–17) is an incomplete anecdote associated with Ḥajjāj ibn Yūsuf, who, as governor of ʿIrāq, ordered the undesirable classes of the population expelled from his newly founded provincial capital of Wāsiṭ. The common link is the language or behavior of an undesirable person referred to as غرابى (see comment on lines 3–4). The individual so characterized, however, is not the same person in the two anecdotes.

Lines 3–4. The unvoweled word غرابي is clearly pointed in line 3 but unpointed in lines 4 and 13 and also in the plural form الغراب in line 13. The noun *ghurāb* (plural *ghurb*, from which a double plural *ghirāb* is possible) is defined as the sharp edge of something or the sharpness of anything, including sharpness of the tongue and thence meaning sharpness of temper or the like, passionateness, irritability or vehemence of a man or a youth or a horse (see Lane, p. 2241). Furthermore, *ghurb* and the possible plural *ghirāb*, said of a person or of language, means strange or far from being intelligible or difficult to understand or obscure or the state of being a stranger or a foreigner (see Lane, pp. 2240 and 2242). The last meaning could apply to the furtive stranger in the Bedouin camp of lines 3–4 and to the strangers or foreigners of line 13 who were expelled from Wāsiṭ.

Again, assuming that the dot over the *ghain* in line 3 is an accidental speck and reading عرابي and also stretching a point of grammar and lexicography by virtue of analogy, *qiyās* (a device still somewhat fluid in both sciences in young Aṣmaʿī's day), one could associate this assumed reading with رجل عَرَابة, a brisk, lively, or sprightly man, or with عِرَابة, foul or obscene speech or talk (see Lane, pp. 1991 and 1995). All of these meanings, depending on one's idea as to what constitutes sprightliness or vulgarity, could be applied to the men and the language of both parts of the papyrus text because of their partly parallel and closely related anecdotes that are reported in the sources. Amended readings (ا)عرابي and الاعراب are not admissible, especially in line 13, on either paleographic or historical grounds. For all our sources are agreed that Ḥajjāj ibn Yūsuf's edict of expulsion of some people from Wāsiṭ was not aimed primarily at the vulgar boors or clowns among the Bedouins, let alone at all of the Bedouins. An amended reading عزابي in line 3 has a bare paleographic possibility since dots are not always carefully placed with the letters to which they belong, as for example in قد of line 11. Associated with a bachelor or a solitary distant herder (see Lane, p. 2033), the term might apply to the main character in lines 3–4 of our first anecdote but would not apply to line 13 for the same historical reason that is given above against the reading اعرابي.

The desert setting in which we find Aṣmaʿī reporting a personal anecdote is readily explained by his well known frequent visits and some lengthy sojourns with the Bedouins in search of knowledge of classical Arabic and its poetry. Not so well known is his marriage to a Bedouin woman. The *qaum* of line 3 could refer to any Bedouin group he was staying with at the time or to the people of his Bedouin wife (see pp. 104 f.).

Lines 5–6. The familiar theme of an amorous swain seeking his beloved's camp or tent needs no comment. Lazy people disinclined to timely action or physical exertion were to be found in all walks of life, as reflected in several proverbs on this and related themes (see e.g. Bakrī, *Faṣl al-maqāl fī sharḥ kitāb al-amthāl lī Abī ʿUbaid*, p. 276; Ṭāshkuprīzādah, *Kitāb miftāḥ al-saʿādah* I 15–17, 31; *Rauḍ al-akhyār*, pp. 250–53).

Lines 7–12. The lazy lover who claimed these five verses would seem to be a plagiarist if we accept the identification of verses 1, 3, and 4 as those of Walīd II (125–26/743–44) as reported by Ibn ʿAbd Rabbihi (*ʿIqd* IV 454), the only identification provided so far in the available sources. The *ʿIqd* text reads as follows:

لعل اللـــه يجمعني بسلمى   اليس الله يفعل ما يشاء
وياتي بي ويطرحنى عليها   فيوقضني وقد قضى القضاء
ويرسل ديمة من بعد هذا   فتغسلنا وليس بنا عنـــاء

For يجمعني of the first verse, some of the *ʿIqd* manuscripts have ان ياتى, which could be a slight variant if not an error for ياتيني of line 7 of our text, where the remaining variants are self-explanatory. See Gabrieli, p. 34, No. I, for the fully pointed text of Walīd's three verses.

The phrase ويكشف الكساء of our line 9 alternates in comparable situations with كشف الغطاء and هتاك الستر (*ʿIqd* VI 451 f.; Masʿūdī V 433). The prevalence of this type of amatory verse and Walīd's use of it is discussed below (pp. 92 ff.). Note that the last verse of our poem calls for a *kasrah* as its final vowel as against the *ḍammah* of the preceding four verses—a fault technically known as *iqwāʾ* (see *Shiʿr*, pp. 29 f., for several examples).

Lines 12–17. The script of this second anecdote becomes increasingly cursive, with fewer diacritical points and more careless execution of individual letters. The final *rāʾ* and *mīm* of الامير لم in line 14 look more like final *nūn*. Note also the misformed medial *ṣād* of نصر in line 16, citing Sūrah 110:1. For further comment on the background of the text see pp. 83 ff.

ḤAJJĀJ IBN YŪSUF

Historical Background

I

Muʿāwiyah (41–60/661–80) and his governors of ʿIrāq were able, for the most part, to keep that turbulent province under control by a combination of force and painstaking diplomacy. The subsequent inter-dynastic rivalry that ended with the victory of the Marwānid branch of the Umayyads, the ʿAlīd tragedy at Karbalāʾ, and the counter-caliphate of ʿAbd Allāh ibn al-Zubair (61–73/681–92) roused the several dissident groups, particularly those in ʿIrāq, to intensify their open opposition. Even after the failure of the Shīʿite movement of Ibn al-Ḥanafīyah, the revolt of the Khārijite Mukhṭār, and the fall of Abd Allāh ibn al-Zubair, ʿAbd al-Malik (65–86/685–705) realized that he had still to reckon with the Shīʿites and the Khārijites and to contend with the tribal ambitions of the predominantly South Arab settlers of ʿIrāq, whose wholehearted loyalty to his North Arab dynasty entrenched in Syria could not always be taken for granted. It is, therefore, not surprising that, except for Ḥajjāj ibn Yūsuf, ʿAbd al-Malik found no ready and unconditional takers for the governorship of ʿIrāq.[1]

Force rather than diplomacy, in peace and war, characterized Ḥajjāj's long rule (75–95/694–714) of that restless key province and its eastern dependencies. ʿAbd al-Malik, convinced of Ḥajjāj's loyalty and for the most part also of his indispensability, condoned Ḥajjāj's policy of force though he did, on occasion, warn him against or rebuke him for causing excessive bloodshed.[2] Ḥajjāj's first speech when he took office in Kūfah let the Kūfans know in no uncertain terms that he intended to rule with an iron hand and would assuredly cause rebels to shed blood.[3] Open rebellion by the Khārijites, especially that of Shabīb ibn Yazīd al-Shaibānī (d. 77/696 or 78/697) in ʿIrāq proper and the halfhearted support of Ḥajjāj's ʿIrāqī forces sent against Shabīb, soon gave Ḥajjāj occasion to match his threatening words with gory deeds. Thwarted by Shabīb's guerrilla tactics and suspicious of his own ʿIrāqī forces, Ḥajjāj sent urgent appeals to ʿAbd al-Malik for Syrian troops, which were quickly dispatched.[4] The trusted Syrians fought well,

[1] Masʿūdī V 291 f.: قال (عبد الملك) ويلكم من للعراق فصمتوا وقام الحجاج فقال انا لها. Only after having asked the same question twice more with the same results did ʿAbd al-Malik finally appoint Ḥajjāj.

[2] See e.g. Ṭabarī II 1133 f.; Masʿūdī V 308–12, 389; Ṣūlī, *Adab al-kuttāb*, p. 236; Ibn ʿAsākir IV 66–68.

[3] Jāḥiẓ, *Bayān* I 369 f. and II 142; Yaʿqūbī II 326; Masʿūdī V 293 f.; Ṭabarī II 863–65; Mubarrad, pp. 215 f. See ʿ*Iqd* IV 115–24 for Ḥajjāj's speeches. See also Périer, pp. 70–73.

[4] E.g. Ṭabarī II 943 f.; Masʿūdī V 331 f. See also Périer, pp. 134–36.

turned the tide of the war, and eventually put Shabīb's forces to flight, in the course of which Shabīb himself was drowned.[5]

In the meantime, despite advice for leniency, Ḥajjāj had continued to taunt the ʿIrāqīs in general and the Kūfans in particular,[6] thus further aggravating the discontent of the South Arab population and the resentment of the province's military and religious leaders. Discontent and resentment continued to intensify as Ḥajjāj relied more and more on the largely North Arab Syrians, whom he repeatedly characterized as trustworthy, loyal, and of unquestioning obedience,[7] thus adding fuel to the ever smouldering fires of tribal rivalries and animosities. All these factors were, in part at least, responsible for the poor morale of the ʿIrāqī forces and their non-heroic flights before the enemy, particularly in the case of the general ʿAbd al-Raḥmān ibn Muḥammad al-Kindī, better known as Ibn al-Ashʿath, and his largely South Arab troops who fled before Shabīb.[8] Ḥajjāj's mistrust of and accusations against the ʿIrāqīs lasted throughout his rule[9] and in part contributed to the growing animosity between him and Ibn al-Ashʿath,[10] whose rebellion (80–85/699–704) raised the shadow of a counter-caliphate that all but dislodged Ḥajjāj from his powerful position in ʿIrāq.[11] The tide was first turned against Ibn al-Ashʿath in part by the Syrian forces whom the greatly alarmed ʿAbd al-Malik dispatched posthaste[12] and in part by growing dissension in the rebel's camp. Seeking new allies, Ibn al-Ashʿath fled to Khurāsān, where he was finally betrayed in 85/704, and his head was sent to Ḥajjāj in return for tax remission over a period of seven years.[13]

II

It was during the last phase of the rebellion of Ibn al-Ashʿath that Ḥajjāj first gave thought, in 83/702, to a seat of provincial government other than that of Kūfah or Baṣrah. The immediate reason is sometimes given as an incident involving a drunken Syrian soldier who annoyed a Kūfan bride and was killed by her soldier-groom. The latter was nevertheless set free by Ḥajjāj, who expressed disapproval of the Syrian soldier's conduct and furthermore ordered the Syrian troops, then quartered and moving freely among the population, to move to a new encampment on the outskirts of Kaskar.[14] The incident is reported by Ṭabarī without an *isnād* and without identification of the chief characters. Yet, under the circumstances incidents of this type would not be improbable. Be that as it may, separate encampments for the Syrian troops did offer a solution to such problems. But Ḥajjāj had other and more compelling reasons, political and personal, for the founding of Wāsiṭ as a government seat. As governor not only of ʿIrāq proper but of its fast-growing yet turbulent eastern dependencies and since he was even contemplating an invasion of

[5] Ṭabarī II 975 f.; Masʿūdī V 322; Jumaḥī, p. 163; Périer, pp. 131–47. But see Jāḥiẓ, *Bayān* I 285 and 384 and Masʿūdī V 454 for the rebelling South Arab Yazīd ibn al-Muhallab's low opinion of the Syrians as composed of artisans and people of the lower classes.

[6] See e.g. Ṭabarī II 444–46, 954 f., 957. Later he turned a deaf ear to Jāmiʿ al-Muḥārbī's advice on winning the support of the ʿIrāqīs and their troops by milder measures, saying that the sword will bring them to obedience. Jāmiʿ's courageous answer so angered Ḥajjāj that Jāmiʿ felt it necessary to flee to Syria (Jāḥiẓ, *Bayān* II 140 f.; *ʿIqd* II 179 f. and IV 114). See p. 59 above for a comparable situation when Muʿāwiyah readily accepted and acted upon the advice of ʿAmr ibn al-ʿĀṣ.

[7] As with Muʿāwiyah and ʿAmr ibn al-ʿĀṣ (see pp. 51 f.), Ḥajjāj's favorite term for the Syrians was اهل السمع والطاعة, which was also used at times as a battle cry (see Ṭabarī II 959 f.). For the subsequent use of this and other terms by Ḥajjāj in praise of the Syrians, coupled at times with condemnation of the ʿIrāqīs see e.g. Ṭabarī II 1099, 1134.

[8] Ṭabarī II 930–33, 37–39; see also Périer, pp. 129–33.

[9] E.g. Ṭabarī II 1254, 1258; Masʿūdī V 305–7, 328–30, 336.

[10] Ṭabarī II 1042–46.

[11] *Ibid.* II 1054–67, 1072–77, 1085 f., 1094 f., 1098–1101; Masʿūdī V 302–5.

[12] Ṭabarī II 1059 f.: فرسان اهل الشام يسقطون الى الحجاج في كل يوم مائة وخمسون وعشر واقل على البُرد . . . See also Masʿūdī V 304 and 366, according to which the women of the royal harem had to sacrifice some of their treasures in order to meet the payroll of the Syrian troops sent to Ḥajjāj.

[13] Ṭabarī II 1102–4, 1132–36; Masʿūdī V 305–7; Périer, pp. 224–26.

[14] E.g. Ṭabarī II 1125 f., 1236.

the Chinese border,[15] Ḥajjāj saw the political and military advantage of a provincial capital that was more centrally situated than either Kūfah or Baṣrah. His distrust of the ʿIrāqī forces and of many leading non-military personalities who were critical of his policy of force or who supported Ibn al-Ashʿath impelled Ḥajjāj to seek a secure capital to be peopled by his own loyal supporters. Ibn al-Ashʿath fled to Sijistān, pursued by the Syrians and others, including Ḥajjāj's son Muḥammad, sometime during the winter of 83–84/702–3.[16] His flight left Ḥajjāj and ʿIrāq free from active warfare though the end of the rebellion of Ibn al-Ashʿath could by no means have been taken for granted. Ḥajjāj, as I see it, must have begun building Wāsiṭ in this very winter, which would adequately explain why some sources report it as first built in 83/702 and others in 84/703.[17] Wāsiṭ as completed in 86/705 was a twin city on the shores of the Tigris, the two parts linked by a pontoon bridge. On the western shore was the new Wāsiṭ with its government and public buildings and accommodations for the Syrian troops. The older Kaskar, on the eastern shore, was incorporated into the new capital. Its largely Persian population was later augmented mainly by Turks from the Transoxus and by an earlier colony of Bukhārians whom ʿUbaid Allāh ibn Ziyād had settled in Baṣrah.[18] Both the plan and the settlements of the twin city reflected Ḥajjāj's vigilant eye on the eastern dependencies, his aversion to the ʿIrāqīs, and his reliance on Syrian troops who, like him, were committed to the cause of the Umayyads in general[19] and to that of ʿAbd al-Malik and Walīd I in particular.[20]

Social and Literary Backgrounds

Born at Ṭāʾif in 41/661 to a humble family of schoolteachers, a profession then largely in the hands of the *mawālī* and of Christians and Jews, the ambitious young Ḥajjāj ibn Yūsuf left the schoolroom to seek his fortune in public administration in the Ḥijāz itself. Presently he made his way north to the imperial capital of Damascus, where he served under Rauḥ ibn Zinbāʿ, chief of police for ʿAbd al-Malik.[21] Ḥajjāj was among Rauḥ's men in ʿAbd al-Malik's campaign against Muṣʿab ibn al-Zubair and his ʿIrāqī supporters (70–72/689–91) when he first came to the attention of ʿAbd al-Malik as a strong and resourceful military disciplinarian. With Muṣʿab out of the way, ʿAbd al-Malik next gave the eager Ḥajjāj the task of reducing his brother ʿAbd Allāh ibn al-Zubair, counter-caliph in the Ḥijāz.[22] This Ḥajjāj speedily accomplished the next year (73/692), to become himself the governor of Mecca and then of Medina (73–75/692–94) and presently the strong-handed governor (75–95/694–714) of the more strategic and turbulent province of ʿIrāq and its eastern dependencies.[23]

Ḥajjāj's rapid rise to high office and political power was soon followed by an ambitious climb up the social ladder, primarily through marriage alliances (see pp. 72 f.). In the meantime, he sought a reputation as orator, linguist, and finally as patron of learning and culture, for his rivals, enemies, and at times

15 *Futūḥ al-buldān*, p. 290.

16 E.g. Ṭabarī II 1100–1104.

17 Jāḥiẓ, *Bayān* I 113; Ṭabarī II 1125; Masʿūdī, *Kitāb al-tanbīh wa al-ishrāf* (*BGA* VIII [1894]) p. 360; Ibn Khallikān I 155 (= trans. I 360); Yāqūt IV 883 f. See also Maximilian Streck's *Die alte Landschaft Babylonien nach den arabischen Geographen* II (Leiden, 1901) 318–33 and his article "Wāsiṭ" in *EI* IV 1228–32; Périer, pp. 205–13; G. Le Strange, *The Lands of the Eastern Caliphate; Mesopotamia, Persia, and Central Asia, from the Moslem Conquest to the Time of Timur* (Cambridge, England, 1905) pp. 31 f.

18 *Futūḥ at-buldān*, p. 376; Ibn Rustah, p. 187; Yaʿqūbī, *Kitāb al-buldān*, 2d ed. (in *BGA* VII [1892]) p. 322. See also references in preceding note.

19 Ḥajjāj played a significant role, for example, in the campaign against Muṣʿab ibn al-Zubair (70–72/689–91) in ʿIrāq and in the fall of Muṣʿab's brother the counter-caliph ʿAbd Allāh ibn al-Zubair (d. 73/692) in the Ḥijāz.

20 Ḥajjāj was ever ready to support either caliph against any rival or opposition within or without the Umayyad family, particularly in regard to the heirship and succession (see e.g. Ṭabarī II 1164–68, 1173, 1274 f., 1284; see also Périer, pp. 228 f., 335).

21 E.g. Jāḥiẓ, *Bayān* I 113. For details of Ḥajjāj's family background and youth see Périer, pp. 3–7.

22 Périer, pp. 28–35.

23 ʿ*Iqd* II 79–81; Zambaur, pp. 19, 24.

even his patrons[24] taunted him with his humble origin and background.[25] The combination of great power, high social and cultural ambitions, and the nagging reminders, if not his own resentment, of his humble origin played a role in his high-handed treatment and disposal of those who criticized or dared to defy him, as it did also in his choice of the population for his new capital of Wāsiṭ. The incident reported in lines 13–17 of our papyrus is but one of many symptoms of these several socio-cultural causes at work. Ḥajjāj's concern with correct speech, and particularly with the correct reading and transcribing of the Qur'ān, must have dated back to his schoolteaching days. In addition to his sensitivity to errors in the reciting of the Qur'ān, from which not even he was free,[26] the political and religious overtones of persistent variant readings, particularly those of ʿAbd Allāh ibn Masʿūd (d. 32/653),[27] so alarmed him that he took steps to safeguard the correct reading and transcription of the ʿUthmānic edition of the Qur'ān. It was perhaps no accident that the same year (86/705) saw the completion of Wāsiṭ and of Hajjāj's revision of the ʿUthmānic Qur'ān, copies of which he sent to Damascus and the provincial capitals.[28]

According to some sources it would seem that Ḥajjāj excluded from Wāsiṭ from its very beginning all undesirables, commonly described collectively as the *nabāṭ* or as the *nabīṭ* and the *anbāṭ*.[29] Other sources report that he expelled them when he himself first took up residence in his new capital.[30] Still others report that the expulsion took place when the city was completed.[31] Our papyrus text (line 13) indicates expulsion at some unspecified time rather than initial expulsion or exclusion. The stern Ḥajjāj would hardly have allowed an initial order of exclusion to be ignored. There is also the possibility that some so-called undesirables may have been used as construction workers in the building of Wāsiṭ. We do know that he employed Ḥassān al-Nabaṭī to drain and reclaim the marshes.[32] We read further that, having expelled the *nabāṭ* from Wāsiṭ on taking up his residence in that city, Ḥajjāj wrote his kinsman Ḥakam ibn Ayyūb, deputy governor of Baṣrah, to expel immediately all the *nabāṭ* from Baṣrah also, for they corrupt religion and the (whole) world. When Ḥakam reported that he had expelled all the *nabāṭ* except those who read the Qur'ān and were knowledgeable in religion and world affairs, he received an angry reply for not expelling all of them and was all but accused of being part *nabaṭī* himself.[33]

Whether or not the Nabataeans of the Nabataean kingdom of pre-Islāmic times were originally an ethnic group, Aramaic or Arab, need not detain us here.[34] Yet, mention should be made in passing of their

[24] E.g. ʿ*Iqd* V 20–25; see also *ibid.* p. 38, where ʿAbd al-Malik upbraids him for his conduct and taunts him with his background, and pp. 41 f. for Prince Sulaimān's abusive and threatening letter to Ḥajjāj. See Masʿūdī V 364–67 for the upraiding he received from Umm al-Banīn, wife of Walīd I.

[25] E.g. Mubarrad, p. 290; see also Périer, pp. 3–7.

[26] When Yaḥyā ibn Yaʿmar pointed out, at Ḥajjāj's own insistence, an error in the latter's reading of Sūrah 9:24, Ḥajjāj gave him three days to get out of ʿIrāq and exiled him to Khurāsān, where he served as secretary to its governor, Yazīd ibn al-Muhallab (82–85 A.H.); Jumaḥī, p. 13; *Nuzhah*, pp. 11 f. See ʿ*Iqd* V 20 and 36 for other incidents.

[27] E.g. Masʿūdī V 330 f.

[28] *OIP* L 48–49 and our Vol. II 20; see also Périer, pp. 255–57, esp. n. 3 on p. 256.

[29] E.g. Jāḥiẓ, *Bayān* I 270 and III 318: قال المدائنى سمعت ابا الضمرى يقول كان الحجاج احمق بنىَ مدينة واسط في بادية النَبطَ ثم قال لهم لا تدخلوها فلما مات دلفوا اليها من قريب. For the generally poor opinion of the *anbāṭ* see *ibid.* II 106 and III 47.

[30] E.g. *Muḥāḍarāt* I 220: لما نزل الحجاج واسطا نفى النبط عنه.

[31] Yāqūt IV 886: ولما فرغ الحجاج من بناء واسطا امر باخراج كل نبطى بها وقال لا يدخلون مدينتى فانهم مفسدة فلما مات دخلوها عن قريب (see also Périer, p. 209).

[32] Mubarrad, p. 286; Le Strange, *The Lands of the Eastern Caliphate*, p. 42. Ḥassān al-Nabaṭī outlived Ḥajjāj to intrigue later against Khālid al-Qaṣrī (Ṭabarī II 1779 f.).

Ṭabarī II 1122 gives a dramatic account of the expulsion, in 83 A.H., from Baṣrah and other cities, of recently converted non-Arab villagers who were sent back to their villages.

[33] *Muḥāḍarāt* I 220: الا من قرأ منهم القرآن وتفقه للدين والدنيا. For Ḥakam see e.g. Ṭabarī II 872, 972 f., 1061 f., 1182.

[34] See e.g. Masʿūdī, *Kitāb al-tanbīh wa al-ishrāf*, pp. 31, 35, 38, 78, 95, 184; Ernst Honigmann in *EI* IV 1801–8. It should be noted, however, that Dhū al-Rummah in his several satires on Imru' al-Qais and his tribe refers to them as unwarlike agriculturalists and calls them *anbāṭ* (Macartney, p. xiii and Nos. 44:5, 53:31, 78:44) and pigs and apes addicted to pork and wine (*ibid.* Nos. 23:35 and 29:47).

political and literary contributions to the pre-Islāmic Arab world and particularly to their role in the evolution of the Arabic script.[35] Early in the Islāmic period the villagers and agricultural inhabitants of Syria and ʿIraq were referred to somewhat contemptuously as *anbāṭ*, and they continued to be looked down upon whether or not they converted to Islām. Soon the derisive term came to be applied, regardless of race or religion, to all sorts of people who were considered undesirable. These included indigenous populations such as the inhabitants of the marshlands (*baṭāʾiḥ*) of ʿIrāq, peoples of mixed blood, and "the lowest or basest or meanest sort, the refuse of men and the vulgar sort thereof."[36] All of these types Ḥajjāj would have considered unfit to live in his city of Wāsiṭ. It should be noted further that the undesirable person involved in each of the two anecdotes of our papyrus text could readily represent any one of these types, whether the descriptive term used in the papyrus is derived from *gharaba* or *ʿaraba* or *ʿazaba* (comment on lines 3–4).

The question arises, on the one hand, why the papyrus text does not in this particular context use the words commonly found in the sources, namely *nabaṭī* and its plurals, and, on the other hand, why the papyrus term does not appear in the sources, not even where supplemental terms are appended to *nabāṭ* or to *anbāṭ*. One answer could be that our papyrus respesents a text from a still youthful yet recondite Aṣmaʿī (b. *ca.* 123/741), who was fascinated with rare words and expressions in both prose and verse and who achieved the enviable reputation of being the ranking expert at elucidating the several meanings of a word and its derivatives. The papyrus term in all probability had a limited short-term currency before yielding to the readily understood and more widely used *nabaṭī* and its several plurals.

According to our papyrus text, Ḥajjāj considered inability to recite the Qurʾān sufficient reason for expulsion. Whenever such ability was claimed, it had to be put to the test, in this particular case by the recitation of Sūrah 110, which consists of three short verses. As our text breaks at this point, we do not know whether or not the test was passed. We do know, however, of instances well after the beginning of the first century when such claims failed the test either because of incorrect Qurʾānic citation[37] or because of recitation of poetry mistakenly assumed to be Qurʾānic text.[38] Walīd I (86–96/705–15), who was more influenced by Ḥajjāj than was ʿAbd al-Malik,[39] refused to pay petitioners' debts unless they could recite passages from the Qurʾān.[40] Ḥajjāj must have changed his mind about allowing Qurʾān-reading *nabāṭ* to remain in Wāsiṭ since he soon ordered all the *nabāṭ*, including those who read the Qurʾān and were knowledgeable in religion and world affairs, expelled even from the older Baṣrah.[41] The Bedouins (*aʿrāb*), however, were not so categorically disliked and excluded. Aṣmaʿī reports the case of an ill-mannered and vulgar *aʿrābī* who was imprisoned in Wāsiṭ until, after Ḥajjāj's death, he and many other prisoners were set free.[42] Ḥajjāj, like many rulers and scholars, had a keen appreciation of the innate intelligence and ready wit found among the Bedouins, literate or otherwise.[43] Several anecdotes are reported, frequently by Aṣmaʿī, in which Ḥajjāj overlooked insolence or even defiance of his orders by an outspoken

[35] See *OIP* L.

[36] See Lane, pp. 2759 f., and references in n. 34 above.

[37] Jumaḥī, p. 562.

[38] *Fihrist*, p. 91; *ʿIqd* III 479.

[39] E.g. *ʿUyūn* II 49: قال الوليد ألا إن امير المومنين عبد الملك كان يقول الحجاج جلدة ما بين عينيى ألا وإن الحجاج جلدة وجهى كلّه. For Walīd's even stronger appreciation of Ḥajjāj as expressed on the latter's death see n. 85 on p. 90 below.

[40] Walīd made one such supplicant recite 10 verses each from Sūrahs 8 and 9 (Ṭabarī II 1271).

[41] *Muḥāḍarāt* I 220 cites Muḥammad without an *isnād* as follows: روى في الخبر ان النبي صلعم قال اذا تفيهقت الانباط ونطقت بالعربية وتعلمة القرآن فالهرب الهرب منهم فانهم أكلة الربا ومعدن الشر واهل غش وخديعة. This passage is followed by sayings of such leading Companions as ʿUmar I and Ibn ʿAbbās in condemnation of the *nabāṭ*.

[42] *ʿIqd* III 481 and V 46.

[43] *Ibid.* III 424, 444, 477 f. See *ibid.* III 418–98 for the character and behavior of Bedouins and their witty sayings and anecdotes about them (pp. 477–83 citing Aṣmaʿī as often as not) and p. 10 for Abū Tammām's contrast of the intelligence, prudence, or sagacity of the Bedouins with the tyranny, cruelty, and lack of manners of the *ahl al-Jazīrah*.

but quick-witted Bedouin, including cases that involved severe criticism of the rule of Ḥajjāj himself and that of his brother Muḥammad as governor of the Yemen. Ḥajjāj appreciated the sagacity of his illiterate Bedouin cousin whom he appointed, sometime during the reign of Walīd I, as governor of Isfahān, where taxes were in arrears. The taxpayers thought they could outwit this ignorant Bedouin only to find themselves caught in his trap.[44] Furthermore, Ḥajjāj himself married a Bedouin woman versed in Bedouin speech and poetry to round out the talents of his full quota of four wives (see p. 72

There were a few who dared to point out to Ḥajjāj that the site of Wāsiṭ offered no personal advantage to him or his family,[45] and a few others, including Ibn al-Qirrīyah, echoed the opinion.[46] There were also those who considered his policy of excluding the indigenous *nabāṭ* from Wāsiṭ foolish and doomed to ultimate failure, since the city was in their territory (see n. 29 above). Events proved them right, for soon after the death of Ḥajjāj the *nabāṭ* moved into the forbidden city. Thereafter, as Ḥajjāj had feared, the quality of Wāsiṭ's population deteriorated rapidly, so that the city and its people became the butt of the cutting satire of Bashshār ibn Burd and other poets.[47]

However, in the dozen years or so that Ḥajjāj lived and ruled in Wāsiṭ, he strove to give the city an air of artistic and cultural distinction. The bridge of boats joining the two parts of the city, the two congregational mosques, the government buildings, and especially his own palace with its green cupola (*qubbat al-khaḍrā'*), which he proudly displayed, were show places that profited in part from materials stripped from buildings in other cities.[48] He chose his administrative staff, his personal secretaries, and his few close associates as much for their loyalty as for their intelligence and culture. He recommended Muḥammad ibn Yazīd al-Anṣārī to ʿAbd al-Malik as the perfect private secretary, because he was trustworthy, virtuous, wise, even tempered, and a keeper of secrets.[49] Hājjāj was so keenly aware of literary style that he rightly suspected gifted ghost writers to be the drafters of some letters from his officials in Khurāsān.[50] He was greatly annoyed if he was caught in any grammatical error whatever and distressed if he failed to grasp the meaning of a literary or historical allusion, especially when it came in a curt letter from ʿAbd al-Malik.[51] His own conversation and correspondence were generally brief, clear cut, and apt, while his public speeches, threatening or otherwise (see p. 81, n. 3), frequently give the impression of a veritable literary tour de force.

But Ḥajjāj was ever suspicious of groups of scholars, orthodox or otherwise, who exerted politico-religious influence, the *ʿulamā'* and *fuqahā'*, that is, Qur'ānic-readers, judges and jurists, and traditionists. He pointedly humiliated a great number of rebel *fuqahā'* and *mawālī* in these professions by grouping them, despite their learning and culture, among the villagers and the *anbāṭ*[52] and thus no doubt helped to drive

[44] Masʿūdī V 390–93; Périer, pp. 285 f. Aṣmaʿī reports a sequel in which this Bedouin, named Zaid, is approached by a brotherly Bedouin who seeks his favor in verse but in vain (Rabaʿī, pp. 38 f.).

[45] Jāḥiẓ, *Bayān* II 140; ʿ*Iqd* II 179 f. and IV 114 f.:
قال العتبي دخل جامع المحاربي على الحجاج وكان جامع شيخا صالحا لبيبا جريئا على السلطان وهو الذى قال للحجاج إذ بنى مدينة واسط بنيتها على غير بلدك وتورثها غير ولدك فجعل الحجاج يشكو سؤ طاعة اهل العراق.
One word led to another and Jāmiʿ al-Muḥārbī turned against Ḥajjāj and fled to Syria (see n. 6 on p. 82 above).

[46] *Futūḥ al-buldān*, p. 290; Masʿūdī V 341 f.; ʿ*Iqd* VI 223.

[47] See e.g. ʿ*Uyūn* II 47; Ṭabarī III 290; Yāqūt IV 886 f. Yāqūt himself had some kind words for the Wāsiṭ of still later days (Yāqūt IV 886–88). Deterioration of some elements of city population was not limited to Wāsiṭ (see e.g. Mubarrad, pp. 285 f.; Claude Cahen, *Mouvements populaires et autonomisme urbain dans l'Asie musulmane du moyen-âge* [Leiden, 1959]).

[48] Yāqūt IV 882–86; Périer, pp. 205–8 and references there cited; see also Le Strange, *The Lands of the Eastern Caliphate*, p. 39.

[49] Ṭabarī II 1168.

[50] E.g. Ṣūlī, *Adab al-kuttāb*, p. 235; Jumaḥī, p. 13; *Nuzhah*, p. 12.

[51] *Fāḍil*, p. 51; Masʿūdī V 277 f., 344 f., 387 f.

[52] Mubarrad, p. 286: فاحب (الحجاج) ان يزيلهم عن موضع الفصاحة والآداب ويخلطهم باهل القرى والانباط وقال انما الموالى علوج.
Ḥajjāj drew a distinction between Arab and non-Arab *mawālī* and permitted the former but not the latter to lead in prayers (ʿ*Iqd* II 233). Later we find Marwān II preferring the manumitted *mawlā* to the allied one (see Ṭabarī II 1852: مولى عتاقة افضل من مولى تباعة). See our Vol. I 28 f. for the role of learned *mawālī*.

several of them into the arms of such colorful rebels as Shabīb ibn Yazīd al-Shaibānī and especially Ibn al-Ashʿath.[53] But Hajjāj did not hesitate to harass and persecute the most prominent scholars of these groups, *mawālī* or not, if they opposed his views and threatened the success of his policy of iron rule. Some of them, for instance Anas ibn Mālik, ʿAbd Allāh ibn ʿUmar ibn al-Khaṭṭāb, and Ḥasan al-Baṣrī, were rescued from his wrath by ʿAbd al-Malik.[54] Ḥajjāj's vengeful wrath was vented on the *ʿulamā*ʾ who had joined Ibn al-Ashʿath and had the misfortune to be sent as prisoners to Wāsiṭ. Except for the few who managed to escape, such as Ibrāhīm ibn Yazīd al-Nakhaʿī, they were either left to die in prison, as was Ibrāhīm ibn Yazīd al-Taimī, or were summarily executed.[55] Saʿīd ibn Jubair managed to elude Ḥajjāj for many years of hiding but was captured in 94/713 and brought before Ḥajjāj, who upbraided him for his disloyalty and finding him still firm and defiant ordered his immediate execution.[56] But not even repentance and humility had been enough to save the life of his former friend Ibn al-Qirrīyah (see p. 73). The encyclopedic Shaʿbī, on the other hand, who had alerted the haughty Ibn al-Ashʿath to Ḥajjāj's murderous hate and then joined him,[57] escaped execution and even punishment because of the friendly advice of both the secretary and the son of Ḥajjāj himself and by a combination of studied prudence and sustained humility.[58] Soon thereafter Ḥajjāj sent Shaʿbī to the aging and surfeited ʿAbd al-Malik, who wished for a well rounded and entertaining scholar to inform and amuse him with lively conversation and ready citations from the poets.[59] After an initial disciplinary coolness the caliph was more than pleased with the scholar, whom he appointed as tutor to his sons (see p. 136, n. 165) and took for a favorite companion. Shaʿbī amused ʿAbd al-Malik for some two years and comforted him with reassuring verse on his deathbed.[60]

On his arrival as governor of ʿIrāq, Ḥajjāj was not inclined to encourage the poets with prizes until ʿAbd al-Malik ordered him to do so.[61] Yet, the poets as a class were more acceptable to Ḥajjāj than were the *ʿulamā*ʾ as a group. Several factors contributed to this attitude. There was the time-honored role of the poet as the voice of his tribe to broadcast its heroic achievements and defend its honor, and there was also the role of the poet as propagandist or critic for or against Muḥammad and his cause. Several poets of Muḥammad's time outlived him and, along with a few others, continued the role of propagandist despite a Qurʾānic condemnation of poets,[62] which was interpreted for a brief span by the ultra-pious as con-

[53] Ṭabarī II 1076 f., 1085 f., 1100 gives lists of leading Qurʾānic-readers and traditionists who took to the field with Ibn al-Ashʿath at Dair al-Jamājim and Maskan, where their several speeches were aimed at keeping up the soldiers' morale. Several of them fell in battle, and others fled with Ibn al-Ashʿath to Kirmān. In order to prevent further united support of Ibn al-Ashʿath on the part of the *mawālī*, Hajjāj dispersed the latter to their villages of origin and impressed on the hand of each the name of his village (see e.g. *ʿIqd* III 416 f.).

[54] Jāḥiẓ, *Bayān* I 262; Ṭabarī II 854 f. and III 2490 f.; Masʿūdī V 295, 323, 389; *ʿIqd* V 35, 36–39, 53–55; Mawardī, *Adab al-dunyā wa al-dīn*, pp. 42 f. See also Périer, pp. 89–91, and our Vols. I 16 and II 21, 148, 172, 249.

[55] Masʿūdī V 393 f. See also our Vol. II 21.

[56] Ṭabarī II 1261–66 gives details of several versions of Saʿīd's wanderings, capture, and execution and of the subsequent death of Ḥajjāj himself. See also Masʿūdī V 376 f.; *ʿIqd* V 55; our Vol. II 21.

[57] Ṭabarī II 1043. The sentiment was returned by Ibn al-Ashʿath, who considered Ḥajjāj below him socially.

[58] Shaʿbī was among those of Ibn al-Ashʿath's partisans whom Ḥajjāj had promised amnesty if they joined the forces of Qutaibah ibn Muslim in Khurāsān (Ṭabarī II 1111–13; Masʿūdī 334 f.; *ʿIqd* V 32, 54 f.).

[59] *Aghānī* IX 168 f.; *ʿIqd* II 77; *Irshād* I 30; Périer, p. 304.

[60] Abū Ḥātim al-Sijistānī, *Kitāb al-muʿammarīn* (Ignaz Goldziher, *Abhandlungen zur arabischen Philologie* II [Leiden, 1899]) pp. 68–70; *Majālis al-ʿulamā*ʾ, pp. 208 f.; *Aghānī* IX 169–71, XIV 100, and XVI 165; *ʿIqd* II 77 f. See also our Vols. I 17, 44 and II 228. Masʿūdī V 368–71 details another deathbed scene, in which ʿAbd al-Malik surrounded by his family gives his sons his final instructions (*waṣiyah*) including the advice to regard Ḥajjāj well, since it was he who had facilitated this affair (i.e., the succession) for them: اكرموا الحجاج فانه الذى وطاء لكم هذا الامر (cf. n. 39 on p. 85 above).

[61] *Muḥāḍarāt* I 46.

[62] Sūrah 26:224–26. See also Sūrah 36:69: وما علمناه الشعر وماينبغى له ان هو إلا ذكر وقرآن مبين.

demnation of all poets and poetry.[63] Some poets attached themselves to the cause of ʿAlī, others to the cause of Muʿāwiyah. Subsequently, the Shīʿites, the Khārijites, the Zubairids, and the two branches of the Umayyads themselves all needed the poet to flatter and amuse in time of peace and as a mouthpiece and propagandist in time of war. Yet the poet was not, as a rule, a steady retainer or formal appointee. His flattering praise and scathing satire had at least to appear as self-initiated if not spontaneous. Fortunate was the ruler who could attract and hold a first-class poet, and rare was the poet who did not expect a rich reward in recognition of his service and superior talent. He had always to mind his tongue and on occasion to swallow his pride. If out of conviction or in a moment of pique he antagonized his patron, he would seek safety in the desert or take refuge with some new but powerful patron not necessarily of the same religious or political persuasion. If an offending poet on being captured stood his ground, he then risked his life for his convictions. Though fewer poets than *ʿulamāʾ* were prepared to take such a course, a poet in such circumstances was on occasion likely to be summarily executed. On the other hand, a first-class poet who was loyal to his patron and effective against the enemy, spirited yet discreet, though at times reproved for a passing minor offense, was on the whole more likely to be frequently humored and richly rewarded.

It is in the light of such established and accepted practices that one must view Ḥajjāj's relationship with the poets. ʿIrāq was already on the way to leadership in the fields of language and literature. The large Tamīmite population no doubt took pride in the two leading poets of the day, Jarīr[64] from the Najdian Yamāmah and Baṣrah-born Farazdaq, who locked horns in turbulent ʿIrāq. Jarīr was early identified with Baṣrah, where he met frequently with Muḥammad ibn Sīrīn, while Farazdaq preferred Ḥasan al-Baṣrī.[65] The two poets staged poetry tournaments for empire-wide acclaim, each against the other[66] and both of them against most other poets, including for Jarīr a third famed poet, the Taghlibid and Christian Akhṭal, favored poet of ʿAbd al-Malik (see p. 111). In restless and rebellious ʿIrāq we find Jarīr favoring the rebel governor Muṣʿab ibn al-Zubair[67] while Farazdaq leaned at first to the ʿAlīds. Yet, being secular poets and not religious *ʿulamāʾ*, they both readily served the next Umayyad governor, the pleasure-loving Prince Bishr ibn Marwān (71–74/690–93),[68] who was given to stirring up jealous rivalries among the poets, especially those who waited on him.[69] In view of the rapidly changing attitudes of these leading poets, it is understandable that Ḥajjāj on taking office as governor of ʿIrāq in 75/694 did not wish to encourage the poets as a group. But the force of tradition, the poets' persistence in waiting at his door,[70] the order from ʿAbd al-Malik to receive and reward them, and Ḥajjāj's own love of poetry, at which both he and ʿAbd al-Malik took a turn from time to time,[71] all combined to cast him eventually in the role

[63] The literature on this theme is considerable and varied, being related to Sūrah (26:221–26 and 36:69) that Muḥammad was a prophet and not a poet with demonic inspiration. Tradition distinguishes between the truthful and the lying poet, whether he is panegyrist or satirist, and recommends the former but condemns the latter (see e.g. *Concordance* III 135 f. شعر, III 139 f. esp. حين انزل الله في الشعر, VI 181 f. مدح, and VII 68 f. هجاء, اهجوا قريشا, and هجاء المشركين. For discussions of the theme see e.g. Bukhārī IV 146–48; Muslim XV 11–15 with Nawawī's commentary; *Muzhir* II 469–73, which draws heavily on Ibn Fāris and Ibn Rashīq. See also *Sīrah* I 882; Jāḥiẓ, *Bayān* I 281 and III 333–36; *Fāḍil*, pp. 13 f.; Sīrāfī, p. 73; *ʿUmdah* I 9 f. and II 138; *Muḥāḍarāt* I 46 f.; Muṣṭafā Ṣadīq al-Rāfiʿī, *Taʾrīkh adāb al-ʿArab* (Cairo, 1953) II 223–31; Yaḥyā al-Jabbūrī, *Shiʿr al-mukhaḍramīn* (Baghdād, 1383/1964) pp. 40–49. For a survey of treatment of the theme by Western scholars and a fresh approach to the relationship of Muḥammad and the poets see Irfan Shahid, "A contribution to Koranic exegesis," *Arabic and Islamic Studies in Honor of Hamilton A. R. Gibb*, ed. George Makdisi (Cambridge, Mass., 1965) pp. 563–80.

[64] He satirized the North Arab Banū Qais, as did Akhṭal (Jumaḥī, pp. 429, 443 f.).

[65] *Fāḍil*, pp. 110–12; *ʿIqd* V 383; Périer, p. 288.

[66] Their respective merits were current topics of conversation even in the opposing military camps (*Aghānī* VII 55; see also Nicholson, *A Literary History of the Arabs*, p. 239).

[67] Jumaḥī, p. 357.

[68] See Zambaur, pp. 39 and 41, for his governorship of Kūfah, to which the governorship of Baṣrah was added in 73 A.H.

[69] *Fāḍil*, pp. 106–9; Masʿūdī V 253–57; *Aghānī* VII 67 f.; Ibn ʿAsākir VI 69–71.

[70] E.g. *Amālī* II 265 f.

[71] For samples of Ḥajjāj's verse see e.g. Ṭabarī II 1058 and Masʿūdī V 311 f.; for that of ʿAbd al-Malik see Ṭabarī II 1054–57 and Masʿūdī V 309 f., 368 f., 380; for both see Ibn ʿAsākir IV 66–68 and Périer, pp. 287 and 330.

of patron of poets,[72] from a personal and political as from a literary point of view. He is known, for instance, to have written to Qutaibah ibn Muslim, who was reputed to be a transmitter of poetry (*rāwiyat li al-shiʿr*) and whom Ḥajjāj had appointed in 83/702 as governor of Rayy,[73] asking him to name the ranking poets of the *jāhilīyah* and of his own day. Qutaibah named Imruʾ al-Qais and Ṭarafah ibn al-ʿAbd for the pre-Islāmic period and Farazdaq, Jarīr, and Akhṭal as the ranking tribal poet or self-eulogist, satirist, and descriptive poet respectively.[74] And while all these poets humored and praised Ḥajjāj, Jarīr on the whole proved to be Ḥajjāj's most effective and preferred panegyrist[75] even though he had at one time satirized him and composed romantic verses in reference to his wife Hind bint Asmāʾ and had come close to being executed by Ḥajjāj for his offenses.[76] Other poets who had either satirized Ḥajjāj or composed romantic verses to a woman of his family, such as ʿUdail ibn al-Farkh and Muḥammad ibn ʿAbd Allāh ibn Numair respectively, sought refuge in flight.[77] Aʿshā Hamdān, who supported the caliphal ambition of Ibn al-Ashʿath and had satirized Ḥajjāj, had the misfortune to be captured and brought before the latter, who ordered his immediate execution.[78] On the other hand, Aʿshā Banī Rabīʿah offended Ḥajjāj with an elegy on the rebel Mundhir ibn al-Jārūd but later repented and eulogized Ḥajjāj and was forgiven.[79] Still other poets he sent on political missions to and for ʿAbd al-Malik.[80]

Of all the poets, Jarīr became most closely associated in literature as in life with Ḥajjāj as his favorite panegyrist. His verses were so moving in both sentiment and style that they aroused the envy of even ʿAbd al-Malik, which may or may not have induced Ḥajjāj to present Jarīr to that caliph. Just when and by whom Jarīr was presented at the Damascus court is somewhat controversial. Jumaḥī[81] reports Jarīr as accompanying Ḥajjāj on his only visit to Damascus, and Masʿūdī informs us that this visit took place soon after the victory at Dair al-Jamājim (83/702) but does not mention Jarīr among those who accompanied Ḥajjāj.[82] Somewhat later sources, with a family *isnād* tracing back to Jarīr himself, report that Ḥajjāj sent ʿAbd al-Malik a delegation headed by his son Muḥammad accompanied by Jarīr, thus affording the latter a greater opportunity for richer rewards.[83] Inasmuch as Jarīr was with Ḥajjāj in Wāsiṭ, his meeting and service with ʿAbd al-Malik fell within the last two or three years (84–86 A.H.) of that caliph's reign. ʿAbd al-Malik's initial coolness toward Jarīr because of his earlier support of Muṣʿab ibn al-Zubair and his extravagant praise of Ḥajjāj, that undaunted poet's challenging encounters with the Damascus court poets, especially Akhṭal and ʿAdī ibn al-Riqāʿ, and the caliph's final wholehearted approval of the "Baṣran" poet will be considered in connection with Document 5.

Ḥajjāj's more cordial relationships with the poets as contrasted with his harassment of the *ʿulamā*ʾ

[72] Périer, pp. 287–304, covers Ḥajjāj's personal relationship with several poets in more detail than is called for here.

[73] Their first meeting was in 77 A.H. (Ṭabarī II 962 f., 1083, 1119). Jāḥiẓ, *Ḥayawān* I 333, explains how a transmitter's function was comparable with that of a camel as a carrier and why Qutaibah came to be called a *rāwiyah*: الراوية هو الجمل نفسه وهو حامل المزادة فسميّت باسم حامل المزادة ولهذا المعنى سمّوا حامل الشعر والحديث راوية (cf. Lane, روى, p. 1196, col. 2).

[74] *Muzhir* II 481: واما شعراء الوقت فالفزدق افخرهم وجرير اهجاهم والاخطل اوصفهم.

[75] See Périer, pp. 287 f., 295–97, and references there cited.

[76] Jumaḥī, p. 429; Masʿūdī V 351–55; Périer, p. 292. The chronology of these events is not too clear. Most probably Jarīr's offenses dated back to the time of his support of Muṣʿab ibn al-Zubair, and the threatening interview with Ḥajjāj and Hind was probably Jarīr's first meeting with Ḥajjāj as governor of ʿIrāq. The date of the interview is not stated, and the occasion for it is controversial. Jumaḥī, p. 346, and *Aghānī* VII 70 f. point to their first meeting in Baṣrah; others place it in Wāsiṭ, which I am not inclined to accept since it is not likely that Jarīr and Ḥajjāj would have ignored each other for the first several years of Ḥajjāj's governorship (see Périer, p. 288, and also pp. 114–16 below). Furthermore, according to *Aghānī* VII 70 f., Ḥajjāj took Jarīr to task only for entering Wāsiṭ without permission but otherwise received him cordially.

[77] See Périer, pp. 297 f. and 278 respectively, and references there cited; see also Yāqūt I 239 f.

[78] Ṭabarī II 1113–18; Masʿūdī V 355–58; Périer, pp. 196 f.

[79] *Aghānī* XVI 162; Périer, p. 299.

[80] Ṭabarī II 1165–68; *Amālī* II 265 f.

[81] Jumaḥī, p. 357.

[82] Ṭabarī II 1138 f.; Masʿūdī V 348 f.

[83] *Aghānī* VII 66, 181; *ʿIqd* II 82–84; *Amālī* III 43–46; Périer, p. 295.

is reflected in the reactions to his death. We find, to begin with, Yaʿlā ibn Makhlad rebuking the dying Ḥajjāj as he enumerates his political sins[84] while Farazdaq comforted him with verses. Among the scholars who felt a great sense of relief or joy at the news of Ḥajjāj's death were Ḥasan al-Baṣrī, Abū ʿAmr ibn al-ʿAlāʾ, and Prince ʿUmar ibn ʿAbd al-ʿAzīz.[85] Among those who praised and mourned him were Walīd I, the orator-governor Khālid al-Qaṣrī,[86] and Jarīr and Farazdaq, though Farazdaq did so under pressure from Walīd I and in more restrained terms than those in which he eulogized the living Ḥajjāj. And later he satirized the dead Ḥajjāj to please the caliph Sulaimān.[87]

WALĪD II

Prince and Caliph

The brief golden era of the Umayyads was all but over with the death of Walīd I in 96/715. The divisive tribal rivalries and religio-political parties had undermined its political strength. The new conquests during the reigns of ʿAbd al-Malik and Walīd I had brought an influx of foreign elements as *mawālī* of all degrees of culture and especially as slaves of both sexes. They had brought also an increasing flow of general and state income through expanded trade and commerce and imperial taxation. These social and economic influences resulted in an affluent and hedonistic society at court and among the upper classes which overshadowed the warnings of a new generation of religious scholars who lacked both the authority and the courage of their predecessors among the Companions and the Successors, whose ranks were so depleted by death by 96/715 that the year itself became known as the year of the passing of the *ʿulamāʾ* and *fuqahāʾ*.[88] The poets continued to flourish at court though more and more in competition with singers and musicians of both sexes. Yazīd II (101–5/720–24), who had married Ḥajjāj ibn Yūsuf's niece, the mother of Yazīd's son Walīd,[89] reversed the cautious tribal policy of ʿUmar II (99–101/717–19) who, though he had imprisoned the South Arab Yazīd ibn al-Muhallab, drew the line at torture and assassination.[90] Yazīd II now placed the Muhallabids at the mercy of their North Arab enemies, including his Thaqafite relatives by marriage who had previously suffered at the hands of the Muhallabids. In 102/721 he appointed as his heirs his brother Hishām to be succeeded by his son Walīd, then eleven years old—a move that he later regretted, as did Walīd still later.[91] Yazīd II won the unenviable reputation of being the least capable of the Umayyad caliphs and the first of that dynasty to degrade the dignity of the court and of the upper class by openly flaunting a life of wine, women, and song.[92] He died of grief a few days after the death of his favorite songstress, Ḥabābah.[93] Hishām (105–25/724–43), the practical merchant-caliph, slowed down the several forces of disintegration at work in the empire but could not halt, let alone reverse, their course.[94] His own life was circumspect, and the tone of his court was com-

[84] *Amālī* III 175; Ibn Khallikān I 156 f. (= trans. I 362 f.). See Périer, pp. 328–35, and *ʿIqd* V 46 for details of the illness and death of Ḥajjāj and the general reaction to these events. Jāḥiẓ, *Bayān* III 160, gives the reaction of an old woman of Ḥajjāj's household.

[85] *ʿIqd* V 49, 55; *Nuzhah*, p. 17. See Mubarrad, p. 294, and *Aghānī* VII 73, 181, for Prince ʿUmar's adverse opinion of the living Ḥajjāj. For Walīd's reaction to his death see Aṣmaʿī, *Khalq al-insān*, ed. A. Haffner (Leipzig, 1905) p. 174: خرج الوليد وهو مشعان الشعر وهو يقول هلك الحجاج بن يوسف وقرة بن شريك والله لاشفعن لهما الى ربي وهو يتفجع عليهما.

[86] *ʿIqd* V 30 f.

[87] *Ibid.* II 177 f. and V 56 f.; Périer, pp. 333 f.

[88] Ṭabarī II 1266; see *ibid.* III 240 for a listing of these scholars.

[89] See *ibid.* II 1359–1417 for the revolt of the Muhallabids.

[90] *Ibid.* II 1346.

[91] *Ibid.* II 1740; Yaʿqūbī II 376 f., 393; *Aghānī* VI 103.

[92] Jāḥiẓ, *Tāj*, pp. 30–33.

[93] *ʿIqd* VI 61 f.; see also Abbott in *JNES* I 357 f. and references there cited.

[94] See Nabia Abbott, "A New Papyrus and a Review of the Administration of ʿUbaid Allāh b. al-Ḥabḥāb," *Arabic and Islamic Studies in Honor of Hamilton A. R. Gibb*, pp. 27–35.

paratively somber.[95] Walīd, on the other hand, had inherited his father's love of ease and pleasure.[96] The personal incompatibility of uncle and nephew was further aggravated when Hishām sought to set aside Walīd's succession in favor of his own son Maslamah or failing that to have Maslamah appointed as Walīd's heir, but Walīd refused to consider either proposition.[97] Thereafter, the relationship between caliph and heir deteriorated to the point of open animosity, and Walīd's hostility could not be overcome even after the death of Hishām.[98]

Walīd left Damascus to hold princely court at his Blue Palace beside the spring of Aghdāf in the Jordanian desert, where he gathered around him congenial poets, singers, and musicians for whom he was not only a patron but a fellow professional.[99] Hishām, in the meantime, lost no opportunity to discredit Walīd's friends and partisans and to publicize Walīd's excesses.[100] Walīd, in turn, denounced Hishām and satirized him in verses that anticipated and eventually celebrated his uncle's death.[101] Walīd as caliph (125–26/743–44), already a victim of his passions of pleasure and hate and now drunk with both wine and power and further corrupted by the possession of Hishām's immense treasury, lived faster, spent more freely,[102] and directed his vengeance against Hishām's family.[103] Heedless of dynastic and imperial consequences he soon alienated his other Umayyad cousins by appointing his two minor sons, born of concubines, as heirs.[104] He committed an even worse blunder by antagonizing the powerful South Arab Yemenites, the military backbone of the Syrian army, by selling their fallen representative Khālid al-Qaṣrī to his enemies, who tortured him to death and persecuted his family.[105] To make matters still worse, he indulged in outbursts of sacrilegious words and deeds that alarmed the religious groups and thus hastened their co-operation with the Yemenites and his rival cousins. It was his cousin Yazīd, son of Walīd I, who first thought of making a bid for the throne, even against the advice of his brother, ʿAbbās, by calling for Walīd's abdication and then raising a hue and cry against him and demanding his deposition.[106] Again, it was Yazīd rather than the religious leaders who persistently accused Walīd, both before and after his assassination, of heresy and moral delinquency.[107] Even with allowance for some exaggera-

[95] Aṣmaʿī transmits an incident which gives some insight into Hishām's personality (Rabaʿī, p. 27, No. 52).

[96] Mubarrad, p. 386; *Shiʿr*, pp. 427, 485; Ṭabarī II 1741, 1775; Masʿūdī VI 4, 13 f. Francesco Gabrieli gives a detailed account of the life and reign of Walīd II (Gabrieli, pp. 1–33) and appends a collection of 102 fragments of his poetry (*ibid.* pp. 34–64). Khalīl Mardam, *Dīwān al-Walīd ibn Yazīd* (Damascus, 1355/1937), reproduced Gabrieli's collection of these fragments, omitting the first and thus creating a discrepancy of one in the otherwise parallel numbering of the poems. In his introduction Khalīl Mardam gives a lively picture of the life of Walīd but without documentation except general references mostly to Ṭabarī's *Taʾrīkh*, the *Aghānī* of Abū al-Faraj al-Iṣfahānī, and Ibn ʿAsākir's *Taʾrīkh al-kabir.*

[97] Ṭabarī II 1742, 1745; Gabrieli, pp. 4 f. and 46, No. XLIV.

[98] E.g. Ṭabarī II 1751; *Aghānī* VI 103 f. Maslamah sought to soften Hishām's attitude toward Prince Walīd, who therefore spared Maslamah on his accession and eventually mourned his death.

[99] Ṭabarī II 1795; Mubarrad, p. 386; Khalīl Mardam, *Dīwān al-Walīd ibn Yazīd,* Intro. pp. 17–24.

[100] E.g. Ṭabarī II 1744 f.

[101] *Ibid.* II 1751 f.; Masʿūdī VI 5; *Aghānī* VI 106, 1098; Gabrieli, pp. 9 f., 26, and 41, No. XXVIII, 47, No. XLVIII, 49, No. LV, 51, No. LX, 58 f., Nos. LXXXII and LXXXVI, 62, No. XCVI. (Gabrieli's numbers should be decreased by one for Khalīl Mardam's *Dīwān al-Walīd ibn Yazīd.*) Walīd would not allow treasury funds for Hishām's burial (Yaʿqūbī II 394).

[102] Ṭabarī II 1751 f., 1754, 1791 f.

[103] *Ibid.* II 1768, 1776.

[104] *Ibid.* II 1775 f.; Yaʿqūbī II 397.

[105] Ṭabarī II 1778, 1783 f., 1809, 1936 f.; Yaʿqūbī II 396 f., 400; Dīnawarī, pp. 347–49, 365, 397. For Khālid's long governorship of ʿIrāq under Hishām and his subsequent removal and imprisonment see e.g. Ṭabarī II 1812–22. See Jumaḥī, p. 298, for the role of the Yemenites as arch rebels.

[106] Ṭabarī II 1784 f., 1787, 1797; *Aghānī* VI 136 f. See also Ṭabarī II 1785 and 1791 and n. 109 below. ʿAbbās ibn al-Walīd remained loyal to Walīd II, fought on his side, was taken prisoner and persecuted along with his family (Ṭabarī II 1800, 1809, 1826).

[107] Ṭabarī II 1777:
فرماه بنو هاشم وبنو الوليد بالكفر وغشيان امهات اولاد ابيه . . . وبالزندقة وكان اشدهم فيها قولا يزيد بن الوليد وكان الناس الى قوله اميل لانه كان يظهر النسك ويتواضع حتى حمل الناس على الفتك به.

tion on the part of Yazīd and his closest supporters,[108] it is generally agreed, that the defiant Walīd supplied his enemies with plenty of fuel for their fire up to a few days before his murder.[109] Yet, when he realized all was lost, he implied a belated if not last-minute repentance by some of his verses and by taking hold of the Qur'ān in imitation of the about-to-be-murdered ʿUthmān and to make amends for having made the Book a target for his arrows.[110] Following the assassination, which was quick but savage, Yazīd piously, some say hypocritically,[111] took credit for ridding the Muslims of Allāh's enemy (see references in n. 106), and Yemenite poets celebrated their avenging of Khālid al-Qaṣrī.[112] The murder, far from solving any of the major problems of the empire, served only to intensify the interdynastic civil war and afford further opportunities for Yemenite revolts and thus to pave the way for the ʿAbbāsid victory of 132/750, which put an end to Umayyad rule in the Muslim east.

Poet and Lover

We return to Aṣmaʿī's first anecdote of our papyrus text. Erotic poetry cast in a similar vein is readily found in Arabic poetry from pre-Islāmic days to the time of Aṣmaʿī and after, and much of it is less restrained than our text. Satirists and amorous poets were often too blunt and vivid in their statements regardless of whether or not their verses, in reference to others or to themselves, were backed with facts and deeds.[113]

The deterioration of the moral tone of the Umayyad court and of the upper classes becomes apparent when we recall that ʿUmar I exiled Naṣr ibn al-Ḥajjāj ibn ʿIlāṭ for being too attractive to the ladies of Medina (see p. 46), that ʿUmar ibn ʿAbd al-Azīz, as governor of that city, ordered the aged Jarīr publicly punished for his scathing satire,[114] and that Ḥajjāj ibn Yūsuf would not tolerate vulgarity in his new

[108] See *ibid.* II 1799–1801, where the cornered Walīd protests the exaggeration of his sins and misdeeds: قال الوليد فلعمري لقد اكثرت واغرقت وان فيها أحِلّ لى لسعة عما ذكرت . . . اما والله لا يُرتق فتقكم ولا يلم شعثكم ولا تجتمع كلمتكم. See *ibid.* II 1744 and Gabrieli, p. 45, No. XXXIX, for a similar defense of his tutor and intimate companion ʿAbd al-Ṣamad al-Shaibānī.

[109] See Ṭabarī II 1854 and 1844, where Yazīd as caliph refers to the dead Walīd as فان عد و الله لم يكن يرى من شرايع الاسلام شيئا الا اراد تبديله والعمل فيه بغيرما انزل الله وكان ذلك منه شائعا شاملا عريان لم يجعل الله فيه سترا ولا لاحد فيه شكا. See *ibid.* II 1741 and 1775 for brief references to Walīd's unorthodox views and statements. Masʿūdī VII 11 says more specifically ذكر المبرد ان الوليد الحد في شعر له ذكر فيه البنى صلعم وان الوحى لم ياته من ربّه and cites two of Walīd's verses

تلّعب بالخلافة هاشمى   بلا وحى اتاه ولا كتاب
فقل لله يمنعنى طعامى   وقل لله يمنعنى شرابى

on the authority of Mubarrad, but these verses have not been found in the latter's works, and Masʿūdī's translator suggests they have been suppressed for religious reasons. See Gabrieli, p. 35, No. VI, where a third verse has been added on the authority of Sibṭ ibn al-Jauzī.

[110] See Gabrieli, p. 44, No. XXXVII; Masʿūdī VI 10 f.; *Aghānī* VI 125.

[111] See e.g. Tabarī II 1777, 1791, 1874, where Walīd is accused of being a Qādirite. See *ibid.* II 1780 f., 1801, and 1806 f. for details of the murder and disposal of the severed head and body (cf. Yaʿqūbī II 400; *Aghānī* VI 139 f.).

[112] Mubarrad, p. 736:

فان تقتلوا مناكريما فاننا   قتلنا امير المومين بخالد
قتلنا بالفتا القسرى منهم   وليدهم امير المومنينا
ومرونا قتلنا عن يزيد   كذالك قصاونا المعتدينا

The Yazīd of the last verse is Yazīd ibn al-Muhallab. See also Tabarī II 1809, 1817, 1822–24, 1935.

The fall of the Umayyads did not put an end to the deadly rivalry between the North and South Arabs. In two other verses the South Arabs expressed pride in the defeat and death of the ʿAbbāsid caliph Amīn and stated that it was their religious duty to dispose of all offending caliphs.

[113] One need only mention the *dīwān*'s of, for example, Imru' al-Qais, Farazdaq, ʿUmar ibn Abī Rabīʿah, Bashshār ibn Burd, and Abū Nuwās. See e.g. Aḥmad Muḥammad al-Hūfī, *Al-ghazal fī al-ʿaṣr al-jāhilī*, pp. 218–56, for the influence of this type of pre-Islāmic poetry on Islāmic poets. See also Jabbūr's *ʿUmar ibn Abī Rabīʿah*.

[114] *Aghānī* VII 75 f. Masʿūdī V 428–30 relates a dramatic episode in which ʿUmar, having first removed a judge of Medina from office for possessing a singing girl, was nevertheless so affected by her performance that he restored her master to his judgeship. *Aghānī* VIII 6 f. reports a case of successful resistance to the songstress Sallāmah's temptation.

capital of Wāsiṭ. In the second half of the first century the flourishing schools of music in ʿIrāq and the Ḥijāz were well stocked with local and foreign professional singers of comparatively loose morals.[115] The sober-minded scholar ʿUrwah ibn al-Zubair (d. 93/712) no longer felt at home in Medina because of the conduct of its people, nor did his son ʿAbd Allāh[116] and, not much later, Zuhrī.[117] In contrast, we find Farazdaq boasting of his sexual powers in terms that shocked the pleasure-loving Sulaimān into quoting Sūrah 24:2: "The fornicatress and the fornicators, scourge each one of them a hundred stripes . . .." The poet countered with Sūrah 26:226, "the poets . . . they say that which they do not," and departed with a reward.[118] ʿUmar ibn Abī Rabīʿah, who also sought refuge in this Qurʾānic verse, improvised romantic poetry addressed to high-born ladies on their way to a pilgrimage and even during the circuit of the Kaʿbah, which once led an angry Prince Sulaimān to order the poet away to Ṭāʾif for the duration of the Ḥajj ceremonies.[119] Khālid al-Qaṣrī, Hishām's governor of ʿIraq, met with the jurists of Kūfah and during the meeting asked them for a romantic tale but found it necessary to caution them against lewdness and vulgarity.[120] Hishām tolerated the blunt verses of the libertine ʿIrāqī poet ʿAmmār dhī Kināz, whom he rewarded and even protected against the regularly stipulated flogging for drunkenness.[121] There were, of course, men and women in all walks of life who, out of piety and innate decency, shunned objectionable word and deed, in private and in public. Jāḥiẓ recorded and documented the swift decline of the moral standards of the court and the upper classes following the reign of Yazīd II (101–5/720–24),[122] and he is reinforced by the numerous off-color anecdotes that run through the literary sources and involve both the lower and the upper classes.[123] Such deterioration of the moral fiber did not go without some protest and condemnation,[124] which nevertheless made due allowance for the scientific and medical description and study of sex and its problems.[125]

We turn next to Walīd's romantic life and poetry and their bearing on the first anecdote of our papyrus. While yet prince and heir, Walīd had married the ʿUthmānid Suʿdā (vars.: Suʿdah, Suʿād) bint Saʿīd and had later fallen in love with her sister Salmā (vars.: Sulaim, Sulaimah, Sulam).[126] He divorced Suʿdā so that he could marry Salmā, but the proud and indignant father of the two girls would not permit such a marriage. Later, Walīd regretted having divorced Suʿdā and attempted a second courtship, but Suʿdā

115 Jabbūr I 44–71; see also Abbott in *JNES* I 351 f.

116 Abū Ḥayyān al-Tawḥīdī, *Risālah fī al-ṣadāqah wa al-ṣadīq*, pp. 97, 393.

117 See Vol. II 35.

118 ʿ*Uyūn* IV 107; Ibn Khallikān II 264 (= trans. III 620). Jumaḥī, pp. 36–39, compares Jarīr favorably to Farazdaq in such matters; see also Thaʿālibī, *Thimār*, pp. 511 f.

119 *Muwashshaḥ*, p. 203; Jabbūr II 85.

120 *Amālī* III 205: حدثونا بحديث عشق ليس فيه فحش.

121 *Aghānī* XX 174–80.

122 Jāḥiẓ, *Tāj*, pp. 30–33, 151 f.

123 See e.g. Jāḥiẓ, *Bayān* II 371 and III 180 f.; Jāḥiẓ, *Mufākharat al-jawārī wa al-ghilmān*, ed. Charles Pellat (Beirūt, 1957); ʿ*Uyūn* IV 87–113; Jumaḥī, pp. 34–39; ʿ*Iqd* VI 139–63; *Amālī* I 230–36 and III 202 f.; Ibn Abī ʿAwn, *Kitāb al-tashbīhāt*, Chapters 44–45; *Inbāh* III 300; *Rauḍ al-akhyār*, Chapter 30. For numerous instances of such anecdotes see also *Aghānī* and Tanūkhī, *Nishwār al-muḥāḍarah*, ed. D. S. Margoliouth (Oriental Translation Fund of Great Britain and Ireland, "Publications" n.s. XXVII–XXVIII [London, 1921–22]). The list, which could be extended, indicates marked tolerance of this phenomenon.

124 See e.g. ʿ*Uyūn* IV 84–87 and 101, which warns against the lustful eye and begins with a quotation attributed to Jesus, reflecting Matt. 5:27–29, which in turn is reflected in Sūrah 24:30. See also *Inbāh* II 266 f.; ʿUbaid Allāh ibn Muḥammad ibn Abī al-Dunyā, *Dhamm al-malāhī*, ed. James Robson (London, 1938).

125 E.g. Aṣmaʿī, *Khalq al-insān*, pp. 158–60, 222–25; Jāḥiẓ, *Ḥayawān* I 258 f. and II 105; ʿ*Uyūn* I, pp. L, 72, 74. Obscenity in national literature is not limited to that of the Arabs, nor has its presence and the problems it presents escaped the attention and study, on both a national and a comparative basis, of past and present scholars of the East and the West.

126 The variants of the girls' names are used to accommodate the meter of each poem. Concurrent marriage to sisters is forbidden, but adultery with a sister-in-law does not nullify her sister's marriage.

emphatically rejected him.[127] In the meantime Walīd satirized the girls' father[128] and continued to address amorous verses to Salmā, implying in some that she returned his love.[129] There is ample evidence, however, that she shunned his attentions and avoided meeting him, so that once he even disguised himself as an oilseller in order to get to see her.[130] Furthermore, he scandalized all in still other verses that all but deified her.[131] Once he became caliph, Walīd tacitly forced her father's hand and married Salmā, perhaps against her will since she died shortly after.[132] Walīd mourned her deeply in a number of his poems,[133] she having been perhaps his only true love.[134] Fully a third of the 102 of his poems collected by Francesco Gabrieli are either about her or addressed to her, using the several variants of her name. Ḥammād al-Rāwiyah, who recited about a thousand odes to Walīd, noted his marked preference for the lighter and more risqué verses of ʿUmar ibn Abī Rabīʿah and Bashshār ibn Burd.[135] Walīd ordered his musicians to set his verses to music, especially those on Salmā, and took pride in their widespread popularity in the desert and in the cities and himself joined in singing them.[136] The poets among Walīd's intimate companions mentioned Salmā in their verses, some of which were also set to music. Yazīd ibn Ḍabbah's ode of fifty verses started with two of Walīd's own verses in which Salmā was mentioned. The poem so delighted Walīd that he ordered the verses to be counted and rewarded the poet with 1,000 dirhems for each verse, thus setting a record for later caliphs to follow.[137] The story of Walīd and Salmā could hardly have escaped the attention of the popular storytellers of his day and after. It must have formed the central theme of *Kitāb Salmā wa Suʿād* as listed by Nadīm among a dozen such anonymous romantic tales.[138]

[127] See *Aghānī* I 59 f., where Salmā is confused with her sister Suʿdā, and VI 113–15, 117 f., 122, 141; *ʿIqd* IV 452–54 and VI 123; Jabbūr I 78 f. See Paul Schwarz, *Der Dīwān des ʿUmar ibn Abī Rebiʿa* II (Leipzig, 1902) No. 211, for the full ode, which begins with طال ليلى وتعنّاني الطرب and from which the verses that caught Walīd's fancy are cited.

[128] *Aghānī* VI 117 f., 122; Gabrieli, pp. 34 f., No. III.

[129] *Aghānī* VI 122; Gabrieli, p. 43, No. XXXIV.

[130] *Aghānī* VI 114 f.; Gabrieli, p. 40, No. XXIII.

[131] Gabrieli, pp. 35, No. V, and 46, No. XLII.

[132] *Aghānī* VI 116, 132. No cause is given for her death, which is said to have taken place seven or forty days after their marriage; both numbers I suspect to be approximations.

[133] Gabrieli, pp. 42, Nos. XXIX–XXX, and 50, No. LVI.

[134] See *ibid.* pp. 42, No. XXXIII, and 60 f., Nos. XC and XCIV.

[135] *Aghānī* I 21, 50, 59 f. and III 29, 43.

[136] *ʿIqd* IV 453 f.; Gabrieli, p. 46, No. XLII:

شاع شعرى في سلمى واشتهر   ورواه الناس بادٍ وحضر
وتهادته العذارى بينها   وتغنين به حتى اشتهر
قلت قولا في سلمى معجبا   مثل ما قال جميل وعمر

The *ʿIqd* version has الغوانى instead of العذارى in verse 2. The poets referred to in verse 3 are the Bedouin Jamīl ibn Maʿmar al-ʿUdhrī and the city dweller ʿUmar ibn Abī Rabīʿah al-Makhzūmī, who were considered by some to be respectively the most and the least truthful of their contemporaries as to romantic verse (*Muwashshaḥ*, p. 205; see also *Aghānī* I 133 f. and VII 102–4). For some two dozen of Walīd's verses on Salmā and others on wine and the hunt that were set to music see *Aghānī* VI 116–22, 136 f., 139, 141, 143.

[137] See *Aghānī* VI 146 and 147 f. for parts of the ode, which starts with

سلمى تلك في العير   قفى اسالك او سيرى

(cf. Mubarrad, p. 12, and Gabrieli, p. 39, No. XVIII, for variants of expression and echos of meaning).
The tendency to exaggerate the amount of a poet's reward is frequently met with in later reports.

[138] *Fihrist*, p. 307; this list is followed by a list of 27 entries of romances between humans and genii. The tendency to fictionize the lives of the more romantic caliphs still prevails, as seen in Jurjī Zaidan's numerous such tales and more recently in the story of Walīd II by ʿAlī al-Jārim, *Maraḥ al-Walīd* (Cairo, 1948).

We turn finally to the specific content and moral tone of the five verses in the first anecdote of our papyrus text. Of these, verses 1, 3, and 4 are credited to Walīd II by Ibn ʿAbd Rabbihi (see p. 80). The second verse (lines 8–9) could be assigned to either Walīd or the lazy lover of Aṣmaʿī's anecdote, but the fifth verse (lines 11–12) I would assign to the lazy lover. Neither as prince nor as caliph did the energetic Walīd have need to wish for a life of ease in an equable climate, for such a life was in fact at his command, and he made every effort to enjoy it. The fifth verse is much more in keeping with the circumstances and character of the furtive and slothful lover of the papyrus text, who obviously appropriated some of Walīd's widely known and sung verses and later recited them to Aṣmaʿī with some variations. The moral tone of the piece reflects the accepted practices of the time. In its implicit meaning, as in its language, it is more restrained than some products of several of Walīd's and later of Aṣmaʿī's contemporaries who were seemingly oblivious to the numerous Qurʾānic injunctions against vulgarity and obscenity of thought, word, and deed.[139] Anecdotes and poems of a wishful or an actual lover dwelling on a nightlong rendezvous with the beloved are readily found.[140] Walīd himself bragged of his verses to Salmā in the style of Jamīl ibn Maʿmar al-ʿUdhrī and of ʿUmar ibn Abī Rabīʿah al-Makhzūmī (see n. 136 above). The Quraish were exceedingly proud of ʿUmar as their poet and tolerated in him that which they condemned in other poets, asserting that in his objectionable verse he, being a poet, says what he does not do.[141] Yet the Umayyad caliphs and their governors found it necessary on several occasions to threaten and restrain him from addressing his romantic verses to the women of their families, especially those on their way to and from a pilgrimage or those performing the Ḥajj ceremonies.[142] Ḥammād al-Rāwiyah reported that Walīd's favorite poets were ʿAdī ibn Zaid and ʿUmar ibn Abī Rabīʿah, famed for their verses on wine and women respectively, but added that Walīd was not much impressed with even the best product of the poets, including that of the Quraishite ʿUmar ibn Abī Rabīʿah. Most of Walīd's verses to or about Salmā are tender and touching enough to recall the poetry of Jamīl ibn Maʿmar al-ʿUdhrī and some of the poetry of ʿUmar ibn Abī Rabīʿah al-Makhzūmī.[143] But neither the *dīwān* of ʿUmar[144] nor that of Walīd[145] is free from verses that are blunt in their expression or in their intended meaning, some of which are akin to those of our papyrus text. When questioned about or reprimanded for such poetry ʿUmar and his friends, especially the Quraish, relegated the offending verses to fiction and, like Farazdaq, claimed Sūrah 26:226 as their defense (see p. 93). But, when old and repentant, ʿUmar himself is said to have acknowledged the verses as being autobiographical.[146] If the wine-loving Walīd was more blunt at times than the usually sober ʿUmar,[147] the reason may well have been Walīd's addiction to wine, women,

[139] See e.g. Sūrahs 2:164, 268, and 271, 6:151, 7:27 and 32, 16:90, 24:219–21. The Qurʾān stipulates only half the regular punishment for slaves of both sexes (Sūrah 4:25), which may account in part for the greater laxity of that class. Furthermore, the Qurʾān promises Allāh's merciful forgiveness of the repentant sinner and libertine (Sūrahs 3:135 and 24:19–21), barring the deathbed repentance of a lifelong transgressor (Sūrah 4:18). See also Qurʾānic concordances under e.g. زنى, فاحشة, and فسق and *Concordance* IV 79–81 فحش. For the misuse of Qurʾānic and *ḥadīth* citations in the time of Hārūn al-Rashīd and Aṣmaʿī see e.g. ʿ*Iqd* VI 404 and *Rauḍ al-akhyār*, pp. 184 f.

[140] See e.g. Jāḥiẓ, *Maḥāsin*, pp. 352 f.; ʿ*Iqd* VI 52; *Aghānī* III 64 and 170, VIII 6 f., *Muwashshaḥ*, pp. 161, 170; Khālidīyān, *Al-mukhtār min shiʿr Bashshār* (ʿAlīkarah, 1353/1934) p. 295.

[141] *Aghānī* I 52 f. and VIII 101; *Muwashshaḥ*, pp. 202, 205; Jabbūr II 142.

[142] Jabbūr II 96–104, 127–36. ʿUmar was so much in his element during the pilgrimage season, when high-born and attractive women from all the provinces came to his home province of the Ḥijāz, that he wished pilgrimages would take place every two months instead of once a year.

[143] Jabbūr II 179 f.

[144] See Schwarz, *Der Dīwān des ʿUmar ibn Abī Rebiʿa* II, No. 6, lines 12–23; Jabbūr II 181–88, esp. p. 186.

[145] See Gabrieli, pp. 35, No. IV, 41, No. XXV, 52 f., No. LXVI, 63, No. XCIX; ʿ*Iqd* VI 52.

[146] Mubarrad, pp. 570–72; *Aghānī* I 67 and 89, II 146; Jabbūr II 119–21, 174, 181–88.

[147] Jabbūr II 16–26.

and song,[148] the combination of which he himself declared leads to immoral conduct.[149] Walīd's observation was confirmed by the more sober of his older contemporaries, even when wine was not explicitly specified, as illustrated by the request of the leading Quraish and Anṣār of Medina to their newly arrived governor ʿUthmān ibn Ḥayyān (93–96/711–15) to give first priority to the forbidding of singing and fornication. The governor's readily given promise to act on the request favorably within three days was foiled by the wiles of still another Quraishite of that city, Ibn Abī ʿAtīq, patron of the famed songstress Sallāmah and intimate companion of ʿUmar ibn Abī Rabīʿah. Ibn Abī ʿAtīq contrived a meeting between the governor and the songstress, who confessed her past sins, declared her repentance, and chanted verses from the Qurʾān. Touched by her performance, ʿUthmān yielded to Ibn Abī ʿAtīq's suggestion that he should hear her as a professional singer. So charmed was the governor with her dulcet voice that he permitted her to continue to sing and then felt obliged to permit the other songstresses to continue.[150]

The fact that Walīd II was interested in the manuscript collections of Ḥammād al-Rāwiyah and Jannād suggests that he probably committed most if not all of his own poetry to writing. Though we have no evidence that he did so regularly and systematically, we do know that he included some of his poetry in his correspondence with Hishām, with the Medinans on his accession, and with Naṣr ibn Sayyār.[151] The inclusion in letters of citations from the poets or of one's own verses dated back to the time of Muḥammad[152] and the Companions, as illustrated by the correspondence of ʿUmar I and his ʿIrāqī governor, of ʿAlī and Muʿāwiyah, and of ʿAbd al-Malik and Ḥajjāj ibn Yūsuf. This practice was not limited to rulers and their officials but was fast becoming widespread among the lettered upper classes. Still another growing practice was the exchange of original verses between the sexes, such as the verses written by an absent husband seeking to rouse his wife's jealousy but receiving in answer seven verses which so roused his jealousy that he hastened back home,[153] or the verses of a needy and outraged wife upbraiding her absent husband for failing to provide bread for her while he himself lived in luxury and grew fat at Ḥajjāj ibn Yūsuf's court.[154] Men seeking reconciliation with an estranged songstress, concubine, or wife did so in written verse.[155] Others sought to win back even a divorced wife with written verses, as did Farazdaq,[156] Walīd himself (vainly), and still later even Aṣmaʿī,[157] who, though a ranking critic

[148] Gabrieli, pp. 40, No. XXII, 52 f., No. LXVI, 61, No. XCII.

[149] *Aghānī* VI 134 f.; Khalīl Mardam, *Dīwān al-Walīd ibn Yazīd*, Intro. p. 18. Walīd was a great if not perhaps a compulsive drinker. He drank "seventy cups" of wine the night he heard of Hishām's death, an event which put him into a retrospective and resentful mood for the wasted years of his life during Hishām's long reign (Ṭabarī II 1811 f.). See Gabrieli, pp. 46, No. XLIII, 47, Nos. XLV–XLVI, 51, No. LX, 59, No. LXXXVI, 62, No. XCV, for Walīd's love of wine and his views on drinking.

[150] *ʿIqd* VI 49 f. *ʿIqd* VI 1–82 is devoted to statements and anecdotes that illustrate the differing attitudes of individuals, social classes, religious groups, and geographic regions toward music and song. Sallāmah's sweet voice and blunt speech fell short of the conquest of an admirer who resisted her temptation by citing the Qurʾān to her (*Majālis Thaʿlab* I 6 f.; *Aghānī* VIII 6 f.). See n. 114 on p. 92 above for the effect of a singing girl on ʿUmar ibn ʿAbd al-ʿAzīz. Gifted male singers were also considered a threat to morals, especially for women, and Sulaimān, who had his favorite male and female singers, took severe measures against some of the males (*ʿIqd* VI 50, 66–69).

[151] E.g. Ṭabarī II 1742, 1749 f.; *Aghānī* VI 107 f., 111.

[152] *Maṣādir*, pp. 126 f.

[153] Ibn Abī Ṭāhir Ṭaifūr, pp. 119 f.

[154] *Amālī* II 138:

أتهدى لي القرطاس والخبز حاجتى   وانت على باب الامير بطين
اذ غبت لم تذكر صديقا ولم تقم   فـانت على ما في يدك ضنين
فانت ككلب السوء جوّع اهله   فيُهزل اهل البيت وهو سمين

[155] *Akhbār al-quḍāt* I 185, 192; see also Lane, p. 243.

[156] *ʿIqd* VI 124.

[157] *ʿUyūn* IV 125 gives four lines of mediocre verse in which the scholar expressed disappointment in his divorced wife's successor, regretted the divorce, but left the reconciliation up to her. See *ʿIqd* VI 120 and 122–26 for several more instances of more or less prominent men who regretted having divorced their wives, some of them expressing their regret in verse.

of poetry, knew that he was no poet.[158] The delivery of written verses by messenger in the time of ʿAbd al-Malik is instanced in a four-verse proposal of marriage by a warrior poet who was turned down because he portrayed himself as a lion while the object of his attentions saw herself as a gazelle seeking her kind.[159] ʿUmar ibn Abī Rabīʿah sent written verses to some of the ladies.[160] Abū ʿAmr ibn al-ʿAlāʾ's large collection of manuscripts[161] contained some contemporary poetry along with that of pre-Islāmic poets. Some of his older contemporaries lent an ear to a youth reading poetry from a *daftar*.[162] Bashshār ibn Burd, whose blindness did not prevent his appointment to a government bureau,[163] had secretaries and several transmitters to whom he dictated official business and his poetry respectively.[164] Twice a week he dictated his poetry to an assembly of women.[165]

A number of poets of the Umayyad period committed at least some of their verses, not necessarily romantic ones, to writing. These include, in more or less chronological order, Yazīd ibn Rabīʿah ibn Mufarragh al-Ḥimyarī (d. 69/689),[166] Jabīr ibn ʿAbd Allāh al-Anṣārī,[167] the Khārijite poets Sumairah ibn al-Jaʿd and Qaṭarī ibn al-Fajāʾt (d. 77/696 or 697),[168] Abū Kaladah,[169] the three leading poets of the period, namely Akhṭal, Jarīr, and Farazdaq.[170] A copy of Abū Ṭālib's ode in praise of Muḥammad which was made in this period later came into the hands of Jumaḥī (see n. 205 below). The schoolteacher-poet Dhū al-Rummah could hold his own with Ḥammād al-Rāwiyah in the poetry and accounts of the battle days of the Arabs.[171] The schoolteacher-poet Kumait ibn Zaid and his companion Ṭirimmāḥ both wrote down materials from Ruʾbah ibn al-ʿAjjāj which they worked into their own verses.[172] Dhū al-Rummah appreciated accurate letter forms, corrected careless execution in the manuscripts of Shuʿbah ibn al-Ḥajjāj ibn Ward al-Azdī and ʿĪsā ibn ʿUmar[173] and Ḥammād al-Rāwiyah, whose plagiarism of pre-

158 For some of the rare samples of Aṣmaʿī's verse see e.g. *Marātib*, p. 83, and ʿ*Iqd* I 175 and VI 58.

Khalīl despaired of Aṣmaʿī's understanding of meters, and both scholars knew their own limitations in composing poetry; see e.g. ʿ*Iqd* V 308: قال الخليل الذى اريده من الشعر لا اجده والذى اجده منه لا اريده . . . وقيل للاصمعى ما منعك من قول الشعر قال نظرى لجيده. Aṣmaʿī sought instruction on meters (ʿ*arūḍ*) from Khalīl, who, losing patience with Aṣmaʿī's lack of comprehension of the subject, asked him to scan the verse

ان لم تستطيع شيئـــا فـــدعـــه وجـــاوزه الى مـــا تستطيع

and Aṣmaʿī, taking the hint, refrained from bringing up the subject again with Khalīl (*Khaṣāʾiṣ* I 361 f.). Ibn al-Muqaffaʿ and Mufaḍḍal ibn Muḥammad al-Ḍabbī also are said to have known better than to compose verses (ʿ*Umdah* I 75).

In contrast to these four scholars, their contemporaries Ḥammād al-Rāwiyah and Khalaf al-Aḥmar were known as expert versifiers who did not hesitate to attribute their own compositions to some of the classical poets or to plagiarize the latter. They were exceptions to the rule that poets were poor critics and critics poor poets (ʿAskarī, *Maṣūn*, pp. 5 f.; *Shiʿr*, pp. 10 f., 496; Marzūqī I 14, 18–20). The credibility of both these Kūfan transmitters, particularly that of Ḥammād, was damaged by the accusations of rivals, questioned by most Baṣran scholars, and has remained controversial despite some staunch defenders, both past and present (see e.g. Jāḥiẓ, *Bayān* I 143; *Aghānī* V 164 f.; *Marātib*, pp. 72 f.; *Irshād* IV 140; *Mufaḍḍalīyāt* II, Intro. pp. 16–21; *Maṣādir*, pp. 368–72 and 438–50).

159 Ibn Abī Ṭāhir Ṭaifūr, p. 151: فلما قرأت الشعر قالت للرسول قل له فدينك انت اسد فاطلب لنفسك لبؤة فاني ظبية احتاج الى غزال. See *Amālī* III 47 for a girl's more caustic verses written in refusal of her cousin's proposal of marriage.

160 Mubarrad I 413; *Aghānī* I 38, 63, 82, 90; Jabbūr II 104, 106, 153, 159. See also Blachère, *Histoire de la littérature arabe des origines à la fin du XVᵉ siècle de J.-C.* I 96–98.

161 See Vol. I 23 and p. 27 above.

162 Jāḥiẓ, *Ḥayawān* I 61.

163 ʿ*Umdah* I 6.

164 *Aghānī* III 32 f., 43, 44 f., 62 f.

165 *Ibid.* III 34, 50, 52, 67; see *Dīwān Bashshār ibn Burd*, ed. Muḥammad al-Ṭāhir ibn ʿĀshūr, I (Cairo, 1369/1950) 30–35 for the poet and the women.

166 *Aghānī* XVII 57–59; *Khizānah* II 216.

167 Masʿūdī V 266.

168 *Ibid.* V 312–17; *Khizānah* II 438 f.

169 *Aghānī* X 114.

170 These three poets and their writing-down of poetry are discussed below in connection with Document 5.

171 *Shiʿr*, p. 368; *Aghānī* V 212–14; *Muwashshah*, pp. 172, 191 f.

172 Ṣūlī, *Adab al-kuttāb*, p. 62; ʿ*Iqd* IV 194; *Muwashshah*, pp. 170–72, 208; ʿ*Umdah* II 194; *Muzhir* II 349 f.

173 *Muwashshah*, pp. 171 f., 177 f., 192.

Islāmic poetry he claimed he could detect.[174] Four poets at the court of Yazīd II brought their written verses to him for appraisal, and Yazīd expressed himself in verse jotted down on the back of each poet's composition.[175] In Walīd's own court there were the poet-musician and author Yūnus al-Kātib, who was also a bureau secretary credited with a *Kitāb al-aghānī*, and Ṭaraiḥ (or Ṭuraiḥ) ibn Ismāʿīl, who referred in his verses to Walīd's written poetry and to his own care in composing his eulogy on Walīd himself.[176] The ode of Yazīd ibn Ḍabbah so pleased Walīd that he ordered its verses counted, which implies a manuscript on hand, before he rewarded the poet lavishly, 1,000 dirhems for each of its fifty verses. Bashshār ibn Burd dictated his materials to scholars who sought him out for the purpose.[177] His poem in praise of Abū ʿAmr ibn al-ʿAlā' was sent to the latter by the hand of Bashshār's pupil Salm al-Khāsir, who as a youth bought poetry manuscripts (*dafātir al-shiʿr*) and as a full-fledged poet wrote elegies on papyrus in anticipation of the death of certain notables, including his benefactress Queen Zubaidah.[178] The poetry book of Salm's contemporary Abū al-Shamaqmaq was written on Kūfan parchment in a wonderful script and bound in fine leather of Ṭā'if.[179] Bashshār's cutting satire and blunt verse drew protests from Ḥasan al-Baṣrī and Malik ibn Dīnār.[180] Mahdī eventually forbade him the recitation of romantic verse,[181] and powerful enemies whom he had satirized finally brought about his downfall on the charge of heresy (*zandaqah*),[182] though an examination of his manuscripts after his death failed to substantiate the charge.[183] Among the younger intellectuals who served the early ʿAbbāsids in ʿIrāq were poets and secretaries who took manuscripts in book form for granted, as witnessed in Sayyid al-Ḥimyarī's collection of *faḍā'il* of ʿAlī, which he put into verse,[184] and in Abān al-Lāḥiqī's translation and versification of *Kalīlah wa Dimnah* and other originally Persian books.

Assuming that Walīd II likewise wrote down his poetry, we can point to several factors, some generally and others specifically related to his life and poetry, that worked against the survival of his output in its entirety. Among these were the confusion and civil war that followed his death and his own reputation for a fast and sacrilegious life, which provided the opportunity and the motive for the destruction or suppression of his offending verses in reference to religion or morality or racial prejudice.[185] Since he had no brothers interested enough to defend him and no adult sons to cherish his memory and since he had alienated his first cousins, the preservation of his poetry depended on the efforts of poets and musicians who had been his intimate companions and had abetted him in his way of life. Most of these, fearing for their own lives of this close association, lay low after Walīd's death. Some of them, however, and most other poets of the Umayyad period emerged later to court favor with the newly established ʿAbbāsids.[186] Under such circumstances, most of Walīd's verses that had been set to music and were already widely and orally popular in his lifetime, whether credited to him or not, had a better chance of survival than his

[174] *Aghānī* V 172; see also p. 173 below.

[175] Ibn ʿAsākir VI 344–36.

[176] *Ibid.* VII 53–55; *Aghānī* IV 114–18 and XVII 167.

[177] *Aghānī* III 44 f.

[178] *Ibid.* XXI 111, 121; Khaṭīb IX 136. See also Abbott, *Two Queens of Baghdad*, pp. 85, 172.

[179] Jāḥiẓ, *Ḥayawān* I 61: هو في جلود كوفية ودفتين طائفتين بخط عجيب.

[180] *Aghānī* III 35, 41.

[181] *Ibid.* III 41, 55, 65, 68.

[182] *Ibid.* III 42, 70–73.

[183] Mubarrad, pp. 546 f. Heresy, open or overt, was so rife at the time that in 163/780 Mahdī took severe measures against the heretics and shredded their manuscripts with knives (cf. e.g. *Dīwān Bashshār ibn Burd* I 16–30; Ṭāha Ḥusain, *Ḥadīth al-arbaʿā'* I [Cairo, 1925] 191–212).

[184] Which he had his four daughters recite (see Vol. II 260).

[185] The numerous odes of the anti-Arab Yazīd ibn Ḍabbah were fragmented and scattered by the Arabs (see *Fuḥūlat al-shuʿarā'*, pp. 500 and 513).

[186] A notable exception was Abū al-ʿAbbās Sā'ib ibn Farrūkh, the blind poet at the court of Marwān II. He was faithful to the Umayyads despite threats and enticements from Manṣūr, who was eventually (in 141 A.H.) touched by his loyalty (*Aghānī* XV 59–62).

more serious and more offensive poems. This factor may in part account for the small number of his surviving poems, as for their predominant themes and the fragmentary nature of most of them. The survival of these poems and of anecdotes associated with them, like much of the information that has come down to us on the Umayyads, must be credited to the efforts of such early genealogist-historians as ʿAbd al-Malik ibn ʿUmair (see p. 76), to anthologists who collected *akhbār* and speeches, such as Khālid al-Qaṣrī, and to collectors of poetry such as Ḥammād al-Rāwiyah and Mufaḍḍal ibn Muḥammad al-Ḍabbī. Their successors, the emerging "encyclopedists" of the second century, included private collectors,[187] family historians, and representatives of the various racial, religious, and political groups. Among these may be mentioned Haitham ibn ʿAdī, who was known as a pupil and transmitter of Ḥammād al-Rāwiyah,[188] Abū ʿUbaid, Abū ʿUbaidah, and Aṣmaʿī. Their numerous works covering a wide variety of subjects were fully exploited by the succeeding generations of scholars and historians.

The source materials for Umayyad history and culture were the manuscript collections of prominent families, such as the poetry and *ḥadīth* collections of Ḥassān ibn Thābit and other Anṣār which were known and sought after.[189] The papers and correspondence of ʿUmar I and ʿAmr ibn al-ʿĀṣ were passed on, in part at least, to their sons and grandsons, as detailed in Volume II of these studies. So also were those of ʿAlī and his family. Ḥusain ibn ʿAlī carried two saddleloads of his correspondence with the Kūfans and other ʿIrāqīs which he displayed as evidence of their promise to help him in his fight for the caliphate.[190] There was also Muʿāwiyah's brother ʿUtbah ibn Abī Sufyān, whose offspring included a succession of family historians and poets. Their materials were passed on by their distinguished member ʿUtbī.[191] Some of the first-century collectors of *akhbār* had access to government archives which often if not always included the correspondence and the literary collections of the caliph, as in the case of the state bureaus (*dīwān*'s) of Muʿāwiyah, ʿAbd al-Malik, Walīd I, and Hishām.[192] Governors who had a literary bent and who were patrons of poets and scholars, such as Bishr ibn Marwān, Ḥajjāj ibn Yūsuf, and Khālid al-Qaṣrī,[193] had literary manuscripts kept either in their state bureaus or in their personal libraries.[194] As we have already seen above, a grandson of ʿAbd Allāh ibn ʿAbbās, namely ʿAbd Allāh ibn ʿAlī, collected the *dīwān*'s of the Marwānids. Even court records occasionally included some poetry, for we read that Muḥammad ibn ʿImrān al-Ṭalḥī, the last Umayyad judge of Medina, ordered his court secretary to write some edifying verses that took his fancy at the bottom of a legal document for the benefit of future readers.[195] We may note in passing that ʿAbd Allāh ibn ʿAbbās, Zuhrī, Ibn Isḥāq, and Shāfiʿī were all preoccupied with poetry and that they all used and produced manuscripts,[196] some of which included poetry.

There was, furthermore, steady supplementation of manuscript sources through oral information

[187] See Jumaḥī, p. 204; see also our Vol. I 4, 22, 29.

[188] *Aghānī* V 164; *Irshād* IV 140. For Haitham ibn ʿAdī see *GAL* I 140 and II 77, 213.

[189] Vol. II 259 f.; Jumaḥī, pp. 125, 396; *Maṣādir*, pp. 125–28, 157 f., 205.

[190] Ṭabarī II 298 f.: . . . فاخرج خرجين مملوين صحفا فنشرها بين ايديهم.

[191] See p. 77 and Baihaqī, p. 12.

[192] See Vols. I 10, 18, 23 and II 181 f. and p. 13 above.

[193] Khālid's family was well rooted in the art of poetry and written composition (see e.g. *Aghānī* XIX 54: اعراقهم في الشعر). Khālid and his father were both private secretaries, and Khālid as governor commissioned Zuhrī to compose a genealogical work and a biography of Muḥammad; only the first of these projects was begun, and it was not finished (*ibid.* XIX 57, 59).

[194] See Vol. I 17.

[195] *Akhbār al-quḍāt* I 185. The judge was confirmed in his office by the ʿAbbāsids. In Manṣūr's reign we find him ordering his secretary to write down some amusing verses that Aṣmaʿī was reciting, and he added that the nobles were zealous for witticisms (*ibid.* I 187: ويحك الاشراف همتهم الملاحة). Judges and jurists, like caliphs, occasionally indulged in composing verses of their own (e.g. ʿ*Umdah* I 12–19).

[196] See e.g. Vols. I, Document 6, and II 54–56, 98, 100; *Aghānī* IV 49; Yūsuf ibn ʿAbd Allāh ibn ʿAbd al-Barr, *Jāmiʿ bayān al-ʿilm wa faḍlihi* I 77: قلت للزهري اخرج التى كتبك فاخرج الى كتب فيها شعر; Samʿānī, *Adab al-imlāʾ wa al-istimlāʾ*, p. 70.

received from knowledgeable city dwellers and Bedouins, much of which was first committed to writing by enterprising second-century scholars. Foremost among those who drew heavily on the memory, knowledge, and experience of the Bedouins were Abū ʿAmr ibn al-ʿAlāʾ and his devoted pupil and loyal transmitter Aṣmaʿī, to whom we owe a Bedouin's version of Walīd's three verses that appear in our papyrus text.

There is some evidence of early traffic in poetry manuscripts among poets and scholars. The demand was met through copies made, for a fee, from oral dictation or from other manuscripts or even through purchase of a poem itself. An ode written by a Bāhilī in praise of Marwān II was sold after the caliph's death for 300 dirhems to Marwān ibn Abī Ḥafṣah, who, by making changes in the first two verses, turned it into a eulogy of Maʿn ibn Zāʾidah (d. 152/769).[197] That a considerable market existed for manuscripts of poetry and music (*dafātir al-shiʿr wa al-ghināʾ*) is indicated by the fact that the sale of such manuscripts became a point of controversy between Mālik ibn Anas and his pupils. Mālik, whose linguistic and literary interests were less pronounced than those of either Abū Ḥanīfah or Shāfiʿī, disapproved of the sale of such manuscripts even more emphatically than he disapproved of the sale of religious knowledge.[198]

First-century Muslim scholars struggled with specific criteria for evolving a system of literary criticism though they were concerned at first primarily with pre-Islāmic poetry and poets, including poets who lived into Islāmic times. First-century poets appraised their fellow poets. The approach of both poet and scholar was more or less subjective and in some respects traditional, being somewhat reminiscent of the pre-Islāmic poetry contests staged at Sūq ʿUkkāẓ. However, some first-century poets' appreciative critiques of some verses of their fellow poets contain as much substance as the authoritative judgment of Nābighah al-Dhubyānī at Sūq ʿUkkāẓ.[199] Of the scholars, it was Abū ʿAmr ibn al-ʿAlāʾ who first approached the problem of standards of criticism on the more inclusive basis of both the quantity and the quality of a poet's total product, rather than quick and changing judgments based on a verse or two or even an entire poem. Some of his views have survived mainly in Aṣmaʿī's *Fuḥūlat al-shuʿarāʾ*, where he is frequently cited and approved by the author, who was his admiring and faithful pupil. Torrey, editor and translator of the *Fuḥūlat*, has shown effectively that Aṣmaʿī himself fell short of evolving an organized system of literary criticism.[200] Yet Aṣmaʿī does put emphasis on a poet's need to know the poetry, history, and genealogy of the Arabs[201] and on the less tangible qualities of originality, literary style, and a measure of natural poetic talent, as also on the quantity of a poet's output. Aṣmaʿī's contemporary Abū ʿUbaidah also emphasized quantity.[202] But even the standard of quantity is fluid, as it ranges from five or six to twenty or more odes for qualifying among the first-rank poets, the *fuḥūl*,[203] a title reserved almost exclusively in Aṣmaʿī's day for the pre-Islāmic poets, including those who lived into Islāmic times.[204]

[197] *Aghānī* IX 42; *Muwashshaḥ*, pp. 252 f.

[198] Saḥnūn ibn Saʿīd al-Tanūkhī, *Al-mudawwanah al-kubrā* (Cairo, 1324/1906) III 396 f. The controversy extended at the same time to the loaning of books, including poetry manuscripts, for a fee (*Muḥāḍarāt* I 71–73). It should be noted that the activities of the bookseller (*warrāq*) were as extensive in the fields of language and literature as in those of Qurʾānic commentary and *ḥadīth* (see our Vols. I 22 and 24 f. and II, esp. pp. 16, 46–49, 228 f.; see also pp. 13 f. and 35 above and 149 below).

[199] See e.g. *Shiʿr*, pp. 78, 197 f.; *Aghānī* I 51 f., VIII 194 f., and IX 163; *Muwashshaḥ*, pp. 39 f., 47, 60, 205; ʿAskarī, *Maṣūn*, pp. 3 f.; ʿ*Iqd* V 397. Some of these poets developed a more tangible critical ability, which is dealt with in detail below (see pp. 122–43 and 187–92).

[200] See *Fuḥūlat al-shuʿarāʾ*, pp. 488 f.

[201] ʿ*Umdah* I 132 f.

[202] See *Shiʿr*, p. 141.

[203] See *Fuḥūlat al-shuʿarāʾ*, pp. 495, 497, 498; *Muwashshaḥ*, pp. 80 f.; ʿ*Umdah* I 132 f.

[204] For Islāmic poets Aṣmaʿī expresses his opinion negatively by stating that a given poet, for example Dhū al-Rummah, does not rank among the *fuḥūl*, or, influenced by his earlier training, he resorts to terms used in *ḥadīth* criticism such as حجة (see pp. 103 and 192, n. 186), or he refrains from giving a clear-cut opinion (see *Fuḥūlat al-shuʿarāʾ*, pp. 495–98; *Marātib*, p. 73; ʿ*Umdah* I 138).

However, the more systematic and inclusive *Ṭabaqāt fuḥūl al-shuʿarāʾ* of Aṣmaʿī's younger contemporary Jumaḥī (d. 231/845) gives about equal attention to the pre-Islāmic and the Islāmic poets.[205]

We have no specific reference to Walīd's total output of poetry, and the quantity which has survived would not qualify him for high rank among the Islāmic poets. As for the quality of his poetry, his intimate companions and court poets declared, on occasion, that as a poet he surpassed them, though allowance should be made for flattery and the hope of sizable rewards. In the early years of the "Blessed Dynasty" few poets or scholars would risk their own fortunes by bringing up the subject of the Umayyads, let alone mentioning Walīd II, who was considered a heretic, unless to denounce him. The first unfavorable reference to Walīd was made by Bashshār ibn Burd in a pro-ʿAlīd poem with racial overtones. The poem was originally intended as a satire on Manṣūr but was altered, after the failure of the ʿAlīd cause, to a satire on Abū Muslim al-Khurāsānī, who had played a major role in the establishment of the ʿAbbāsid dynasty. The poet reminds the new rulers of the fates of such crowned tyrants as Khusrau II, Marwān II, and Walīd II, points out that they are following the same course, and suggests the course they should follow.[206] Other derogatory references to Walīd originated with some of the early ʿAbbāsids themselves. The first such reference was made by Jaʿfar ibn Sulaimān, governor of Medina (146–50/763–67), to the poet Rummāḥ ibn Yazīd ibn Maiyādah, a favorite of Walīd, whom he had rewarded richly and who had eulogized Walīd in glowing terms at the time of his death.[207] Jaʿfar took the poet to task for praising him in less glowing terms than he had used for Walīd the libertine (*fāsiq*). The poet retorted that he did not say Walīd was a libertine and, besides, the measure of praise is in proportion to the liberality of the praised—an answer that pleased the governor as to the poet's loyalty and induced him to match Walīd's liberality.[208] When the question of Walīd's heresy was later raised at Mahdī's court, the judge and jurist Ibn ʿUlāthah refuted it on the theory that Allāh would not have permitted him to be caliph had he in truth been a heretic—an argument that put Allāh's mark of approval on the ʿAbbāsids as well.[209] The first forthright defense of Walīd as a ruler and appreciation of him as a poet came at the request of Hārūn al-Rashīd from the pro-Marwānid poet Marwān ibn Abī Ḥafṣah[210] after Hārūn had assured him that nothing he said would be held against him. The poet then described Walīd as one of the most elegant and vigorous of men and also as one of the best poets and one of the most liberal of men.[211] Hārūn al-Rashīd next asked Marwān to cite some of Walīd's verses, and the poet recited Walīd's verse on the dead Hishām, which Hārūn ordered a secretary to write down.[212] Hārūn is further reported as having cursed Walīd's assassins.[213] Poets of the ʿAbbāsid period appropriated many of Walīd's verses on romance and especially on wine. Abū Nuwās was considered the ablest adapter of Walīd's poetry, in its style as in its basic

205 See Jumaḥī, pp. 21 f., 42, and Intro. pp. 15, 34–36. The assumed permanent superiority of the "ancients" over the "moderns" was successfully challenged thereafter as literary criticism developed further and new poets asserted their claim to superiority. This is readily seen in Ibn Qutaibah's introduction to his *Al-shiʿr wa al-shuʿarāʾ* and in Ibn al-Muʿtazz's *Kitāb al-badīʿ* as forerunners in this phase of literary criticism.

206 *Aghānī* III 28 f.; ʿAskarī, *Maṣūn*, pp. 162 f.

207 *Shiʿr*, p. 485; *Aghānī* II 92, 106–9.

208 Ibn al-Muʿtazz, *Ṭabaqāt*, pp. 106 f. This source reports Jaʿfar as governor of Baṣrah, which is an error (see Zambaur, pp. 24, 40). Jaʿfar's second governorship of Medina (161–66/777–82) was later than this episode since Rummāḥ ibn Yazīd ibn Maiyādah died early in the reign of Manṣūr (*Aghānī* II 120).

209 See *Aghānī* VI 140 f., where two different accounts are given for Ibn ʿUlāthah; see also e.g. Ṭabarī III 462 and *Akhbār al-quḍāt* III 251 f.

210 See e.g. *Shiʿr*, pp. 481 f.; Ibn al-Muʿtazz, *Ṭabaqāt*, pp. 42–54; *Muʿjam al-shuʿarāʾ*, pp. 396 f.; *Muwashshaḥ*, pp. 251–54; Khaṭīb XIII 142–45.

211 *Aghānī* VI 109 and IX 41: كان من اجمل الناس واشدهم واشعرهم واجودهم.

212 See preceding note and Gabrieli, p. 35, No. V.

213 *Aghānī* VI 140.

meaning.[214] The sources on hand yield no second-century critical estimate of Walīd as a poet, perhaps because of neglect by the Yemenite Abū ʿAmr ibn al-ʿAlāʾ and the politic Aṣmaʿī, neither of whom would have been particularly interested in the fallen anti-Yemenite Walīd of disrepute. They did, however, express opinions on several Islāmic poets, including a goodly number of Walīd's contemporaries, such as ʿUmar ibn Abī Rabīʿah, ʿAdī ibn al-Riqāʿ, and Dhū al-Rummah. Jumaḥī, Ibn Qutaibah, and Mubarrad likewise seem to have refrained from expressing critical opinions of Walīd, as far as their extant works indicate. He does not seem to have fared any better at the hands of the early anthologists, for only Buḥturī cites him, and once only.[215] It was not until after the ʿAbbāsids themselves had lost both political power and literary luster following the assassination of Mutawakkil in 247/861[216] that historians and literary scholars, predominantly non-Arabs, searched seriously into the life, reign, and poetry of Walīd II. Ṭabarī, Masʿūdī, Abū al-Faraj al-Iṣfahānī, Ibn ʿAbd Rabbihi, and possibly Aḥmad ibn Ibrāhīm ibn al-Jazzār[217] have, among them, preserved practically all that is extant of Walīd's poetry. Later authors who do pick up Walīd's history and story have little except a few fragments of his verse[218] to add to the picture given by these third- and fourth-century authors. Lesser known or still unpublished works of third/ninth-century scholars are more promising as sources of additional fragments, though I have so far discovered but one such fragment, namely two verses cited by Muḥammad ibn al-ʿAbbās al-Yazīdī (d. 310/922),[219] who drew on oral and written sources that trace back to Ḥammād al-Rāwiyah, Ḥammād ʿAjrad, Haitham ibn ʿAdī, ʿUtbī and his father, Madāʾinī, Abū ʿUbaidah, Jāḥiẓ, and other second-century collectors and authors to whom sufficient attention has already been drawn above. Because the collection of Walīd's poetry was at first neglected it is remarkable that we have as much of it as we do. Though his personal reputation and his corrupt rule, followed by the fall of the Umayyads, contributed to the early neglect of his poetry, his royal birth and colorful yet tragic life helped to keep alive a certain amount of interest in the man and his poetry.[220] Nevertheless, the serious study and appraisal of his surviving poetry had to await modern times and scholarship.

Carl Brockelmann listed Walīd II among Umayyad poets of second rank.[221] Some quarter of a century later Ṭāha Ḥusain[222] touched briefly on the tragic life of Walīd and the literary quality of his poetry. Francesco Gabrieli collected and edited his poetry, related much of it to the events of his life, and ventured an opinion as to its literary quality.[223] Gabrieli was followed by Khalīl Mardam, who saw fit, as already pointed out (p. 91, n. 96), to omit the first poem of Gabrieli's edition, on which he otherwise relied

[214] *Ibid.* VI 109 f.: له في الخمر وصفتها اشعار كثيرة قد اخذها الشعراء وادخلوها في اشعارهم سلخوا معانيها وابو نواس خاصة فانه سلخ معانيه كلها وجعلها في شعره فكررها في عدة منه. See Ḍiyāʾ al-Dīn Naṣr Allāh ibn Muḥammad ibn al-Athīr, *Al-mathal al-sāʾir fī adab al-kātib wa al-shāʿir* (Cairo, 1282/1865) p. 469, on the three degrees of poetry theft ranging from outright theft of a poem lifted from a book (*naskh*) to rewording a verse but retaining some of its basic sense (*salkh*) to scoffing at or vilifying a verse or poem (*maskh*). There is also allusion to the sense of a verse, either to expand on it or to reverse its meaning.

[215] See Buḥturī *Al-ḥamāsah*, ed. L. Cheikho (Beirūt, 1910) p. 160, No. 854, which consists of only two lines.

[216] See Nabia Abbott, "Arabic papyri of the reign of Ǧaʿfar al-Mutawakkil ʿala-llāh (A.H. 232–47/A.D. 847–61)," *ZDMG* XCII (1938) 88–135.

[217] I.e., as the suggested author of *Al-ʿuyūn wa al-ḥadāʾiq fī akhbār al-ḥaqāʾiq*, third part edited by M. J. de Goeje and P. de Jong, *Fragmenta historicorum Arabicorum* I (Lugduni Batavorum, 1869).

[218] See Gabrieli, pp. 35, Nos. IV–V, and 42, No. XXXII.

[219] Yazīdī, p. 117:

الاليت انى منكم حيث كنتم　　مكان سهيل من جميع الكواكب
راهن اصحابا وهن يريـــنـــه　　ويسرء اذا يسرين غير مصاحب

[220] It is to be noted that Walīd is not included in a list of five leading Quraishite poets of the Umayyad period (*Aghānī* III 101). It is conceivable, however, that Aḥmad ibn Muḥammad al-Murthadī (d. 286/899) may have included him in his *Shuʿarāʾ Quraish* (see *GAL* S I 219 and *Irshād* II 57 f.).

[221] *GAL* I 60 and S I 96.

[222] *Ḥadīth al-arbaʿāʾ* I 174–79.

[223] See Gabrieli, esp. pp. 25–33.

heavily both for the texts of the poems and for his introduction.[224] Ṭāha Ḥusain, Gabrieli, and Khalīl Mardam are agreed that Walīd favored lighter themes and the shorter meters that usually go with them—such as the *wāfir* meter of our papyrus text—over weightier topics and the longer and more difficult meters that they call for. Again, all three are rightly agreed that his verses lack a measure of artistic refinement and that final touch of literary polish expected of first-rank poets. Being blessed with natural poetic talent, he was content to use it, usually in extemporaneous verse when he was under the influence of wine or under emotional stress. That is, Walīd lacked the professional poet's incentive to achieve high literary polish as he competed with his peers for professional recognition and financial rewards. Nevertheless, Walīd's poetry is appreciated for its easy flow, its spontaneity, and its forthrightness. Incomplete as the extant collection is, it still yields enough firsthand information to provide an insight into his character and motivation. Though some of his verses are shocking enough to tempt one to suppress them even in our permissive twentieth century, more of his poems arouse sympathy for this high-spirited poet and caliph who fell victim to the fatal combination of his own strong-headedness and unfortunate family and political circumstances.

DATING OF THE DOCUMENT

Several questions arise to which the sources on hand give no definite answer. When did Aṣmaʿī encounter the Bedouin lover? Did he then recognize the verses of our text as Walīd II's poem with some variation? My considered guess is that the encounter with the Bedouin occurred early in Aṣmaʿī's literary career, and it seems possible that he did not at that time associate the verses with Walīd II.

Aṣmaʿī's first subjects of serious study were the Qur'ān and *ḥadīth*. His interest in the Qur'ān was probably stimulated by family tradition since his grandfather was employed by Ḥajjāj ibn Yūsuf to record and recite the corrections ordered by Ḥajjāj to be made in the ʿUthmānic edition of the Qur'ān.[225] Aṣmaʿī transmitted some information (*akhbār*) on Umayyad times and personalities, including several of the early Marwānids and also Ḥajjāj, on the authority of his father on that of his grandfather,[226] but he used the family *isnād* rarely in contrast to his extensive use of other sources of information for his numerous interests. From the study of the Qur'ān to that of Tradition and law was the usual path for young aspirants to scholarship in the religious sciences. Most of the leading traditionists who were still active until about the mid-second century of Islām are listed among the young Aṣmaʿī's teachers. They included Ḥammād ibn Salamah ibn Dīnār, Misʿar ibn Kidām, and Shuʿbah ibn al-Ḥajjāj ibn Ward al-Azdī,[227] all of whom committed their *ḥadīth* collections to writing.[228] Such traditionists grounded him in their method of parallel oral and written transmission, and it was to their terminology that he resorted in expressing critical opinions on Islāmic poets (see p. 100, n. 204). Just when Aṣmaʿī decided that his professional career lay not in the religious sciences is hard to say. His decision to specialize in the secular field of language and literature was undoubtedly influenced by Abū ʿAmr ibn al-ʿAlā', the leading Qur'ānic-

[224] See Khalīl Mardam, *Dīwān al-Walīd ibn Yazīd*, esp. pp. 22–26.

[225] *Marātib*, p. 65; Sīrāfī, p. 69. For the nature of the changes ordered by Ḥajjāj see p. 84 above. Little is known of Aṣmaʿī's family besides the names of his grandfather and father, a paternal uncle, and a maternal uncle who seems to have been remembered only for his parsimony, a characteristic associated with Aṣmaʿī himself. Stranger still is the lack of information on any literary activity of his brother ʿAlī and his own son Saʿīd. What we know of his nephew ʿAbd al-Raḥmān ibn ʿAlī (d. 231/846) as the only member of the family who transmitted Aṣmaʿī's books does not indicate a close personal relationship between the two.

[226] See e.g. *Majālis Thaʿlab* II 615 f. and Ibn ʿAsākir IV 62, 82.

[227] See e.g. Sīrāfī, p. 60 and Khaṭīb X 410.

[228] See *Inbāh* II 197 f.; see also our Vol. II 45, 50, 52–54, 67–69, and pages listed in index under their separate names. See, further, Rabaʿī, Intro. pp. 2 f., citing Ibn ʿAsākir on the authority of Mubarrad, for Aṣmaʿī's own reference to the numerous scholars, jurists, traditionists, and long list of poets and eloquent men from whom he learned, memorized, and transmitted and to whom collectively he gave the credit for his own accurate knowledge, which in turn brought a delegation of Khurāsānian scholars seeking him as the ranking Baṣran scholar.

reader of his day and the foremost authority on language and literature. It is also possible that Aṣmaʿī's serious interest in poetry may have been first aroused by Shuʿbah ibn al-Ḥajjāj, who was interested mainly in poetry before he specialized in *ḥadīth*,[229] much as Zuhrī and Shāfiʿī just before and after him were interested in poetry before they decided to specialize in *ḥadīth* and *fiqh*. Furthermore, it was probably the aging Abū ʿAmr ibn al-ʿAlāʾ who first directed the younger scholar to seek out the knowledgeable among the Bedouins, on whom he himself had relied so heavily for his knowledge of correct Arabic and pre-Islāmic poetry. Be that as it may, we do know that Aṣmaʿī soon formed a lifelong habit of periodic visits to the desert. In his earlier days he lived and moved freely enough among the Bedouins to marry one of their women and to be rejected by another.[230] His insatiable curiosity covered every phase of Bedouin life, private and public. His informants, both men and women, came from every level of Bedouin society.[231] His reputation among them was so well known and widespread that a Bedouin woman who met him as a stranger could guess his identity from his lively conversation or from a display of his memory, which was matched at least once by a Bedouin woman.[232] Bedouins who could not supply the information he sought would readily direct him to those among them who could.[233] Prying into all sorts of Bedouin experiences, he was apt to ask, as in line 6 of our papyrus text: "Have you said anything (of poetry) about that?" And the Bedouin being questioned would be just as apt to recite verses that he considered his own.[234] The character of the anecdotes he reported about Bedouin men and women and about his personal experiences among them ranged from innocuous[235] to highly edifying[236] to extremely shocking,[237] and the papyrus episode comes close to this last. It should be added here that in moral tone Aṣmaʿī was no better and no worse than many of his contemporaries of high or low degree.

It is at the time of the youthful Aṣmaʿī's intensive contacts with the Bedouins that I would place his encounter with the Bedouin lover of our papyrus text. This was not too far removed from the time of Walīd II, whose verses on Salmā, whether credited to him or not, would still have been popular in the desert, where dynastic change and political power lay not so heavy as they did on the city dwellers. It was also the time when Aṣmaʿī was collecting and storing up information and experiences in his extraordinary memory, which apparently was both auditory and photographic[238] but which he nevertheless aided by much writing while he was still among the Bedouins.[239] Back among the city dwellers, he would sort,

[229] Khaṭīb X 411.

[230] Sarrāj, *Kitāb maṣāriʿ al-ʿushshāq* (Istanbul, 1301/1883) pp. 375 and 404.

[231] See *Marātib*, p. 40 (cited also in *Muzhir* II 401 f.), for a list of knowledgeable and literate Bedouins who contributed much to Abū Zaid al-Anṣārī, Abū ʿUbaidah, and Aṣmaʿī; see *Fihrist*, pp. 43–50, for entries on these and other Bedouins, several of whom are well known authors.

[232] *Amālī* I 265 f.

[233] *Muzhir* II 307.

[234] Inquiry about original verses was addressed to city dwellers as well. See e.g. *Aghānī* XIV 62; *Irshād* VII 303: هل قلت في ذلك شيئا.

[235] E.g. *ʿUyūn* IV 5; *Marātib*, pp. 52 f.; Khaṭīb VI 179; Ibn Abī Ṭāhir Ṭaifūr, pp. 105, 107, 108, 162; Ibshīhī II 152, 213 f.

[236] E.g. *Amālī* I 225 f. and 265 f., III 29; *ʿIqd* IV 151 f.; Sarrāj, *Kitāb maṣāriʿ al-ʿushshāq*, p. 404.

[237] E.g. Jāḥiẓ, *Maḥāsin*, pp. 202 f., 352 f.; *Muwashshah*, pp. 12, 77 f.; *ʿUyūn* IV 26; Khaṭīb VI 281; Ibn Abī Ṭāhir Ṭaifūr, p. 117; Ibshīhī II 214; *Rauḍ al-akhyār*, pp. 194, 242. The Qurʾān is severe on the Bedouins, as on the hypocrites (*munāfiqūn*), but does not categorically condemn all Bedouins as ignorant or as godless and mercenary (Sūrah 9:90, 97 f., 99–102).

[238] His claim to phenomenal feats of memory such as memorizing 10,000 to 16,000 *arjūzah* was at one time politely questioned, and on one occasion it was, at his suggestion, put to the test, which, we are told, fully proved his claim (*Marātib*, pp. 51, 57; Zubaidī, pp. 185, 188; Khaṭīb X 415 f.; *ʿIqd* V 306; *Inbāh* I 90 f. and II 198; Ibn Khallikān I 362 [= trans. II 124]; *Bughyah*, p. 313). See our Vol. II 52 f. for memory testing of religious scholars.

Among the first- and second-century scholars who were known for their remarkable memories may be included Ibn ʿAbbās (e.g. *Khizānah* II 421–24), Shaʿbī (Aḥmad Farīd Rifāʿī, *ʿAṣr al-Maʾmūn* I 315), Abū ʿAmr ibn al-ʿAlāʾ, Shāfiʿī, and the poets Ḥammād al-Rāwiyah, Abū Nuwās (*Inbāh* I 350), and Abū Tammām. Yet all these men, proud as they were of their memories, used manuscripts and acquired sizable libraries, and most of them composed books of their own. The early ʿIrāqī scholars in the fields of language and literature became known as *aṣḥāb al-kutub* (*Marātib*, p. 98; *Fihrist*, p. 47).

[239] Sīrāfī, pp. 66 f.; *Muzhir* II 307–9.

augment, and classify his materials that were in time to take the form of monographs on a surprisingly wide range of subjects.[240] Meanwhile his Bedouin anecdotes, artfully presented in conversation, attracted attention and enhanced his reputation for serious scholarship and an entertaining personality.[241] Reports of his fame soon reached Mahdī and Hārūn al-Rashīd. The latter summoned Aṣmaʿi to the court, marveled at his extensive knowledge of Arabic and poetry[242] and his store of information on the Umayyads,[243] and greatly enjoyed his company and stories, especially those relating to the Bedouins. To keep up his stock of entertaining material with which to amuse Hārūn and others, Aṣmaʿī would make occasional trips to the desert on the city's outskirts in search of Bedouin anecdotes, some of which no doubt quickly gained oral currency before they were included in his *Nawādir al-aʿrāb*.[244] It is regrettable that his serious students who became his editor-transmitters overdid the editing of at least some of his books and that others drew freely on his materials but failed to safeguard the identity of his works as separate units. One famous pupil, Abū ʿUbaid (d. 223/838), who served as a private tutor and became a prolific author patronized by the Ṭāhirid family of generals and governors, organized Aṣmaʿī's works into chapters and supplemented them with materials from Abū Zaid al-Anṣārī and from Kūfan sources, using only manuscripts for the most part.[245] Still another gifted pupil, Abū Naṣr Aḥmad ibn Ḥātim al-Bāhilī (d. 231/846), was preferred by Aṣmaʿī above all others,[246] and is said to have transmitted all of Aṣmaʿī's works. He expanded Aṣmaʿī's *Nawādir* (not to be confused with his *Nawādir al-aʿrāb*) by something like a third, which Aṣmaʿī himself deleted before he permitted others to copy Abū Naṣr's manuscript.[247] A third pupil, ʿAlī ibn al-Mughīrah al-Athram (d. 232/847), who became a professional transmitter and bookseller,[248] was in demand for his accurate manuscripts and was credited with transmitting all of Aṣmaʿī's works as well as those of Abū ʿUbaidah. Aṣmaʿī's nephew ʿAbd al-Raḥmān ibn ʿAlī, a less congenial pupil, is said to have possessed some of his uncle's original manuscripts, from which he transmitted presumably after Aṣmaʿī's death.[249] Many other pupils transmitted Aṣmaʿī's materials less exhaustively.[250] Aṣmaʿī's works that have survived as units give evidence of variation and supplementation by their transmitters.

240 E.g. *Fihrist*, p. 55; *Inbāh* II 202 f. Aṣmaʿī considered five steps essential to genuine scholarship: quietness, attentive listening, retention, composition, and publication (*ʿIqd* II 215). He acquired a sizable library, borrowed manuscripts, composed and dictated his works, and permitted pupils to copy and transmit them (see *Fuḥūlat al-shuʿarāʾ*, p. 500; Jāḥiẓ, *Bayān* II 97; Jumaḥī, p. 204; Karl Vilhelm Zetterstéen, "Aus dem Tahḏīb al-luġa al-Azharī's," *Le monde oriental* XIV [1920] 14 f.; *Muzhir* I 160).

241 Abū Nuwās, among others, compared Aṣmaʿī to a nightingale because he charmed his listeners into giving him the victory in conversation or debate with his better informed but less amusing competitors (Sīrāfī, pp. 61 f.; Khaṭīb X 414, 417; *Inbāh* II 201; Ibn Khallikān I 362 [= trans. II 124]; *Bughyah*, pp. 395, 400). For a less flattering comment on Aṣmaʿī's materials, style, and delivery see *Nuzhah*, p. 68, and Ibn Khallikān I 390 (= trans. III 390), which expands the passage, the gist of which is that Aṣmaʿī's style made the worst appear good while Abū ʿUbaidah expressed himself badly but furnished much useful knowledge.

242 *Marātib*, pp. 54 f., 56 f.; Zubaidī, p. 186; Khaṭīb X 417; Ibn Fāris, *Ṣāḥibī*, p. 44; *Nuzhah*, p. 69.

243 Masʿūdī V 401 f.; Ibn Khallikān I 364; see our Vol. II 47 and 54 and p. 99 above for sources on the Umayyads that were available in Aṣmaʿī's lifetime. Aṣmaʿī's knowledge of the life and times of Ḥajjāj ibn Yūsuf and Khālid al-Qaṣrī is amply illustrated by Ibn ʿAsākir's entries on both governors. The accounts cover their interest in and encounters with Bedouins as reported repeatedly by Aṣmaʿī (see e.g. Ibn ʿAsākir IV 52, 62, 72, 82 and V 70, 74–77, 78). Furthermore, Aṣmaʿī's interest in history was such that he has been credited, rightly or not, with a *Taʾrīkh al-mulūk al-ʿArab wa al-ʿAjam* (see our Vol. II 90, n. 33, and p. 13 above).

244 Khaṭīb X 412 f.; *Inbāh* II 200 f. See Abbott, *Two Queens of Baghdad*, pp. 147–49, 171, 174, 180, 187, for Aṣmaʿī as Hārūn's courtier-companion. Not much later, Saʿīd ibn Salm al-Bāhilī was to relate a truly amusing story of a Bedouin who would not have anything to do with a Bāhilī, not for love of life or money (Khaṭīb IX 74).

245 *Marātib*, p. 93:

ذكر اهل البصرة ان اكثر ما يحكيه عن علمائهم غير سماع انما هو من الكتب . . . فاخذ كتب الاصمعى فبوب ما فيها واضاف اليه شيئا من علم ابي زيد وروايات عن الكوفيين.

246 *Marātib*, pp. 82 f.; Zubaidī, p. 198; Khaṭīb IV 114; *Irshād* I 406; *Inbāh* I 36 f.; *Muzhir* II 408.

247 See Zetterstéen in *Le monde oriental* XIV 14 f.

248 *Fihrist*, p. 56; Khaṭīb XII 107 f.; *Irshād* V 421 f. and VII 304.

249 *Marātib*, pp. 49, 82 f.; Sīrāfī, pp. 62 f.; *Fihrist*, p. 56; *Muzhir* II 408.

250 See e.g. Zubaidī, p. 104; *Bughyah*, p. 400.

Though his *Nawādir al-aʿrāb* has not survived as a unit in any contemporary or subsequent transmission, its contents are nevertheless repeatedly met with in practically every work on Arabic language and literature, along with Bedouin anecdotes attributed to one or another of Aṣmaʿī's contemporaries,[251] none of whom is credited specifically with a *nawādir al-aʿrāb*, though several of them collected and published *nawādir* of a number of different categories.

The first anecdote of our papyrus text clearly belongs with the *nawādir al-aʿrāb*, and the second anecdote is associated with the first by virtue of the boorishness of the chief character in each of them. The papyrus fragment is probably a student's notation made from Aṣmaʿī's dictation or copied from his manuscripts. Again, it could be a notation made from the dictation of any one of the above-mentioned chief transmitters of Aṣmaʿī's works or from manuscripts of others of Aṣmaʿī's many pupils. I am inclined to believe that it was made by indirect transmission through a pupil, rather than by direct transmission from Aṣmaʿī himself, on the basis of the script, which resembles available specimens of the early third century more than it does those from the second century of Islām.

The fact that our papyrus comes from Egypt presents, as I see it, no problems. For even in Aṣmaʿī's lifetime his fame and at least some of his works had reached Khurāsān in the east and Spain in the west. Visitors from Khurāsān sought him out,[252] and shortly after his death Abū Naṣr Aḥmad ibn Ḥātim traveled to Iṣfahān carrying with him his copies of Aṣmaʿī's works, including the collections of the poetry of pre-Islāmic and Islāmic poets.[253] Before leaving on a pilgrimage, Abū Naṣr intrusted his manuscripts to a friend who made them available for copying during Abū Naṣr's absence. On his return, Abū Naṣr's anger for the loss of his expected gain from the transmission of Aṣmaʿī's works was appeased by the gift of a large sum of money from the citizens and their leader.[254] Though Khurāsān of the second and third centuries surpassed Egypt in linguistic studies, Egypt and the west were not too far behind. The nature and extent of Egypt's progress has been detailed above (pp. 33–40), particularly her role from about the mid-second century onward as a half-way center for North African and Spanish scholars seeking knowledge in the eastern provinces, first in the Ḥijāz and then in ʿIrāq. Thus, at least some of the works of such prominent scholars as the Kūfan Kisāʾī and the Baṣran Aṣmaʿī were introduced into Egypt and the west during their authors' lifetime[255] and continued to be sought after, like Sībawaih's *Kitāb*, by succeeding generations of traveling scholars and to be studied, taught, and circulated by native Egyptians and by new settlers in Egypt.

Considering the combined factors of Walīd II's reputation, the popularity of his verses and of Bedouin anecdotes, Aṣmaʿī's career and his numerous transmitters, and, finally, the script of our papyrus, it seems safe enough to conclude that the text dates probably from about the mid-second century but that the papyrus itself is more probably from the early third century of Islām. The third century was richly productive in practically every phase of history, literature, and other cultural fields—a period when Jāḥiẓ, Ibn Qutaibah, Mubarrad, Yaʿqūbī, Ṭabarī, and Masʿūdī were studying the lives and co-ordinating and expounding upon the works of their predecessors. The many second-century and the more numerous third-century sources were freely used by Abū al-Faraj al-Iṣfahānī and Abū ʿAlī al-Qālī, who spiced their

[251] For example, Kisāʾī likewise spent much time among the Bedouins and wrote down all sorts of linguistic information that was incorporated in his series of three *nawādir* works, which may have included incidental Bedouin anecdotes (see *Fihrist*, pp. 65 f.; Khaṭīb XI 404; *Inbāh* II 258, 273 f.). Haitham ibn ʿAdī related some of his experiences among the Bedouins at the request of Mahdī, who was already intrigued with the variety of the Bedouin tales; see *Inbāh* III 365–67: قال لى المهدى يا هيثم ان الناس يخبرون عن الاعراب شحاً ولؤما وكرما وسماحا وقد اختلفوا في ذلك فما عندك.

[252] Rabaʿī, Intro. pp. 2 f., and n. 228 on p. 103 above.

[253] *Irshād* I 406: نقل معه مصنفات الاصمعى واشعار شعراء الجاهليه والاسلام مقروة على الاصمعى.

[254] *Ibid.* I 406 f. Abū Naṣr returned to Baghdād in 220/835.

[255] Khaṭīb XIV 222 f.

works with numerous Bedouin anecdotes, as the *Aghānī* of the former and the *Amālī* of the latter so readily attest. By their time any political reason for ignoring Umayyad cultural achievements had long been dissipated and all but forgotten. It is not suprising that the *Aghānī* has yielded more of Walīd's surviving poetry than any other single source. Nor is it surprising that the encyclopedic Spanish scholar Ibn ʿAbd Rabbihi (246–328/860–940), who lived in the golden age of the Umayyads of Spain, alone identified three of the five verses that we find in our papyrus poem as those of Walīd II (see pp. 80 and 95). His failure to identify the transmitter was in keeping with his stated policy of omitting the *isnād*'s of well known and well attested materials in the interest of brevity.[256] It has remained for our papyrus fragment to identify Aṣmaʿī as a transmitter of this particular poem of Walīd's, which, through the accident that its end rhyme is the first letter of the alphabet, comes first in Gabrieli's collection of what has survived of Walīd's poetry. The papyrus fragment likewise gives us Aṣmaʿī's illustration of Ḥajjāj ibn Yūsuf's well known policy of excluding the boorish and the vulgar from his new capital of Wāsiṭ.

[256] ʿ*Iqd* I 3 f.: وحذفت الاسانيد من اكثر الاخبار للاستخفاف والايجاز وهربا من التثقيل والتطويل لانها اخبار ممتعه وحكم ونوادر لا ينفعها الاسناد باتصاله ولايضرها ما حذف منها (see also p. 78 above).

DOCUMENT 5

A BEDOUIN'S OPINION OF JARĪR'S POETRY AS EXPRESSED TO THE CALIPH HISHĀM

PERF No. 636. First half of third/ninth century.

Papyrus fragment, 18.5 × 3.5 cm. (Pl. 6). The text is on the back of an earlier document of accounts in Greek figures and traces of text in a small cursive script commonly used in the third century.

Script.—Small cursive script written with well formed letters in a steady hand that is readily legible. Diacritical points are used sparingly, mostly for *ba'* and its sister letters *nūn* and *yā'* and occasionally for *khā'* and *zā'*. The *hamzah* is omitted. The circle indicates the end of a verse of poetry.

TEXT

1 زعموا ان اعرابي دخل على هشام وعنده الفرزدق وجرير فقال ه[شام يا اعرابي هل تعرف]

2 من الشعر شيئا قال ما سقط عنى الا ازد له قال فهل تعرف من هذا احدا قال لا قال فاخبرني امدح بيت قيل

3 قال قول جرير يا امير المومنين فيكم الم قال السمّ خير من ركب المطاي واندى العلمين بطون راح ○

4 قال فاخبرني بهجا المر شيئا قيل قال جرير يا امير المومنين فغض الطـرف انك من نمير فلا كعب بلغت ولا كلابا ○

5] انما يهجو [

Comments.—No literal parallels are available in the sources on hand, although several comparable texts and occasions are recorded and are discussed below.

Line 1. The reconstruction of the last two words is based on consideration of space and suggested by the same phrase in line 2. Alternative phrases in the sources are هل تروى or simply أتروى.

Lines 3–4. The two verses of Jarīr's poetry quoted here are frequently cited in most of the sources. Their history and long-sustained popularity are discussed below.

HISTORICAL BACKGROUND

I

A full and firm chronology of the lives and poetry of even the three ranking poets of the Umayyad period, Akhṭal, Jarīr, and Farazdaq, is not available from the sources. More often than not we have little more to guide us in dating than the reign of a caliph or the duration of the rule of a governor. When a reign or governorship covers some two decades, as in the case of ʿAbd al-Malik and Ḥajjāj ibn Yūsuf, other clues must be sought for dating a specific event of their time. Briefer reigns or governorships, though they narrow the period, fail to fix the date of a specific personal or literary event. The period widens again when the same person serves more than once as governor of a given province. It widens still further when an Umayyad personage is named without indication of his status at the time—governor, prince, or caliph—as happens quite frequently in reference to the four sons of ʿAbd al-Malik who succeeded him and to a lesser extent in reference to ʿUmar ibn ʿAbd al-ʿAzīz, who served as governor and caliph.

The scholars most indifferent to a poet's chronology were the grammarians and the lexicographers, who cited verses out of context to serve their specific fields. Even the literary critics of the Umayyad and ʿAbbāsid periods were more concerned with hair-splitting arguments pertinent to their respective literary tastes and theories than with an integrated view of the life and work of a poet whose odes and verses they literally dissected. Some of the more historically minded commentators were more apt to furnish information significant for the dating of an ode. Internal evidence from a poet's *dīwān* cannot always be trusted for fixing a specific date for a given ode since some verses may have been added or eliminated by the poet himself or by his *rāwiyah* or by subsequent transmitters and commentators, each for a reason of his own (see e.g. p. 190). More fruitful are the major annalists, Ṭabarī in particular. For, though Ṭabarī had to contend with contradictory birth dates even for some of the Umayyad caliphs, he did ascertain and record more dates of caliphs, governors, judges, and leaders of pilgrimages, not to mention rebellions, wars, and battles, than are to be found in the available historical works of his predecessors. He lived in the same century as did such poets as Abū Tammām, Buḥturī, and Ibn al-Muʿtazz, philologists, such as Mubarrad and Thaʿlab, littérateurs such as Ibn Qutaibah and Muḥammad ibn al-Qāsim ibn al-Anbārī, and such commentators as Ibn al-Sikkīt and Sukkarī, all of whom were preoccupied, each group in its own way, with their rich heritage of pre-Islāmic and Islāmic poetry. Gifted with a powerful intellect and a man of encyclopedic knowledge and prodigious industry, Ṭabarī made good use of most of the leading Islāmic poets to judge from his frequent citations of their verses in his *Taʾrīkh.* Ibn Isḥāq before him and Masʿūdī among others after him did much the same, but Ṭabarī and those after him stood on firmer ground and were more discriminating in their choice of citations than Ibn Isḥāq. However, inasmuch as Ṭabarī and Masʿūdī cite poetry primarily in relation to historical and political events or in reference to a given poet's direct relationship to those in power, they too are of not much help for establishing a full chronology of a poet's life and work. All in all, even after we correlate pertinent statements from the above-mentioned varied sources, the net result is apt to be no more than a few specifically dated events, some probable date limits for a few others, and a rough relative chronology for a few more. Chronological problems will confront us as we seek to follow the historical and literary backgrounds of the texts of Documents 5 and 6, both of which revolve around the three ranking poets of the Umayyad period, Akhṭal, Jarīr, and Farazdaq.

II

Though the anecdote of Document 5 dates from the reign of Hishām, the two verses of poetry cited in lines 3 and 4 are from two separate odes which Jarīr (d. 110/728 at age of over 80) actually composed in the reign of ʿAbd al-Malik. The verse in line 3 is from the first ode that Jarīr composed in praise of ʿAbd al-Malik. We have previously covered (p. 89) the relationship between Jarīr and Ḥajjāj ibn Yūsuf, who sent the poet, highly recommended, to the court of ʿAbd al-Malik sometime during the last two or three years of that caliph's reign. There are several versions of Jarīr's reception at the Damascus court. The most complete and detailed account comes with a family *isnād* that traces back to Jarīr himself.[1] There are no meaningful discrepancies between this account and the shorter and partial accounts that are scattered in several earlier and some later sources.

ʿAbd al-Malik showed no eagerness to receive Jarīr since he had favored the Zubairids.[2] When ʿAbd al-Malik finally did receive the poet, he addressed him as Ḥajjāj's poet and permitted him to recite only his odes in praise of Ḥajjāj. Angered at a verse that referred to Ḥajjāj as valiantly stemming the tide of rebellion against the Umayyads, ʿAbd al-Malik informed Jarīr that Allāh did not give him victory through Ḥajjāj but made victorious His faith and His representative. He dismissed the poet abruptly

[1] *Amālī* III 43–46.

[2] Jumaḥī, p. 357; *Aghānī* VII 66.

and without a reward.[3] Jarīr was determined that he would not leave Damascus until he had won the caliph's favor and a reward, without which both his reputation and his fortune would be ruined. When, on the intercession of Muḥammad ibn al-Ḥajjāj, Jarīr was finally permitted to recite an ode in praise of ʿAbd al-Malik the poet began with an unfortunate verse referring to himself, which the superstitious ʿAbd al-Malik considered an ill omen.[4] As the caliph listened peevishly, the alarmed Jarīr, concerned with the future of his fame and fortune, improvised, as he himself reported,[5] the verse cited in line 3 of our papyrus. ʿAbd al-Malik was so delighted with this high praise of his openhanded generosity that he kept asking the poet to repeat the verse and awarded him the royal gift of one hundred of the best camels. Jarīr, taking advantage of the caliph's mood, then boldly asked for equipment and camel drivers, among other requests, for the journey back to ʿIrāq.[6] Ḥajjāj was so pleased with ʿAbd al-Malik's acceptance of Jarīr and the latter's poetic brilliance that, had he not feared offending the caliph, he would have matched the royal reward instead of actually awarding the poet but half that gift.[7]

During a ten-day visit as a member of the ʿIrāqī delegation to ʿAbd al-Malik, Jarīr met the older and well established court poet Akhṭal. The latter had at first considered Jarīr a better poet than Farazdaq but had been induced under pressure from the governor of ʿIrāq Bishr ibn Marwān and his agents and against his own better judgment to reverse himself in favor of Farazdaq.[8] Though Akhṭal regretted his involvement, yet he rejected friendly advice to desist from further antagonizing Jarīr.[9] Thereafter the personal and professional pride of both poets goaded them to the exchange of satire until the death of the

[3] *Aghānī* VII 66 gives the verse

من سد مطلع النفاق عليكم   او من يصول كصول الحجاج

and the caliph's remark: ان الله لم ينصرني بالحجاج وانما نصر دنيه وخليفته (cf. *ibid.* VII 181: ان الله لم ينصر الحجاج).

[4] The inauspicious verse reads

اتصحو ام فوادك صاح   عشية هم صحبك بالرداح

(see Jāḥiẓ, *Tāj*, p. 133; *Aghānī* VII 66 f.; *Amālī* III 45). For the complete ode of 22 verses see *Dīwān Jarīr*, ed. Karam al-Bustānī (Beirūt, 1379/1960) pp. 76–78, and *Sharḥ dīwān Jarīr*, pp. 96–99. For another instance of verses considered ominous by ʿAbd al-Malik see Ibn Ṭabāṭabā, p. 123; Ibn al-Jauzī, *Akhbār al-ḥamqā wa al-mughaffalūn*, ed. Khāẓim al-Muẓaffar (Najaf, 1386/1966) pp. 57–60, records this and other instances when ʿAbd al-Malik and Hishām found verses ominous though not so intended by the poets involved. ʿAbd al-Malik once dreamt that he was physically overpowered by ʿAbd Allāh ibn al-Zubair and nailed to the ground with four pegs. He sent a messenger to Muḥammad ibn Sīrīn in Baṣrah for an interpretation of the dream and was told to expect victory over his enemy and the succession of four of his sons (see Tanūkhī's *Nishwār al-muḥāḍarah* as translated from an unpublished manuscript by D. S. Margoliouth, "The table-talk of a Mesopotamian judge," Part II, *Islamic Culture* VI [1932] 195). This episode brings to mind the report that Jarīr's mother dreamt that she gave birth to a black rope that wound itself around the necks of many and choked them and she was told she would give birth to a son and a poet "full of acrimony and violence, who would be an affliction to men." And, therefore, when her seven-month son was born she named him Jarīr, which means "halter" (*Aghānī* VII 58 f.; Ibn Khallikān I 128 [= trans. I 296]). Both dreams may well have been fabricated after the actual events (see *Aghānī* VII 59, 72). Superstitions of all sorts had a strong hold on most Arabs of pre-Islāmic and Islāmic times. Men and women in all walks of life, including rulers and scholars, saw good and bad omens in a variety of happenings. Diviners and dream interpreters had a large following. Augury, especially from the call or flight of birds, was widespread. Even a slip of the tongue could suggest an omen to one with a lively imagination. All were not equally affected, and some frowned on such practices. Poets and their critics were familiar with this phenomenon and would-be poets were cautioned against verses that might be considered as bad omens. For a sampling of instances of and attitudes toward such practices, drawn for our purposes largely from the first two centuries of Islām, see e.g. Jāḥiẓ, *Bayān* I 105 and II 212; *ʿUyūn* I 144–53; Ṭabarī II 1163; *Aghānī* X 132; Māwardī, *Adab al-dunyā wa al-dīn*, pp. 285–88; *ʿIqd* II 300–303; Ibn Ṭabāṭabā, pp. 122–24; Baihaqī, pp. 343–59, 363, 617; Khaṭīb X 49 f., 54, 60. See our Vol. II 169 for Muḥammad ibn Sīrīn and the interpretation of dreams and *Concordance* IV 70 f. تطير.

[5] *Amālī* III 45, lines 8–10.

[6] *Ibid.* III 45; cf. Jāḥiẓ, *Tāj*, pp. 133 f.; *Aghānī* VII 66 f.; *ʿIqd* II 83 f.; *Sharḥ dīwān Jarīr*, pp. 98 f.; Ibn Khallikān I 129 (= trans. I 297 f.). See also Nicholson, *A Literary History of the Arabs*, pp. 244 f.

[7] *Amālī* III 45 f.

[8] Jumaḥī, pp. 386 f., 408 f.; Bevan I 494 f.; Ṣāliḥānī, *Naqāʾiḍ Jarīr wa al-Akhṭal*, pp. 148, 197, 207; *Aghānī* VII 44, X 2 f., and XX 170.

[9] Bevan I 496; *Aghānī* VII 173.

older Akhṭal. It is, therefore, not surprising that when the two met at the court of ʿAbd al-Malik they quickly exchanged insults.[10] ʿAbd al-Malik amused himself at the expense of first one and then the other. He dismissed both poets from his presence to fight it out in the courtyard, knowing that if they came to blows Jarīr would win over the older Akhṭal; but the latter, knowing his disadvantage, remained at a distance out of sight of the younger poet.[11] At another time ʿAbd al-Malik threatened to have Akhṭal mount on the back of Jarīr in order to humiliate the latter, but he refrained from carrying out his threat when several of those present, including Jarīr himself, protested that it would not be fitting for a Christian to so humiliate a Muslim.[12] Nevertheless, Jarīr's short visit to the imperial court helped, though indirectly, to bring about the greatest public honor Akhṭal achieved under the Umayyads. For, having seen and heard ʿAbd al-Malik's ultimate pleasure in and rich reward for Jarīr's panegyric, Akhṭal had reason for concern for his own status. He therefore pointed out to ʿAbd al-Malik that Jarīr claimed he had composed his ode in three days while he himself had spent a whole year composing an ode to satisfy all of the caliph's wishes, and Akhṭal was promptly ordered to recite this new ode.[13] The poet stepped out to fortify himself with drink and returned to recite what was soon to become his most famous ode. As the recitation proceeded, ʿAbd al-Malik's pleasure mounted and reached a peak at the forty-first verse

شمس العداوة حتى يستقاد لهم   واعظم الناس احلاما اذا قدروا

stressing the Umayyads' determined opposition to the enemy until the latter surrenders and accepts their rule, which the poet says is most compassionate. The rest of this ode of eighty-four verses, recounting the services of Akhṭal and the Banū Taghlib to the Umayyads and satirizing their enemies and also Jarīr and his tribe, so pleased the caliph that he exclaimed: "This is (indeed) sweet (to the ear)! Were it, by Allāh, to be placed on a piece of iron it would melt it down." Akhṭal was rewarded with money and was all but smothered with gifts of rich clothing as ʿAbd al-Malik declared him the poet of the Umayyads and according to one account had him paraded in public with a crier proclaiming: "This is the poet of the Commander of the Faithful. This is the best poet of the Arabs."[14] For his year's effort on this his most famous ode Akhṭal, as the poet of the Umayyads, reveled thereafter in all the professional and financial rewards that that honor entailed.[15]

Jarīr was at the court of ʿAbd al-Malik on at least one more occasion, when he found himself in competition with ʿAdī ibn al-Riqāʿ al-ʿĀmilī, the favorite court poet of Prince Walīd. Nevertheless, Jarīr proved to be a match for ʿAdī in the presence of ʿAbd al-Malik when of all the poets at the gate only he and ʿAdī were admitted to celebrate the wedding of Walīd's son ʿAbd al-ʿAzīz to Umm Ḥakīm. ʿAdī won much praise for his three verses that referred to the bride and the groom as the sun and the moon in constant association in which he wished them lifelong happiness.[16] Jarīr followed with six verses, two each

[10] Jumaḥī, pp. 409 f.; *Aghānī* VII 181; *ʿIqd* V 296 f.

[11] *Aghānī* VII 64 f. and 69: قال (عبد الملك) قاتل الله جريرا ما افحله اما والله لو كان النصراني برز اليه لاكله.

[12] *Amālī* III 44; but see *ʿUmdah* I 21 f. and *Khizānah* I 221, where ʿAbd al-Malik is said to have carried out his threat.

[13] *Aghānī* VII 172; Ṣāliḥānī, *Shiʿr al-Akhṭal*, pp. 98–112, esp. p. 104.

[14] *Aghānī* VII 172 f., 175 f.; *ibid* 181: هذه المزمرة والله لو وضعت على زبر الحديد لاذابتها. For the entire ode see *Akhtal, Encomium Omayadarum*, ed. M. Th. Houtsma (Lugd. Batavorum, 1878); Ṣāliḥānī, *Shiʿr al-Akhṭal*, pp. 98–112; Ṣāliḥānī, *Naqāʾiḍ Jarīr wa al-Akhṭal*, pp. 79–85.

[15] *Aghānī* VII 172 f., 181.

[16] *Aghānī* XV 49 f.:

قمر السماء وشمسها اجتمعا   بالسعد ما غابا وما طلعا
ما وارت الاستار مثلهما   ممن راى هذا ومن سمعا
دام السرور له بها ولها   وتهنيا طول الحياة معا

(cf. *ʿUyūn* III 69).

in praise of the bride and the groom and the last two expressing congratulations and sincere good wishes.[17] ʿAbd al-Malik rewarded each poet with 10,000 dirhems.

Later Jarīr found himself again in competition with ʿAdī ibn al-Riqāʿ, this time at the court of Walīd I, probably at his accession, when we know that Jarīr warned Ruʾbah ibn al-ʿAjjāj and his father not to take sides against him and that Walīd rebuked Jarīr for his biting satires.[18] Like ʿAbd al-Malik, Walīd showed his displeasure with Jarīr and other poets who had supported the Zubairids by refusing to receive them at his private sessions with the poets. But Jarīr and the others had access to the caliph at his public audiences, and Jarīr seized one such occasion to make a dramatic entry and boldly requested Walīd's permission to challenge ʿAdī as a poet. The surprised Walīd answered: "May Allāh not inflict the people with many of the likes of you." And the unabashed Jarīr replied: "O Commander of the Faithful, I alone have kindled the community! Were there to be many like me, they would devour the people completely." A broad smile spread over Walīd's face in amused astonishment at Jarīr's ready retort and his great self-confidence, and then Walīd seated him among the court poets.[19] When Jarīr finally came face to face with ʿAdī, he either did not or more likely pretended not to recognize him.[20] When Walīd named ʿAdī ibn al-Riqāʿ al-ʿĀmilī, Jarīr played on the words *riqāʿ*, "ragged clothes," and *ʿāmilah*, "laboring," and in connection with the latter cited Sūrah 88:3–4, which refers to those laboring in hell-fire, and concluded with a vituperative verse. ʿAdī answered with a verse in kind and then took refuge at Walīd's feet. Walīd angrily rebuked Jarīr for his misuse of the Qurʾān and threatened to humiliate him and degrade him among his fellow poets by having a foreign client (*ghulām*) saddle and mount him. Like ʿAbd al-Malik before him, Walīd was dissuaded from carrying out this threat because some who were present pointed out the inappropriateness of a foreign client so humbling a ranking Muslim Arab poet. Jarīr was then dismissed with the warning that should he dare to satirize ʿAdī he would have to face severe consequences at the hands of Walīd himself. Jarīr did nevertheless satirize ʿAdī but did not explicitly name him and thus escaped any consequences.[21] But on another occasion, during the pilgrimage of the year 91/709, the satires of Jarīr and ʿUmar ibn Lajāʾ so angered Walīd that he ordered his governor of Medina, Abū Bakr ibn Muḥammad ibn ʿAmr ibn Ḥazm al-Anṣārī, to have both poets flogged.[22]

Upon ʿUmar II's accession several persistent poets hastened to congratulate him but were kept waiting for a long time before they managed to gain an audience either alone or in groups. Among them we find Jarīr, Farazdaq, Kuthaiyir,[23] Nuṣaib,[24] and Dukīn.[25] Though all were disappointed in their expectation of rich rewards such as they had become accustomed to, yet ʿUmar's motives and his desire to conserve

[17] *Aghānī* XV 50. See Thaʿālibī, *Thimār*, p. 239, for a second version, according to which Jarīr recited his verses first; this version gives several textual variants for the verses of both poets and does not mention the equal rewards they received from ʿAbd al-Malik but adds that Walīd preferred ʿAdī's fewer verses and rewarded him with double the reward he gave Jarīr: فقال له وليد لئن اقللت فلقد احسنت وامر له بضعف ما امر لجرير. The marriage was unhappy and ended in divorce.

[18] *Aghānī* XVIII 123 f. and XXI 88; see also Ibn ʿAsākir V 394 f.

[19] *Aghānī* VII 72: قال جرير انما انا واحد قد سعرت الامة فلو كثر امثالى لاكلوا الناس اكلا . . . فتبسم وليد حتى بدت ثناياه تعجبا من جرير. Akhṭal, too, considered Jarīr a calamity; see Jumaḥī, p. 316: سل الاخطل عن جرير بالكوفة وجلده ثم امره فجلس فقال دعوا جريرا اخزاه الله فانه كان بلاء على من صُبّ عليه.

[20] *Aghānī* VII 73; *Muwashshaḥ*, pp. 129 f. See ʿ*Iqd* V 296 f. for Jarīr's non-recognition of Akhṭal and for Kuthaiyir's and Akhṭal's non-recognition of each other, both instances being in the presence of ʿAbd al-Malik.

[21] Jumaḥī, pp. 324 f.; *Aghānī* VII 73 and VIII 179 f.; *Muwashshaḥ*, pp. 129 f.

[22] Jumaḥī, p. 369; *Aghānī* VII 69.

[23] For Jarīr's interview while Farazdaq and others waited outside see *Aghānī* VII 57 f. *Shiʿr*, pp. 317–21, and *Aghānī* VIII 152–54 give the fullest accounts, with *isnād*'s that trace back to Ḥammād al-Rāwiyah on the direct authority of Kuthaiyir (see also ʿ*Iqd* II 86–96).

[24] See preceding note and ʿ*Iqd* V 292.

[25] *Shiʿr*, pp. 387 f.; cf. ʿ*Iqd* II 84–86.

community funds for the purposes for which they were intended were appreciated by both Jarīr[26] and Kuthaiyir.[27]

The verse cited in line 4 of our papyrus text is from the only ode in which Jarīr satirized yet another poet and his tribe, namely ʿUbaid ibn Ḥuṣain al-Numairī (d. 90/709),[28] better known as Rāʿī, "camel-herder," for his excellent descriptions of camels. Jumaḥī classed him with Jarīr, Farazdaq, and Akhṭal though he among others considered him somewhat inferior to the other three.[29] The older Rāʿī, like Akhṭal, was drawn into taking sides in the rivalry between Jarīr and Farazdaq and expressed himself in verse in favor of the latter.[30] Jarīr convinced him that it would be to his best interest to desist and to take a neutral position and Rāʿī promised to do so. But under pressure from his tribe and powerful friends, and some add under the influence of drink, Rāʿī broke his promise. Warned once more by Jarīr, Rāʿī was about to apologize and renew his promise of neutrality. At this moment Rāʿī's hot-headed son Jandal rushed in to prevent Rāʿī from doing so. He struck his father's mount while reciting a verse satirizing Jarīr. The mule brushed past Jarīr and knocked off his headgear. Rāʿī drove off without returning to make amends for his foolish son's conduct, and Jarīr tells us that had Rāʿī done so he would not have satirized him.[31] With mounting anger as he picked up his headgear, Jarīr answered Jandal's verse with an obscene one of his own, using the same meter and rhyme. Rāʿī soon regretted the incident, rebuked his son, and warned him of worse satire yet to come from Jarīr, who would not spare the honor of their women. And so it was. For Jarīr hurried home and, accompanied by a secretary-transmitter and fortified with food and drink, sat up all night drafting an ode of eighty verses in the same meter and rhyme as the verses already exchanged between Jandal and himself.[32] The verse that pleased Jarīr most is the one cited in line 4 of our papyrus, which in Nicholson's apt translation reads: "Cast down thine eyes for shame! for thou art of Numayr—no peer of Kaʿb nor yet Kiláb."[33] The next day Jarīr, well groomed[34] and mounted on a

[26] *Aghānī* VII 58: قال جرير لاصحابه وفيهم الفرزدق خرجت من عند رجل يقرب الفقراء ويباعد الشعراء وانا مع ذلك عنه راض.
Back home Jarīr summarized his reaction in the verse

تركت لكم بالشام حبل جماعـــة　　　امين القوى مستحصد العقد باقيا

(*ibid.*). See *Fragmenta historicum Arabicorum* I 63 for his verses in appreciation of the new uses to which ʿUmar II put some of the money.

[27] Kuthaiyir reported to his companions that the caliph was other-world minded: فان الرجل آخروى ليس بدنيوى (*Shiʿr*, p. 318) and فليس الرجل بدنيوى (*Aghānī* VIII 153; *ʿIqd* II 87). They took note of the fact in the odes which they recited to him and received a modest reward from his private purse.

[28] Modern editors give this death date without indicating its source, which I have not so far found; see e.g. Yāqūt VI 426 (Index); Jāḥiẓ, *Bayān* II 295; Qudāmah (1963) p. 45; Nāṣir al-Ḥānī, *Shiʿr al-Rāʿī al-Numairī wa akhbāruh* (Damascus, 1964) pp. 7 f.

[29] Jumaḥī, pp. 249–51; *Aghānī* VII 38.

[30] Jumaḥī, pp. 372 f.; *Aghānī* VII and 49 f., XX 169 f.; Bevan I 428. All of these sources indicate that

يا صاحِبىّ دنا الرواح فسيرا　　　غلب الفرزدق في الهجاء جريرا

is the verse that caused trouble for Rāʿī.

[31] *Aghānī* XX 169.

[32] Jumaḥī, pp. 273 f.; *Aghānī* VII 49 and XX 169. The account of this whole episode as found in these two sources is repeated in parts and supplemented, in both *isnād*'s and content, in Bevan I 427–51, the ode itself (No. 53) having grown to 112 verses with a composite commentary. See also *Dīwān Jarīr* (1960) pp. 58–66 and *Sharḥ dīwān Jarīr*, pp. 64–80. Jarīr seems regularly to have had on hand a secretary to whom he dictated his poetry (see *ʿIqd* III 186).

[33] Nicholson, *A Literary History of the Arabs*, p. 246; see *ibid.* pp. 245 f. for a lively translation of *Aghānī* VII 49 f.

[34] See Bevan I 320 and II 624 and 650 for dress and grooming and see *Khizānah* IV 172 for a satirist's costume and grooming, including that of Labīd, in pre-Islāmic times.

See Bevan II 546–76 (No. 61) and *Aghānī* XIX 38 f. for an episode involving Farazdaq that in several respects parallels the episode of Jarīr and Jandal. This time the foolish son of the highly placed and highly respected Abū Bakr ibn Muḥammad ibn ʿAmr ibn Ḥazm al-Anṣārī challenged Farazdaq's claim that he was *the* poet of the Arabs and demanded that he prove his claim by producing an ode to match one of Ḥassān ibn Thābit which he, the son, recited. That night Farazdaq roamed hill and dale until inspiration came and enabled him to compose a long ode of 113 verses (Bevan II, No. 61) and, having first groomed himself, recited it the next day.

stallion, presented himself at the circle of Rāʿī and Farazdaq in the Mirbad of Baṣrah and recited his long ode to the dismay and shame of both poets. The aging Rāʿī, we are told, never recovered from the shock, professionally or otherwise, and the shame was to haunt his family and his tribe, the Banū Numair, long after his death despite the fact that Rāʿī himself made a brief answer to Jarīr and Farazdaq defended Rāʿī and his tribe in a satire composed in answer to Jarīr.[35]

Though the affair of Jarīr and Rāʿī became widely known in considerable detail, none of the sources actually date it. Little is heard of Rāʿī after his humiliation. Some say he died of grief on the spot, but others report that he and his people left Baṣrah in great haste and departed to their tribal settlement only to find that the news of Rāʿī's humiliation had preceded him and that he died soon after.[36] His son Jandal reports that his father, in order to discipline him, had vowed he would not answer Jarīr for a year but that he died before the year was out.[37] If we accept 90/709 as Rāʿī's death date (see p. 113, n. 28) then it must follow that his clash with Jarīr took place no earlier than 89 A.H. But this conclusion is contradicted by reports that the verse cited in line 4 of our papyrus and another verse from the same ode were cited to ʿAbd al-Malik (d. 86/705) by a Bedouin as the best verse of satire and the best heroic verse of the Arabs (see pp. 117–19). Knowing that the sources show discrepancies of as much as four years for the death dates of Rāʿī's more successful and better known contemporaries Akhṭal, Jarīr, and Farazdaq, I am more inclined to suspect Rāʿī's death date as given by modern editors or else to reject the statement that he died within a year after his bitter experience with Jarīr than I am inclined to suspect the report that verses from this specific ode of Jarīr's were recited to ʿAbd al-Malik. Several other bits of evidence reinforce my position. For most of some seven years before Ḥajjāj ibn Yūsuf took office as governor of ʿIrāq, Jarīr had been away from Baṣrah with his people in their settlement of Marrūt, while back in Baṣrah Farazdaq intensified his attacks on Jarīr and the Banū Kulaib. Soon after Ḥajjāj's arrival in ʿIrāq, Jarīr, at the insistence of his people, returned to Baṣrah in order to be in a better position to counterattack Farazdaq.[38] Jarīr, while trying to persuade Rāʿī to be neutral in respect to his rivalry with Farazdaq, pointed out to Rāʿī that he, Jarīr, had been seven years in the province parrying satirical attacks against his people.[39] Inasmuch as Jarīr had been an acknowledged poet and dreaded satirist for some three decades before Ḥajjāj's appointment as governor of ʿIrāq, Jarīr must have been here referring to seven years spent in Baṣrah after his return to the city early in Ḥajjāj's governorship. Furthermore, we learn from a composite and much abbreviated account that Ḥajjāj one night summoned Jarīr to the governor's palace, but there is no mention of the time or of the city in which this summons took place. What Ḥajjāj wished was to know why Jarīr abused the people with his satires. Jarīr's reply was that he did so only in retaliation for their having satirized him first—an explanation that he once gave to Abū ʿAmr ibn al-ʿAlāʾ in answer to the same question.[40] Jarīr then added: "What have I to do with Ibn Umm Ghassān or with Baʿīth or with Farazdaq or Akhṭal or Ibn Lajāʾ?" And he continued to name poets he had satirized. Said Ḥajjāj: "I know not what you have to do with these; you tell me." Jarīr gave some details of why and how each of the twenty poets named had satirized him first and of how he had answered in each case, beginning with the above-named five poets and in that order, which is known to be generally chronological. As Jarīr

[35] Jumaḥī, pp. 373 f., 435; Jāḥiẓ, *Bayān* III 334 f.; *Aghānī* VII 50 and XX 171. For Farazdaq's ode see Bevan I 451–78 (No. 54). *Khizānah* I 35 gives Rāʿī's 3-verse answer to the verse cited in line 4 of our papyrus text (cf. *Aghānī* VII 45 and XX 170).

Similarly, members of Akhṭal's tribe, the Banū Taghlib, experienced a deep sense of humiliation at some of the verses of Jarīr's satire of Akhṭal (see e.g. Jāḥiẓ, *Bayān* III 371 f.; *Sharḥ dīwān Jarīr*, pp. 448–53, from which the fourth verse of the *Bayān* text is missing).

[36] Jumaḥī, p. 374; *Aghānī* XX 171.

[37] Jumaḥī, p. 374; *Aghānī* XX 172. See also Nāṣir al-Ḥānī, *Shiʿr al-Rāʿī*, pp. 64 and 119, but on p. 53 this author is misled by a misreading of the words ابنه and ابيه into accepting the statement that Rāʿī outlived Jandal.

[38] *Shiʿr*, pp. 286 f.; *Amālī* III 43.

[39] Bevan I 431.

[40] *Aghānī* VII 43; *ʿIqd* V 296.

finished with each poet, Ḥajjāj asked *thumma man*, "then who?" Thus, we have clear indication of a chronological sequence for this list of poets, a list that was cut short only by the break of day.[41] Rāʿī is eighth in this list, which, it should be noted, does not include ʿAdī ibn al-Riqāʿ (d. 95/713 or 714), whom Jarīr first met late in the reign of ʿAbd al-Malik.

If we assume that the conversation between Jarīr and Ḥajjāj took place at the latter's palace in Baṣrah,[42] then we must assume that it occurred shortly before Ḥajjāj moved to his new capital of Wāsiṭ in the winter of 83/84 A.H. (see pp. 82 f.) in order to allow for the seven years Jarīr claimed to have been in Baṣrah at the time of his conversation with Rāʿī and for some lapse of time between that event and his conversation with Ḥajjāj. If, on the other hand, the conversation with Ḥajjāj took place later in Wāsiṭ, it would have to be placed before the competition between Jarīr and ʿAdī which began late in ʿAbd al-Malik's reign (65–86/685–705) and climaxed early in the caliphate of Walīd I (86–96/705–15), probably soon after Walīd's succession, when it was customary for the poets to wait on the monarch in order to congratulate and praise him in the hope of receiving his patronage.[43] In either case, Jarīr's abusive satire of Rāʿī had ample time and opportunity to reach the ear if not, indeed, the hand of ʿAbd al-Malik and of his heir and successor, Walīd I. For we know that news of such events traveled fast by direct word of mouth, by special messenger,[44] or even by imperial post as in the case of an ode of Akhṭal's.[45] We know that Jarīr had several literate transmitters to whom he dictated his poems, especially the longer ones such as his satire of Rāʿī,[46] and that Farazdaq also had secretary-transmitters.[47] Their poetry had ready and

[41] *Aghānī* VII 43–49 and XX 170. There is no convincing reason to assume, as does Aḥmad al-Shāyib, *Taʾrīkh al-naqāʾiḍ fī al-shiʿr al-ʿarabī* [Cairo, 1946] pp. 209–13), that this interview between Ḥajjāj and Jarīr is a fabrication of Abū al-Faraj al-Iṣfahānī. One has to keep in mind constantly the uncertain relative chronology of some of the events and that Abū al-Faraj's account is a condensation of two earlier lengthy accounts. Jarīr claimed at various times in his long career to have overcome 43, 50, and 80 poets (*Aghānī* VII 40 and 59).

[42] Ḥajjāj did once order both Jarīr and Farazdaq to appear, dressed in their pre-Islāmic tribal costumes, at the governor's palace in Baṣrah, but here again the event is not dated (Jumaḥī, pp. 346, 368; *Aghānī* VII 71).

[43] Maḥmūd Ghināwī al-Zuhairī in his *Naqāʾiḍ Jarīr wa al-Farazdaq* (Baghdād, 1954), pp. 62–121, makes a commendable contribution to the chronology of the *naqāʾiḍ*. He has, however, been misled into dating Jarīr's satire of Rāʿī, for whom he gives no death date, after the year 96 A.H. (see *ibid.* pp. 105 f. and 112) because of a marginal note that has crept into the Bevan edition of the *naqāʾiḍ*, where it appears in parentheses and reads وذلك بحدثان قتل وكيع قتيبه بن مسلم فباهلة ونمير غضبان على بنى يربوع, which refers to the fall and death in 96 A.H. of Muslim ibn Qutaibah al-Bāhilī, governor of Khurasān (see Ṭabarī II 1283; Bevan I 427 f., 432).

[44] Bishr ibn Marwān as governor of ʿIrāq (71–74/690–93) sent by messenger a copy of Surāqah al-Bāriqī's satire of Jarīr and demanded an immediate written answer to it (Jumaḥī, pp. 377–80; *Aghānī* VII 44, 66 f.; *Sharḥ dīwān Jarīr*, pp. 300–303).

Jarīr himself complained that Akhṭal and fifty able poets, none inferior to Akhṭal himself, would draft a satire of Jarīr and that Akhṭal would then claim the draft as his own and send the finished product to Jarīr (*Aghānī* VII 40; *Muwashshaḥ*, pp. 138 f., 141).

Farazdaq during his several imprisonments wrote poems seeking his freedom and sent them by messengers to friends and persons in power (see e.g. Jumaḥī, p. 296; *Aghānī* XIX 24, 61). He even conducted family affairs and correspondence with his wife Nawār in written verse (see e.g. *Majālis al-ʿulamāʾ*, pp. 294 f.; *Aghānī* XIX 23 f.; *ʿIqd* VI 95, 124 f.; Ibn Khallikān II 266 f. [= trans. III 624 f.]). He also sometimes forced scholar-transmitters to write down his *naqāʾiḍ* and memorize and transmit them (see n. 137 on p. 131 below). Farazdaq himself claimed an instant and tenacious memory (*Aghānī* XIX 34).

[45] ʿAbd al-Malik ordered Akhṭal to write an ode in praise of Ḥajjāj, and it was forwarded by post to Ḥajjāj in ʿIrāq (*Aghānī* VII 174). For the ode see Ṣāliḥānī, *Shiʿr al-Akhṭal*, pp. 73–76 and 82, note *d*.

[46] The names of at least five of Jarīr's transmitters, in addition to several of his sons, have come down to us: Ḥusain al-Kātib, Ashʿab the musician and singer, Jarīr's grandsons Mishal and Ayyūb (sons of Kusaib by Jarīr's daughter Zaidāʾ [Bevan III 122]), and Marbaʿ (see e.g. Jumaḥī, p. 349; Bevan I 430 and II 975; *Shiʿr*, p. 307; *Aghānī* VII 42; *Fihrist*, p. 159; *ʿUmdah* I 138).

[47] ʿUbaid of the Banū Rabīʿah and an unnamed fellow tribesman, ʿAbd Allāh ibn Zālān al-Tamīmī, and Ibn Mattawaih seem to have been his chief professional transmitters (see Jumaḥī, p. 471; Bevan II 907 f., 1049; *Shiʿr*, p. 486; *Aghānī* XIX 26; *ʿUmdah* I 132). Farazdaq was not so fortunate as Jarīr in his several sons, since all but Labaṭah died young. Not much is known of Labaṭah except that he was more politic than Farazdaq, was dominated by his wife, and resisted and neglected his father but had some poetic ability and transmitted from Farazdaq to Aṣmaʿī among others (Jumaḥī, pp. 294 f.; Yazīdī, pp. 56 f.; *Aghānī* XIX 23; *Muʿjam al-shuʿarāʾ*, p. 357 and reference there cited). Farazdaq and Jarīr had a common transmitter, ʿAbd Allāh ibn ʿAṭiyah (*Aghānī* XIX 32).

At least some of Kuthaiyir's poetry was committed to writing possibly by a transmitter son-in-law whose manuscripts were passed on to his family (*Aghānī* VIII 30: . . . عن ولد جمعة بنت كُثيّر انه وجد في كتب ابيه التى فيها شعر كثير).

widespread circulation, and some of their lighter and easily quotable verses were put to music and sung by ranking musicians and singing girls.[48]

Furthermore, Jarīr, the poet and the man, was more favored than Farazdaq by the Bedouins and the Quraish and their clients, both Arabs and foreigners.[49] Moreover, ʿAbd al-Malik had a lifelong interest in poets and poetry and developed a keen critical sense for the latter (see p. 136, n. 165). In his last years he found his most relaxing pleasure in conversation with scholars and littérateurs of the caliber of Shaʿbī and with Bedouins knowledgeable in poetry. There is therefore no valid reason to question Madāʾinī's report, tracing back through a double *isnād* to ʿAbd al-Malik ibn ʿUmair and to ʿAwānah ibn al-Ḥakam (see below), that a Bedouin in answer to questions put to him by ʿAbd al-Malik as to the best poetry recited some of the most famous verses of Jarīr,[50] including the one cited in line 4 of our papyrus from an ode satirizing both Rāʿī and Farazdaq.

Each of the two verses of our papyrus text is frequently cited, in early and later sources, either alone or in combination with comparable verses of Jarīr or other poets. The panegyrists dwelt on the qualities most admired by the Arabs and particularly flattering to their rulers, such as noble descent, generosity, forebearance, and courage. The following illustrative citations are verses from the four contemporary and comparable poets with whom we are primarily concerned—Jarīr, Farazdaq, Akhṭal, and Rāʿī. Jarīr's

الستم خير من ركب المطاى　　　واندى العالمين بطون راح

is more apt than not to be found in association with Akhṭal's equally famous

شمس العداوة حتى يستقاد لهم　　　واعظم الناس احلاما اذا قدروا

since the two verses were addressed in close succession to ʿAbd al-Malik.[51] The qualities directly opposed to those lauded in panegyric were most apt to be attacked by the satirists, who seldom overlooked low or base descent, miserliness, vindictiveness, and cowardice among other personal or tribal shortcomings. Jarīr's

فغض الطرف انك من نمير　　　فلا كعب بلغت ولا كلاب

is the verse cited in line 4 of our papyrus, belittling the descent of Rāʿī and his tribe, and echoed in part by Rāʿī's

تـابى قضاعة ان تعرف لكم نسبا　　　وابنــا نزار بيضــة البلــد

in his satire of ʿAdī ibn al-Riqāʿ.[52] Jarīr's above-cited verse was in some competition as his most effective satire with another of his verses, in which he attacked Farazdaq's character

وكنت اذا نزلت بدار قوم　　　اطعنت بخزية وتركة عارا

and which Farazdaq himself confessed was the verse that disquieted him most.[53] Akhṭal more than matched this with the verse which is considered the most vulgar in Arabic poetry

قوم اذا استنبح الاضياف كلابهم　　　قالوا لامهم بولى على النــار

[48] For the active role of the transmitter of poetry see e.g. *Shiʿr*, p. 307; *Aghīnī* I 116 f., VII 42, and XVII 98; ʿ*Iqd* VI 24, 46 f.; Bevan II 1048. The role of a poet's personal transmitter as secretary-editor in the 1st century of Islām is significantly illustrated by the individual and group activities of several direct transmitters from Jarīr and Farazdaq (see *Aghānī* IV 53 f.; *Muwashshaḥ*, pp. 116 f.; cf. Jumaḥī, p. 305, n. 1).

[49] See e.g. Jumaḥī, pp. 319 f., 347 f.; *Muwashshaḥ*, p. 115; *Aghānī* VII 6 f., 65.

[50] *Aghānī* VII 54 f.; Qurashī, pp. 36 f.

[51] E.g. Jumaḥī, p. 426; Ṣāliḥānī, *Shiʿr al-Akhṭal*, pp. 96–112; *Shiʿr*, p. 311. See also pp. 111 f. above.

[52] Jumaḥī, p. 435; *Aghānī* XX 172; Tabrīzī, *Sharḥ ʿalā dīwān ashʿār ḥamāsat Abī Tammām* (Bulāq, 1296/1879) II 31. In Ibn Qutaibah, *Kitāb al-maʿānī al-kabīr*, ed. Fritz Krenkow (Ḥaidarābād, 1368/1949) I 575 f., the first half of the verse reads تابى قضاعة ان ترضى دعاوتكم.

[53] Jumaḥi, p. 353; Bevan I 251, 397; *Aghānī* XIX 36; Masʿūdī VI 155; ʿAskarī, *Maṣūn*, p. 20; Ibn Khallikān II 261 (= trans. III 616).

accusing Jarīr and his people of extreme miserliness and inhospitality.[54] Jarīr himself pointed out the four-barbed thrust of Akhṭal's verse and its elaboration in the next two verses as being the most damaging to him and his people.[55] Also associated with one or the other of the verses already cited is a famous verse of Akhṭal which cuts across praise and blame as its first half lauds the Quraish for their clemency and generosity and its second half satirizes the Anṣār as wholly base—no small literary feat. One version reads

ذهبت قريش بالسماحة والندى واللوم تحت عمائم الانصار

and a second version is translated by Nicholson as follows:

"Quraysh have borne all honour and glory,
And baseness alone is beneath the turbans of the Anṣár."[56]

The two words that survive at the end of line 5 of our document give no clue as to the content of that line but do indicate that still another line followed it. The search for parallels for Jarīr's two verses cited in lines 3 and 4 soon convinced me that the papyrus text is part of a unit account expressing a speaker's choice of the best verse in each of at least three of the four major categories of Arabic poetry, namely panegyric (*madīḥ*), satire (*hijā'*), erotica (*nasīb*), and heroic (*fakhr*). To these should be added elegiac (*rithā'*) and description (*ṣifah*), the latter cutting across all the other categories. Continued search revealed, first, that of all the poets of the Umayyad period only Jarīr is credited with verses of supreme quality in at least four of these categories and, second, that in three of the four such accounts available the opinion is expressed by a Bedouin to ʿAbd al-Malik, instead of to the caliph Hishām as in the papyrus text, while in the fourth account it is expressed directly to Jumaḥī (d. 231/845) by a Bedouin of the Banū Usayyid who claimed that Jarīr excelled Farazdaq in heroic, panegyric, satiric, and romantic poetry.

In the Jumaḥi account four of Jarīr's verses are cited by the Bedouin in support of his opinion.[57] The first verse

اذا غضبت عليك بنو تميم حسبت الناس كلهم غضابا

is from Jarīr's ode satirizing Rāʿī and his tribe, in which he expressed also his own pride in the overpowering effect of the influence of the Banū Tamīm, to which both Jarīr and Farazdaq belonged. Farazdaq himself confirmed the excellence of the verse and wished he had been its author.[58] The next two verses cited by the Bedouin to Jumaḥī are those of lines 3 and 4 of our papyrus, and in the same order, both of which have been dealt with above. The fourth is the romantic verse

ان العيون التى في طرفها حورٌ قتلتنا ثم لم تحيين قتلانا

and is frequently cited in later sources.[59]

[54] Jumaḥī, p. 428; Ṣāliḥānī, *Naqā'iḍ Jarīr wa al-Akhṭal*, p. 134; *ʿUyūn* II 195; *Muwashshaḥ*, pp. 140 f. In ʿAskarī, *Maṣūn*, p. 21, the first half of the verse reads قوم اذا طرف الاضياف دارهم.

[55] See Bevan II 1053 f. for these verses and for Jarīr's verses that Farazdaq considered most damaging to him personally. Akhṭal was fully aware of the effect of his verses on Jarīr (*Muwashshaḥ*, p. 140). See *Shiʿr*, p. 312, and *ʿIqd* V 298 for two verses of Baʿīth that hurt Jarīr as severely.

[56] See Jumaḥī, p. 397; Ṣāliḥānī, *Shiʿr al-Akhṭal*, p. 314; Ṣāliḥānī, *Naqā'iḍ Jarīr wa al-Akhṭal*, p. 158; Jāḥiẓ, *Bayān* I 79; *Shiʿr*, p. 302; Mubarrad, p. 101; *Aghānī* XIII 148 (المكارم والعلا) and XIV 122 (بالمكارم كلها); *ʿIqd* V 321; Ibn al-Shajarī, *Kitāb al-ḥamāsah*, ed. Fritz Krenkow (Ḥaidarābād, 1345/1926) pp. 108 f. Despite the several textual variants in these sources, the character of the verse and its basic concepts are clear in all. For Nicholson's translation see *A Literary History of the Arabs*, p. 241. The religious, political, and personal motivation for the verse has been touched on elsewhere in these studies (see our Vol. II 260 and p. 139 below).

[57] Jumaḥī, pp. 319 f. See Ibn Khallikān I 127 f. (= trans. I 295) for a parallel account and a prose translation of the four verses. See also Ibn Qutaibah, *Kitāb al-maʿānī al-kabīr* I 285 f.; Ibn Ṭabāṭabā, p. 48; Thaʿālibī, *Ījāz*, p. 41.

[58] *Aghānī* VII 41: قال الفرزدق وقد قال (جرير) بيتا لان اكون قلته احب الى مما طلعت عليه الشمس (cf. p. 144 below). For ʿAbbās ibn Yazīd al-Kindī's 3-verse satirical retort to Jarīr's verse see Qudāmah, p. 46, Qudāmah (1963) pp. 105 f. and *Aghānī* VII 46.

[59] See Jumaḥī, p. 320, and cf. *ibid.* pp. 39 and 352. See also *Sharḥ dīwān Jarīr*, p. 595; *Aghānī* VII 53 f.; Tabrīzī, *Sharḥ ʿalā dīwān ashʿār ḥamāsat Abī Tammām* III 14; Mubarrad, p. 161; Thaʿālibī, *Ījāz*, p. 41.

Two later and separate accounts trace back to two authorities earlier than Jumaḥī. The first of these accounts is found in Qurashī's *Jamharat ashʿār al-ʿArab* on the authority of ʿAwānah ibn al-Ḥakam (d. 158/775), a fourth-generation member of a scholarly family, whose son or brother ʿIyāḍ carried on the family's scholarly tradition.[60] The second account is found in Abū al-Faraj al-Iṣfahānī's *Aghānī* as reported by Madā'inī on the direct authority of ʿAwānah alone and, through a second *isnād,* as transmitted directly to Madā'inī by Abū ʿImrān on the authority of his father, ʿAbd al-Malik ibn ʿUmair (d. 136/753 at age 103), who had access to early sources, including the library of Muʿāwiyah (see p. 76, n. 253). Though both accounts are abridgements of earlier reports, they are, so far as we are here concerned, point by point identical in sequence and content except for a few minor variants.[61] The occasion was a large public banquet at the court of ʿAbd al-Malik. Among those present were Jarīr and a knowledgeable Bedouin of the Banū ʿUdhrah. ʿAbd al-Malik, impressed with the Bedouin's conversation, asked him if he was versed in poetry and was told to ask anything about poetry that he wished. Then began the familiar question-and-answer method of eliciting a critical literary opinion. What ʿAbd al-Malik wished to know was the best verse in each of the four major categories of Arabic poetry, and he received in answer the same four verses that are cited in Jumaḥī's account but with the order of verses one and two reversed. However, the two accounts continue with a fifth question by ʿAbd al-Malik. He wished to know the verse of Arabic poetry with the best simile, and the Bedouin recited a fifth verse of Jarīr's:

سرى لهم ليل كانه نجومه   قناديل فيهن الذبال المفتل

Still other details are provided in both accounts. Jarīr's attention was caught when the Bedouin recited the first of his verses, and his pleasure became increasingly evident as the Bedouin recited each successive verse. His delight was so great that he turned over his own regular reward of 400 dirhems[62] and some gift cloth to the Bedouin, which prize ʿAbd al-Malik then matched.

The fourth account of this episode is reported on the authority of ʿAwānah ibn al-Ḥakam and Hishām ibn Muḥammad ibn al-Sā'ib al-Kalbī.[63] ʿAbd al-Malik addressed the same five questions to the Bedouin of the Banū ʿUdhrah and received the same answers as in the preceding two accounts. But there are some differences too. Akhṭal and Farazdaq also were present at the banquet. After the Bedouin had cited the five verses of Jarīr ʿAbd al-Malik asked him if he knew Jarīr and the Bedouin said that he did not but that he longed to meet him. ʿAbd al-Malik then pointed out the three poets to the Bedouin, who responded with two verses praising Jarīr and satirizing the other two, whereupon first Farazdaq and then Akhṭal angrily accused the Bedouin, in verse, of falsehood, ignorance, and low degree. Angered, Jarīr then came to the defense, also in verse, of the Bedouin, leaped to place a kiss on his head, and relinquished his reward of 500 dirhems, which ʿAbd al-Malik matched.

That Farazdaq was ever present at the court during the reign of ʿAbd al-Malik or, indeed, prior to the reign of Sulaimān seems to have been erroneously questioned by Marzubānī.[64] We know that Jarīr was at the court late in ʿAbd al-Malik's reign on more than one occasion. It is not likely that Farazdaq, with Akhṭal already a friend at the court of ʿAbd al-Malik, would not compete with Jarīr for that liberal monarch's favor, even though Ḥajjāj ibn Yūsuf did not see fit to recommend him. Ḥajjāj's attitude may have given Jarīr the notion that Farazdaq would not visit Damascus while he, Jarīr, was there.[65] But Farazdaq did just that, though here again the time is not stated. The last account cited above would

[60] Zubaidī, p. 246; see also p. 35 above.

[61] See Qurashī, pp. 36 f.; *Aghānī* VII 54, line 18, to p. 55, line 12; *Sharḥ dīwān Jarīr*, p. 456: سرى نحوكم ليل كان نجومه الخ.

[62] Jarīr still expected to receive this amount as his regular reward even from ʿUmar II (see pp. 112 f.).

[63] *Dīwān Jarīr* (Cairo, 1313/1896) II 189–91.

[64] *Muwashshaḥ*, pp. 164–66; but see Ibn ʿAsākir VII 52 f. and Blachère in *EI* II (2nd ed.) 788 f.

[65] Jāḥiẓ, *Bayān* II 323: لما قدم الفرزدق الشام قال له جرير ما ظننت انك تقدم بلدا انا فيه قال الفرزدق انى طالما خالفت راى العجزة (cf. *Aghānī* XIX 39 f.).

indicate that Farazdaq's visit and the episode itself took place sometime in the last two or three years of ʿAbd al-Malik's reign.

There seems to have been no parallel attempt to claim for either Farazdaq or Akhṭal supremacy in all of the above-specified five categories. Akhṭal did claim supremacy for himself in erotica, satire, and panegyric.[66] But his claim was quickly refuted when he was accused of even confusing satire with panegyric.[67] Of younger contemporary poets, Bashshār ibn Burd was credited by Abū ʿAmr ibn al-ʿAlāʾ with supreme excellence in panegyric and satire and in the new style (*badīʿ*) of poetry.[68] But Aṣmaʿī, though he considered Bashshār the last of the classical poets, reserved high praise for the verses of Jarīr and Akhṭal. For when in the usual question-and-answer literary dialogue Hārūn al-Rashīd asked him for the best verse each in heroic, panegyric, and satire Aṣmaʿī cited Jarīr's

اذا غضبت عليك بنو تميم   حسبت الناس كلهم غضاباً

and his

الستم خير من ركب المطاى   واندى العالمين بطون راح

and Akhṭal's

قوم اذا استنبح الاضياف كلابهم   قالوا لامهم بولى على النار

respectively. Hārūn al-Rashīd promptly countered in each instance with verses from Bashshār which he considered even better.[69]

Bedouin partiality for Jarīr cannot be explained entirely by the fact that his outlook and verse, rather than the outlook and poetry of such city dwellers as Akhṭal and ʿAdī ibn al-Riqāʿ, typified their poetry, for Farazdaq's poetry reflected much of the same Bedouin approach. Farazdaq's overbearing personality in contrast to that of the more congenial Jarīr may have accounted in part for the latter's popularity among contemporary Bedouins.

With the passing of time and the rise of a new generation of poets, some knowledgeable Bedouins still proclaimed Jarīr superior to all the Arab poets[70] while others were considering the possibility that Sayyid al-Ḥimyarī had surpassed him.[71] On the whole, however, even non-Bedouin literary scholars and critics of the second century and after were remarkably loyal to and appreciative of the poetry of Jarīr, Farazdaq, and Akhṭal, whom they ranked in this order it would seem, though only an exhaustively programmed computer could yield a final answer to the question of the relative merit of Jarīr and Farazdaq. Nevertheless, the order assumed above is repeatedly indicated if we judge by the number and the frequency of citations of their respective verses as representative of the best in the major categories of Arabic poetry and in a growing list of other themes that lent themselves to poetic expression.[72] Celebrated verses of ranking poets were usually grouped together under such headings as *muqalladāt al-shuʿarāʾ* or *qalāʾid al-shuʿarāʾ* and were further characterized as apt, or readily quotable, or proverbial, or unmatchable.[73]

[66] See *Aghānī* VII 177, where he cites verses in each category to support his claim.

[67] *Shiʿr*, pp. 305 f.; Jumaḥī, pp. 404 f.; *Aghānī* VII 183 f.; *Muwashshaḥ*, pp. 133–36.

[68] *Aghānī* III 26. See Ḍiyāʾ al-Dīn Naṣr Allāh ibn Muḥammad ibn al-Athīr, *Al-mathal al-sāʾir fī adab al-kātib wa al-shāʿir*, p. 489, for Bashshār's exalted opinion of his own poetic talent; for his opinion of our three poets, which places Jarīr first and Akhṭal last, see e.g. Jumaḥī, pp. 315 and 319 f., *Aghānī* VII 40, *Muwashshaḥ*, pp. 115 f., and 138, Ibn ʿAsākir V 426.

[69] See *Dīwān Bashshār ibn Burd*, ed. Muḥammad al-Ṭāhir ibn ʿĀshūr I 70 f. and 110, III (1376/1957) 270 f.

[70] The statement is credited to Abū Mahdīyah (or Abū Mahdī), a Bedouin philologist of Baṣrah, who is also credited with praying that Allāh would forgive Jarīr for his satire of the Banū Qais (*Aghānī* VII 69 f.; *Maʿārif*, p. 271). For Abū Mahdīyah see e.g. *Marātib*, p. 40, Zubaidī, pp. 38 f. and 175, *Fihrist*, p. 46.

[71] *Aghānī* VII 6 f.

[72] See e.g. Ibn Abī ʿAwn, *Kitāb al-tashbīhāt*, pp. 415–19, for a list of 99 topics which is not even exhaustive; see also ʿAskarī, *Maṣūn*, pp. 14–51 *et passim*.

[73] For representative groupings of such celebrated verses see e.g. Jumaḥī, pp. 305–12, 349–55, and 425–33, for Farazdaq, Jarīr, and Akhṭal respectively; *Shiʿr*, pp. 7–9, for all three poets; *ʿUyūn* II 191–97, esp. pp. 195 f. for Jarīr and Akhṭal; Ibn Ṭabāṭabā, pp. 24–31, 48, 58 f.; *Muwashshaḥ*, pp. 115–32, for the three poets; *Muʿjam al-shuʿarāʾ*, pp. 486 f.; Thaʿālibī, *Ījāz*, pp. 41–43; *ʿUmdah* II 138 f.; *Irshād* VII 259 f.

The Christian Akhṭal, so definitely associated with the Umayyads, came to be neglected under the ʿAbbāsids. Farazdaq's verses, on the other hand, were more likely than not to be apt, but they were just as likely to be so obscene or vituperative that, for reasons of decency, they were practically unquotable.

No parallel has yet come to light for the conversation between the caliph Hishām and a Bedouin[74] that is reported in our papyrus text—a conversation which has, so far as it goes, much in common with that of ʿAbd al-Malik and the Bedouin of the Banū ʿUdhrah (as seen above). In all probability, the account represented by our papyrus text included at least two more citations from Jarīr, that is, the heroic verse and the erotic verse cited by the Bedouin to ʿAbd al-Malik. Prince Hishām, who was fourteen years old when ʿAbd al-Malik died in 86/705,[75] may or may not have been present at the public banquet which was the occasion for the conversation between that caliph and the Bedouin. In any case, Akhṭal praised the young prince and received the disappointing reward of only 500 dirhems, which he distributed to some youths.[76] We first hear of Hishām's personal association with Akhṭal, Jarīr, and Farazdaq when he was nineteen years old,[77] that is, in 91/710 and therefore in the reign of his brother Walīd I. Hishām confronted the three poets with a she-camel and the first hemistich of a verse which he asked each poet to complete—a common literary pastime. The camel was to be the reward for the best second half of the verse. Akhṭal won, yet the prince begrudged him the promised prize.[78] We learn on the authority of ʿUtbī, whose manuscripts were available after his death (see p. 77), that Hishām was again with our three poets, still in the reign of Walīd I since Akhṭal died before that caliph, when his interest in their poetry was on a much higher level. Having first scolded them for their unending rivalries and the disturbing effects on their families and tribes, the prince asked for opinions on the three poets first from a kinsman of Farazdaq, whose answers merely echoed a current opinion on the comparative merits of the three.[79] Present on this occasion was Khālid ibn Ṣafwān, on whom the prince now called for more meaningful opinions. Khālid's lengthy statement is illustrative of his perception, prudence, and rhymed-prose style. Four lines of printed text are devoted to Farazdaq, one and a half to Jarīr, and only one line to Akhṭal, yet Khālid managed to please not only Hishām and his half-brother Maslamah, who likewise expressed his appreciation in rhymed prose, but also each of the three poets.[80] Hishām's interest in poetry, especially in the pre-Islāmic heritage, grew as he reached maturity. His personal interest in the contemporary poets was less marked and hardly comparable to that of his father, ʿAbd al-Malik, or his brothers Walīd I and Yazīd II. The renowned poets of his early days, including Akhṭal and Kuthaiyir, had passed on before his caliphate began, and the careers of Jarīr and Farazdaq were soon to end in death. Hishām was overly sensitive to personal

[74] Anecdotes involving Hishām and Bedouins seem to be scarce. Hishām, being a recluse by nature, was not likely to have had much use for the Bedouins, and thus our papyrus text is rather exceptional in this respect. Ṣūlī, *Adab al-kuttāb*, p. 65, reports a chance encounter, on the pilgrimage road, of Hishām and an illiterate Bedouin whose graphic description of each of the letters of the word خمسة on a milestone told Hishām that he had 5 miles still to go.

[75] Hishām must have been born in 72/691 or 692 though his age at death is variously given as 52, 54, and 55 (Ṭabarī II 1729; Ibn al-Athīr, *Al-kāmil fī al-taʾrīkh* IV 517 and V 122).

[76] *Aghānī* VII 180: قال هشام قبحه الله ما ضرَّ الا نفسه.

[77] *Ibid.*

[78] *Ibid.*: فقال هشام اركبها لا حملك الله.

[79] *Aghānī* VII 73, lines 13–14: اما جرير فيغرف من بحر واما الفرزدق فينحت من صخر واما الاخطل فيجيد المدح والفخر (see p. 141 below for the full text). There is some confusion as to the name and identity of this speaker, who was either Farazdaq's paternal cousin and brother-in-law Shabbah (or Sabbah) ibn ʿAqqāl (or ʿIqāl) or the latter's son ʿAqqāl ibn Shabbah (see Ṭabarī II 1731; Jumaḥī, pp. 387, n. 5, and 391; cf. ʿ*Uyūn* IV 75). Dhahabī, *Al-mushtabih fī al-rijāl*, ed. ʿAlī Muḥammad al-Bajāwī (Cairo, 1962) II 465, specifies ʿAqqāl ibn Shabbah as the correct form of the name.

[80] *Aghānī* VII 73, lines 15–21; *Irshād* IV 160 f.; Baihaqī, pp. 458 f. Khālid came from a family of orators (*Shiʿr*, p. 402); for further samples of his prose see p. 141 below. Prince Maslamah (d. 122/740) was better known as a general and a governor who took interest in archeology (see our Vol. I 55).

remarks[81] and less tolerant than ʿAbd al-Malik of a poet's religious and political allegiances.[82] His increasing aloofness and miserliness did not encourage the poets to persist in seeking him when a warmer welcome and richer rewards could be had first at the court of Yazīd II and then at that of Hishām's alienated nephew and heir Prince Walīd ibn Yazīd (see pp. 91–93), not to mention the patronage of rival governors and generals. Yet, Hishām could be touched by a poet's sincere verses, as in the case of the Medinan ʿUrwah ibn Udhainah, who, when accused by Hishām of economic motives only, left before the rewards were distributed. Convinced that he had misjudged the poet, Hishām sent him double the reward that the others had received.[83] He was annoyed at Nuṣaib's delay in coming to congratulate him on his accession, but on learning that illness had been the cause of the delay Hishām rewarded Nuṣaib well.[84] Even his rage against the Shīʿite schoolteacher-poet Kumait ibn Zaid for his bold *Hāshimīyāt*[85] was dispelled by that poet's touching elegy on Hishām's recently deceased son Muʿāwiyah, which brought tears to the caliph's eyes and a pardon and rich reward for the pro-ʿAlīd poet.[86] He could relent enough in his antagonism to replace earlier threats with cordiality and patronage, as in the case of Ḥammād al-Rāwiyah. Hishām as prince had threatened Ḥammād for partiality to his brother Yazīd II, but as caliph he summoned Ḥammād from ʿIrāq to the court in Damascus so that he could be informed and entertained with Ḥammād's vast knowledge of Arabic poetry, history, and especially the characteristics of the pre-Islāmic period.[87]

The quarter-century following Hishām's reign saw the transition from Umayyad to ʿAbbāsid rule and climaxed in the literary career of Abū ʿAmr ibn al-ʿAlāʾ, whose influence left a pervasive and lasting effect on the entire field of Arabic language and literature. His own somewhat belated conviction that Islāmic poetry such as that of Dhū al-Rummah, whom he considered the last of the classical poets,[88] and that of Akhṭal, Jarīr, and Farazdaq merited study and inclusion in his teaching program[89] did not go far enough for either Abū ʿAmr or his pupil and transmitter Aṣmaʿī to place Islāmic poets on a par with those of pre-Islāmic times.[90] Though in his old age Abū ʿAmr saw fit to destroy his large private library, his theories and personal views were nevertheless quickly propagated by his earlier pupils such as ʿĪsā ibn ʿUmar and Yūnus ibn Ḥabīb and his still younger pupils Abū ʿUbaidah, Aṣmaʿī, and Abū Zaid al-Anṣārī.[91] They

[81] For example, he was angered at Abū al-Najm al-ʿIjlī for referring to him as squint-eyed, which he was (*Shiʿr*, pp. 382 f.; *Aghānī* IX 79 f.).

[82] For instance, he imprisoned Farazdaq for his praise of Ḥasan ibn ʿAlī, better known as Zain al-ʿĀbidīn, during the pilgrimage of the year 90/709 (*Aghānī* XIX 40 f.; Ibn Khallikān I 264 f. [= trans. III 621 f.]). He resented the allegiance of both Ḥammād al-Rāwiyah and Nābighah al-Shaibānī to his brother Yazīd (see e.g. *Aghānī* V 166 and VI 152 respectively).

[83] See e.g. *Shiʿr*, pp. 367 f.; *Aghānī* XXI 165; *ʿIqd* II 183–85.

[84] *Aghānī* I 148. See also p. 112 above.

[85] Autograph copies must have been available since the caliph ordered the poet's tongue and hand cut off, but the order could not be executed because the poet escaped from prison and went into hiding (*Aghānī* XV 114 f.; Jumaḥī, pp. 268 f.).

[86] *Aghānī* XV 116 f., 121; *ʿIqd* II 183; Zubaidī, p. 278.

[87] *Aghānī* V 166 f. and XX 174 f.; Ibn Khallikān I 206 f. (= trans. I 471 f.).

[88] Jāḥiẓ, *Bayān* III 372 f.; *Aghānī* XVI 113; Qurashī, p. 35; *ʿUmdah* I 56.

[89] Jāḥiẓ, *Bayān* I 308: كان ابو عمرو بن العلاء يقول لقد كثر هذا المحدث وحسن حتى هممت ان آمر فتياننا بروايته (cf. *Shiʿr*, p. 5 and *ʿUmdah* I 56 f., which uses the term هذا المولد and gives Ibn Rashīq's comment on its literary significance). Abū ʿAmr's earlier attitude was quite different, as indicated by Aṣmaʿī's report that he had studied for ten years under Abū ʿAmr without having heard him cite a single Islāmic verse as *ḥijjah*, i.e. authoritative (Jāḥiẓ, *Bayān* I 308). Furthermore, Abū ʿAmr's earlier opinion, as expressed to Abū ʿUbaidah, was that the contemporary poets were at best no more than imitators and at worst originators of abominable poetry: كل على غيرهم ان قالوا حسنا فقد سبقوا اليه وان قالوا قبيحا فمن عندهم (*Aghānī* XVI 113). See Ibn Khallikān I 513 (= trans. II 451) for a different version which reads مرقعون مهذبون انما هم كلّ على غيرهم and has been translated "They are patchers and botchers and a burden to all but themselves."

[90] See *Fuḥūlat al-shuʿarāʾ* pp. 495 f.; *Aghānī* VII 172.

[91] *Marātib*, pp. 21–23, 39 f.

became increasingly interested in Islāmic poetry, and their personal views of the respective merits of the poets of the Umayyad period, particularly Akhṭal, Jarīr, and Farazdaq, formed the basis of a comparatively more objective view of Islāmic poetry as a whole and of its relation to the pre-Islāmic product. We find, for instance, the linguist and poet Ibn Munādhir, an admirer of ʿAdī ibn Zaid al-ʿIbādī, whom he took for a model, cautioning Abū ʿUbaidah to judge his poetry and that of ʿAdī not by its period but on its merit.[92] A new turn to the controversy over the relative merits of the "ancients" and the "moderns" developed as Islāmic poetry presently found advocates in such critics as Jumaḥī,[93] Jāḥiẓ,[94] and Ibn Qutaibah.[95] Furthermore, the activities of Ḥammād al-Rāwiyah and Mufaḍḍal ibn Muḥammad al-Ḍabbī in collecting and preserving some at least of the earlier poetry, reinforced by the collections of the Kūfan Abū ʿAmr al-Shaibānī and his followers, supplied much of the material for a nascent scheme but hardly yet for a theory of literary criticism. Nevertheless, these scholars and their contemporaries provided much of the source material for the increasingly complex and comprehensive commentaries of the third century and after for the *dīwān*'s of both pre-Islāmic and Islāmic poets.

MODES OF EARLY LITERARY CRITICISM

I

We had occasion in connection with Document 3 to discuss at some length the basic characteristics of Arabic secular prose as illustrated in the categories of public speaking and descriptive composition from the eve of Islām to about the mid-second/mid-eighth century (see pp. 56–78). The linguistic and stylistic qualities which were generally accepted throughout that period were precision, clarity, economy of words, and a sense of rhythm. That these same qualities were demanded in other types of prose literature can be readily seen from a liberal sampling of the speeches and aphorisms of the Christian Quss ibn Sāʿidah of Najrān, whom Muḥammad and Abū Bakr were said to have heard in Sūq ʿUkkāẓ, and from the sermons and sayings on many phases of life that were accepted as his and came to be admired in early Islāmic times.[96] Though he was confused with an earlier legendary figure, Quss's aphorisms and literary style were referred to in proverbially superlative terms.[97] From the samplings of prose literature, other than

[92] *Aghānī* XVII 12: اتق الله واحكم بين شعرى وشعر عدى بن زيد ولا تقول ذلك جاهلي وهذا محدث فتحكم بين العصرين ولكن احكم بين الشعرين ودع العصبية. See *ibid.* XVII 15 and 27 f. for further relationship between Ibn Munādhir and Abū ʿUbaidah. Ibn Munādhir was rebuffed by Khalaf al-Aḥmad for comparing himself to the ranking classical poets (*ibid.* XVII 11 f.). For Aṣmaʿī's opinion of this ʿAdī ibn Zaid see *Fuḥūlat al-shuʿarā'*, p. 494. For the life and times of ʿAdī see *OIP* L 5 f., 13.

[93] See Jumaḥī, Intro. pp. 15 f. and 21 f.

[94] Jāḥiẓ, as usual, saw the two sides of the controversy. He gave due recognition to the "ancients" but denied the concept that they could not be surpassed or even equaled: قال الجاحظ ما على الناس شى اضرّ من قو لهم ما ترك الاول للآخر شيئا (*Khaṣā'iṣ* I 190 f.); قال الجاحظ اذا سمعت الرجل يقول ما ترك الاول لآخر شيئا فاعلم انه ما يريد ان يفلح (*Irshād* VI 58).

[95] *Shiʿr*, pp. 5 f.; see also n. 205 on p. 101 above and Abū Ḥātim al-Sijistānī, *Kitāb al-muʿammarīn* (Goldziher, *Abhandlungen zur arabischen Philologie* II) pp. 122–74, esp. pp. 143–74.

[96] Jāḥiẓ, *Bayān* I 57 f., 76–78, 297, and 343, II 276; Abū Ḥātim al-Sijistānī, *Kitāb al-muʿammarīn*, pp. 76–78; Baihaqī, pp. 351–56, 426; *ʿIqd* II 254 and IV 128; *Aghānī* XIV 41–43; *Amālī* II 39 f.; Thaʿālibī, *Thimār*, pp. 94 f., 99, 185; ʿAskarī, *Maṣūn*, p. 179; Ibn ʿAsākir I 356–60; *Khizānah* I 267. *Fihrist*, p. 63, mentions Ibn Durustawaih's *Khabar Quss ibn Sāʿidah*, which has survived in four folios; see Arthur J. Arberry (ed.), *The Chester Beatty Library: A Handlist of the Arabic Manuscripts* VII (Dublin, 1964) 151, No. 5498 (8).

[97] See e.g. ʿAbd al-Raḥmān ibn ʿĪsā al-Hamadhānī, *Kitāb al-alfaẓ al-kitābīyah*, ed. Louis Cheikho (Beirūt, 1913) p. 298: تقول العرب انطق من قس بن ساعدة (see also Abū Ḥātim al-Sijistānī, *Kitāb al-muʿammarīn*, p. 76); Masʿūdī, I 133 f.: قال اعشى قيس احكم من قس. Thaʿālibī, *Thimār*, pp. 94 f., repeats these two proverbs and adds three more beginning with اخطب, اعقل, and ابلغ respectively. Maidānī, *Al-majmaʿ al-amthāl* I 117 has ابلغ من قس (see also Ḍiyā' al-Dīn Naṣr Allāh ibn Muḥammad ibn al-Athīr, *Al-jāmiʿ al-kabīr*, pp. 73 f.).

descriptions of maidens and women, of such stylists as ʿAmr ibn al-ʿĀṣ, Ṣaʿṣaʿah ibn Ṣūḥān, Aḥnaf ibn Qais, Ibn al-Qirrīyah, and Khālid ibn Ṣafwān—all cited in connection with Document 3—it is clear that the basic literary qualities that were admired by the first generation of Muslims continued to be admired into early ʿAbbāsid times. For apart from the leading Umayyad secretarial essayists, namely the Arab ʿAbd al-Ḥamīd ibn Yaḥyā and the Persian Ibn al-Muqaffaʿ, whose essays reflected Persian influence in practice and style, none made an effort to develop a formal system of literary critique of prose during this period. Their contemporaries were, for the most part, content to follow the taste and example of the eloquent among the Bedouins, as Khālid ibn Ṣafwān expressly affirmed.[98]

Turning our attention now to pre-ʿAbbāsid Islāmic poetry, we again find no system of formal literary critique in the period under consideration. Nevertheless, there are some patterns that indicate a reaching-out for forms of criticism and a number of individual statements by scholars and poets that were meaningful enough to form collectively a tentative base for a later theory of literary criticism. This development was to be expected in view of the longer history of Arabic poetry and the fact that there was much greater preoccupation with poetry than with prose, alike on the part of rulers and rebels, linguists and literary scholars, and the cultured and affluent upper classes. There was, therefore, greater incentive for the poets of the period to produce and to compete for the power, prestige, and economic rewards that the imperial and provincial courts and high society held out to them, especially to the forerunners among them. The role of the early Islāmic linguists as literary critics has received considerable attention from modern scholars while that of the professional poets has been comparatively neglected, no doubt, in part at least because of the belief that literary critics made poor poets and poets made poor literary critics. Despite the several grains of truth in this concept, there are exceptions, more perhaps in the case of poets than in the case of scholar-critics.[99] Furthermore, except for Abū ʿAmr ibn al-ʿAlāʾ, the period under consideration produced no philologists who were deeply involved with the literary criticism of poetry. But it did produce many master poets, some of whom were vocal critics of their fellow professionals and at times ventured or were prodded into self-criticism. The subjective element in their criticism could hardly have been avoided in a society marked by tribal, political, and religious rivalry, from which the poets' patrons and the scholar-critics also were not exempt. Therefore, in order to examine the role of poets in early literary criticism, we present the texts of representative statements from several leading poets of the Umayyad period, selected to give a closer view of both the continuity with the past and the emergence of new approaches to and modes of poetry criticism. Analysis of these and similar statements in the light of the earliest extant work on the subject, namely Aṣmaʿī's *Fuḥūlat al-shuʿarāʾ*, should enable us to relate to models and theories of Arabic literary criticism of the third/ninth century and after.

Oral literary criticism of Arabic poetry dates back to pre-Islāmic times and antedates that of prose. For our purpose we need to go no farther back than the eve of Islām. Accounts of poets' contests held in Sūq ʿUkkāẓ name the winner but tell us little or nothing of the bases on which the contests were judged. The judge was usually a sage or a poet, or he combined the two functions as in the case of Hind bint al-Khuss, who was tested in both prose and poetry (see p. 64). More fruitful is the account of a contest presided over by the poet Nābighah al-Dhubyānī, who ranked Aʿshā Maimūn and the poetess Khansāʾ ahead of the still heathen Ḥassān ibn Thābit. Ḥassān challenged the verdict and demanded to know the basis on which it was made. Nābighah's answer is reported in two accounts, one that traces back through Aṣmaʿī to Abū ʿAmr ibn al-ʿAlāʾ and a somewhat fuller one whose *isnād* goes no farther back than Ibn Qutaibah and

[98] Jāḥiẓ, *Bayān* I 184 (see also n. 239 on p. 74 above); *Adāb al-Shāfiʿī*, pp. 316 f. Jāḥiẓ, *Bayān* I 102 gives a number of definitions for *balāghah*.

[99] Khalaf al-Aḥmar, for example, was considered a good scholar-critic and poet while his famous contemporaries Khalīl ibn Aḥmad and Aṣmaʿī were credited with little or no poetic ability (see p. 97, n. 158).

includes Khansāʾ's protest against Nābighah for allowing sex discrimination to influence his decision.[100] Ibn Qutaibah's account as reported in the *Aghānī* of Abū al-Faraj al-Iṣfahānī reads as follows:

أن نابغة بنى ذبيان كان تضرب له قبة من أدم بسوق عكاظ يجتمع اليه فيها الشعراء فدخل اليه حسّان بن ثابت وعنده الاعشى وقد انشده شعره وانشدته الخنساء قولها — قذى بعينك ام بالعين عوّار — حتى انتهت الى قولها

وانّ صخراً لتأتم الهداة به   كانه علَمٌ فى راسه نار
وانّ صخرا لمولانا وسيّدنا   وان صخرا إذا نشتو لنحار

فقال (النابغة) لولا ان ابا بصير (الاعشى) انشدنى قبلك لقلت انك اشعر الناس انت والله اشعر من كل ذات مثانة فقالت والله ومن كل ذات خصيتين فقال حسّان انا والله اشعر منك ومنها قال حيث تقول ماذا قال (حسان) حيث اقول

لنا الجفنات الغُرّ يلمعن بالضحى   واسيافنا يقطرن من نجدة دما
ولدنا بنى العنقاء وابنى محرّق   فاكرم بنا خالا واكرم بنا ابنما

فقال (النابغة) انكَ لشاعر لولا انك قللت عدد جفناك وفخرت بمن ولدت ولم تفخر بمن ولدك. وفى رواية اخرى فقال له انك قلت الجفنات فقللت العدد ولو قلت الجفان لكان اكثر وقلت يلمعن فى الضحى ولو قلت يبرقن بالدجى لكان ابلغ فى المديح لان الضيف بالليل اكثر طروقا وقلت يقطرن من نجدة دما فدللت على قلة القتل ولو قلت يجرين لكان اكثر لانصباب الدم وفخرت بمن ولدت ولم تفخر بمن ولدك فقام حسّان منكسرا منقطعا

Note in particular Nābighah's specific and factual criticism, point by point, of Ḥassān's poor choice of words, his lack of emphasis on pride of ancestry, and his failure to use sufficiently strong hyperbole in heroic poetry.

Our next specimen comes from the time of ʿAbdah ibn al-Ṭabīb, who, along with Zuhair ibn Abī Sulmā, was favored by ʿUmar I. ʿUmar was himself a knowledgeable and respected critic of contemporary poetry[101] though both he and Abū Bakr, among other leading Companions, favored and cited only such verses as were compatible with Islām. Before their conversion to Islām, ʿAbdah and several of his fellow Tamīmite poets would gather for a festive outing with wine flowing freely. After all had recited some of their poetry, they would call for an exchange of candid opinions or seek a verdict on the respective merits of their verses from any knowledgeable person present. Their opinions, particularly that of ʿAbdah, are of interest, despite their subjectivity, for their frankness, for their positive as well as their negative approach, and for the literary quality of their brief yet succinct prose with its household and desert similes. These characteristics emerge despite the lapse of time and the different versions available. Some versions are

[100] For the account that traces back to Abū ʿAmr see *Muwashshaḥ*, pp. 60 f., and see also *Aghānī* IX 163; for Ibn Qutaibah's account see *Shiʿr*, pp. 197 f., and *Aghānī* VIII 194 f. See also *Amālī* III 118 and *Khizānah* III 432. *Muwashshaḥ*, p. 60, records Ṣūlī's admiration of Nābighah's critical acumen: قال الصولى فانظر الى هذا النقد الجليل الذى يدل على نقاء كلام النابقة وديباجة شعره. Ḥassān was envious of Nābighah's poetry and the rich rewards it brought him from Nuʿmān ibn al-Mundhir (see e.g. Qurashī, pp. 27 f.). For a more recent appreciation of Nābighah see ʿAbd Allāh ʿAbd al-Jabbār and Muḥammad ʿAbd al-Munʿim Khafājā, *Qiṣṣat al-adab fī al-Ḥijāz* (Cairo, 1377/1958) pp. 392–406, 637–74.

The ode that Khansāʾ recited at Sūq ʿUkkāẓ expressed praise and mourning for her brother Ṣakhr and is cited in the sources only in parts which when combined yield a poem of more than 36 verses. See e.g. Mubarrad, p. 737; *Shiʿr*, p. 201; *ʿIqd* III 267 f.; *Aghānī* XIII 138; *Dīwān al-Khansāʾ*, ed. Karam al-Bustānī (Beirūt, 1960) pp. 47–50. See also *GAL* I 40 and *GAL* S I 70.

The manuscript collection of Mr. H. P. Kraus of New York contains a 2nd/8th-century papyrus fragment (No. P129) written in small but fine Kūfic-*naskhī* script and consisting of a 7-verse ode of Khansāʾ in praise and mourning for her brother Ṣakhr. This short ode with some variation is found in the sources but sometimes with a verse or two missing or a verse added.

[101] Jāḥiẓ, *Bayān* I 243 f.; *Aghānī* IX 162; Thaʿālibī, *Ījāz*, p. 41. See *Maṣādir*, pp. 204–14, for the lively interest of ʿUmar I and his contemporaries in poetry.

condensed, others are composite accounts, while still others include transmitter's or author's comments, mostly glosses, and most are well fortified with multiple *isnād*'s. Abū al-Faraj al-Iṣfahānī's account, which traces back to Aṣmaʿī, Muḥammad ibn Ḥabīb, Muḥammad ibn al-ʿAbbās and other members of the Yazīdī family, reads as follows:

اخبرنا ابن زيد عن عبد الرحمن عن عمه (الاصمعى) واخبرنا محمد بن العباس اليزيدى قال حدثنى عمى عبيد الله عن (محمد) بن حبيب واخبرنى عمى قال حدثنا الكرانى قال حدثنا العمرى عن لقيط قالوا اجتمع الزبرِقان بن بدر والمخبل السعدىّ وعَبْدة بن الطبيب بن عمرو بن الأهتم قبل أن يُسلِموا وبعدَ مبعث النبى صلى الله عليه وسلم فنَحَروا جَزُوراً واشترَوا خمراً ببعير وجلسوا يشوون ويأكلون فقال بعضهم لو أنّ قوماً طاروا من جَودة أشعارهم لِطرْنا فتحاكموا إلى أوّل من يَطْلُعُ عليهم فطلع عليهم ربيعة بن حُذار الأسدىّ وقال اليزيدى فجاءهم رجل من بنى يربوعٍ يسأل عنهم فدَلّ عليهم وقد نزلوا بطن وادٍ وهم جلوس يشربون فلما رأوه سرهم وقالوا له أخبرا أينُا أشعرُ قال أخاف أن تغضبوا فآمَنُوه من ذلك فقال أمّا عمرو فشعره برودٌ يمنية تنشر وتطوى وأما أنت يا زبرقان فكأنك رجل أتى جزورا قد نُحِرت فأخذ من أطايبِها وخلطه بغير ذلك وقال لقيط فى خبره قال له ربيعة بن حُذار وأمّا أنت يا زبرقان فشعرك كلحم لم ينضج فيؤكلَ ولم يُترَك نيئا فيُنْتفَعَ به وأما أنت يا مخبَّلُ فشعرك شُهُب من نار الله يلقيها على من يشاء وأما أنت يا عبدة فشعرك كمزادةٍ أُحكِم خزرها فليس يقطر منها شىء

And Marzubānī's account, with other *isnād*'s, reads:

كتب الىّ أحمد بن عبد العزيز أخبرنا عمربن شبة قال حدّثنى عبد الله بن محمد بن حكيم الطائى قال حدّثنا خالد بن سعيد بن عمرو بن سعيد عن أبيه قال تحاكم الزِّبْرِقانُ بن بدر وعمرو بن الأهتم وعَبْدَةُ بن الطبيب والمخبَّل السعدى الى ربيعة بن حذار الاسدى فى الشعر أيهم أشعر فقال للزبرقان أما أنت فشعرك كلحم أسخن لا هو أُنصج فأكل ولا ترك نيئاً فينتفع به وأما أنت ياعمرو فان شعرك كبرود حبر يتلألأ فيها البصر فكلما أعيد فيها النظر نقص البصر وما أنت يامخبل فان شعرك قصّر عن شعرهم وارتفع عن شعر غيرهم وأما أنت يا عبدةُ فان شعرك كمَزادةٍ أُحكم خرزُها فليس تقطر ولا تمطر حدثنا ابن دريد قال حدثنا السكن بن سعيد عن محمد بن عباد عن ابن الكلبى قال ابن دريد وأخبرنى عمى يعنى الحسين بن دريد عن أبيه عن ابن الكلبى قال حدثنى خالد بن سعيد عن أبيه وكتب الى أحمد بن عبد العزيز أخبرنا عمر بن شبة قال حدّثنى عبد الله بن محمد بن حكيم الطائى قال حدثنا خالد بن سعيد بن عمرو بن سعيد عن أبيه قال اجتمع الزبرقان بن بدر وعمرو ابن الأهتم وعبدة بن الطبيب والمخبَّل التميميون فى موضع فتناشدوا أشعارهم فقال لهم عبدة والله لو أن قوما طاروا من جودة الشعر لطرتم فاما أن تخبرونى عن أشعاركم وإما أن أخبركم قالوا أخبرْنا قال فانى أبدأُ بنفسى أما شعرى فمثل سقاء وكيع — وهو الشديد يصطنعه الرجل فلا يسرب عليه أى لا يقطر — وغيره من الاسقية أوسع منَه وأما أنت يا زبرقان فانك مررت بجزور منحورة فاخذت من أطايبها واخابثها وأما أنت يامخبل فان شعرك العلاط والعِراض قال العلاط مِيسَم الابل فى العنق والعواض سمة فى عرض الفخذ [102]

Ḥuṭai'ah (d. 30 or 59 or 69 A.H.), because of his roving life, sharp tongue, and unsociable personality,[103] was not disposed to lengthy critical discourses with others on poetry or any other subject. He displayed considerable originality and spent much time polishing his odes to achieve the high degree of uniform

[102] For these two accounts see *Aghānī* XII 44 (= *Aghānī* [1927——] XIII 197 f.) and *Muwashshaḥ*, pp. 75 f., respectively. See also *Iṣābah* III 199 f. For some of ʿAbdah's poems see e.g. *Shiʿr*, pp. 456 f., and *Mufaḍḍalīyāt* I 268–304 and 575, II 92–104. For 2nd-century evaluation of ʿAbdah as a poet see e.g. Jāḥiẓ, *Bayān* II 362 f., and *Aghānī* XVIII 163 f.

[103] See e.g. *Aghānī* II 52; cf. Ignaz Goldziher, "Der Dîwân des Ǧarwal b. Aus Al-Ḥuṭej'a," *ZDMG* XLVI (1892) 1–53, esp. pp. 1–31.

proficiency on account of which he and several other poets were characterized as the "slaves of poetry" and their poetry was faulted by Aṣmaʿī and others for its monotony of labored excellence.[104] Ḥuṭai'ah, despite his mercenary motives, was so wholly involved with his art that he is credited with statements in verse and prose that reflect his thoughts on the temperament and effort needed to produce and preserve effective and accurate poetry. He expressed his fourfold classification of poets[105] in verse:

الشعراء فـــاعلمن اربعة   فشاعر لا يرـ تجي لمنفعـــه
وشاعر ينشد وسط المجمعه   وشاعر يجري ولا يجرى معه
وشاعر يقال خمر في دعه

We have a dramatic account from Abū 'Ubaidah of Ḥuṭai'ah's deathbed scene, when, despite the urgings of those around him to express his last wishes and prepare to meet his God, he persisted in reciting verses from some of the best poets and concluded with his own verses

الشعر صعب وطويل سُلمه   والشعر لا يطيعه من يضلمه
اذا ارتقى فيه الذى لا يعلمه   زلت به الى الخضيض قدمه
يريد ان يعربه فيعجمه

and added وليل للشعر من راوية السوء.[106]

We turn next to Baʿīth, who ranked high among his contemporaries and among later critics as both orator and poet.[107] His bold but well founded and point-by-point criticisms of older and well established poets, including Akhṭal, Jarīr, and Farazdaq, won the admiration of Walīd I and his half-brother Maslamah. For the young but stout-hearted poet referred to his professional elders derisively. He called Farazdaq a fool and Jarīr a dog, playing on the latter's tribal affiliation. He spoke derisively of the Christian Akhṭal's faith and called Ibn Rumailah a betrayer of his own brother. He displayed precise knowledge of weaknesses in their verses that not only missed their aim but boomeranged on points of literary or moral defect in each instance. Walīd I was both surprised and pleased and rewarded Baʿīth well. We read as follows:

وكتب الى أحمد بن عبد العزيز أخبرنا عمر أن شبة قال يقال انه اجتمع على باب الوليد بن عبد الملك الفرزدق وجرير والاخطل والبعيث والاشهب بن رُميلة فدخل عليه داخل فقال يا أمير المؤمنين لقد اجتمع على بابك شعراء ما اجتمع مثلهم على باب ملك قط ثم سماهم فأمر بالفرزدق فأدخل أولهم فاستنشده وحادثة ثم أمر بالباقين فأدخلوا وأخّر البعيث فقيل له فى البعيث فقال انه ليس كهؤلاء فقيل له ما هو بدونهم فأمر به فأدخل ثم استنشده فقال يا أمير المؤمنين ان من حضرك ظنوا أنك انما قدمتهم علىّ لفضل وجدته عندهم لم تجده عندى قال أولست تعلم أنهم أشعر منك قال كلا والله ولأنشدنك من أشعارهم ما لو هجاهم أعدى الناس لهم ما بلغ منهم ما بلغوا من أنفسهم أما هذا الشيخ الاحمق وأشار الى الفرزدق فانه قال لعُبيد بنى كليب هذا وأشار الى جرير

بأىّ رِشاء ياجريرُ ومـــاتـــح   تدلَّيْتَ فى حَوْمات تلك القماقم

فجعله تدلى عليه وعلى قومه وأما عُبيد بنى كليب وأشار الى جرير فقال لهذا الشيخ

[104] Jāḥiẓ, *Bayān* I 210 f. and II 8–13; *Muzhir* II 498. See also Goldziher in *ZDMG* XLVI 42 and Goldziher, *Abhandlungen zur arabischen Philologie* I (Leiden, 1896) 129–34.

[105] See Jāḥiẓ, *Bayān* II 9, editor's note. For other contemporary and later fourfold classifications of poets see e.g., Jāḥiẓ, *Bayān* II 8 f., '*Umdah* I 72–74, and *Muzhir* II 489–91.

[106] *Aghānī* II 59; '*Umdah* I 74; *Muzhir* II 490.

[107] Jāḥiẓ, *Bayān* I 210 f. and III 372 f.; *Shiʿr*, p. 313; '*Umdah* I 67 f.

لَقومِی أحمَی للحقیقة منکمُ　　وأضربُ للجبّار والنّقع ساطعُ
وأوثقُ عند المردفات عشيّةً　　لَحاقاً اذا ماجرّد السيف لامعُ

فجعل نساءه سبايا بالغداة قد نكحن ووثقن فى عشيتهن باللحاق وأما هذا ابن النصرانية يعنى الأخطل فانه قال

لقد أوقعَ الجحّافُ بالبِشر وقعة　　الى الله منها المشتكى والمعوّلُ

فأقرّ بما أقرّ به وهناً وجبناً وضعفاً وأما ابن رُميله الضعيف فانه قال

ولما رأيتُ القومَ ضُمّت حبالهم　　وَنى وَنيةً شرّى وما كان وانيا

فأقر أن شره ونى عنه وقت الحاجة اليه فقال له الوليد لعمرى لقد عبت معيبا ثم استنشده وأحسن جائزته قال الشيخ أبو عبيد الله المرزبانى رحمه الله تعالى وذكرُ الفرزدق فى هذا الحديث غلط لانه ما ورد على خليفة قبل سليمان بن عبد الملك[108]

The literary-minded Prince Maslamah once asked Baʿīth to name the best poets of the Arabs. Baʿīth replied in bold and far from complimentary terms naming Jarīr and Farazdaq and the two sons of Rumailah, Ashhab and Zabāb, as the best poets of the time but again pointed out specific weaknesses in some of their verses that he himself would not have been glad to have said, not even for love of a fortune in camels. We read:

. . . حدثنا لقيط بن بكير المحاربي قال قدم البَعيث على مَسْلَمة بن عبد الملك . . . ثم قال مسلمة للبَعيث حدثنى من أشعر العرب قال أعْيارٌ تركتها بالصَّمّان من بنى حنظلة يكتدمون قال ومن هم قال الفرزدق وجرير وابنا رُمَيلة — يعنى الاشهب وزَبابا ابنى رميلة — والله أصلح الله الأمير ما منهم رجل الا قد قال بيتا ما يسرني أني قلته ولي حمر النعم قال وما قالوا قال قال الفرزدق

لقد طَوَّفتْ فى كل حىّ فلم تجدْ　　لعَورتها كالحىّ بكر لن وائل
أعفّ وأوفى ذمّةً يعقدونها　　وخيراً اذا وازى الذرى بالكواهل

فكيف يفخر على بكربن وائل بعد هذا وما يقول لقومه واما جرير فقال

رُدّى جمالَ البَين ثم تحمّلى　　فمالكِ فيهم من مُقام ولا ليا

فأين يقيم ابن المراغة اذا لم يُقم فى عشيرته وقومه وأما ابن رميلة فقال

ولما رأيتُ القومَ نالتْ رماحُهم　　زَباباً وَنى شرّى وما كان وانيا

وكان أحرى أن لاينى شرُّه حين شك القوم زَباباً يعنى ابن رميلة اخا الاشهب بن رميلة[109]

The next poet to draw our attention in respect to modes of early literary criticism is the part-Negro slave Nuṣaib, who first came into public view when his owner's family in the Ḥijāz, on discovering his talent for poetry, decided to sell him. For they feared that he would address erotic verses to their women or satirize their men and so bring shame and dishonor to all of them.[110] The young Nuṣaib wished to have

108 *Muwashshaḥ*, pp. 165 f.; cf. *ʿIqd* V 368 f. and Ibn ʿAsakir V 123 f. See p. 118 above for Marzubānī's reaction concerning Farazdaq's presence at court prior to the reign of Sulaimān and my comment on his statement.

109 *Muwashshaḥ*, pp. 164 f.

110 Jumaḥī, pp. 545 f.: قد نبغ (نصيب) بقول الشعر ونحن منه بين شرّين اما ان يهجونا فيهتك اعراضنا او يمدحنا فيشبّب بنسائنا وليس لنا في شىء من الخلتين سيرة (see also Jāḥiẓ, *Bayān* I 221; *Shiʿr*, p. 242; *Aghānī* I 135). The Negro slave and poet Suḥaim, a contemporary of ʿUthmān ibn ʿAffān, was eventually put to death for bringing dishonor to his owners' families through his verses though he had once proclaimed his own moral virtue in the following among other verses:

وان كنتُ عبدا فنفسى حرة كرما　　او اسود اللون انى ابيض الخُلق

(see Jumaḥī, pp. 77 f., 143, 156 f.; *Aghānī* XXI 2–5; cf. *Fuḥūlat al-shuʿarāʾ*, p. 499).

ʿAbd al-ʿAzīz ibn Marwān, then governor of Egypt, for his owner and patron. He therefore made his way to that governor's palace and recited verses in his praise but refrained from accepting the prize of 1,000 dinars, pointing out that he as a slave was not entitled to prizes. There followed a dramatic slave-market scene in which Nuṣaib was being auctioned. From an initial bid of 50 (or 30) dinars for the man as a laborer, his price rose steadily as his specific abilities for taking good care of weapons and of camels were enumerated and finally reached 1,000 dinars, bid by ʿAbd al-ʿAzīz' agent as Nuṣaib's ability to compose poetry in perfect form was mentioned.[111] Thus began a mutually rewarding relationship between royal patron and emancipated poet. Nevertheless, the patronage of ʿAbd al-ʿAzīz and of several other members of the royal family after him did not suffice to remove the stigma of Nuṣaib's black color, particularly among contemporary poets competing for the same royal patronage. The first such poet to belittle Nuṣaib because of his color was Aiman ibn Khuraim, early in the eighth decade of Islām and in the presence of ʿAbd al-ʿAzīz himself. Asked by the governor what he thought of the poetry of Nuṣaib, Aiman replied pointedly that Nuṣaib was the best poet of all of the color of his skin. Enraged by this remark, ʿAbd al-ʿAzīz retorted "by Allāh he is a better poet than you are." Aiman, resentful of Nuṣaib and realizing that he himself was no longer welcome, requested that he be allowed to join the governor's brother Bishr ibn Marwān, then governor of ʿIrāq (71–74/690–93), and the request was granted.[112] This episode did not deter other poets, including Jarīr and Farazdaq, from expressing the same opinion later, but it did encourage Nuṣaib to resort to ʿAbd al-ʿAzīz' reply to Aiman and, further, to claim superiority over all.[113] This color prejudice once caused Prince Sulaimān, to whom ʿAbd al-ʿAzīz had commended Nuṣaib for protection, to dismiss Farazdaq without reward at the same time that Nuṣaib received a handsome prize, which in turn led the indignant Farazdaq to improvise the verse

وخير الشعر اشرفه رجالا   وشر الشعر ما قال العبيد

as he departed.[114] Kuthaiyir, himself physically unprepossessing, composed the verses

وايتُ ابا الحجناء في الناس جائزا   ولون ابي الحجناء لون البهائم
تراه على ما لاحه من سواده   وان كان مظلوما له وجه ظالم

to express his reaction to Nuṣaib's color and features.[115] Nuṣaib himself, when he was among well-wishers, was not reluctant to refer to his color and low origin. When ʿAbd al-ʿAzīz wished to include him in his inner circle of companions, the poet drew attention to these in terms that outdid Kuthaiyir's two verses:

اصلح الله الامير اللون مرمّد والشَعر مفلفل ولم اقعد اليك بكريم عنصر ولابحسن منظر وانما هو عقلي ولساني فان رايتَ ان لا تفرق بينهما فافعل[116]

[111] Jumaḥī, pp. 546 f.: انه شاعر عربي لا يطوى ولا يقوى ولايُساند; for the terms see e.g. *ibid.* pp. 56–64, Bevan II 1026, and *Aghānī* I 131 f. For definitions of these technical terms and illustrative verses of Dhū al-Rummah (see p. 190 below), Farazdaq, Jarīr, and ʿAdī ibn al-Riqāʿ among others see *Muwashshaḥ*, pp. 13–26, 99 f., and 132. *Shiʿr*, pp. 29 f. and 145 f., and *Muwashshaḥ*, p. 59, report that Bishr ibn Abī Khāzim was corrected by his brother for his error of *iqwāʾ*, an error committed by Nābighah al-Dhubyānī also.

[112] *Aghānī* I 131 f. and XXI 11 f.: قال ايمن هو اشعر اهل جلدته فقال (عبد العزيز) هو والله اشعر منك (see also *Fuḥūlat al-shuʿarāʾ*, p. 499).

[113] Jumaḥī, pp. 544 f.: قال جرير لنصيب اذهب فانت اشعر اهل جلدتك – وكان نصيب اسود – فقال وجلدتك يا ابا حزرة (see also *Aghānī* I 134 f., 142; ʿ*Umdah* I 44).

[114] Jumaḥī, pp. 547 f.; *Shiʿr*, pp. 242 f.; Mubarrad, p. 106; *Aghānī* I 134 f.; *Amālī* III 41; Ibn Khallikān II 261 (= trans. III 615); note that اكرمه alternates with اشرفه.

[115] *Shiʿr*, p. 242, and ʿ*Uyūn* IV 40. *Aghānī* I 140 has حائرا for جائزا. Kuthaiyir himself was ugly and short, and even ʿAbd al-ʿAzīz joked about his short stature (see e.g. *Shiʿr*, p. 262; *Aghānī* VIII 28, 30). Kuthaiyir seems to have enjoyed the company of Nuṣaib, some of whose verses and successes he envied (see e.g. Mubarrad, pp. 103, 201; *Aghānī* I 142–44).

[116] ʿ*Iqd* II 131 f.

When ʿAbd al-Malik took Nuṣaib to task for his infrequent visits he replied that he, a black slave, was not fit company for kings and when he was offered some drink (*nabīdh*) he refused it saying that he would not have his intellect, through which he had attained to the caliph's company, destroyed by drink.[117] He concluded with some verses on color as against ability and character.

Nuṣaib was intelligent enough to understand the racial and class prejudices of the Arab society of his day. He considered it the better part of wisdom not to protest loudly against these prejudices nor yet to challenge them, preferring instead to conduct himself with dignity and make the best of his situation. His attitude and conduct fit well the sober man's idea of the intelligent and wise man.[118] For he refrained from satire, wishing, as he said, neither to dishonor the noble nor to blackmail the mean and hence be himself more deserving of satire.[119] Again, except when pointedly goaded, he refrained from claiming superiority over all other poets, as many of his contemporaries were quick to do, though he did hold a high opinion of himself.[120] He did have preferences for and opinions of some of these poets. For instance, he preferred Jarīr to Farazdaq.[121] When asked to give an opinion on his fellow Ḥijāzian poets in comparison to himself, he did so briefly: "Jamīl is our imām (in poetry), and ʿUmar ibn Abī Rabīʿah is our best descriptive poet of the mistresses of the curtained canopies, and Kuthaiyir is quickest to move one to tears about beautiful but lowly women and is our best in the praise of kings. And as for me, I say what you have heard."[122]

Unlike Nuṣaib, Kuthaiyir, despite his own physical handicaps, was bolder and more vocal in his criticism of his fellow Ḥijāzian poets, most of whom conceded his poetic superiority, as did also ʿAbd al-Malik and even at one time Walīd I and still later several literary critics.[123] We have some quite lengthy accounts that tell of Kuthaiyir's self-confidence, professional pride, and critical competence. In an encounter with ʿUmar ibn Abī Rabīʿah, Aḥwaṣ, and Nuṣaib, Kuthaiyir displayed intimate knowledge of the poetry of all three as he quoted first some of each poet's commendable verses and then verses illustrating each poet's weaknesses. He thus humiliated and silenced each poet in turn as he criticized both the form and the content of verses on the very themes in which each poet was supposed to excel. The several versions of this episode, some of them composite accounts, are too lengthy to reproduce here.[124] But Kuthaiyir's bases and methods of literary criticism are equally well-illustrated in a comparatively brief account of his encounter with the Syrian poet ʿAdī ibn al-Riqāʿ at the court of Walīd I. ʿAdī recited his ode in praise of Walīd in which he referred also to his own labored method of composition and asserted that because of his professional self-sufficiency he had no need to seek further knowledge from

[117] *Amālī* III 128: انا اسود البشر قبيح المنظرة وانما وصلت الي مجلس امير المومنين بعقلي فان راى امير المومنين ان لا يدخل عليه ما يزيله فعل فاعفاه ووصله (cf. Jāḥiẓ, *Bayān* I 221, n. 2). See also *Aghānī* I 140 and ʿ*Iqd* II 245 for some of Nuṣaib's verses on his color. That a man is not to be judged by his color is implied by a saying of the Prophet: كرم الرجـــل دينه ومرؤته عقله وحسبُه خـُلقه (ʿ*Iqd* II 247).

[118] ʿ*Iqd* II 240: على العاقل ان يكون عالما باهل زمانه مالكا لسانه مقبلا على شانه.

[119] Jumaḥī, p. 545: ادَعُ الهجاء لخلتين اما اهجو كريما فاهتك عرضه واما اهجو لئيما لطلب ما عنده فنفسى احق بالهجاء اذ سوّلت الى لئيم (see *Aghānī* I 137 and 142 for somewhat different versions).

[120] Jumaḥī, p. 348.

[121] *Aghānī* VII 63.

[122] *Aghānī* I 142 (= *Aghānī* [1927——] I 355): جميل امامنا وعمر بن ابي ربيعه اوصفنا لربات الحجال وكثيّر ابكنا على الدمن واما انا فقد قلتُ ما سمعتَ. But *Muwashshaḥ*, p. 205, has جميل اصدقنا شعرا وكثير ابكنا على الظُعن وابن ابي ربيعه اكذبنا وانا اقول ما اعرف. See also *Aghānī* VII 95, where Kuthaiyir declares Jamīl the best poet.

[123] E.g. Jumaḥī, pp. 542 f.; *Shiʿr*, p. 330; *Aghānī* IV 43; *Khizānah* I 232.

[124] See e.g. Mubarrad, pp. 320–22, and *Muwashshaḥ*, pp. 162–64; ʿ*Iqd* V 372 f. gives a shorter version. See Thaʿālibī, *Ījāz*, pp. 44 f., for some of the best representative verses of the three poets.

others.[125] Kuthaiyir challenged and silenced ʿAdī on these points. Abū al-Faraj al-Iṣfahānī's account[126] reads as follows:

اخبرنى عيسى بن الحسين الورّاق قال حدثنى احمد بن الهيثم بن فراس قال حدثنى العُمرى عن الهيثم بن عدى قال انشد عدى بن الرقاع الوليد بن عبد الملك قصيدته التى اولاها — عرف الديار توهّمًا فاعتادها — وعنده كثيّر وكان يبلغه عن عدى انه يطعن على شعره ويقول هذا شعر حجازى مقرور اذا اصابه قر الشام جمد وهلك فانشده (عدى) اياها حتى الق على قولة

وقصيدة قد بتُ اجمع بينها حتى اقوّم مَيلها وسِنادها

قفال له كثيّر لوكنتَ مطبوعا وفصيحا وعالما لم تاتِ فيها بميل وسناد فتحتاج الى ان تقوّمها ثم انشد (عدى)

نظر المثقّف فى كُعوب قَناته حتى يُقيم ثِقافُه مُنادها

فقال له كثيّر لا جرم ان الايام اذا تطاولت عليها عادت عوجاء ولأن تكون مستقيمة لا تحتاج الى ثقاف اجودُ لها ثم انشد

وعلمتُ حتى ما أُسائل واحدا عن علم واحدة لكى ازدادها

فقال كثيّر كذبت ورب البيت الحرام فليمتحنك امير المومنين بان يسالك عن صغار الامور دون كبارها حتى يتبين جهلك وماكنت قط احمق منك الان حتى تظنّ هذا بنفسك فضحك الوليد ومن حضر وقُطع بعدى بن الرقاع حتى ما نطق

Verses from the above-mentioned ode of ʿAdī are frequently cited, particularly the three that Kuthaiyir criticized but usually without reference to the latter's criticisms.[127] Nevertheless, the technical terms in these verses and Kuthaiyir's reaction to them have significant bearing on the use and interpretation of these and related technical terms in the formative stages of Arabic literary criticism.[128]

ʿAbd al-Malik was much impressed with the sensitive and magical qualities of Kuthaiyir's poetry, which he frequently recited and of which he had a copy[129] that was used for the instruction of the princes.[130] ʿAbd al-Malik sent Kuthaiyir to ʿIrāq during the governorship of Bishr ibn Marwān to recite some of his tribal and politically oriented poems in the congregational mosques of Baṣrah and Kūfah.[131] The poet was given a cool reception by the ʿIrāqī scholars and poets, who considered all Ḥijāzī poetry inferior to the ʿIrāqī product.[132] But Kuthaiyir was wary enough, then and later under Yazīd II,[133] to resist satirical entanglement with any of the ʿIrāqī poets, let alone with either Jarīr or Farazdaq, both of

[125] For the whole ode of 38 verses see Nuwairī IV 246–50. On the basis of verses 10, 18, and 21 (*ibid.* pp. 248 f.) ʿAdī would be classified as a *mutakallif* rather than a *maṭbūʿ*, i.e., as a slavish craftsman rather than a natural-born poet (see e.g. *Shiʿr*, p. 17). See also Marzūqī I 4 f., 9 and 12 f. on the two types of poets.

[126] *Aghānī* VIII 183 f. (= *Aghānī* [1927——] IX 316 f.). See also *Muwashshaḥ*, pp. 190 f.

[127] See e.g. Jumaḥī, pp. 558 f.; Jāḥiẓ, *Bayān* III 213 f.; *Shiʿr*, pp. 392 f.; *ʿUyūn* II 128; *ʿIqd* II 219, V 314, and VI 81; *Muwashshaḥ*, pp. 190 f.

[128] See e.g. Qudāmah, Intro. pp. 20 f., 34 f., 43 f. and text pp. 109–11; Qudāmah (1963) pp. 209–12. See also n. 111 on p. 128 above.

[129] As did the poet's family (*Aghānī* VIII 30).

[130] *Ibid.* VIII 36. See also n. 165 on p. 136 below.

[131] *Ibid.* VIII 30 f.; Jumaḥī, p. 377.

[132] Jumaḥī, pp. 452, 457. But Ibn Abī Isḥāq considered Kuthaiyir the best of the Islāmic poets (*ibid.* p. 44).

[133] See e.g. *ibid*, p. 542.

whom had at one time or another commented on the weakness of Ḥijāzī poetry.[134] The same criticism was used against Kuthaiyir's poetry by Akhṭal[135] and ʿAdī.[136]

Most of the leading poets of the Umayyad period proclaimed their own superiority over their contemporary fellow poets. The claim was based more often than not on one or two of a given poet's own verses—a basis used also, as seen above, by contemporary and later literary critics. More interesting are claims of superiority based on specific qualities or characteristics of a poet's whole output, whether stated matter-of-factly or figuratively. Rāʿī, for instance, claimed general superiority over his uncle in the following terms: انك تقول البيت وابن اخيه واقول البيت واخاه.[137] ʿUmar ibn Lajā claimed superiority over his cousin, a fellow poet, in the slightly different expression لاني اقول البيت واخاه ولانك تقول البيت وابن عمه, and Ibn Qutaibah explained "a verse and its paternal cousin" as البيت مقرونا بغير جاره ومضموما الى غير لفقه.[138] Ru'bah ibn al-ʿAjjāj asserted his superiority over his son ʿUqbah because the latter's poetry had no companion, ليس للشعره قران, in explanation of which Ibn Qutaibah added يريد انه لا يقارن البيت بشبهه.[139] Still later we find Mubarrad preferring the poetry of Farazdaq to that of Jarīr because "Farazdaq produces a verse and its brother, while Jarīr produces a verse and its paternal uncle."[140] Thus, while both the syntactical and the conceptual independence of each verse of Arabic poetry as complete in itself has long been widely recognized, the early emphasis on the various degrees of the conceptual interrelationship of consecutive verses has been for the most part overlooked by students of the early history of Arabic literary criticism.[141] Such interrelationship did not imply that a given verse should depend on the next verse for the completion of its basic meaning. The distinction is illustrated in Majnūn Lailā's verses

وادنيتني حتى اذا مـــا سبيتني بقول يُحلّ العصم سهل الاباطح
تجافيت عني حين لا لي حيلة وغادرت ما غادرت بين الجوانح

that were recited by Abū ʿAmr ibn al-ʿAlā' to Jarīr on his return from Syria. These two verses so affected Jarīr in ʿIrāq that he exclaimed that were it not unseemly for an old man like himself to shout for joy he would let out a scream that would be heard by Hishām on his throne in Syria. Ibn ʿAbd Rabbihi commented that these verses would be considered among the most subtle and elegant of poetry were it not for the *taḍmīn*, that is, the dependence of the first verse on the second for completion of its meaning, and then he cited the single verse of ʿAbbās ibn al-Aḥnaf

اشكو الذيـن اذاقـوني مودتهـــم حتى اذا ايقظوني بالهوا رقـــدوا

[134] See e.g. *Aghānī* I 71 f. and *Muwashshaḥ*, pp. 202 f., for Jarīr's comment on the poetry of ʿUmar ibn Abī Rabīʿah: شعر تهامي اذا انجد وجد البرد. And see *Muwashshaḥ*, p. 206, for Farazdaq's comment on the poetry of the same poet: ارى شعرا حجازيا ان انجد اقشعر.

[135] See *Fuḥūlat al-shuʿarā*, pp. 502 f., سئل الاخطل عن شعر كثير فقال حجازي يكد البرد, and Mubarrad, p. 322, شعر حجازي مجوّع مقرور (see also *Aghānī* VII 173).

[136] *Aghānī* VIII 183: كان عدي يطعن في شعره ويقول هذا شعر حجازي مقرور اذا اصابه قر الشام جمد وهلك. From all of the comments cited it is clear that the ʿIrāqīs and the Syrians considered Ḥijāzī poetry inferior because, as they claimed, its thinness of substance and its insipidity rendered it dull and unappealing.

[137] *Muwashshaḥ*, p. 157.

[138] *Shiʿr*, pp. 25 f.; Jāḥiẓ, *Bayān* I 212; ʿ*Uyūn* II 184. See *Muwashshaḥ*, pp. 362 f., for similar statements and explanations in somewhat different terms.

[139] *Shiʿr* p. 26. *Muwashshaḥ*, pp. 365 f., justifies Ru'bah's poor opinion of his son's poetry, which had failed to survive for want of merit.

[140] *Muwashshaḥ*, p. 121, with examples on pp. 111 f.

[141] See Qudāmah, Intro. pp. 10 f. and text pp. 73–75 (= Qudāmah [1963] pp. 154–56), under the somewhat related terms صحة المقابلة and صحة التفسير (see also ʿ*Umdah* II 28–31 and Marzūqī I 18).

as conveying the full meaning of the two verses of Majnūn Lailā.[142] Ibn Qutaibah's account[143] adds a second verse of ʿAbbās ibn al-Aḥnaf

واستنهضونى فلما قمت منتهضا   بثقل ما حملونى فى الهوا قعدوا

and his two verses could be considered as illustrative of consecutive verses that are as closely related as are a person and his brother, nephew, or paternal cousin. The closer the relationship of two consecutive verses, the better is the poetry.

II

That Umayyad and later literary critics agreed that Akhṭal, Jarīr, and Farazdaq were the leading poets of the Umayyad period but could not arrive at a generally acceptable relative ranking for them is a fact too well known to detain us here. And we need not dwell on the numerous occasions when each of the three poets claimed superiority over one or both of the other two on the basis of only one or a few of his verses.[144] What does interest us at this point is the self-appraisal and mutual criticism of these three poets among others on the basis of the over-all characterization of their poetry, particularly as to meaningful content and forceful effectiveness. We read, for instance, that Akhṭal on being asked by Prince ʿUmar, son of Walīd I, who was the best of poets answered "who when he praises exalts and when he satirizes debases" and on being ordered to name three such poets named Aʿshā Maimūn, Ṭarafah ibn al-ʿAbd, and himself in that order.[145] Akhṭal's statement reflects his admiration of the two earlier classical poets and his own pride in the effectiveness of his praise of the Umayyads and his satires first of the Anṣār and later of Jarīr and the Banū Kulaib among others. Jarīr and his admirers used the same criterion, claiming that Jarīr's praise of his lowly father raised him up[146] while his satires of Rāʿī and others debased them. Farazdaq considered himself no less forceful in his panegyrics and more than a match for any other in his satires. He claimed that he and Jarīr had the same demon but that this demon spoke more wickedly through his tongue than through Jarīr's.[147] And, inasmuch as such wickedness was usually expressed in extremely vulgar and vituperative verse, it rendered Farazdaq on the whole more feared rather than more appreciated than Jarīr and Akhṭal.[148] Soon after Akhṭal and Farazdaq had joined forces against Jarīr, they

[142] See ʿ*Iqd* V 378 for the entire episode, including Ibn ʿAbd Rabbihi's comment:
وهذا من ارق الشعر كله والطفه لو لا التضمين الذى فيه والتضمين ان يكون البيت معلفا بالبيت الثانى لا يتم معناه الا به وانما يحمد البيت اذا كان قايما بنفسه.
See ʿ*Umdah* II 68–72 for discussion and illustrations of *taḍmīn*.

[143] See ʿ*Uyūn* III 78, which cites all four verses with some variants but with no comments. See also *ibid.* IV 139; *Shiʿr*, pp. 363, 525; *Aghānī* VIII 21; Ibn al-Muʿtazz, *Ṭabaqāt*, p. 255.

[144] See e.g. *Aghānī* VII 177, where Akhṭal claims superiority in panegyric, satire, and erotica on the basis of two and three verses in each category. See Qurashī, p. 36, where Akhṭal and Farazdaq claim over-all superiority, yet each concedes he could not match some few verses of some other poet. See *Muwashshaḥ*, p. 136, where Akhṭal is faced by his critics with four serious errors, and *ibid.* p. 131, where Jarīr is reported to have acknowledged the superiority of Akhṭal's one-verse answer to a verse of his own but then recited a second verse that he considered superior to the one verse of Akhṭal; see our Document 6, comment on recto 8–13, for Jarīr's second verse.

[145] See *Aghānī* VII 175: الذى اذا مدح رفع واذا هجاء وضع. See Qurashī, p. 35, for Abū ʿUbaidah's application of this critical approach to Akhṭal, Jarīr, and Farazdaq, and see Ṣāliḥānī, *Shiʿr al-Akhṭal*, pp. 345–48, for Akhṭal's opinion of himself.

[146] *Aghānī* VII 58 f.

[147] Thaʿālibī, *Thimār*, p. 57: قال الفرزدق شيطان جرير هو شيطاني الا انه من في اخبث (cf. *Aghānī* VII 15; Ibshīhī I 59 f.). Abū al-Najm al-ʿIjlī considered his demon to be masculine and that of ʿAjjāj to be feminine (*Aghānī* IX 79).

[148] *Aghānī* VII 178 draws attention to Akhṭal's greater meanness couched, however, in less offensive terms.

expressed admiration for each other not only in their *naqā'iḍ* but in their personal relationships.[149] Though they continued to proclaim their own superiority over Jarīr, they agreed, in a moment of truth and mellowed by drink and recitation of their own poetry, that Jarīr excelled them in the ready and smooth flow of his verses, which were apt and gained quick and widespread appeal among high and low society. Akhṭal pointed out further that his own satire, which he considered superior to that of Jarīr and others, was transmitted by only the few who were wise in the art of poetry. The complete account which follows[150] reveals the full extent of the admiration of Akhṭal and Farazdaq for each other.

اخبرنى احمد بن عبيد الله قال حدثنى يعقوب بن اسرائل قال اخبرنى اسمعيل ابن ابى محمد اليزيدى قال اخبرنى ابو محمد (يحى بن المبارك) اليزيدى قال خرج الفرزدق يؤم بعض الملوك من بنى امية فرفع له فى طريقه بيت احمر من أدم فدنا منه وسأل فقيل له (بيت) الاخطل فاتاه فقال له انزل فلما نزل قام اليه الاخطل وهو لا يعرفه الا انه ضيف فقعدا يتحدّثان فقال له الاخطل ممن الرجل قال من بنى تميم قال فانك اذا من رهط اخى الفرزدق فقال تحفظ من شعره شيأ قال نعم كثيرا فما زالا يتناشدان ويتعجب الاخطل من حفظه شعر الفرزدق الى ان عمل فيه الشراب وقد كان الاخطل قال له قبل ذلك انتم معشر الحنيفية لا ترون ان تشربوا من شرابنا فقال له الفرزدق خفض قليلا وهات من شرابك فاسقينا فلما عملت الراح فى ابى فراس قال انا والله الذى اقول فى جرير فانشده فقام اليه الاخطل فقبل راسه وقال لا جزاك الله عنى خيرا لِمَ كتمتنى نفسك منذ اليوم واخذا فى شرابهما وتناشُدهما الى ان قال له الاخطل والله انك واياى لاشعر منه ولكنه أُتِـى من سير الشعر ما لم نُوتِـه قلت انا بيتا ما اعلم ان احدا قال اهجى منه قلت

قوم إذا استنبح الاضياف كلبهم   قالـو لامهم بـولى على النارِ

فلم يروه الا حكماء اهل الشعر وقال هو (جرير)

والتغلبـــى إذا تنحنـــح للقرى   حـــك استه وتمثل امشـــالا

فلم تبق سُقاة ولا امثالها الا رووه فقضيا له انه اسيرُ شعرا منهما

The conversation between Akhṭal and Farazdaq as recorded above amounts to an admission that Jarīr was more of a natural poet (*maṭbū'*) than either of them and hence also more self-sufficient. And, in fact, their poetry though more polished is also more labored (*mutakallaf*).[151] We have seen (p. 111) how Akhṭal was annoyed when 'Abd al-Malik was so greatly pleased with an ode which Jarīr had composed in a few days, while he himself had been working for a whole year on an ode in praise of that same caliph. Moreover, Akhṭal received help from several poets in the composition of at least some of his satires against Jarīr. Furthermore, he is reported as saying: "We the poets are greater thieves than even the goldsmiths."[152] As for Farazdaq, he was reported as saying that there were times when it was harder for him

[149] *Aghānī* VII 178 reports that Akhṭal, on first recognizing Farazdaq, kneeled in admiration and Farazdaq followed suit فسجد لي وسجدت له (see also Ṣāliḥānī, *Shi'r al-Akhṭal*, p. 354, and references and comment in n. 150 below). *Aghānī* XIV 98 states that Farazdaq knelt on hearing a verse of Labīd recited in a mosque and when questioned on this said: انتم تعرفون سجدة القرآن وانا اعرف سجدة الشعر. But see *Fuḥūlat al-shu'arā'*, p. 498, for Aṣma'ī's doubts about the quality of Labīd's poetry, an opinion that must be reflected in the change in Labīd's poetry and in the elegies of Ḥassān ibn Thābit after their conversion to Islām (*Muwashshah*, p. 62: قال الاصمعي طريق الشعر اذا ادخلته في باب الخير لانَ).

[150] *Aghānī* VII 186 f. (= *Aghānī* [1927——] VIII 317 f.) gives the most detailed account of this episode, on the authority of Abū Muḥammad al-Yazīdī, and it is condensed in *Muwashshah*, pp. 131 and 140 f. '*Umdah* II 146 f. gives a fragmented account with no *isnād*, in which direct reference to Farazdaq is missing but which ends with فلم يبق سقاء ولا امة حتى روتـه . . . قال الاصمعى فحكما له بسيرورة الشعر. See also Ṣūlī, *Akhbār Abī Tammām*, ed. Khalīl Maḥmūd 'Asākir *et al.* (Cairo, 1356/1937) pp. 219 f., where Jarīr relishes his widespread popularity with the public (cf. pp. 116 and 119 above).

[151] Kuthaiyir pointed out to 'Adī ibn al-Riqā' that a natural-born poet would not have committed the errors that 'Adī had in his verses (see *Aghānī* VIII 184 and p. 129 above).

[152] *Muwashshah*, pp. 138 f., 141: نحن معاشر الشعراء اسرق من الصاغة.

to compose a single verse than to have a tooth extracted.[153] But he was adroit at lifting ideas from several ancient and contemporary poets and actually appropriated verses of several of his contemporaries.[154] In fact, Aṣmaʿī considered that nine-tenths of Farazdaq's poetry was stolen as against only one half-verse stolen by Jarīr,[155] a statement to be suspected with respect to both poets. For though direct plagiarism was frowned on by all, the less obvious stealing of ideas (*sirqat al-maʿānī*) to be expressed in one's own words in prose or verse was so ancient and widespread a practice that hardly an orator or a poet was not guilty of it. Controversial at first, the practice became tolerated among the "moderns" and even admired when a new expression of an old idea adorned with a new style in richer and more modern metaphoric speech was considered more effective. This type of plagiarism looms large in Arabic literary criticism and dovetails into the concept of literary originality, especially in respect to the *badīʿ* poetry that had a good start with Bashshār ibn Burd and found its most effective champion in Ibn al-Muʿtazz and his *Kitāb al-badīʿ*.[156]

The statement most often cited on the respective merits of Jarīr and Farazdaq is said to be Akhṭal's comment جرير يغرف من بحر والفرزدق ينعت من صخر, "Jarīr draws from the sea and Farazdaq carves from stone." This comment has recently given rise to a controversy as to when, by whom, and where it was first used. One set of statements credits its first use not to Akhṭal himself but to his son Mālik. Briefly, this view is based on a report that Akhṭal in Syria, having heard of the reputation and rivalry of Jarīr and Farazdaq in ʿIrāq, sent his son to ʿIrāq to listen to and appraise their poetry. On his return, the son's report (or perhaps only what has survived of it) consisted solely of the figurative statement cited above, on the basis of which Akhṭal declared Jarīr to be the better of the two poets.[157] He then reinforced his verdict with his own two verses

اني قضيت قضاء غير ذى جنف   لما سمعت ولما جاءني الخبر
انّا الفرزدق قد شالت نعماته   وعضه حيـــة من قومه ذكـــر

declaring his impartiality on the basis of what he had heard and elaborating on his verdict in other forceful figures of speech.[158]

[153] Jāḥiẓ, *Bayān* I 216; *Aghānī* XIX 36; *ʿIqd* V 327; ʿAskarī, *Maṣūn*, p. 13; *Muwashshaḥ*, pp. 111 f.

[154] *Aghānī* XIX 22: كان الفرزدق يقول خير السرقة ما لا يجب فيه المقطع يعنى سرقة الشعر. See also *Muwashshaḥ*, pp. 106–12, esp. p. 108: كان الفرزدق مهيبا تخافه الشعراء.

In addition to Farazdaq's reputation for vituperative verse his very physique and appearance roused fear in his victims and opponents; see n. 205 on p. 142 below for a physical comparison of Jarīr and Farazdaq.

[155] *Fuḥūlat al-shuʿarāʾ*, p. 502. *Marātib*, p. 49, and *Muwashshaḥ*, pp. 105 f., take exception to this opinion as an impossible exaggeration for both poets. For definitions, distinctions, and examples of the technical terms *ikhtirāʿ wa ibtidāʿ*, originality of idea and expression, and of *akhdh*, borrowing and improving on an idea, as against *sirqah*, outright theft of idea and expression, see e.g. *ʿUmdah* I 175–78 and II 215–26. See p. 144 below for ʿAdī's improvement on a simile of Jarīr's.

[156] ʿAbd al-Raḥmān ibn ʿĪsā al-Hamadhānī, *Kitāb al-alfāẓ al-kitābīyah*, p. ix (من اخذ (معنى) عاريا وكساه من عنده لفظا فهو احق به ممن اخذه عنه); *ʿIqd* V 338–40; Jurjānī, *Al-wasāṭah*, ed. Muḥammad Abū al-Faḍl Ibrāhīm and ʿAlī Muḥammad al-Bajāwī (Cairo, 1364/1945) pp. 183–99 *et passim*; Āmidī, *Al-muwāzanah baina shiʿr Abī Tammām wa al-Buḥturī* (1961) pp. 124 (من ادركته من اهل العلم بالشعر لم يرون سرقات المعاني من كبير مساوي الشعراء وخاصة المتاخرين), 139 f., *et passim*; *ʿUmdah* I 177 f. (الاختراع للمعنى والابداع للفظ فاذا تم للشاعر ان ياتي بمعنى مخترع في لفظ بديع فقد استولى على الامر); Ibn Rashīq, *Quraḍat al-dhahab fī naqd ashʿār al-Arab* (Cairo, 1344/1926). See *Inbāh* II 204 f. for *sirqat al-maʿānī* from Arabs and non-Arabs.

[157] Jumaḥī, pp. 386 f.; Jāḥiẓ, *Bayān* II 119, 280; Bevan I 494; *Aghānī* X 2 f. Cf. A. Caussin de Perceval in *Journal asiatique*, series 2, Vol. XIII (1834) 307–9.

[158] E.g. Jumaḥī, p. 387; Bevan II 879 f. Cf. Ṣāliḥānī, *Naqāʾiḍ Jarīr wa al-Akhṭal*, p. 197; *Aghānī* VII 185. Maḥmūd Ghināwī al-Zuhairī, *Naqāʾiḍ Jarīr wa al-Farazdaq*, pp. 224–26, questioned this whole episode mainly on the basis that Akhṭal's son Mālik was not known as either a poet or a critic, that Jarīr made no reference to Akhṭal's decision in his favor, and that these two verses of Akhṭal do not appear in the early transmission of his *dīwān*. These objections in turn may be questioned on the reasonable assumptions that Akhṭal was the best judge of his son's abilities, that the son's report and Akhṭal's remark and two verses were made in a private conversation between the two since Akhṭal had no reason as yet to declare himself publicly for either Jarīr or Farazdaq, and that the two verses in question were suppressed once Akhṭal, under pressure and temptation, declared himself publicly in favor of Farazdaq—a declaration that was bound to receive widespread publicity.

In a second set of statements Akhṭal himself subsequently and for the first time in ʿIrāq expresses the "sea-and-stone" verdict under persistent pressure from the governor, Bishr ibn Marwān, and some of his intimate associates. Careful analysis of two accounts of Akhṭal's statement to Bishr led me to suspect some error or tampering in both accounts. The first reads قال (الاخطل) الفرزدق ينعت من صخر وجرير يغرف من بحر فلم يرض بذلك جرير وكان سبب الهجاء بينهما and, in view of the context, should have pleased Jarīr and displeased Bishr.[159] The other account reads فلما دخل عليه الاخطل ساله (بشر) عن الفرزدق وجرير فقال له الاخطل اصلح الله الامير اما الفرزدق فاشعر العرب and is clearly incomplete since the use of اما and فاشعر calls for a preceding comparative statement on both poets.[160] In view of Jumaḥī's account it seems reasonable to suspect that Akhṭal, reluctant to change his opinion but anxious not to offend the governor, hedged with a statement that must have read in full اصلح الله الامير الفرزدق ينعت من صخر وجرير يغرف من بحر اما الفرزدق فاشعر العرب فلم يرض بذلك جرير and would have been satisfactory enough for Bishr while supplying an understandable reason for Jarīr's displeasure. Though Bishr may have been satisfied,[161] there were others, particularly Muḥammad ibn ʿUmair ibn ʿUṭārid, Farazdaq's intimate companion and kinsman, who induced Akhṭal to produce his first ode satirizing Jarīr and the Banū Kulaib and praising Farazdaq and his forebears.[162] Farazdaq could not resist expressing his delight in an ode that praised Akhṭal and Muḥammad ibn ʿUmair. Jarīr soon answered in a lengthy ode referring to Bishr's role and satirizing Akhṭal, Farazdaq, and Muḥammad that contained two verses

يا ذا العباية ان بشرا قد قضى ان لا تجوز حكومة النشـــوان
فدعوا الحكومة لستم من اهلها ان الحكومة في بنى شيبـــان

refuting their verdict.[163] Bishr and Muḥammad coerced and tempted other poets to declare Farazdaq superior to Jarīr but prevailed on only Surāqah al-Bāriqī, whose verses to that effect

ابلغ تميـما غثها وسمينهـــا والقول يقصد تارة ويجـــورُ
ان الفرزدق برزت حلبـــاته عفوا وغودر في الغبار جرير
هذا قضاء البارقي وانــــه بالميل في ميزانكم لجديـــر

were part of an ode which Bishr sent to Jarīr by a messenger who was ordered to bring back Jarīr's answer in writing. Jarīr's reply consisted of a lengthy ode which contained the significant verses

يا صاحبى هل الصباح مُنير ام هل للوم عواذلي تفتـــير
يا بشر انك لم تزل في نعمـــة ياتيك من قبل العلى بشير
يا بشر حق لوجهك التبشير هلا غضبت لنا وانت امير
قد كان حقك ان تقول لبارق يا آل بارق فيما سبَّ جرير

and which he worked the night long to produce.[164]

159 Jumaḥī, p. 408, lines 5–6.

160 Bevan II 880.

161 See *Aghānī* VII 52 f., according to which Bishr once called on both Jarīr and Farazdaq for impromptu heroic verse (*fakhr*), a category in which the social standing of Farazdaq's family gave him the edge over Jarīr. After three rounds of one verse each, Bishr declared Jarīr the winner and rewarded both poets. For other instances when either Jarīr or Farazdaq is declared the winner or claims the victory see e.g. Jumaḥī, pp. 329 f., and *Aghānī* I 71 f.

162 Jumaḥī, pp. 387 f.; Bevan I 494–96; Ṣāliḥānī, *Naqāʾiḍ Jarīr wa al-Akhṭal*, pp. 197, 223; Ṣāliḥānī, *Shiʿr al-Akhṭal*, pp. 273 f.; *Sharḥ dīwān Jarīr*, pp. 569–77, especially the first two verses on p. 573.

163 Jumaḥī, pp. 388 f., 408; Bevan II 879–907 (= Nos. 94–95), esp. p. 897, verses 42–43; Ṣāliḥānī, *Naqāʾiḍ Jarīr wa al-Akhṭal*, pp. 207 f., verses 48–49; *Sharḥ dīwān Jarīr*, pp. 569–77, esp. p. 573. See also *Aghānī* VII 185 and X 2 f.

164 For these and the three verses of Surāqah al-Bāriqī see Jumaḥī, pp. 377–80; *Aghānī* VII 67 f. For the entire ode see *Sharḥ dīwān Jarīr*, pp. 300–303. The relative timing of Bishr's pressure on Akhṭal and that on his own court poets is not too clear, but the order in which the episodes are described above seems the more likely. See Bevan II 966 f. and 1014 f. for Jarīr's verses satirizing Surāqah in odes Nos. 101 and 106, which satirize other poets as well.

Another example of the figurative use of the sea and stone to indicate literary virtuosity is provided by ʿAbd al-Malik in a report that traces back through Abū ʿUbaidah to Shaʿbī. ʿAbd al-Malik was a great admirer of Aʿshā Bakr, whose poetry he ordered included in his sons' curriculum as he instructed the royal tutor in the following terms: ادبهم بروايه شعر الاعشى فان لكلامه عذوبة قاتله الله ما كان اعذب بحره واصلب صخره فمن زعم ان احدا من الشعراء اشعر من الاعشى فليس يعرف الشعر.[165]

Jarīr, Farazdaq, and many of their critics readily appropriated the sea metaphor in reference to their poetry, while the stone one was seldom used even by Farazdaq himself—a fact which could be interpreted as tacit recognition of Jarīr's superiority. Both Jarīr and Farazdaq elaborated on the basic sea metaphor, each in his own interest. Farazdaq is reported as saying اني واياه لنغترف من بحر واحد وتضطرب دلاوه عند طول النهر, implying conceptual thinness in Jarīr's lengthy odes.[166] Jarīr was given to short odes of praise and long ones of satire, though his reason is not convincing since brevity was more desirable in both categories for quick memorizing and ready recall: قال يا بنى اذا مدحتم فلا تطيلوا الممادحة فانه ينسى اولها ولا يحفظ آخرها فاذا هجوتم فخالفوا.[167]

That Jarīr made the most frequent use of the sea metaphor, in public and in private,[168] is readily understandable as is his lengthy elaboration of the significance of the term itself and of terms closely related to it in their literal or derived meanings.[169]

[165] Qurashī, pp. 29 ff. *Muzhir* II 309 f. reports ʿAbd al-Malik's instructions to Shaʿbī to teach the princes poetry and to watch their diet, behavior, and associations: فقال علمهم الشعر يمجدوا وينجدوا واطعمهم اللحم تشد قلوبهم وجزّ شعورهم تشد رقابهم فجالس بهم عليه الرجال يناقضوهم الكلام. Muʿāwiyah ibn Abī Sufyān and ʿUmar I before him had also stressed the moral and social benefits of knowing poetry (*ʿUmdah* I 10).

ʿAbd al-Malik and his brothers, especially Bishr and to a lesser extent ʿAbd al-ʿAzīz, were well versed in pre-Islāmic and contemporary poetry. ʿAbd al-Malik was a lifelong student of poetry, much of which he memorized and manuscripts of which he stocked in his library (see pp. 72, 88, 130). He took care to see that his sons were well instructed in the subject by their tutors, including Shaʿbī. He himself developed a keen sense of literary criticism as attested by several poets and scholars. Occasionally in an informal family setting, in the presence of their tutors, he gave the young princes an object lesson in the art of literary criticism. His four heir-designates—Walīd, Sulaimān, Yazīd, and Hishām—and their half-brother Maslamah often attended the caliph's numerous sessions with scholars and poets. As each heir in turn became caliph, his brother-heirs and his sons were more apt than not to attend his literary sessions and to contribute to the discussion when called upon. While this practice created for future scholars problems of chronology as to whether these royal personages made certain literary statements as princes or as caliphs, it did on the other hand render them not only political patrons of poets but also students of poetry. While their role as students, which involved the use of the postal service for obtaining literary information from leading ʿIrāqī scholars, has not been completely overlooked (see e.g. Jumaḥī, pp. 51 f., and cf. Jabbūr I 151–55), its full extent has not been appreciated, particularly in respect to the leading role of ʿAbd al-Malik. The political motivation of ʿAbd al-Malik's patronage of scholars and poets is fairly well known, but not so well known is his great desire to impress these same groups, particularly those from ʿIrāq, that ʿIrāq had no monopoly on literary knowledge and its dissemination. For though he had ordered Ḥajjāj ibn Yūsuf to send him the ʿIrāqī Shaʿbī he kept that scholar waiting for an audience and gave him a cool reception. He then baited him with literary questions and tested his knowledge of poetry and, having first refuted his answers, he addressed him thus: يا شعبى انما اعلمتك هذا لانه بلغنى ان اهل العراق يتطاولون على اهل الشام يقولون ان كانوا غلبوا على الدولة فلم يغلبوا على العلم والروايه واهل الشام اعلم بعلم اهل العراق من اهل العراق (*Aghānī* IX 171). See p. 87 above for the continued relationship of scholar and caliph.

ʿAbd al-Malik as scholar and literary critic is an intriguing subject, and the pertinent source materials are copious enough to yield a rewarding study.

[166] Jumaḥī, p. 318; Bevan II 1047; *Aghānī* VII 40. Farazdaq preferred shorter odes (*Aghānī* XIX 33).

[167] *ʿUmdah* II 103, where Farazdaq also is accused of too lengthy poems. See also Jāḥiẓ, *Bayān* I 213, *ʿUyūn* II 184, *ʿIqd* II 269, and *ʿUmdah* II 103–14, where the argument is against odes of great length and in favor of shorter but more compact ones rich in striking verses that are readily memorized and recalled, these being more desired by a poet's powerful patrons and more dreaded by his enemies. A comparison of the *naqāʾiḍ* of our three poets confirms that Jarīr indulged in lengthier odes than the other two and reveals that Akhṭal was the most restrained in this respect, thus illustrating the latter's practice of pruning and condensing his odes to about a third of the original draft (see e.g. Jumaḥī, pp. 420 f.; *Aghānī* VII 171).

[168] Expressed at first mostly at the court of ʿAbd al-Malik or of Prince Walīd and later in response to questions from one or another of ʿAbd al-Malik's several sons (see *Aghānī* VII 51; Jumaḥī, pp. 53 f.; *ʿUmdah* I 61; nn. 190 and 194 on p. 139 below.

[169] Variants and related terms used by Jarīr are فاني سبحت الشعر تسبيحا and فاني نحرت (بحرت) الشعر نحرا, meaning briefly that he had delved deeply into the subject of poetry and acquired a vast knowledge and expertness in the field (see Lane, بحر and نحر). Later, he who attempted to master the *Kitāb* of Sībawaih was said to ride the sea or ocean (see e.g. Sīrāfī, p. 50).

We learn from accounts that trace back to Jarīr himself through the family *isnād* of ʿUmārah on the authority of his father ʿAqīl on the authority of his father Bilāl on the authority of his father Jarīr that when Jarīr was asked by one of the caliphs, either ʿAbd al-Malik or Walīd I (the former more likely), to explain some of these terms he had a ready and expansive answer. Short versions of such accounts are given by Abū ʿUbaidah[170] and Abū al-Faraj al-Iṣfahānī[171] with some variations. The fullest account is that of Abū ʿAlī al-Qālī on the authority of Abū Bakr ibn al-Anbārī on the authority of Abū Ḥātim al-Sijistānī on the authority of the above-mentioned family *isnād*. Jarīr, according to all three versions, was asked first for his opinion on several ranking earlier and contemporary poets, including Akhṭal and Farazdaq, for each of whom he had some high praise. The caliph in question then remarked that Jarīr had reserved no praise for himself only to discover that Jarīr ranked himself above all the others. The full account reads:

حدثنا ابوبكر قال حدثنـا ابو حاتم قال حدثنى عُمارة بن عُقيل قال حدثنى ابى يعنى عقيل بن بلال قال
سمعت ابى يعنى بلال بن جرير يقول سمعت جريرا يقول دخلتُ على بعض خلفاء بنى أميّة فقال الاتحدثنى
عن الشعراء فقلت بلى قال فمن أشعر الناس قلت ابن العشرين يعنى طرفه قال فما تقول فى ابن ابى سلمى
والنابغة قلت كان يُنيران الشعر ويُسديانه قال فما تقول فى امرى القيس بن حُجر قلت اتخذ الخبيث الشعر
نعلين يطوهما كيف شاء قـال فما تفول فى ذى الرمة قلت قَدر من الشعر على ما لم يقدر عليه احد قال فما تقول
فى الاخطل قلت ما باح بما فى صدره من الشعر حتى مات قال فما تقول فى الفرزدق قلت بيده نبعة الشعر قابضاً
عليها قال فما ابقيت لنفسك شيئا قلت بلى والله يا امير المومنين انا مدينة الشعر التى يخرج منها ويعود اليها ولأنا
سبحت الشعر تسبيحا ما سبحه احد قبلى قال وما التسبيح قلت نسبت فاطرفت وهجوت فارذيت ومدحت فاسنيت
ورملت فاغزرت ورجزت فابحرت فانا قلت ضروبا من الشعر لم يقلها احد قبلى[172]

The next item in this speech that calls for comment is Jarīr's opinion of Dhū al-Rummaḥ, which is cited in other sources also and which stresses his excellent similes.[173] More often than not another comment of Jarīr, whether coupled with the first or not, stresses the paucity of Dhū al-Rummah's themes and hence the monotony of his verses, which soon begin to pall.[174] Since this comment, نقط عروس وابعار ضباء, with slight variations and with or without an accompanying gloss, is credited to Farazdaq and Abū ʿAmr ibn al-ʿAlāʾ also, it is difficult to tell with certainty who was the first to use it. It or a different version of it may have been used first by Farazdaq and said directly to Dhū al-Rummah himself,[175] but it is

[170] Bevan II 1047 f. See p. 147 below for ʿUmārah.

[171] *Aghānī* VII 60. See also *ibid.* VII 130, where the conversation is said to have taken place with "one of the Umayyad rulers."

[172] *Amālī* II 181 f. The two short versions (Bevan II 1047 f. and *Aghānī* VII 60) have the following variations.
Line 5: Both short versions refer to two sons of Abū Sulmā and omit Nābighah al-Dhubyānī.
Line 8: Bevan has فانجرت; both short versions have ارديت.
Line 9: Bevan has فانا قلت ضروب الشعر كلهـا, and *Aghānī* VII 60 has فانا قلت ضروب الشعر كلها وكل واحد منهم قال نوعا منها قال صدقت.

The phrases ضروب الشعر and سيرورة الشعر in relation to Jarīr's proficiency as claimed by himself and conceded by other poets (see pp. 133 above and 139 below) could be extended to include the wider and readier use of meters and rhymes by a natural-born poet.

[173] See e.g. Jumaḥī, pp. 46, 465; *Aghānī* VII 60 and 130, XVI 113 f.

[174] *Muwashshah*, pp. 170–72; see also p. 191 below.

[175] *Muwashshah*, p. 171: ارى شعرا مثل بعر الصبيان. Cf. *ibid.* pp. 64 f., where Farazdaq characterizes Nābighah al-Jaʿdī and his poetry as a clothier who stocks both good and poor materials, which opinion was cited approvingly by Aṣmaʿī: صاحب خلقان يكون عنده مطرف بالف وخمار بواف وقال الاصمعى صدق الغرزدق.

more probable that the expression and its gloss originated with Abū ʿAmr and was then given currency first by both Jarīr and Farazdaq and later by others, including Aṣmaʿī and his contemporaries.[176]

Farazdaq was an even greater admirer of the earlier poets than was Jarīr. He considered them his models and looked upon himself and some of his contemporaries as their professional heirs. He expressed his admiration in both prose and poetry. He compared poetry itself to a dismembered camel whose best parts had been appropriated by earlier poets, who left nothing worthwhile but the forelimbs and the contents of the abdomen to be distributed among the poets of his own generation.[177] In one of his odes[178] Farazdaq named a score of earlier leading poets who served as his models[179] and claimed that he inherited their poetry, which was shared by only a few others, including Akhṭal and Rāʿī but not Jarīr.[180] Jarīr and his family are satirized outrageously in the rest of this lengthy ode.[181]

Jarīr's opinion as expressed in Abū ʿAlī al-Qālī's account (given above) in admiration of Akhṭal's inexhaustible productivity until his death is cited in other sources, where the Christian Akhṭal is referred to as "the son of the Christian woman."[182] More frequently cited is Jarīr's more candid opinion expressed initially in private to his son Nūḥ, who saw no reason to suppress it despite the fact that it amounted to all but an outright acknowledgment of the older Akhṭal's superiority—a superiority conceded by several scholars.[183] After Akhṭal's death Nūḥ asked his father which of the two was the better poet, that is, Jarīr or Akhṭal. The question disturbed Jarīr, who nevertheless answered thus: "My son, I reached Akhṭal when he had but one canine tooth; had he had one other, he would have devoured me. Two factors gave me the advantage over him, his advanced age and his corrupt faith."[184] Jarīr on various occasions expressed other favorable opinions of Akhṭal, acknowledging especially his excellence in praising royalty and in the description and praise of wine.[185]

Akhṭal was fully aware of the religious bias against him but refused to be deterred by it. Sure of his

176 Bevan II 1048; Jumaḥī, p. 467; *Shiʿr*, pp. 29, 333; *Aghānī* XVI 115; *Muwashshaḥ*, pp. 171 f., 362; Ibn Khallikān I 513; *Khizānah* I 52.

177 Qurashī, p. 24; *Muwashshaḥ*, p. 363. For Jāḥiẓ' opposite view see p. 122, n. 94. See n. 149 on p. 133 above for Farazdaq's high opinion of a verse of Labīd, and see the Arabic passage quoted on p. 125 for an earlier use of the camel metaphor.

178 Bevan I 181–211, No. 39.

179 *Ibid.* I 200 f., verses 51–60. Verse 57 reads

والجعفرى وكان بشر قبلـــه   لى من قصائده الكتاب المجْمَلُ

180 *Ibid.* I 201 f., verses 61–64. Verse 61 reads

دفعـــوا كتابهـــن وصـــيـــة   فورثتُهن كانهن الجَنـــدلُ

and can and has been interpreted to mean that they willed him in writing their poetry. However, the verse could refer to Farazdaq's possession of copies of their poetry since he indicates in verse 57 (cited in n. 179 above) that he did have manuscripts of the poetry of Labīd ibn Rabīʿah al-Jaʿfarī and Bishr ibn Abī Khāzim.

181 *Ibid.* I 202–11, verses 65–104.

182 Ṣāliḥānī, *Takmilah*, p. 15; Bevan II 1048; *Aghānī* VII 60. The phrase ابن النصرانية was applied in a discriminatory sense to Christians and Muslims whose mothers were Christians, as in the case of Khālid al-Qaṣrī, and even to Muslims whose grandmothers or more distant forebears were Christians, as in the case of Farazdaq's Bedouin wife (see e.g. Bevan II 705, verse 45, and 807, verse 4).

183 Both Abū ʿAmr ibn al-ʿAlāʾ and Yūnus ibn Ḥabīb and Aṣmaʿī after them ranked Akhṭal first among the Islāmic poets (*Fuḥūlat al-shuʿarāʾ*, p. 496; *Aghānī* VII 174; see also pp. 140 and 146 below).

184 Bevan I 498: يا بنى ادركت الاخطل وله ناب واحد ولو ادركته وله ناب آخر لاكلنى اعاننى عليه خصلتان كبر سنه وخبث دينه (see also *Aghānī* VII 171, 177; *Muwashshaḥ*, pp. 130, 131, 227; Jumaḥī, p. 419 and editor's note 4). For other references to the devouring of a rival, as used by ʿAbd al-Malik in reference to Jarīr and by Jarīr himself, see pp. 111, n. 11, and 112 above. Jarīr frequently referred in his verses to Akhṭal's Christian faith and used the diminutive form of the poet's name, Ukhaiṭal (see e.g. Bevan I 496 and 506, verses 44–47 and II 936, verses 9–13, and 1041, verse 5, which refers to Akhṭal's daughters mourning for their father). See also *Sharḥ dīwān Jarīr*, pp. 199 f., and Ṣāliḥānī, *Shiʿr al-Akhṭal* (1905) p. 13, lines 5–10.

185 Jumaḥī, p. 420; *Aghānī* VII 69; *Muwashshaḥ*, p. 171; ʿ*Umdah* I 61.

own great gift of poetry and of its appreciation among the most powerful and the most learned[186] and secure in the avowed protection of Muʿāwiyah and ʿAbd al-Malik, he flaunted his talent and his faith in the face of opposition with impunity[187] but not without a few narrow escapes such as he experienced when he satirized the Anṣār and Jāḥḥāf ibn Ḥukaim.[188]

Jarīr's opinion of Farazdaq as holding firmly in his hand the spring-source of poetry is frequently cited.[189] Once, for the benefit of his son ʿIkrimah, Jarīr ranked Zuhair ibn Abī Sulmā and Farazdaq first among pre-Islāmic and Islāmic poets respectively.[190] Such high praise for his two leading rivals again brought the remark "but you have left nothing for yourself," to which Jarīr had one of two answers, though sometimes the two were combined. One answer used the sea metaphor (see pp. 134–36), and the other answer was "I am the city (i.e., citadel) of poetry," used generally without comment[191] but elaborated upon on at least one occasion by Jarīr himself and later by others. Jarīr's initial expansion of the phrase seems to have been "I am the city of poetry from which it emerges and to which it returns."[192] This appears in Abū ʿAlī al-Qālī's text presented in full above with Jarīr's further elaboration and elucidation of his thought, and it appears also in the short versions of Abū ʿUbaidah and Abū al-Faraj al-Iṣfahānī (see p. 137). In the full account Jarīr claims excellence in all of the major categories and forms of poetry, including the *rajaz* forms,[193] and in abundant quantities—an accomplishment, he concluded, that no other had matched.[194] Except for his claim to excellence in the *rajaz* meter, this self-assessment was heartily confirmed by knowledgeable Bedouins as detailed above in connection with the discussion of Jarīr's verses that are cited in lines 3 and 4 of our papyrus text.

Another forceful phrase applied to Jarīr and Farazdaq is "Farazdaq constructs and Jarīr demolishes." Its origin is not clear, but Maslamah ibn ʿAbd al-Malik, who favored Farazdaq, used the phrase only to reject it with the added comment "and nothing arises from ruins,"[195] which twist was ignored by Jarīr

[186] Cautioned by a friend to desist from further satirizing Jarīr, Akhṭal declared himself equal to taking on Jarīr and the Banū Kulaib and added ثم اعلم ان العالم بالشعر لا يبالى وحق الصليب اذا مر به البيت العائر السائر الجيد امسلم قاله ام نصراني (*Aghānī* VII 173, 177). See Ṣūlī, *Akhbār Abī Tammām*, ed. Khalīl Mahmūd ʿAsākir *et al.* p. 174, for the opinions of Ḥammād al-Rāwiyah and Ṣūlī on this view.

[187] See Jumaḥī, pp. 417 f., for Akhṭal's appearance before the mosque of Kūfah, *Aghānī* VII 175 for his encounter with Rāʿī, *Shīʿr*, pp. 303 f., and ʿ*Uyūn* IV 34 f. for an encounter with a Muslim host. ʿ*Umdāh* II 22 f. and *Khizānah* I 220 f. sum up some of these and other situations. See also Nicholson, pp. 221, 240–42.

[188] See e.g. Bevan I 401 f.; Jumaḥī, pp. 411–15; Mubarrad, pp. 286 f.; *Aghānī* XI 59–61; *Muwashshaḥ*, pp. 136–38, 166. On the whole, the Umayyads were tolerant of Christians who were in their service and even of heterodox Muslim poets, as seen in the case of the Shīʿite Kuthaiyir, provided they did not champion religio-political causes; see e.g. *Aghānī* VIII 27: كان كُثير غاليا في التشيع . . . وكان آل مروان يعلمون بمذهبه فلا يغيرهم ذلك له لجلالته في اعينهم ولطف محله في انفسهم وعندهم.

[189] E.g. Jumaḥī, p. 251; Bevan II 1048; Ṣāliḥānī, *Takmilah*, p. 15; *Aghānī* VII 51, 60, 130; ʿ*Iqd* V 271, 325; ʿ*Umdah* I 61.

[190] *Shiʿr*, pp. 57 f.; *Aghānī* VII 51. See also ʿ*Umdah* I 61, where Jarīr concludes with نبغة الشعر فى يد الفرزدق . . . فاني نحرت الشعر نحرا.

[191] E.g. Ṣāliḥānī, *Takmilah*, p. 15; Bevan II 1048 f.; Qurashī, p. 35; *Aghānī* VII 69; ʿ*Iqd* V 271; *Muwashshaḥ*, p. 171.

[192] See Percival in *Journal asiatique*, series 2, Vol. XIV (1834) 13 f., 22 f.

[193] Jāḥiẓ, *Bayān* I 215; *Aghānī* VII 55; *Muwashshaḥ*, p. 127. See n. 155 on p. 188 below for references on the uses of the *rajaz* meter.

[194] For still other candid statements of Jarīr on his two leading rivals namely Akhṭal and Farazdaq, see e.g. *Muwashshaḥ*, p. 130: اخبرنا ابن دريد . . . حدثني الاصعي قال . . . حدثني نوح بن جرير قال قلت لابي يا ابت من اشعر الناس قال قاتل الله قرد بني مجاشع يعنى الفرزدق فعلمت انه قد فضله قلت ثم من قال قاتل الله نصراني بنى تغلب فما انق شعره وابين فضلـه قال قلت فما لك لا تذكر نفسك قال انا مدينة الشعر.

See also *Aghānī* VII 172, as transmitted by Ibn al-Sikkīt on the authority of Aṣmaʿī on the authority of Abū ʿAmr ibn al-ʿAlāʾ, سئل جرير اي الثلاثة اشعر فقال اما الفرزدق فتكلف منى ما لا يطيق واما الاخطل فاشدّنا اجتراء وارمانا للفرائض واما انا فمدينة الشعر.

[195] *Muwashshaḥ*, p. 117: قيل لمسلمة بن عبد الملك اي الشاعرين اشعر اجرير ام فرزدق قال ان الفرزدق يبنى وجرير يهدم وليس يقوم مع الخراب شيء.

The concept of the builder as always either superior or inferior to the demolisher as generally applied to poetry and poets was rejected by later critics (see e.g. Jāḥiẓ, *Bayān* I 213 f.; *Shiʿr*, pp. 28 f.; ʿ*Uyūn* II 184 f.; Ḥuṣrī, *Zahr al-ādāb wa thamar al-albāb* on margins of Ibn ʿAbd Rabbihi, *Al-ʿiqd al-farīd* [Cairo, 1293/1876] II 253 f.).

and his admirers. For Jarīr's sons were proudly aware of the demolishing effect of his satirical counter-thrusts against those who had attacked him. They therefore wished to know why he had restrained himself, comparatively speaking, in his counterattacks against ʿUmar ibn Lajā' al-Taimī. Jarīr's answer, in its briefest form, is reported as "I did not find among them nobility to humiliate nor a structure to demolish."[196] Other statements add that the Banū Taim were shepherds and that the poets among them would each compose a few verses which ʿUmar would appropriate and use in answer to Jarīr's satires.[197] Contemporary women who were knowledgeable in poetry and its criticism, and there were quite a number of them, generally preferred Jarīr, the poet and the man, to Farazdaq because of the latter's obscenities.[198] Some of these women did not hesitate to point out to Farazdaq himself that Jarīr had indeed demolished what he, Farazdaq, had built, as they compared verses of the two poets.[199]

Finally, we find Akhṭal, Jarīr, and Farazdaq described as or compared to three horses in a race. The metaphor or simile may have been suggested by Farazdaq's heroic verses about his family's horsemen, swift and victorious in battle, and Jarīr's verses demolishing that image in terms in part similar to those used by the critics.[200] The first to use the simile seems to have been Maslamah ibn ʿAbd al-Malik, who claimed to know the three poets better than anyone else and placed Akhṭal always first, Farazdaq now first and now second, and Jarīr first, second, or third—a scheme which allows multiple ties.[201] The simile was used also by a group waiting at the gate of the same Maslamah, which placed Akhṭal consistently first, Farazdaq consistently second, and Jarīr either first or third.[202] The use of the simile was reported later to Jumaḥī, whose explanatory comment conveys the idea of a longlasting contest with many races in different fields and with no decision reached as to an over-all winner.[203]

[196] *Aghānī* VII 51: لم اجد حسبا (شرفا) اضعه ولابنا اهدمه (cf. ʿ*Iqd* V 271, 328). See also Jāḥiẓ, *Bayān* III 335: فليس يسلم من مضرة الهجاء الا خامل جدا اونبيه جدا.

[197] *Aghānī* VII 72; *Muwashshaḥ*, p. 129. After ʿUmar ibn Lajā' and his tribe made their peace with Jarīr, he continued to satirize "the mean lot" but claimed the verses were composed during the period of their feud (Jumaḥī, p. 371).

[198] See e.g. Bevan I 181 f., No. 39, and Jarīr's answer on pp. 211 f., No. 40; *Aghānī* VII 56 f.; *Muwashshaḥ*, pp. 160–62.

[199] The literary role of Muslim women in early Islām has been noted occasionally but for the most part briefly. Women of all ages and classes, Bedouins or city dwellers, high-born members of society or low-born but well trained songstresses, displayed on numerous occasions memories well stocked with pre-Islāmic and contemporary poetry. Several of the leading poets of the Umayyad period had sisters or daughters who gave evidence of poetic talent which they seldom fully developed owing in part to a sense of loyalty to fathers or brothers and in part to social discouragement. Where such talent could not be smothered, it found acceptable outlet mainly in elegies, in which the gentler sentiments and the more refined phrases prevailed (see p. 143, n. 213). Nevertheless, the ranking poetesses of the period and such high-born patronesses of culture as Sukainah bint al-Ḥusain ibn ʿAlī did not hesitate to face the poets, including Jarīr and Farazdaq, with the technical shortcomings of their verses, or the vulgarity of their expressions, or the falsity of their egotistical professional claims. Sukainah's perceptive literary criticism, fully documented with liberal citations from the ranking poets, so impressed the poets themselves that they sought her judgment in their own contests and seldom questioned her verdict. She, too, as a rule preferred Jarīr's verses to those of Farazdaq, despite the latter's Shīʿite leanings (see e.g. *Aghānī* VII 53 f., XIV 173–75 and 177, XIX 40 f.; *Muwashshaḥ*, pp. 159 f., 166–69; Ibshīhī I 58). When a young poetess of Akhṭal's own people dared to satirize him, the poet threatened her family in verse with sharp reprisals. The threat silenced the girl and induced her family to placate the poet (Ṣāliḥānī, *Shiʿr al-Akhṭal*, p. 362).

The source material bearing on the literary role of women in early Islām is plentiful though for the most part disorganized and widely scattered. Ibn Abī Ṭāhir Ṭaifūr and later a few others have brought together some of the earlier materials. Their aim was more to amuse the reader than to enlighten him as to the literary role of women. Some modern students of the history of Arabic literature have shown interest in this theme, which, nevertheless, still awaits a thoroughly analytical and critical study.

[200] See e.g. Bevan II 566, No. 61:67–70, and Jarīr's answer on p. 590, No. 62:27, which reads

عرفتم لنا الغرّ السوابق قبلكم   وكان لقينيك السُّكيت المخلَّف

(cf. *Dīwān Jarīr* [1313/1896] II 2–12 and *Sharḥ dīwān Jarīr*, p. 376).

[201] *Shiʿr*, p. 301.

[202] Jumaḥī, pp. 315 f.; *Aghānī* VII 178.

[203] Jumaḥī, pp. 315 f. Cf. *Aghānī* VII 63 f., 172; *Muwashshaḥ*, p. 115.

The critics did use similes of their own that were in part reminiscent of those used in *ḥadīth* criticism. They compared themselves to artists such as musicians and singers, to such artisans as jewelers, clothiers, and carpenters, and to money changers, horse traders, and slave traders, whose judgments were based on professional knowledge and practical experience (see e.g. Jumaḥī, pp. 6–8; Qudāmah, p. 5; *Muwashshaḥ*, pp. 64 f.; ʿ*Umdah* I 75–77). See also our Vol. II 74.

Self-appraisal and mutual criticism among poets contemporary with Akhṭal, Jarīr, and Farazdaq were neither as vocal nor as colorful as the opinions of this trio and, with the exception of those of Kuthaiyir and Baʿīth, seem to have made a less forceful impression on the scholar-critics of their day and after. The extent to which the opinions of our three poets engaged the attention of their contemporaries and successors is attested by the frequent citation of these opinions in both early and later sources, as our footnote documentation readily reveals. Furthermore, most of their opinions, expressed in their own words or in somewhat modified phraseology, were incorporated by their contemporaries into the emerging apparatus of criticism by which the three poets themselves and others were judged then and later.

Instructive evidence of this process is seen in statements made in the presence of the three poets and therefore before the death of Akhṭal late in the reign of Walīd I. Opinions on the three poets were solicited by Prince Hishām and his half-brother Maslamah, and the speakers were a kinsman of Farazdaq and the orator-scholar Khālid ibn Ṣafwān. The princes concurred heartily in Khālid's judgment, which Hishām considered impartial enough to satisfy all three poets and thus to escape their satire. The account as recorded by Abū al-Faraj al-Iṣfahānī, which should be read carefully with a view to both the ideas and the phraseology of the three poets as detailed above, reads as follows:

قال هشام بن عبد الملك لشبّه بن عقّال وعنده جرير والفرزدق والاخطل وهو يومئذ اميرٌ ألاتخبر نى عن هولاء الذين
قد مزّقوا اعراضهم وهتكوا استارهم واغروا بين عشائرهم فى غير خير ولابرّ ولانفع ايهم اشعرُ فقال شبه اما جرير
فيغرِف من بحر واما الفرزدق فينحِت من صخر واما الاخطل فيُجيد المدح والفخر فقال هشام ما فسّرت لنا
شيئا نحصِّله فقال ما عندى غير ما قلت فقال (هشام) لخالد بن صفوان صِفهم لنا يأبن الأهتم فقال اما اعظمُهم
فخرا وابعدهم ذكرا واحسنهم عذرا واسيرهم مثلا واقلّهم غزلا واحلاهم عِللا الطامى إذا زخر والحامى إذا زأر
والسامى اذا خطر الذى إن هدر قال وان خطر صال الفصيُح اللسان الطويلَ العِنان فالفرزدق واما احسنُهم
نعتاً وامدحهم بيتا واقلّهم فوتا الذى إن هجا وضع وان مدح رفع فالاخطل واما اغزرهم بحراً وارقهم شعرا
واهتكهم لعدوّه سترا الاغر الابلق الذى إن طلب لم يُسبق وان طُلب لم يُلحق فجرير وكلهم ذكى الفواد
رفيع العماد وارِى الزناد فقال له مسلمة بن عبد الملك ما سمعنا بمثلك ياخالد فى الاولين ولارايناقى الاخرين
واشهد انك احسنهم وصفا والينهم عِطعا واعظمهم مَقالا واكرمهم فعالا فقال خالد أتم الله عليك نِعمه واجزل
لديك قِسمه وانس بكم العربة وفرّج بكم الكربة وانت والله ما علمتُ ايها الامير كريم الغراس عالم بالباس
جواد فى المحل بسام عند البذل حليم عند الطيش فى ذِروة قريش ولبـاب عبد شمس ويومك خير من امس
فضحك هشام وقال مارايتُ كتخلصك يأبن صفوان فى مدح هولاء ووصفهم حتى ارضيتهم جميعا وسلمت
منهم [204]

Shabbah's routine repetition of Akhṭal's often-quoted appraisals speaks for itself and need not detain us. Khālid's well informed and shrewdly diplomatic appraisal of the three poets is understandable enough considering his own literary talents and the company present on the occasion.

[204] *Aghānī* VII 73 (= *Aghānī* [1927——] VIII 81); cf. Ḥuṣrī, *Zahr al-ādāb wa thamar al-albāb* on margins of Ibn ʿAbd Rabbihi, *Al-ʿiqd al-farīd* (1293/1876) II 252 f. Baihaqī, pp. 458 f., gives an *isnād*-less account of Khālid's speech in which Hishām is not mentioned. The speech itself differs considerably from that of the *Aghānī* account in the order of its main parts, in the transfer of some of its descriptive phrases from one poet to another, and in a few additional phrases. Most of the changes favor Farazdaq. The following discrepancies between the *Aghānī* account and that of Ḥuṣrī may be noted.
Lines 1–4: Ḥuṣrī omits Shabbah (see n. 79 on p. 120 above for confusion as to name and identity) and his speech and refers to Hishām as caliph, which is an error since Akhṭal died before Hishām became caliph.
Line 5: Ḥuṣrī has البحر الطامي and دعر instead of زأر.
Lines 7–8: Ḥuṣrī supplies واقهمهم شعرا واكثرهم ذكرا and omits واهتكهم لعدوة سترا.
Line 11: Ḥuṣrī omits وانس بكم . . . الكربة.
Line 12: Ḥuṣrī has من اشراف عبد شمس.

Khālid's comparatively lengthy characterization of Farazdaq actually does no more than stress that poet's addiction to heroic verse and saber-sharp satire. The rest is but word embroidery stemming on the one hand from Khālid's own predilection for rhymed prose and intended on the other hand to avoid rousing the quickly angered, sharp-tongued, and powerfully built Farazdaq.[205]

Khālid's opinion of Akhṭal must have been indeed gratifying to that poet, who was not only the panegyrist of the Umayyads but who originated the very phrase used by Khālid (see p. 132). Furthermore, Akhṭal had characterized himself and the other two in much the same terms as did Khālid.[206]

Finally, Khālid's appraisal of Jarīr reinforces some of the very factors on which Jarīr himself based his claim to superiority, namely his use of many meters and greater coverage of themes, his easily flowing and more refined verse, readily conceded by his rivals also, and his ability to defeat and humiliate numerous rivals. Furthermore, in placing Jarīr, in the racing metaphor, as either the sole winner or sharing that honor in a tie with another, Khālid not only added to Jarīr's pleasure but avoided offending the other two poets and further gratified Maslamah, who placed Akhṭal always as the winner.

Clearly, Khālid's appraisal, though relatively more comprehensive in its totality, contains no basic point of criticism that was not already current among poets and scholars along with a few points that were missed by Khālid. Furthermore, these points, in their concepts as in their phraseology, continued to be repeated faithfully, if not indeed slavishly, among generations yet to come as one can readily see from the numerous parallel citations presented in this study. For instance, Bashshār ibn Burd, a younger contemporary of both Jarīr and Khālid, was disappointed because Jarīr had not considered him important enough to satirize.[207] Later, in a conversation with Jumaḥī, he declared Jarīr superior to both Akhṭal and Farazdaq on the basis of Jarīr's own claim of proficiency in more categories of poetry than either of his rivals.[208] Still later, prior to and during the reign of the ʿAbbāsid Mahdī, Marwān ibn Abī Ḥafṣah was asked about the three poets. He expressed his opinion in mediocre verse, for ready citation,

ذهب الفرزدق بالفخار وانّما   حُلو الكلام ومرّه لجريــــر
ولقد هجا فامض اخطل تغلب   وحوى اللّـهى بمديحه المشهور
كل الثلاثة قد اجاد فمدحـــه   وهجاؤه قد سار كلّ مسير

and recalled it later, in the reign of Amīn, for the benefit of Jumaḥī and others.[209] Of interest at this point is that the second hemistich of the first verse was current in the poet's lifetime and was first said to Farazdaq himself by his wife Nawār, who considered Jarīr superior as man and poet.[210] Marzubānī

[205] Khālid was short and physically unprepossessing. For his own description of himself and of his personality see pp. 73 f. The slender and somewhat tense Jarīr, with melodious voice, was no physical match either for the big, heavy-set, broad-chested, leonine Farazdaq (see Ibn al-Jarrāḥ, *Al-waraqah*, ed. ʿAbd al-Wahhāb ʿAzzām [Cairo, 1953] p. 75: اما جرير فكان طويلا مضطربا أعن . . . واما الفرزدق فكان عصنفرا عظيم الهـامة رحب الصدر عظيم القصرة كانه اسد). The contrast between the two poets in physique no doubt added to Farazdaq's embarrassment when both were ordered by Sulaimān to strike off the heads of Greek prisoners and Jarīr's partisans saw to it that Farazdaq was handed a blunt sword as against Jarīr's sharp one. Farazdaq's failure and Jarīr's success gave the latter one more episode with which to taunt Farazdaq (see e.g. Bevan II 1035, No. 108; Jumaḥī, pp. 340–42; Ṭabarī II 1338–40; Qurashī, pp. 37 f.; *Muwashshah*, p. 102; Thaʿālibī, *Thimār*, p. 175; Māwardī, *Adab al-dunyā wa al-dīn*, pp. 6 f.).

[206] See e.g. Bevan I 497.

[207] *Aghānī* III 143; *ʿUmdah* I 70. Cf. Jumaḥī, p. 380.

[208] Jumaḥī, pp. 115, 315, 391; *Muwashshah*, pp. 106, 115 f. See also pp. 117–19 and 137 above.

[209] Jumaḥī, p. 318; Mubarrad, p. 416; *Aghānī* IX 46; Ibn al-Muʿtazz, *Ṭabaqāt*, p. 46. Marwān ibn Abī Ḥafṣah like Aṣmaʿī, was known to change his opinion of poets on the spur of the moment (see e.g. *Shiʿr*, p. 20, and *Muwashshah*, p. 121, and cf. *Fuḥūlat al-shuʿarāʾ*, pp. 488 f.).

[210] *Fuḥūlat al-shuʿārāʾ*, p. 503, has شَرَكَك فى حلوه وغلبك فى مره, but Jāḥiẓ, *Bayān* II 184, has اما انه قد غلبك في حلوه وشاركك في مره. See also *Fāḍīl*, p. 108, and *Muwashshah*, pp. 106 and 115, where several others transmit the phrase as شركك في مره وغلبك في حلوه (i.e., the two poets were equal in satire but Jarīr was superior in panegyric and erotica), which on the basis of all that is known of the character and poetry of the two poets has to be the right word order of the phrase. See Bevan I 126 for Nawār's early admiration of Jarīr's poetry, which increased Farazdaq's determination to satirize Jarīr.

rejected Nawār's opinion on account of her stormy life with Farazdaq.[211] For Nawār had been tricked out of her choice of a suitor by Farazdaq, who then persuaded her to marry him. But the good and religious Nawār soon found Farazdaq's way of life distasteful and scolded him constantly about it.[212] We, in turn, should discount Marzubānī's opinion fully for the "sweet" part of the phrase and to a lesser degree for the "bitter." For Farazdaq himself, among others, confirmed Jarīr's claim to superiority in delicate romantic and other categories of touching verse.[213] Furthermore, Farazdaq envied Jarīr his famous heroic verse

اذا غضبت عليك بنو تميم حسبت الناس كلهم غضبانا

whereby Jarīr stole a double march on Farazdaq in praise of their common tribe, the Banū Tamīm, in the very category of poetry in which Farazdaq claimed and was generally accorded superiority.

III

The *naqā'iḍ* of our trio of poets display not only their literary virtuosity but also their most egotistical and competitive characteristics. In the heat of literary combat, decency and truth were sacrificed in the interest of victory and its promise of fame. When Farazdaq greatly magnified the comparatively low social status of the family of Jarīr, the latter did not hesitate to cast doubt on Farazdaq's Arab descent.[214] Neither of these two poets spared the reputation of the women of the other's family or of any other rival's family. Yet they were but following the widely accepted idea in literary circles that "the best of poetry is that which lies most."[215] However, the sources do give us glimpses of other facets of the personality and character of the poets of the time. Here again, what is revealed concerning our three poets is based largely

[211] *Muwashshaḥ*, p. 106: لا يقبل قول النوار على الفرزدق لمنافرتها اياه.

[212] Jumaḥī, pp. 282 f.; *Aghānī* VIII 190: فكانت لاتزال تشارّه وتخالفه لانها كانت صالحة حسنة الدين وكانت تكره كثيرا من امره (cf. *Aghānī* XIX 9). For the dramatic and stormy married life of Farazdaq and Nawār, which finally ended in divorce but during which Nawār appealed to Jarīr against Farazdaq's verses satirizing her and praising a Bedouin co-wife, see e.g. Bevan I 166 f. and II 803–8, Jumaḥī, pp. 267 f. and 280–83, *Aghānī* VIII 187–92 and XIX 6–12, and Richard Boucher, *Divan de Férazdak* (Paris, 1870) text pp. 2–5 and translation pp. 4–8. Farazdaq regretted the divorce and was a repentant mourner at Nawār's funeral ceremonies performed by Ḥasan al-Baṣrī (Jumaḥī, pp. 267 f., 283; *Aghānī* XIX 47).

[213] Bevan II 1048: قال الفرزدق قاتل الله ابن المراغة ما احوجه مع عفته الى جزالة شعرى وما احوجنى مع فجوري الى رقة شعره. *Shi'r*, p. 29, gives a somewhat different version: كان العرزدق يقول ما احوجه مع عفته الى صلابة شعرى وما احوجنى الى رقة شعره لما ترون.

Jumaḥī, in a conversation with Mu'āwiyah ibn Abī 'Amr ibn al-'Alā', compared Jarīr's السمّ خير من ركب المطايا الخ with Akhṭal's شمس العداوة حتى يستفاد لهم الخ in the following terms: بيت جرير احلى واسير وبيت الاخطل اجزل وارزن, to which Mu'āwiyah added صدقت وهكذا كانا فى انفسهما عند الخاصة والعامة (Jumaḥī, p. 426; *Aghānī* VII 180). For Jarīr's comparatively more sensitive and refined references to women see e.g. Jumaḥī, p. 39, *Aghānī* VII 41 and 55, '*Iqd* V 300 f. and VI 25. Farazdaq's poetry was so lacking in sensitivity that when Nawār died it yielded no verses appropriate for the occasion, and the professional mourners resorted to Jarīr's touching and widely known elegies on his own son and wife (Jumaḥī, pp. 391–93; Mubarrad, p. 723; *Shi'r*, pp. 208 f.; *Aghānī* VII 40, 53; '*Iqd* III 256; *Sharḥ dīwān Jarīr*, pp. 199 f.

It was thought that elegies, especially for women, were the most difficult category of poetry for men to compose and therefore that only the best of poets could sincerely eulogize or elegize a woman. Again, it was generally conceded that a poetess was at her best in elegies; see n. 199 on p. 140 above and e.g. '*Umdah* I 30 f. and 79 f.: اصعب الشعر الرثاء لانه لا يعمل رغبة ولارهبه . . . اشعر الناس من تخلص من مدح امراة ورثاها. See also '*Umdah* II 117–26, where Ibn Rashīq expounds and illustrates both of these observations.

[214] Jāḥiẓ, *Bayān* III 78.

[215] See e.g. Qudāmah, Intro. pp. 1, 9, 38 f. and text pp. 26 f.: احسن الشعر اكذبه. See also '*Iqd* V 328 and 335–38 (اشعر الناس الذى يصور الباطل في صورة الحق والصق في صورة الباطل); Baihaqī, p. 461 (ليس انطق بالكذب من الشعراء); Abū Hilāl al-Ḥasan ibn 'Abd Allāh al-'Askarī, *Kitāb al-ṣinā'atain al-kitābah wa al-shi'r*, pp. 136 f. (يراد من الشاعر حسن الكلام والصدق يراد من الانبياء), 138 f.; *Muzhir* II 470. See further pp. 93, 95, and 133, n. 149, above. It is interesting to note in connection with the role of truth and falsehood in poetry a related concept, as stated by Aṣma'ī, that the quality of poetry deteriorates when it depicts good or gentle themes: قال الاصمعى طريق الشعراء اذا ادخلته في خير لان الاترى ان حسان بن ثابت كان علا في الجاهليه والاسلام فلم دخل شعره في باب الخير في مراثي رسول الله صلعم . . . لان شعره (*Muwashshaḥ*, p. 65). But see Marzūqī I 11 f. for a different approach to truth and falsehood in poetry.

on their own statements. Their extreme egotism is forgotten in moments of truth when one acknowledges the effectiveness of another's barbs even though pointed at himself or when they envy verses of other poets regardless of the nature or target. Akhṭal, for instance, proclaimed his love of wine and his aversion to outrageous indecencies in poetry and claimed that his own satires were such that not even a virgin would hesitate to recite them to her father.[216] Once Akhṭal had satirized a person, he refused later to praise him or, having first praised a person, refused thereafter to satirize him. The same was true of Jarīr but for the rare cases when he praised Ḥajjāj and Farazdaq after having satirized them (pp. 89 and 145). In contrast, Farazdaq did not hesitate to praise and later satirize or to satirize and later praise a person—practices which both Akhṭal and Jarīr held against him.[217] Jarīr explained that his lampoons on women were counterthrusts made in self-defense against an aggressor or rival who spared not the women of his own family and tribe.[218] Not only Farazdaq's wife Nawār but also Farazdaq himself confirmed on more than one occasion the truth of Jarīr's statement.[219] Farazdaq went a step farther and condemned others for baiting Jarīr only to find him more than their match in the battle of words.[220] Farazdaq and Akhṭal each envied some of the verses of the other.[221] Jarīr was even more forthright in expressing pity as ʿAdī ibn al-Riqāʿ recited the first half of a verse. But this changed to admiration as ʿAdī recited the second hemistich, and Jarīr felt pity for himself, which soon turned into a strong sense of envy, for ʿAdī, in describing the horns of a gazelle, had actually improved on one of Jarīr's own similes.[222]

ʿAbd al-Malik once asked Akhṭal and Jarīr if they wished they had authored some verses of other poets. Their negative answers were followed in each case with a strong expression of admiration for some verses of an as yet little known younger poet in whom they had detected talent. Akhṭal's choice was his fellow tribesman Quṭāmī,[223] and Jarīr's choice was Muzāḥim al-ʿUqailī.[224]

Akhṭal had the honesty to admit his regret for having taken sides in the verbal duels of Jarīr and Farazdaq.[225] Jarīr spoke with feeling of the one time he regretted having satirized the Banū Numair.[226]

[216] *Aghānī* VII 178: قال الاخطل ما هجوت احدا قط بما تستحى العذراء تنشده اباها (see also Ṣāliḥānī, *Shiʿr al-Akhṭal*, p. 344).

[217] Bevan II 1048 f. But see *Fragmenta historicum Arabicorum* I 83 and 88, where ʿUmar ibn Hubairah admired Farazdaq for satirizing him as governor and praising him later as a prisoner. See also Ṭabarī II 1433.

[218] Jāḥiẓ, *Bayān* III 149 f.; see also p. 114 above.

[219] Jāḥiẓ, *Bayān* II 184: قال الفرزدق لنوار كيف رايت جريرا قالت رايتك ظلمتة اولا ثم شغرت عنه برجلك اخرا قال انا أنى قالت نعم اما انه قد غلبك في حلوه وشاركك في مره; Jumaḥī, pp. 312 f.: قال بعض الخلفاء لهما حتى متى لا تنتزعان فقال جرير يا امير المومنين انه والله يظلمنى قال الفرزدق صدق انا اظلمه ووجدت ابي يظلم اباه (see *Aghānī* XIX 7, where the caliph in question is identified as Yazīd II).

[220] *Aghānī* VII 41: هزوه فوجدوه عند الهراش نابحا وعند الجراء قارحا وقد قال بيتا لان اكون قلته احب الى مما طلعت عليه الشمس (see p. 117 above for the verse envied by Farazdaq). See also ʿ*Umdah* II 60, where Jarīr is considered among the best of all poets when angered.

[221] Qurashī, p. 36.

[222] Mubarrad, p. 514; *Aghānī* VIII 182; *Muʿjam al-shuʿarā*ʾ, p. 253. See also ʿ*Umdah* I 176 f., where Ibn Rashīq cites and comments on the two verses involved:

قول جرير يصف الخيل

يخرجن من مستطير النقع داميهً كان آذانها اطراف اقـــلام

فقال عدى بن الرقاع يصف الغزال

تزجى أغنّ كان ابرة روقـــه قلم اصاب من الدواة مـــدادهـــا

ʿAdī's verse is frequently cited for its more apt and novel simile (see e.g. Jumaḥī, p. 558; *Shiʿr*, p. 392; ʿ*Iqd* V 313; Ṣūlī, *Adab al-kuttāb*, pp. 78 f.; Thaʿālibī, *Thimār*, p. 239).

[223] See e.g. *Aghānī* XX 118 f. and 130 f.; see also n. 182 on p. 191 below for differing opinions of Akhṭal and Shaʿbī as to the best verses of this as yet little known poet. For Quṭāmī see e.g. Jumaḥī, pp. 452–57, *Shiʿr*, pp. 453–56 and *Aghānī* XX 118–31.

[224] See e.g. *Aghānī* XVII 152; Jumaḥī, p. 583, where Muzāḥim's poetry is characterized in terms similar in part to those used for Jarīr's; ʿAskarī, *Maṣūn*, pp. 25, 173. See also Henri Lammens, "Le chantre des Omiades," *Journal asiatique*, series 9, Vol. IV (1894) 402–4 and references there cited for other occasions when ʿAbd al-Malik plied his courtiers, poets, and scholars with evaluative questions, and n. 165 on p. 136 above for ʿAbd al-Malik as a student and critic of poetry.

[225] Bevan II 496.

[226] *Aghānī* VII 74: فانصرفتُ وانا اندم الناس على ما سلف منى الى قومه (see Bevan I 432–51, No. 53).

Farazdaq, having first sharply criticized Kumait ibn Zaid's *Hāshimīyāt* in praise of the ʿAlīds, encouraged the younger poet with the highest praise, assuring him he was the best of all.[227] In their old age Jarīr and Farazdaq dwelt more on their affinities than on their differences. When Khālid al-Qaṣrī, Hishām's governor of ʿIrāq, imprisoned Farazdaq, Jarīr to the surprise and admiration of the caliph pleaded for his release. In his statement, as reported by Abū ʿUbaidah,[228] Jarīr regretted and negated the false vanities of their *naqāʾiḍ* in terms that are worth quoting in full:

قال هشام يا جرير ان الله قد اخزى الفاسق قال أيَّ الفُساق يا اميرالمدمنين قال الفرزدق ثم قال يا امير المومنين ان اردت أن تتَّخذ يدا عند حاضرة مُضرو باديتها فاطلق لهم شاعرهم وسيدهم وابن سيدهم فقال هشام يا جرير أما يسرّك ان يخزى الفرزدق قال لا والله يا امير المومنين الا ان يخزى بلساني قال فاين ما تقول له ويقول لك قال ما اقول ولا يقول الا الباطل فلما انصرف جرير اتبعه هشام بُصرّةٍ وقال ويحه اىُّ امرئُ هو عند حسبه

When the news of Farazdaq's death in Baṣrah reached Jarīr in the Najdian Yamāmah, he expressed a premonition of his own soon-to-follow demise, though he was a decade or so younger than Farazdaq. As tears filled his eyes to the amazement of those present, he explained that he was mourning for himself as well. For he felt that seldom do two kinsmen or two friends or a husband and wife whose lives have been so intertwined as had his and Farazdaq's outlive for long one the other.[229] He died some six months later but not before he had left the Arab literary world several touching elegies on his erstwhile rival Farazdaq.[230]

IV

The leading philologists and grammarians of the late Umayyad period were primarily professional Qurʾānic-readers, as were also the majority of their pupils. As such they pursued their linguistic studies as a means to the understanding and interpretation of the Qurʾān. There were a few exceptions, the most notable being Abū ʿAmr ibn al-ʿAlāʾ, who included the collection and study of pre-Islāmic poetry among his objectives. It was with the Arab Khalīl ibn Aḥmad's *Kitāb al-ʿarūḍ* and his *Kitāb al-ʿain*, even if he only began it, and the *Kitāb* of the Persian Sībawaih that specialized linguistic studies first achieved professional recognition in their own right. From among the contemporaries and pupils of Khalīl and Sībawaih came the first littérateurs of Islām—the collectors, transmitters, commentators, and finally the emerging critics of Arabic literary prose and poetry, but mostly the latter, both pre-Islāmic and Islāmic. This was the period of Ḥammād al-Rāwiyah[231] and Mufaḍḍal ibn Muḥammad al-Ḍabbī, who have crossed our path so often that they need not detain us here. It was also the period of Muḥammad ibn al-Sāʾib al-Kalbī (d. 146/763), genealogist and Qurʾānic commentator, who transmitted from choice a hundred odes of Jarīr and was intimidated by Farazdaq into transmitting an equal number of his *naqāʾiḍ*, having first read them out to Farazdaq himself—an indication of possession of *naqāʾiḍ* manuscripts by one or both of these men.[232] A similar episode involved the Kūfan Khālid ibn Kulthūm

[227] Masʿūdī VI 36–39: قال الفرزدق يا بنى اصبت واحسنت . . . وانت والله اشعر من مضى واشعر من بقى.

[228] Bevan II 984 f.

[229] *Ibid*. II 1045 f.; *Aghānī* XIX 45.

[230] Bevan II 1046 f.; *Aghānī* XIX 45 f. These elegies are in contrast to his verse in anticipation of Farazdaq's death and to his first single verse of impulse when he heard of his rival's death (see Thaʿālibī, *Thimār*, p. 107).

[231] See *Aghānī* VII 52 for a conversation between Ḥammād and Farazdaq on the respective merits of the latter and Jarīr.

[232] *Maʿārif*, pp. 266 f.: فقال لى (الفرزدق) اتروى شيئا من شعرى قلت لا ولكني اروى لجرير ماية قصيدة فقال تروى لابن المراغة والله لاهجونّ كلبا سنة او تروى لى كما رويت لجرير فجعلت اختلف واقرا عليه النقائض خوفا منه وما لي في شى منها حاجة. For Muḥammad ibn al-Sāʾib al-Kalbī's works and manuscripts and the patronage of booksellers by himself and his son Hishām see our Vols. I, 25, 45, 48, 55 and II 47, 99, 104–6.

Farazdaq was quick to satirize scholars who criticized his grammar or preferred Jarīr to himself (see e.g. Zubaidī, p. 24). For his encounters with ʿAnbasat al-Fīl see Sīrāfī, pp. 23 f., and *Muwashshaḥ*, pp. 100 f., 104 f. See also p. 26 above.

al-Kalbī (n.d.), who had collected and written down the poetry of several tribes and some of the *naqā'iḍ* of Jarīr and Farazdaq but memorized and recited only those of Jarīr. Farazdaq threatened to satirize the Banū Kalb unless Khālid wrote down, memorized, and recited Farazdaq's responses to Jarīr's odes.[233] Khālid concludes his account thus: فقلت افعل فلزمته شهرا حتى حفظت نقائضها وانشدته خوفا من شره.

The period of these first littérateurs was overlapped by that of Akhfash al-Akbar, Khalaf al-Aḥmar, Yūnus ibn Ḥabīb, Abū Zaid al-Anṣārī, Abū 'Ubaidah, and Aṣma'ī, all of whom displayed insight into various phases of literary criticism. Inasmuch as satire was the most widely used weapon against literary rivals or political and personal foes, the scholars for the most part tended to judge the poets by their effectiveness in that category. Though opinion was unanimous that our three poets were the most effective of the pre-'Abbāsid Islāmic poets, individual critics presented plausible reasons for their preference of one of the three over the other two. Their reasons reflected their own fields of intellectual interest as well as aesthetic and moral values and involved such aspects as range of vocabulary, variety of satirical themes, degree of obscenity and of truthfulness. Yūnus ibn Ḥabīb, who preferred Farazdaq to Jarīr, is reported as saying that were it not for Farazdaq's poetry one-third of the Arabic language would have been lost.[234] Akhfash al-Akbar and, after him, Abū 'Ubaidah pointed out the paucity and falsity of Jarīr's satirical themes aimed at Farazdaq as against some hundred such themes used against Jarīr by Farazdaq.[235] Yūnus ibn Ḥabīb favored Akhṭal over the other two for his greater number of long odes, his greater accuracy, and his aversion to obscenity.[236] Abū 'Ubaidah admired all three poets but criticized Farazdaq for lack of intellectual honesty as did also Aṣma'ī, who admired Jarīr's originality and on the whole preferred Akhṭal to both Farazdaq and Jarīr in confirmation of the opinion of Abū 'Amr ibn al-'Alā'.

Abū al-Faraj al-Iṣfahānī recorded repeatedly the divergent opinions of the "ancients" and the "moderns" on the ranking of our three poets. His statement that all of the "ancients" ranked Akhṭal third is certainly misleading but may reflect at least in part the general opinion of the "transmitters" of his day on Akhṭal's rank (see pp. 119 f.). He himself, to judge by his initial oration, favored Farazdaq. Nevertheless, he summed up rather well, barring some exceptions, the subjective factors that influenced a critic's over-all preference by classifying the critics themselves in two groups. Those who incline to strong language and haughty poetry that takes firm hold of them rank Farazdaq first; those who incline to the poetry of born poets and to gentle, easily flowing, gallant verse rank Jarīr first.[237] Abū al-Faraj, it should be noted, omits any reference to moral factors. Therefore, it is readily understood why such born poets as Bashshār ibn Burd and Ibn Munādhir (d. 199/815) were great admirers of Jarīr (see p. 119, n. 68).[238] Ibn Munādhir's answer to the familiar question as to who was the best poet may be here summarized in the words "he who is playful and serious at will" and "he who is beyond reach both in his sportive mood and

[233] *Aghānī* XIX 11 f. For Khālid's activities see *Fihrist*, pp. 66 and 157, *Inbāh* I 352, and *Bughyah*, p. 241. Farazdaq himself memorized a great deal of his own and others' poetry and preferred short to longer odes (*Aghānī* XIX 33 f.; see also p. 136 above).

[234] *Aghānī* XIX 48: قال ابو عبيدة سمعت يونس يقول لولا شعر الفرزدق لذهب ثلث لغة العرب. Yūnus was generally partial to Farazdaq (*ibid.* p. 6: وكان يونس فرزدقيا) as in fact was Jarīr, excepting always himself (see Qurashī, p. 35: قال جرير كذب من قال انه اشعر من الفرزدق . . . وقال انا مدينة الشعر).

[235] *Muwashshaḥ*, pp. 121–24.

[236] *Aghānī* VII 174 and Yazīdī, p. 80; cf. Ṣāliḥānī, *Shi'r al-Akhṭal*, pp. 343 f. Yūnus cited in support of his preference five early grammarians, including Ibn Abī Isḥāq and Abū 'Amr ibn al-'Alā', all five of whom he described as having beaten a path for progress in speech in contrast to others' cited authorities who were neither Bedouins nor grammarians: هولاء طرّقوا الكلام وماشوه لا كمن تحكمون عنه لا بدويين ولا نحويين.

[237] *Aghānī* XIX 48: هم في ذلك طبقتان اما من كان يميل الى جزالة الشعر وفخامته وشدة أسره فيقدم الفرزدق واما من كان يميل الى اشعار المطبوعين والى الكلام السمح السهل الغزل فيقدم جريرا. See pp. 125 f. and 130, n. 125, above for the natural-born as against the laboring poet.

[238] See *Aghānī* III 25 for Aṣma'ī's preference for Bashshār, a born poet, as against Marwān ibn Abī Ḥafṣah and his labored poetry.

in his lofty thoughts." He then named Jarīr as the supreme example and reinforced his opinion with citations from Jarīr's poetry.[239] Buḥturī, on the other hand, reports that his father, a contemporary of Ibn Munādhir, was similar in temperament to Jarīr yet such an extreme admirer of Farazdaq's poetry that he did not even wish to speak to anyone who preferred Jarīr to Farazdaq, nor would he count such a one among those knowledgeable in poetry.[240]

It seems fitting at this point to refer to Jarīr's great-grandson ʿUmārah ibn ʿAqīl ibn Bilāl ibn Jarīr, a poet and a scholar in his own right[241] who surpassed the several other poets of Jarīr's family. To him and his line back to Jarīr himself we owe much of our information on Jarīr the man and on his relationships with some of his contemporaries (see p. 115, n. 45, and p. 137). ʿUmārah was court poet to several of the early ʿAbbāsid caliphs, including Maʾmūn.[242] He was much sought after by scholars of ʿIrāq, beginning with Abū ʿUbaidah and including his own younger contemporaries Mubarrad and Thaʿlab,[243] to whom he dictated not only his own poetry but also that of other members of his family, particularly that of Jarīr.[244] It is interesting to note both the conformity and the divergence in literary criticism as reflected in remarks of Salam, great-grandson of Abū ʿAmr ibn al-ʿAlāʾ, who recalled the latter's statement that poetry had ended with Dhū al-Rummah but added that he wished Abū ʿAmr could see how much more advanced was ʿUmārah.[245] Salam also remarked that ʿUmārah's poetry was more uniformly good and faultless than Jarīr's, to which ʿUmārah himself added that the greater part of Jarīr's poetry cannot be matched by anyone. And there were some who agreed with both statements, especially Mubarrad, who is quoted as saying that "the eloquence of the modern poets ended with ʿUmārah ibn ʿAqīl."[246]

The information in this section has been brought together at the risk of some repetition for the purpose of stressing the general character and level of literary criticism during the second/eighth century as indicated by the scholars' criticism of our trio of poets. For I have gathered from numerous references to many other poets, particularly Dhū al-Rummah (see Document 7), that the same type of literary criticism was applied to the contemporaries and predecessors of our three, though to a much lesser extent to the pre-Islāmic poets, who as a group were accepted and extolled as models of excellence. Much of the scholars' criticism, apart from a flexible quantitative element, was centered on the mechanics of grammar and prosody, with some attention paid to permissible poetic license.[247] So far as criticism was focused on the niceties of style and on aesthetics, the scholars of the second half of the second century contributed

239 *Aghānī* III 154 f. and VII 63; see also Ibn Khallikān I 128 f. (= trans. I 296 f.), which combines the two *Aghānī* accounts and gives a literal translation.

240 *Muwashshaḥ*, p. 124.

241 *GAL* S I 122; Ibn al-Muʿtazz, *Ṭabaqāt*, pp. 316–18.

242 *Aghānī* XX 183 f., 186; *Muʿjam al-shuʿarāʾ*, p. 247. See also Ṭabarī III 1659.

243 Bevan III 170; *Dīwān Salāmah ibn Jandal*, ed. Louis Cheikho (Beirūt, 1910), p. 22; *Fāḍil*, p. 62.

244 E.g. *Aghānī* XV 101 and XX 183 f., 185 f.; *ʿIqd* V 368; Khaṭīb XII 282 f. ʿUmārah himself had written down his teacher's materials and had dictated all of his own *dīwān* to his *rāwiyah* Ibrāhīm ibn Saʿdān ibn al-Mubārak, who later refused to let the aged ʿUmārah use his manuscripts unless he promised to share his reward with him (*Aghānī* XX 187; Sīrāfī, pp. 80, 85 f.; *Marātib*, p. 39). See pp. 14 and 30 above for other members of Ibrāhīm's family of scholars.

For Zuhair ibn Abī Sulmā's and Jarīr's remarkable families of poets in both the ascending and descending lines see e.g. *Fihrist*, p. 159, and *ʿUmdah* II 236.

245 *Aghānī* XX 183.

246 *Ibid.*: قال المبرد ختمت الفصاحة في شعراء المحدثين بعمارة بن عقيل (cf. *Muwashshaḥ*, p. 119). ʿUmārah seems to have been the last ranking poet of Jarīr's remarkable family. He was, so he said, ugly but sagacious. He married a beautiful but foolish woman in the hope that his offspring would inherit her beauty and his sagacity, but they inherited her foolishness and his looks (Khaṭīb XII 282 f.; *Nuzhah*, p. 108). His own *dīwān*, however, continued to circulate. Among those who memorized some of his poetry was a woman client of the descendants of Ḥajjāj ibn Yūsuf. She memorized poetry and taught it to the daughters of the house (*Amālī* II 62).

Farazdaq's sons died young except Labaṭah, who supplied some personal information about his father (see n. 47 on p. 115 above). Farazdaq himself claimed that he inherited his poetic talent from his maternal uncles (*Aghānī* XIX 49; cf. Jumaḥī, p. 152).

247 See e.g. *Shiʿr*, pp. 6, 29–35; Jumaḥī, pp. 181–88, 299 f., 362; *ʿUmdah* II 208–15; *Muzhir* II 471 f.

little that was basically different in character from what had already been displayed by the scholars of the first half of the century and by the leading Umayyad poets themselves in their mutual criticism and self-appraisal and by a few of their poetically inclined patrons. Literary criticism on this level remained for the most part a matter of passing impulse for some and of intuitive knowledge for others and was for all more or less subjective.

Aṣmaʿī's natural inclination to be an entertaining raconteur and his ambition to be a favored courtier may or may not have hindered him, despite his prodigious talent and vast knowledge, from undertaking a more formal and analytical approach to literary criticism than one finds in his *Fuḥūlat al-shuʿarāʾ*. Nevertheless, anyone who delves deeply into the sea of Arabic literature, as Jarīr would say, soon realizes that Aṣmaʿī and his outstanding contemporaries do reflect the level of literary criticism reached in the age of Abū ʿAmr ibn al-ʿAlāʾ and that in so doing they have reduced for us the effects of the loss of that great scholar's large library and the loss of the manuscript collections of that age. They spent much time and energy in collecting, digesting, and preserving their literary heritage. Their pupils had at their disposal the record of this heritage, which was clarified and augmented through their personal contact with these masters. The scholars of the next generation were exposed to new cultural and literary influences from within and without their society. They were, therefore, in better position, as either traditionists or eclectics, to begin producing the more formal and increasingly analytical works of literary criticism, for both prose and poetry, that so greatly enriched the literature of the third/ninth century and left their mark on Islāmic culture for several centuries thereafter.

DOCUMENT 6

PARTS OF TWO ODES OF AKHṬAL

Oriental Institute No. 17642. Late third/late ninth century.

Paper book folio, 28.2 × 19.2 cm. (Pls. 7–8). The paper, of fine quality and medium thickness, is of the type that became increasingly common for literary purposes in ʿIrāq from the beginning of the third/ninth century onward. It came into use much earlier in the provinces farther to the east, where it continued to be the main writing material. The bitter and lengthy complaint which Jāḥiẓ addressed to Muḥammad ibn ʿAbd al-Malik al-Zayyāt (d. 233/847), who for his own ulterior motives had persuaded Jāḥiẓ to use leather and parchment for the manuscripts in his large library instead of Chinese or Khurāsānian paper, is indicative enough of the rapidly increasing use of paper in the first half of the third/ninth century. Jāḥiẓ, furthermore, pointed out the advantages of rag paper (*waraq quṭnī* and *dafātir al-quṭnī*) as writing material because of its smoothness and light weight, especially for use by book copyists and booksellers and by traveling scholars, as against the rough and heavier leather or parchment.[1] Attention has been drawn above to several extant literary works written on paper and dated in the second half of the third/ninth century (see p. 11). Their scripts are comparable in several respects with that of our Document 6, which is well preserved except for a minor break at the bottom. Note the *basmalah* and part of the *ḥamdalah* scribbled later in the two lines on the lower half of the left margin of the recto.

Script.—*Naskhī* book hand of medium quality. It lacks consistency, especially for the several forms of the separate *alif*, other than the straight perpendicular, as in recto 6 and 9 and verso 1–2. The script shows a few irregular Kūfic features such as the forms of the initial and final *kāf*, as in recto 5 and 8, the *ḥā*ʾ or *khā*ʾ with a beam, as in recto 14, and the large semi-angular *ṭā*ʾ, as in verso 2. Diacritical points are freely used. The letters *dāl* and *rā*ʾ each have a dot below to distinguish them from *dhāl* and *zāy*, and *sīn* has three dots in a row below (as in verso 5 and 7) to distinguish it from *shīn* with three dots above. A small letter corresponding in each case to the letter itself is placed under *ḥā*ʾ (as in recto 19), *ṣād* (recto 14 and 20), *ṭā*ʾ (recto 14), and *ʿain* (recto 14 and 17). Final *yā*ʾ and the *alif maqṣūrah* interchange. Vowels are used freely but not fully. The *hamzah* is used in recto 5 and verso 7, 11, 17, and 20, more often than

[1] See Jāḥiẓ, *Rasāʾil*, ed. ʿAbd al-Sālam Muḥammad Hārūn (Cairo, 1384/1964–65) I 252–54, for the following excerpt from which I have omitted Jāḥiẓ' refutation of the supposed advantages of leather:

وما عليك ان تكون كتبي كلها من الورق الصيني ومن الكاغذ الخراساني قل لي ولمَ زينت النسخ في الجلود ولم حثثتنى على الأدم . . . وقد علمت ان الورّاق لا يخط في تلك الايام سطرا ولا يقطع فيها جلدا . . . وقلت لي ليس لدفاتر القطني أثمان في السوق . . . وزعمت ان الارضية الي الكاغذ اسرع . . . فكنت سبب المضرّة في اتخاذ الجلود والاستبدال بالكاغذ وكنت سبب البلية في تحويل الدفاتر الخفاف في المحمل الى المصاحف التى تثقل الايدى وتحطم الصدور وتقوس الظهور وتعمى الابصار.

Thereafter, Jāḥiẓ and his secretary-copyist no doubt used paper for his own compositions and bought paper manuscripts for his library from booksellers, some of whom were known specifically as his bookseller (*warrāq al-Jāḥiẓ*), for example Zakariyā ibn Yaḥyā (*Fihrist*, p. 220; Jāḥiẓ, *Ḥayawān* I, Intro. pp. 12 f.; *Amālī* I 248; *Irshād* VI 75) and ʿAbd al-Wahhāb ibn ʿĪsā (Khaṭīb XI 28 f., 163). We find Jāḥiẓ also in the company of the poet-bookseller Maḥmūd al-Warrāq, who recites some of his verses to him (Jāḥiẓ, *Rasāʾil* [1964–65] II 36). For instances of close association between second/eighth-century booksellers and scholars and poets—not to mention such powerful patrons as the caliphs and the Barmakids and some eager bibliophiles (*jammāʿat lil-kutub*)—see e.g. our Vols. I 3 f., 24, 91, n. 3, and II 46 f., 127. To these we can add the association of Mufaḍḍal ibn Muḥammad al-Ḍabbī with Ḥabīb ibn Busṭām al-Warrāq (*Inbah* III 300). That so few early manuscripts on paper or other writing materials have survived is due in large part to the nature of the soil of the eastern provinces of Islām.

not in conjunction with *yāʾ*. The *shaddah* is used in recto 14 and 17–18 and verso 12. The *sukūn* is not indicated. The circle is used, though not regularly, to mark a break in the verse text and occasionally at the end of a comment, as in recto 6 and 16. No space or other device marks off the hemistichs. That the same shade of ink, heavier in some parts than in others, is used for the consonantal text and the orthographic devices indicates that the latter are original and not, as in many cases, later additions. The orthographic system is that devised by Khalīl ibn Aḥmad for use especially in poetry (see pp. 7–9).

TEXT

Recto

1 والحفيرة لها ويفعل باللغزين ما يفعل بالنافقاء
2 وتراب اللغزين يسما النافقاء
3 فلا تدخل بيوت بنى كليب ولا تقرب لهم ابدا رحالا
4 ترى [م]نها لوامع مُبرقات يكدن ينِكن بالحدق الرجالا
5 قصيرات الخطى عن كلّ خير الى السؤات مسمحة رعالا
6 ○ الرعال السراع ○
7 وقـــال
8 كذبتك عينُك ام رايت بواسط غلس
9 الظلام من الرباب خَيالا
10 اراد الاستفهام واكذبتك
11 فالقا الالف ويقال اتيته غلس الظلام
12 وملس الظلام وملث الظلام وقد يكون
13 ذلك فى اول الليل واخره
14 وتعرضت لك بالابالخ بعد ما قطعت بابرق خُلّة ووصالا
15 الابرق الجبل المختلط بالرمل وهى البُرقة
16 والخلة الصداقة ○
17 وتغوّلت لتروعنا جِنيّة والغانيات يرينك الاهوالا
18 التغوّل التلوّن والغانيات الجوارى
19 واحدتهن [غا]نية والاهوال الاخواف
20 يمدُدن من هفواتهن الى الصبا سببا يصدن به الغُواة طوالا

Verso

1 الهفوة الجهل يقال هفا يهفوا هفوة ويُهفا
2 والطول الطويل والصبا العشق يقال
3 صبا صبوا صبوة وصباً
4 وما رايتُ كمكرهن اذا جرى فينا ولا كحبالهن حبالا
5 المهديات لمن هوين مسبة والمحسنات لمن قلين مقالا
6 يقال قليته اقليته قِلا وقلان وقليه قلاه قِلاة

7 يرعين عهدك ما رأينك شاهدا واذا مذلتَ يصرن عنك مذال
8 المنذل العرض بالشى والاطراح له نذل بماله
9 ومذل بعرضه ومذل بمضجعه اذا عرض منه وتركه
10 مذلا ومذاله وهو مذلته ومذيل
11 واذا وعدنك نأيلا اخلفنه ووجدت عند عداتهن مطالا
12 واذا دعونك عمَّهن فانه سبب يزيدك عندهن خبالا
13 الخبال الفساد يقال خبلته اخبله خبلا
14 وخبالا
15 واذا وزنت حلموهن الى الصبا رجع الصبى بحلومهن فمالا
16 اهى الصريمة منك ام مُحلم ام ذا الدلال فطال ذاك دلالا
17 ولقد علمت اذا العشار تروحت هدج الرئال تكبُّهن شمالا
18 العشار النوق التى قد اتت على عشر اشهر
19 من ملقحها او قاربت به [ويقال عش]رة الناقة
20 اذا بلغت ذلك الوقت والرئال النعام وتكبهن يريد
21 الريح وهن للنعام قوله شمالا يريد هابة شمالا

Comments.—The two odes represented in our document are to be found in published collections of Akhṭal's poetry (see Ṣāliḥānī, *Shiʿr al-Akhṭal*, pp. 41–51, 163–65; Ṣāliḥānī, *Takmilah*, p. 7, Nos. 10 and 13; Ṣāliḥānī, *Naqāʾiḍ Jarīr wa al-Akhṭal*, pp. 70–73, 189–91; Griffini, pp. 49 f.), but the commentary differs markedly from those in these sources, which in turn differ among themselves. The order of verses also differs, and three verses of the published editions are missing in our fragment though they may have been included in the manuscript it represents. However, the familiar phenomenon of different manuscripts of the same ode varying not only in verse order but in number of verses is correctly understood to have stemmed, to begin with, from the very nature of Arabic poetry, which demands syntactic independence for each verse. This in turn facilitated changes in verse order and the deletion or addition of verses in revisions made by the poet himself or by his secretary (*kātib*) or by his personal transmitter (*rāwiyah*), who functioned at times as secretary, editor, and critic. Again, but perhaps to a lesser extent, additions and deletions of verses may have been the work of persons who because of failure of memory or for other reasons of their own tampered with certain poems.

The original commentaries in the above-cited editions of Akhṭal's poetry are supplemented by comments of their modern editors. These two sets of comments provide mainly linguistic aids so far as our text is concerned and, along with the historical and literary background of the *naqāʾiḍ* of Akhṭal, Jarīr, and Farazdaq as already presented in connection with our Documents 4 and 5, eliminate the need for detailed line-by-line comments here. Attention is drawn mainly to scribal errors, to the order or omission of verses, to uncommon textual variants, to any marked differences in the original commentaries of the several editions, and to some rather interesting citations of these verses.

Recto 1–6. From an ode of nine verses satirizing Jarīr and the women of his tribe. The comments in lines 1–2 refer to the last verse on the page which preceded our folio. This verse in the printed text reads

تسدّ القاصعآءُ عليه حتى   ينفق اويموت بهـــا هـُزالا

but is cited by Mubarrad, p. 153, with the variant عليك, which changes the verbs following to the second person singular. The verse is cited in explanation of يا اهل العراق as used by Ḥajjāj ibn Yūsuf in addressing a severe rebuke to the people of ʿIrāq (see p. 81 above and see also Ṣāliḥānī, *Shiʿr al-Akhṭal*, pp. 163–65, and Ṣāliḥānī, *Naqāʾiḍ Jarīr wa al-Akhṭal*, pp. 190 f.).

Recto 3–6. The dot below the *rāʾ* of the last word of line 3 is either omitted in the printed editions or placed under the following *ḥāʾ*, thus giving the incorrect reading رجالا. The two verses of lines 4–5 are cited with the variation فان بها for the first and second words of line 4 by Ibn Qutaibah, who credited the two verses to Farazdaq and related them to the lustful eye (see *ʿUyūn* IV 84 and n. 124 on p. 93 above). See Ṣāliḥānī, *Naqāʾiḍ*, pp. 190 f. for lexical comments on these two verses and pp. 191–97 for Jarīr's 42-verse answer to the ode from which they are drawn.

Recto 7–verso 21. Recto 7 introduces an ode of Akhṭal in answer to a satire of him by Jarīr. For the twelve verses of our folio see Ṣāliḥānī, *Shiʿr*, pp. 41–43, Ṣāliḥānī, *Takmilah*, p. 7, No. 10, Ṣāliḥānī, *Naqāʾiḍ*, pp. 70–73, and Griffini, pp. 49 f. Ṣāliḥānī realized that it is not always possible to tell with certainty which of Jarīr's *naqāʾiḍ* were in direct answer to which ones of Akhṭal, and vice versa, since the two poets usually used the same meter and rhyme and at times the same themes in answering one another; however, he cites a number of Jarīr's poems that were in direct answer to specific ones of Akhṭal (Ṣāliḥānī, *Naqāʾiḍ*, pp. iii–v, ix–xi). He also points out that some of Farazdaq's verses were credited to Akhṭal for the same reasons (*ibid.* p. 219). See Ṣāliḥānī, *Takmilah*, p. 5, for a verse of Akhṭal that was credited to Zaid ibn Bishr.

In these twelve verses Akhṭal, like other poets (see p. 131), dwells on the wiles of women.

Recto 8–13. Note the poetic license in the omission of the *alif* of interrogation in line 8, as explained in the commentary (see also Abū ʿUbaidah, *Majāz al-Qurʾān*, ed. M. Fuad Sezgin, I [Cairo, 1374/1954] 56 and references there cited). The Wāsiṭ of line 8 is not to be confused with Ḥajjāj's new provincial capital of ʿIrāq, for it is Wāsiṭ al-Jazīrah in the tribal grounds of the Banū Taghlib (see Ṣāliḥānī, *Shiʿr*, p. 41, and Yāqūt IV 882, where the verse itself is cited, and Yāqūt IV 888). Some comments in Griffini's Yemenite manuscript come very close to those of our folio, as in the present instance, but are not wholly identical with the latter. The differences are mainly brief additions or omissions and suggest the possibility that the Yemenite manuscript drew on our text or that both manuscripts drew on a common source; see Griffini, Preface pp. 5 f., for his discussion of the possible sources of the Yemenite manuscript.

Jarīr acknowledged the superlative quality of this satire against him but declared that there was no match for his own verse

والتغلبي اذا تنحنح للقرى   حك استه وتمثل الامثالا

(see *ʿIqd* V 273, *Muwashshaḥ*, p. 131, and n. 144 on p. 132 above). For the whole ode see *Sharḥ dīwān Jarīr*, pp. 448–53, but note esp. line 1 on p. 451.

Recto 14–16. In Ṣāliḥānī, *Naqāʾiḍ*, p. 70, line 14 starts with the verse corresponding to our تخيلت. Ṣāliḥānī, *Shiʿr*, p. 41, cites اباطح as a questionable variant for ابالخ. The Yemenite commentary uses phrases identical with those of our text and adds وتعرضت يعنى الرباب اى تعرضت لك فى المنام (Griffini, p. 49). For a fuller commentary and illustrative citations from Jamīl ibn Maʿmar al-ʿUdhrī and an unnamed poet see Ṣaliḥānī, *Naqāʾiḍ*, pp. 70 f.

Recto 17–19. In Ṣāliḥānī, *Naqāʾiḍ*, p. 70, the verse corresponding to our line 17 starts with تعرضت instead of تعولت. The published commentaries among them cover our text; that of Ṣāliḥānī, *Shiʿr*, is briefer and that of the Yemenite text is fuller, but both are lexical glosses.

Recto 20–verso 3. The commentary of our folio up to this point is largely a gloss devoted to possible variants mostly in the nature of synonyms. Here and in several of the comments that follow there is emphasis on the parts of the verb, perhaps chiefly because these verbs are either weak or doubled. Such emphasis is not found in the other commentaries on this section (see Ṣāliḥānī, *Shiʿr*, p. 42; Ṣāliḥānī, *Naqāʾiḍ*, p. 71; Griffini, pp. 49 f., where the الا of طوالا was overlooked by the copyist).

Verso 4. A uniform variant for وما is إنْ in all the parallel sources.

Verso 5–6. Note the form قال ان, perhaps intended for قالآن. The marginal comment اذا ابغضه is a later addition.

Verso 7–10. The commentary of lines 8–9 appears in the Yemenite text with minor variation, but the verbal forms of line 10 are omitted (see Griffini, p. 50). The brief commentary in Ṣāliḥānī, *Shiʿr*, p. 42, cites an illustrative verse of Rāʿī, and the much fuller comment in Ṣāliḥānī, *Naqāʾiḍ*, pp. 71 f., cites no less than five poets.

Verso 11. This verse is preceded in Ṣāliḥānī, *Shiʿr*, p. 43 by

ان الغوان ان رايتك طاويـــــا   بُـرد الشباب طوين عنك وصالا

and in the Yemenite text by

ويجدنارديـــة الشباب لذيذة   ويردن من لبس المشيب خبالا

(Griffini, p. 50).

Verso 12–14. One comment on the verse of line 12 adds that Zuhair ibn Abī Sulmā was the first to express its sense, thus:

وقال الغواني انما انت عمنـــــا   وكان الشباب كالخليط تـُزَايلـــه

(see Ṣāliḥānī, *Naqāʾiḍ*). *Shiʿr*, p. 312, cites our verse and compares it favorably with two verses of Quṭāmī which convey the same meaning. *ʿUyūn* IV 121 cites the four verses of our verso 5, 7, 11, and 12 in a section dealing with the wiles of women. The last of these is followed in Ṣāliḥānī, *Naqāʾiḍ*, by a verse

واذا دعونك يا اخى فانــــــــه   ادنـــا اليـــك مودّة ووصالا

which is missing in our folio. For these two verses see also Nuwairī III 77 and Ibn Khallikān II 11 f. (= trans. III 136), where they are cited by the Spanish Ibn Zuhr.

Verso 15. This verse in Ṣāliḥānī, *Naqāʾiḍ*, follows our recto 20.

Verso 16. The Yemenite text has a brief comment and breaks off at this point (Griffini, p. 50). A brief comment in Ṣāliḥānī, *Naqāʾiḍ*, provides the variant قطاب for قطال.

The verse was admired by critics for its compactness (see Jumaḥī, pp. 420 f., and *Aghānī* VII 172).

Verso 17–21. Ṣāliḥānī, *Shiʿr*, and Ṣāliḥānī, *Naqāʾiḍ*, each present a commentary somewhat similar to that of our text, but the latter cites two illustrative verses. Ṣāliḥānī's own comments in both of these works are rich in the elucidation of the poetry and in the references provided.

THE DEVELOPMENT OF LITERARY COMMENTARY IN EARLY ISLĀM

The commentary of our document, as indicated above, is not identifiable with any of the other available commentaries on the poetry of Akhṭal. We shall, therefore, consider briefly the general field of the development of literary commentaries in early Islām in search of clues that may lead at least to an informed guess as to a probable date or author of our commentary.

The first step in the development in early Islām of secular commentaries is linked to that in the development of Qurʾānic commentaries. For the citation of a classical verse to explain a word or phrase of the Qurʾānic text constituted a sort of reverse comment on the verse itself. This was but one phase of the intensive linguistic studies that centered from the start and continued to evolve around both the wording (*alfẓ*) and the intrinsic or hidden meaning (*maʿna*) of the Qurʾānic text as explained through *tafsīr*.

We have pointed out above (p. 145) that the leading early philologists and grammarians were primarily Qur'ānic-readers and that some continued to concentrate on the Qur'ān while others expanded their linguistic efforts into the secular field, in which poetry was at first the major literary component. The first interesting clue to catch my attention for the present purpose was the use of the term *tafsīr* for both sacred and secular commentaries through the third/ninth century. The Qur'ānic *Tafsīr* of Ibn 'Abbās (d. 68/688),[2] known as the father of all such works, was primarily linguistic and mostly lexical to judge by what little of the original work has come down to us through his pupils, especially his secretary-transmitter 'Ikrimah. Differentiation in the Qur'ānic sciences (*'ulūm al-Qur'ān*) to include four types of commentaries, namely lexical (*qirā'āt*), grammatical (*i'rāb*), interpretive (*ma'ānī*), and historical, that is, the occasion for the revelation of a given passage (*tanzīl*), was already recognized by 'Umar I, who encouraged Ibn 'Abbās in his *tafsīr* activity.[3] The interest of both these leaders in poetry probably led them to use the term *tafsīr* for their comments on poetry as well. The term was so used throughout the second/eighth century by such outstanding scholars as Zuhrī,[4] Mufaḍḍal ibn Muḥammad al-Ḍabbī (see n. 18 on p. 156), Akhfash al-Akbar,[5] Shāfi'ī,[6] Abū 'Amr al-Shaibānī,[7] and Aṣma'ī, who, unlike his rival Abū 'Ubaidah, refrained from *tafsīr al-Qur'ān* and from *tafsīr* of satirical poetry.[8] Again Aṣma'ī and his younger rival Ibn al-A'rābī claimed to be and were recognized as experts at elucidating the meaning of poetry (*ma'ānī al-shi'r*) and its correct grammar (*i'rāb al-shi'r*) respectively.[9] Each of these authors wrote a work titled *Ma'ānī al-shi'r*, though Ibn al-A'rābī was more knowledgeable as to the meaning of the strange or rarely used words occurring in poetry: دواوين الشعر وتفسير غريبها.[10] It should be noted that the *Aṣma'iyāt* met with a cool reception among scholars because of the comparative obscurity, or perhaps brevity, of its selections and the paucity of its unusual elements.[11]

As the term *ilm al-tafsīr* came to connote Qur'ānic interpretation and was expanded to include commentaries on other religious subjects, the term *tafsīr* was less readily applied to secular literary fields but at the same time came into general use by translators and commentators of the "foreign sciences."[12] Just when the term *sharḥ* came to be used, sometimes as an alternative to *tafsīr*, is hard to say. One notes, however, that Qudāmah ibn Ja'far uses *tafsīr* for the intra-verse interpretation

فله بلا حَزَن ولا بمسرة   ضحك يُراوح بينه وبكاءُ

with the second hemistich said to be the *tafsīr* of the first and gives examples of a whole verse as the

[2] See Vol. II 99.

[3] See Vol. II 110 and note that some written *tafsīr* accompanied the Qur'ān as early as the reign of 'Umar I.

[4] See e.g. Vol. I 17.

[5] See Bevan II 1026, where Akhfash expresses his conviction that the average Bedouin is not knowledgeable enough to explain or interpret poetry: عامة اهل البدو ليس تفهم مايريد الشاعر ولا يحسنون التفسير.

[6] See *'Umdah* I 18: كان الشافعي احسن التاس افتفانا في الشعر. See also Khaṭīb II 63; *Irshād* VI 369 f., 380, 383; *Muzhir* I 160: كان اصحاب الادب ياتونه فيقرون الشعر عليه فيفسره وكان يحفظ عشرة الاف ابيت من شعراء هذيل باعرابها وغريبها ومعانيها.

[7] Either Abū 'Amr al-Shaibānī or a contemporary asked 'Umārah ibn 'Aqīl ibn Bilāl, great-grandson of Jarīr, for his *tafsīr* of a verse (see *Dīwān Salāmah ibn Jandal*, ed. Louis Cheikho, p. 7, and for 'Umārah, pp. 13 and 22. See *Marātib*, p. 19, for تفسير ابو عمرو الشيبانى فى نوادره.

[8] *Marātib*, pp. 41 and 48: كان لا يفسر شيئا من القران ولاشيئا من اللغة له نظير او اشتقاق فى القرآن وكذلك الحديث تحرجا وكان لا يفسر شعرا فيه هجاء (but see our Vol. II 113).

[9] See e.g. *Inbāh* III 129, 133 f. For Aṣma'ī see also Sīrāfī, p. 62, *Majālis al-'ulamā'*, pp. 33 f., and Ibn Fāris, *Ṣāḥibī*, p. 44.

[10] See e.g. *Inbāh* II 203 and III 131 respectively. Zajjājī, *Al-īḍāḥ fī 'ilal al-naḥw*, p. 92, defines *gharīb* as الغريب هو ما قل اسماعه في اللغة ولم يدر في افواه العامة كما دار في افواه الخاصة and then gives several illustrations.

[11] ليست بمرضيّة عند العلماء لقلة غريبها واختصار روايتها (see e.g. *Fihrist*, p. 56; *Inbāh* II 203; *Maṣādir*, pp. 571 f.). Aṣma'ī was, on the other hand, strong in dialects, as can be readily seen from his several surviving works (see *Amālī* II 203 and cf. *GAL* I 104 f. and *GAL* S I 163–65).

[12] See e.g. Ḥājjī Khalīfah II 328–32 and Carra de Vaux in *EI* IV 603. This development is reflected also in Brockelmann's long list of *tafsīr* works (*GAL* S III 1108 f.).

tafsīr of an immediately preceding one and that he introduces the subsection with من انواع المعانى صحة التفسير.[13] But about a half-century later Ibn Jinnī titled his commentary on the *Ḥamāsah* of Abū Tammām *Al-tanbīh ʿalā sharḥ mushkilāt al-ḥamāsah*.[14] It should be noted further that even thereafter *tafsīr* and *sharḥ* were occasionally used interchangeably for both Qurʾānic and literary commentaries.

One notes that in his long list of the more prolific second- and third-century poetry editors and commentators, Nadīm uses neither *tafsīr* nor *sharḥ*, or their verbal forms, but uses regularly the more general and less specifically descriptive verbs *ʿamila*, "he did, made, or wrought," and *ṣanaʿa*, "he made or wrought skillfully." Since he interchanges the two verbs at times, it is not always possible to ascertain from the *Fihrist* text alone just what a given poet, transmitter, or commentator actually did with the poetry in question. We read for instance that Dhū al-Rummah himself did (*ʿamila*) his own ode, that Mufaḍḍal ibn Muḥammad al-Ḍabbī *ʿamila al-ashʿār* for the caliph Mahdī, that Abū ʿUbaidah did (*ʿamila*) the *naqāʾiḍ* of Jarīr and Farazdaq, that Aṣmaʿī's transmission (*riwāyah*) of the same *naqāʾiḍ* was inferior to that of Abū ʿUbaidah, and that Sukkarī did (*ʿamila*) the poetry of Akhṭal and the *naqāʾiḍ* of Jarīr and Farazdaq and improved them. The verb *ṣanaʿa*, too, at times implies more than composition or more than collection and simple transmission. For we read that the poetry manuscript of Ibrāhīm ibn Harmah consisted of some two hundred folios but was expanded into a manuscript of some five hundred folios in Sukkarī's version.[15] No doubt the expansion was due, at least in part, to Sukkarī's commentary. That is, while *rawā* is simple transmission with perhaps some minor editing, *ʿamila* and *ṣanaʿa* imply a greater degree of literary contribution, including authorship of the poetry or collection and transmission of it with or without a commentary. On the whole the *Fihrist* terminology conveys the impression that Nadīm was concerned more with the survival and the quantity of the poetry itself than with the types of commentaries which, as we know from other extant sources, frequently accompanied poetry editions. More explicit and significant for the increasing volume of literature, in both the composition and the study of poetry, is Nadīm's use of the verb *ṣannafa*, which definitely indicates written composition of organized literary works of both prose and poetry.[16]

The several branches of *ilm al-tafsīr* in the Qurʾānic and related fields began to emerge shortly before the appearance of formal commentaries on poetry and were well advanced in the first half of the second century. This is readily seen from a comparison of the meager linguistic comments in what has survived of the *Tafsīr* of Ibn ʿAbbās with the several *tafsīr* works of Muqātil ibn Sulaimān. The latter varied in both type and content from the brief and strictly linguistic comments of the *Wujūh wa al-naẓāʾir* to the *Tafsīr al-kabīr* with its expanded and varied commentary, a feature that characterized also the *Tafsīr al-Qurʾān* of Muqātil's contemporary Muḥammud ibn al-Sāʾib al-Kalbī (d. 146/763).[17]

The philologists and grammarians of the first half of the second century commented freely on individual verses which they cited as a conclusive illustration (*shāhid*) in proof of some point raised in their discussions. Abū ʿAmr ibn al-ʿAlāʾ's comments of this type were frequently cited by his pupils. But there seems to be no clear evidence that he undertook a sustained commentary on any poet's *dīwān* or on any anthology of poetry. The same observation holds for Ḥammad al-Rāwiyah. The Kūfan Mufaḍḍal ibn

[13] Qudāmah, pp. 73–77; Qudāmah (1963) pp. 154–56. See *ʿUmdah* II 28–31, titled *bāb al-tafsīr*.

[14] Marzūqī I, Intro. p. 11. See *GAL* I 126 and *GAL* S I 192, No. 10, for Ibn Jinnī's *Sharḥ aṣmaāʾ shuʿarāʾ al-ḥamāsah*.

[15] *Fihrist*, p. 159: ابراهيم بن هرمة وشعره مجرد نحو مائتى ورقة وفي صنعة ابي سعيد السكري نحو خمسمائة ورقة وقد صنعه الصولي ولم يات بشىء.

[16] See *ibid*. pp. 157–59, with the heading اسماء ما صنفوه من الكتب وتحتوى على الشعر والشعراء . . . ومقادير ما خرج من اشعارهم and such typical terms as صنعه من جميع الرو يات, عمله فزاد فيه, and عمله فقصر او فجوّد. For more on the niceties of these basic terms see Lane, صنع, صنف, and عمل.

[17] See Vol. II, Document 1, esp. pp. 105 f. and 112.

Muḥammād al-Ḍabbī deliberately refrained from commenting on the poems he collected and transmitted, being aware of his weakness in language rareties, grammatical points, and the interpretation of poetry.[18]

The second half of the second century—the era of Sībawaih, Khalīl, Kisā'ī, Abū 'Ubaidah, and Aṣma'ī—saw a heightened interest in pre-Islāmic poetry as a discipline in its own right. This interest more than matched the interest in that poetry for its use as a linguistic tool and was expanded to include the output of the poets of Islāmic times. Thus, in turn, collectors, transmitter-editors, and scholar-commentators were induced to broaden their activities to include some aspects of the biographical, social, and historical backgrounds of poets and their poetry. This half-century could well have been the time when the term *sharḥ* became more closely associated with poetry and secular fields, as *tafsīr* had earlier become associated with Qur'ānic and other religious subjects. It might be of interest that though basically the verbs *fasara* and *sharaḥa* both mean "to explain," "to interpret," or "to disclose" only the second term includes among its several meanings "to expand," in which sense it is used in Sūrah 94:1. Certainly, in the further development of *shurūḥ* literature, not only did the field expand in that more *dīwān* commentaries were produced, but many of the ranking commentators of the third century and after offered increasingly complex and voluminous commentaries. However, the earlier type of brief and primarily linguistic commentary was not neglected in either the Qur'ānic or the poetic field. We have traced in the linguistic field itself the simultaneous production of elementary and advanced grammars, frequently both types by the same ranking scholar. A somewhat similar situation seems to have prevailed in connection with poetry commentaries to meet the needs of the young scholar and also the demands of the aspiring professional and the cultured layman. Any of the numerous linguist-educators from the second half of the second century onward who for one reason or another produced an elementary grammar (see pp. 29–31) could have found it necessary to produce also an elementary gloss and scholia as bare essentials for the understanding of the poetry he collected or taught. Whether the emphasis was on lexical or grammatical points would depend on whether the particular scholar's field of specialization was *lughah* or *naḥw*.[19] It is both interesting and instructive to note here that Qudāmah ibn Ja'far, writing for fellow scholars and cultured laymen, complained of the excessive emphasis laid by his predecessors on the lexical and grammatical elements in their study of poetry to the comparative neglect of a comprehensive system of critical analysis, which deficiency his *Naqd al-shi'r* was meant to remedy.[20] At about the same time his contemporary Ṣūlī (d. 335/946), who shared several of Qudāmah's professional and literary interests, produced a commentary on the *Dīwān Abī Tammām* that was all but void of lexicography and grammar but rich in information (*akhbār*) about and in defense of Abū Tammām as a competent poet, especially as compared to Buḥturī, a theme that Ṣūlī expanded in his *Akhbār Abī Tammām*.[21] A commentator's intellectual bent and his professional status and duties inclined him to study or produce one type of commentary rather than another or even to compose several types, each to serve a different purpose. The effects of such personal factors are reflected in Jāḥiẓ' comment that he found Aṣma'ī knowledgeable in only the strange elements

[18] *Marātib*, p. 71: كان يقول اني لا احسن شيئا من الغريب ولا من المعاني ولا تفسير الشعر وانما كان يروى شعرا مجردا ولم يكن عالما بالنحو ولا كان يشدُو منه شيئا (cf. *Muzhir* II 405 f.). Mufaḍḍal was, nevertheless, credited with a *Ma'ānī al-shi'r* (*Fihrist*, p. 69; *Inbāh* III 302; *Nuzhah*, p. 33). See Qudāmah (1963) pp. 13 ff. for his fivefold division for the study of poetry.

[19] Zubaidī, who stresses this distinction, lists only three scholars as specialists in both of these fields, namely the Baṣrans Abū 'Amr ibn al-'Alā' (Zubaidī, pp. 28–34 and 176) and 'Īsā ibn 'Umar (*ibid.* pp. 35–41 and 176) and the Kūfan Muḥammad ibn Ḥabīb (*ibid.* pp. 153 f. and 216).

[20] Qudāmah, Intro. p. 8 and text pp. 1 f. (= Qudāmah [1963] pp. 13 f.):
فأما علم جيد الشعر من رديه فان الناس يخبطون في ذلك منذ تفقهوا في العلم فقليلا ما يصيبونه ولما وجدت الامر على ذلك وتبينت ان الكلام في هذا الامر اخص بالشعر من سائر الاسباب الاخر وان الناس قد قصروا في وضع كتاب فيه رايت ان اتكلم في ذلك بما يبلغه الوسع.

[21] See pp. 59–140 in edition of Khalīl Maḥmūd 'Asākir *et al.* See *Dīwān Abī Tammān bi sharḥ al-Khaṭīb al-Tabrīzī*, ed. Muḥammad 'Abduh 'Azzām, I (Cairo, 1951) Intro. pp. 13–16, for a brief survey of early *dīwān* commentaries as a background for the numerous and increasingly lengthy *shurūḥ* on the *Dīwān Abī Tammām* by Ṣūlī and later commentators.

in poetry and Akhfash al-Awsaṭ in only its grammar and Abū ʿUbaidah in only what touches it of historical background and genealogical information.[22] From the second half of the second century onward there must have been a steady demand for all types of commentaries on the numerous poetry *dīwān*'s and anthologies, classical and contemporary alike, that were being compiled or composed. These would range from single-purpose commentaries stressing the lexical aspect (*lughah*), grammar (*iʿrāb*), strange or foreign words and phrases (*gharīb*), the basic significance (*maʿānī*) of verses or poems, or pertinent bits of information (*akhbār*) to commentaries involving various combinations of these elements or even eventually including all of them as did, for instance, a work by Tabrīzī (d. 502/1109), who wrote three different commentaries (*shurūḥ*) on the *Ḥamāsah* of Abū Tammām, varying from a brief one to an exhaustive one.[23] Whether or not poetry was taught in the elementary mosque schools probably depended on the equipment and inclination of the teacher (*muʿallim*). More mature students attending public sessions of linguists and grammarians in mosque circles (see p. 25) or elsewhere were constantly exposed to some phase of poetry study and discussion. Poetry was included in the curriculum of the palace school and in that of the children of the nobility and the wealthy who were taught by private tutors.[24] Brief primarily lexical and grammatical commentaries, similar to that of our folio text, served the needs of young scholars of these three groups. Lengthier and more complex *shurūḥ*, such as flowed from the pen of Abū ʿUbaidah and increased steadily to climax in such exhaustive commentaries as most of those by Tabrīzī, were intended for cultured laymen (*udabāʾ*) and linguistic and literary professionals (*ʿulamāʾ*) whose wide intellectual interests generally overlapped.

The production of formal scholarly commentaries on the output of a given poet or tribe could hardly have started very long before the later part of the life of Abū ʿAmr ibn al-ʿAlāʾ (d. 154/771). Mufaḍḍal ibn Muḥammad al-Ḍabbī's specific statement that his collection of poetry was void of any comment implies that the collections of some of his contemporaries did include some sort of commentary. Foremost among his younger contemporaries who were most likely to have provided their collections with commentaries is the Kūfan Abū ʿAmr al-Shaibānī, scholar, tutor, and tireless collector of tribal anthologies, whose life all but spanned the second century. He is certainly cited more frequently than is the Baṣran Abū ʿAmr ibn al-ʿAlāʾ in many of the commentaries of the third century and after, no doubt in part because several of the leading commentators of the third century had been his pupils and in part because several of his sons and grandsons transmitted his works.[25] That a number of Abū ʿAmr al-Shaibānī's Baṣran contemporaries provided some sort of commentary for their poetry collections is indicated by the statement that Akhfash al-Awsaṭ was the first to dictate his comments on *gharīb al-shiʿr* after the verses which called for them instead of dictating all comments at the end of an ode according to the earlier prac-

[22] ʿ*Umdah* II 84:
قال الجاحظ طلبت علم الشعر عند الاصمعي فوجدته لا يحسن الا غريبه فرجعت الى الاخفش فوجدته لا يتقن الا اعرابه فعطفت على ابي عبيدة فوجدته لا ينقل الا ما اتصل بالاخبار وتعلق بالايام والانساب فلم اظفر بما اردته الاعند أُدباء الكتّاب كالحسن بن وهب ومحمد بن الزيات.

Nadīm credits Ḥasan ibn Wahb with a manuscript of his own poetry consisting of 100 folios averaging 20 lines to the page (*Fihrist*, pp. 159) and devotes a long section to the poetry of secretaries (*ibid.* pp. 166–68). See also Marzūqī I 16–20 for this commentator's thesis that the professional state secretaries of the ʿAbbāsid period were on the whole more knowledgeable and eloquent than the poets as a group. Cf. Ṣūlī, *Akhbār Abī Tammām*, pp. 108 f., where Ḥasan ibn Wahb reacts to the statement اذا كانت دولة بنى اميه حلبة الشعراء فدولة بنى هاشم حلبة الكتاب by favoring the eloquence of the ʿAbbāsid secretaries and the poetry of Abū Tammām. For Jāḥiẓ' criticism of the conduct of the state secretaries of both the Umayyad and ʿAbbāsid dynasties see his *Dhamm al-kuttāb* (Jāḥiẓ, *Rasāʾil* [1964–65] II 183–209).

[23] See Marzūqī I, Intro. p. 12 and references there cited.

[24] See e.g. Jāḥiẓ, *Bayān* I 68 f.; *Majālis Thaʿlab* I 82 f.; *Aghānī* II 191 f.; *Fihrist*, p. 6. See also our Vol. I 17 and p. 136 above. See our Vol. II 13 f. for city mosques as centers for religious education and civic life and culture.

[25] See e.g. *Marātib*, pp. 91 f.; *Fihrist*, p. 68; *Irshād* II 234; *Inbāh* I 221–30, esp. pp. 227–29.

tice.[26] Akhfash's method gained acceptance and prevailed thereafter as being more conducive to the listener's and the reader's understanding of any verse that called for a comment.[27] Because of his vast knowledge of the Arabic language, its grammar, and its poetry Akhfash was classed among the leading second-century transmitters in these fields. His audiences were large enough to require a dictation master, in which capacity he employed, in Baghdād, the younger Kūfan scholar ʿAlī ibn ʿAbd Allāh al-Ṭūsī.[28] It should be noted that Akhfash stressed the collation of manuscripts at every stage of copying in order to preserve their accuracy.[29] Nevertheless, it is known that Akhfash deliberately refrained from providing full and clear presentation of his materials so that there would be need for his lucrative personal services (see p. 28).

PROBABLE AUTHOR AND DATE OF THE DOCUMENT COMMENTARY

We have already indicated above that our commentary is not identifiable with that in any known extant edition of the poetry of Akhṭal. Inspection of some two dozen third- and fourth-century commentaries by such leading commentators as Abū ʿUbaidah, Ibn al-Aʿrābī, Ibn al-Sikkīt, Muḥammad ibn Ḥabīb, Sukkarī, Thaʿlab, and Muḥammad ibn al-Qāsim ibn al-Anbārī on the *dīwān*'s of mostly pre-ʿAbbasid poets served only to dramatize the wide difference between them and our folio commentary. For these commentaries are generally longer and grow progressively more complex and composite as each successive commentator draws on the commentaries and related works of his predecessors, frequently citing verses of other poets to explain those in the particular *dīwān* that is the object of his commentary. It seemed reasonable, therefore, to look for a probable author of our text among the scholars who functioned also as teachers or tutors of the young, especially as we recall that Abū ʿAmr ibn al-ʿAlāʾ finally approved the poetry of Akhṭal, Jarīr, and Farazdaq for the instruction of the young (see p. 121). Our commentary, if we assume that it is typical of the entire manuscript which it represents, readily suggests Akhfash al-Awsaṭ, who was tutor to the sons of Kisāʾī, as a probable author by reason of its brevity, its lexical and grammatical nature, and its placement after the verses involved. The sources, however, do not associate Akhfash with the transmission (*riwāyah*), with or without a commentary, of the poetry of either Jarīr or Akhṭal. Yet, in his capacity as tutor he might have produced such a work for his pupils or for the lucrative book market.

Among Akhfash's outstanding contemporaries Aṣmaʿī comes readily to mind because he is credited with editing and transmitting the poetry of some two dozen poets from pre-Islāmic times through the Umayyad period. Unfortunately, none of his editions has survived in its original form. The list includes a *Naqāʾiḍ Jarīr wa al-Farazdaq* and a *Shiʿr Jarīr*,[30] to both of which Aṣmaʿī's contribution is fully reflected in the composite commentaries of the Bevan edition of the *naqāʾiḍ* of Jarīr and Farazdaq. The fact that Aṣmaʿī seems to be nowhere credited with editing and transmitting the collected poetry of Akhṭal could account for his being either bypassed or cited very rarely in the available recensions of *Shiʿr al-Akhṭal*

[26] Zubaidī, p. 76; *Inbāh* II 39. Confusion of the several scholars named Akhfash occurs in the sources and in the works of some modern scholars. See *Inbāh* II 36 for a list of eleven scholars so named and *Muzhir* II 453 f. and 456 for the statement that when an Akhfash is not further identified the scholar referred to is Akhfash al-Awsaṭ.

[27] Some three centuries later Tabrīzī wished to revert to the older practice but found that his students preferred Akhfash's method, which he then followed (*Dīwān Abī Tammām bi sharḥ al-Khaṭīb al-Tabrīzī*, ed. Muḥammad ʿAbduh ʿAzzām, I, Intro. pp. 14 f.).

[28] *Marātib*, pp. 48, 68; Zubaidī, p. 76. See also *Fihrist*, p. 71; *Irshād* V 229 f.; *Inbāh* II 285. See our Vol. II 48 and 125 for the qualification and duties of a dictation master (*mustamlī*) in *ḥadīth* and other fields.

[29] See Suyūṭī, *Tadrīb al-rāwī fī sharḥ Taqrīb al-Nawawī*, p. 154: قال الاخفش اذا نسخ الكتاب ولم يعارض ثم نسخ ولم يعارض خرج اعجميا.

[30] See e.g. *Fihrist*, pp. 157 f., esp. lines 30–32 on p. 158. See also *Muwashshaḥ*, p. 125, where Khalaf al-Aḥmar corrects Aṣmaʿī's reading of verses of Jarīr as he heard them from Abū ʿAmr ibn al-ʿAlāʾ. For Aṣmaʿī and the poetry of Dhū al-Rummah see pp. 198–200 below.

and in the incomplete version of *Naqā'iḍ Jarīr wa al-Akhṭal* believed to be the edition of Abū Tammām. It does, nevertheless, seem strange that Aṣma'ī, who held such a high opinion of Akhṭal's poetry (see p. 119 above), should have neglected it at the same time that he was involved with the poetry of both Jarīr and Farazdaq. Recently 'Abd al-'Azīz al-Maimanī al-Rajkūtī questioned Abū Tammām's authorship of *Naqā'iḍ Jarīr wa al-Akhṭal* and suggested either Aṣma'ī or, in his opinion, more likely Sukkarī as the probable editor-commentator, on the basis primarily of internal commentary citations from an Abū Sa'īd, which is the patronym (*kunyah*) of both of these scholars.[31]

In any case, our commentary, if it is typical of the entire manuscript which it represents, could hardly have come from the hand of Aṣma'ī, to judge from liberal samplings of his readily available comments.[32] The samplings revealed a pattern, if not a style, for Aṣma'ī's comments, whether they are in works stemming directly from him, such as *Dīwān shi'r Ṭufail* as transmitted by Abū Ḥātim al-Sijistānī directly from Aṣma'ī, or in surviving works stemming from his contemporaries, such as his Baṣran rival Abū 'Ubaidah or the Kūfan scholars Abū 'Amr al-Shaibānī and Ibn al-A'rābī, as transmitted by their pupils. It is interesting to note that Aṣma'ī is quoted frequently and sometimes at great length in the *dīwān* recensions of these other scholars, especially if he and one or more of them are credited with an edition of the same *dīwān*, as in *Dīwān Labīd* as transmitted, with added commentary, by the Kūfan scholar 'Alī ibn 'Abd Allāh al-Ṭūsī from Abū 'Amr al-Shaibānī and Ibn al-A'rābī[33] and in the Bevan edition of the *naqā'iḍ* of Jarīr and Farazdaq, which is based largely on the recension of Abū 'Ubaidah. Other commentaries tested for more light on Aṣma'ī's comments include those on the poetry of 'Urwah ibn al-Ward,[34] 'Ajjāj,[35] and Dhū al-Rummah.[36] On the whole, Aṣma'ī's *dīwān* comments substantiate the literary historians' and critics' appraisals of the type and scope of his linguistic and literary gifts (see p. 154) and the extent of his dependence on Bedouin sources. For his comments center first on explanation of the literal as well as the intrinsic meaning of a phrase or verse (*ma'ānī al-shi'r*), next on dialects and strange words (*lughāt* and *gharīb*), and to a lesser extent on pertinent bits of information (*khabar*) relating to geography, genealogy or background, and least of all on simple lexical and grammatical points, including broken plurals and weak or irregular verbs such as are found in our folio text. Furthermore, our sampling of commentaries revealed that the Kūfan transmitters were more apt than the Baṣran transmitters to stress such grammatical points as those mentioned above and that the pattern in this respect was emphasized by the Kūfan tutor, philologist, and poetry commentator Ibn al-A'rābī and sustained by his leading pupils and transmitters, especially 'Alī ibn 'Abd Allāh al-Ṭūsī and Muḥammad ibn Ḥabīb.[37]

[31] Abū Tammām, *Kitāb al-waḥshīyāt*, ed. 'Abd al-'Azīz al-Maimanī al-Rajkūtī (Cairo, 1963) Intro. p. 5. I find an Abū Sa'īd cited only four times for lexical comments (*ibid.* pp. 3, 28 f., 62 f., and 153) and only once for pertinent information, i.e., *khabar* (pp. 13 f.), all of which are inconclusive in one way or another as to Abū Tammām's authorship. It should be noted, however, that if Abū Tammām is indeed the editor-commentator, he would have to be citing Aṣma'ī and not his own much younger contemporary Sukkarī. On the other hand, Aṣma'ī was seldom cited simply as Abū Sa'īd, while Sukkarī was frequently so cited. Scholars have continued to credit *Naqā'iḍ Jarīr wa al-Akhṭal* to Abū Tammām (see e.g. *Dīwān Abī Tammām bi sharḥ al-Khaṭīb al-Tabrīzī*, ed. Muḥammad 'Abduh 'Azzām, Intro. p. 13; see also H. Ritter in *EI* I [1960] 154).

[32] Where no more than about two dozen references to Aṣma'ī were indicated in a given source, all were checked and his comments analyzed; and at least that many references were checked and analyzed where the indexes indicated three or more dozen references to Aṣma'ī.

[33] See *Sharḥ dīwān Labīd ibn Rabī'ah*, ed. Iḥsān 'Abbās (Kuwait, 1962).

[34] See *Dīwān 'Urwah ibn al-Ward*, ed. Mohammed Ben Cheneb (Alger, 1926).

[35] See Maximilian Bittner (ed.), *Das erste Gedicht aus dem Dīwān des arabischen Dichters al-'Aǵǵāǵ* (Wien, 1896).

[36] See pp. 198–200 for references to Aṣma'ī's comments in Macartney.

[37] For Ibn al-A'rābī's lengthy lexical comments and his stress on singulars and plurals see e.g. Ṣāliḥānī, *Shi'r al-Akhṭal* (1905) pp. 2, 4, 6, 10, 14, 17, 22, 26, *et passim*; for his emphasis on verbals and the multiple significance of given verbs see *ibid.* pp. 3, 4–6, 8, 13, 19, 30, 32, 34, 35, 38, *et passim*. For Muḥammad ibn Ḥabīb's usually briefer comments on such points of grammar see e.g. Yazīdī, pp. 22, 39, 53, 66, 68, 69, 70, 74. Some of the stress on grammatical points in the commentaries on the *naqā'iḍ* of Jarīr and Farazdaq may have been passed on by Muḥammad ibn Ḥabīb, though it is not possible to ascertain that from the Bevan edition (see e.g. Bevan I 1, 7, 8, 12, 13, 26, 36, and 37, line 12: قال ابن حبيب من هاهنا روى المفضل).

Among the contemporaries of Akhfash al-Awsaṭ and Aṣmaʿī, Yaḥyā ibn al-Mubārak al-Yazīdī (d. 202/817), scholar and tutor of Prince Ma'mūn, poet and transmitter of poetry,[38] comes to mind as a possible author of our text. Also possible are several of his sons, particularly Ismāʿīl (d. 275/888), himself a poet who is credited with a *Ṭabaqāt al-shuʿarā'*[39] and who reported that his father before his death destroyed all the manuscripts of his own poetry about Hārūn al-Rashīd and Jaʿfar al-Barmakī.[40] Yaḥyā's great-grandson Muḥammad ibn al-ʿAbbās al-Yazīdī (d. 310/922) preserved this famed family's literary heritage (see p. 29) and composed the *Akhbār al-Yazīdiyīn*.[41] He too was a royal tutor and a poet, and that he was a transmitter-commentator of *Shiʿr al-Akhṭal* is revealed by the St. Petersburg manuscript copy which has been so painstakingly edited by Ṣāliḥānī and which has for its title and *isnād* شعر الاخطل رواية ابي عبد الله محمد بن العباس اليزيدى عن ابي سعيد السكرى عن محمد بن حبيب عن ابن الاعرابي. The *isnād* spans the third/ninth century and draws on both Baṣran and Kūfan sources as was becoming a common practice among scholars of the third-century mixed school of Baghdād. The commentary of our folio text is different from that of Muḥammad ibn al-ʿAbbās al-Yazīdī but is close to it in a few instances. The similarities suggest the possibility that our text represents that of any one of his three sources—Sukkarī, who alone is credited with "having done the poetry of Akhṭal and improved it,"[42] Muḥammad ibn Ḥabīb, and Ibn al-Aʿrābī—not one of whom is specifically credited in the available sources with the transmission of Akhṭal's poetry. But, then, neither do these same sources mention Muḥammad ibn al-ʿAbbās al-Yazīdī's transmission of *Shiʿr al-Akhṭal*, which transmission came to light only with the discovery of the St. Petersburg manuscript copy published by Ṣāliḥānī.[43] Nor do these same sources mention Muḥammad ibn al-ʿAbbās al-Yazīdī's transmission of the *naqā'iḍ* of Jarīr and Farazdaq though several manuscripts of their *naqā'iḍ* have come to light. The initial *isnād* of the Bevan edition of these *naqā'iḍ* reads in full قال ابو محمد عبد الله بن العباس اليزيدي قال الحسن بن الحسين السكرى قال ابو جعفر محمد بن حبيب حكى عن ابي عبيدة and is confirmed at the end.[44] Bevan has drawn attention to the very numerous comments of Muḥammad ibn al-ʿAbbās al-Yazīdī that run through the recension of Abū ʿUbaidah in contrast to the comparatively few comments of Muḥammad ibn Ḥabīb and even of Sukkarī,[45] both of whose independent transmissions are mentioned in the sources.[46]

A second chain of transmission of the *naqā'iḍ* of Jarīr and Farazdaq begins with the Kūfan Saʿdān ibn al-Mubārak, founder of a family of scholars, royal tutors, bibliophiles, and booksellers (see pp. 14 and 30). Saʿdān transmitted these *naqā'iḍ* from Abū ʿUbaidah, presumably with the latter's commentary, to his son Ibrāhīm (see p. 147, n. 244), who in turn transmitted them to Sukkarī.[47] Saʿdān is frequently cited

[38] See e.g. Ibn al-Muʿtazz, *Ṭabaqāt*, pp. 273–75; Sīrāfī, pp. 40–47; Zubaidī, pp. 60–64, 142; Khaṭīb III 412 f.; *Nuzhah*, pp. 15, 51 f. See *Aghānī* XVIII 72–94 for more of Yaḥyā's poetry and that of some of his sons and grandsons.

[39] *Fihrist*, p. 51; Zubaidī, pp. 38, 78; Khaṭīb VI 283; *Inbāh* I 213.

[40] Ibn al-Jarrāḥ, *Al-waraqah*, pp. 4 f., 27: قال اسمعيل كان لابي اشعار كثيرة في الرشيد وجعفر بن يحيى وغيرهما فقبل ان يموت حرقها واخذ علينا الا نخرج له غير المواعظ. Zubaidī, p. 64, reports the same but omits حَرقها, which could also be read as خرقها.

[41] Zubaidī, p. 65: كان عالما بالعربية حاملا لعلم سفله اديبا فاضلا. He was a valued teacher of Abū al-Faraj al-Iṣfahānī, who praised him highly and transmitted much material from him directly; see *Aghanī* XVIII 73: كان آخر من بقى من علماء هذا البيت وكان فاضلا عالما ثقة فيما يرويه منقطع الى القرين في الصدق وشدة التوقى فيما ينقله وقد حملنا نحن عنه وكثير من طلبة العلم ورواته علما كثيرا فسمعنا منه سماعا جما.

[42] *Fihrist*, p. 158: شعر الاخطل عمله السكرى وجوده.

[43] See Ṣāliḥānī, *Shiʿr al-Akhṭal*, Intro. pp. 3 f.

[44] See Bevan I xi and 1, II 1054; see also *Fihrist*, p. 158.

[45] Bevan I xi; see also the listings under Sukkari (*ibid.* III 127).

[46] See below for Muḥammad ibn Ḥabīb and *Fihrist*, p. 158, for Sukkarī: نقائض جرير والفرزدق عملها ابو عبيدة معمر بن المثنى ورواها الاصمعى دون تلك الرواية وعملها ابو سعيد بن الحسين السكري وجودها.

[47] *Fihrist*. pp. 71, 79; *Irshād* I 59 f.; *Inbāh* I 185 and II 55.

in the Bevan edition of these *naqā'iḍ*, much oftener than Muḥammad ibn Ḥabīb, who is cited twice as often as Sukkarī, as a glance at their index entries readily reveals. Sa'dān's son 'Uthmān had a personal copy of the *Naqā'iḍ Jarīr wa al-Farazdaq*, and he and his copy are cited several times in the Bevan edition, in which his brother Ibrāhīm is not mentioned at all. Analysis of the citations from the transmissions of Sa'dān and Muḥammad ibn Ḥabīb readily revealed, first, that brief lexical glosses predominate in both while there are only a few points of grammar and, second, that lengthy immediate background information or more remote historical accounts are much more favored in Sa'dān's transmission, which in this respect stays closer on the whole to Abū 'Ubaidah's initial and basic commentary.

A third work of Muḥammad ibn al-'Abbās al-Yazīdī, the *Amālī*, remained unknown until Fritz Krenkow discovered the Constantinople manuscript, the only known extant copy, which traces back to the years 368–70/978–81.[48] Analysis of the *Amālī*'s several major *isnād*'s, family or otherwise, and of the commentary on poetry citations of various lengths revealed that Muḥammad ibn al-'Abbās al-Yazīdī leaned heavily on both the transmission and the comments of Muḥammad ibn Ḥabīb[49] and that the commentary throughout is on the whole brief, a characteristic also of his commentary on *Shi'r al-Akhṭal* as revealed by the St. Petersburg manuscript copy published by Ṣāliḥānī. As to the nature of the *Amālī* comments, apart from a few informative notes (*akhbār*)[50] and brief elucidating comments (*ma'ānī*),[51] they are linguistic and mainly lexical. More significantly, there is some emphasis on rarely used and broken plurals and comments on the parts of verbs similar to those found in our folio text (see p. 152). Though it is not always clear whether such comments stem from the author himself or from one of his sources, yet Muḥammad ibn Ḥabīb is more frequently specified than any other as the direct source.[52] This is not surprising in view of the fact that Abū 'Amr ibn al-'Alā' and Muḥammad ibn Ḥabīb are two of the only three language scholars whom Zubaidī included in both his list of philologists and his list of grammarians (see p. 156, n. 19) and the fact that Muḥammad ibn Ḥabīb was, to begin with, a teacher and a private tutor, functions which, however, he apparently did not particularly like.[53] We read also that Sukkarī took a great deal of material from him.[54] The *Fihrist* entry which concentrates on Sukkarī's transmission of and commentary on specified poetry *dīwān*'s, *naqā'iḍ*, and anthologies does not reveal the great extent of Muḥammad ibn Ḥabīb's earlier and parallel literary activity, which is, however, clearly revealed in the main entry on Muḥammad ibn Ḥabīb himself.[55] Among the long list of books credited to him are *Akhbār al-shu'arā' wa ṭabaqātihim, Al-shu'arā' wa ansābihim, Kunā al-shu'arā', Alqāb al-qabā'il*, and *Kitāb al-qabā'il*, the last being an autograph copy written on Khurāsānian Ṭalḥī paper for Mutawakkil's bibliophile wazir Fatḥ ibn Khāqān. These titles indicate continued interest in genealogy and tribal and literary history for their own sake as well as for their bearing on Muḥammad ibn Ḥabīb's several collections of the poetry of specific tribes and individual poets. He is credited with the transmission of the poetry of

[48] See Yazīdī, Intro. p. 13 and text p. 154.

[49] See e.g. *ibid.* pp. 21, 26, 31, 38, 44–79.

[50] See e.g. *ibid.* pp. 17, 44, 47 f., 68, 80, 81, from several of Muḥammad ibn al-'Abbās al-Yazīdī's major sources, which include two of his uncles, Isḥāq ibn Ibrāhīm al-Mauṣalī, and Abū al-'Abbās Muḥammad ibn al-Ḥasan al-Aḥwal.

[51] *Ibid.* pp. 17, 24, 53.

[52] See *ibid.* pp. 4, 39, 53, 59, 66, 68, and 118 for plurals and pp. 22, 69, 70, and 74 for verbs, the first from Ibn al-A'rābī and the rest from Muḥammad ibn Ḥabīb, who is frequently cited as Abū Ja'far.

[53] *Fihrist*, p. 106; *Irshād* VI 473. *Inbah* III 121 records this attitude in his verses:

ان المعلم لا يزال معلما   لو كان علم آدم الاسماء
من علم الصبيان اصبوا عقله   حتى بني الخلفاء والخلفاء

[54] *Irshād* VI 474: اكثر اخذه عنه ابو سعيد السكرى. This source cites Marzubānī, who accuses Muḥammad ibn Ḥabīb of plagiarism (cf. *Inbāh* III 121).

[55] See *Fihrist*, pp. 157 f. for Sukkarī and p. 106 for Muḥammad ibn Ḥabīb: كان من علماء بغداد بالانساب والاخبار واللغة والشعر والقبائل وكان مؤدبا وكتبه صحيحة (cf. Khaṭīb II 277; *Inbāh* III 119).

at least the Banū Hudhail and the Banū Shaibān.[56] His transmission of the collected poetry of individual poets, probably all with some of his own commentary includes that of no less than eleven specified poets, beginning with Imru' al-Qais and ending with Jarīr and Farazdaq,[57] but overlooks that of Akhṭal. His transmission of Akhṭal's poetry, however, is indicated in the full *isnād* of the St. Petersburg manuscript copy of *Shiʿr al-Akhṭal*, published by Ṣāliḥānī, and brings the list of Muḥammad ibn Ḥabīb's *dīwān*'s to a full dozen, which I suspect is still incomplete. His *Naqā'iḍ Jarīr wa ʿUmar ibn Lajā'*, *Naqā'iḍ Jarīr wa al-Farazdaq*, and *Ayyām Jarīr al-latī dhakrahā fī shiʿrihi* would seem to indicate that he had a greater interest in the poetry of Jarīr than in that of either Farazdaq or Akhṭal and possibly a greater interest in *naqā'iḍ* than in other categories of poetry. This, too, I begin to suspect since we do have the *Shiʿr al-Akhṭal*, which includes most of Akhṭal's *naqā'iḍ*.

Starting with Muḥammad ibn al-ʿAbbās al-Yazīdī, fourth-generation member of a famous family of scholars, poets, and royal tutors, we have come in a roundabout way to Muḥammad ibn Ḥabīb, himself a royal tutor, a multitalented linguistic scholar, and a leading poetry transmitter-commentator, as a possible author of the manuscript represented by our folio. Furthermore, as we look again at the above-cited *isnād* of *Shiʿr al-Akhṭal* and integrate each successive transmitter with pertinent bits of information already gathered about him this possibility is repeatedly reinforced. For we know now that the Kūfan transmitters Ibn al-Aʿrābī and his pupils ʿAlī ibn ʿAbd Allāh al-Ṭūsī and Muḥammad ibn Ḥabīb were more likely than others to stress grammatical points in their commentaries, that Muḥammad ibn Ḥabīb was both a philologist and a grammarian, that he transmitted from both Ibn al-Aʿrābī and Abū ʿUbaidah to Sukkarī, who is classified primarily as a transmitter of the poetry texts of specified *dīwān*'s, *naqā'iḍ*, and anthologies as well as the commentaries on them. We know also that Sukkarī transmitted from Muḥammad ibn Ḥabīb to Muḥammad ibn al-ʿAbbās al-Yazīdī and that the latter, though known to have made a personal contribution to scholarship, was even better known and appreciated as the preserver and transmitter of his scholarly family's literary heritage along with some materials from others. His personal contribution is confirmed by his numerous comments in the Bevan edition of the *naqā'iḍ* of Jarīr and Farazdaq but is not so clearly defined in the St. Petersburg manuscript copy of *Shiʿr al-Akhṭal*. For, apart from the *isnād* of this work, the contribution of each transmitter is only rarely indicated, as Ṣāliḥānī realized and as his index of scholars mentioned in the manuscript copy indicates.[58] On the other hand, Muḥammad ibn al-ʿAbbās al-Yazīdī's dependence on the contributions of his family members and others is readily apparent in his *Amālī*. In both the Bevan edition of the *naqā'iḍ* of Jarīr and Farazdaq and the *Amālī* we find that Muḥammad ibn Ḥabīb is cited specifically more often than Sukkarī. Moreover, Muḥammad ibn Ḥabīb is more apt to indicate broken plurals and even the singulars of such words and to give the parts of weak and irregular verbs. Nevertheless, despite all the points in favor of Muḥammad ibn Ḥabīb, I am still not inclined to consider him as *the* probable author of the manuscript represented by our folio on the strength of this single folio alone. For there is ample evidence in the *dīwān*'s cited that the nature, frequency, and length of poetry comments vary repeatedly within a given commentary. Hence, it would be futile to pursue this line of thought in respect to Muḥammad ibn Ḥabīb's contemporaries, especially since none of them seems to have been associated significantly with the transmission of the poetry of Akhṭal. But as a result of our limited survey of poetry commentaries it seems safe enough to indicate the probability that comments of the type found in our folio were prevalent from at least as early as the time of Abū ʿAmr ibn al-ʿAlā' until that of Muḥammad ibn Ḥabīb, when linguistic studies, particularly those devoted to grammar, were still fluid, if not controversial, enough to demand the attention of the mature

[56] *Maṣādir*, pp. 546, 556, 565.

[57] See *Fihrist*, pp. 106 f.; *Irshād* VI 475 f.; *Inbāh* III 121, n. 1. See also Maḥmūd Ghināwī al-Zuhairī, *Naqā'iḍ Jarīr wa al-Farazdaq*, pp. 13 f. and references cited.

[58] See Ṣāliḥānī, *Shiʿr al-Akhṭal*, pp. 373, 565 ff.

scholar, the cultured reader, and the young learner. That such comments are found more frequently in commentaries that trace back to Kūfans than in those that derive from Baṣran scholars of this early period is due in part to the fact that the Kūfans began earlier to collect and transmit both classical and contemporary poetry. One has but to recall the rich careers in this respect of such Kūfans as Ḥammād al-Rāwiyah and Mufaḍḍal ibn Muḥammad al-Ḍabbī and their younger contemporaries and literary heirs, especially Abū ʿAmr al-Shaibānī and Ibn al-Aʿrābī, to realize why the last two mentioned are cited freely and frequently in poetry collections and commentaries that stem in the main from Baṣran scholars of their day and after. In the mid-third century, as the cultured and more sophisticated intelligentsia of Baghdād leaned toward formal literary criticism, the earlier poetry commentators were subject to criticism for overemphasis on lexical and grammatical elements, as demonstrated in Qudāmah ibn Jaʿfar's literary criticism and Ṣūlī's commentary on the *Dīwān Abī Tammām* (see p. 156). But it was not to be expected that such linguistic elements would be generally neglected thereafter. They are indeed to be found in the lengthier and more varied and complex commentaries of the fourth century and after as illustrated by those of Marzūqī and Tabrīzī.

DOCUMENT 7

VERSES FROM AN ODE OF DHŪ AL-RUMMAH

Michigan Arabic Papyrus No. 6748. Third/ninth century.

Two joined book folios of fine light-colored papyrus, 28 × 21.5 cm., with 13 lines to the page (Pls. 9–10). This type of format was preferred for Qur'ānic codices and other prized manuscripts.[1] The unusually wide outer margins vary between 6 and 8 cm., and the inner margins range from 4 to 7 cm. The text is well preserved except for the lower part of each folio, where large lacunae and several small breaks occur. The upper part of the outer margin of the first page has, at its edge, what seems to be a single illegible word and a vertical notation which could be read في سلة عما[ل] or more likely في سنة ثمان[ين وم]اية. The latter would indicate that the papyrus had been used, at least in part, for an earlier but washed-out text, which would in turn explain a few dots that are not accounted for in the script, though most such dots that appear in our reproductions are but very small breaks in the papyrus itself.

Script.—Best described as a fair sample of large book *naskhī* with irregular use of a few Kūfic letter forms. Kūfic forms are *ḥā'* and *jīm* with a beam (as on pages 1:7, 2:7, 3:4, 4:4), the angular initial *kāf* (as on pages 1:4, 2:5, 3:5, 4:2), *ṣād* and *ḍād* (as on pages 1:2 and 8, 2:2–3 and 8, 3:2 and 11, 4:7), *ṭā'* and *ẓā'* (as on pages 1:7, 3:4, 4:2), and the open medial *'ain* and *ghain* (as on pages 2:2, 8, and 10, 3:8 and 12, 4:5). Diacritical points are freely but not fully used. The position of the dots varies according to the space available from three dots in a horizontal row for *shīn* to three dots in a vertical row for *thā'* (as on page 2:6). The two dots of *tā'*, *qāf*, and *yā'* are usually placed vertically or slanted slightly (as e.g. on page 1:1–3). The letters *dāl* and *dhāl* are not carefully differentiated, though occasionally *dāl* has a dot below it and *dhāl* a dot above it (as on page 2:2 and 9 respectively). Small letters are placed below *ḥā'* (as on pages 2:6, 3:3, 4:2 and 6) and *'ain* (as on pages 3:2 and 4:5), but there is a *muhmalah* over the *ḥā'* of حين on page 2:4, the *ḥā'* of جموح on page 3:12, and the *'ain* of العدي on page 4:1. *Sīn* has three dots in a horizontal row below it (as on page 1:5 and 13) and sometimes a ˅ above it (as on pages 2:2 and 5 and 3:5). The simple *alif* alternates with the hooked form (as e.g. on page 1:1–4). The ligatured *alif* and *lām*, regardless of their position in a word, were written downward and thus called for much lifting of the pen, which resulted frequently in a lower extension with a slight turn, mostly to the left, of the final *alif* (as e.g. on page 1:1–4). The reversed *yā'* alternates with the more regular form (as e.g. on pages 1:7, 2:2, 3:1–2). Medial *ḥā'* and its sister letters are sometimes placed partially or fully below a preceding letter (as on pages 1:3 and 10, 2:3, 3:3, 5, and 8, 4:3 and 8). Final *alif* alternates with *alif maqṣūrah*. Letter extensions are used unevenly and only at the ends of lines. A peculiarity of the scribe was to place a letter over a preceding extension as in the open *ghain* of الغزال on page 2:10 and افتعل on page 4:5 and the *ḍād* of عضالا on page 4:6. These could be later insertions of omitted letters. Omission of a word and a letter are indicated on pages 1:2 and 2:2. Another careless scribal practice was the insertion of a long dash between non-extendable letters in an attempt, not always successful, to even out the lines (as on pages 2:1 and 4 and 3:11). A misplaced extension is on page 1:8, where the final *tā'* of تفرعت instead of the *bā'* of الجبال is extended. The widening of the written area beginning on page 1:7 was probably done to avoid overcrowding of the text, and the indentation of lines 9–13 resulted in a better balance between

[1] See Vol. II 91.

the inner and outer margins. The unevenness of the written area on page 2 is another indication of the scribe's carelessness.

The orthographic system used here and in Document 6 is that of Khalīl ibn Aḥmad, which, it will be recalled, he devised with poetry particularly in mind but which spread rapidly to other fields of secular literature (see pp. 7–10). Freely used are the three basic vowels, *fatḥah, kasrah,* and *ḍammah,* and the doubled forms of the *fatḥah* and *kasrah* for the *tanwīn.* The *sukūn* is indicated by the old sign >, which is carelessly written. The only other orthographic devices used are the small truncated *shīn* and *ʿain* for the *shaddah* and *hamzah* respectively. The placing of the *hamzah* is of particular interest in that it reflects the influence of the earlier Qur'ānic orthography, in which position and color were used to distinguish the dot or point indicating the *hamzah* from the dots used for the three basic vowels.

The *hamzah* in its initial, medial, and final positions is used rather freely, usually without its accompanying vowel, which is nevertheless frequently indicated by the placing of the *hamzah* itself. Thus أَ, أ, and أْ generally indicate the later stabilized أَ, أُ, and إِ. Note, however, that أْ indicates the أُ of أُغنى on page 1:2. Medial *hamzah* alternates with *yā'* (as on pages 1:9 and 3:4 and 7; see also p. 24). Note the use of both the *hamzah* and the two dots of the *yā'* in غرائيب of page 4:5. The independent final *hamzah* is written on the line with its accompanying vowel indicated as in برءَ and برءُ of page 2:11. The *hamzat al-waṣal* and the *maddah* have no specific symbols. However, the *maddah* is not entirely neglected. Medial آ is written with two *alif*'s as in مااثر of page 4:13. Final آ is indicated as أَ as in عليأَ of page 1:3 and appears as أـِ as in الصباءِ of page 1:11. Note also that آً is indicated as أء as in دأءً of page 2:3 or as أً as in اعبأً of page 3:9.

No punctuation or collation signs are used and, as in Document 6, no space or other device marks off the hemistichs.

The more liberal use of more of Khalīl's orthographic symbols in this early poetry manuscript than in early prose works is not surprising since the system was designed to meet the needs of written poetry more adequately than could the cumbersome orthographic system used for Qur'ānic manuscripts, as we have indicated more fully above in the discussion of orthography and scripts, where attention is drawn to the influence of the new system on even Qur'ānic manuscripts. Our papyrus is of interest in that it illustrates the reverse, that is, the influence of the Qur'ānic system on the newer one in non-Qur'ānic manuscripts, especially as to the position of the *hamzah,* in a period of overlapping use of the two systems in both Qur'ānic and non-Qur'ānic manuscripts. The copy of Abū ʿUbaid's *Gharīb al-ḥadīth* dated 252/866 provides an instructive illustration of this process (see p. 11) as does the paper manuscript of the *Dīwān al-Mutanabbī* dated 398/1008 (see p. 12).[2] Indispensable for our understanding of the complexity of the placement of orthographic signs in early Qur'ānic manuscripts, including the various regional practices, and of the progressive transfer of these signs into the more manageable system of Khalīl, with some later modifications, is Dānī's *Muḥkam,* with its copious illustrations of the placing of the vowels and especially of the *hamzah.*

TEXT

Page 1

1 فكـــدتُ اموت من حزن عليهم ولم ار ناوى الاظعان بـــالا

2 فاشرفت الغزالـــة راس حـَوضى اراقـــبهـم ومـا أغنى قبـــالا

[2] For other illustrations of this process within this period of overlapping see e.g. Moritz, *Arabic Palaeography,* Pls. 19–21, and *Namādhij,* Pls. 16 and 64; see also *Le djâmiʿ d'Ibn Wahb,* ed. David-Weill, I iv–vii and 84–106. For additional examples of the use and placement of orthographic signs in both systems see *OIP* L 39 f., 44, 63 and our Vols. I 1–3 and II 87–91; see also pp. 5–11 above and references there cited.

3	كاني اشهل العينين باز	على علياء شبّه فاستخالا
4	رايتهم وقد جعلوا فتاخاً	واجرعة المقابلة شمالا
5	وقد جعلوا السبيّه عن يمين	مقاد المهر واعتسفوا الرمالا
6	كأنّ الآل يرفع بين حزُوى	ورابية الخوىّ بهم سيالا
7	وفى الاظعان مثل مها رماح	علته الشمس فادّرع الظلالا
8	تجوّف كل ارطاة ربوض	من الدّهنا تفرّعت الحبالا
9	أُولاك كانهن اولاك إلّا	شوا لصواحب الارطى ضئالا
10	وان صواحب الاخدار جُمٌّ	وانّ لهن اعجازا ثقالا
11	واعناق الظباء رأين شخصا	نصبن له السـ[والف ا]و خيالا
12	رخيمات الكـ[لام مبطّنا]ت	جواعل في البُرى قصبا خدالا
13	جمعن ملاحة و[خلو]ص عتق	وحسنا بعد ذلك واعتدالا

Page 2

1	كأنّ جلودهن مموهّات	على ابشارها ذهبا زلالا
2	ومـ[يـّه في ا[لظ]عاين وهى شكـّت	سواد القلب فاقتتل اقتتالا
3	عشيّة طالعت لتكون داءً	جوا بين الجوانح او سلالا
4	تريك بياض لبّتها ووجها	كقرن الشمس افتق حين زالا
5	أصاب خصاصة فبدا كليلا	كلا وانغلّ سائره انغلالا
6	وأشنب واضحاً حسن الثنايا	ترا بين ثنيّته خلالا
7	كان رضابهُ من ماء كرم	ترقرق في الزجاج وقد احالا
8	يشج بما سارية سقته	على صمّانة رصفا فسالا
9	وميّه احسن الثقلين وجها	وسالفة واحسنَهُ قذالا
10	ولم ار مثلها نظرا وعينا	ولا ام الغزال ولا الغزالا
11	هي الد[سقم الذى] لا بُرءَ منه	وبرءُ السقم لو رضحت نوالا
12	كذاك الغانيات فرغن منّا	على الغ[فـ]لات رميا واخت[يا]لا
13	فعدّ عن الصبّا وعليكَ شماً	[توقش] في فؤادك وا[ختبـ]ـالا

Page 3

1	فبتُّ اروض صعب الهم حتى	اجلت جميع مرّته مجالا
2	الي ابن العامري الي بلال	قطعت بنعف معلقة العدالا
3	قريت بها الصريمه لا شخاتا	غداة رحيلهنّ ولا حيالا
4	نجايب من نتاج بنى غرير	طوال السمك مفرعة نبالا
5	مضبَّرة كانّ صفا مـ[ـا]سيل	كسا اوراكها وكسا المحالا
6	يخذن بكل خاوية المبادى	ترى بيض النعام بها حلالا
7	كان هويّهنّ بكل خرق	هوىٌّ الربد بادرت الريالا
8	مذببة اضرَّ بها بكوري	وتهجيري اذا اليعفور قالا

9	وادلاجي اذا ما الليل القى	على الضعفاء اعباءً ثقالا
10	اذا خفقت بأمقه صَحصحان	رؤ[و]س القوم واعتنقوا [الا]رحالا
11	فـ[لم] تهبط على [سـ]فوان حتى	وضعن سخالهنّ وصرن آلا
12	[وربَّ مفازة قذف] جموح	تغول منحَّب القرب اغَتيالا
13	[قطعتُ اذا تجوفت] العواطى	ضروب السدر عبريا وضالا

Page 4

1	على خوصاء تذرف ماقياها	من العيدىّ قد لقيت كلالا
2	اذا بركت طرحتُ لها زمامي	ولم اعقد بركبتها عقالا
3	وشعر قد ارقتُ له غريب	أُجنِّبه المُساند والمحالا
4	فبتُّ أُقيمه وأقدُّ منه	قوافيِ ما ايدُ لها مثالا
5	غرائب قد عرفن بكل افق	من الافاق تفتعلُ افتعالا
6	فلم اقدف لمؤمنة حصان	بحمد الله موجبة عضالا
7	ولم امدح لارضيه بشعرى	لئيما ان يكون اصاب مالا
8	ولكن الكرام لهم ثنائى	فلا اخزا اذا ما قيل قالا
9	رايتُ الناس ينتجعون [غيـ]ثا	فقلت لصيدح انتجعى بلالا
10	تناخى عند خير فتا يمان	ا[ذا] النكباء ناوحت الشمالا
11	ندا وتكرُّما ولباب لب	اذا الاشياء حصَّلت الرجالا
12	وابعدهم مسافة غور عقل	اذ ما الامر ذو الشبهات عالا
13	وخيرهم مآثر اهل بيت	وا[كرمهم] ا[ذ] قطعت الاخوّقبالا

Comments.—The papyrus text parallels ode No. 57:6–58 in Macartney's edition of *Dīwān Dhī al-Rummah* and in Muṭīʿ Babbīlī's edition, which retains the Macartney order of odes and verses. The order of verses in our text is the same, but verse 27 of the printed texts is missing. There are a number of lexical and grammatical variants for our text, most of which are indicated by Macartney either in the commentaries (*shuruḥ*) accompanying the text or in his numerous footnotes citing lexical and literary sources in connection with individual verses. The *shuruḥ* most cited for this particular ode are those of the manuscripts of *Dīwān Dhī al-Rummah* that are in the Khedivial Library in Cairo and the India Office Library, which Macartney refers to as "C" and "D" respectively.[3] The *shuruḥ* of these two manuscripts, being for the most part identical or very similar, are cited together in all but seventeen of the hundred verses of the ode, while alone C is cited five times (verses 8, 15–16, 81–82) and D only twice (verses 10 and 58). Supplementary comments, mostly from British Museum and Constantinople manuscripts, are cited in the editor's footnotes. Muṭīʿ Babbīlī's more recent edition is based largely on the Macartney text but has all the cited comments, variants, and literary references indicated in the footnotes along with some added editorial comments.[4] It is not likely that the several extant manuscripts of *Dīwān Dhī al-Rummah* that are not used in either of these two rich editions contain other variants which are significant for our text. In the Landberg Collection of the Yale University Library is one such manuscript, a recent and incomplete copy, a microfilm of which was kindly provided me.[5] Folios 19–21 contain the ode from which our

[3] See Macartney, p. v.

[4] Muṭīʿ Babbīlī, Intro. pp. 1–3 and text pp. 517–37.

[5] Leon Nemoy, *Arabic Manuscripts in the Yale University Library* ("Transactions of the Connecticut Academy of Arts and Sciences" XL [New Haven, 1956]) p. 44, No. 279 (L–750), dated *ca.* A.D. 1888.

papyrus text is drawn, but, apart from scribal errors and the familiar discrepancies of verse count and verse order, there is hardly a variant that is not already covered in the Macartney and Muṭīʿ Babbīlī editions. On the other hand, some of the known but still unstudied manuscripts with early commentaries could prove significant for additional odes, for background information on individual odes, and possibly also for some biographical items. Such a manuscript, not available to me, is one from Ṣanʿāʾ, judged from its script alone to be probably from the third/ninth century.[6]

Page 1:1. Muṭīʿ Babbīlī parallels our text but Macartney has شوق instead of حزن and حادى instead of ناوى. See pp. 184 f. below for the background of the text of pages 1–2.

Page 1:2. The scribe overlooked راس but inserted it later between the lines.

Page 1:4. Macartney and Muṭīʿ Babbīlī have الشمالا.

Page 1:5–6. The order of these verses is reversed in the Yale manuscript.

Page 1:8. Note the repetition of تفرعت and the letter extensions.

Page 1:10. Macartney and Muṭīʿ Babbīlī have الاضعان for الاخدار, the latter along with الاحداج being indicated in the footnotes of both editions.

Page 1:12. Note the variant in the margin, which reads ويروى رخيات الكلام نعامة[ه], and is written in a smaller and more cursive script.

Page 1:13. Our reproduction (Pl. 9) shows at this point many small breaks which can be mistaken for diacritical points. Macartney and Muṭīʿ Babbīlī have فخامة instead of ملاحة, the latter being indicated in the commentary and the footnotes. The *waw* of وعتق is missing in both of the printed editions and in the Yale manuscript.

Page 2:1. Note the peculiar placing, on the line, of the two short diagonal strokes after the *tāʾ* of مموّهاتٌ. Early Qurʾānic usage called for placing two such strokes over the "head" or the initial vertical stroke of the *tāʾ* to indicate its diacritical "points," as it called for the placing of two dots, one over the other on the line, to indicate the *ḍammah* with the *tanwīn*. We have here either compounded confusion of the Qurʾānic and non-Qurʾānic systems of orthography or, more likely, scribal carelessness. Since this is the only instance where our text calls for the double *ḍammah*, the scribe's practice in this respect cannot be checked.

Page 2:2. Note the omission of the medial *ẓāʾ* of الظعائن and the use of *yāʾ* instead of *hamzah*.

Page 2:4. Macartney parallels this verse; Muṭīʿ Babbīlī prefers ثُمّ for حين.

Page 2:5. The last word of the line was first written اعلالا and then changed to انغلالا with the added *nūn* ligatured to the initial *ʿain* without the latter being changed to the medial form. The second half of the line reads in the Yale manuscript لنا وانغل جانبه انغلالا, a variant which is indicated in Macartney's notes.

Page 2:6. Macartney and Muṭīʿ Babbīlī have من بين for بين, but Muṭīʿ Babbīlī prefers نَبتَتـه to the definitely indicated ثنيّتـه of the papyrus and the Macartney text.

[6] Fuʾād Sayyid, "Makhṭūṭāt al-Yemen," *Majallat maʿhad al-makhṭūṭāt al-ʿarabīyah* I (Cairo, 1955) 197; see also Dar al-kutub al-miṣrīyah, *Fihrist al-makhṭūṭāt*, ed. Fuʾād Sayyid, II (Cairo, 1382/1962) 31. It is not clear to me what the relationship of this Ṣanʿāʾ manuscript is to the Ṣanʿāʾ manuscript which Griffinī turned over to the Ambrosian Library in Milan and which was freely used by Macartney, who refers to it as "Ambr." and indicates that it does not contain ode No. 57, the ode of our papyrus text (see Macartney, pp. vi f. and xxxix).

Page 2:8. Verse 27 of Macartney and Muṭīʿ Babbīlī reads

واسحم كالاساود مسبكرا   على المتنين منسدلا جفالا

but is missing between lines 8 and 9 of our text.

Page 2:9. Macartney and Muṭīʿ Babbīlī have خدا for وجها; Muṭīʿ Babbīlī has واحسنهم.

Page 2:10. See n. 120 on p. 184.

Page 2:12. The last word of the line, اختيالا, is reconstructed from the Macartney text, where the variants اختبالا and احتبالا are also given.

Page 2:13. Scribal confusion is indicated in the first half of the verse, where ما and an illegible word following it should be deleted. Macartney, Muṭīʿ Babbīlī, and the Yale manuscript have هما for شيا. Variants for اختبالا are اختيالا and احتبالا, and the latter is preferred by Muṭīʿ Babbīlī.

Page 3:1. See pp. 172–74 for the background of the text of pages 3–4.

Page 3:2. Note the raised *alif* of ابن. Some early manuscripts omit this *alif*, as, for example, in the case of بن شهاب (see Vol. II 166). The marginal note reads ويروى الى ابن العامرين الى بلال, which is indicated also in Macartney's footnotes.

Page 3:3. Macartney's text reads قروت for قريت.

Page 3:7. Macartney's text omits the article of الخرق.

Page 3:8. The papyrus text is identical with that of the Macartney edition, where commentaries of manuscripts C and D yield اقرابى and ارتحالى for تهجيرى and C adds واونة اي حيانا, which suggests ويروى واونة for the marginal notation in the papyrus.

Page 3:9. Macartney's text omits the *alif* of اثقالا.

Page 3:10. Macartney and Muṭīʿ Babbīlī have التزموا for اعتنقوا. Macartney adds references to lexical sources, all of which cite the verse with the reading of the papyrus text. The papyrus marginal notation also reads ويروى التزموا الرحالا.

Page 3-11. Macartney and Muṭīʿ Babbīlī read طرحن سخالهن وإضن آلا, and the commentaries add قذفن سخالهن and صرن as variants; a footnote adds حتى وضعن as the reading of the text of the Constantinople manuscript No. 1677. The marginal note in the papyrus reads ويروى طرحن سخالهن.

Page 3:12–13. The reconstructions in both lines follow the Macartney text, which is also that of Muṭīʿ Babbīlī. Macartney's footnotes indicate طموح, تعول, and اعتيالا as variants for جموح, تغول and اغتيالا of line 12. Footnote variants for line 13 are تجوبت and تخوفت for تجوفت and صدور for سدر. Obviously some of these variants and others indicated above stem from copying from manuscripts instead of writing from dictation.

Page 4:2. Macartney and Muṭīʿ Babbīlī have زماما for زمامى and أعقل for أعقد. This verse is missing in the Yale manuscript, as are also verses 70, 73, and 89 of this ode, which has 100 verses in the two printed editions as against 96 in the Yale manuscript.

Page 4:3. Macartney and Muṭīʿ Babbīlī have لا أعدُّ for ما أيد.

Page 4:4–6. Muṭīʿ Babbīlī's فيث is a scribal error for فبتُ of line 4. Note that lines 3–5 reflect Dhū al-Rummah's appraisal of himself as a poet (see pp. 189 f. below), while in line 6 he declares his aversion to scandalizing virtuous believing women (see p. 188 below).

Page 4:7. The full line parallels the Macartney text, but the footnotes yield لبيبا for لثيما and the variant reading ولست بمادح ابدا لئيما بشعرى. The variant reading is preferred by Muṭīʿ Babbīlī, as is also the variant افاد for اصاب. Note that lines 7–13 of our text and the rest of this long ode are devoted to the poet's justification of his praise of Bilāl ibn Abī Burdah and his family and to the panegyric itself (see pp. 173 f. below).

Page 4:9. Macartney and Muṭīʿ Babbīlī have سمعت for رايت.

Page 4:12–13. The reconstruction of the damaged text follows in part the Macartney and Muṭīʿ Babbīlī editions. The definite article of الشهاب is missing in both editions. Before the last word of line 12 there seems to be an illegible word which disturbs the meter. The confused text could be due in part to the several breaks in the papyrus and in part to scribal carelessness, perhaps resulting from a belated effort to align the extensions at the ends of the two lines. The plural الاخوّ of line 13 can refer to brothers and close kin as well as close friends. Dhū al-Rummah could, therefore, be referring to some of his relatives, especially to his brother Hishām (see pp. 174 f. below), but hardly to his earlier failure to win a reward from ʿAbd al-Malik. The second hemistitch of line 13 deviates markedly from both the Macartney and Muṭīʿ Babbīlī texts, which are the same as the Yale manuscript, and which read: واكرمهم وان كَرُموا فعالا. Inasmuch as neither Macartney nor Muṭīʿ Babbīlī indicates the version found in our text as a variant in any of the manuscripts or the copious literary sources they cite, it could well be that our text is Dhū al-Rummah's original version, which was later edited either by the poet himself or by one of his leading transmitters.

HISTORICAL BACKGROUND

I

Dhū al-Rummah's comparatively short life spanned the last part of the reign of ʿAbd al-Malik through most of the reign of Hishām and thus coincided in part with the lives of Jarīr and Farazdaq. The major political and literary background of this period has been considered above at some length in connection with Documents 4–6. We note, to begin with, that inclination and circumstances seem to have turned Dhū al-Rummah away from playing an active political role comparable to that of Jarīr and Farazdaq among other poets. Reading through his *Dīwān,* one has to conclude that his first and lasting passion was for nature in its desert setting. Little of the desert's hardships, its dunes and water sources, its flora and fauna escaped his sharp eye and receptive mind. But, like most poets of his day, he was drawn to the flourishing cities of Baṣrah and Kūfah (see p. 201, n. 255), alternating between them and the desert. He learned the rudiments of reading and writing from an itinerant city dweller and later taught school in the desert (*bādiyah*). He preferred to have his poetry written down,[7] as did other poets of his day whose literary activities have been covered above.[8]

A number of Dhū al-Rummah's verses reveal his familiarity with formal manuscripts, old and contemporary, and with the act of writing itself, as in the following verses from Macartney, the last verse being from an ode that the poet recited to ʿAbd al-Malik.

No. 1:4: من ذمنة نسفت عنها الصبا سفعا كما تنشر بعد الطية الكتــب
No. 18:1: كأنّ ديار الحى بالزرق خلقةُ من الارض ام مكتوبةُ بمدادِ

[7] Jāḥiẓ, *Ḥayawān* I 41 (see p. 197 below); *Aghānī* XVI 121; Ṣūlī, *Adab al-kuttāb*, p. 62; *Muwashshaḥ*, pp. 172, 178, 192; *Khaṣāʾiṣ* III 296; *Muzhir* II 349 f. See also p. 155 above.

[8] Particularly instructive are references, direct or indirect, to manuscripts of Akhṭal, Jarīr, and Farazdaq and the court poets of the poet-caliph Walīd II (see e.g. pp. 97 f., 113, 115 f., 145 f.).

No. 38:1: أأن ترسمت من خرقآء منزلــة كالوحى فى مصحف قدمح منشور

No. 51:1: ألـلأربع الدهم اللواتى كانهـا بقيات وحى فى متون الصحآئف

No. 66:4: كأنّ قرا جرعائها رجعت به يهودية الاقـلام وحى الرسآئل

No. 71:3: دياراً لمىّ قد تعفّت رسومهـــا أخالُ نواحيها كتابا معجـــما

No. 73:2: كأن أُنوف الطير فى عرصاتها خراطيم أقـــلام تخطُّ وتعجمُ

No. 81:6: أربَّت بها الامطار حتى كأَنها كتاب زبور فى مهاريق معجمُ

Furthermore, most of the early sources on hand report that he dictated his poetry and at times corrected the resulting manuscript.[9]

Teaching school in a desert settlement could have involved little more than reading, writing, and the recitation of the Qurʾān. Dhū al-Rummah makes frequent allusions to Qurʾānic phrases and terms, at times in justification of his own views and conduct. Nevertheless, he did not play an active role in the religious controversies of his day, though some sources refer to him as a Qādirite and a Muʿtazilite.[10] He seems to have been preoccupied primarily with his poetry, which, despite his natural talent, he sought constantly to polish and perfect (see p. 190). But, like most poets of his day, he aspired to fame and fortune and hoped to achieve both through royal patronage.[11] We find him very early in his career reciting a long ode to ʿAbd al-Malik supposedly in praise of that royal patron of poets, but the ode turned out to be mostly in praise of the poet's she-camel Ṣaidaʿ. Displeased and disappointed, ʿAbd al-Malik told the young poet to seek his reward from his mount and dismissed him empty handed.[12] Thereafter the poet apparently was disinclined to seek royal favor and was content instead with the patronage of local officials and provincial governors, with whom he fared more favorably. Among these were Muhāzir ibn ʿAbd Allāh, governor of the Najdian Yamāmah,[13] ʿUmar ibn Hubairah, governor of ʿIrāq (103–5/721–23),[14] and particularly Bilāl ibn Abī Burdah. Bilāl started as chief of police in Baṣrah and rose to be judge, to which office was soon added the deputy-governorship of Baṣrah under Khālid al-Qaṣrī, Hishām's governor of ʿIrāq (105–20/723–38).[15]

It is possible that Dhū al-Rummah sought and received the patronage of ʿAbd al-Malik ibn Bishr ibn Marwān, deputy-governor of Baṣrah during the governorship of Maslamah ibn ʿAbd al-Malik, who was removed from that office along with his appointees, including ʿAbd al-Malik ibn Bishr, by Yazīd II in 103/721.[16] Dhū al-Rummah does mention an Ibn Bishr, whom Macartney correctly suspected was this ʿAbd al-Malik ibn Bishr, for he is referred to as Ibn Bishr by Farazdaq and in the sources also.[17] In the poet's only other reference to a Marwānid[18] he could well mean either Maslamah or this Ibn Bishr.

[9] See e.g. Jāḥiẓ, *Ḥayawān* I 41, 63, 65 (this entire section up to p. 104 being instructive for its numerous references to early writing and to books); *ʿIqd* IV 194; *Muwashshah*, pp. 177 f.; *ʿUmdah* II 194.

[10] *Majālis al-ʿulamāʾ*, p. 74, but see *Aghānī* XVI 122. It should be recalled that Walīd II also was considered a Qādirite (see n. 111 on p. 92 above).

[11] Poets considered it beneath their dignity and a disgrace to accept rewards from other than heads of state and their chief administrators, i.e., primarily caliphs, governors, and wazirs (see e.g. *ʿIqd* I 275; *ʿUmdah* I 52–54; n. 49 on p. 175 below).

[12] *Aghānī* X 158. See Macartney, No. 81, for this ode of 48 verses, the first 17 of which are devoted to Mayya, verses 18, 22–23, and 25 to the caliph, and the rest to the camel.

[13] See e.g. Macartney, Nos. 31, 33, 62.

[14] See e.g. *ibid.* No. 25.

[15] See e.g. Jumaḥī, p. 14; Ṭabarī II 1506, 1526, 1593. Another patron of Dhū al-Rummah, mentioned in passing, was Ibrāhīm ibn Hishām al-Makhzūmī (see Macartney, No. 78:1, 19–22, 25–27).

[16] Jumaḥī, pp. 287 f.; Mubarrad, pp. 288, 479; Ṭabarī II 1417, 1433 f., 1436; *Aghānī* XIX 16 f.

[17] Macartney, p. xiii and No. 48:66–69; Jumaḥī, p. 288; *Aghānī* XIX 17. See *Irshād* IV 124 and 126–28 for this Ibn Bishr as a patron of poets.

[18] See Macartney, No. 5:67:

تؤمُّ فتى من آل مروان اطلقت يداه وطابت فى قريش مضاربُهْ

There is, furthermore, a curious account with no *isnād* that reports Dhū al-Rummah as congratulating the caliph Marwān II (127–32/744–50) on his accession. The poet is described as decrepit and bent low with age.[19] Marwān made a pointed comment to the effect that he did not expect the poet to be able to produce any verse in his praise after all the praise he had lavished on Mayya (or Mayyah) and his she-camel Ṣaidaʿ. Dhū al-Rummah assured him he could indeed and recited

فقلت لها سيرى امامك سيّدٌ   تغرَّع من مروان ومن محمدِ

which again included his she-camel. And the poet then recited

طويت غدائرها ببُرد بَلِىَ   ومحا الترب محاسن الخـدِ

in response to Marwān's wish to know what Mayya was doing.[20]

Marwān was impressed with the matched rhyme of these two verses and ordered the poet to be rewarded with 1,000 dinars for each of his ancestors whom the poet had named in the first verse. Said Dhū al-Rummah: "Had I known this, I would have mentioned your forebears back to ʿAbd Shams."[21] This episode is improbable since there is general agreement that Dhū al-Rummah died no later than 117/735. On the other hand, the poet could have visited Prince Marwān on his appointment in 114/732 to the governorship of Mauṣil along with that of Armenia and Adhrabījān.[22] The description of the poet as being decrepit and bent low with age gains some support from other reports of his physical appearance (see pp. 181–83). But his description of Mayya, who was probably not much older than he, as a gray-haired old woman with no trace of beauty left in her face needs further support.

Mayya, beloved of Dhū al-Rummah, and Bilāl ibn Abī Burdah are the objects of praise in our papyrus text. We turn our attention first to the latter. Bilāl's character and reputation as a public official left much to be desired. To gain consideration for high office he relied in part on the reputation of his grandfather Abū Mūsā al-Ashʿarī, conqueror of much of ʿIrāq, judge and governor of Baṣrah and Kūfah during most of the reigns of ʿUmar I, ʿUthmān, and ʿAlī.[23] He relied more on his own guile and strong hand to win and hold such office. We find him congratulating ʿUmar II on his accession and striving through lengthy public prayers to impress the pious ʿUmar with his own piety while secretly offering a year's salary for help in securing the appointment as governor of ʿIrāq. The attempt boomeranged, for ʿUmar himself had set his confidant to test Bilāl's display of piety. And when the bribery was revealed to ʿUmar, he instructed the then governor of ʿIrāq not to employ Bilāl in any official capacity.[24]

Bilāl's big opportunity came during Khālid al-Qaṣrī's governorship of ʿIrāq, when as deputy-governor of Baṣrah he acquired direct and full control of most of its civic offices, including the police department, the judgeship, and the leadership of public worship.[25] There seems to be general agreement that Bilāl's strong hand grew progressively oppressive and his temper extremely intolerant of criticism,[26] so that complaints against his avarice, injustice, and autocratic rule went directly to Hishām, who then ordered

[19] ʿ*Iqd* I 319: ثم هدم ذو الرمة متحانيا كبرة.

[20] Taken literally, this verse could mean that Mayya was already dead and buried. But, since it is known that she outlived the poet, the verse could mean that she was clothed in rags and that destitution had erased all beauty from her face. Furthermore, it is known that Mayya was married to a stingy man and that she did not retain her good looks in her old age (see pp. 179 and 183).

[21] ʿ*Iqd* I 319 f. Neither verse appears in Macartney and Muṭīʿ Babbīlī, and so far I have found no references in other sources to this probably fictionized episode.

[22] See Zambaur, pp. 3, 36, 177.

[23] See Zambaur, pp. 39, 42; *EI* I (1960) 695 f. For Abū Mūsā's role in the First Civil War of Islām and his inept handling of the arbitration when he was outwitted by ʿAmr ibn al-ʿĀṣ see pp. 49 f. above.

[24] Mubarrad, pp. 258 f.; Ibn ʿAsākir III 319.

[25] Ṭabarī II 1506, 1526, 1593: شرطة البصرة واحداثها وقضائها والصلاة باهلها (cf. *Akhbār al-quḍāt* II 21).

[26] *Akhbār al-quḍāt* II 21; Ibn ʿAsākir III 319 f.

Khālid to remove Bilāl from office and hold him as house prisoner. Khālid did so rather reluctantly in 118/736, some two years before his own downfall and the death of Bilāl in 120/738.[27]

Bilāl, like most others of his class and position, was well versed in poetry[28] and was also a patron and a tolerable critic of poets. Both Jarīr and Farazdaq were too old to be actively seeking court favor except that Khālid al-Qaṣrī was still a desirable subject for poets of their caliber and fame. Farazdaq is known to have called on Bilāl, who in turn visited the poet during his last illness.[29] Jandal ibn al-Rāʿī sought Bilāl's favor and met with mediocre success.[30] On the whole Bilāl seems to have preferred the company of loose and wanton poets such as the Kūfan Ḥamzah ibn Bīḍ, whose friendship with Bilāl dated back to their youth.[31] Ḥammad al-Rāwiyah also sought Bilāl's favor, and he received it even though Dhū al-Rummah pointed out Ḥammād's attempt to pass off some pre-Islāmic verses in praise of Bilāl as his own (see pp. 97 f.). The incident led to Ḥammād's acknowledgment of Dhū al-Rummah's expert knowledge of the difference between pre-Islāmic and Islāmic idiom.[32] Ḥammād supplemented this opinion with complimentary statements on Dhū al-Rummah's wide knowledge and eloquence and compared him to Imru' al-Qais in his masterful use of simile.[33] Dhū al-Rummah's rival Ru'bah ibn al-ʿAjjāj, who accused him of plagiarizing his verse,[34] was on familiar enough terms with Bilāl to ask him why he still rewarded Dhū al-Rummah despite the accusation. Bilāl's answer implies a preference for the personality of our poet, regardless of his compositions.[35] Nevertheless, it was not Ru'bah but the more serious and sober Dhū al-Rummah who came to be recognized as the panegyrist of Bilāl, who outlived Dhū al-Rummah by some three years. Patron and poet proved congenial enough despite their marked difference in personality and character.

Bilāl was in a position to take advantage of the poet, whom he declared to be not a good panegyrist. Like ʿAbd al-Malik, Bilāl was annoyed at Dhū al-Rummah's preoccupation with his she-camel Ṣaidaʿ in odes that were intended to praise him. When the poet recited

رايت النـاس ينتجعون غيثا   فقلت لصيدع انتجعى بلالا

Bilāl exclaimed: "So no one seeks me except Ṣaidaʿ!" He then ordered one of his men to give Dhū al-Rummah feed for his camel and thus shamed the poet.[36] Bilāl sometimes criticized Dhū al-Rummah's verses unjustly when not even Abū ʿAmr ibn al-ʿAlā', fearful of Bilāl's anger and vengeance, dared to declare Dhū al-Rummah in the right.[37] For fearful indeed was Bilāl's vengeance, as exemplified by his

27 Ṭabarī II 1657 f., 1779 f.; Ibn ʿAsākir III 319 f. For Ḥassān al-Nabaṭī, who was involved in Khālid's downfall, see p. 84 above.

28 See e.g. Jumaḥī, p. 473; *Aghānī* XVI 122; *Akhbār al-quḍāt* II 30.

29 *Aghānī* XIX 32 f., 44.

30 *Ibid.* XX 172.

31 *Ibid.* XV 15, 25 f.

32 *Akhbār al-quḍāt* II 34; *Aghānī* V 172, 174: قال حمّاد عرف (ذو الرمة) كلام اهل الجاهلية من كلام اهل الاسلام. See also Jumaḥī, p. 41, where Bilāl, himself an expert in the poetry of Ḥuṭai'ah, detects Ḥammād's plagiarism of Ḥuṭai'ah's verses in praise of Abū Mūsā al-Ashʿarī (see e.g. *Aghānī* II 506 and XI 29). Nāṣir al-Dīn al-Asad defends Ḥammād and presents evidence of his general reliability as transmitter of pre-Islāmic poetry (*Maṣādir*, pp. 440–50).

33 *Aghānī* XVI 113: لم ار افصح ولا اعلم بغريب منه . . . كان احسن الجاهليه تشبيها امرو القيس وذو الرمة احسن اهل الاسلام تشبيها (cf. Jāḥiẓ, *Bayān* I 154).

34 *Shiʿr*, pp. 338–40, stresses Dhū al-Rummah's borrowing or elaborating of other poets' ideas (كان كثير الاخذ) as against outright theft (*sirqah*), of which Ru'bah accused him (*Aghānī* XVI 121: قال روبه كلما قلتُ شعرا سرقه ذو الرمة).

35 *Aghānī* XVI 123: قال روبه لبلال بن ابي بردة علام تعطى ذا الرمة فوالله انه ليعمد الى مقطعاتنا فيصلها فيمدحك بها فقال (بلال) والله لو لم اعطيه الا على تاليفه لا عطيته (note the contraction of على ما into علام and see Lane, على, p. 2145, col. 2, for further instances).

36 Mubarrad, p. 259; *Akhbār al-quḍāt* II 41; *Jumal*, p. 160; *Muwashshaḥ*, p. 178.

37 See *Aghānī* XVI 121 f. and *Akhbār al-quḍāt* II 25 and 37 f. for accounts that trace back to Aṣmaʿī; see also Jumaḥī, pp. 483 f., and Ibn ʿAsākir III 320. For Abū ʿAmr's general attitude toward those in power see p. 26 above.

treatment of the poet-scholar Khālid ibn Ṣafwān, who had dared to protest his oppressive rule.[38] It is therefore not surprising that Dhū al-Rummah was questioned as to why he praised Bilāl above all others. His reported answer ignores completely Bilāl's reputation and stresses his own code of conduct. "Because," said he, "he (i.e., Bilāl) has smoothed my couch, regarded my company, and rewarded me handsomely, I find it only right, because of his great favor, that he should fully command my gratitude."[39] As it happens, both question and answer and the sentiments they convey are reinforced in Dhū al-Rummah's poetry, particularly in the ode which is represented in our papyrus text and from which the following verses[40] are drawn

ولم امـــدح لارضيـــه شعرى   لئيما ان يكون اصابا مـــالا
ولكن الكرام لهـــم ثنـــآئى   فلا اخزى مـــا قيل قـــالا
رايتُ الناس ينتجعون [غيـ]ثـــا   فقلت لصيدع انتجعى بلالا

بنى لك اهل بيتك يا ابن قيس   وانت تزيدهم شرفا جـــلالا
مكارم ليس يحصيهن مـــدح   ولا كذبا اقول ولا انتحـــالا

In the rest of this long ode Dhū al-Rummah continues to lavish high praise on Bilāl and his ancestors, as he does in several other long odes.[41] Careful reading of this material in the light of this family's historical record leads me to conclude even after allowing for poetic hyperbole and even if the poet, as he claims, is not lying that he is at best telling but part of the truth—a practice followed by a goodly number of his profession.

II

Little is known of the personal history of Dhū al-Rummah and his immediate family, particularly his parents. He was raised by his oldest brother, Hishām ibn ʿUqbah,[42] and he had two other brothers, the younger[43] of whom preceded him in death while the older, Masʿūd, outlived the others.[44] All four brothers were poetically gifted, but Dhū al-Rummah surpassed the other three in output and reputation. He is, nevertheless, accused of exploiting some of their ideas and appropriating some of their verses, which because of his established reputation were then attributed to him.[45] However, there seems to have been no *dīwān* of the poetry of either Hishām or Masʿūd, both of whom are mentioned in the sources primarily in connection with Dhū al-Rummah himself.

The family fortunes apparently declined on more than one occasion. The Muhallabids are said to have defrauded and ill-treated the family.[46] Dhū al-Rummah is referred to, perhaps as a youth, as a *ṭufailī*, that is, a parasitic adventurer who was habitually an intruder at festive parties or at mealtime.[47] Again, we find

[38] *Akhbār al-quḍāt* II 25, 37 f. When Bilāl was deposed and imprisoned, Khālid was then set free and pleaded for the freedom of Bilāl (*ibid.* II 38 f.). For Khālid's literary style and personality see e.g. pp. 73–75 above.

[39] *Akhbār al-quḍāt* II 34; Baihaqī, p. 131: قيل له لما خصصت بلال بن ابى بردة بمدحك فقال لانه وطاء مضجعى واكرم مجلسى واحسن صلتى فحق لكثير معروفه عندى ان يستولى على شكري (cf. Ibn ʿAsākir III 320).

[40] Macartney, No. 57:52–54 (= page 4:7–9 of our text) and 59–60.

[41] See Macartney, Nos. 32, 35, 59, 87.

[42] E.g. Mubarrad, p. 148.

[43] The name of this brother is given as خرفاس or جرفاس and as اوفى, which latter is believed to be confused with a cousin's name (see *Aghānī* XVI 111; Jumaḥī, pp. 480 f.).

[44] *Aghānī* XVI 114; Macartney, p. 157.

[45] *Aghānī* XVI 111: كان لذي الرمة اخوة ثلاثة مسعود وجرفاس وهشام كلهم شعراء وكان الواحد منهم يقول الابيات فيبني عليها ذو الرمة ابياتا اخر فينشدها الناس فيغلب عليها (ذو الرمة) لشهرته وتنسب اليه (cf. *Jumal*, pp. 63 f.; Sarrāj, *Kitāb maṣāriʿ al-ʿushshāq*, pp. 351 f.).

[46] *Aghānī* V 155; cf. Macartney, No. 81:1

[47] *Aghānī* XVI 112.

him accusing his brother Hishām of being jealous of him and keeping him at a distance when Dhū al-Rummah's own fortunes were low.[48] He seems to have been closer to his brother Masʿūd despite the latter's pointed criticism of his tearful verses (see p. 186). Perhaps Bilāl, who was reckoned a miser, did not always reward the poet handsomely. But the poet himself was in truth a spendthrift, as his daughter realized (see below). For shortly before his death and after taking counsel with his brother Masʿūd, he started reluctantly on a trip to seek the caliph Hishām's favor.[49] He rode his aged she-camel and met with a fatal accident, probably on the way out though one account places it on the return trip and describes the poet as wearing a robe of honor supposedly received from the caliph.[50] His chief mourners were his brothers Hishām[51] and Masʿūd, especially the latter to judge by his several dirges ending in different rhymes.[52]

Of Dhū al-Rummah's private life next to nothing is known. He does not seem to have married, and no specific concubine is romantically associated with him unless there was a one-sided sentiment on the part of Kathīrah (see p. 179). He was proud of his *kunyah*, Abū al-Ḥārith,[53] which may have been just a nickname since there is no specific mention of a son named Ḥārith. Some credit the poet with a son named ʿAlī, who is said to have been in love with Salmā, a daughter of Mayya, but others question this.[54] He did have a daughter, Lailā, who was so identified by his brother Masʿūd as sharing his grief, though she had deplored her father's free spending.[55] There is mention of a niece, Tumāḍir, the daughter of Masʿūd,[56] but no reference to nephews. It would seem therefore that the survival of Dhū al-Rummah's poetry was due in the first place to his own efforts in having it written down, secondly to the efforts of his several transmitters, and eventually to generations of scholars and musicians who were fascinated with his similes and his romantic odes.

DHŪ AL-RUMMAH AND MAYYA

I

Though the sources on hand contain many references to Dhū al-Rummah's romances, the information they provide is for the most part spotty, often inconsistent, and at times quite contradictory. The poet early became the object of literary and anecdotal monographs titled *Akhbār Dhī al-Rummah* by such second- and third-century littérateurs as Isḥaq ibn Ibrāhīm al-Mauṣalī and his son Ḥammād[57] and Hārūn ibn Muḥammad ibn al-Zayyāt.[58] These works are frequently cited in literary sources, especially in Abū

48 *Ibid.* XVI 111 f.; cf. Macartney, No. 47:12–18. See also Mubarrad, p. 148, where Hishām is described as a sensible man: كان من عقلاء الرجال.

49 Dhū al-Rummah's decision to seek out Hishām, under such circumstances, must be related to his proud boast that he accepted gifts from none but the chief rulers; see ʿ*Umdah* I 52: كان ذو الرمة لا يقبل الا صلة الملك الاعظم وحده (cf. n. 11 on p. 171 above).

50 *Aghānī* XVI 126 f.: قال يا مسعود اجدني قد تماثلت وخفت الاشياء عندنا واحتجنا الى زيارة بنى مروان فهل لك بنا فيهم فقال (مسعود) نعم . . . وركب ذو الرمة ناقته فقمصت به وكانت قد اعفيت من الركوب وانفجرت النوطه التي كانت به.
Details of Dhū al-Rummah's accident and subsequent death and burial vary considerably. The most probable version is the above, namely that he suffered from a tumor or an ulcer (*nūṭah*) which broke open with his fall and hastened his death; but, again, the same source (*ibid.*) reports that he died of smallpox (*judarī*).

51 Mubarrad, p. 48; ʿ*Uyūn* III 67; *Aghānī* XVI 111. For a lengthy ode of Hishām see *Shiʿr*, pp. 336 f.

52 See references in n. 51; Jumaḥī, pp. 480 f.; *Muʿjam al-shuʿarāʾ*, p. 371, and *ibid.* ed. ʿAbd al-Sattār Aḥmad Farrāj (Aleppo, 1379/1960) p. 284; Ibn Khallikān I 513 (= trans. II 450). Note that some of the verses quoted in these citations are credited now to Hishām and now to Masʿūd.

53 *Aghānī* XVI 110; *Shiʿr*, p. 333; Ibn Khallikān I 510 (= trans. II 447); *Muzhir* II 422.

54 See Macartney, No. 70:51 and editor's comment.

55 *Aghānī* XVI 111, 128; Macartney, No. 5:69. See also *ibid.* No. 22:73–77, where the poet refers to his daughter's reactions to his spending, and verses 78–83, where he defends his actions.

56 Yāqūt IV 153.

57 *Fihrist*, pp. 142, 143.

58 *Ibid.* p. 123.

al-Faraj al-Iṣfahānī's *Aghānī*, where a particular *khabar* is often introduced with a full *isnād* tracing back to the author or with the statement "I copied from the book of So-and-So," one of the above-mentioned authors among others being named.[59] Furthermore, Dhū al-Rummah's romance with Mayya caught the imagination of some writer(s) of historical tales along with the famous romances of Jamīl and Buthainah, Kuthaiyir and ʿAzzah, Majnūn and Lailā, Yazīd and Ḥabābah, and many others.[60] The great majority of romantic tales were anonymous, and all seem to have been popular with the general public. Some were written by second-century scholars who were reasonably reputable in other fields, such as ʿĪsā ibn Dāb (d. 171/787 or 788) of Medina, schoolteacher and poet knowledgeable in genealogy and general information (*ansāb wa akhbār*), who composed historical tales and fictional stories and found favor with the caliphs Mahdī and Hādī.[61] The *Fihrist* list of authors of such fictionized historical romances includes ʿĪsā and the still better known second-century Hishām ibn Muḥammad ibn al-Sāʾib al-Kalbī and Haitham ibn ʿAdī.[62] Significant for us is the fact that the historical and literary accounts as well as the fictionized romances circulated in the second century and that both types are reflected in the subsequent literature on hand beginning with the works of Jumaḥī and Jāḥiẓ and including the works of a good number of their successors for centuries thereafter. While this accounts for some of the inconsistencies and contradictions noted in the sources, it provides no sure means for detecting the thin line between historical fact and literary fiction. Such being the case, the *Dīwān* of Dhū al-Rummah, though incomplete, must be our first guide to his romances and particularly to his romance with Mayya, to whom the first part of our papyrus text is devoted.

II

Among the facts that emerge from the heterogeneous sources on hand is that there were at most four women who at one time or another caught and held, for varying periods of time, the poet's fancy. Furthermore, all four women were Bedouins whose home grounds were in the Najdian Dahnāʾ, the home district of the poet himself. One gathers from his *Dīwān* that the poet's family headquarters were not far from those of the women, which in turn were not far each from the other. The locality in which three of the women and, for the most part, the poet himself lived and moved was the town of Ḥuzwā and its environs—a comparatively firm and fertile region nestling in a valley of the seven-hilled dunes of the Dahnāʾ.[63] It is in Ḥuzwā and occasionally a few other places in this general locality that the poet places the fourth woman. Furthermore, the scenic beauty of the Dahnāʾ dunes so affected Dhū al-Rummah that he is said to have chosen its highest hilltop, near Ḥuzwā, for his burial place.[64]

It is not possible to determine with certainty who was Dhū al-Rummah's first love nor yet to what extent his love affairs overlapped. The *Dīwān* mentions a certain Ṣaidāʾ in one ode only,[65] with no reference to another woman as a possible rival, which suggests an early passing infatuation. It mentions Umaimah, known also as Umm Sālim,[66] less frequently than the other two. The affair with her may have

[59] E.g. *Aghānī* XVI 110–14, 117–19, 122, 125–27; see also *Muwashshah*, pp. 108, 178, 194.

[60] *Fihrist*, p. 306.

[61] See e.g. Jāḥiẓ, *Bayān* I 68, II 62, III 250 and 252; Jāḥiẓ, *Tāj*, p. 116. See also *Marātib*, pp. 99 f., where Aṣmaʿī accuses ʿĪsā of forging poetry and *akhbār* and of false attribution of linguistic information to the Bedouins, which opinion is repeated in *Irshād* VI 104–11 and *Muzhir* II 414. Such false attribution reflects the Bedouins' reputation for linguistic knowledge.

[62] *Fihrist*, p. 306; see *ibid*. pp. 90, 95 f., and 99 f. for these authors' main entries and list of their works.

[63] Yāqūt II 61, 262 f., 635 f., III 619 and 850, IV 43. See also Macartney, e.g. Nos. 30:9, 39:11, 60:5, 66:1, 10–11, 13, 17, and 21 (all referring to both Mayya and Kharqāʾ), 67:1, 3, and 23, 70:6, 86:3–4 and 8.

[64] Yāqūt II 635 f. and III 885; Macartney, No. 75:16. See also *Aghānī* XVI 126 f.

[65] Macartney, No. 11:1, 11–12, 16, 21–22, 26. A variant for هوى صيداء of line 11 is هوى خرقاء, which suggests the possibility that Ṣaidāʾ was a pseudonym for Mayya during the poets' early secret infatuation.

[66] *Ibid*. Nos. 15:1 and 3, 50:5, 79:10 and 44, 84:2–6; in Nos. 23:5–6 and 72:1–4 both she and Mayya are mentioned, and in No. 48:1–15 an actual meeting of the poet and Umm Sālim is mentioned. See also ʿ*Uyūn* IV 143.

preceded the poet's public declaration of his love for Mayya, as can be deduced from the following verses:[67]

لقد كنتُ اخفى حب مىَّ وذكرهـا   رسيس الهوى حتى كـأن لا اريدها
كما كنت اطوى النفس عن ام سالم   وجاراتها حتى كـأن لا اهيدها

The ode continues with more verses on Mayya. And in the only other ode in which the two are named, again only passing reference is made to Umm Sālim while the rest of this short ode of eight verses is devoted to Mayya.[68] Otherwise, Umm Sālim fades out of the picture so far as both the sources and the *Dīwān* are concerned.

Of the several accounts of Dhū al-Rummah's first meeting with Mayya, the most reliable seems to be that given by the poet himself as he recalled it some twenty years later. Thirsty in the desert, Dhū al-Rummah along with an older brother and a cousin sight a large encampment. Dhū al-Rummah, then only a boy, is sent to ask for a skinful of water. An elderly woman calls on Mayya to fill his container. The boy loses his heart to Mayya on first sight and is so affected that he neglects to hold steady the container and the water spills to the left and the right of it. Mayya comments on the thoughtlessness of taking such a young boy on a desert trip. Her comment inspires him to recite his very first five verses—in the *rajaz* meter—to which he added later. "Thereafter," concluded the reminiscing poet, "I have remained desperately in love with her for these twenty years."[69]

A number of unusually clear-cut statements in several of the poet's verses tell us that he was but a boy of ten when he first saw and fell in love with Mayya and that he kept his feelings secret, even from his immediate family, for ten years. Thereafter, he could no longer suppress or hide his love for her:[70]

فلم ار عذرا بعد عشرين حجـــة   مضت لى وعشرين قد مضين الى عشر
فـــاخفيت شوقى من رفيقى وانـــه   لذو نسب دان الىّ وذو حجـــر

Supplementary accounts, with or without an *isnād*, of this first meeting add some details which seem far-fetched indeed and others which could be authentic. Among the latter, we note that the boy asked Mayya to mend his waterskin. She said she could not do so because she was a *kharqā*ʾ, that is, a cherished young maiden who does no menial labor. But, on her mother's order, she did give him a drink of water. Thereafter, Dhū al-Rummah named her "Kharqā'" and often so referred to her.[71] The *kharqā*ʾ detail is particularly important because it has led to the confusion of Mayya, who was of the Banū Minqar, with a woman who came later into the poet's life and whose given name was Kharqāʾ. She was of the Banū al-Bakkāʾ ibn ʿĀmir and is therefore referred to as the Bakkāʾīyah and the ʿĀmirīyah. Corroboration of these bits of information about the poet's first meeting with Mayya is found in his verse

تلك الفتاة التى علقتهـــا عرضـــا   انّ الكريم وذا الاسلام يُختلـــبُ

that refers to their chance meeting while both were young and in his verse

اصابتك مىّ يوم جـــرعآء مـــالك   بـواجـــة من غُلّـــة وكـــبـــاد

that indicates that it was thirst and the need for water that had brought him to her people's place.[72]

[67] Macartney, No. 23:5–6.

[68] *Ibid.* No. 72. For other reference to Umm Sālim see *ibid.* comments on No. 48:1–15, which deal with linguistics rather than with information about her.

[69] *Aghānī* XVI 114; cf. Macartney, No. 22, esp. verses 21–25.

[70] See Macartney, No. 35:1–4 and 12–16.

[71] *Aghānī* XVI 110. The often-repeated statement that it was she who first hailed him as "Dhū al-Rummah," must be disregarded. More reliable are the statements of scholars who link the name to his verse

وغير مرضوخ القفاء موتود   أشعث بـــاق رُمّة التقليـــد

(see Macartney, No. 22:7; Jumaḥī, pp. 481 f.; *Shiʿr*, p. 334; *Aghānī* XVI 110 f.; Ibn Khallikān I 448 [= trans. II 45]; Yāqūt II 822; *Muzhir* II 440; *Khizānah* I 51 f.).

[72] Macartney, Nos. 1:22 and 18:4; cf. No. 22:21–23.

As I see it, the second meeting between Mayya and the poet must have taken place several years later, when the boy was no longer readily recognizable in the grown young man. In the meantime, Dhū al-Rummah's reputation as a poet had been established and his verses on Mayya had become well known. The salient points in the account of this meeting are as follows. A group of travelers, including Dhū al-Rummah, alighted at the encampment of Mayya's father. The guests were refreshed with a drink of milk, but Dhū al-Rummah was for some reason overlooked, whereupon Mayya herself gave him a drink of fresh milk. When the company left, her father revealed Dhū al-Rummah's identity as "the man who has been saying all those things about you." The embarrassed girl exclaimed: "Oh how awful! Oh how wicked!" She then went into her tent, and her father did not see her for three days.[73] In this context Mayya's exclamations could not possibly refer to Dhū al-Rummah's appearance. They must refer, therefore, to the entire situation, that is, to the poet's numerous romantic verses about her, to his visit to her father, and to her waiting on him without recognizing him.

Another meeting with Mayya, if it indeed took place, must have occurred after this incident. This time, Dhū al-Rummah comes upon Kharqā' (= Mayya[74]) and a company of her young women at a watering place. He orders them to unveil, and all but Kharqā' oblige. "He then said to me," reports Kharqā', "if you do not unveil, I will scandalize you. So I unveiled. He did not cease to recite and recite (his poetry) until he foamed at the mouth. I did not see him thereafter."[75]

There is an account of still another meeting between Mayya and Dhū al-Rummah. This meeting, if it took place at all, must be placed considerably later than their second meeting at her father's place. For Mayya is now no longer a sensitive girl in her father's household but a young woman of independent action and, if the tale is to be believed, of immodest behavior. The story is that Mayya, not having seen Dhū al-Rummah for some time, yet having heard his verses recited, vowed to sacrifice an animal on the day she sees him. When she does see him, he is ugly, short, and swarthy while she herself is among the most beautiful of women. Disappointed in his appearance, she exclaims: "Oh how ugly! oh how horrid! My sacrifice is indeed wasted!" Angered, Dhū al-Rummah recites the verses

على وجـــه ميّ مسحة من ملاحـــة   وتحت الثيـاب الشين لوكانـــا باديـــا
الم تر ان الماء يخبث طعـــمـــــه   وان كان لون المـــاء ابيض صافيـــا

to the effect that she is deceptive and that her clothing hides her physical defects.[76] To these verses she responds, so the story goes, by disrobing and taunting him further with her faultless body. The two part in anger.[77] This episode has the earmark of fiction.

Mayya's desire to see Dhū al-Rummah, her vow, their meeting, and her disappointment in his physical appearance are possible enough, though, from the several other available descriptions of both of them, theirs was no case of "beauty and the beast" except in the imagination of some fictionist. The remaining details of the account are negated by several factors. First, Dhū al-Rummah denied vehemently that he

[73] *Aghānī* XVI 124: فقال لها ابوها اتعرفين الرجل الذى سقيته صبوحك قالت لا والله قال هو ذو الرمة القائل فيك الاقاويل فوضعت يدها على راسها وقالت واسواتاه وابؤساه ودخلت بيتها فما راها ابوها ثلاثا.

Note that the exclamations واسواتاه وابؤساه can be translated in more than one way, depending on the contexts in which they occur, as here and in n. 77 below.

[74] From what is known of Kharqā' al-ʿĀmirīyah, such an episode could not possibly have involved her.

[75] *Aghānī* XVI 124: فقال لئن لم تسفرى لافضحنك فسفرت فلم يزل يقول حتى ازبد ثم لم اراه بعد ذلك. The episode is reported by Hārūn ibn Muḥammad ibn al-Zayyat (mentioned above) on the authority of Ibn al-Sikkit on the authority of his father. See also n. 103 below.

[76] Variants are الخزى, يخلُف, and في العين for الشين, يخبث, and ابيض respectively. See, further, nn. 77 and 80 below and references there cited.

[77] *Shiʿr*, pp. 334 f.: فلما راته رجلا دميما اسود وكانت من اجمل النساء فقالت واسوتاه وابواساه (cf. ʿ*Uyūn* IV 39; *Aghānī* XVI 120; Ibn Khallikān I 513 [= trans. II 447 f.]; *Khizānah* I 52).

had ever uttered the verses[78] that supposedly induced Mayya to disrobe. Second, Kathīrah, a jealous cousin or slave girl of Mayya's family, eventually acknowledged that she had composed the verses and attributed them to Dhū al-Rummah.[79] Again, the verses in question are out of tune not only with the great amount of poetry that Dhū al-Rummah devoted to Mayya but also with the poetry he devoted to other women. For one can readily gather from his *Dīwān* that he was much more apt to address women, to chide or to flatter, in language that was more chaste and circumspect than bold and audacious (see p. 187). It should be noted further that the two verses in question, though often cited in the sources,[80] do not appear in the available copies of his *Dīwān*.

Lovers' quarrels Dhū al-Rummah and Mayya no doubt had, if not before, then certainly after, her marriage to her paternal cousin 'Āṣim. On one occasion Dhū al-Rummah and a company of riders stopped to greet Mayya, who in return greeted all except, pointedly, Dhū al-Rummah. The poet, angered at being so humiliated publicly, departed as he recited two verses of his own to the effect that Mayya had broken for good the tie that was between them and ended with

الم تــر اذ المــاء تخلــف طعمــه   وان كان لــون المــاء ابيض صافيا

which is the second of Kathīrah's verses with a slight variation.[81] The *Dīwān* corroborates a meeting when Mayya did not return Dhū al-Rummah's greeting, though without the other details. The poet pleads with his companions to go out of their way with him to Mayya's abode. They arrive and greet her. She returns their greetings but does not answer that of the speaker, that is, Dhū al-Rummah himself:[82]

خليلى عوجــا بارك الله فيكمــا   على دار مىّ من صــدور الركائب
وقفنا فسلمنــا فردّت تحـيــة   علينــا ولم ترجع جواب المخاطب

Mayya's marriage greatly distressed the poet, who could not bear the thought of her being married to a stingy man. He expressed his feelings in four verses,[83] the second of which does play on the idea of Mayya disrobed.

لئن زوّجت مىّ خسيسا لطال مــا   بغى منذر ميّا خليــلا يهينهــا
تزينك ان جرّدتهــا من ثيــبهــا   وانت اذا جرّدت يومــا تشينهــا
فيا نفس ذلّى بعد مىّ وسامحــى   فقد سامحت مىّ وذّل قريــنهــا
ولمّا اتــانى ان ميّا تزوجــت   خسيســا بكى سهل المعــا وحزونها

In other verses he implies that the marriage was a family arrangement rather than one of love on Mayya's part and describes her husband as insecure and jealous and the least worthy of her.[84] Furthermore, as a distressed and jealous lover himself, Dhū al-Rummah vented his feelings in verses that expressly wished for 'Āṣim's death.[85]

[78] *Aghānī* XVI 119: قال ذو الرمة وكيف اقول هذا وقد قطعت دهرى وافنيت شبابي بها وامدحها ثم اقول هذا.

[79] Jumaḥī, pp. 475 f.; *Aghānī* XVI 119, 121. Macartney, No. 81:16 reads

تغيرتِ بعدى ام وشى الناس بيننا   بما لم اقله من مُسدّى وملحمِ

and could well refer to this Kathīrah episode.

[80] See Macartney, pp. 675 f., Addendum 99, which is an ode of 8 verses including the two verses specifically denied by Dhū al-Rummah, three more verses in elaboration of the theme, and two verses of regrets that he wasted so much poetry on Mayya (cf. *Aghānī* XVI 120; Ibn Khallikān I 511 [= trans. II 448]).

[81] *Aghānī* XVI 119. See also Macartney, p. 675, Addendum 99:3.

[82] See Macartney, No. 7:1 and 5. The poet often made such a request of his traveling companions (see *ibid.* e.g. Nos. 58:1, 71:1, 66:1, 83:1, and p. 673, Addendum 82).

[83] *Ibid.* No. 86:15–18.

[84] *Ibid.* No. 10:30–34.

[85] Jumaḥī, p. 349; Macartney, No. 8, esp. verses 13–14.

The lovelorn poet was drawn to Mayya's dwelling by his desire to see and talk with her. One dark night he contrived to fall in step with her husband in the hope that he would not be recognized and would be invited in as a house guest. The ruse failed, for 'Āṣim did recognize him and offered him some food but left him in the outer inclosure. Mayya, too, recognized him. At midnight the poet sang out loud

اراجعـــة يا مىّ ايامنـــا الـــــتى   بذى الرمث ام لا ما لُهن رجوعُ

with a reference to their previous meetings[86] which so enraged the jealous husband that he ordered Mayya to abuse the poet and deny his statement.[87] She strove in vain to calm her husband by reminding him of his duty as a host and of the fact that a poet says what he wishes and not what he actually does (see pp. 93 and 95). Under threat of death Mayya did as her husband ordered, whereupon the incensed Dhū al-Rummah rode away determined to transfer his affection to another.[88]

It is at this point that Kharqā' al-Bakkā'īyah, who was better known as Kharqā' al-'Āmirīyah, enters Dhū al-Rummah's life to become repeatedly and at times hopelessly confused in most of the sources on hand with Mayya, who was, we know, also frequently referred to as Kharqā'. But after much sorting and sifting of the sources, including Dhū al-Rummah's *Dīwān*, a plausible picture of Kharqā' al-'Āmirīyah and her distinct personality begins to appear. Her first meeting with the poet was not long before his death. The object of his first visit was not romance but treatment of his sore eye, for she was known as an oculist (*kaḥḥālah*). She was advanced enough in age to be concerned about her diminishing beauty. Rather than accept a fee of some sort for treating Dhū al-Rummah's eye, she asked that he compose ten romantic verses about her and the remaining evidence of her beauty so that people would continue to seek her out for herself as well as for her trade. The poet obliged,[89] for he saw an opportunity to rouse Mayya's jealousy. However, he composed but two or three romantic odes about Kharqā' al-'Āmirīyah before death overtook him.[90] This bit of information also is substantiated by the *Dīwān* of Dhū al-Rummah, which contains only three sustained references to her[91] and some half-dozen passing mentions of her name, some of them in competition with Mayya's.

Kharqā''s vanity sustained her concern for the loss of her beauty, for some time later she requested her fellow tribesman Quḥaif al-'Uqailī to compose some romantic verses about her. He responded with

لقد ارسلت خرقـــآء نحوى جريهــّا   لتجعلنى خرقآء فيمـــن أضـــلّت
وخرقآء لا تزداد إلا مـــلاحـــــة   ولو عمّرت تعمير نـــوح وجلّـــــت

and thus gallantly assured her of increasing beauty though she were to live to be as old as Noah.[92]

Kharqā' continued to ply her trade at Faljah, a stop on the pilgrimage road from Baṣrah through the Najdian Ḥujr,[93] where people alighted presumably for eye treatment as well as for her entertaining

[86] See *Aghānī* XVI 114 with variants and Macartney, No. 47:4; see also Macartney Nos. 43:5, 46:5, and 60:5–6, which express similar nostalgic sentiments of recalling the past.

[87] The *Dīwān* has numerous references to their meetings by day or by night (see e.g. Macartney, Nos. 46:9–10, 47:4, 49:3–5, 51:7, 67:37, 68:15, 78:10, 83:9, 87:8 and 13). See p. 95 above for references to night meetings with the beloved.

[88] *Aghānī* XVI 114: فانصرف عنها مغضبا يريد ان يصرف مودته عنها الى غيرها.

[89] *Aghānī* XVI 123: شبب ذو الرمة بخرقآء العامرية بغير هوى وانما كانت كحّالة فداوت عينه من رمد كان بها فزال فقال لها ما تحبين فقالت عشرة ابيات تشبب بي ليرغب الناس فى اذا سمعوا ان فى بقية للتشبيب ففعل.

[90] شبب بخرقآء العامريّه يكيد مىّ بذلك فما قال فيها الا قصدتين او ثلاثا حتى مات (see *Aghānī* XVI 123 but see also *ibid.* p. 114 and *Shi'r*, pp. 335 f.).

[91] Macartney, Nos. 51:6–13, 66:5–22, and 70:1–16.

[92] Jumaḥī, pp. 479 f.; *Aghānī* XVI 124. See also *Aghānī* XX 140 f. and *Khizānah* IV 250. Mubarrad, p. 342, identifies Quḥaif as an 'Āmirī. The name قحيف is misread in some sources as جحيف. Jumaḥī places Quḥaif last in his last of ten groups of four poets each (see Jumaḥī, pp. 583, 592–99). See *Aghānī* XX 140–43 for the main entry on Quḥaif. Noah is said to have lived 950 years (Sūrah 29:13).

[93] Yāqūt I 81 and III 911.

conversation, for she was knowledgeable in genealogy and ready with poetry citations.[94] Among those who visited her on the way to or from a pilgrimage was Mufaḍḍal ibn Muḥammad al-Ḍabbī, who described her as tall and still beautiful and active despite her age. She berated him for not having visited her on earlier pilgrimages and cited a verse attributed to Dhū al-Rummah:[95]

تمام الحج ان تقف المطايا   على خرقاء واضعة اللثام

She recited this same verse and the second of the two above-cited verses of Quḥaif al-ʿUqailī to Muḥammad ibn al-Ḥajjāj al-Usayyidī,[96] who had stopped to visit her when she was eighty years old.[97] She then recalled Dhū al-Rummah, gave a touching description of him (see below), called Allāh's blessing on his soul, recited five verses of her own composition in praise of him, and finally expressed her gratitude to him for making her name famous—the last a sentiment she is said to have expressed in prose also.[98]

III

The greater number of source references to Mayya's beauty and Dhū al-Rummah's physical unattractiveness lack specific details and were intended, it would seem, to heighten the contrast. The several more or less detailed descriptions of Mayya and Dhū al-Rummah at various periods of their lives narrow this contrast and enable us to gain at least a sketch of their basic physical endowments and yield in addition some clues as to their personalities. That the poet's general appearance left something to be desired is indicated by his mother's reaction to a description of him, probably as a youth, as being small, short, ugly, and humpbacked. "Listen to his poetry," said she, "and look not at his face."[99] He could not have improved with the years of exposure to desert life and the hot sun. For when Mayya is supposed to have seen him as a man, she was repelled, as this highly romanticized tale goes, as much by his color as by his general physique. Still another unflattering description of Dhū al-Rummah, based largely on Bedouin hearsay and referring probably to a still later period in his life, presents a picture of a "diseased yet fleshy man, square built and short, with a nose that was not beautiful."[100]

There are, however, other descriptions of the poet that seem to deserve as much if not, indeed, more credit than the preceding accounts. These trace back, as a rule, through more reliable *isnād*'s to persons who knew the poet more intimately and for long periods. They are of especial interest in that they mention several attractive features of his person and comment on some traits of his personality.

There is a description of the poet as Kharqāʾ al-ʿĀmirīyah recalled him when she was well advanced in age. "He was," reminisced Kharqāʾ, "of a clear complexion and spoke sweetly, was compactly built, excellent at description, and chaste of eye."[101] A fuller and more balanced description of the poet and

[94] *Aghānī* XVI 124 f.; *Khizānah* I 52.

[95] *Shiʿr*, p. 336; *Aghānī* XVI 124; Ibn Khallikān I 512 (= trans. II 448 f.); *Khizānah* I 52. For the verse see Macartney, p. 673, Addendum 87.

[96] *Aghānī* XVI 125 and 127 have الاسدى for tribal identifications, but p. 119 has الاسيدى من بنى أُسيد بن عمرو بن تميم. The voweling of الأُسيِّدى is provided in *Maʿārif*, p. 37, and Dhahabī, *Al-mushtabih fī al-rijal* I 26.

[97] *Aghānī* XVI 124 f. See Jāḥiẓ, *Maḥāsin*, pp. 204 f., for other occasions on which she cited these verses. She retained her good looks in her old age, but she could not have been 80 years old when Dhū al-Rummah first saw her.

[98] *Aghānī* XVI 125. See p. 184 below for a similar sentiment expressed by Mayya.

[99] *Aghānī* XVI 112: كان دميما شختا أجناء فقالت امه اسمعوا الى شعره ولا تنظروا الى وجهه. The nature of the deformity of the poet's back may have been a degree of curvature rather than a pronounced hump that would have made him readily recognizable at all times. The only other related term associated with him is "his back bent low with age" (متحانيا كبرة), applied to him possibly some two or three years before his death, in a report that seems questionable (see p. 172 above).

[100] *Aghānī* XVI 112: قال أُسيد الغنوي سمعت ببايدتنا من قوم هضبوا الحديث ان ذا الرمة كان قد عيه وكان كناز اللحم مربوعا قصيرا وكان انفه ليسى بالحسن.

[101] *Aghānī* XVI 126: كان رقيق البشرة وعذب المنطق حسن الوصف مقارب الرصف عفيف الطرف (see pp. 93 and 152 above for reference to the lustful eye).

some traits of his personality is transmitted by Abū al-Faraj al-Iṣfahānī from three of his contemporaries on the authority of Ibn Shabbah on the authority of Isḥāq ibn Ibrāhīm al-Mauṣalī on the authority of Masʿūd ibn Qand, who heard it from ʿIṣmah ibn Mālik, a leading direct transmitter of Dhū al-Rummah's poetry who once accompanied the poet on a visit to Mayya's home grounds. They come upon Mayya and the women when the men are away. ʿIṣmah recites one of Dhū al-Rummah's longer odes, the first twenty-seven verses of which relate to Mayya, and is interrupted by comments now by one of the women and now by Mayya herself. ʿIṣmah and the women retire a short distance while Mayya and Dhū al-Rummah converse, and she accuses the poet of false sentiments. When ʿIṣmah sights the dust raised by the mounts of the returning men, he alerts the poet and they depart, as they had come, both riding on ʿIṣmah's pedigreed she-camel used especially for the occasion since the men could detect the footprints of Dhū al-Rummah's own mount.[102] There is no way of knowing how much of this tale is fact and how much fiction. It is of interest because ʿIṣmah and not the poet himself is said to have recited the ode, and ʿIṣmah's description of Dhū al-Rummah indicates the reason: "He has nice eyes and a good melodious voice; when he speaks, you sense no impediment in his speech, but when he recites poetry he sputters and his voice grows hoarse."[103] On a later and last visit of the two men to the then deserted site of Mayya's abode, ʿIṣmah, sensing the poet's deep emotion, comments that he never saw anyone gain such mastery over his passion, and the poet adds "I am indeed (a man) of great endurance and patience."[104] Dhū al-Rummah himself refers frequently to his physical and health handicaps in his verses, but it is not possible to time such references. One may assume, however, that physical symptoms of lovesickness belonged more to his mature days than to his early youth. A few citations will suffice. Such verses as

واسواتاه ثمّ يا ويلى ويا حرَبى   انى اخو الجسم فيه السقم والكربُ

رأتْ شُجونى ورات تخديدى   من مُجحفات زمن مريِّد
نقحن جسمى عن نضار العود   بعد اهتزاز الغصن الاملود

ولكن عذابى أَن اكون أتيته   عقآئل اوصاف يُشبهن بالخيل
اتتنى كلاب الحى حتى عرفننى   ومدت نسوج العنكبوت على رحلى

فتى مسلهم الوجه شارك حبها   سقام السرى فى جسمه بسقام

وان كنتَ قد هيّجت لى دون صُحبتى   رجيع هوى من ذكر ميَّة مسقم

recall in part Mayya's reaction to his appearance and in part his own awareness of his generally deteriorating health.[105]

Apart from the general statement that Mayya was a woman of great beauty, the sources provide comparatively few details as to her features and figure. Our one description of her as a young woman

[102] *Aghānī* XVI 129 f. Jāḥiẓ, *Maḥāsin*, pp. 204 f., and *Amālī* III 125 f. add more details, such as Mayya giving the poet a jar of ointment and a string of beads for his mount. See also Macartney, No. 5:1–27, esp. verses 20–22.

[103] *Aghānī* XVI 129: كان حلو العنين حسن النعمة ان حدث لم تسأم حديثه واذا انشدك بربر وجش صوته. *Amālī* III 124 adds that he was thin-bearded, had bright teeth, a broad forehead, and was of good speech: خفيف العارضين براق الثنايا واضح الجبين حسن الحديث.

[104] *Amālī* III 126: ما رايتُ رجلا اشد صبابة ولا احسن عزا فقال ذو الرمة اننى لجلدٌ على ما تَرى واني لصبور (cf. Macartney, e.g. Nos. 24:1, 29:13–15, 30:5 and 15, 32:5).

[105] Macartney, Nos. 1:27, 22:17–20, 64:36–37, 78:14, and 81:3 respectively. Such verses, along with the prose descriptions already cited, may explain why the poet, although he was not yet forty years old, could have been described as decrepit and bent low with age.

comes from ʿIṣmah ibn Mālik, who recalled her appearance when he accompanied Dhū al-Rummah on a visit to her. According to ʿIṣmah, she was then a tawny-colored, delicately built young woman with long hair, pretty and witty though not, in this context, as pretty and witty as some of the women who were with her.[106]

Mayya as a mother of young sons was described to Jumaḥī by Abū Sawwār al-Ghanawī as smooth complexioned, long of face and cheeks, with aquiline nose, and still with traces of beauty.[107] Asked by Jumaḥī if she had recited to him any of Dhū al-Rummah's verses, Abū Sawwār answered: "Yes, by Allāh! She gives long sustained recitations the likes of which no one has seen."[108]

A third account comes from Abū al-Muhalhil, who had gone to considerable trouble to find Dhū al-Rummah's famed Mayya. Disappointed on seeing her, practically a toothless old woman (see p. 172, with n. 20), he wondered aloud why Dhū al-Rummah had been so deeply enamored of her. "Wonder not," she is reported as saying, "I will show you his convincing reason." She then summoned her young daughter and ordered her to unveil. Dazzled by the young girl's beauty and perfection, the man exclaimed: "May Allāh accept his (i.e., Dhū al-Rummah's) reason and have mercy upon him!" Mayya then informed him that Dhū al-Rummah was first attracted to her when she was of the girl's age (and presumably as beautiful). And, in answer to her visitor's request, Mayya dictated some of Dhū al-Rummah's poetry to him.[109]

In a somewhat similar but more detailed interview Muḥammad ibn al-Ḥajjāj al-Usayyidī, on seeing the aged Mayya, said to her: "O, Mayya, I can't help but see that Dhū al-Rummah has wasted his two verses on you":

أما انتَ عن ذكراك ميّة مقصر ولا انت ناسى العهد منها فتذكرُ
تهيم بها ما تستفيق ودونهـــــا حجاب وابواب وستر مســـتّرُ

Mayya laughed as she pointed out that he sees her now that her beauty has vanished and added: "May Allāh have mercy on Ghailān! He said these verses about me when I was more beautiful than a glowing fire on a cold night to the eyes of a man suffering from the cold." Then she summoned her daughter, who is here named Asmāʾ. The gist of the rest of the interview is about the same as that with Abū al-Muhalhil except that there is no mention of Mayya reciting any of Dhū al-Rummah's poetry.[110] There is also the report that when a man who was blind in one eye saw Mayya, he too wondered aloud what Dhū al-Rummah had seen in her to admire and added: "I do not see that you are as he has described you." She retorted "He saw me with two eyes and you see me with but one."[111]

Women also were curious about Dhū al-Rummah's Mayya. One woman who had long wanted to see her

106 *Amālī* III 126: كانت ميّ صغراء أُملودا واردة الشعر حلوة ظريفة وانّ في النساء اللاتى معها لأحسن منها. For descriptions of her by Dhū al-Rummah, for whom she was الحسناء, see Macartney, No. 68:5.

107 Jumaḥī, p. 476: اخبرنى ابو سوار الغنوى وكان فصيحا قال رايتُ ميّ ورايت معها بنين لها صغار قلت فصفها قال مسنونة الوجه طولية الخدين شمّاء الانف عليها وسم جمال (cf. *Shiʿr*, p. 335; *Aghānī* XVI 120; Ibn Khallikān I 311 [= trans. II 447]).

108 Jumaḥī, p. 476: اي والله تسح سحا ما رأى مثله احدٌ. But *Shiʿr*, p. 335, and *Aghānī* XVI 120 render this phrase as قال نعم كانت تسح سحا ما راى ابوك مثله. Ibn Khallikān I 311 (= trans. II 447) relied on the *Shiʿr* version alone and assumed that the report had been given directly to Ibn Qutaibah, thus leading De Slane to point out the impossibility of such transmission. Note that Ibn Khallikān names the reporter as Abū Ḍirār as against Jumaḥī's direct source, Abū Sawwār, for whom see *Fihrist*, p. 45.

109 ʿ*Uyūn* IV 40: فقالت علقنى والله وانا فى سنها فقلتُ عذره الله ورحمه فاستنشدتها فجعلت تنشد وانا اكتب. Cf. ʿ*Iqd* VI 423, which concludes with قالت علقنى ذو الرمة وانا فى سن هذه وكل جديد الى بـَلى.

110 *Aghānī* XVI 119 f. See Macartney, p. 666, Addendum 40, for the two verses cited by Muḥammad ibn al-Ḥajjāj al-Usayyidī. Ṭabarī I 2382 mentions a Muḥammad ibn al-Ḥajjāj who was a transmitter from ʿAbd al-Malik ibn ʿUmair, for whom see pp. 62 and 76 above.

111 Jāḥiẓ, *Maḥāsin*, p. 205.

did not think much of her when she finally met her until she heard Mayya speak and express her appreciation of the fame that the poet had brought her. Impressed with Mayya's eloquence, the woman realized that Dhū al-Rummah had not done her full justice,[112] an indication that this woman knew some at least of Dhū al-Rummah's poetry on Mayya. Be that as it may, there is evidence that Mayya herself had memorized much of his poetry and transmitted it to others, for both Abū Sawwār and Abū al-Muhalhil bore witness to her good memory and ready transmission.

Dhū al-Rummah's physical descriptions of Mayya as found in his *Dīwān* confirm and surpass those of the sources, which is not surprising since he was a poet-lover. He nowhere gives a complete picture of Mayya at any one period of her life. Yet, no detail of her features and figure seems to have escaped him, though some features are more frequently mentioned than others in the numerous and at times repetitious verbal sketches of her that are scattered in more than fifty of some eighty odes published by Macartney. Though Mayya's physical attractions loom large in most of these references, articles associated with her such as her attire, jewelry, and perfume[113] as well as the furnishings of her dwelling and the litters in which she and her women traveled also receive the poet's attention.[114] And her women companions are not overlooked.[115] Dhū al-Rummah's visits to Mayya and his nostalgic recollections of them, as well as his generally tearful return to the deserted sites, take up many of the traditionally romantic verses (*nasīb*) of the introductions to most of his odes.

Little is to be gained from a list of all the references to each item of Mayya's physical attractions and traits of personality, though I have noted and analyzed all of them in order to gain a sufficiently representative sketch of Mayya as Dhū al-Rummah actually saw her or as he more often pictured her in a lover's fantasy. A goodly number of his odes, including the verses in the first part of our papyrus text, give comparatively full descriptions which should be consulted by readers curious about the actual texts. The descriptions are as a rule rich in the metaphors and particularly the similes on which Dhū al-Rummah's literary reputation as a poet largely rests. Nevertheless, their profuse use in rapid succession tends at times to distract attention from rather than illuminate the subject.[116]

From the copious *Dīwān* materials on hand we gather that young Mayya was tall and slender, yet small boned and well rounded.[117] She had an oval face with a silken-smooth unblemished complexion comparable to the yellow-red glow of the rising sun.[118] She had large bright brown eyes rimmed with long black lashes, a color combination expressed in a verse

كحلاء فى برج صفراء فى نعج   كانها فضة قد مسها ذهب

that is one of the poet's verses most often cited for its literary quality.[119] Her eyes were, moreover, comparable to the eyes of gazelles for their beauty and magic appeal.[120] The poet dwells on the sensitive

[112] *Fāḍil*, p. 115: فخرجت مىّ وهى تقول شهرنى غيلان شهره الله قالت المرأة فلم اكبّرها حين رايتها فلمّ تكلمت ورايتُ فصاحتها علمت ان ذا الرمة قصر فى وصفها (see p. 181 above for Kharqā' al-ʿĀmirīyah's expression of gratitude to Dhū al-Rummah).

[113] See e.g. Macartney, Nos. 1:4 and 17, 10:16, 19, and 22, 30:16–22, 35:32–33, 64:11 and 17.

[114] See e.g. *ibid.* Nos. 5:8 and 16–17, 25:23, 40:13, 41:24–28, 78:8.

[115] See e.g. *ibid.* Nos. 5:8 and 16–17, 51:8–9, 57:6–20 and 31–32 (= pages 1:1–2:2 and 2:12–13 of our papyrus text), 64:14–19.

[116] See e.g. *ibid.* Nos. 1:6–29, 5:19–23, 10:15–25, 24:10–15, 25:14–17, 35:20–34, 52:11–19, 57:20–30 (see page 2:2–11 of our text), 64:11–19, 78:10–13.

[117] *Ibid.* Nos. 1:13, 35:23–25, 57:18 (= page 1:13 of our text), 64:12–13.

[118] *Ibid.* No. 52:16; see, further, Nos. 1:15, 10:20, 24:11, 29:24, 35:30, 57:22–23 and 28 (= page 2:4–5 and 9 of our text).

[119] *Ibid.* No. 1:20; note the many variants of this verse, some of which perhaps originated with the poet himself. For more verses on the eyes see e.g. *ibid.* Nos. 24:12, 29:23, 30:16–17, 64:16, and p. 668, Addenda 49:2 and 52.

[120] *Ibid.* No. 52:17 (see p. 187 below for citation of this verse and two other such verses). Dhū al-Rummah was opposed to comparing any feature of a woman with that of a cow, as was commonly done, especially in respect to large passive eyes (see e.g. *ibid.* No. 25:14). He much preferred to compare women to gazelles and at times reversed the simile and compared gazelles to one or the other of his lady loves; see e.g. *ibid.* Nos. 1:19, 5:19, 10:11–15, 24:10, 52:16–17, 57:14, 16 and 29 (= pages 1:9, 1:11, and 2:10 of our text, where the poet's sentiment is that not even a gazelle can be compared to Mayya), 66:17. See also *Aghānī* V 63 and 126 f., X 163, XVI 119; Mubarrad, pp. 420, 509; *Muwashshaḥ*, p. 169; Yāqūt III 198; *Khizānah* IV 597.

mouth,[121] the highly colored lips,[122] and the even and bright white teeth.[123] She had a firm chin and long slender neck.[124] Her braided, heavy, long black hair covered parts of her back and chest.[125] She had small wrists and slender hands and feet.[126] Her walk, when she was a heavier mature woman, was slow and swaying.[127] The poet is enamored of her captivating smile[128] and enchanted with her soft, sweet, sensible, and elegant speech[129]—speech that he longed to hear whether or not it cured his lovesickness[130] and even when she questioned his sentiments,[131]

وقد حلفتْ بالله ميّةُ ما الذى   احدثها الا الذى انا كاذبـــهْ

لمىّ شكوت الحبّ كيما تثيبنى   بودّى فقالت انما انت تمـــزحُ

On the other hand, he speaks of her as being generally patient and understanding,[132] but he also implies that she was too sparing of her attention so far as he was concerned, so that he was delighted even if she disagreed with him:[133]

اذا نازعتك القول ميّة اوبدا   لك الوجه منها او نضا الدرع سالبه

The poet's superlatives are lavished on her whom he sees as a true free-born Arab lady[134]—a paragon such as is not to be found among Arabs or non-Arabs:[135]

ديار ميّة اذا مىّ تساعفنـــا   ولا يرى مثلها عجم ولاعربُ

All in all, as we are told in the following verse, Dhū al-Rummah would have us believe that were even Luqmān the Sage to cast an eye upon the unveiled Mayya, he would be dazed and utterly bewildered:[136]

ولو أنّ لقمان الحكيم تعرضت   لعينيه مىٌ سافراً كاد يَبرقُ

IV

Was Dhū al-Rummah sincere in his avowed love for Mayya or was he merely using her name as a literary motif to enhance his reputation?[137] We note that some of his romantic verses addressed to the three other women in his life, beginning with Ṣaidā', convey at times sentiments similar to those expressed about Mayya. But we note also that thoughts of Mayya intrude even in the odes that start with praise of Umaimah, or Umm Sālim, and Kharqā'. The over-all implications of the *Dīwān* so far as Mayya is concerned indicate that she had an ever increasing hold on the poet's mind and heart during some thirty of the forty years of his life. If his interest in Mayya started as a youthful venture, it persisted through his

121 Macartney, Nos. 1:19, 25:16, 57:22 (= page 2:4 of our text).
122 *Ibid.* Nos. 25:16 and 64:14.
123 *Ibid.* Nos. 1:19, 10:25, 24:13, 35:26–27, 57:24 (= page 2:6 of our text).
124 *Ibid.* Nos. 24:14–15, 25:17, 52:16.
125 *Ibid.* Nos. 35:28, 57:27 (which is missing in our text), 78:11–12.
126 *Ibid.* Nos. 30:20, 52:15, 64:12–13.
127 *Ibid.* No. 30:21–22.
128 *Ibid.* Nos. 22:11, 25:16–17, 29:24, 34:12, 35:20–21, 46:12, 52:18, 83:10.
129 *Ibid.* Nos. 1:25, 25:17, 29:22, 35:20–22, 57:17 (= page 1:12 of our text).
130 See e.g. *ibid.* Nos. 73:5 and 82:8, where her conversation only aggravated his condition, and p. 676, Addendum 101.
131 *Ibid.* Nos. 5:20 and 10:36.
132 Macartney, No. 1:24.
133 *Ibid.* No. 5:22; cf. *Aghānī* XVI 130 and *Amālī* III 125, 126.
134 Macartney, No. 14:14; see also No. 68:5, where she is referred to as الحسناء.
135 *Ibid.* No. 1:10; cf. Mubarrad, p. 452, and *Khizānah* I 378.
136 Macartney, No. 52:12.
137 *Ibid.* No. 1:18 reads

تزداد للعين ابهاجـا اذا سفرت   وتحرجُ العين فيها حين تنتقبُ

and *'Umdah* I 137 f., for example, touches on this controversial point.

maturity despite the remonstrances of friends and family, including his brother Mas'ūd, as indicated by the following two pairs of verses:[138]

عشيّة مسعود يقول وقد جرى   على لحيتى من عبرة العين قاطرُ
أَفى الدار تبكى أَن تفرّق اهلها   وانت أمرو قد حلّمتك العشائر

فهلا لا تزد جهلا وتأمرِ   به وتطاوع العين الهمولا
فانّك لست معذورا بجهلٍ   وقد اصبحت شايعت الكهولا

Expressions of his deep and abiding though hopeless love occur time and again in his *Dīwān,* and it is possible to trace through some of the verses the likely course of his affection from his first youthful attraction on and on,[139]

وقد كانت الحسنآء مىّ كريمة   علينا ومكروها الينا زيالها
لقد علقت مىّ بقلبى علاقة   بطيئا على مَر الشهور انحلالها

فما حب ميّه بالذى يكذبُ الفتى   ولا بالذى يُزهى ولايتملقُ

دعانى الهوى من نحو مىّ وشاقنى   هوى من هواها تالدٌ ونزيعُ

and on to love's hold on the very core of his heart,[140]

وميّ فى الضعائن وهى شكت   سواد القلب فاقتل اقتالا

and love's continued growth until it crowded out everything and everyone:[141]

اذا القلب لا مستحدث غير وصلها   ولا شغله عن ذكر ميّه شاغلة

اذا خطرت من ذكر ميّة خطرة   على النفس كادت فى فوادك تجرحُ
تصرّف اهواء القلوب ولا أرى   نصيبكِ من قلبى لغيرك يمنحُ

His love was never a case of out-of-sight, out-of-mind, for absence makes his pierced heart grow fonder,[142]

وبعض الهوى بالهجر يمحى فيمتحى   وحبكِ عندى يستجيد ويربحُ

and his love could grow no further:[143]

فما زال يغلو حبّ ميّه عندنا   ويزداد حتى لم نجد ما يزيدها

He loves even the ground on which she treads. Breezes blowing from her people's quarters agitate his heart with a passion that brings tears to his eyes, but everyone loves the place where his loved one dwells,[144]

اذا هبّت الارواح من اى جانب   به أهل مىّ هاج قلبى هبوبها
هوى تذرف العينان منه وانما   هوى كل نفس حيث كان حبيبها

and, finally, Allāh knows that he loves her with a strong and enduring affection:[145]

ويعلم ربى ان قلبى يحبها   على تلك من حال متين العلائقِ

[138] Macartney, Nos. 32:3–4 (cf. No. 62:6 ff.) and 58:6–7 (cf. Ibn Khallikān I 512 f. [= trans. II 450]) respectively.
[139] Macartney, Nos. 68:2 and 12, 52:6, 47:8 respectively.
[140] *Ibid.* No. 57:20 (= page 2:2 of our text).
[141] *Ibid.* Nos. 62:12 (cf. p. 661, Addendum 5) and 10:8–9 respectively.
[142] *Ibid.* No. 10:10 (cf. Nos. 17:28, 25:4–5, 40:8, 41:6–7; *Aghānī* XVI 122 f.).
[143] Macartney, No. 23:8.
[144] *Ibid.* No. 8:8–9 (cf. *Aghānī* XVI 130 and Ibn Khallikān I 511 [= trans. II 448]).
[145] Macartney, No. 53:14.

Thoughts of Mayya haunt him in his dreams as in his waking hours.[146] They intrude even on his prayers—and he was a reasonably religious man[147]—to confuse and confound him to the point that he knows not what he is doing, even to losing count of his forenoon prayers:[148]

وانصب وجهى نحو مكة بالضحى　　اذا كان من فرط الليالى بداليا
اصلى فما ادرى اذا ما ذكرتها　　اثنتين صليت الضحى ام ثمانيا

Perhaps yet another indication of his sincerity is the generally chaste language he employs throughout in reference to Mayya even when he is angered or frustrated, as in the following verses:[149]

أميّة ما أحببت حبّك أيّما　　ولا ذات بعل فاحلفى لى بذلكِ
وما ذكرككِ الشى الذى ليس راجعا　　به الوجد إلا ضلّة من ضلالكِ

This characteristic of all his romantic odes and sundry verses led Aṣmaʿī to consider Dhū al-Rummah the most decent and serious minded of all the lovers he knew.[150]

All things considered, it would seem that Dhū al-Rummah while yet a precocious boy of ten was first struck with the young Mayya's sweet charms and touched by her concern for his tender age as she supplied him with water. He then and there adopted her as his secret talisman for his budding genius.[151] He came later to use her name as a literary device much as a gallant young medieval knight used his exploits to praise and pay homage to his lady fair. But he was soon bewitched, only to endure the pangs of unrequited love:[152]

فتلك التى يعتادنى من خبالها　　على النأى داءُ السحر او شبه السحرِ
وعين كعين الرئم فيها ملاحة　　هى السحر او ادهى التباسا واعلقُ
هى السحر إلّا ان للسحر رقية　　واننّى لا القى لما بى راقيا

and finally realized that he was indeed genuinely and deeply in love with her and with her only. But, the sources being what they are, it seems fitting to conclude this line of thought with the familiar "and only Allāh knows best."

DHŪ AL-RUMMAH THE POET

I

Dhū al-Rummah, like many another poet, began his career as a transmitter of poetry. And, like many a nephew, he was first directly influenced by an uncle, ʿUbaid ibn Ḥuṣain al-Numairī, better known as Rāʿī, "camel-herder" (see pp. 113–16), whose poetry he transmitted.[153] Rāʿī had a tangible effect on the

[146] See *ibid.* Nos. 1:30 40:8, 46:1–12, 49:1–11, 52:4–5, 55:24–26, 82:1–11, and p. 661, Addendum 41.

[147] See e.g. *ibid.* Nos. 7:30, 30:14, 57:51 (= page 4:6 of our text), and Addenda 47 and 63 on pp. 667 and 670 respectively. See also *Aghānī* XVI 128: كان ذو الرمة حسن الصلاة حسن الخشوع فقال ان العبد اذا قام بين يدى الله لحقيق ان يخشع and (on the authority of ʿĪsā ibn ʿUmar as reported by Aṣmaʿī) الاصمعى عن عيسى بن عمر قال كان ذو الرمة ينشد الشعر فاذا فرغ قال والله لاكسعنك بشى ليس فى حسابك سبحان الله والحمد لله ولا اله الا هو والله اكبر (cf. Jāḥiẓ, *Maḥāsin*, p. 183).

[148] Macartney, No. 87:21–22.

[149] *Ibid.* No. 55:25–26.

[150] *Aghānī* XVI 113: قال الاصمعى ما اعلم احد من العشاق الحاظرين وغيرهم شكى حبّا احسن من شكوى ذى الرمة مع عفة وعقل رصين. Abū ʿUbaidah (*ibid.*) noticed the same qualities in the poet's general attitude and conversation: فيحسن التخلص مع حسن انصاف وغفاف فى الحكم (see also p. 179 above and p. 188 below).

[151] See *Aghānī* XVI 114, esp. lines 13–4 : فلما انحطت (ميّة) على القربة رايت مولى لم ار احسن منه.

[152] Macartney, Nos. 35:34, 52:17, 87:26. It should be noted that Kuthaiyir's affection for ʿAzzah paralleled that of Dhū al-Rummah for Mayya in that eventually both romances progressed from a professional to an emotional phase (see e.g. *Shiʿr* pp. 321 f.).

[153] Jumaḥī, p. 467; *Muwashshaḥ*, pp. 170, 183.

young poet's style and theme orientation, particularly in the description of camels,[154] but not to the point of stifling the younger poet's inclination or originality.

Dhū al-Rummah's first attempts at versification centered on the *rajaz*, a comparatively primitive meter that was all but pre-empted at the time by ʿAjjāj and his son Ru'bah.[155] The latter, a rival of Dhū al-Rummah, accused him of plagiarizing some of his verses (see p. 173), as he accused Ṭirimmāḥ and Kumait ibn Zaid (see p. 97) of plagiarizing his language materials and even his father of stealing some of his verses.[156] It should be recalled that Dhū al-Rummah was accused of appropriating some of his brothers' ideas and verses. However, Dhū al-Rummah himself early realized that he could not compete with such *rajaz* experts as Ru'bah and his father, and thereafter he concentrated on a limited number of other meters that were more suitable for regular odes[157] and used mostly the *ṭawīl, basiṭ, wāfir* and *mutaqārib* varieties.[158]

Just as Dhū al-Rummah knew his limitations as to the *rajaz* meter, he knew also when to refrain from satire. He refused to satirize the Banū Ḥabtar, who had found fault with some of his verses, because he knew them to be transmitters of poetry and knowledgeable in that art.[159] He must have sensed his weakness in this major category of Arabic poetry, which he nevertheless attempted occasionally though, by the accepted standard of the time, not very successfully. He countered criticism of his ineffective satire by claiming that he did not wish to damage the reputations of believing women, who were as a rule the satirist's most vulnerable target in attacks on family and tribal honor.[160] But his excuse was no more acceptable to the critics than were similar excuses of ʿAjjāj and others who were weak in satire (see p. 139, n. 195).

Dhū al-Rummah could hold his own even in satire against lesser poets but not against such master satirists as Jarīr and Farazdaq. This is neatly illustrated in his involvement with Hishām al-Mara'ī, whose poetry was mostly in the *rajaz* meter and hence not conducive to effective satire. Dhū al-Rummah attacked Hishām and his people for their lack of hospitality and his verses hit their mark. Jarīr, suspecting

[154] When critics preferred Rāʿī's descriptions of camels to those of Dhū al-Rummah, the latter pointed out that Rāʿī described royal mounts while he himself was more concerned with working camels of the desert and the market place (see Jumaḥī, pp. 468 f.; *Muwashshaḥ*, pp. 174–76.

[155] For a definition of this meter see Lane, pp. 1036 f. For its origin and development see e.g. Sībawaih I 147 and 155 and ʿ*Umdah* I 121–24, 126; see also Goldziher, *Abhandlungen zur arabischen Philologie* I 76–83 and 120, and for early leading poets who used it see *GAL* S I 90–92. For its later development and for its humble use by Arabs and its exalted use by Persians see *EI* Supplement, pp. 178–81, and A. J. Arberry (ed.), *The Legacy of Persia* (Oxford, 1953) pp. 211 f.

Numerous bits of personal and literary information and rare anecdotes (*akhbār* and *nawādir*) are told of ʿAjjāj, Ru'bah, and Abū al-Najm al-ʿIjlī, whose rivalries were almost as marked as those of Akhṭal, Jarīr, and Farazdaq. An anecdote about Ru'bah and some of his verses are included in the text of *PERF* No. 864, which Karabacek dated to the 3rd/9th century—a date likely enough for the text itself but hardly for the papyrus copy. The latter I would place in the first half of the 4th century, largely on the basis of its script and the fact that it is written on a fragment of a palimpsest which retains remnants of an earlier, 3rd-century script. For parallels, with variants, of the Ru'bah anecdote and some of the verses see e.g. Jumaḥī, p. 581, and *Aghānī* XVIII 125 and XXI 91.

[156] *Aghānī* X 156; *Muwashshaḥ*, p. 209. Ru'bah's Bedouin diction, as well as that of Farazdaq, was held in very high esteem by Abū ʿAmr ibn al-ʿAlā' (see *Khizānah* I 152: قال ابو عمرو بن العلاء لم ار بدويا اقام فى الحضر الا فسد لسانه غير روبه والفرزدق). Ru'bah's eloquent speech became almost proverbial, while that of Ḥasan al-Baṣrī and that of Ibrāhīm al-Sindī were compared to it (Ibn Saʿd VII 1, p. 121; Jāḥiẓ, *Bayān* I 321 f.; see also *Khaṣā'iṣ* III 305). For Ru'bah's accusation against his father see Sīrāfī, pp. 91 f., and Ibn ʿAsākir VI 395.

[157] *Muwashshaḥ*, p. 174. This report traces back to Thaʿlab on the authority of Abū ʿUbaidah on the authority of Muntajiʿ ibn Nabhān al-Aʿrābī, one of Dhū al-Rummah's leading transmitters. See also p. 200 below.

[158] As readily confirmed by the meters of his *Dīwān*, which includes also his earlier *rajaz* pieces, some of them of considerable length (e.g. Macartney, Nos. 12–14 and Addenda 11, 21, 26, 31, 51, 60, 93 on pp. 662 ff.).

[159] *Muwashshaḥ*, pp. 180 f.: نسخت من خط ابي موسى الحامض قيل لذى الرمة الا تهجو بنى حبتر قال لا لانهم قوم رواة رماة اى يرون الشعر ويرمون الرجل بمعايبه ويصيبون ما فيه (see *Aghānī* VII 78 f. for Abū Ḥabtar and Kuthaiyir).

[160] See Macartney, No. 57:51 (= page 4:6 of our text), which reads

فلم اقذف لمومنة حصان　　　بحمد الله موجبة عضالا

that Dhū al-Rummah favored Farazdaq,[161] injected himself into the quarrel by aiding Hishām with verses in Dhū al-Rummah's meter and rhyme in answer to Dhū al-Rummah's attack. But Dhū al-Rummah detected the verses as those of Jarīr and took him to task for it, explaining that he did not favor Farazdaq against Jarīr. He himself then accepted help from Jarīr against Hishām. This was so effective[162] that Hishām and his people eventually prevailed on Jarīr to help them again with satirical verses. Jarīr's aid resulted in victory for Hishām shortly before the death of Dhū al-Rummah.[163]

Dhū al-Rummah seems to have been generally more tolerant of criticism from his fellow poets than from scholars, as is well illustrated by his relationships with Jarīr and Farazdaq, whose opinions he deliberately sought, in contrast to his resentful attitude toward Abū ʿAmr ibn al-ʿAlā', whose opinions were unsolicited. Abū ʿAmr even though he initiated the statement that "poetry began with Imru' al-Qais and ended with Dhū al-Rummah" (see pp. 121 and 147) did on occasion find fault with specific verses of Dhū al-Rummah on points of grammar and meaning—a type of criticism with which Farazdaq at times agreed[164] and other poets paralleled though not always justifiably.[165]

Dhū al-Rummah's desire to impress and win the approval and praise of his fellow poets is indicated also by the fact that he sought the opinions of Kumait and Ṭirimmāḥ, to whom he recited some verses that he considered among his best. The more amiable and generous Kumait[166] exclaimed that what they had heard was indeed "brocade" rather than the "muslin" of their own verses. The less impressionable and more critical Ṭirimmāḥ would not go that far but conceded that what they had heard was good enough. Then Dhū al-Rummah recited two of his verses and asked if Ṭirimmāḥ could produce anything to match them. Ṭirimmāḥ recognized them as verses from the ode which had displeased ʿAbd al-Malik, who had refused to reward Dhū al-Rummah for it (see p. 171). Kumait urged Ṭirimmāḥ to give Dhū al-Rummah his due, and in the end Ṭirimmāḥ apologized and conceded that the reins of poetry were in the palm of Dhū al-Rummah's hand.[167]

That Dhū al-Rummah protected himself from what he recognized as his weakness is in itself a point of strength. It is instructive to note his own appraisal of what he considered his several strong points as a

[161] See Jumaḥī, p. 469. Dhū al-Rummah's leaning toward Farazdaq may be explained in part by the latter's repeated favorable mention at court of the younger and as yet little known poet; see e.g. *Aghānī* X 113, where both Jarīr and Farazdaq mention Dhū al-Rummah favorably, and *ibid.* XVI 119, where Farazdaq alone does so.

[162] *Aghānī* XVI 117 f. gives a vivid description of Hishām's reaction at this point. He beat on his head and wailed قتلنى جرير قتله الله هذا والله شعره الذى لو نقطت منه نقطة فى البحر لكدرته. In their exchange of satire Dhū al-Rummah and Hishām could not bypass their respective sub-tribes, the Banū ʿAdī and the Banū Imrī al-Qais. These latter were characterized as unwarlike agriculturalists and inhospitable eaters of pork and drinkers of wine (see Macartney, No. 29:44–55, esp. verses 47–48, and references under Imru' al-Qais on p. xiii). For a sample of Dhū al-Rummah's restrained allusion to their women, even in satire, see *ibid.* No. 29:56–60.

[163] See Jumaḥī, pp. 471–75; *Aghānī* VII 61–63 and XVI 116–18. Macartney, Nos. 27:17–19, and 68:78–84, incorporate most of Jarīr's verses in aid of Dhū al-Rummah. The claim that had Dhū al-Rummah lived longer he would have wrested the victory from Hishām should be discounted since the real victor was not Hishām but Jarīr, for whom Dhū al-Rummah was no more a match than Rāʿī had been (see pp. 113 f. above) and a similar claim had been made for Rāʿī. See, further, *Aghānī* VII 61 and *ʿUmdah* II 219 f. *Khizānah* I 51 f. reports that Dhū al-Rummah refused an invitation from Jarīr to exchange satire because he did not wish to attack women.

[164] *Majālis al-ʿulamā'*, p. 337. See also Macartney, No. 29:3, and *ʿUmdah* I 181.

[165] *Muwashshaḥ*, pp. 178–85, is devoted largely to this type of criticism by various poets and scholars of specific verses of Dhū al-Rummah. See e.g. *Aghānī* XVI 122 f. for a criticism that was itself challenged. Criticism pointing out the errors of poets (اغاليط الشعراء) was a type which hardly any poet or transmitter escaped (see e.g. *ʿUmdah* II 191–96; *Muzhir* II 497–505).

[166] He not only readily conceded Dhū al-Rummah's superiority at description but volunteered the reason for it, namely that Dhū al-Rummah's descriptions, unlike his own, were made from personal observation (see *Aghānī* X 157 and XV 125: لانك تصف شيئا رأيته بعينك وانا أصف شيئا وصف لى وليس المعانية كالوصف). *Aghānī* I 139 reports Kumait's silent acceptance of repeated criticism of his verses by Nuṣaib who preferred in each instance a verse of Dhū al-Rummah (cf. *Muzhir* II 499 f.).

[167] *Aghānī* X 157 f.: قال الكميت هذا والله الديباج لا نسجى ونسجك الكرابيس . . . فقال له الطرماح معذرة اليك انّ عنان الشعر لفى كفك. See also *The Poems of Ṭufail ibn ʿAuf al-Ghanawī and aṭ-Ṭirimmāḥ ibn Ḥakīm aṭ-ṭā'yī*, ed. and trans. F. Krenkow ("'E. J. W. Gibb Memorial' Series" XXV [London, 1927]) pp. xxv f. and pp. 166 f., Ṭirimmāḥ No. 47:18 and commentary.

poet. To begin with, as some of his verses reveal, he considered himself a good and careful technician in his art and extraordinarily effective in his use of uncommon words and phrases that then became ever so widely known:[168]

وشعر قد ارقت له غريـــــب   اجنبه المـــساند والمحــــــالا
فبتُ اقيمه واقــدّ منـــــه   قوافى لا ايــدّ لهــا مثـــالا
غرائب قد عرفن بكل أفــق   من الافاق تفتعل افتعـــالا

He worked hard on revisions, including the addition of new verses, which led one of his several transmitters to protest the confusion caused thereby in his own transmission.[169] Dhū al-Rummah acknowledged his debt to Rāʿī, his first direct mentor, but claimed that he had surpassed him by far.[170] He was perfectly aware of his facility with excellent similes.[171] He realized from experience that poetic inspiration was not always at one high level. He classified his odes in three categories, giving an example for each group: those in the composition of which he experienced an easy flow and play of words, those in which he had to exert himself more energetically, and those during the composition of which he was as one completely possessed.[172] He illustrated his third category with his famed ode which begins with the verse:

ما بال عينك منها الماء ينسكب   كانه من كلى مفرية سربُ

and which is the one ode that Jarīr envied Dhū al-Rummah for and wished that he himself had composed.[173] And Jarīr is reported as saying that had Dhū al-Rummah become dumb after this one ode he would have been the greatest poet among men.[174] Dhū al-Rummah was asked: "What would you do should poetry be locked away from you?" He answered: "How can it be locked away from me when I have its keys?"[175]

[168] Macartney, No. 57:48–50 (= page 4:3–5 of our text). See also Jāḥiẓ, *Bayān* I 153 f. and *Khaṣāʾiṣ* I 325; cf. n. 111 on p. 128 above.

[169] *Aghānī* XVI 118 and *Muwashshaḥ*, p. 184: قال بعض رواة ذى الرمة له افسدت علىّ شعرك وذلك ان ذا الرمة كان اذا استضعف الحرف ابدل مكانه. Such confusion probably accounts for some of the more numerous variants for some of his verses, such as Macartney, p. 5, draws attention to in respect to No. 1:20. For the role of the transmitter as editor, whether he was right or wrong, see e.g. Jumaḥī, pp. 20, 40 f.; Jāḥiẓ, *Bayān* I 269; Ibn Ṭabāṭabā, p. 124; see also p. 151 above.

[170] *Aghānī* XVI 121: قيل لذى الرمة انما انت راويه الراعى فقال اما والله لئن قيل ذاك ما مثلى ومثله الا شاب صحب شيخا فسلك به طرقا ثم فارقه فسلك الشاب بعده شعابا واودية لم يسلكها الشيخ قط. But see Zubaidī, p. 210, where this claim is questioned by Mufaḍḍal ibn Muḥammad al-Ḍabbī. Dhū al-Rummah apparently was resented by his cousin Jandal ibn al-Rāʿī (see Macartney, No. 19:6–7).

[171] Ibn Shubrumah reported that he heard Dhū al-Rummah say اذا قلت كانه ثم لم اجد مخرجا فقطع الله لسانى (*Aghānī* XVI 113). He once criticized a verse of Dhū al-Rummah and caused the latter to change a word in it only to have Abū al-Ḥakam ibn al-Bakhtarī fault first Ibn Shubrumah and then the poet for making the change (*ibid.* XVI 122 f.; *Muwashshaḥ*, p. 180). Ibn Shubrumah was a minor poet and critic who later served as judge in Baṣrah and for the Sawād of Kūfah and was known as a good and wise judge (see e.g. *Majālis Thaʿlab* II 483; *ʿIqd* II 365, IV 124, VI 335; *Akhbār al-quḍāt* III 36–129, esp. pp. 95–108 for his relations with poets).

[172] *Aghānī* XVI 118; *Khizānah* I 379. For the odes with which Dhū al-Rummah illustrated his first and second categories see Macartney, Nos. 66 and 38 respectively.

[173] *Aghānī* XVI 118. For the entire ode with commentaries see e.g. Macartney, No. 1, and Qurashī, pp. 177–87. *Aghānī* XVI 123 reports that Dhū al-Rummah, dressed in expensive clothing and with tears streaming down his bearded face, stood and recited this long ode in the Mirbad of Baṣrah, the meeting place of poets and orators. See, further, e.g. Ibn Ṭabāṭabā, p. 19, for glowing praise of the similes in this ode, and pp. 27, 56 f., 109 f., for more praise of some of Dhū al-Rummah's verses (cf. Jurjānī, *Al-wasāṭah* [1364/1945] p. 190).

Dhū al-Rummah's demonic inspiration is indicated in his expression ما جننت به جنونا and in Jarīr's reason for his envy: فان شيطانه كان له فيها ناصحا. The "demon" must have made frequent visits since Dhū al-Rummah continued to add to this ode until his death (*Aghānī* XVI 118). See n. 147 on p. 132 above for the demons of Abū al-Najm al-ʿIjlī and ʿAjjāj and of Jarīr and Farazdaq. For the theme of demonic inspiration in respect to Arab poets see Ḥamīdah ʿAbd al-Razzāq, *Shayaṭīn al-shuʿaraʾ* (Cairo, 1956) pp. 85–107.

[174] *Muwashshaḥ*, pp. 171, 185; Ibn Khallikān I 513 (= trans. II 451). *Muwashshaḥ*, pp. 174 f., notes the several criticisms of individual verses even in this ode.

[175] *ʿUmdah* I 137 f.

Dhū al-Rummah, however, was either unwilling or more probably unable to accept and hence to profit from the major criticism against his poetry such as was voiced by Jarīr and Farazdaq, whose status and approval he coveted.[176] For though both of these ranking poets appreciated Dhū al-Rummah's several strong points to the extent that Jarīr envied Dhū al-Rummah for his famous ode mentioned above and Farazdaq appropriated some of his verses,[177] neither hesitated to point out his several weaknesses. Both pointed to the paucity of his meters and his weakness in several categories of poetry, to the monotony of his themes and his preoccupation with camels and cattle, and to the doleful and lachrymose features of his poetry, all of which, they explained, disqualified him for first rank.[178] They expressed the totality of their criticism, favorable or otherwise, in the phrase *nuqat ʿarūs wa abʿār ghizlān*, which, along with its gloss, probably originated with Abū ʿAmr ibn al-ʿAlāʾ (see pp. 137 f.). De Slane's translation reads thus: "Dhū al-Rummah's verses are like sugar-plums scattered at a marriage feast; they disappear quickly; or they are like the dung of gazelles; at first, it has an odour, but it soon becomes mere dung."[179] This combination of admiration mixed with a greater part of severe criticism of Dhū al-Rummah led Ṣāliḥ ibn Sulaimān, one of his several transmitters, to accuse both Jarīr and Farazdaq of jealousy.[180] Dhū al-Rummah had other admirers among the poets, but they were neither so outspoken nor yet such powerful opinion makers as either Jarīr or Farazdaq. They included Kumait and Ṭirimmāḥ, whose favorable opinions have been discussed above, and the Negro slave poet Nuṣaib, who preferred a series of Dhū al-Rummah's verses over a comparable number of the verses of the ʿAlīd Kumait.[181]

That Dhū al-Rummah was even less willing to accept criticism from scholars is indicated by his reaction to the suggestions of Abū ʿAmr ibn al-ʿAlāʾ for improvement of a verse in praise of Bilāl which had displeased the latter (see p. 173, n. 36) much as similar verses had earlier displeased ʿAbd al-Malik. "O Abū ʿAmr," said Dhū al-Rummah, "you are unique in your knowledge, and I, in my knowledge and poetry, am the same."[182]

Dhū al-Rummah sustained both his faith and his high self-esteem to the last. For when he realized that death was near he expressed the concept that "man proposes, God disposes," and asked that he be buried not in some pit in the lowlands but on the highest hilltop of his beloved dunes. His wish was granted, and

176 *Aghānī* VII 60 and 130, XVI 113 f.; but see p. 137 above for Jarīr's high praise of Dhū al-Rummah's similes.

177 Jumaḥī, pp. 470 f.; *Aghānī* XVI 116 and XIX 23. See also Macartney, No. 19:1–5. Farazdaq was given to such thefts, and Aṣmaʿī, it should be recalled, considered nine-tenths of Farazdaq's poetry as stolen (see pp. 133 f. above). Farazdaq was often accompanied by one of his secretaries (see p. 115, n. 47) who was ordered to take down the verses that particularly impressed him.

178 See e.g. Jumaḥī, pp. 468 f.; *Shiʿr*, p. 333; *Aghānī* VII 62 and XVI 115, 117, 129; *Muwashshaḥ*, pp. 172 f.; Ibn Khallikān I 511 (= trans. II 447). It should be noted that Ibn Khallikān himself considered Dhū al-Rummah of first rank (*Khizānah* I 52).

179 Ibn Khallikān trans. II 451 f.

180 *Aghānī* XVI 112: قال صالح بن سليمان كان الفرزدق وجرير يحسدانه واهل الباديه يعجبهم شعره.
Jarīr and Farazdaq had early recognized the talents of the youthful and still little-known Dhū al-Rummah, whom each considered second only to himself when recommending him to ʿAbd al-Malik, who then sent for Dhū al-Rummah (see *Muwashshaḥ*, p. 239).

181 *Aghānī* I 138 f.; *Muzhir* II 499 f. For Nuṣaib as a critic of poetry see pp. 127–29 above.

182 *Muwashshaḥ*, p. 179. Earlier, Akhṭal had rebuffed Shaʿbī in the presence of ʿAbd al-Malik in somewhat the same manner in respect to the relative quality of some of the verses of Quṭāmī and poetry in general; see *Aghānī* IX 170 f. for the account as told by Shaʿbī himself: قال لى الاخطل يا شعبى لك فنونا فى الاحاديث وانما لنا فى واحد فان رايتَ ان لا تحملنى على اكتاف قومك فادعهم حرضا فقلت لا اعرض لك فى شى من الشعر ابدا فاقلنى فى هذه المرة. Note Shaʿbī's ready apology despite his high estimate of his own great knowledge of poetry, much of which he claimed he could recall in month-long recitation without repeating a single verse; see *ʿIqd* V 275: قال الشعبى ما انا لشىء من العلم اقلّ منى رواية للشعر ولو شئت أن انشد شعرا شهرا لا أُعيد بيتا لفعلت.

the record, which traces back through Abū ʿUbaidah to Muntajiʿ ibn Nabhān, adds that his tomb can be seen from a distance of three days' journey.[183]

II

We turn our attention now to the post-contemporary critics of Dhū al-Rummah's poetry, the foremost of whom seems to have been Aṣmaʿī, some of whose opinions have already been covered. As these are recalled and related to some of his other statements, it soon becomes clear that Aṣmaʿī was in fact little more than a transmitter of the body of criticism, favorable or otherwise, that was already current in Dhū al-Rummah's lifetime—opinions expressed by Jarīr and Farazdaq among others which were sustained beyond the poet's short life primarily by Abū ʿAmr ibn al-ʿAlāʾ and Ḥammād al-Rāwiyah. The latter believed that the poet was neglected partly because of his youth and partly because of jealousy.[184] To begin with, Aṣmaʿī, like the earlier critics, did not consider Dhū al-Rummah among the poets of first rank (*al-fuḥūl*) nor yet noteworthy (*mufliq*) except for his similes,[185] though he did consider him on the whole linguistically authoritative (*ḥijjah*) because he was a Bedouin.[186] On one occasion Aṣmaʿī placed Dhū al-Rummah among the best poets for his ability to convey the meaning of a verse before its rhyme word and then to make meaningful use of this word itself. He readily cited two verses in illustration and commented on them.[187] He held Dhū al-Rummah superior to Kumait[188] but reiterated the opinion that Dhū al-Rummah was not good in either panegyric or satire.[189] He echoed Jarīr's opinion that most of Dhū al-Rummah's poetry had better remained unsaid[190] and approved and transmitted the "sugar-plum" metaphor.[191] One does run across other criticisms by Aṣmaʿī of words, phrases, or verses of Dhū al-Rummah and other poets which are not all accepted, in their narrow sense and implication, by later critics.[192] Thus, Aṣmaʿī's contribution was mainly one of collecting and transmitting not only the poetry of Dhū al-Rummah but also all the previous major criticism (*naqd*) of his poetry. The contribution of Abū ʿUbaidah, on the other hand, was one of recording the background and the setting (*akhbār*) of some of the poetry and of most of this criticism. Furthermore, such few opinions as he did express convey

[183] *Aghānī* XVI 127: قال اردنا شيئا واراد الله شيئا . . . لما احتضر ذو الرمة قال انى لست ممن يدفن فى الغموض والوهاد . . . فاين انتم من كثبان حزوى وهما رملتان مشرفتان على ما حولهما من الرمال (cf. Yāqūt II 635 f., and III 885: قال ان مثلى لم يدفن فى البطون والوهاد . . . اين انتم عن الفرنداذين). And the account ends with فانت اذا رايت موضع قبره رايته من مسيرة ثلاث فى اعلا فرنداذين وهما رملان بالدهنا مرتفعان جداً. See also Macartney, No. 75:16, and p. 176 above.

[184] *Aghānī* XVI 113: ما أخر القوم ذكره الا احداثة سنه وانهم حسدوه (cf. *ibid.* XVI 122). See p. 173 above for more of Ḥammād's opinions and p. 191 for an accusation of jealousy.

[185] *Ibid.* XVI 114: قال الاصمعى كان ذو الرمة اشعر الناس اذا شبّه ولم يكن مفلق.

[186] *Fuḥūlat al-shuʿarāʾ*, p. 503: قال ذو الرمة حجة لانه بدوى ولكن ليس يشبه شعر العرب ثم قال الا واحدة التى تشبه العرب وهى التى يقول فيها والباب دون ابى غسّان مسدل (cf. Macartney, No. 17:13). See also ʿAskarī, *Maṣūn*, pp. 173 f., where Aṣmaʿī credits various poets with a specialty and says of Dhū al-Rummah: ومن اراد الغريب من شعر المحدث ففى اشعار ذى الرمة. Ḥammād al-Rāwiyah had already expressed an even stronger appreciation in this respect: وكيع عن حمّاد بن اسحاق (الموصلى) قال قال حمّاد الراوية قدم علينا ذو الرمة الكوفة فلم ار افصح ولا اعلم بالغريب منه (*Aghānī* XVI 113, lines 18–19). See p. 190 above for Dhū al-Rummah's own estimate of his proficiency in the use of unusual words and phrases.

[187] Qudāmah, p. 94 (= Qudāmah [1963] pp. 194 f.). For the two verses in question see Macartney, No. 67:1–2.

[188] *Fuḥūlat al-shuʿarāʾ*, p. 503; *Muwashshaḥ*, p. 171.

[189] *Aghānī* XVI 121.

[190] *Muwashshaḥ*, p. 185: قال الاصمعى لو ادركتُ ذا الرمة لاشرت عليه ان يدع كثيرا من شعره فكان ذلك خيرا له.

[191] *Ibid.* p. 179.

[192] E.g. *Muwashshaḥ*, p. 180, reports that Aṣmaʿī gives his severest criticism of Dhū al-Rummah's use of زوجة for "wife" instead of the Qurʾānic زوج, "mate," used for both sexes; cf. *Muzhir* II 376. Jurjānī, *Al-wasāṭah* (1364/1945) p. 480, takes exception to Aṣmaʿī's criticism. *Irshād* III 15 reports Abū ʿAlī al-Fārisī's objection to Aṣmaʿī's criticism of a verse of Dhū al-Rummah (cf. *Khizānah* IV 239).

an air of personal conviction rather than of mere transmission.[193] His best praise is for the elegance and refinement of Dhū al-Rummah's romantic verses, an opinion shared by Aṣmaʿī (see p. 187). In this category Abū ʿUbaidah considered Dhū al-Rummah the equal of Jarīr, despite some objections by others.[194] Poets and critics who were contemporaries of these two outstanding scholars had little to add on Dhū al-Rummah and his poetry. We do read, however, that Abū Bakr ibn ʿAyyāsh al-Khayyāṭ (d. 193/809) and some of his contemporaries found solace in weeping after hearing a Bedouin recite some of Dhū al-Rummah's tearful verse.[195] We read further that Salam, great-grandson of Abū ʿAmr ibn al-ʿAlāʾ, took exception to the latter's categoric statement that poetry ended with Dhū al-Rummah. But it was left for the Syrian Buṭain ibn Umayyah al-Ḥimṣī, himself a minor poet of limited output,[196] to summarize hastily most of the previous criticisms of Dhū al-Rummah. He compared him unfavorably with Jarīr. Farazdaq, and Akhṭal and summarily dismissed him as being but one-fourth of a poet since he fell short in panegyric, satire, and heroic verse and excelled only in his use of similes—the main categories of poetry according to Buṭain.[197]

Thus we have here an equally instructive parallel to the evolution of literary criticism in respect to Jarīr, Farazdaq, and Akhṭal (see pp. 147 f.). For third-century poets down to Ibn al-Muʿtazz, who greatly admired Dhū al-Rummah particularly for his excellent metaphors and similes such as those used in his description of the last stage of a sunset,[198] add nothing that had not already been expressed in the second century. Nor, in fact, do the linguists, grammarians, and critics, including Jāḥiẓ, Ibn Qutaibah, Mubarrad, and Thaʿlab, show any originality in this respect though most of them dwell, some at considerable length, on Dhū al-Rummah's apt use or his misuse of words, on points of grammar, and occasionally on a misplaced simile. On the whole these scholars and critics and their successors of the fourth century and after give this poet due credit for his excellent figures of speech, especially his similes, by citing them in great numbers and in illustration of practically every category of his poetry.[199]

III

While second- and third-century scholars dissected Dhū al-Rummah's poetry, splitting hairs over its diction and grammar or admiring its linguistic rarities and elegance and its superb similes, the Bedouins recited and sang his verses, as they did Jarīr's, in appreciation of their apt desert themes and romantic

[193] This is well illustrated by the collection of intermixed *naqd* and *akhbār* in *Aghānī* XVI 113 f. and especially in *Muwashshaḥ*, pp. 169, 173–76, 178–79, 183.

[194] See e.g. *Muwashshaḥ*, p. 176: قال ثعلب قال ابو عبيدة كان ذو الرمة اذا اخذ فى النسيب ونعت فهو مثل جرير وليس ورا ذلك شى فقيل له ما تشبه شعره الا بوجوه ليست لها اقفاء وصدور ليست لها اعجاز فقال كذا هو.

Furthermore, Abū ʿUbaidah admired Dhū al-Rummah himself for his sincerity, conciliatory attitude, and refined speech; see *Aghānī* XVI 113, lines 11–12:
قال ابو عبيده ذو الرمة يخبر فيحسن الخبر ثم يرد على نفسه الحجة من صاحبه فيحسن الرد ثم يعتذر فيحسن التخليص مع حسن وانصاف وعفاف في الحكم.

[195] See Mubarrad, p. 52; *Aghānī* V 97; *Irshād* II 374, 377; Macartney, No. 66:1–2. See also pp. 194–97 below. The ode in question is the one Dhū al-Rummah cited as an example of his quick and ready compositions as against his odes that required greater degrees of effort (see p. 190 above).

[196] See *Fihrist*, p. 163. Tabarī III 1090 f. reports that Buṭain was handsomely rewarded for his ode in praise of ʿAbd Allāh ibn Ṭāhir, whom he accompanied to Egypt in 210/825, and that he died in Alexandria soon thereafter.

[197] *Muwashshaḥ*, p. 172:
قيل للبطين أكان ذو الرمة شاعرا متقدما فقال البطين اجمع العلماء بالشعر على أن الشعر وضع على اربعة أركان مدح رافع او هجاء واضع او تشبيه مصيب او فخر سامق وهذه كله مجموع فى جرير والفرزدق والاخطل فاما ذو الرمة فما احسن قط أن يمدح ولا احسن ان يهجو ولا احسن ان يفخر يقع فى هذا كله دونا وانما يحسن التشبيه فهوربع شاعر (cf. *ibid.* p. 176).

[198] ʿ*Umdah* I 185: كان ابن المعتز يفضل ذا الرمة كثيرا ويقدمه بحسن الاستعارة والتشبيه (cf. Macartney, No. 48:36).

[199] His similes are readily cited by such leading authors from the early 3rd to the 11th century as Jumaḥī, Ibn Qutaibah, Mubarrad, Thaʿlab, Qudāmah, Ibn Ṭabāṭabā, Jurjānī in his *Wasāṭah*, Marzubānī, Ibn Rashīq, Ibn Munqid in his *Al-badīʿ fī naqd al-shiʿr*, Ibn Khallikān, and ʿAbd al-Qādir ibn ʿUmar al-Baghdādī in his *Khizānah*.

sentiments. There was, therefore, no break in either the availability or the circulation of Dhū al-Rummah's poetry. Still a third group, the musicians and singers of the second half of the second century, paid tribute to this poet and his verse. The setting was mainly the early ʿAbbāsid court and the palaces of the Barmakids. First among the musicians to discover the lyrical qualities of Dhū al-Rummah's verse was the adventurous, sophisticated, and highly gifted Ibrāhīm al-Mauṣalī (125–88/742–804),[200] companion and court musician to Mahdī, Hādī, and Hārūn al-Rashīd.[201] Hārūn, we learn, was already enamored of Dhū al-Rummah's verse. Jaʿfar al-Barmakī pointed out to Ibrāhīm how he could capitalize on Hārūn's admiration of Dhū al-Rummah's poetry to enhance his own prestige and win himself a fortune by requesting a monopoly on the singing of Dhū al-Rummah's verses at court.[202] Ibrāhīm followed Jaʿfar's advice, and the monopoly was readily granted, bringing in its wake a veritable fortune to this enterprising musician, who composed over a hundred melodies for the poet's verses.[203] Ibrāhīm's even more gifted and famous son Isḥāq (150–235/767–849), who was his successor at the court,[204] reported that his father composed some nine hundred melodies which he, Isḥāq, classified neatly into three groups of three hundred each as comparable in value and quality to the gold, silver, and copper currency of the realm. Isḥāq eliminated from circulation the three hundred "copper" melodies because they were no more than passing pleasures but retained the "silver" ones, which were good though their quality was shared by others, and cherished the "golden" ones, which he considered matchless.[205] Since Dhū al-Rummah's verses do not readily lend themselves to levity, we may concede that two-thirds of Ibrāhīm's musical scores for the poet's verses were indeed among his "silver" and "golden" compositions. To these Isḥāq added some melodies of his own. But even the best songs sometimes fade in popularity and are forgotten, and such was eventually the fate of most of the melodies composed by father and son for Dhū al-Rummah's verses. For our fullest source, the *Aghānī*, specifies only six such melodies—considerably fewer than the number of melodies composed by the Mauṣalīs for their own poetry.[206] And we should not overlook other poets whose verses attracted these cosmopolitan musicians.[207]

[200] See *GAL* S I 223 f. for Ibrāhīm al-Mauṣalī and his son Isḥāq.

[201] *Aghānī* V 2–49, VIII 162–65, and XVI 128 f. yield the fullest of the early accounts of the life, character, and artistic endowments of Ibrāhīm, and *ibid.* V 53–131 is fuller in these respects for his son Isḥāq. Abū al-Faraj al-Iṣfahānī relies mainly on the several *akhbār* monographs authored by Isḥāq, who drew on Abū ʿUbaidah and Aṣmaʿī among others. The monographs were supplemented and transmitted by his comparatively lackluster son Ḥammād to several 3rd-century authors interested in Dhū al-Rummah (see pp. 175 f. above) and directly or indirectly to Abū al-Faraj's older contemporaries such as Qudāmah and Wakīʿ.

Ibrāhīm is reported as saying that he was first alerted to the lyrical qualities of Dhū al-Rummah's verse in a dream, after which he acquainted himself with the life and verse of the poet as he composed his melodies (*Aghānī* V 38 f.).

[202] *Ibid.* V 39:

قال جعفر بن يحى البرمكى . . . انّ امير المومنين يحفظ شعر ذى الرمة حفظ الصبا و يعجبه و يُؤثره فاذا سمع فيه غناء أطربه اكثر مما يطربه غيره مما لا يحفظ شعره . . . فقل له تقطعنى شعر ذى الرمة اغنى فيه ما اختاره وتحظر على المغنين جميعا أن لا يداخلونى فيه فانى احب شعرة واستحسنه.

[203] *Ibid.* V 39 f.: فغنيتُ مايه صوت وزيادة عليها فى شعر ذى الرمة . . . فاخذت والله بها الف الف درهم والف الف درهم.

[204] *Ibid.* V 48 reports that Hārūn consoled Isḥāq on his father's death, transferred Ibrāhīm's pay to his children, and doubled Isḥāq's remuneration as his father's successor at the court. This happy relationship between courtier-musician and caliph was threatened only once, when Isḥāq, in answer to the caliph's question as to current public talk, informed him that the people were expecting him to order the downfall of the Barmakids (*ibid.* V 113).

[205] *Ibid.* V 17:

قال حمّاد قال لى ابي صنع جدّك تسعمايه صوت منها ديناريه ومنها درهمية ومنها فلسية وما رأيتُ اكثر من صنعته فامّا ثلثماية منها فانه تقدّم الناس جميعا فيها وامّا ثلثماية فشاركوه وشاركهم فيها وامّا الثلثماية الباقية فلعب وطرب قال ثم أسقط ابي الثلثمايه الاخرة بعد ذلك من غناء ابيه فكان اذا سئل عن صنعة ابيه قال هي ستماية صوت.

See *ibid.* V 61 f. and 79 f. for Isḥāq's aversion to levity and careless performance. Father and son played significant roles, at the request of Harūn al-Rashīd and Wāthiq respectively, in the selection of the best 100 tunes current in their day (*ibid* I 5 f.).

[206] See *ibid.* V 6, 23, 32, 58, 81 for Ibrāhīm and *ibid.* V 40, 74, 75, 82, 87, 103, 104, 106, 107, 114 for Isḥāq.

[207] The list of such poets is long. Occasionally mentioned are some of Dhū al-Rummah's contemporaries, such as Jarīr, Akhṭal, Rāʿī, Walīd II, and Bashshār ibn Burd, and poets contemporary with the musicians themselves, such as Marwān ibn Abī Ḥafṣah, ʿAbbās ibn al-Aḥnaf, and Abū al-ʿAtāhiyah (*ibid.* V 20, 40, 56, 82 f., 90 f., and *passim*).

There was yet another, though indirect, tie between Dhū al-Rummah and Isḥāq, namely the latter's interest in the Bedouins and their diction. For the multitalented Isḥāq, so highly praised in the sources[208] and so well understood and appreciated by Henry George Farmer for his musical genius and contributions to the theory and practice of Arabian music,[209] was also a lexicographer. Isḥāq, like many a leading scholar of his day, including the courtier Aṣmaʿī, with whom both he and his father clashed at times,[210] and Ibn al-Aʿrābī (see pp. 75 f.), whom he subsidized with a liberal pension,[211] sought out Bedouin men and women and wrote down their diction and poetry. Isḥāq composed melodies for some of their verses[212] and was accused of attributing some of his own verses to them.[213] He was even admired for his ability to imitate the verses of Dhū al-Rummah, and an instance is given in which his imitation of four verses was so perfect that none could detect it except one who had acquired and transmitted all of Dhū al-Rummah's poetry.[214]

It is interesting, though not surprising, to note that all of Dhū al-Rummah's verses that the *Aghānī* reports as having been set to music are drawn from his romantic odes or romantic introductions to odes of other categories. They are verses of intense longing for the beloved and of weeping over her deserted dwelling, that is, verses of the very type that Dhū al-Rummah's foremost fellow poets and critics believed helped to disqualify him for inclusion among the poets of first rank. Again, it is interesting to note that not only did Ibrāhīm and Isḥāq at times shed tears freely[215] but that Hārūn al-Rashīd also was quickly moved to tears by a sad verse or a pious preachment.[216]

The main *Aghānī* entries on Ibrāhīm al-Mauṣalī have yielded four selections of Dhū al-Rummah's verses that were set to music by this musician. Ibrāhīm informs us that the first verses of Dhū al-Rummah which he set to music and sang before Hārūn al-Rashīd were the following two:[217]

ألا يااسلمـِي يا دار ميّ على البلى ولا زال منهلّا بجرعائك القطـرُ
فـإن لم تكونى غير شام بقفرة تجرُّ بها الأذيال صيفيـّة كدرُ

[208] E.g. *ibid.* V 46, 54, 57, 86, 102 f., 104, 109, 115; *Fihrist*, pp. 140–42; Ibn Khallikān I 81 f. (= trans. I 183–87).

[209] See e.g. Henry George Farmer, *Historical Facts for the Arabian Musical Influence* (London, 1930) pp. 27 f., 241–44, 247–55. Farmer covers the contributions of both Ibrāhīm and Isḥāq to Arabian music in several of his numerous works on the subject. His own sustained effort to understand and interpret Arabian music to the West is particularly noteworthy.

[210] See e.g. *Aghānī* V 56, 68, 75 f., 107 f.; cf. *Marātib*, pp. 59 f.

[211] *Aghānī* V 55: كان اسحاق يجرى على ابن الاعرابي فى كل سنة تلثماية دينار (cf. *Irshād* II 217). For Isḥāq as musician and language scholar see e.g. *Fihrist*, pp. 140–42; *Nuzhah*, pp. 65, 104–6; *Inbāh* I 215–19; *Irshād* II 197–225.

[212] See e.g. *Aghānī* V 44, 56, 83, 90, 100, 120.

[213] *Ibid.* V 77.

[214] *Ibid.* V 109 f.: فلم يشك احد سمعه انه له ولا فطن لما فعل احد الا من حصا شعر ذى الرمة كله ورواه.
See Ibn Khallikān I 82 (= trans. I 185) for a reference to the *dīwān* of Isḥāq and a sample of his poetry addressed to Hārūn al-Rashīd.

[215] See e.g. *Aghānī* V 15, 17, 22, 93; p. 106 cites two verses on old age and adds كان اسحاق اذا غنى هذا الصوت ياخذ بلحيته و يبكى ; p. 82 cites two verses of Isḥāq's own poetry and melody and adds كان اسحاق اذا غناه تفيض دموعه على لحيته و يبكى احرّ بكاء .

[216] See e.g. Ibn Qutaibah, *Al-imāmah wa al-siyāsah* (Cairo, n.d.) p. 126; Abū Nuʿaim, *Ḥilyat al-awliyāʾ wa ṭabaqāt al-aṣfiyāʾ* VIII 105; Khaṭīb V 372 and XIV 8; Ibn Khallikān I 525 (= trans. II 278 f.). See also Thaʿālibī, *Khāṣṣ al-khāṣṣ* (Beirūt, 1966) pp. 83 f., which cites many of Dhū al-Rummah's lachrymose verses as among his very best poetry.

[217] *Aghānī* V 38 f. and XVI 128; note the dream element in both versions. See also Macartney, No. 29:1–2. For criticisms of the first verse see e.g. *Muwashshaḥ*, p. 185. The *Aghānī* text is not so reliable as that of Macartney, which is therefore used here for all the citations involved. Macartney gives, as a rule, numerous references to the cited verses in both lexigraphical and literary works and draws attention to significant textual variants.

The next *Aghānī* selection, cited in two versions, each with a separate melody,[218] consists of four verses from a single ode:

امنزلتى ميّه سلام عليكمـــــا   هل الازمن اللاءى مضين رواجعُ
وهل يرجع التسليم اويكسف العمى   ثلاث الأثافى والرسوم البلاقـــع
توهمتها يومـــا فقلت لصاحبى   وليس بها إلا الظباء الخواضـــع
وموشيـَّةٌ سحم الصياصى كانها   مجلَّلـــة حوٌّ عليهـــا البراقـــع

These, like Ibrāhīm's other melodies for Dhū al-Rummah's verses, were first composed and sung by him and by him alone at the court of Hārūn al-Rashīd. The third *Aghānī* selection consists of three verses from the same ode:[219]

قف العيسَ ننظر نظرة فى ديارها   فهل ذاك من دآء الصبابة نافعُ
فقال امـــا تغشى لميّه منـــزلا   من الارض إلا قلتَ هل انتِ رابع
وقلَّ الى أطلال مىّ تحيـَّـــــة   تحيّى بهـــا أو أن ترشَّ المدامـــع

It was after Dhū al-Rummah had finished reciting this very ode of 44 verses that Farazdaq pointed out to him that his doleful verses kept him from achieving first rank as a poet.[220] The fourth of Ibrāhīm's melodies indicated in the *Aghānī*[221] was composed for the following two verses:

اذا هبت الارواح من نحو جانب   به اهل مىّ هاج شوقى هبوبها
هوى تذرق العينان منه وانمـــا   هو كل نفس حيث كان حبيبها

The *Aghānī* specifies only two selections of Dhū al-Rummah's verses as having been set to music by Isḥāq. The first was composed for five verses

ذكرتُكِ إذ مرّت بنا امّ شاذن   امام المطايـــا تشرئبٌّ وتسنـــحُ
من المولَفات الرمل ادماءُ حرّة   شعاع الضحى فى متنها يتوضَّح
هى الشبه أعطافا وجيدا ومقلةً   وميـَّة أبهى بعد منهـا وامـــلـح
كان البرى والعاج عيجت متونهُ   على عـُشر نهّى به السيل أبـَطح
لئن كانت الدنيا علىّ كما أَرى   تباريح من مىّ فللموت أروح

and sung by Isḥāq and others for Ma'mūn.[222]

Though Isḥāq was in high favor with the caliphs from Hārūn al-Rashīd to Mutawakkil,[223] it was with Wāthiq (227–32/842–47) alone that he had an amicable professional rivalry, which was in marked contrast to his better known professional rivalry with Prince Ibrāhīm ibn al-Mahdī. For Wāthiq, as prince and caliph, composed numerous melodies which were committed to writing and some of which he submitted to Isḥāq for criticism and correction. He enjoyed Isḥāq's masterly performances,[224] especially those

[218] *Aghānī* V 39 and XVI 129; Macartney, No. 45:1–4; cf. *Muwashshaḥ*, pp. 172 f.

[219] *Aghānī* XVI 129; Macartney, No. 45:7–9.

[220] Jumaḥī, p. 468. See, further, p. 191 above and other references cited in n. 178.

[221] *Aghānī* XVI 130; Macartney, No. 8:8–9.

[222] See *Aghānī* V 63, which reports that Isḥāq first heard these verses recited to one man by another who introduced the set with still another verse, which has to be an earlier version of Macartney, No. 10:34. The above five verses are drawn from the same ode (Macartney, No. 10:11, 12, 15, 17, 38). See also *Aghānī* V 126 f.

[223] Isḥāq's relationship with Muʿtaṣim became strained because he began his ode in celebration of the completion of Muʿtaṣim's palace with verses bewailing the ruins of a habitation and these verses were considered ominous by the caliph and those assembled; see *Muwashshaḥ*, pp. 301 f.: فتطيّر المعتصم وتغامر الناس وعجب كيو ذهب هذا على اسحاق مع فهمه وعلمه وطول خدمته للموك . . . وخرج المعتصم الى سُر من راى وخرب القصر (cf. n. 4 on p. 110 above).

[224] Isḥāq's one professional weakness was the poor quality of his voice (see *Aghānī* V 104: لم يكن في اسحاق شى يعاب الا حلقه وكان يغلب الناس جميعا بطبعه وحذقة).

occasioned by contests among leading composers and singers of his day, several of whom Wāthiq himself instigated to the competition, as other caliphs had done before him. He made great demands on Isḥāq's energy and time, took him on his travels, and kept him for long periods at his court. On one occasion Isḥāq, lonesome for home and family, recalled two verses of Dhū al-Rummah

خليلى عوجا من صدور الرواحل   بجمهور حُزوى فابكيا فى المنازلِ
لعل انحدار الدمع يعقب راحةً   من الوجد او يشفى نجىَّ البلابـلَ

which he had heard recited by a Bedouin and for which first he and then Wāthiq had composed melodies, though that of the caliph was for the second verse only.[225]

Still other verses of Dhū al-Rummah set to music by Ibrāhīm al-Mauṣalī and his son Isḥāq and by other musicians of their day are likely to be met with in the sources, and such verses are just as likely to be of the same category as those cited above. Be that as it may, we have learned that Bedouins, poets, scholars, musicians, and caliphs helped to keep Dhū al-Rummah's poetry, both oral and written, in circulation throughout the second/eighth century. Thus, in turn, it was possible for third/ninth-century compilers and commentators such as Abū al-ʿAbbās Muḥammad ibn al-Ḥasan al-Aḥwal and Sukkarī to pay tribute to Dhū al-Rummah by preserving his poetry for posterity.

EARLY EDITIONS OF DHŪ AL-RUMMAH'S POETRY

The numerous references to poetry manuscripts possessed or generated by Umayyad scholars, poets, and caliphs already cited in the present volume came as no surprise to me. Particularly instructive are the several dramatic episodes in which Akhṭal, Jarīr, and Farazdaq are reported as writing down or dictating some of their longer odes, such as Akhṭal's ode, written on the order of ʿAbd al-Malik, in praise of Ḥajjāj ibn Yūsuf and Jarīr's writing and dictating of his satire on Rāʿī and the contemporary manuscripts of the *naqāʾiḍ* of Jarīr and of Farazdaq. Thus, irrespective of Dhū al-Rummah's own writing ability, I see no reason to question his desire, a desire common to these his older contemporaries and associates, to preserve his own poetry accurately and in writing. And, indeed, this desire is indicated in a passage[226] which reports his explicit instructions to ʿĪsā ibn ʿUmar:

قال ذو الرمة لعيسى بن عمر اكتب شعرى فالكتاب احب الى من الحفظ لان الاعرابى ينسى الكلمة وقد سهر في طلبها ليلة فيضع فى موضعها كلمة فى وزنها ثم ينشدها الناس والكتاب لا ينسى ولايبدل كلام بكلام

One of Dhū al-Rummah's younger contemporaries, the anthologist Mufaḍḍal ibn Muḥammad al-Ḍabbī, gave evidence of the increasing production and availability of poetry manuscripts from which one could select what he considered best for study and for memorizing,[227] as he himself did in his famed *Mufaḍḍalīyāt*. One would expect that the family, admirers, and professional direct transmitters of Dhū al-Rummah attempted to keep his poetry in circulation by word of mouth or in writing or by a combination of both methods. His brother Masʿūd probably did so in one or another of these ways, and after Dhū al-Rummah's death Mayya, who had memorized his numerous odes or parts of odes on his love for

[225] See e.g. *Aghānī* V 57 f., 60, 63 f., 83 f., 91–97 and VIII 162–65 for Isḥāq and Wāthiq; for the verses see *Aghānī* V 96 f. and Macartney, No. 66:1–2. Cf. p. 193 above, with n. 195).

[226] Jāḥiẓ, *Ḥayawān* I 41. ʿ*Umdah* II 194 omits any reference to Jāḥiẓ but repeats this passage and attributes it erroneously to a Mūsā ibn ʿAmr. See pp. 170 f. above for Dhū al-Rummah as one among other literate poets.

[227] *Muwashshaḥ*, p. 358: اخبرنا محمد بن الحسين ابن دريد قال اخبرنا ابو حاتم عن ابي زيد قال سمعت المفضل يقول ما لم يكن من الشعر حسنا عينا فبطون الصحف احمل لموونته من صدور عقلاء الرجال. Note the direct unbroken strong *isnād* which traces back through Ibn Duraid to Abū Ḥātim (al-Sijistānī) to Abū Zaid (al-Anṣārī), who heard the statement from Mufaḍḍal himself. ʿ*Uyūn* II 130 reports Yaḥyā ibn Khālid al-Barmakī as saying: الناس يكتبون احسن ما يسمعون ويحفظون احسن ما يكتبون ويحدثون باحسن ما يحفظون.

her, dictated many of them at length to Abū al-Muhalhil (see p. 183). But credit for the first-known formal edition of Dhū al-Rummah's poetry belongs to one of his direct transmitters, the eloquent Muntajiʿ ibn Nabhān, who was also a source of linguistic and biographical materials transmitted to the ever receptive Abū ʿAmr ibn al-ʿAlāʾ, Aṣmaʿī, and Abū ʿUbaidah.[228] A second direct transmitter, Aswad ibn Ḍubʿān (or Ḍibʿān), transmitted Dhū al-Rummah's verses to Ibrāhīm ibn Mundhir,[229] who seems at one time to have been secretary to Ibn Munādhir, poet, critic, and defender of early and contemporary Islāmic poetry (see pp. 122 and 147). We know of at least two other direct transmitters of Dhū al-Rummah's poetry, the faithful ʿIṣmah ibn Mālik and Ṣāliḥ ibn Sulaimān.[230] To the collections, written or oral, of these several direct transmitters should be added that of Abū ʿAmr ibn al-ʿAlāʾ, the foremost admirer of Dhū al-Rummah. The collecting and editing of the output of individual poets, with or without commentary, progressed rapidly in the second half of the second/eighth century, as amply illustrated by the activities of Abū ʿAmr al-Shaibānī, Abū ʿUbaidah, and Aṣmaʿī. I have so far found no clear-cut statement in the sources to the effect that Aṣmaʿī collected, edited, transmitted, or commented on the poetry of Dhū al-Rummah.[231] But indirect evidence strongly implies that he did all of these at one time or another for the greater part if not for the whole of the poet's output. He was, to begin with, fully aware of Abū ʿAmr ibn al-ʿAlāʾ's high esteem for Dhū al-Rummah's poetry, and though he himself did not rank that poet among the *fuḥūl* he did nevertheless consider him, as a true Bedouin, to be authoritative in his knowledge and use of the language. Again, Aṣmaʿī's statement that had he met Dhū al-Rummah he would have advised him to destroy most of his poetry implies that he had the whole *dīwān* on which to base his judgment.[232] Furthermore, Aṣmaʿī's interest in and comments on the poet's *dīwān* are reflected in the Macartney edition in citations credited to Aṣmaʿī directly[233] or through his most trusted pupil and transmitter, Abū Naṣr Aḥmad ibn Ḥātim al-Bāhilī (see pp. 105 f. above), who in turn provided some of his own comments.[234] While most of these citations are introduced with the familiar *qāla* and *rawā*, the comment on one verse[235] reads *wa fī riwāyat al-Aṣmaʿī* and is supplemented with *wa qāla Abū ʿAmr*, which in this instance has to refer to the Baṣran Abū ʿAmr ibn al-ʿAlāʾ, Aṣmaʿī's avowed and revered mentor, rather than the Kūfan Abū ʿAmr al-Shaibānī as Macartney assumed for this and all other references to an Abū ʿAmr who is not further identified. On the strength of this assumption Macartney wrote: "In fact, I think we may conclude that the original text was that of al Aṣmaʿî and that the glosses were largely based upon the commentary of ash-Shaibânî, and finally, that the account given in the colophon of Const. of the provenance of the text is substantially worthy of belief."[236] I am in agreement with Macartney's view of

[228] ʿ*Iqd* V 233; *Muwashshaḥ*, p. 174; Bevan I 487; *Mufaḍḍalīyāt* I 327.

[229] See *Aghānī* XVIII 24 and Macartney, pp. vii f. and xiii, and note the variant spelling of the name اسود بن ضبعان. Still another transmitter of Dhū al-Rummah about whose name there is some confusion is mentioned in Macartney, No. 27:53–54.

[230] *Aghānī* XVI 112 and 124. See p. 190 above for the role of one of Dhū al-Rummah's transmitters.

[231] The *Fihrist* references to both Dhū al-Rummah and Aṣmaʿī do not mention the latter in respect to such activities. *Inbāh* II 202 f. lists the works of Aṣmaʿī but is silent on this point, as is the editor's considerable supplementation of the already long list of Aṣmaʿī's works.

[232] See pp. 192 f. for Aṣmaʿī as a critic of Dhū al-Rummah's poetry.

[233] Macartney does not index either Aṣmaʿī or Abū ʿAmr al-Shaibānī in full. The following references for Aṣmaʿī's comments concentrate on ode No. 57, to which our papyrus text belongs, with supplementary references for the other odes: Macartney, No. 57:20, 21, 24, 44, 73, 91, and 93, and Nos. 1:5, 78, and 97, 10:27 and 54, 17:26, 21:3, 5, and 23, 29:23, 30:45, 75:81, 78:4 and 35, 81:43.

[234] See *ibid.* Nos. 35:32 and 57:31, 40, 67. Macartney, following some sources, accepted Abū Naṣr as the nephew and son-in-law of Aṣmaʿī and a transmitter from Abū ʿAmr al-Shaibānī and thence was misled to accept the comments as those of Abū ʿAmr al-Shaibānī (*ibid.* pp. vii, xii). That this Abū Naṣr was Aṣmaʿī's nephew is emphatically denied by other sources; see e.g. *Marātib*, p. 82, which is reproduced in *Muzhir* II 408: زعموا هو ابن اخت الاصمعى وليس هذا بثبت رايت جعفر بن محمد ينكره كان اثبت من عبد الرحمن (بن اخى الا صمعى) واسن.

[235] Macartney, No. 1:78.

[236] See *ibid.* p. vii, where Abū ʿAmr ibn al-ʿAlāʾ is not even mentioned.

the very informative colophon of the Constantinople manuscript with its multiple *isnād*'s but not with his statement that the glosses were largely based on Shaibānī's commentary. It is known that when Baṣrans cited simply Abū ʿAmr with no further identification they invariably meant the Baṣran Abū ʿAmr ibn al-ʿAlāʾ but when they referred to the Kūfan Abū ʿAmr they identified him as Abū ʿAmr al-Shaibānī.[237] I therefore scanned Macartney's edition of the *Dīwān* for all references to Abū ʿAmr and found first that only one reference specifies Abū ʿAmr al-Shaibānī. It is drawn from the Ṣanʿā' manuscript of the Ambrosian Library and from its wording could well be not the main comment but a confirmatory one.[238] The second and only other reference that Macartney indexed specifically under Abū ʿAmr al-Shaibānī turned out to be simply Abū ʿAmr[239] and from its context in two other verses of the same ode points rather to Abū ʿAmr ibn al-ʿAlāʾ, since the comment on each quotes Aṣmaʿī[240] and the second in its wording وغير الاصمعى يقول clearly indicates that the initial comment was that of Aṣmaʿī. All the other references to Abū ʿAmr occur likewise in odes in which Aṣmaʿī also is mentioned.[241] But the ode from which our papyrus text is drawn is even more illuminating since the comments on it draw repeatedly on Abū ʿAmr,[242] Aṣmaʿī,[243] and Abū Naṣr Aḥmad ibn Ḥātim,[244] all introduced with either *qāla* or *rawā*, and in one instance simply on the Baṣrans.[245] In other words, the comments on this particular ode can be said to be drawn mainly from Baṣran sources best represented by these three leading and closely associated scholar-transmitters.

Our papyrus, to judge by its script and orthography, dates from the third/ninth century. There is, however, no way of knowing whether the text itself represents a third- or a second-century version, perhaps stemming initially from Abū ʿAmr ibn al-ʿAlāʾ, who had direct and close contact with Dhū al-Rummah himself (see p. 191). Unfortunately, neither Abū ʿAmr nor Aṣmaʿī specifies any direct transmitter as his source. But there is indirect evidence that either or both of these scholars could have received the text of Dhū al-Rummah's poetry from one of his leading direct transmitters, namely Muntajiʿ ibn Nabhān, who is cited by both Abū ʿAmr[246] and Aṣmaʿī[247] as eloquent and knowledgeable.

We are on firmer ground in respect to Muntajiʿ's close relationship with Abū ʿUbaidah, Aṣmaʿī's leading Baṣran rival for professional recognition and court patronage. Nadīm, in a section that reports Sukkarī's numerous editions of pre-Islāmic and early Islāmic poetry,[248] mentions Abū ʿUbaidah in connection with Muntajiʿ's edition of Dhū al-Rummah's poetry in the following brief statement: و(عمعله) المتجع بن نبهان روى عنه ابو عبيده.[249] Read out of context the second sentence could be misinterpreted to mean that Abū ʿUbaidah transmitted, for the most part, only general information from Muntajiʿ. But the statement must be read in the light of Nadīm's specific purpose and terminology and of his

[237] This early manner of distinguishing between the two Abū ʿAmr's soon gained general currency among scholars, as repeatedly illustrated in the *Fihrist* (pp. 157 f.) list of transmitters and editors of poetry.

[238] See Macartney, No. 52:29, footnote: كذالك يقول ابو عمرو الشيبانى.

[239] See *ibid.* No. 10:16.

[240] See *ibid.* No. 10:27 and 54, footnotes.

[241] See *ibid.* No. 1:78, which cites both Abū ʿAmr and Aṣmaʿī, and No. 29, which cites Abū ʿAmr alone in verses 6, 17, 25, and 29 and Aṣmaʿī in verse 23.

[242] *Ibid.* No. 57:21, 35, 50, 64.

[243] *Ibid.* No. 57:20, 21, 24, 44, 73, 91, 93.

[244] *Ibid.* No. 57:31, 40, 67.

[245] *Ibid.* No. 57:39: واهل البصرة يقولون.

[246] *Majālis al-ʿulamāʾ*, pp. 2–4, 7; Zubaidī, pp. 38 f.; *Amālī* III 40; *Inbāh* III 323; *Muzhir* II 278.

[247] *Shiʿr*, p. 428; *ʿIqd* II 289; Zubaidī, p. 175; *Mufaḍḍalīyāt* I 391.

[248] *Fihrist*, pp. 157 f.

[249] *Ibid.* p. 158, lines 21–22.

overly abbreviated style for the entire section. Nadīm specifies a dual purpose, namely "to list the names of poets whose poetry Sukkarī "did" (*'amil*) and at the same time to mention also others who "did" the same poetry."[250] However, in the main body of this section he mentions also those who transmitted (*rawā*) a given poet's output. Again his reference to Dhū al-Rummah's poetry starts briefly with ذو الرمة عمله جماعة ورووه.[251] He mentions the progressively exhaustive editions of Abū al-'Abbās Muḥammad ibn al-Ḥasan al-Aḥwal and Sukkarī ahead of the edition of the earlier Muntaji'. I therefore conclude that the term *rawā* in the first passage quoted above is either a scribal or a typographical error and that the second sentence of the statement should read ورواه عنه ابو عبيده. For it would seem strange indeed if a scholar of the caliber and reputation of Abū 'Ubaidah, whose house was said to contain *dīwān al-'Arab*,[252] who had done (*'amil*) the *naqā'iḍ* of Jarīr and Farazdaq (see p. 160), and who was an avowed admirer of Dhū al-Rummah and his poetry (see pp. 192 f.), had overlooked the edition of that poet's best known direct transmitter.

Copies of Muntaji''s edition could have reached Hārūn al-Rashīd and his court musicians Ibrāhīm al-Mauṣalī and his son Isḥāq, all three well known as great admirers of Dhū al-Rummah's poetry, through either Aṣma'ī or Abū 'Ubaidah or through both of these Baṣran scholars. We know that Ibrāhīm and Isḥāq were interested in the life of Dhū al-Rummah and that Isḥāq and his son Ḥammād each wrote a monograph titled *Akhbār Dhī al-Rummah* (see pp. 175 f.). Furthermore, we know that Isḥāq was himself a poet, that he could and did imitate Dhū al-Rummah's poetry expertly (see p. 195) and that though he drew for literary materials on both Aṣma'ī and Abū 'Ubaidah (see p. 194, n. 201) he preferred the company of the latter. We read further that it was Isḥāq who was instrumental in bringing the Baṣran Abū 'Ubaidah to the court at Baghdād. Angered at Aṣma'ī's arrogance and his miserliness with his literary materials, Isḥāq convinced the wazir Faḍl ibn al-Rabī' of the undesirability of these qualities and at the same time praised Abū 'Ubaidah's extensive and profound knowledge of all the sources of the Arabs and his generosity with his materials. Isḥāq's enthusiastic recommendation induced Faḍl ibn al-Rabī' to invite Abū 'Ubaidah, in 188/804, to Baghdād and the court of Hārūn al-Rashīd.[253]

In view of the considerable evidence of a close relationship between Abū 'Ubaidah and Isḥāq, both prolific authors with sizable libraries[254] and both great admirers of Dhū al-Rummah's poetry, it seems highly probable that Isḥāq sought and received a copy of Abū 'Ubaidah's transmission of Muntaji''s edition of Dhū al-Rummah's poetry.

The several second/eighth-century collections and transmissions of Dhū al-Rummah's poetry must have been available for the most part to the third/ninth-century editor Abū al-'Abbās Muḥammad ibn

[250] *Ibid.* p. 157: واذكر فى هذا الموضع ايضا من عمل ما عمله السكرى.

[251] See *ibid.* p. 158, lines 20–23, for the full entry.

[252] Zubaidī, p. 195: قد اجتمع له علم الاسلام والجاهليه وكان ديوان العرب فى بيته.

For long lists of Abū 'Ubaidah's own works see e.g. *Fihrist*, pp. 53 f.; *Irshād* VII 168–70; *Inbāh* III 285–87. Abū 'Ubaidah's son 'Abd Allāh dictated poetry for a fee and charged 30 dinars for dictating the poetry of Kuthaiyir (*Aghānī* VIII 28). One of Abū 'Ubaidah's several pupil-secretaries, 'Alī ibn al-Mughīrah al-Athram, who is credited with transmitting all the works of both Abū 'Ubaidah and Aṣma'ī, was also a professional bookseller (see e.g. *Irshād* V 421 f. and VII 304; *Inbāh* II 319 f.).

[253] *Aghānī* V 107 f. and *Irshād* VII 166 give full accounts of these events with an *isnād* that traces back to Isḥāq ibn Ibrāhīm al-Mauṣalī. For briefer references to some of these events see e.g. Jāḥiẓ, *Bayān* I 331; Khaṭīb XIII 253 f.; *Inbāh* III 277 f.

[254] For the libraries of Aṣma'ī and Isḥāq see e.g. *Fihrist*, pp. 55 f. and 141 f., and Kūrkīs 'Awwād, *Khazā'in al-kutub al-qadīmah fī al-'Irāq*, pp. 194–96; for that of Abū 'Ubaidah see *Fihrist*, pp. 53 f., and Zubaidī, p. 195. For libraries of other scholars of the Umayyad and early 'Abbāsid periods see Kūrkīs 'Awwād, *op. cit.* pp. 191–96.

al-Ḥasan al-Aḥwal, whose edition drew on the previous transmissions.[255] Abū al-ʿAbbās al-Aḥwal, a language scholar and also a professional copyist, flourished in the mid-third/mid-ninth century.[256] One of his younger transmitters, the scholar and poet Ibrāhīm ibn Muḥammad, better known as Nifṭawaih (d. 323/935), reported that Abū al-ʿAbbās al-Aḥwal collected (*jamaʿ*)[257] the poetry of 120 poets and that he, Nifṭawaih, did (*ʿamil*) the poetry of fifty poets,[258] including the *naqāʾiḍ* of Jarīr and Farazdaq and the poetry of Dhū al-Rummah, all of which he memorized.[259]

The most exhaustive edition of Dhū al-Rummah's poetry reported by Nadīm is that of Sukkarī, the outstanding transmitter and editor of literary works and especially of poetry.[260] Though listed among the Baṣran philologists and considered the foremost transmitter from Baṣran scholars,[261] he did not neglect the Kūfans, especially those whose transmission derived initially from Baṣran scholars. His transmission of the *naqāʾiḍ* of Jarīr and Farazdaq traces back to the Baṣran Abū ʿUbaidah, in one version through the Kūfan Muḥammad ibn Ḥabīb and in another version through the Kūfan Saʿdān ibn al-Mubārak (see p. 160). Sukkarī's main contribution, like that of ʿAlī ibn ʿAbd Allāh al-Ṭūsī (see p. 158), was thought by some to be not that of a ranking philologist but that of a transmitter from both Baṣran and Kūfan scholars.[262] Apart from his own compositions, Sukkarī's primary function was that of editor and publisher of the works of many scholars and the output of many poets,[263] much of which survived in his accurate handwriting to Nadīm's day.[264]

The text of our third/ninth-century papyrus could represent the transmission or an edition of any one of the scholars considered above. It is probably from either a copy of Abū ʿUbaidah's transmission or the edition of either Abū al-ʿAbbās al-Aḥwal or Sukkarī. In any case, the sources give evidence of continuous written transmission of Dhū al-Rummah's poetry from his own time onward, as was the case with the poetry of his ranking contemporaries Akhṭal, Jarīr, and Farazdaq and several of their contemporaries whose poetry was transmitted by Abū ʿAmr ibn al-ʿAlāʾ.[265]

255 See *Fihrist*, pp. 72 and 158: عمله ابو العباس محمد بن الحسن الاحول من جميع الروّايات. *Fihrist*, p. 158, lines 21–23, mentions ahead of the edition of Muntajiʿ one of Hilāl ibn Mayyās, who is not further identified in our sources. There is, however, a bare possibility that he is Hilāl al-Ḍabbī, a contemporary of Jarīr (see *Aghānī* VII 65). The *Fihrist* passage concludes with four transmitters: والليث بن ضمّام يرويه عن ابن المرضى والقاسم بن قاسم يرويه عن ابى جهمة العدوى. Of the four, only the last named is further identified in the sources. He is the Kūfan poet Abū Juhmah al-Mutawakkil ibn ʿAbd Allāh al-Laithī, who eulogized the caliph Muʿāwiyah and his son Yazīd (*Aghānī* XI 39–44; *Muʿjam al-shuʿarāʾ*, pp. 109 f.). The aged Abū Juhmah could have met the youthful Dhū al-Rummah during one of the latter's frequent visits to Kūfah (*Aghānī* XVI 112: كان ذو الرمة كثيرا ما ياتى الحضر فيقيم بالكوفة والبصرة). No meeting of these two poets is reported in the earlier sources on hand, but *Khizānah* I 379 does actually report that Abū Juhmah heard Dhū al-Rummah when he classified his odes in three categories (see p. 190 above).

Since the above-mentioned four transmitters are named in chronological order, the three still unidentified would have to be younger contemporaries of either Abū Juhmah or Muntajiʿ, i.e., 2nd-century men whose transmission along with that of Muntajiʿ among others (see pp. 194 f. above) contributed to the more exhaustive editions of the 3rd/9th century.

256 For his biographical entries see e.g. Khaṭīb II 185; *Irshād* VI 482 f.; *Inbāh* III 191 f.; *Bughyah*, p. 33.

257 See Vol. I 21 f. for the usage of the verb *jamaʿ* and its derivatives.

258 *Irshād* VI 482 f.

259 Zubaidī, p. 172; *Inbāh* I 178. For Nifṭawaih's biographical entries see e.g. *Fihrist*, pp. 81 f.; Khaṭīb VI 159–62; *Irshād* I 307–15; *Inbāh* I 176–82.

260 For biographical entries see e.g. Zubaidī, p. 200; *Fihrist*, pp. 78, 157 f.; Khaṭīb VII 296 f.; *Irshād* III 62–64; *Inbāh* I 291–94.

261 *Nuzhah*, p. 129.

262 اما الطوسى والسكرى فانهما راويان وليس امامين وقد رويا عن ابى حاتم والرياشى وغيرهما من علماء البصريين وكان السكرى كثير الشكوك (*Marātib*, p. 92). During scholarly sessions Sukkarī used books regularly in contrast to Thaʿlab, who relied on his memory (*Irshād* II 134).

263 انتشر عنه من كتب الادب ما لم ينتشر عن احد من نضرائه (*Irshād* III 62). انتشر عنه من كتب الادب شى كثير (Khaṭīb VII 296); See also *Inbāh* I 291.

264 See *Fihrist*, pp. 55, 69, 78, 100, 106, 145, 157, 159, 160. See also *Inbāh* I 292.

265 See *Fihrist*, p. 158.

After what has been learned from the studies presented in Volumes I and II of the widespread use of writing in early Islām from about the mid-first century onward in the steadily developing fields of Qur'ānic studies, Tradition, and history and also of the emergence and rapid growth of the book market and of court and private libraries,[266] it is not at all surprising to find the same accelerated developments in the fields of language and literature. For lexicography and grammar were basic to both the religious and the secular fields. Literature proper, whether prose or poetry, served also to inform and entertain,[267] particularly poetry since it was still considered by scholar and ruler alike as the *dīwān al-ʿArab*. Furthermore, the objectives, attitudes, and interactions of rival Umayyad poets, outstanding linguistic scholars, and demanding but generous royal and other powerful patrons combined to yield genuinely early Arab modes of literary criticism. Poets and critics alike placed uneven emphasis on linguistic elements, rhetoric, and aesthetics, features that were incorporated later, under the ʿAbbāsids, into a more heterogeneous, analytical, and formal theory of poetics.

[266] See Vols. I 3 f., 20, 23–25, 29 and II 44, 46 f. (esp. n. 133), 49–57, 69, 126 f., 181 f., 229.
[267] See Vol. I 10, 14–19.

INDEX

PLATES

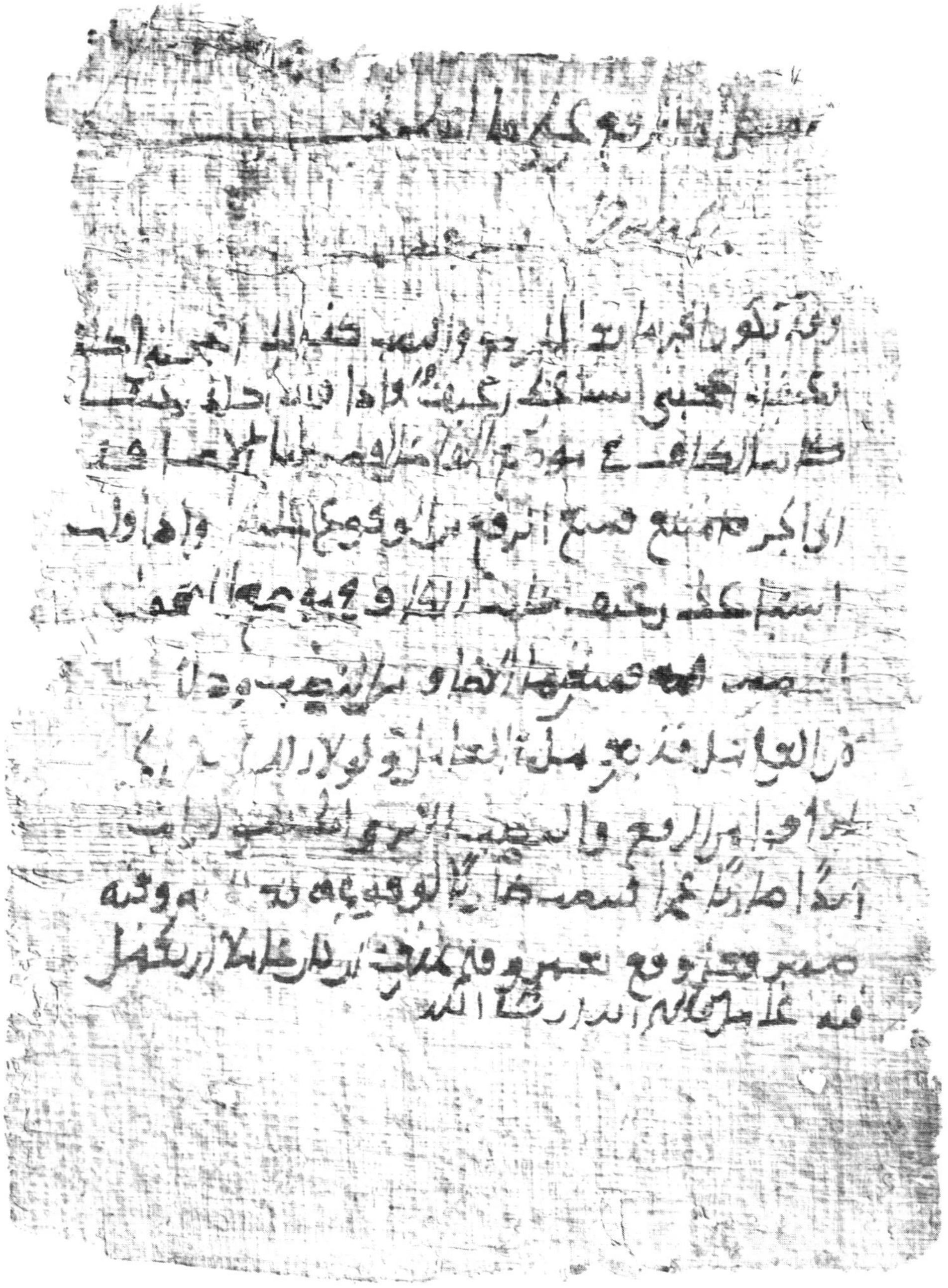

Document 1

RECTO

VERSO

DOCUMENT 2

Courtesy of the Österreichische Nationalbibliothek, Wien

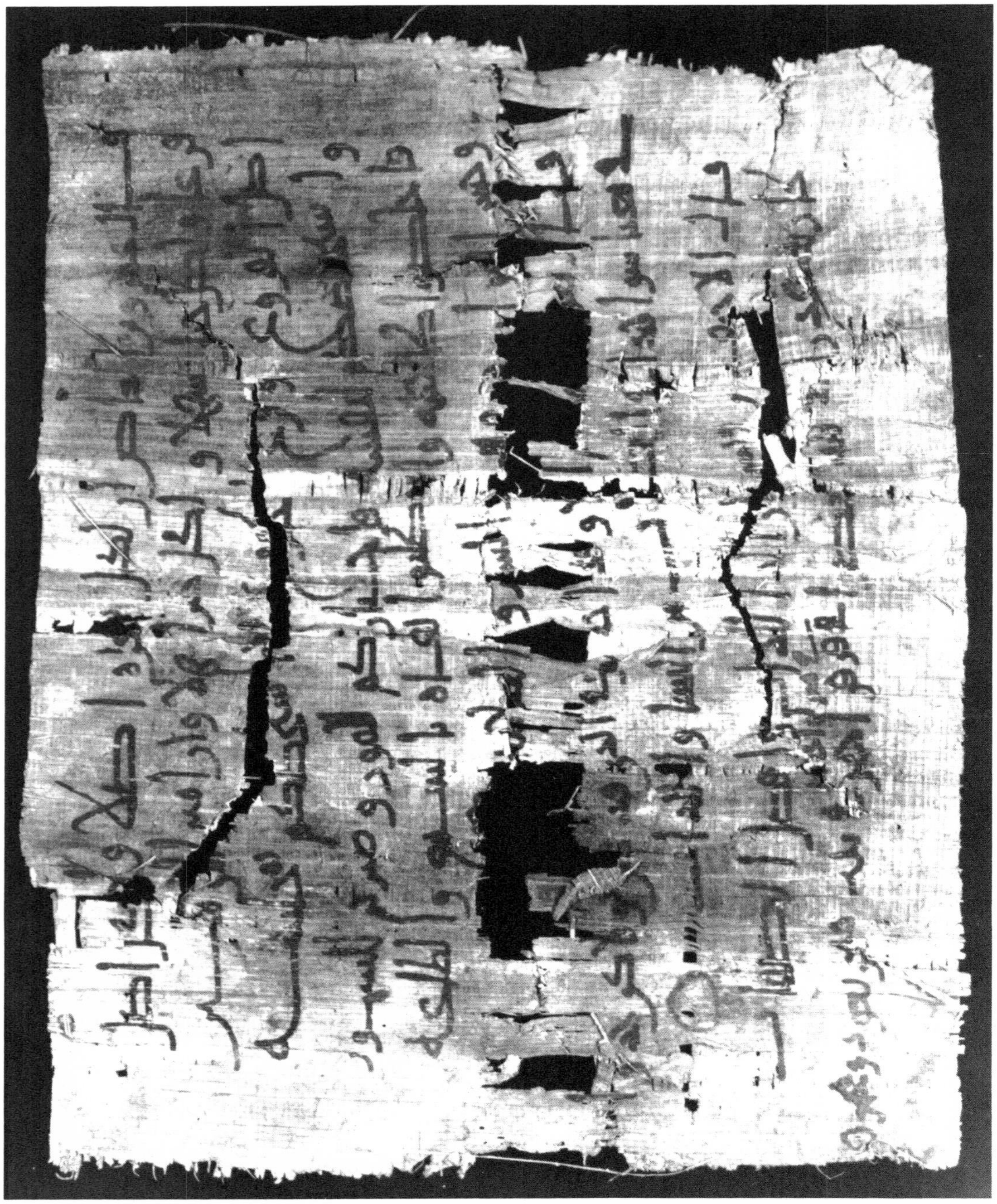

RECTO

DOCUMENT 3

Courtesy of the Österreichische Nationalbibliothek, Wien

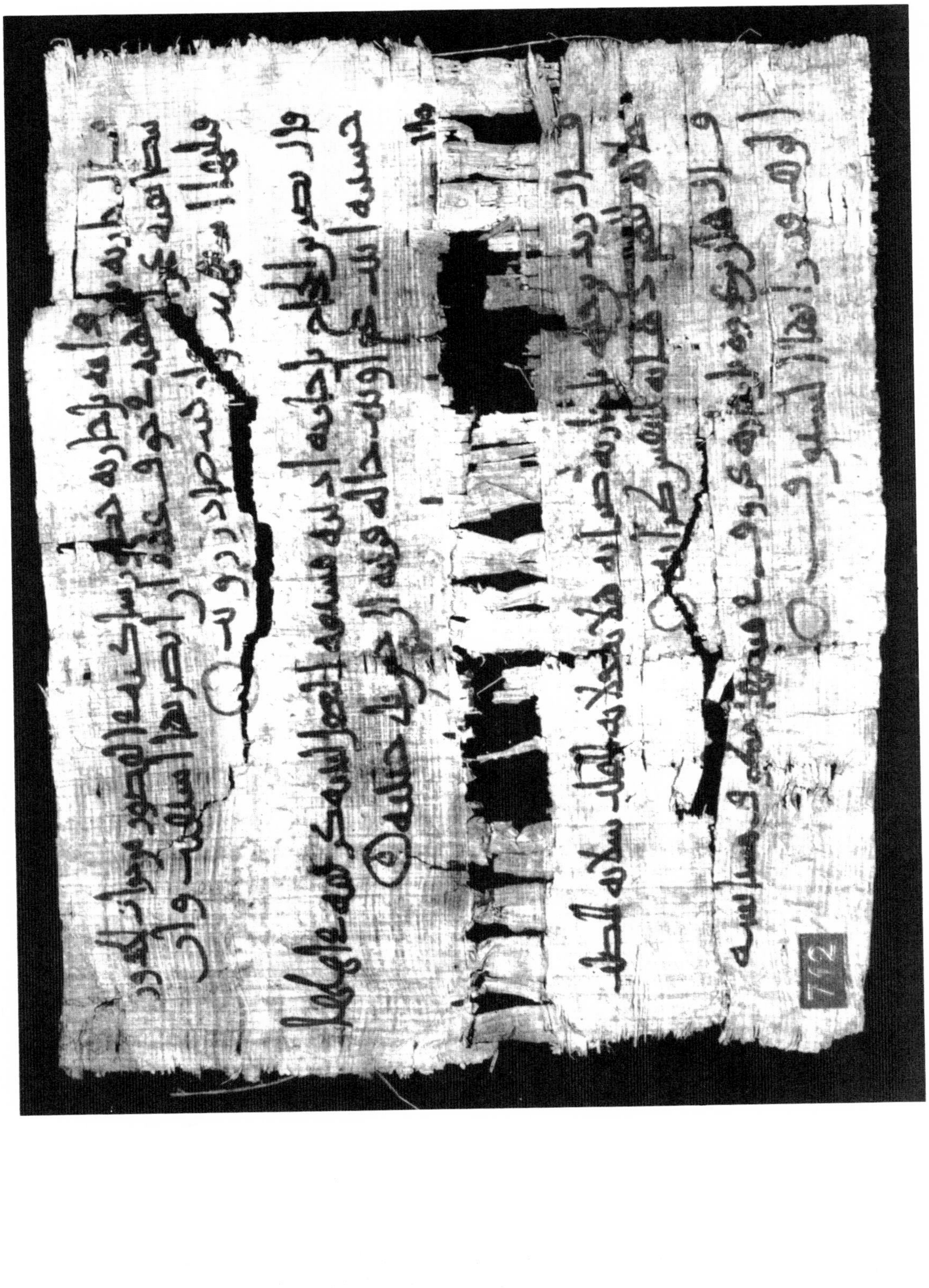

VERSO

DOCUMENT 3

Courtesy of the Österreichische Nationalbibliothek, Wien

PLATE 5

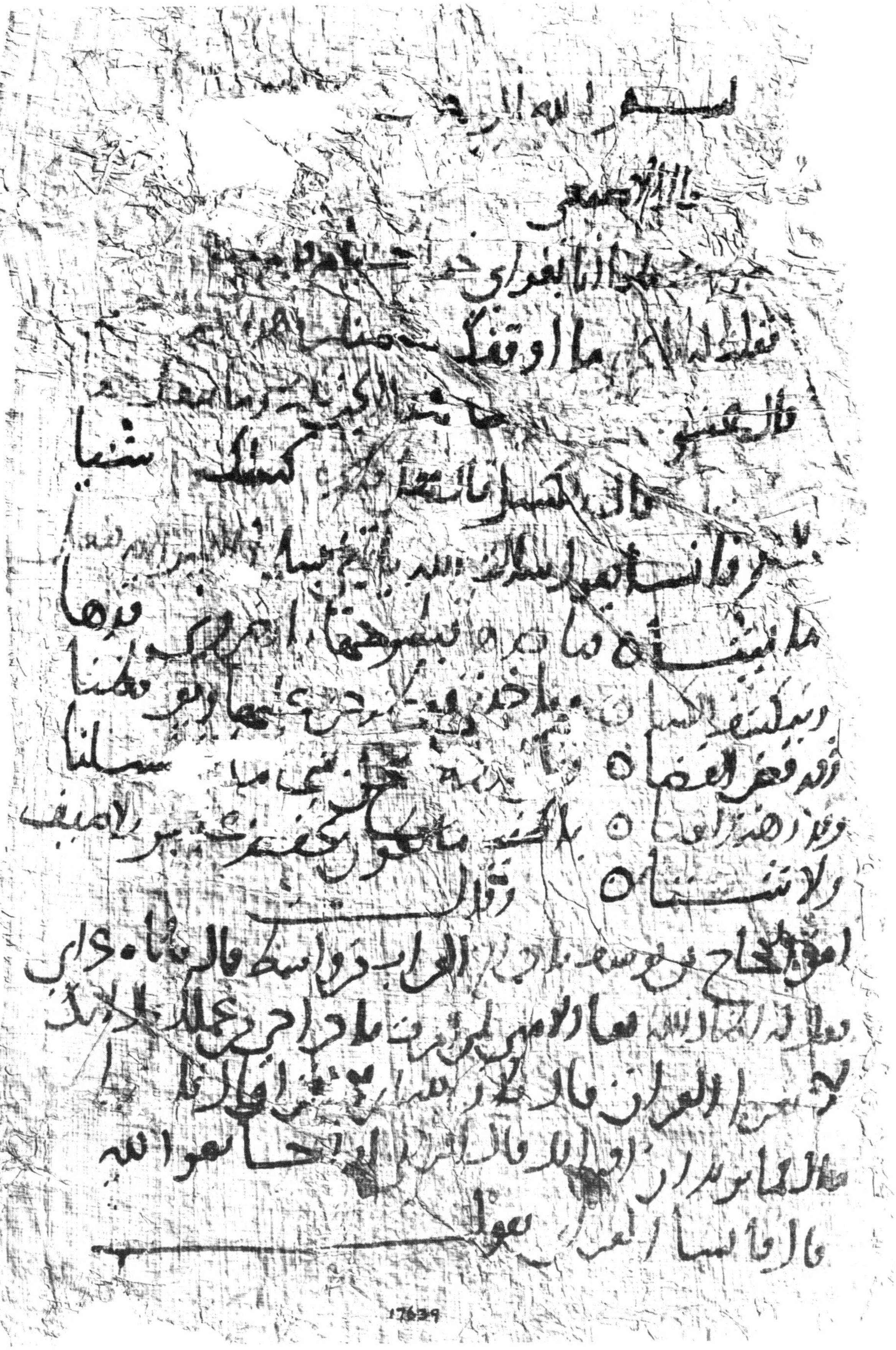

Document 4

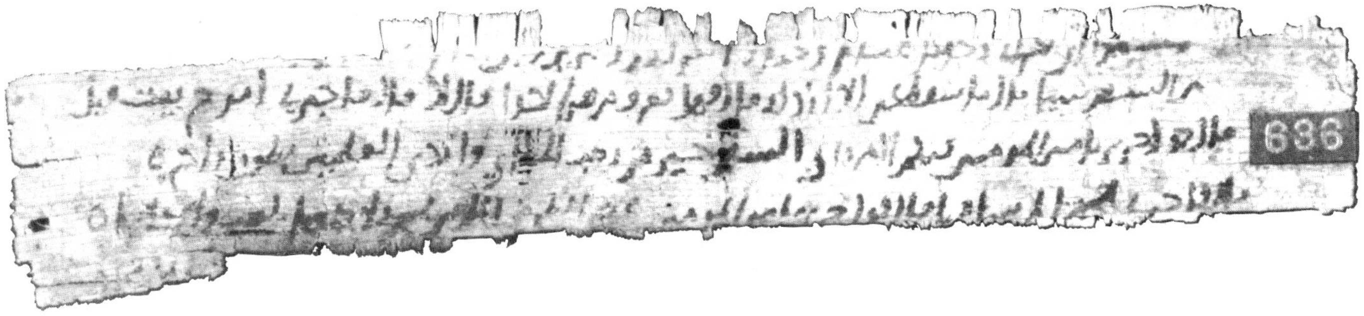

DOCUMENT 5

Courtesy of the Österreichische Nationalbibliothek, Wien

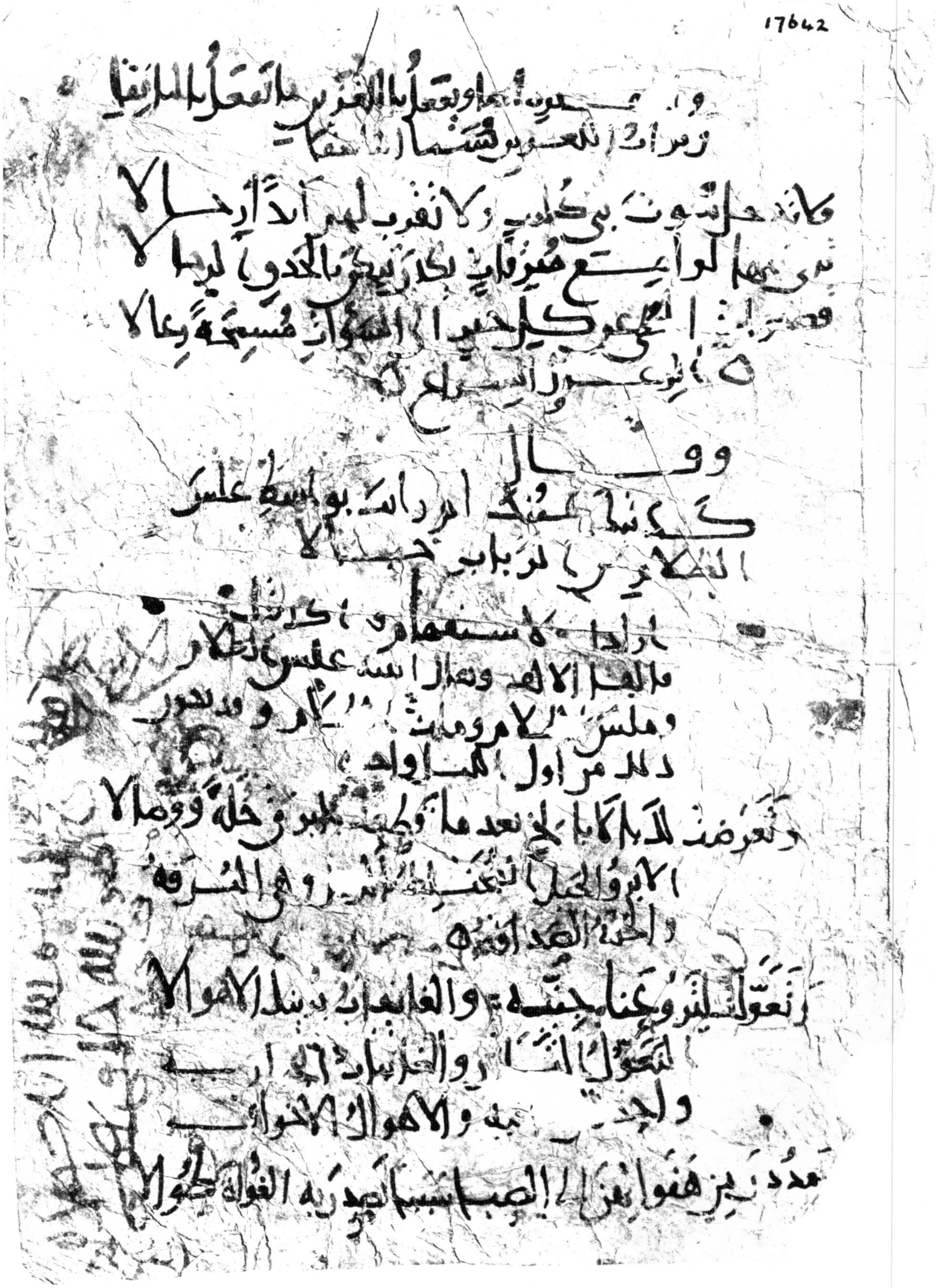

RECTO

Document 6

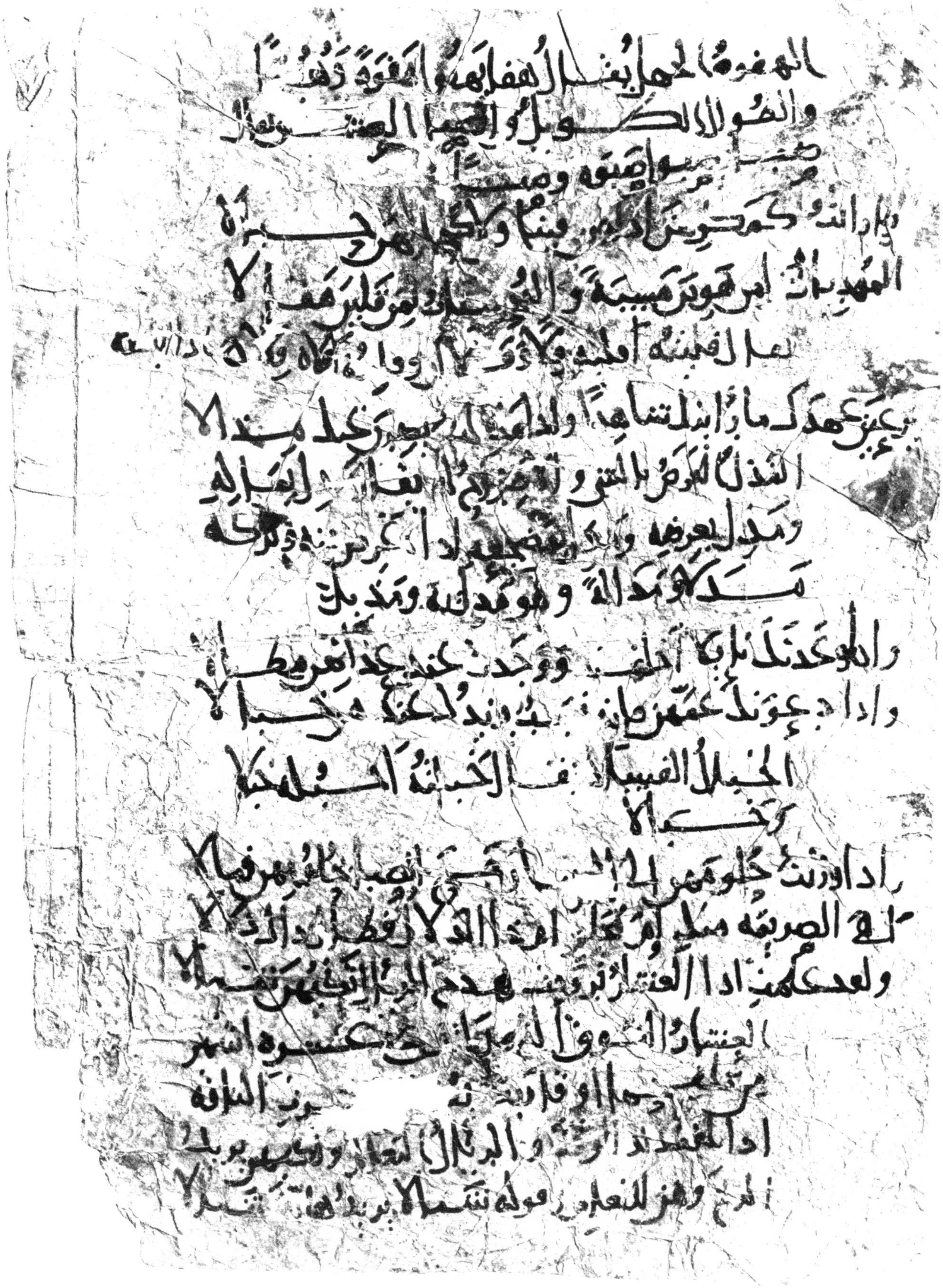

VERSO

Document 6

PAGE 4

PLATE 10

PAGE 3

Document 7

Courtesy of the University Library, University of Michigan, Ann Arbor

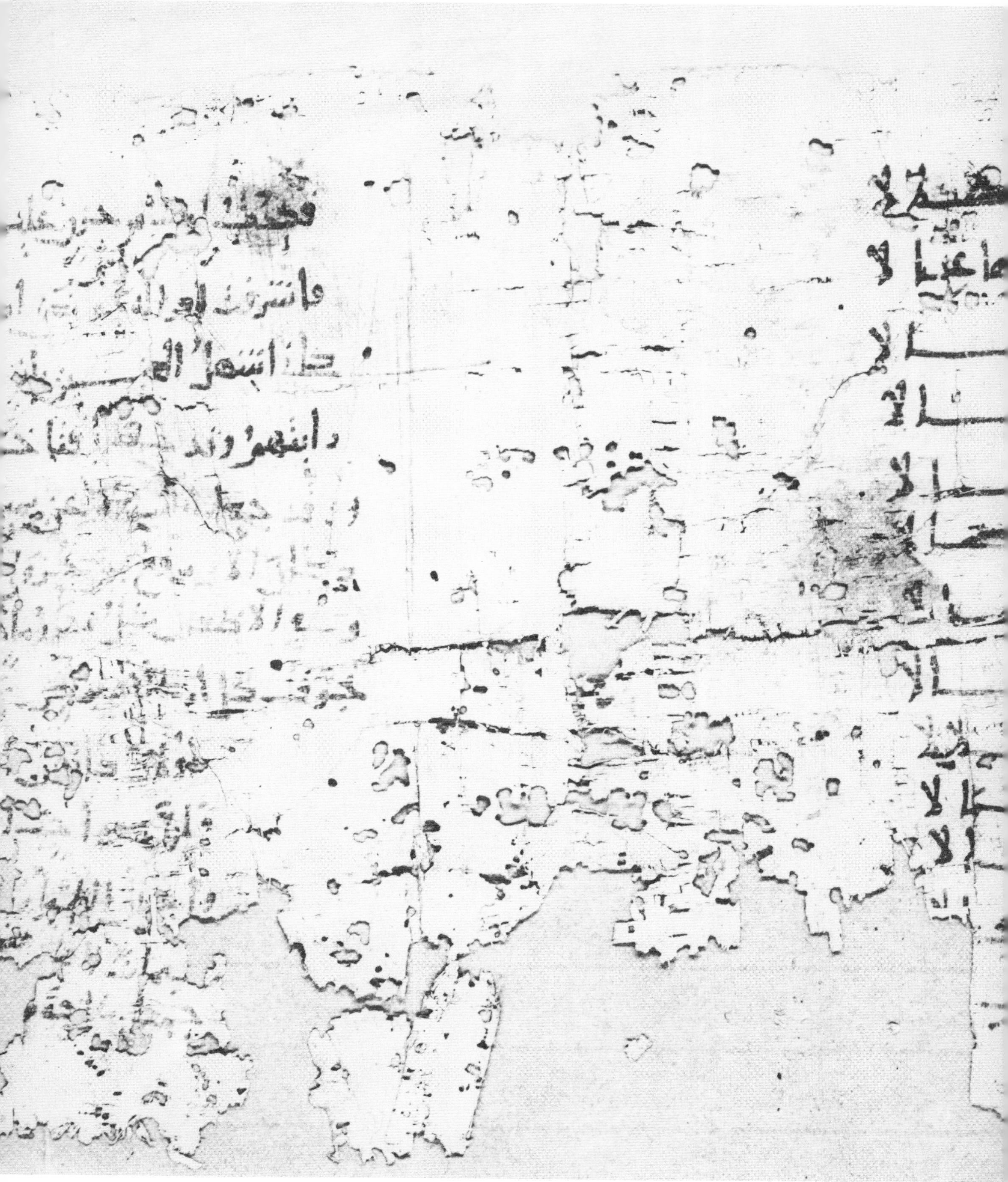

DOCUMENT 7

Courtesy of the University Library, University of Michigan, Ann Arbor

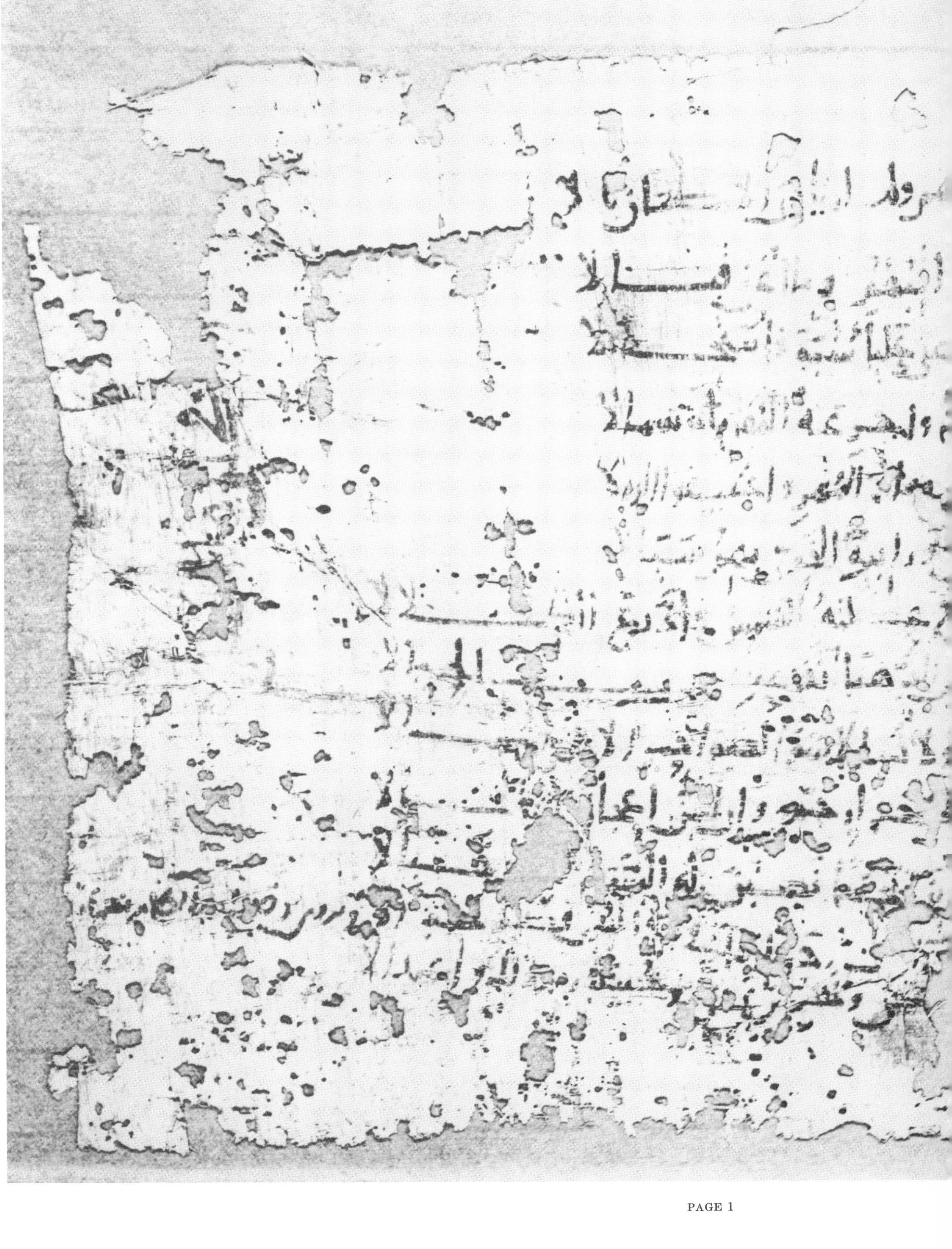

PAGE 1

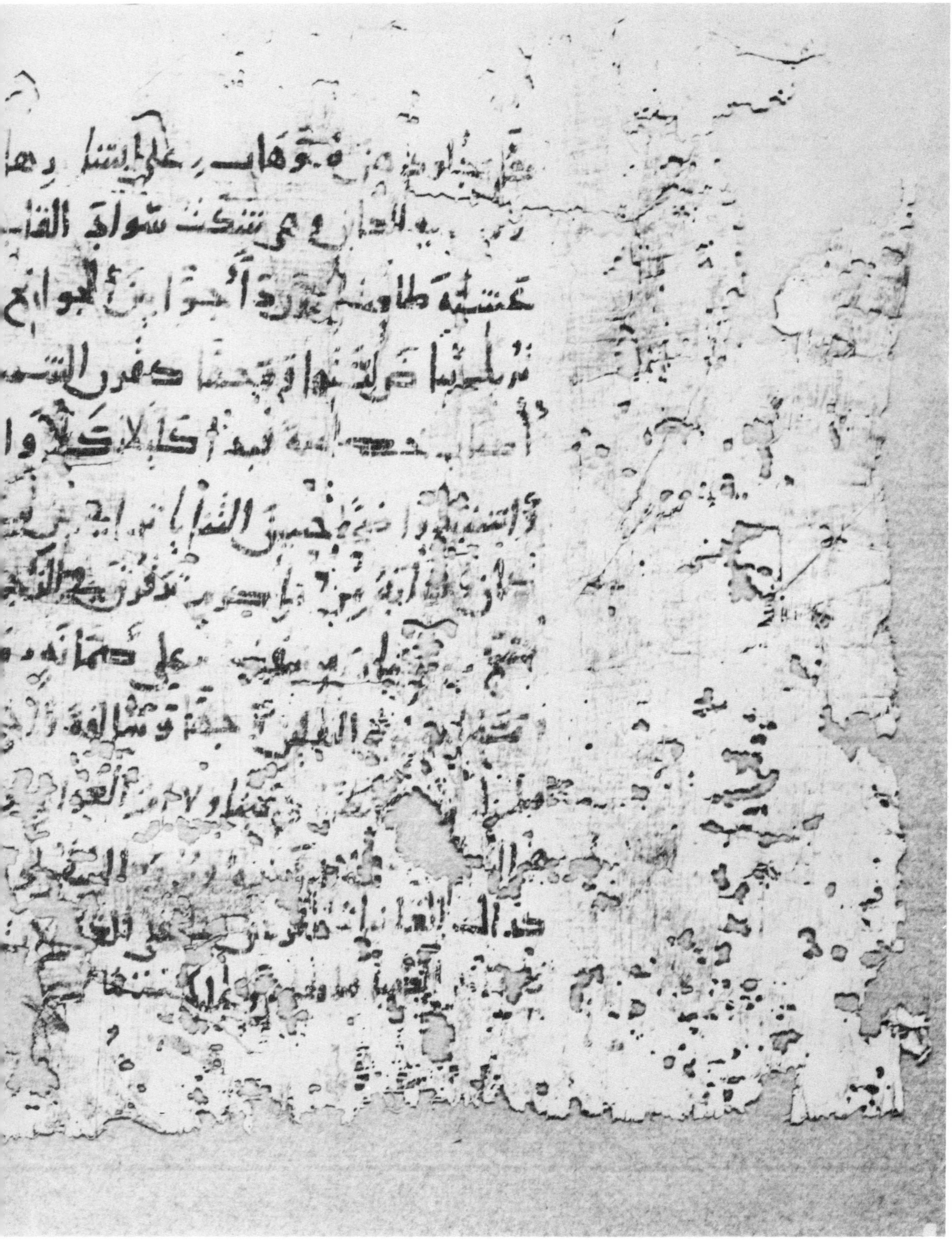

PAGE 2